Advances in Automatic Text Summarization

Advances in Automatic Text Summarization

edited by Inderjeet Mani and Mark T. Maybury

The MIT Press
Cambridge, Massachusetts
London, England

Chapter 2 was originally published in the *IBM Journal of Research & Development* 2(2):159–165, 1958. Reprinted by permission. © 1958 International Business Machines Corporation.

Chapter 3 was originally published in the *Journal of the Association for Computing Machinery* 16(2):264–285, 1969. Reprinted by permission. ©1969 Association for Computing Machinery.

Chapter 4 was originally published in the *Journal of Chemical Information and Computer Sciences* 15(4):226–232, 1975. Reprinted by permission from the author and the American Chemical Society. © 1975 American Chemical Society.

Chapters 5 and 24 were originally published in the *Proceedings of the 18th ACM-SIGIR Conference*, pp. 68–73, 74–82 (respectively), 1995. Reprinted by permission. © 1995 Association for Computing Machinery.

Chapter 14 was originally published in *Strategies for Natural Language Processing*, eds. W. G. Lehnert and M. H. Ringle, pp. 223–244 (Hillsdale, NJ: Erlbaum), 1981. Reprinted by permission. ©1981 Lawrence Erlbaum Associates.

Chapters 16, 17, and 19 were originally published in *Information Processing and Management* 31(5):703–733, 735–751, 675–686 (respectively), 1995. Reprinted by permission from Elsevier Science. © 1995 Elsevier Science.

Chapter 18 was originally published in *American Documentation* 12(2):139–143, 1961 (now entitled *Journal of the American Society for Information Science*). Reprinted by permission from the American Society of Information Science. © 1961 American Society of Information Science.

Chapter 20 was originally published in *Information Systems Research* 3(1):17–35, 1992. Reprinted by permission. © 1992 The Institute of for Operations Research and the Management Sciences (INFORMS), 901 Elkridge Landing Road, Linthicum, Maryland 21090 USA.

Chapter 22 was originally published in *Information Processing and Management* 33(2):193–207, 1997. Reprinted by permission from Elsevier Science. © 1997 Elsevier Science.

Chapter 23 was originally published in *Information Retrieval* 1(1):1–23, 1999. Reprinted by permission from Kluwer Academic Publishers. © 1999 Kluwer Academic Publishers, Boston.

Library of Congress Cataloging-in-Publication Data

Advances in automatic text summarization / edited by Inderjeet Mani and Mark T. Maybury.
   p. cm.
 Includes bibliographical references and index.
 ISBN 0-262-13359-8 (hc : alk. paper)
 1. Automatic abstracting. 2. Computational linguistics. I. Mani, Inderjeet. II. Maybury, Mark T.
P98.5.A87A34 1999
025.4'0285—dc21
                                                     99-22688
                                                         CIP

Contents

Preface

With the rapid growth of the World Wide Web and on-line information services, more and more information is available and accessible on-line. This explosion of information has resulted in a well-recognized information overload problem. There is no time to read everything, and yet we have to make critical decisions based on whatever information is available. In recognition of this need, the research and development of systems to automatically summarize text has become the focus of considerable interest and investment in both research and commercial sectors. *Advances in Automatic Text Summarization* is the first book to capture the current state and principal trends and influences in this exciting and vital field.

This book is intended to serve multiple purposes. First, it is intended to motivate and define the field of text summarization. Second, it is intended to serve as a standard reference for key developments in this field. Third, it can be used for continued research into many remaining problems that remain. The book can be used as a reference for students, researchers and practitioners, or a collection of papers for use in undergraduate and graduate seminars. To facilitate multiple uses, the introduction includes a content overview as well as a list of resources including Web links to bibliographic databases, workshops, and commercial products.

This book began as an idea which was first aired at the ACL'97/EACL'97 Workshop on Intelligent Scalable Text Summarization (ISTS) held in Madrid, Spain, in July 1997. The consensus among those present at that workshop (which was chaired by the editors and which drew prominent representatives from government, academia, and industry from 3 continents) was that there was a need for a book that would collect and present in an integrated framework some of the key results in the field to date and identify promising research issues for the benefit of students, corporate researchers, and research program managers interested in learning more about this field.

While there is much excellent material in the published literature, it appears scattered across many professional societies or shared only in very limited, specialized forums (e.g., workshops, conferences, journals). There is no single "state of the art" collection of papers in this important field for use as supplements for graduate level courses or for professional, commercial and government researchers. The book is especially timely as there now exist new approaches to old problems as well as unique opportunities for cross fertilization of this field (e.g., integration of statistical and symbolic processing). Finally, as fundamental innovations in summarization begin to find their way into commercial systems (e.g., Alta Vista, Oracle's Context, Microsoft Word's AutoSummarize), there is an increased need for a book of this kind.

Advances in Automatic Text Summarization represents the best classical and contemporary research in the field. While in a book of this size it is not possible to represent all relevant research, the 26 articles in the book represent the work of 54 authors, from sites in 5 different countries. In response to our Call for Papers for the book, we received 18 submissions, of which 11 were extensive rewrites of papers presented at the ISTS workshop (15 papers were presented at the workshop altogether), and 7 were new submissions. Of the 11 rewritten workshop papers, 9 were accepted, as well as 4 of the remaining 7 new submissions, giving a total of 13 acceptances out of 18 submissions. The review process was stringent, incorporating 3 phases of anonymous peer review by the editors, contributors, and external reviewers. In addition to the 13 new papers, the book includes 13 reprints of influential papers published in journals or books.

The book begins with an introduction that discusses the background to text summarization, focusing on a framework and architecture for summarization, along with essential terminology. After a brief historical overview, the introduction goes on to provide a summary of each of the six sections of the book, offers a guide to the content and a link to additional resources, and identifies the key remaining problems. It is followed by a position paper by Dr. Karen Spärck Jones (a distinguished scholar in the fields of text summarization, information retrieval and language processing) that provides a framework for text summarization. The remainder of the book is organized into six sections, representing key areas of research and development.

Advances in Automatic Text Summarization	
Section 1	Classical Approaches
Section 2	Corpus-based Approaches
Section 3	Exploiting Discourse Structure
Section 4	Knowledge-rich Approaches
Section 5	Evaluation Methods
Section 6	New Summarization Problem Areas

Each section contains an introduction by the editors that offers concise summaries of the papers, placing them in the perspective of the fundamental framework for text summarization, along with a discussion of relationships to other papers in the book and in the literature at large. In addition, each section introduction offers a critical assessment of the remaining problems and challenges in that particular area.

We hope this book will help promote the development of further advances in automatic text summarization, making it possible for humans to more effectively and efficiently exploit the vast and growing information resources increasingly accessible to us as we enter the new millennium.

Acknowledgments

We would like to thank the MIT Press (especially our editor Douglas Sery) as well as The MITRE Corporation for their support and cooperation. Thanks are of course due to the authors and reviewers for their painstaking efforts, without which this book would not have been possible. Among the external reviewers, we are especially grateful to Dr. Eric Bloedorn, Dr. Gary Klein, and Dr. Kent Wittenburg. Special recognition is deserved for our longsuffering secretarial assistants, Anne Roemer in Reston and Paula MacDonald in Bedford. We are also thankful to David Shumaker and Phyllis Jones at the MITRE Library, for assistance in obtaining high-quality reprints. Finally, we are eternally indebted to our families (Asha, Kailash and Parvati Mani, and Michelle, Zachary, and Max Maybury) for their unqualified support and their willingness to forego our company on the many evenings and weekends that we dedicated to this endeavor.

Inderjeet Mani and Mark Maybury
September, 1998

Introduction

Background

With the rapid growth of the World Wide Web and on-line information services, more and more information is available and accessible on-line. This explosion of information has resulted in a well-recognized information overload problem. There is no time to read everything, and yet we have to make critical decisions based on whatever information is available. The technology of automatic text summarization is indispensable for dealing with this problem.

In recognition of this need, there has been an increase in the research and development budgets devoted to automatic text summarization. The United States (e.g., DARPA), the European Community and Pacific Rim countries have identified text summarization as a critical research area, and are beginning to invest in it. Text summarization is also increasingly being exploited in the commercial sector, in the telecommunications industry (e.g., BT's ProSum), in data mining of text databases (e.g., Oracle's Context), in filters for web-based information retrieval (e.g. Inxight's summarizer used in AltaVista Discovery), and in word processing tools (e.g., Microsoft's AutoSummarize). In addition to the traditional focus of automatic indexing and automatic abstracting (of scientific and technical text) to support information retrieval, researchers are investigating the application of this technology to a variety of new and challenging problems, including multilingual summarization ("tell me what the Spanish, Japanese, and Russian press is saying about the Lewinsky affair") (Cowie et al. 1998), multimedia news broadcasts ("watch the news and tell me what happened while I was away") (e.g., Merlino and Maybury's article in section 6), providing physicians with summaries of on-line medical literature related to a patient's medical record ("summarize and compare the recommended treatments for this patient") (McKeown et al. 1998), and audio scanning services for the blind ("scan in this page and read it quickly") (Grefenstette 1998). As the information overload problem grows, and people become increasingly mobile and information-hungry, new applications for text summarization can be expected.

Motivation, Framework and Terminology

Text summarization is *the process of distilling the most important information from a source (or sources) to produce an abridged version for a particular user (or users) and task (or tasks).* There are many uses of summarization in everyday activities, which are indicative of the types of functions that summarization can perform. We are all familiar with summaries such as:

- headlines (from around the world)
- outlines (notes for students)
- minutes (of a meeting)
- previews (of movies)
- synopses (soap opera listings)
- reviews (of a book, CD, movie, etc.)
- digests (TV guide)
- biography (resumes, obituaries)
- abridgments (Shakespeare for children)
- bulletins (weather forecasts/stock market reports)
- sound bites (politicians on a current issue)
- histories (chronologies of salient events)

In general, humans are extremely capable summarizers. We have an incredible capacity to condense information down to the critical bit, as revealed in the following quote (Bartlett 1983)[1]:

"He said he was against it."

> -- *Calvin Coolidge, on being asked what a clergyman preaching on sin had said.*

With this inspiration in mind, we now turn to summarization by machines.

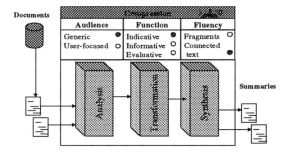

Figure 1. Architecture of a Text Summarization System

Figure 1 illustrates a high level architecture of an automatic text summarization system. Input to the summarization process could be a single document or multiple documents, text or multimedia information such as imagery, audio, or video. Text summarization has traditionally focused mainly on text input (which of course may represent information from some other media). The summary may be an *extract* of the source, or an *abstract*; it can stand in place of the source as a surrogate, or it could be linked to the source, or even be presented in the context of the source (e.g., by highlighting source text).

---

[1] We are grateful to Dr. Graeme Hirst for this quotation.

As also shown in Figure 1, an important parameter to summarization is the level of *compression* (ratio of summary length to source length) desired (sometimes, the complement of this measure is used instead). Note that while this measure is defined in terms of length, which is easily measured, it could also perhaps be defined in terms of information content. As the compression decreases, more information is lost. Traditionally, compression rates range from 1% to 30%. The type of summary output desired could be relatively polished, *connected text*, or else more *fragmentary* in nature (e.g., a list of phrases).

Traditionally, *generic* summaries aimed at a broad readership community and written by authors or professional abstractors served as surrogates for full-text. However, as our computing environments have continued to accommodate full-text searching, browsing, and personalized information filtering, *user-focused* summaries have assumed increasing importance. Such summaries rely on a specification of a user information need, such as an area of interest, topic, or query. It should be borne in mind that the notion of a truly generic summary is problematic, since some background assumptions of an audience are involved in every case.

Finally, the intended function of the summary is usually taken into consideration. Unfortunately, terminology here is not entirely satisfactory. A broad distinction is usually drawn between *indicative* summaries, which are used to indicate what topics are addressed in the source text, and thus can be used to alert the user as to the source content, and *informative* summaries, which are intended to cover the concepts in the source text to the extent possible given the compression rate. These types of summaries are often contrasted with *evaluative* or *critical* summaries, which offer a critique of the source.

As shown in Figure 1, the process of automatic text summarization can be decomposed into three phases: *analyzing* the input text, *transforming* it into a summary representation, and *synthesizing* an appropriate output form. These three phases (discussed further by Sparck Jones in her paper in this book) include three basic *condensation operations* used in summarization:

1. *selection* of more salient or non-redundant information
2. *aggregation* of information (e.g., from different parts of the source, or of different linguistic descriptions)
3. *generalization* of specific information with more general, abstract information.

The above condensation operations can apply in various phases of the summarization task. For example, in the analysis phase, *selection* may rely on *aggregation* at the term level, corresponding to different ways of normalizing terms, and elimination of particular regions of text. In the transformation phase, *selection* may involve *aggregation* of information by merging together representations of similar entities. *Generalization* may involve taking concepts, topics, or events in the source and inferring a more general concept (e.g., a paragraph discussing hard drives being about computer peripherals, or a birthday party inferred from a sequence of events). In the synthesis phase, *aggregation* can involve fusing multiple linguistic descriptions into a single one (e.g., describing Mars, in an appositive phrase, as the fourth planet from the Sun). *Selection* here may involve compaction of text, by removing less salient phrases or words from sentences.

There are several ways in which one can characterize different approaches to text summarization. One useful way is to examine the level of processing. Based on this, summarization can be characterized as approaching the problem at the *surface*, *entity*, or *discourse* levels.

Surface-level approaches tend to represent information in terms of shallow features which are then selectively combined together to yield a salience function used to extract information. These features include:

- Thematic features (presence of statistically salient terms, based on term frequency statistics)
- Location (position in text, position in paragraph, section depth, particular sections)
- Background (presence of terms from the title or headings in the text, the initial part of the text, or a user's query)
- Cue words and phrases (e.g., in-text summary cues such as "in summary," "our investigation," emphasizers such as "important," "in particular," as well as domain-specific "bonus" and "stigma" terms).

Entity-level approaches build an internal representation for text, modeling text entities and their relationships. These approaches tend to represent patterns of connectivity in the text (e.g., graph topology) to help determine what is salient. Relationships between entities include:

- Similarity (e.g., vocabulary overlap)
- Proximity (distance between text units)
- Co-occurrence (i.e., words related based on their occurring in common contexts)
- Thesaural relationships among words (synonymy, hypernymy, part-of relations)
- Coreference (i.e., of referring expressions such as noun phrases)
- Logical relations such as agreement, contradiction, entailment, and consistency
- Syntactic relations (e.g., based on parse trees)
- Meaning representation-based relations (e.g., based on predicate-argument relations).

Discourse-level approaches model the global structure of the text, and its relation to communicative goals. This structure can include:

- Format of the document (e.g., hypertext markup, document outlines)
- Threads of topics as they are revealed in the text
- Rhetorical structure of the text, such as argumentation or narrative structure.

These are pure examples of the approaches, and many systems adopt a hybrid approach (e.g., taking a discourse-level approach where the smallest segments are surface strings or entities). There are also instances of summarization systems which start from a source of structured data, where there is no associated full-text source (though in some of these instances, the structured data could have been constructed from a full-text source or sources as a result of an information extraction process). Such approaches are characterized as being at the entity-level.

The Roots of Text Summarization

Here we briefly sketch the history of the field. Early systems were developed in the late 1950's, characterized by a surface-level approach, for example exploiting thematic features such as term frequency, e.g., Luhn's paper in Section 1, and Rath et al. in Section 5. Whereas the first entity-level approaches based on syntactic analysis appeared in the early 1960s, (Climenson et al. 1961), the use of location features was not developed until somewhat later (see Edmundson's 1969 paper in Section 1). In the early 1970s, there was renewed interest in the field, with extensions being developed to the surface-level approach to include the use of cue phrases (bonus versus stigma items), and which resulted in the first commercial applications of automated abstracting, see Pollock and Zamora in Section 1.

The late 1970s saw the emergence of more extensive entity-level approaches (Skorokhodko 1972) as well as the first discourse-based approaches based on story grammars (vanDijk 1980, Correira 1980). The 1980s enjoyed an explosion of a variety of different work, especially entity-level approaches based on artificial intelligence such as the use of scripts (Lehnert 1981) in Section 4, (DeJong 1982), logic and production rules (Fum et al. 1985), semantic networks (Reimer and Hahn 1988), as well as hybrid approaches, e.g., (Rau et al. 1989), see also (Aretoulaki 1994).

The current period (late 1990s) represents a renaissance of the field, with all three types of approaches being explored very aggressively, heightened by government and commercial interest. Recent work has almost exclusively focused on extracts rather than abstracts, along with a renewed interest in earlier surface-level approaches. This focus on extracts is likely to change in the next few years, however, as more natural language generation work begins to focus on text summarization. In addition, we are seeing the emergence of new areas such as multi-document summarization, multilingual summarization, and multimedia summarization.

Studies of Abstracting Behavior

In conjunction with research on automatic text summarization, there have been two other strands of work which have influenced the field. The first is the psychological study of human summarization in the laboratory (Kintsch and van Dijk 1978; van Dijk 1979). The insights here are based on memory recall experiments and behavior protocols. Subjects in these experiments have been found to use conceptual structures (schemata) for text comprehension; they also interpret texts in the light of previous experience (episodic memory). Experiments reveal that humans create a hierarchical discourse organization, which provides retrieval cues for memory; they restore missing information through inference-based reconstruction processes. What is particularly striking is the tendency of subjects to inject their own comments, opinions, and attitudes in the course of constructing summaries.

The other important influence on automatic text summarization has been the study of professional abstractors who construct abstracts of scientific text for a living. Abstractors are taught to follow prescriptions and guidelines to generate effective abstracts. They aim at producing informative summaries, and they have knowledge of the subject matter being summarized. Cremmins (1996) found that professional abstractors do not attempt to fully "understand" the text, but use surface-level features such as headings, key phrases, and position in paragraphs; they also use discourse features such as overall text structure to organize abstracts. In addition, they revise and edit abstracts. Liddy studied a corpus of 276 abstracts and found that they were structured in terms of canonical components such as *Background, Purpose, Methodology, Results,* and *Conclusions* (Liddy 1991). In her seminal studies of professional abstractors, Endres-Niggemeyer et al. (1995) and Endres-Niggemeyer (1998) found that professional abstractors take a top-down strategy, exploiting discourse structure. They build topic sentences, consider beginnings and ends of units as relevant, exploit in-text summaries, prefer top-level segments of documents, utilize structural organization of documents, examine passages and paragraphs before individual sentences, exploit document outlines, pay attention to document formatting, and paraphrase relations between theme and in-text summaries.

Overview of the Book

This book is organized around solutions to the key elements introduced in the architecture outlined at the beginning of this chapter in Figure 1: input analysis, transformation, and output synthesis. We briefly describe each of the sections in turn, referring the reader to the section introductions for summary overviews of the included papers.

Sparck Jones initiates the volume with a position paper that outlines the challenges facing the field. Her contribution discusses the framework for summarization in terms of the three-phase architecture: interpretation (i.e., analysis), transformation, and generation (i.e., synthesis). She stresses the need to carefully examine factors such as the nature of the input, output, and the purpose for which summaries are being used. After assessing where we stand today, she suggests a near-term strategy for the field of text summarization, aiming (conservatively) at the goal of producing "sufficient for the day" indicative summaries using a variety of linguistic processing methods.

Section 1 (*Classical Approaches*) begins with work dating back 40 years. It is classic in the sense that it serves as a fundamental basis for both modern practical applications as well as motivating subsequent research. These papers all exploit a surface-level approach. Luhn's (1958) paper describes a statistical approach to text summarization, relying on selection of salient information based on term frequency. The next paper, by Edmundson (1969), compares the use of term frequency with other features, including cue phrases (e.g., "significant," "impossible," "hardly"), title and heading words, and sentence location. The paper by Pollock and Zamora (1973) describes an abstracting program at Chemical Abstracts Service which relies on the use of cue-phrases specific to chemistry subdomains; these are used as positive (bonus word) and negative (stigma word) tests for selection of sentences, which are then compacted based on shallow linguistic analyses.

Section 2 (*Corpus-based Approaches*) follows up on Edmundson's work by describing corpus-based methods that can be used to obtain term statistics and to decide on an appropriate combination of features. These papers also involve mainly a surface-level approach. The first paper by Kupiec, Pedersen, and Chen (henceforth, KPC) describes the use of a Bayesian classifier to extract sentences; the classifier is trained on feature-vectors constructed from full-text sentences which are labeled as extract-worthy based on comparison with abstracts. As with Edmundson's paper in Section 1, KPC found that on their data, location was the best individual feature; in their

feature mix, location, cue phrase, and sentence length was the best combination. The next paper, by Myaeng and Jang, describes a variant of the KPC method applied to technical texts in Korean, where the authors found that using a combination of cue words, sentence location, and presence of title words in a sentence led to the best results. The third paper, by Aone, Okurowski, Gorlinsky, and Larsen, reveals that in using term-based statistics along with a KPC approach, different ways of aggregating terms based on recognizing morphological, synonym, and proper name variants can impact summarization performance. The final paper in this section by Hovy and Lin discusses a further instantiation of the three-phase approach, and introduces a new method for identifying location-relevant information. In addition, the paper reports on a thesaurus-based method for aggregating and generalizing concepts in the text, as well as a data-driven method which derives "topic signatures" for text.

Section 3 (*Exploiting Discourse Structure*) While the earlier sections focus on surface-level approaches, this section begins the focus on the other approaches. The papers in this section all exploit models of discourse structure, while maintaining a relatively domain-independent and knowledge-poor approach.

The first two papers use an entity-level approach, exploiting relationships based on text cohesion. In the first paper in this section, Boguraev and Kennedy aggregate and select phrasal terms based on robust syntactic parsing and resolution of anaphoric relationships between the terms. In the second paper, Barzilay and Elhadad aggregate terms into lexical chains based on relationships such as synonymy and hypernymy; these chains are used to select sentences.

The remaining papers in this section build a global discourse-level model of macro-level relations in the text. Marcu uses a rhetorical parser for unrestricted text that exploits cue-phrases to build rhetorical structure theory (RST) trees out of clauses in the text. The tree structure is then used to construct a salience function for selecting clauses. The paper by Strzalkowski et al. treats summarization as a problem of passage ranking given a query, where the "query" is constructed out of the user's query if any, terms in the title, and frequently occurring terms in the text. They use a simple rhetorical model of the discourse structure of news story summaries to combine query-relevant information with the contextual information needed to deal with out-of-context extracts. The final paper by Teufel and Moens breaks down the summarization task into two stages: extraction of sentences, and identification of rhetorical roles (from a set of seven roles) for each extracted sentence. Both stages use Bayesian classifiers modeled on KPC's approach.

Section 4 (*Knowledge-rich Approaches*) emphasizes approaches which model the rich knowledge requirements for summarization in particular domains. All of the papers in this section assume that a relatively rich structured representation has been built, which the summarization process uses as input. While the previous sections focus mainly on the analysis phase of summarization, this section looks in much more detail at the transformation (the first two papers) and synthesis phases (the next two).

The first paper, by Lehnert, describes an inference-based technique (unimplemented) for summarizing narratives, based on structural relations in narratives constructed around "plot units." The second paper, by Hahn and Reimer, describes a three-step process for summarization: first, a repertoire of salience operators is applied to paragraphs, second, topic descriptions are determined and aggregated over paragraphs as appropriate, and third, generalization operators are applied across the topic descriptions to create a hierarchical text graph, in effect combining discourse-level and entity-level approaches.

The next two papers focus on methods for synthesis. The paper, by McKeown, Robin, and Kukich, describes techniques for opportunistically packing information into sentences in two different summarizers: STREAK, which generates basketball game summaries using a revision approach, and PLANDOC, which summarizes network planning activity using discourse planning. The linguistic operations implemented by their summarizers are motivated by corpus analysis of human summaries from these two domains. In the final paper in this section, Maybury describes SumGen, a summarizer for military simulations as well as business news, which uses techniques for event selection, condensation (including aggregation and abstraction) and presentation.

Section 5 (*Evaluation Methods*) includes papers which describe both *extrinsic* evaluations, in which the quality of a summary is judged based on how it affects the completion of some other task, and *intrinsic* evaluations, where humans judge the quality of the summarization directly based on analysis of the summary in terms of fluency, coverage, or resemblance to a manually-constructed ideal summary.

The first paper, by Rath et al., provides empirical evidence for the difficulties inherent in the notion of an ideal summary, demonstrating evidence of low agreement across subjects and over time when subjects are asked to select representative sentences from articles. The second paper, by Brandow, Mitze, and Rau, describes an intrinsic evaluation comparing a system based mainly on thematic features of term frequency against a system that just selects the initial part of the text.

The next two papers describe extrinsic evaluations. Morris, Kasper and Adams report on an evaluation involving the task of answering questions in Graduate Management Admission Test (GMAT) reading comprehension exercises. The final paper by Firmin and Chrzanowski describes an initial "dry-run" of the TIPSTER evaluation of text summarization systems, which measures the impact of both generic and user-focused summarization on performance time and accuracy in assessing relevance. These latter two papers demonstrate empirically that summaries can be as effective as full-texts in these tasks.

Section 6 (*New Summarization Problem Areas*) discusses multi-document summarization and multimedia summarization, two new areas that are growing in interest and importance.

The first two papers exploit a connectivity model for text where the more strongly connected a text unit is to other units, the more salient it is. In the first paper on multi-document summarization, by Salton et al., paragraphs from one or more documents are compared in terms of similarity of vocabulary; those paragraphs above a particular similarity threshold are linked to form a "text relationship map" graph, which can then be traversed in various ways to extract summaries. The second paper, by Mani and Bloedorn, constructs user-focused multi-document summaries using a graph representation whose nodes are term occurrences (positions) in the text and whose edges are cohesion relationships (proximity, repetition, synonymy, hypernymy, and coreference) between those occurrences. This representation is used to select information in each document relevant to the query, and then to compare that information to yield similarities and differences. In the third paper, by McKeown and Radev, relationships between different news stories on terrorist incidents are established by operators that aggregate together similar extracted templates based on logical relationships such as agreement and contradiction. In the synthesis phase, these aggregated templates are fed to a sentence generator that constructs descriptions of the templates and their relationships.

The second emerging area is that of multimedia summarization, i.e., summarization where the input and/or output need not be text. The paper by Merlino and Maybury describes an evaluation of single-media and mixed-media presentation techniques for summarization of video news broadcasts in the context of their Broadcast News Navigator, a tool for searching, browsing and summarizing TV news broadcasts. The final paper by Futrelle illustrates possible techniques to select one or more figures from a document (analogous to sentence extraction), distill a figure to simplify it (analogous to elimination by text compaction), merge multiple figures (analogous to merging and aggregation of text representations), and finally construct the graphical form of the summary diagram in the synthesis phase.

Content Index

Because many of the papers address issues which cut across the above section distinctions, in order to facilitate access, Table 1 cross-references the 26 articles in the six sections of this book by approach, type of condensation operations involved, and type of evaluation discussed. Note that Section 5 contains papers whose main focus is evaluation. While many of the papers focus mainly on the analysis phase of summarization, Sections 4 and 6 contain papers which focus on the transformation and synthesis phases of summarization.

	Approach		
	Surface-level	Entity-level	Discourse-level
Condensation Operations			
Selection	1.2-1.4 2.2-2.5 6.5	3.2-3.3 4.2-4.4 6.2-6.6	3.4-3.6 4.5 6.5
Aggregation	1.2 2.4-2.5 6.5	2.4-2.5 3.2-3.3 4.2-4.5 6.2-6.4, 6.6	2.5 3.3 3.5 4.4-4.5
General-ization	2.5	4.2-4.5, 6.4	4.2-4.5
Evaluation			
Intrinsic	1.3, 2.2-2.5, 5.2-5.3	2.4, 3.3 6.2-6.3	3.4, 3.6
Extrinsic	5.3-5.5, 6.5	4.4, 5.5, 6.3	3.5, 5.5

Table 1: Content of articles in book

Resources

There are a number of on-line resources with related information that will be useful for teachers, students and researchers. The editors have maintained an up-to-date list of on-line conference materials, bibliographies, and pointers to available summarization products at the following location:
http://www.mitre.org/resources/centers/iime/aats.html.

Conclusion

Automatic text summarization promises a powerful technology to exploit in our struggle with information overload. Tools which can very quickly digest large quantities of information will enable us to consider a wider and potentially richer set of information to support decision making. In order to realize these benefits, however, we must overcome a variety of remaining challenges, including the need to:
1. Improve summarization capabilities in the synthesis phase, allowing for additional capabilities in generating abstracts. This includes the challenge of developing more scalable natural language generation techniques with reduced knowledge engineering requirements.
2. Further develop empirically-grounded theoretical models of discourse, as well as increased use of corpora with discourse annotations to provide a better understanding of discourse phenomena.
3. Improve capabilities in robust anaphora resolution and topic detection and tracking.
4. Improve formalization of a range of condensation operations.
5. Develop algorithms which scale up to large-size collections (gigabyte-terabyte ranges).
6. Improve availability of meta-information related to non-textual media, as well as improved analysis of such media. Research will obviously benefit from improved methods for cross-media information fusion and integration.

We can make more rapid progress in achieving the above tasks if as a community we:
1. Develop new linguistically annotated summarization corpora in different text genres, containing both full-text and associated extracts and abstracts. These can help develop better comparisons and evaluation of corpus-based methods.
2. Exploit advances in related fields of natural language processing, data mining, information visualization, and information retrieval.
3. Design evaluations which adequately model real-world situations and information needs, and which address a variety of text genres and lengths.
4. Understand the generality and replicability of results of summarization experiments involving specific source genres, domains, users and tasks.

References

AltaVista   Discovery http://discovery.altavista.digital.com/.

Aretoulaki, M. 1994. Towards a hybrid abstract generation system. In *Proceedings of the International Conference on New Methods in Language Processing*, 220-227, Manchester, England.

Bartlett, J. 1983. *Collection of Familiar Quotations*, 15th edition, Citadel Press, 1983.

Climenson, W.D., Hardwick, N.H., Jacobson, S.N. 1961. Automatic Syntax Analysis in Machine Indexing and Abstracting. In *American Documentation*, 12(3):178-183.

Correira, A. 1980. Computing Story Trees. *American Journal of Computational Linguistics*, 6(3-4):135-149.

Cowie, J., Mahesh, K., Nirenburg, S., and Zajac, R. 1998. MINDS – Multilingual Interactive Document Summarization. In *Working Notes of the AAAI Spring Symposium on Intelligent Text Summarization*, Spring 1998, 131-132. Menlo Park, Calif.: AAAI Press.

Cremmins, E. T. 1996. *The Art of Abstracting*. Information Resources Press.

DeJong, G.F. 1982. An Overview of the FRUMP System. In Lehnert, W. G. and Ringle, M.H., eds., *Strategies for Natural Language Processing*, Lawrence Erlbaum Associates, Hillsdale, NJ.

Endres-Niggemeyer, B., Maier, E., and Sigel, A. 1995. How to implement a naturalistic model of abstracting: four core working steps of an expert abstractor. In *Information Processing and Management* 31(5):631-674.

Endres-Niggemeyer, B. 1998. *Summarizing Information*. Springer-Verlag, New York.

Fum, D., Guida, G., and Tasso, C. 1985. Evaluating Importance: A step towards text summarization. In *Proceedings of the International Joint Conference on Artificial Intelligence (IJCAI'85)*, 840-844.

Grefenstette, G. 1998. Producing Intelligent Telegraphic Text Reduction to Provide an Audio Scanning Service for the Blind. In *Working Notes of the AAAI Spring Symposium on Intelligent Text Summarization*, Spring 1998, 111-117. Menlo Park, Calif.: AAAI Press.

Kintsch, W., van Dijk, T. A. 1978. Toward a Model of Text Comprehension and Production. In *Psychological Review* 85(5):363-394.

Liddy, E. D. 1991. Discourse-level structure of empirical abstracts: an exploratory study. In *Information Processing and Management* 27(1):55-81.

McKeown, K., Jordan, D. A., and Hatzivassiloglou, V. 1998. Generating Patient-Specific Summaries of On-Line Literature. In *Working Notes of the AAAI Spring Symposium on Intelligent Text Summarization*, Spring 1998, 34-43. Menlo Park, Calif.: AAAI Press.

Rau, L., Jacobs, P. S., and Zernick, U. 1989. Information Extraction and Text Summarization using Linguistic Knowledge Acquisition. In *Information Processing and Management* 25(4):419-428.

Reimer, U., and Hahn, U. 1988. Text condensation as knowledge base abstraction. In *Proceedings of the Fourth Conference on Artificial Intelligence Applications*, 338-344.

Skorokhodko, E. F. 1972. Adaptive method of automatic abstracting and indexing. In *IFIP Congress*, Ljubljana, Yugoslavia 71, 1179-1182.

vanDijk, T. A. 1979. Recalling and summarizing complex discourse. In W. Burchart and K. Hulker, eds., *Text Processing*, Walter de Gruyter, Berlin.

vanDijk, T. A. 1980. *Macrostructures: An interdisciplinary study of global structures in discourse, interaction, and cognition*. Lawrence Erlbaum, Hillsdale, NJ.

Automatic summarizing: factors and directions

Karen Sparck Jones
Computer Laboratory, University of Cambridge
New Museums Site, Pembroke Street
Cambridge CB2 3QG, England
sparckjones@cl.cam.ac.uk

Abstract

This position paper suggests that progress with automatic summarizing demands a better research methodology and a carefully focussed research strategy. In order to develop effective procedures it is necessary to identify and respond to the context factors, i.e., input, purpose, and output factors, that bear on summarizing and its evaluation. The paper analyses and illustrates these factors and their implications for evaluation. It then argues that this analysis, together with the state of the art and the intrinsic difficulty of summarizing, imply a nearer-term strategy concentrating on shallow, but not surface, text analysis and on indicative summarizing. This is illustrated with current work, from which a potentially productive research program can be developed.

Introduction

This paper addresses two pressing questions about automatic summarizing: given the present state of the art, what are the best directions to take in research methodology, and in strategy development? The paper reviews where we are now in automatic summarizing, and argues that our methodology focus should be on *context factors*, our strategy focus on *shallow processing*. My claims are that we will not be able to develop useful summarizing systems unless we pay proper attention to the context factors, and especially purpose factors, that shape summaries; and that since we cannot expect even in the medium to long term to emulate human summarizing, we should concentrate, in seeking generally applicable procedures, on relatively shallow techniques that are within reach of current NLP technology. My two concerns are related because the limitations of the technology imply a need for careful identification, from a context point of view, of the summary tasks to which even a quite limited technology could add value, and of the conditions under which it could be successfully applied.

The paper is a programmatic one. My report on the present state of the art is therefore designed only to note its salient features, and does not review recent and current work in detail; and my argument for where we should go is intended as a call to arms, and is therefore broadly assertive, with indicative illustrations, but not finely elaborated.

Background

As background, I shall take for granted an initial definition of a *summary* as: *a reductive transformation of source text to summary text through content reduction by selection and/or generalization on what is important in the source.*

I shall also assume that the basic process model is a three-stage one:

I : source text *interpretation* to source text representation
T : source representation *transformation* to summary text representation
G : summary text *generation* from summary representation.

This model (slightly modifying the earlier one presented in Sparck Jones 1995) may appear obvious. But adopting a general framework with distinct processing phases and data types supplies a useful common means for checking the real logic underlying specific systems, making it easier to identify the assumptions on which they are based, and to compare one system with another. Of course, each major stage can subsume several substages; for instance, in interpretation a process for building individual sentence representations, followed by one integrating these into a larger text representation, perhaps followed by a further process modifying the global text representation. The nature of the assumptions on which a summarizing system are based are made clear when it is recognized, as for example with DeJong's FRUMP (DeJong 1982), that the source and summary representations are conflated.

The definition of a summary, though no more than an informal and obvious one, nevertheless serves to emphasize the fact that summarizing is in general a hard task, even if we can find, and expect to automate for, some situations where it is not. Summarizing is hard because we have to characterize a source text as a whole, we have to capture its important content, where content is a matter both of information and its expression, and importance is a matter of what is essential as well as what is salient.

Current state

Research on automatic summarizing, taken as including extracting, abstracting, etc., has a long history, with an early burst of effort in the sixties following Luhn's pioneering work, two subsequent decades with little research and a low profile, and a marked growth of activity since the mid eighties and especially very recently: see Paice (1990), Endres-Niggemeyer et al. (1995), IPM (1995), Mani and Maybury (1997). But virtually all of the work done so far, and especially the more practically-oriented work involving substantial rather than suggestive implementation, falls under two headings: *text extraction* and *fact extraction*.

In text extraction, where 'what you see is what you get', some of what is on view in the source text is transferred to constitute the summary text. Text extraction is an *open* approach to summarizing, since there is no prior presumption about what sort of content information is of importance. What is important for a source text is taken as marked by the source text according to the general, linguistically-based, importance criteria applied in the extraction process. With fact extraction the reverse is the case: 'what you know is what you get', that is, what you have already decided is the sort of subject content to look for in source documents is what you seek to extract. It is a *closed* approach in that the source text does no more than provide some instantiation for previously-established generic content requirements. The text extraction method is intended to let important content emerge, as individually appropriate from each source. The fact extraction method is intended to find individual manifestations of specified important notions, regardless of source status.

(Much recent work has been on generating text summaries from non-linguistic source data (e.g., McKeown et al. 1995). This is practically an important variant of summarizing, and may be far from easy, but I am excluding it here because the critical issue for summarizing in general is the way the (long) source text is interpreted so that important content can be recognized and 'lifted' from it.)

The processing techniques that characterize the two extraction approaches are naturally very different. In text extraction, processing effectively merges the interpretation and transformation stages. Key text segments (usually whole sentences) are identified by some mix of statistical, locational, and cue word criteria; and generation is primarily a matter of smoothing; for example, by incorporating source sentences preceding key ones containing anaphoric references. One possible way of viewing this type of strategy, as it is often implemented, is to say that the source text is taken as its own representation, without any interpretation, and this representation is then subject to a transformation stage which is simply extractive. The output summary is therefore close to the source in linguistic expression,

and also structure as far as presentation order is concerned. In general, with summaries produced with this strategy, the source is viewed through a glass darkly. The selected sentences together usually have some relationship to what would independently be judged as important source content, and allow the reader to infer what it might be. But this dim view of the original is typically also made more obscure because the output summary text, even after smoothing, is itself not very coherent. Even where an explicit derived or abstract representation, e.g., a frequency-annotated word list, is formed and used for sentence extraction, these points about the resulting summary apply.

With fact extraction (and its variants, for example, "message understanding") the interpretation and transformation stages are also essentially merged. The initial text processing is designed only to locate and process the source text expressions that bear on the specified generic concepts, or concept relations, for which particular factual instantiations are sought. There is no independent source text representation, only the direct insertion of source material, with more or less modification of its original expression according to the individual application requirements, in some information representation that is usually of a frame (template, schema) type. Transformation is already all or largely done, via the initial selection of source material and frame filling. In particular, while individual source items may be substantially transformed for frame entry, the invocation of a predesigned frame constitutes the transformation of the source as a whole. Generation on the other hand usually involves the proper production of natural language text from the underlying representation. The essential character of this approach is that it allows only one view of what is important in a source, through glasses of a particular aperture or color, regardless of whether this is a view showing what the original author would regard as significant.

In practice, there is considerable variation in each of these approaches, often associated with the degree of source reduction. Thus for short sources, single key sentence extraction may be reasonable (if risky), and avoids the problem of output coherence. Similarly, with types of short source, it may be appropriate to process virtually all of their factual content, as in Young and Hayes (1985) work on banking telexes. On the other hand, where summary generation within the fact extraction paradigm is from multiple input sources, there may be more transformation of their combined representation, as with POETIC (Evans et al. 1996), where summarizing is dynamically context-dependent.

But overall, the two styles of summarizing that dominate current research are complementary. The text extraction approach has the advantage of generality, but delivers low-quality output because the weak and indirect methods used are not very effective in identifying important material and in presenting it as well-organized text. The fact extraction approach can deliver better quality output, in substance and presentation, as far as the selected material is concerned, but with the disadvantages that the required type of information has to be explicitly (and often effortfully) specified and may not be important for the source itself.

Clearly, it is necessary to get more power in automatic summarizing than text extraction delivers, and more flexibility than fact extraction offers. This applies even if some customization effort is acceptable, as is required for the fact approach, or might assist the text one.

Taking the larger view, it is evident that as summarizing is all about the reduction of extended source text, it is necessary to address the role of large-scale discourse structure in signaling important text content (as well as its role in supporting discourse interpretation in its own right). General advances in automatic summarizing will therefore require methods of capturing this structure in source interpretation, and of deploying it to support the condensing transformation stage, as well as making it available for use in generation. This need would imply, for example, going further in exploiting Rhetorical Structure Theory than the RST-based text selection strategy of Marcu (1997) does, since we have to envisage using large-scale discourse structure to transform source content. The same applies to other approaches to capturing discourse structure, like those presented in Hearst (1994) and Hahn and Strube (1997).

But though understanding how to identify and use large-scale discourse structure is critical for serious summarizing that can deliver summaries of the same quality as human ones, it is a long-term research topic. It involves, for example, exploring alternative views of large-scale discourse structure where, because theories of discourse structure are not well developed, there are many questions to answer even before the attempt is made to apply structural information in summarizing (Endres-Niggemeyer et al. 1995, Sparck Jones 1993). These questions are about: the types of information - linguistic, attentional, communicative, domain - that defines structure; the forms of structure - instantiated, constructed; the indicators of these sorts of structure, their functional roles, their relationships and, of course, their identification and use. Finding their answers will manifestly take time, and it is therefore rational to look, in parallel, for ways of achieving nearer-term progress in automatic summarizing.

Methodology

I believe that in order to make progress in devising effective *general* summarizing strategies, even if only modest ones, we need to pay much more attention to *context factors*, i.e., to identifying the operational factors for any particular application. It is possible, in building a summarizing system for some application, simply to try it and see - taking whatever strategy we have to hand and discovering whether it delivers outputs that users can accept; and this seems to be what is often done in practice. But it is a crude method of working, and determining the operational factors for individual

cases should encourage both a more rational choice of strategy and better understood strategy development.

It is important to recognize the role of context factors because the idea of a general-purpose summary is manifestly an *ignis fatuus*. When the range of summarizing contexts is considered, there is no reason to suppose that any one summary, even a supposedly good one, would meet all the context constraints, even if only moderately well. Why should any one specific technique give the best or even an acceptable result regardless of the properties of the input source or the requirements for the output summary? Similarly, the notion of a *basic* summary, i.e., one reflective of the source, makes hidden factor assumptions, for example, that the subject knowledge of the output's readers will be on a par with that of the readers for whom the source was intended. This is natural for abstracts prefacing papers, but does not always apply, and either way, source properties need identification so their implications for summarizing can be handled. Effective summarizing requires an explicit, and detailed, analysis of context factors, as is apparent when we recognize that what summaries should be like is defined by what they are wanted for, as well as by what their sources are like.

Context factors

It is convenient to distinguish three classes of context factor: *input*, *purpose* and *output* factors. There is a major problem in that all the factors and their various manifestations are hard to define, so capturing them precisely enough to guide summarizing in particular cases, or to provide the foundations to guide strategy development, is very hard. The factor presentation that follows is therefore primarily intended to emphasize the range and richness of the influences on, and hence varieties of, summarizing. I shall first list the factors and their possible realizations, with brief examples, and then give a larger illustration for a single application.

Input factors

These fall into three classes: source *form*, *subject type*, and *unit*.

Input *form* in turn subsumes source text *structure*, *scale*, *medium* and *genre*. Structure includes both explicit organization as marked by subheadings (e.g., Objective, Data, Method ...), and also structure embedded in text like familiar rhetorical patterns (e.g., statement followed by elaboration). It may or may not be appropriate to preserve this structure in the output summary: thus not merely source headings but also the associated grouping of material may be abandoned. Scale, given that we may talk of summarizing a paragraph or a book, is important because it has implications not only for the degree of reduction in summarizing, but also for the possible extent of content transformation. Thus a long novel can be more variously viewed and presented in summary than a short news story. Medium covers both different natural languages and sublanguages: it is not necessarily the case that the source sublanguage should be preserved in the summary, as for example when telegraphese is expanded to normal prose. Genre, an ill and variably defined notion, here refers to literary form rather than content type, for instance description or narrative. While characterizations like these are very vague, we must expect genre to affect summarizing, for example, with a narrative implying a decision either to preserve the presentational sequence or to exhibit the real event sequence, or perhaps to select major events while omitting linking ones.

Thus a specific source text, e.g., a company project progress report, may have a structure defined by task labels, modest scale, much company-specific nomenclature, and descriptive accounts of present task states. Questions for summarizing could then be whether the given task organization be retained or replaced, say by one grouping tasks as complete and incomplete; whether a very brief one-sentence summary can be produced for such a moderate-length source without too much information loss; whether department-level acronyms be spelt out; and whether the simple state description genre of the source should give way to a checklist rhetoric.

Of course, there have to be reasons for answering these questions one way rather than another: this is where the purpose factors considered below play their key part; and there may also be dependencies between the answers. The point here is that there is no mandatory replication of source text properties in summary text ones; but that decisions on the properties that summaries should have, as these are fed by purpose requirements, imply that the properties of the source are recognized. This applies whether or not these properties are to be changed. While it is possible to adopt an essentially passive summarizing strategy, and perhaps to implement this sufficiently effectively without explicitly identifying source text properties, such a strategy carries with it (as noted earlier) assumptions about the context in which the summary is to be used. To meet stated summarizing requirements it is necessary to identify source properties explicitly, so that the summarizing transformations can be properly carried through. This applies in principle even though, as noted earlier for current fact extraction techniques, summarizing to meet output requirements may ride roughshod over sources. Thus *in general* we have to capture source text properties because processing has to respond to them, even if they may in specific cases vanish before the output text is reached; however as we are summarizing unique communicative texts, we would expect to preserve their distinctive properties unless countermanded; and doing this effectively will normally, to avoid distorting transformations, imply that these properties are preserved in the source representation.

Source text *subject type* may be broadly characterized as *ordinary*, *specialized*, or *restricted*, in relation to the presumed subject knowledge of the source text readers. The distinction between specialized and restricted is be-

tween subject matter that depends on knowing what people in many different locations may be assumed to know and subject matter that is limited to some specific local community. Source texts giving chemical analyses as found in journal publications illustrate the specialized case, ones that rely on local names and references the restricted case. Subject matter also of course covers many individual domains with their own particular knowledge, e.g., sport, gardening. The subject matter factor clearly bears on summarizing through the assumptions that are made about background subject knowledge in summary users, as opposed to source readers. For instance heavily technical financial information in a source may be radically simplified for more popular consumption.

The final input factor, *unit*, distinguishes summarizing over a *single* input source from summarizing over *multiple* sources. More particularly, this is a distinction between summarizing where the source, even if it is collection as in an edited book, consists of material previously brought together with design as a whole and summarizing where the sources are independently generated and not brought together with consideration, as for example a succession of press wires on some major event. Though, as with all the previous distinctions, this is not a hard and fast one, the implications for summarizing of single versus multiple sources are in the treatment of information redundancy or of changing data over time. In the latter case it may be further necessary to consider, in the light of summary purpose requirements, whether only the latest data be treated, or the changes themselves indicated.

Purpose factors

These are the most important factors. It may seem obvious that they should be explicitly recognized and their definition applied to guide the choice of summarizing strategy. But in practice in automatic summarizing work they are often not recognized and stated. This may be because it is tacitly assumed that the purpose of summarizing and its implications are obvious, whether this is because summarizing is viewed as requiring 'straight' content condensation as an operation regardless of context, or is taken to be aimed at basic reflective summarizing, or because some processing method or form of output is specified which is already assumed as appropriate for the summary purpose. But since the purpose factors are critical, their implications may be ramified, and as they are the basis for evaluation, it is essential to analyze them properly.

Purpose factors fall under three headings: *situation*, *audience*, and *use*.

Situation refers to the context within which the summary is to be used, which may be labeled *tied* or *floating*. The former refers to cases where the particular environment within which the summaries are to be used - who by, what for, and when - is known in advance so that summarizing can be tailored in a detailed way to meet these context requirements: for example, product description summaries adapted for the use of a company's marketing department for a particular sales drive. A floating situation is where there is no precise context specification. Thus technical abstract journals may be quite narrow in their view of other purpose factors, but nevertheless not be tied to predictable contexts of use.

The second summary factor, *audience*, refers to the class of reader for whom summaries are intended. Audiences may be more or less tightly characterized along a spectrum from *untargeted* to *targeted* in terms of assumed domain knowledge, language skill, etc. Thus the readers of a mass market women's magazine may be deemed untargeted with respect to summarizing a fiction serial, since they will be so varied in experience and interests. The audience for summaries in a professional abstract journal, say in the law, on the other hand, is (at least by comparison) targeted. There are, further, many possible specific audiences with different characteristic interests, for instance implying different summaries of the same manufactured product report. Defining the summary audience is important because, as already noted, it should not be taken as similar to the audience for the source.

The third purpose factor is *use*: what if the summary for? Possible uses for summaries include those as aids for *retrieving* source text, as means of *previewing* a text about to be read, as information-covering *substitutes* for their source text, as devices for *refreshing* the memory of an already-read source, as action *prompts* to read their sources. For example, a lecture course synopsis may be designed for previewing the course, and may therefore emphasize some information e.g., course objectives, over others.

The account of purpose factors just given is, like that of input factors, only a beginning. It is clearly necessary to develop a fuller view and characterization of purpose factors, as a basis for building generic systems with the capacity to meet purpose requirements and for analyzing individual applications in order to determine their requirements; and it is then necessary, for an application, to do this analysis. This can be expected to be much more detailed than the examples above, and to have quite detailed implications for the treatment of source text content in summarizing. Thus if we know that the summarizing audience is a particular scientific community, with a particular type of use for summaries in a particular type of situation, this could imply that one specific kind of scientific claim needs to be identified as the major claim in a source paper. As this also suggests, summarizing may not only rely on background domain knowledge and even import this into a summary where it is presumed but not given in the source (as in some frame-based approaches): it can rely on other forms of background knowledge and also import this, e.g., stating the situation for which a summary is produced.

Output factors

The final major class of factors is output factors. There are at least three major ones, namely *material, format,* and *style*.

The *material* factor refers to the extent to which the summary is intended to capture all of the important content in the source text, or only some aspects of it. The default case is that the summary is a *covering* one (subject to some concept grain level). But summaries may be designed to capture only some types of source information, for instance in astronomy papers what was observed, or for fiction only the plot, as well as only some concept instantiations as considered under fact extraction. These summaries are intentionally *partial*.

For the second output factor, *format*, we can see a broad distinction between summaries that are wholly or primarily *running* text, as in many journal paper abstracts, and those that are *headed*, where the summary material is tagged or organized by fields that may indeed be standardized across summaries, for example, using a 'Test results' heading in biological abstracts.

The third output factor is *style*. For example, a summary may be *informative*, conveying what the source text says about something; *indicative*, noting that the source is about some topic but not giving what it says about it; *critical*, as in a summary that reviews the merits of the source document; or *aggregative*, used here to define summaries where varied sources, including multiple ones of the same type, are deliberately set out in relation to one another, as in a judicial summing up. This is not an exhaustive (or exclusive) list of alternatives, only a start.

These output factors have also just been presented as free properties of an output summary text. But they of course follow from judgments about what the summary should be like given the nature of the input source and the purpose the summary is intended to satisfy. Thus a summary may only partially cover a source text because the purpose of the summary is to supply a certain kind of information, in condensed form, for a certain kind of use, regardless of other elements in the source. The relations between the three factor types can therefore be expressed as defining a summary *function*, which is: given Input Factor data, to satisfy Purpose Factor requirements, via Output Factor devices.

As this suggests, a quite full ground analysis of input and purpose factors is needed to reach the desired output properties for summaries. But at the same time the unavoidable indeterminacy of summary use (because summaries are made for *future* use) implies that the joint input and purpose characterization cannot simply mandate a specific choice of output factor properties. There will be a need for judgment as to the likely best ways of meeting the purpose requirements given the data characteristics, though if the input and purpose analysis has been well done the choices for output will be limited. These are in any case generic choices, they have to be carried through for each individual summary, applying primarily to the summarizing transformation and following through for the output generation.

An illustration

Book review summaries for librarian purchasers (in public libraries).

We assume a library service which distributes information about new books. This consists not only of basic information like bibliographic details and general type, for instance biography, history, fiction, but also summaries of reviews published in e.g., literary weeklies. The aim is to help librarians decide what to buy for their libraries.

The input factor characterization for this application is that the source texts (i.e., original reviews) have a form that is essentially simple running text; are variable in scale; have literary prose as their medium; and are single units. The purpose factors are a floating situation, since the summaries are distributed on a library mailing list without knowledge of their individual readers, or the precise circumstances in which they are used (e.g., what other information is combined with the mailing to determine purchasing); an untargeted audience, since public librarians vary widely though a general and professional education can be assumed; and summary use as a substitute for the original review, to which the librarians may not have ready access. Rational choices for the output summaries that follow from this input and purpose analysis are that the summaries should be covering ones, not selecting only some types of information from the original reviews; be delivered as simple running text attached to the bibliographic header supplemented by a specification of the source review location and writer; and that the style should be indicative of what aspects of the book the review considered and what attitude the reviewer took to it.

Given this starting position, but only from such a starting position, the details of how to produce the required summaries can be addressed.

Evaluation

A context factor analysis like that just listed is needed for appropriate strategy selection and parametrisation. It is also crucial for evaluation. It is impossible to evaluate summaries properly without knowing what they are for.

The two conventional approaches to evaluation, while not without some utility, are much less useful than might be supposed. One is to evaluate summary texts by comparison with their source texts, in an attempt to answer the question: Has the summary captured the important concepts (and concept relations) in the source? The problem with this approach is how to tell whether it has or not. Even if humans are rather better than current machines at identifying important concepts in discourse, it does not follow that they can be laid out or checked against one another in any simple way. or indeed that this human analysis will not introduce its own biases or have its own defects. The expression of the key concepts for comparative purposes gives language objects that are subject to all the variable interpretation that such objectives have, while their relation to their respective source and summary texts is inaccessible and is precisely what the summarizing process is seeking to capture. Manuals for professional abstractors (e.g., Rowley 1982) recommend that abstractors go over the source to check they have got the main points from it, but this assumes the capability we are trying to define.

In any case, as the discussion of factors brought out, the relation between source and summary need not be 'just' a reduced replication of the same key concepts. As the discussion implies, my original definition of summarizing has to be extended to allow for the use of and presentation in the output summary of information not in the original, and of the introduction of new perspectives on the original. More importantly, my definition of summarizing has to be extended, as a general definition, to recognize the role of summary purpose in determining the nature of the content condensation.

Thus while this comparative method of evaluation, setting summary against source, can be helpful as a development, or rapid vetting, tool, it does not provide an adequate base for rigorous evaluation. The same applies to the more limited, albeit more controllable, question method, designed to establish whether questions (about key content) that can be answered from the source text can also be answered from the summary.

The main alternative evaluation strategy is to compare automatically produced summaries with human ones for the same source. But again, even if we assume that the conditions of summarizing are understood and are the same in both cases, when dealing with content rather than extracted text determining that two texts share the same key ideas is far from trivial. This strategy moreover assumes that the human summary is itself the best reference standard, which is not necessarily the case, as many analogous studies of document indexing have shown. Thus automatic index descriptions of quite different types may be as effective for retrieval as manual ones (see e.g., Salton 1972, 1986; Cleverdon 1977). This 'human reference' approach to evaluation should therefore, like the previous one, be treated only as a rough, preliminary evaluation tool.

In either case, moreover, to make proper use even of these tools, it is essential to take into account what the summary conditions are. Comparison between source and summary for key concept capture should be modulo the pertinent context factors, and the same for comparisons between human and automatic summaries. It is evident, therefore, that it is much better to adopt an evaluation strategy that refers directly to the context constraints and in particular is based on summary purpose. This applies even where it may be thought legitimate to see whether one summary is like another, because the latter has already been shown suited to purpose: there is enough latitude in summarizing for it to be better to adopt the direct test for purpose.

This still, however, leaves much to be done not only in specifying the application constraints on summarizing in an individual case, but in the design and execution of the evaluation, notably the precise definition of evaluation goals and methodology including measures, data, procedures and so forth (Sparck Jones and Galliers 1996). For instance with the library purchasing example, evaluation could be from quite different perspectives, and a quite different levels of detail. Thus it could progress from very simple but still useful starting points, for instance answering just the question: Does the output summary include all the administrative information it ought, which can be rather easily checked. Then, making reference to the purpose for which the summaries are intended in a more direct and comprehensive way, an evaluation could be designed to answer the question: Does the summary allow librarians to reach decisions about whether to buy the book in question or not (though this strategy would have to allow for the fact that it could be the original review, and not the summary, that is defective if there is no decision.) Such an evaluation could be done by decision recording, say. It in principle addresses the key issue as to whether the summary transmits the kind of information pertinent to purchasing that could be drawn from the source review, where the first evaluation addresses only the system's ability to transmit supporting administrative data. But the key issue is still addressed only in rather a loose way. It would seem that summary quality (i.e., utility) could properly only be established by whether the librarians' decisions were 'correct', i.e., that decisions based on summaries were the same as those based on their source reviews. But while this might be determined by decision recording, as before, it would require careful sampling design to gather independent decisions, and could require quite a large scale study to compensate for other variables including, for instance, interaction effects with prices.

These are only some illustrative possibilities. The point is that it is always necessary to motivate whatever evaluation is conducted by reference to the ulterior purpose for which the summaries are intended, whatever particular perspective is adopted for the evaluation, and to work it out in detail. This is clearly a challenge for cases where summaries are envisaged as for multiple uses, and varied audiences, perhaps far in the future. The context factor analysis is nevertheless always required, as it is vital to the design and choice of summarizing strategies, even if the devil is in the detail of what follows from this analysis for strategy specification.

But context analysis also has a critical role to play in helping us, with the present state of the art in automatic summarizing to work from, to choose research directions for summarizing that would be both useful and feasible.

Research strategy

What, then, are the implications from the discussion of context factors for an advance on more powerful, general summarizing technology, and specifically for effective NLP techniques and system designs? In particular, while it is overall appropriate to exploit the factor analysis as a basis for developing much better methods of summarizing than we have now, discovering how to apply the analysis as a lever for source text *discourse* interpretation is a major, long-term, research enterprise. There is therefore every reason to pursue a parallel research strategy of a more practically-motivated and realistic sort aimed at developing useful summarizing methods, for at least some types of environment, in the short to medium term. This is subject to the important requirement that these should be general methods, i.e., not require heavy hand customization as exemplified by approaches relying on domain frames. Clearly, given this requirement, there will be types of, or individual, applications for which we cannot expect to supply a system; and we should allow, even with general strategies, for some parametrisation. But we should try to give substance to the idea of systems that at most require a little tailoring, or can be largely assembled from standard parts, rather than built from scratch as far as the central transformation component is concerned.

This implies focusing on environments where indicative, skeletal summaries are useful. That is, on environments where the user has a rather loose or coarsely defined task, has other aids to carrying out the task so high-class summaries of the kind exemplified by scientific journal abstracts are not required, and indeed for which summaries are not essential. Thus we should focus initially on environments where summaries are helpful but not vital. These should also be environments where the user is knowledgeable about the 'information scene', and where the user operates interactively so they can check or enlarge on their interpretation of a summary by reference to the background context, relate the summary to other sources of information, formulate and carry out their task in a flexible way, and so forth.

The goal is therefore to supply summaries that are 'sufficient for the day', for example, where the role of summaries is to facilitate browsing in an interactive information retrieval environment where there are other search tools available, as well as access to the source documents; or to provide notification about source documents where it is not necessary to do more than give some brief lead into source content, but it is desirable to do more substantial than supply an unstructured list of keywords. Both browsing and alerting are generic activities that can figure within many different encompassing task environments; there are many applications where providing users with word lists, or repeating brief document titles (assuming they exist), is not enough and where a short, readable text indicating the substance of a source document is really valuable.

Forward direction

Some work is already underway of this broad kind (e.g., Boguraev and Kennedy 1997). So my proposal that we should embark on it may appear, if not redundant, too unadventurous. But it is not really so. What is required is far from trivial, once the source *text* extraction strategy is abandoned, i.e., steps are taken towards source interpretation; and it can provide a good grounding for progress towards fuller and deeper interpretation. At the same time, as already claimed, success would be very handy right away. Boguraev and Kennedy's approach, and others reported in Mani and Maybury (1997), are still text based; so though they are generally more sophisticated than earlier systems, and may deliver useful outputs, these are still very limited as content summaries. It is clearly necessary to look for something more substantial.

Now to be more specific about the form nearer-term research strategies should take, i.e., about the type of method worth investigating (given current NLP capabilities). It has to be better than surface text extraction; but equally, for a generally-applicable system, cannot seek deep information like 'fact extraction' does.

I believe that the right direction to follow should start with *intermediate* source processing, as exemplified by sentence parsing to logical form, with local anaphor resolution. This is taking source text analysis as far as it can be taken on a linguistic basis, without a reference domain model. But with this initial processing we can still expect to get more manifest discourse entities and relations between them than the source text in itself supplies, and at the same time maintain a more sympathetic account of the original source than with the fact extraction method driven from prescribed selective fact types.

Processing in this way would, if carried no further, give an extremely shallow source representation as a sequence of sentence representations. But these can be linked by common elements to give a more integrated representation. This is still shallow, and unavoidably so, but has important advantages. It embodies some interpretation of the source text as a whole; and it is neutral, i.e., it is not biased towards any particular view of the source's content or prior specification of the form and content of the eventual summary. The general characteristics of such source representations, even on the rather strong assumption that current engines can deliver them reasonably reliably, and that the problem of competing sentence analyses can be finessed, clearly places some limits on what can be done in summarizing: thus without world knowledge, full discourse entity identification is impossible. But there is still large scope for different ways of exploiting the representation for summarizing purposes, and in particular scope for more than in approaches where the source representation is directly constructed as the summary one.

Thus we can seek to derive a summary representation using more than one type of data, notably statistical data about the frequency of entities (rather than just words), and markedness information, as represented by text location, discourse focus, or cue expressions. Markedness data can be associated with the representation and its discourse entities because the source representation is not too divorced from the original text (though precisely how far markedness data are retained during analysis depends in practice on the detailed style of a logical representation). However its value is enhanced by the fact that it is not tied to surface text strings as such, but to their propositional referents.

Then since a summary representation will be some derived logical form structure, it can be taken as an input to an output text generator.

The core argument on which this suggested sensible research strategy is based is that as full source text analysis is impossible at present or in the nearer term, but robust parsing is feasible now, this will get enough logical form predications for summarizing because extended text is *redundant*, especially with respect to key information. If text content is important, and it therefore mattered to the source writer that the source reader should get this information, it will be emphasized and reiterated. Then from the summarizing point of view, we can assume that even if the source representation is incomplete, both because our analyzers are only linguistic and because they are in practice imperfect, it will nevertheless capture most, if not all, of what is important in the source text. This will apply whether the representation is incomplete but so to speak evenly so, through systematic limitations on analysis, or is incomplete and unevenly so, because of specific analysis failures. In the first case, what is important in the source should still be relatively more prominent; in the second, what is important will be retained one way or another.

Clearly, without full source interpretation, we may expect to miss some material detail, for example, the quantification an initial purely linguistic parsing into logical form does not usually deliver or, as mentioned earlier, full co-reference identification. The question is whether enough of the key source content will be captured for a fairly sound if not wholly accurate summary. In particular, will this approach lead to a better, if still somewhat schematic, picture of the source than the text extraction technique?

The challenge for the proposed strategy is in filling in the necessary detail: building the source logical form representations that capture discourse entities, their relations, and their relative status; and deriving the summary representation from this; also, evaluating the resulting summary texts for applications. Evaluation will not be easy: if the summaries are intended to assist tolerant but rational users with rather loosely defined tasks and varied tools for executing these, this can be expected to make evaluation to determine the (comparative) merits of (alternative) summaries more, not less, difficult.

An illustration

To flesh out the proposal, though without claiming that what follows is the only or best individual approach, I shall take work by Richard Tucker in progress at Cambridge. This illustrates the kind of shallow approach advocated, being studied within an experimental rig designed to test a range of detailed particular variations on the generic strategy, with unrestricted news story texts as sources.

In the input interpretation stage of processing, sentences are parsed into quasi-logical forms using the SRI Cambridge Core Language Engine (Alshawi 1992). This delivers predications with as much disambiguation as can be achieved by using purely linguistic resources, but without quantification since this requires domain context information. The sentence representations are then decomposed into their simple, atomic predications, and these are linked to build up the overall source representation as a *cohesion graph*. The graph nodes are the simple predications, and links between them are of different types based on common predicates, common arguments within sentences, or similar arguments across sentences. The last is a relatively weak form of connection, based on having the same semantic head: establishing stronger connections presupposes the ability to determine actual entity relations, which as already noted cannot in general be achieved using only linguistic means and without quantification structure. The weaker, primarily semantic relationships embodied in the cohesion graph may nevertheless be adequate for the level of summarizing being sought: even if the specific discourse entities cannot be identified, the sort of entity that is involved can, and this may be convey sufficient information for summary utility: thus it may be enough to know a source is about films, without knowing whether it is about one or several. There may be a single graph covering the whole source text, or perhaps several graphs. The main desideratum is at least a fair degree of cross-sentence linkage, and if the original is coherent (if only because redundant), this can be expected.

One advantage of the decomposition to atomic predications is that even if there are alternative parsings for whole sentences, they may share these constituents, so limiting representation to just one, possibly incorrect, sentence parsing may not be too damaging.

The transformation step, deriving the summary representation from the source one, identifies the node set, i.e., predication set, forming the summary content. It exploits weights for the graph edge types, applying a scoring function seeking *centrality, representativeness,* and *coherence* in the node set, i.e., a function that considers both the status of a node set in relation to the larger graph and the status of the individual nodes in a set in relation to one another. The node set extraction is done by a greedy algorithm, and can deliver different node sets according to the relative importance attached to the scoring criteria, as well as to their detailed definition.

The generation step synthesizes the output summary text from the selected predications. This may, however, be text only in a rather restricted sense, since the data for doing the synthesis is limited. This is because the individual source predications may be only fragments, whether because source parsing has failed, or because the simple predications derived from the sentence decomposition are incomplete: in some cases atomic predications are more organizational devices than substantial, and in some cases they are partial because referential expressions are not resolved. Thus even assuming that the method of identifying important content has worked correctly, the final output summary is best described as a 'semi-text' indicative summary noting the main topics of the source document. Clearly some method for organizing and ordering the output material is needed, but in the experimental work so far with short sources and brief summaries this issue has not been seriously addressed. Thus the current procedure essentially groups predications with shared arguments, constructs logical forms for these predication clusters and any unattached predications, and applies the CLE to synthesize output. This may consist of sentences or, for fragmentary predications, mere phrases; and the presentation can follow, as far as possible, the original source ordering of the material.

As a whole, the approach to summarizing just described is a new version of an old generic idea, i.e., that of representing a source text as a network and looking for key nodes or node structures (see e.g., Skorohod'ko 1972; Benbrahim and Ahmad 1994), which has also now been explored as a means of summarizing multiple documents (Salton et al. 1997). But this network view has usually been applied at the text level, with links between surface or slightly normalized words or expressions, though there may have been an assumption, especially with the latter, that these were or were approximations to predications. Taylor (see Taylor and Krulee 1977) envisaged using a deeper source text analysis along with graph abstraction from the resulting semantic network, but his approach seems to have been only partially implemented and rather modestly tested. The major step taken in the research just described has been to be much more thorough about the source text interpretation into logical form, and to carry through a computational implementation (if only a laboratory trial one) using modern NLP techniques, as well as to explore the graph-processing possibilities more fully.

Tucker's strategy clearly depends on some assumptions and raises some issues; and both this specific approach to shallow summarizing using intermediate source representations and graph structures, and others in the same broad class, have in particular to be evaluated by comparison with surface text extraction methods, whether these are ones delivering whole sentences or just providing simple key term lists.

The key assumptions are

1. that source text content is intrinsically complex, i.e., involves substantive meaning relations between con-

cepts;

2. that (for many purposes) a summary that 'covers' what is important for a source as a whole is required; and

3. that in order to convey structured content, a summary also has to be a text.

These assumptions may not seem controversial, but at least some work on summarizing rejects them. They imply that summarizing requires text meaning representations; and the argument is that even though general-purpose, purely linguistic text processing can only deliver meaning representations that are weak in principle (as well as defective in practice), these are still superior to source texts themselves for summarizing precisely because they support the identification of local and global topic structure, which is grounded in predicate-argument relational units. The presumption is that topics have structure that has to be captured and conveyed in a more sophisticated and explicit way than by simple word occurrences and co-occurrences; this begins with individual elementary predication units and extends to connected predications. Further, though the basic predications are underspecified, and the graph links between nodes that assume predicate or argument similarity do this only in a non-referential way, this is sufficient to *indicate* topics. The graph operations naturally aggregate information, which is taken further in synthesis by clustering and a preference for more inclusive predication structures; there is also some generalization, in the sense that selection omits detail. Finally, the way logical form decomposes text into multiple predications supplies a better frequency marking for important entities, to anchor the whole process of identifying summary material, than simple word frequency.

Results from the work are currently being evaluated. In the absence of a task context, evaluation is limited to simple acceptability to human readers, and comparisons with statistically-based extraction methods. Thus the system can be used as a way of identifying key sentences, i.e., those manifesting key predicate-argument structures, which can be compared with the output from simpler, purely statistical techniques. Again, since its ordinary output is rather minimal as text, this can be compared, if only informally, with phrases obtained by proximity or very shallow parsing methods. (Whether this type of output is more useful than extracted paragraph-length passages, or than visualizations of underlying graph structures, requires a functional context.) In the work described, there are many system parameters, e.g., the link weighting scheme, the definition of representative subgraph, so many comparative experiments within its own framework are required, as well as tests against outputs from other general-purpose approaches.

But more broadly, to test the general claims that underlie this whole approach, there are many important problems and issues to address. These include

1. coping with analysis limitations (e.g., minimal word sense disambiguation) and failures (e.g., fragmentary representations);

2. incorporating direct content significance markers like cue expressions, and indirect ones like discourse structure indicators;

3. exploiting direct information about lexical frequencies, i.e., statistical data;

4. taking advantage of additional general-purpose resources, e.g., thesauri, term hierarchies;

5. extracting large-scale topic organization from the basic network;

6. addressing output presentation mechanisms, whether referring to source constraints or new summary ones;

7. determining tradeoffs between computational effort and output utility.

It is not evident precisely what may be useful or attainable: for instance the analogy with document indexing suggests that the lack of sense disambiguation may matter less than is assumed, because lexical conjunction achieves it sufficiently for the user, even if word meanings remain broad. But these questions have to be explored. In addition, there is a need for fully functional evaluation.

Conclusion

This research program is feasible, and it will be worthwhile if it leads to better (i.e., more useful) summaries than extraction-based methods, for which Brandow, Mitze and Rau (1995) may be taken as representative. Thus my argument is that pushing forward with shallow summarizing strategies of the kind described has three important advantages. We already have the NLP technology to start; we should get something that is practically valuable; and we can learn from the tougher cases. Thus we may gain insight into discourse structure through using predication networks, and we may be able to gain insight into the best ways of exploiting what in practice may be very limited domain information.

Finally, the approach has the merit of being naturally extensible or adaptable to longer texts, and in particular longer texts than ones often encountered in summarizing aimed at fair source coverage. The claim on which a shallow approach like that described is based is that what is important in a text will 'shine through' rough and partial source interpretation. Longer text summarization has to be addressed, because the need for summaries is stronger, while the challenge for reduction is greater. In the type of approach adopted, statistics and and markedness clues can both be expected to be more in evidence and hence more readily exploitable. Thus there should be a natural route forward for scalable summarizing.

References

Alshawi, H. ed. 1992. *The Core Language Engine.* Cambridge MA: MIT Press.

Benbrahim, M. and Ahmad, K. 1994. Computer-aided lexical cohesion analysis and text abridgement. Report CS-94-11. Computer Sciences Department, University of Surrey, Guildford, England.

Boguraev, B., and Kennedy, C. 1997. Salience-based content characterization of text documents. In Mani, I. and Maybury, M. eds. *Intelligent scaleable text summarization*, 2-9. Proceedings of a Workshop Sponsored by the ACL. Somerset NJ: Association for Computational Linguistics.

Brandow, R.; Mitze, K.; and Rau, L.F. 1995. Automatic condensation of electronic publications by sentence selection. *Information Processing and Management* 31 (5): 675-685.

Cleverdon, C.W. 1977. A computer evaluation of searching by controlled language and natural language in an experimental NASA database. Rep. ESA 1/432. European Space Agency, Frascati, Italy.

DeJong, G.F. 1982. An overview of the FRUMP system. In Lehnert, W.G. and Ringle, M.H. eds. *Strategies for natural language processing*, 149-176. Hillsdale NJ: Lawrence Erlbaum.

Endres-Niggemeyer, B.; Hobbs, J.; and Sparck Jones, K. eds. 1995. *Summarizing text for intelligent communication.* Dagstuhl Seminar Report 79, 13.12-17.12.93 (9350), IBFI, Schloss Dagstuhl, Wadern, Germany, 1995. (Full version: http://www.bid.fh-hannover.de/SimSum/Abstract/)

Evans, R., et al. 1996. POETIC: a system for gathering and disseminating traffic information *Natural Language Engineering*, 1 (4): 1-25.

Hahn, U. and Strube, M. 1997. Centering in-the-large: computing referential discourse segments. *Proceedings of the 35th Annual Meeting of the Association for Computational Linguistics and the 8th Conference of the European Chapter of the Association for Computational Linguistics*, 104-111. Somerset NJ: Association for Computational Linguistics.

Hearst, M. 1994. Multi-paragraph segmentation of expository text. *Proceedings of the 32nd Annual Meeting of the Association for Computational Linguistics*, 9-16. Somerset NJ: Association for Computational Linguistics.

IPM. 1995. Special Issue: Summarizing Text. *Information Processing and Management*, 31 (5): 625-784.

Mani, I. and Bloedorn, E. 1997. Multi-document summarization by graph search and matching. *Proceedings of the Fourteenth National Conference on Artificial Intelligence (AAAI-97)*, Providence, RI, July 27-31, 1997, pp. 622-628. Also available at http://xxx.lanl.gov/abs/cmp-lg/9712004.

Mani, I. and Maybury, M. eds. 1997. *Intelligent scalable text summarization.* Proceedings of a Workshop Sponsored by the ACL. Somerset NJ: Association for Computational Linguistics.

Marcu, D. 1997. From discourse structures to text summaries. In Mani, I. and Maybury, M. eds. *Intelligent scalable text summarization*, 82-88. Proceedings of a Workshop Sponsored by the ACL. Somerset NJ: Association for Computational Linguistics.

McKeown, K.; Robin, J.; and Kukich, K. 1995. Generating concise natural language summaries. *Information Processing and Management*, 31 (5): 703-733.

Paice, C.D. 1990. Constructing literature abstracts by computer: techniques and prospects. *Information Processing and Management*, 26 (2): 171-186.

Rowley, J. 1982. *Abstracting and indexing.* London: Bingley.

Salton, G. 1972. A new comparison between conventional indexing (Medlars) and automatic text processing (SMART). *Journal of the American Society for Information Science*, 23 (2): 75-84.

Salton, G. 1986. Another look at automatic text-retrieval systems. *Communications of the ACM*, 29 (7): 648-656.

Salton, G., et al. 1997. Automatic text structuring and summarization. *Information Processing and Management*, 33 (2): 193-207.

Skorokhod'ko, E.F. 1972. Adaptive method of automatic abstracting and indexing. In Freiman, C.V. ed. *Information Processing 71*, 1179-1182. (Proceedings of IFIP Congress 71), Amsterdam: North-Holland,

Sparck Jones, K. 1993. What might be in a summary? In Knorz, G.; Krause, J.; and Womser-Hacker, C. *Information Retrieval 93: Von der Modellierung zur Anwendung*, 9-26. Proceedings der 1. Tagung, Information Retrieval '93. Konstanz: Universitatsverlag Konstanz. (http://www.cl.cam.ac.uk/public/papers/ksj/ksj-whats-in-a-summary.ps.gz)

Sparck Jones, K. 1995. *Discourse modelling for automatic summarizing*, (Technical Report 290, Computer Laboratory, University of Cambridge, 1993.) In Hajičová. E., et al. eds. *Travaux du Cercle Linguistique de Prague* (Prague Linguistic Circle Papers). New Series, Volume 1, 201-227. Amsterdam: John Benjamins.

Sparck Jones, K. and Galliers, J.R. 1996. *Evaluating natural language processing systems.* Lecture Notes in Artificial Intelligence 1083. Berlin: Springer.

Taylor, S.L. and Krulee, G.K. 1977. Experiments with an automatic abstracting system. *Proceedings of the ASIS Annual Meeting,* Volume 14. Washington DC: American Society for Information Science.

Young, S.R. and Hayes, P.J. 1985. Automatic classification and summarization of banking telexes. *Proceedings, Second Conference on Artificial Intelligence Applications,* 402-408. New York, NY: Institute of Electrical and Electronics Engineers.

Section 1

Classical Approaches

The articles in this first section open the book by outlining simple but powerful techniques for automated summarization. They are classical both temporally, originating with work from 40 years ago, as well as technically, serving as a fundamental basis for both practical applications as well as motivating subsequent research.

In perhaps the first computational paper on automated extraction, Luhn (1958) describes a simple, genre-specific technique that uses term frequencies to weight sentences which are then extracted to form an abstract. Luhn was motivated by the need to deal with the problem of information overload, which may seem ironic more than 40 years later, in our era of a rapidly expanding global information web. Luhn cites some benefits of automatic abstracting: it is inexpensive compared to human effort and, unlike humans, it is consistent and avoids the subjectivity and variability observed in human abstractors (see Rath et al., Section 5).

Luhn's algorithm first filters terms in the document using a stop-list of closed-class words such as pronouns, prepositions, and articles. Next, terms are normalized based on aggregating together orthographically similar terms: Pairs of terms (e.g., "similar" and "similarity") are matched at each character position. Once a mismatch occurs, the number of non-similar subsequent letters of both terms is counted. If this count is less than 6, these terms are aggregated together. The frequencies of these aggregate terms in the document are noted, and low-frequency terms are removed. Sentences are then weighted using the resulting set of "significant" terms and a term density measure. Each sentence is divided into segments bracketed by significant terms not more than four non-significant terms apart. Each segment is scored by taking the square of the number of bracketed significant terms divided by the total number of bracketed terms. The score of the highest scoring segment is taken as the sentence score.

Luhn describes several possible extensions to the basic algorithm, such as varying the length of the abstract, and giving an added premium to words in a domain-specific word list (i.e., "bonus" words). He also mentions the possibility of applying the algorithm to foreign languages in order to create abstracts, which could then be translated to avoid translating the full document. Finally, he also suggests using these techniques to generate index terms for information retrieval.

Luhn's basic idea of a statistical approach to text summarization, relying on ingredients such as term frequency and term normalization, has had a considerable influence on the field. In addition, the problem of text segmentation continues to be of interest. Subsequent progress in the field, however, allows one to identify some aspects of his approach that are no longer ideal. The particular type of term aggregation and normalization Luhn uses has since been supplanted by the use of stemming (Frakes 1992) or (especially for languages with rich morphology) morphological analysis; see also papers by Hovy and Lin and Aone et al. in Section 2 for further varieties of term aggregation. In information retrieval, absolute term frequency by itself is recognized as being less useful than term frequencies which are normalized to take into account document length and frequency in a collection (Harman 1992). Finally, thematic features such as term frequency by themselves are somewhat less useful in summarization compared to other features such as title or location, as shown in Edmundson's paper in this section, and also in the papers by Kupiec in Section 2 as well as Teufel and Moens in Section 3.

The next paper by Edmundson (1969) extends earlier work to look at three features in addition to word frequencies: cue phrases (e.g., "significant," "impossible," "hardly"), title and heading words, and sentence location. Edmundson created programs to weight sentences based on each of the four methods: cue phrase, keyword (i.e., term frequency based), location, and title. He then evaluated each of the programs by comparison against manually created extracts. He used a corpus-based methodology, dividing his set of articles into a training and test set. In the training phase, he used feedback from evaluations to readjust (by hand) the weights used by each of the programs, which were then tested and evaluated on the test data. Edmundson found that the three additional features dominated word frequency measures in the creation of better extracts. He also found that the combination of cue-title-location was the best, with location being the best individual feature and keywords alone the worst-performing algorithm.

The investigations reported by Pollock and Zamora (1975) at the Chemical Abstracts Service (CAS) provide further insight into the effectiveness of automated extraction for particular subject areas. Their system, developed at a time when not much full-text was available on-line, is focused on generating abstracts (compressed at 20% of the original) of chemistry articles. The system relies on the use of cue-phrases specific to chemistry subdomains. Cue phrases are used as positive (bonus word) and negative (stigma word) tests for sentences to be included in the summary. Term frequencies are used mainly to modulate the effects of cue phrases. Since a text which has lots of positive terms could end up having a longer summary, some control over compression is achieved by making positive terms which occur frequently in the text have less positive weight, and having negative terms which occur frequently in the text contribute less negative weight. In addition, the frequency criteria help tune the impact of the word-list for each chemistry subdomain. For example, in articles on photographic chemistry, *negative* would have less of a negative impact.

In contrast to the previous two papers, Pollock and Zamora carry out elimination operations aimed at sentence compaction[1]. The terms in the word-list also have part-of-speech information (noun, verb, etc., unambiguously specified), used mainly in contextual tests to classify commas in the text, the latter in order to identify clause boundaries. Introductory and parenthetical clauses, as well as phrases ending in "that" (likely to be followed by a conclusion) or beginning with "in" (e.g., "in conclusion") are deleted from the final summary. A particularly interesting feature is the normalization of vocabulary in the output, to ensure that the abstracts satisfy CAS standards; these include abbreviation of words or phrases, standardizing non-US spellings, and replacement of chemical compound names with formulas. The authors conclude that while the overall quality of the abstracts is lower than that of good manual abstracts, they believe the automatically generated ones are "functionally adequate."

These early ground-breaking systems started off the discipline of text summarization smartly. The fairly straightforward early systems worked remarkably well. Indeed, extracting sentences on the basis of features such as word-counts, location, and cue phrases remain important techniques especially in commercial extraction systems today. We also see in these early papers a focus on evaluation of both human and machine performance. There are even suggestions in these early works of the importance of tailoring summarization techniques to the source domain and user. Authors of these early works also point to foreign language summary, problems only recently being given new-found attention.

A number of issues that remain concerns today were raised from the very beginning, including: What are the most powerful but also more general features to exploit for summarization? How do we combine these features? How can we evaluate how well we are doing? These questions have attracted the attention of a lot of subsequent research, and are discussed in remaining sections of this book. The corpus-based approaches in Section 2 extend the work of Edmundson to address these and other questions, and the papers in Section 5 address fundamental issues in evaluation.

---

[1] For a recent approach to compaction, see (Grefenstette 1998).

References

Frakes, W.B. 1992. Stemming Algorithms. In Frakes, W.B., and Baeza-Yates, R., *Information Retrieval - Data Structures and Algorithms*, Prentice Hall. 131-160.

Grefenstette, G. 1998. Producing Intelligent Telegraphic Text Reduction to Provide and Audio Scanning Service for the Blind. In *Working Notes of the AAAI Spring Symposium on Intelligent Text Summarization*, Spring 1998, 111-117. Menlo Park, Calif.: AAAI Press.

Harman, D. 1992. Ranking Algorithms. In Frakes, W.B., and Baeza-Yates, R., *Information Retrieval - Data Structures and Algorithms*, Prentice Hall. 363-392.

Harman, D., and Voorhees, E.M. 1996. *The Fifth Text Retrieval Conference (TREC-5)*, Technical Report, SP-500-238, National Institute of Standards and Technology, Gaithersburg, Maryland.

H. P. Luhn

The Automatic Creation of Literature Abstracts*

Abstract: Excerpts of technical papers and magazine articles that serve the purposes of conventional abstracts have been created entirely by automatic means. In the exploratory research described, the complete text of an article in machine-readable form is scanned by an IBM 704 data-processing machine and analyzed in accordance with a standard program. Statistical information derived from word frequency and distribution is used by the machine to compute a relative measure of significance, first for individual words and then for sentences. Sentences scoring highest in significance are extracted and printed out to become the "auto-abstract."

Introduction

The purpose of abstracts in technical literature is to facilitate quick and accurate identification of the topic of published papers. The objective is to save a prospective reader time and effort in finding useful information in a given article or report.

The preparation of abstracts is an intellectual effort, requiring general familiarity with the subject. To bring out the salient points of an author's argument calls for skill and experience. Consequently a considerable amount of qualified manpower that could be used to advantage in other ways must be diverted to the task of facilitating access to information. This widespread problem is being aggravated by the ever-increasing output of technical literature. But another problem — perhaps equally acute — is that of achieving consistence and objectivity in abstracts.

The abstracter's product is almost always influenced by his background, attitude, and disposition. The abstracter's own opinions or immediate interests may sometimes bias his interpretation of the author's ideas. The quality of an abstract of a given article may therefore vary widely among abstracters, and if the same person were to abstract an article again at some other time, he might come up with a different product.

The application of machine methods to literature searching is currently receiving a great deal of attention and now indicates that both human effort and bias may be eliminated from the abstracting process. Although rapid progress is being made in the development of systems using modern electronic data-processing devices,

their efficiency depends on availability of literary information in machine-readable form. It is evident that the transcription of existing printed text into this form would have to be done manually at this time. In the future, however, print-reading devices should be sufficiently developed for this task. For material not yet printed, tape-punching devices attached to typewriters and typesetting machines could readily produce machine-readable records as by-products.

This paper describes some exploratory research on automatic methods of obtaining abstracts. The system outlined here begins with the document in machine-readable form and proceeds by means of a programmed sampling process comparable to the scanning a human reader would do. However, instead of sampling at random, as a reader normally does when scanning, the new mechanical method selects those among all the sentences of an article that are the most representative of pertinent information. These key sentences are then enumerated to serve as clues for judging the character of the article. Thus, citations of the author's own statements constitute the "auto-abstract."

The programs for creating auto-abstracts must be based on properties of writing ascertained *by analysis of specific types of literature.* Because the use of abstracts is an established practice in science and technology, it seemed desirable to develop the method first for papers and articles in this area. A primary objective of the development was to arrive at a system that could take full advantage of the capabilities of a modern electronic data-processing system such as the IBM 704 or 705, while at the same time keeping the scheme as simple as possible.

*Presented at IRE National Convention, New York, March 24, 1958.

Measuring significance

To determine which sentences of an article may best serve as the auto-abstract, a measure is required by which the information content of all the sentences can be compared and graded. Since the suitability of each sentence is relative, a value can be assigned to each in accordance with the quality criterion of significance.

The "significance" factor of a sentence is derived from an analysis of its words. It is here proposed that the frequency of word occurrence in an article furnishes a useful measurement of word significance. It is further proposed that the relative position within a sentence of words having given values of significance furnishes a useful measurement for determining the significance of sentences. The significance factor of a sentence will therefore be based on a combination of these two measurements.

It should be emphasized that this system is based on the capabilities of machines, not of human beings. Therefore, regrettable as it might appear, the intellectual aspects of writing and of meaning cannot serve as elements of such machine systems. To a machine, words can be only so many physical things. It can find out whether or not certain such things are similar and how many of them there are. The machine can remember such findings and can perform arithmetic on those which can be counted. It can do all of this by means of suitable program instructions. The human intellect need be relied upon only to prepare the program.

Establishing a set of significant words

The justification of measuring word significance by use-frequency is based on the fact that a writer normally repeats certain words as he advances or varies his arguments and as he elaborates on an aspect of a subject. This means of emphasis is taken as an indicator of significance. The more often certain words are found in each other's company within a sentence, the more significance may be attributed to each of these words. Though certain other words must be present to serve the important function of tying these words together, the type of significance sought here does not reside in such words. If such common words can be segregated substantially by non-intellectual methods, they could then be excluded from consideration.

This rather unsophisticated argument on "significance" avoids such linguistic implications as grammar and syntax. In general, the method does not even propose to differentiate between word forms. Thus the variants *differ, differentiate, different, differently, difference* and *differential* could ordinarily be considered identical notions and regarded as the same word. No attention is paid to the logical and semantic relationships the author has established. In other words, an inventory is taken and a word list compiled in descending order of frequency.

Procedures as simple as these, of course, are rewarding from the standpoint of economy. The more complex the method, the more operations must the machine perform and therefore the more costly will be the process. But in

this case an even more fundamental justification for simplicity can be found in the nature of technical writing. Within a technical discussion, there is a very small probability that a given word is used to reflect more than one notion. The probability is also small that an author will use different words to reflect the same notion. Even if the author makes a reasonable effort to select synonyms for stylistic reasons, he soon runs out of legitimate alternatives and falls into repetition if the notion being expressed was potentially significant in the first place.

A word list compiled in accordance with the method outlined will generally take the form of the diagram in Fig. 1. The presence in the region of highest frequency of many of the words previously described as too common to have the type of significance being sought would constitute "noise" in the system. This noise can be materially reduced by an elimination technique in which text words are compared with a stored common-word list. A simpler way might be to determine a high-frequency cutoff through statistical methods to establish "confidence limits." If the line C in the figure represents this cutoff, only words to its right would be considered suitable for indicating significance. Since degree of frequency has been proposed as a criterion, a lower boundary, line D, would also be established to bracket the portion of the spectrum that would contain the most useful range of words. Establishing optimum locations for both lines would be a matter of experience with appropriately large samples of published articles. It should even be possible to adjust these locations to alter the characteristics of the output.

The curve for the degree of discrimination, or "resolving power," of the bracketed words in the figure might look something like the dotted line, E. It is apparent that words that cannot be put in the category of common words may sometimes fall to the left of line C. If the program has been properly formulated, the location of these words on the diagram would indicate their loss of discriminatory power. The word "cell" in an article on biology may be an example of this. It may be anticipated that the cutoff line, once established, may be stable over many different degrees of specialization within a field, or even over many different fields. Moreover, the resolving power would increase with the need for finer resolution. The case of a common word falling in the region to the right of line C can be tolerated because of its lesser degree of interference.

Establishing relative significance of sentences

As pointed out earlier, the method to be developed here is a probabilistic one based on the physical properties of written texts. No consideration is to be given to the meaning of words or the arguments expressed by word combinations. Instead it is here argued that, whatever the topic, the closer certain words are associated, the more specifically an aspect of the subject is being treated. Therefore, wherever the greatest number of frequently occurring different words are found in greatest physical proximity to each other, the probability is very high that the information being conveyed is most representative of the article.

The significance of degree of proximity is based on the characteristics of spoken and written language in that ideas most closely associated intellectually are found to be implemented by words most closely associated physically. The divisions of written text into sentences, paragraphs, chapters, et cetera, is another physical manifestation of the graduating degree of association of ideas. These aspects have been discussed in detail in an earlier paper by the writer.*

From these considerations a "significance factor" can be derived which reflects the number of occurrences of significant words within a sentence and the linear distance between them due to the intervention of non-significant words. All sentences may be ranked in order of their significance according to this factor, and one or several of the highest ranking sentences may then be selected to serve as the auto-abstract.

*H. P. Luhn, "A Statistical Approach to Mechanized Encoding and Searching of Literary Information," *IBM Journal of Research and Development*, 1, No. 4, 309-317 (October 1957).

It must be kept in mind that, when a statistical procedure is applied to produce such rankings, the criterion is the relationship of the significant words to each other rather than their distribution over a whole sentence. It therefore appears proper to consider only those portions of sentences which are bracketed by significant words and to set a limit for the distance at which any two significant words shall be considered as being significantly related. A significant word beyond that limit would then be disregarded from consideration in a given bracket, although it might form a bracket, or cluster, in conjunction with other words in the sentence. An analysis of many documents has indicated that a useful limit is four or five non-significant words between significant words. If with this separation two or more clusters result, the highest one of the several significance factors is taken as the measure for that sentence.

A scheme for computing the significance factor is given by way of example in Fig. 2. It consists of ascertaining the extent of a cluster of words by bracketing, counting the number of significant words contained in the cluster, and dividing the square of this number by the

Figure 1 **Word-frequency diagram.**
Abscissa represents individual words arranged in order of frequency.

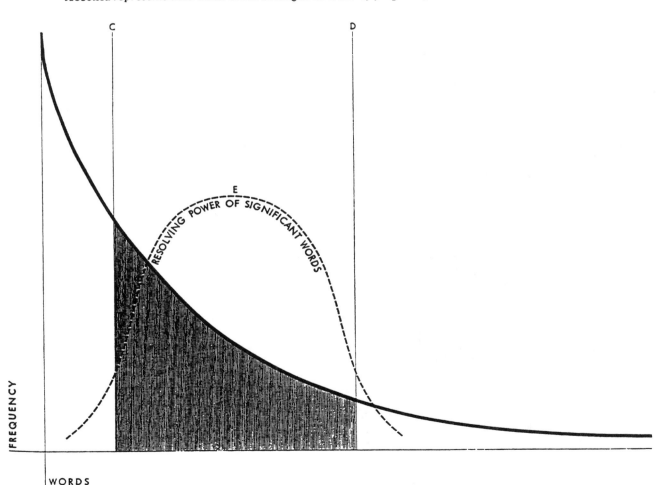

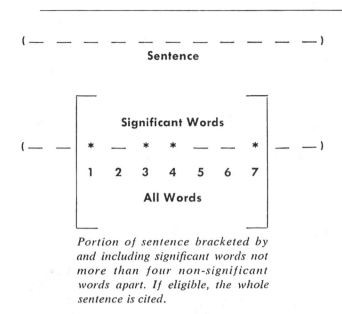

Portion of sentence bracketed by and including significant words not more than four non-significant words apart. If eligible, the whole sentence is cited.

Figure 2 **Computation of significance factor.**
The square of the number of bracketed significant words (4) divided by the total number of bracketed words (7) = 2.3.

total number of words within this cluster. The results based on this formula, as performed on about 50 articles ranging from 300 to 4,500 words each, have been encouraging enough for further evaluation by a psychological experiment involving 100 people. This experiment will determine on an objective basis the effectiveness of the abstracts generated.

The resolving power of significant words derived under the method described depends on the total number of words comprising an article and will decrease as the total number of words increases. In order to overcome this effect, the abstracting process may be performed on subdivisions of the article, and the highest ranking sentences of each of these divisions may then be selected and combined to constitute the auto-abstract. In many cases the author provides such divisions as part of the organization of his paper, and they may therefore serve for the extended process. Where such deliberate divisions are absent they can be made arbitrarily in accordance with some criteria established by experience. These divisions would be arranged in such a way that they overlap each other, for lack of any simple means of mechanically detecting the exact point of the author's transition to a new subject subdivision.

A more detailed account of these and other computing methods, as well as details on programming electronic data-processing machines for this procedure, will be given in subsequent papers.

By way of example, two auto-abstracts are included in this paper. Exhibit 1 shows four selected sentences of a 2,326-word article from *The Scientific American*. A table of word frequency is also given. Exhibit 2 shows the highest ranking sentence of a 783-word article from the Science Section of *The New York Times*. A complete reproduction of this article is given.

Machine procedures

The abstracts described in this paper were prepared by first punching the documents on cards. Punctuation marks in the printed text not available on the standard key punch were replaced by other key-punch characters. The cards thus produced constitute the machine-readable form of the document.

The abstracting process was initiated by transcribing the card record onto magnetic tape by means of an auxiliary card-to-tape unit. The resulting tape was introduced into an IBM 704 data-processing machine, which was programmed to read the taped text to separate it into its individual words, to note the position of each word in the document, the sentence and paragraph in which it appeared, and to note the punctuation preceding and following it. Concurrently, common words such as pronouns, prepositions, and articles were deleted from the list by a table-lookup routine. This operation was followed by a sorting program which arranged the remaining words in alphabetic order.

The next step of the machine operation was a consolidation of words which are spelled in the same way at their beginning, such as *similar* and *similarity*. This procedure was a simple statistical analysis routine consisting of a letter-by-letter comparison of pairs of succeeding words in the alphabetized list. From the point where letters failed to coincide, a combined count was taken of the non-similar subsequent letters of both words. When this count was six or below, the words were assumed to be similar notions; above six, different notions. Although this method of word consolidation is not infallible, errors up to 5% did not seem to affect the final results of the abstracting process. The machine then counted the occurrence of similar words derived in this way. Words of a stipulated low frequency were then deleted from the list and locations of the remaining words were sorted into order. These words thereby attained the status of "significant" words.

The significance factor for each sentence was determined by a computing routine in accordance with the formula previously mentioned. All sentences which scored above a predetermined cutoff value were written on an output tape along with their respective values. The basis for this cutoff value depends on the amount of detailed information needed for a given type of abstract. Results were then printed out from this tape.

Extended applications

Although a standard abstract has thus far been assumed in order to simplify the explanation of the machine process, extracts or condensations of literature are used for diverse purposes and may vary in length and orientation.

Exhibit 1

Source: The Scientific American, Vol. 196, No. 2, 86-94, February, 1957

Title: Messengers of the Nervous System

Author: Amodeo S. Marrazzi

Editor's Sub-heading: The internal communication of the body is mediated by chemicals as well as by nerve impulses. Study of their interaction has developed important leads to the understanding and therapy of mental illness.

Auto-Abstract*

It seems reasonable to credit the single-celled organisms also with a system of chemical communication by diffusion of stimulating substances through the cell, and these correspond to the chemical messengers (e.g., hormones) that carry stimuli from cell to cell in the more complex organisms. (7.0)†

Finally, in the vertebrate animals there are special glands (e.g., the adrenals) for producing chemical messengers, and the nervous and chemical communication systems are intertwined: for instance, release of adrenalin by the adrenal gland is subject to control both by nerve impulses and by chemicals brought to the gland by the blood. (6.4)

The experiments clearly demonstrated that acetylcholine (and related substances) and adrenalin (and its relatives) exert opposing actions which maintain a balanced regulation of the transmission of nerve impulses. (6.3)

It is reasonable to suppose that the tranquilizing drugs counteract the inhibitory effect of excessive adrenalin or serotonin or some related inhibitor in the human nervous system. (7.3)

*Sentences selected by means of statistical analysis as having a degree of significance of 6 and over.
†Significance factor is given at the end of each sentence.

Significant words in descending order of frequency (common words omitted).

46	nerve	12	body	6	disturbance	4	accumulate
40	chemical	12	effects	6	related	4	balance
28	system	12	electrical	5	control	4	block
22	communication	12	mental	5	diagram	4	disorders
19	adrenalin	12	messengers	5	fibers	4	end
18	cell	10	signals	5	gland	4	excitation
18	synapse	10	stimulation	5	mechanisms	4	health
16	impulses	8	action	5	mediators	4	human
16	inhibition	8	ganglion	5	organism	4	outgoing
15	brain	7	animal	5	produce	4	reaching
15	transmission	7	blood	5	regulate	4	recording
13	acetylcholine	7	drugs	5	serotonin	4	release
13	experiment	7	normal			4	supply
13	substances					4	tranquilizing

Total word occurrences in the document: 2326

Different words in document:

Total of different words 741

Less different common words 170

Different non-common words 571

Ratio of all word occurrences to different non-common words . . . . ~4:1

Non-common words having a frequency of occurrence of 5 and over:

Total occurrences 478

Different words 39

Exhibit 2

Source: The New York Times, September 8, 1957, page E11

Title: Chemistry Is Employed in a Search for New Methods to Conquer Mental Illness

Author: Robert K. Plumb

SCIENCE IN REVIEW

Chemistry Is Employed in a Search for New Methods to Conquer Mental Illness

By ROBERT K. PLUMB

By coincidence this week-end in New York City marks the end of the annual meeting of the American Psychological Association and the begining of the annual meeting of the American Chemical Society.

Psychologists and chemists have never had so much in common as they now have in new studies of the chemical basis for human behavior. Exciting new finds in this field were also discussed last week in Iowa City, Iowa, at the annual meeting of the American Physiological Society and at Zurich, Switzerland, at the Second International Congress for Psychiatry.

Two major recent developments have called the attention of chemists, physiologists, physicists and other scientists to mental diseases: It has been found that extremely minute quantities of chemicals can induce hallucinations and bizarre psychic disturbances in normal people, and mood-altering drugs (tranquilizers, for instance) have made long-institutionalized people amenable to therapy.

Money to finance resreach on the physical factors in mental illness is being made available. Progress has been achieved toward the understanding of the chemistry of the brain. New goals are in sight.

At the psychiatrists meeting in Zurich last week, four New York City physicians urged their colleagues to broaden their concept of "mental disease," and to probe more deeply into the chemistry and metabolism of the human body for answers to mental disorders and their prevention.

Blood May Tell

Dr. Felix Marti-Ibanez and three brothers, Dr. Mortimer D. Sackler, Dr. Raymond R. Sackler and Dr. Arthur M. Sackler cited evidence that the blood chemistry of victims of schizophrenia is different from that of normal people. Perhaps multiple biological factors are responsible for this chemical change, they suggested.

Mental disease is a "developmental process" and long duration of a disorder may result in "permanent alteration of anatomy and physiology," they said. They urged that trials of new drugs which affect the brain should be concentrated on complex studies of the mechanism of action of the drugs. The variety of substances capable of producing profound mental effects is a new armory of weapons for use in investigating biological mechanisms underlying mental disease, they said.

The sources of behavioral disturbance are many and they may come from external as well as internal forces, the four reported. This concept has already proven practical, for instances, when it enabled psychiatrists to predict that the administration of ACTH and cortisone could produce psychosis.

"It led some years ago to the development of a blood test which was 80 per cent accurate in the identification of schizophrenic patients," they said. "It permitted us on physiologic grounds to deny that the psychoneuroses and the psychoses were lesser and greater degrees of the same disease process, and, in fact, to affirm that they represented opposite and even mutually exclusive directions of physiologic disturbances," they said.

Chemicals now available should be used not only to bring relief to the mentally sick but also to uncover the biological mechanisms of the disease processes themselves. "Only then will the metabolic era mature and bring to fruition man's long hoped for salvation from the ravages of mental disease," they reported.

Chemistry of the Brain

At the psychologist's meeting here, a technique for tracing electrical activity in specific portions of the animal brain was described by researchers from the University of California at Los Angeles. They reported that deep brain implants in cat brains were used to record electrical discharges created as the animals respond to stimulations to which they had been conditioned. In this way the California group reported, it is possible to track the sequence in which the brain brings its various parts into play in learning. Specific areas of memory in the brain may be located. Furthermore, the electrical pathways so traced out can be blocked temporarily by the use of chemicals. This poses new possibilities for studying brain chemistry changes in health and sickness and their alleviation, the California researchers emphasized.

The new studies of brain chemistry have provided practical therapeutic results and tremendous encouragement to those who must care for mental patients. One evidence that knowledge in the interdisciplinary field is accumulating fast came last week in an announcement from Washington.

This was the establishment by the National Institute of Mental Health of a clearing house of information on psychopharmacology. Literature in the field will be classified and coded so that staff members can answer a wide variety of technical and scientific questions. People working in the field are invited to send three copies of papers or other material — even informal letters describing work they may have in progress—to the Technical Information Unit of the center in Silver Spring, Md.

Exhibit 2 **Auto-Abstract**

Two major recent developments have called the attention of chemists, physiologists, physicists and other scientists to mental diseases: It has been found that extremely minute quantities of chemicals can induce hallucinations and bizarre psychic disturbances in normal people, and mood-altering drugs (tranquilizers, for instance) have made long-institutionalized people amenable to therapy. (4.0)

This poses new possibilities for studying brain chemistry changes in health and sickness and their alleviation, the California researchers emphasized. (5.4)

The new studies of brain chemistry have provided practical therapeutic results and tremendous encouragement to those who must care for mental patients. (5.4)

A condensation of a document to a given fraction of the original could be readily accomplished with the system outlined by adjusting the cutoff value of sentence significance. On the other hand, a fixed number of sentences might be required irrespective of document length. Here it would be a simple matter to print out exactly that number of the highest ranking sentences which fulfilled the requirement.

In many instances condensations of documents are made emphasizing the relationship of the information in the document to a special interest or field of investigation. In such cases sentences could be weighted by assigning a premium value to a predetermined class of words.

These two features of the auto-abstract, variable length and emphasis, might at times be usefully combined. In the case of a long, comprehensive paper, several condensed versions could be prepared, each of a length suitable to the requirements of its recipient and biased to his particular sphere of interest.

Along these same lines, a specificity ranking technique might prove feasible. If none of the sentences in an article attained a certain significance factor, it would be possible to reject the article as too generalized for the purpose at hand.

In certain cases an abstract might be amplified by following it with an enumeration of specifics, such as names of persons, places, organizations, products, materials, processes, et cetera. Such specific words could be selected by the machine either because they are capitalized or by means of lookup in a stored special dictionary.

Auto-abstracting could also be used to alleviate the translation burden. To avoid total translation initially, auto-abstracts of appropriate length could be produced in the original language and only the abstracts translated for subsequent analysis.

Finally, the process of deriving key words for encoding documents for mechanical information retrieval could be simplified by auto-abstracting techniques.

Conclusions

The results so far obtained for technical articles have indicated the feasibility of automatically selecting sentences that will indicate the general subject matter, very much as do conventional abstracts. What such auto-abstracts might lack in sophistication they will more than compensate for by their uniformity of derivation. Because of the absence of the variations of human capabilities and orientation, auto-abstracts have a high degree of reliability, consistency, and stability, as they are the product of a statistical analysis of the author's own words. In many cases the abstract obtained is the type generally referred to as the "indicative" abstract.

Once auto-abstracts are generally available, their users will learn how to interpret them and how to detect their implications. They will realize, for instance, that certain words contained in the sample sentences stand for notions which must have been elaborated upon somewhere in the article. If this were not so for a substantial portion of the words in the selected sentences, these sentences could not have attained their status based on word frequency.

There is, of course, the chance that an author's style of writing deviates from the average to an extent that might cause the method to select sentences of inferior significance. Since the title of the paper is always given in conjunction with the auto-abstract, there is a high probability that it will favorably supplement the abstract. However, there will always be a residue of inadequate results, and it appears to be entirely feasible to establish criteria by which a machine may recognize such exceptions and earmark them for human attention.

If machines can perform satisfactorily within the range outlined in this paper, a substantial and worthwhile saving in human effort will have been realized. The auto-abstract is perhaps the first example of a machine-generated equivalent of a completely intellectual task in the field of literature evaluation.

Received December 2, 1957

New Methods in Automatic Extracting

H. P. EDMUNDSON

University of Maryland, * *College Park, Maryland*

ABSTRACT. This paper describes new methods of automatically extracting documents for screening purposes, i.e. the computer selection of sentences having the greatest potential for conveying to the reader the substance of the document. While previous work has focused on one component of sentence significance, namely, the presence of high-frequency content words (key words), the methods described here also treat three additional components: pragmatic words (cue words); title and heading words; and structural indicators (sentence location).

The research has resulted in an operating system and a research methodology. The extracting system is parameterized to control and vary the influence of the above four components. The research methodology includes procedures for the compilation of the required dictionaries, the setting of the control parameters, and the comparative evaluation of the automatic extracts with manually produced extracts. The results indicate that the three newly proposed components dominate the frequency component in the production of better extracts.

KEY WORDS AND PHRASES: automatic extracting, automatic abstracting, sentence selection, document screening, sentence significance, relevance, content words, key words, pragmatic words, cue words, title words, sentence location, research methodology, parameterization, comparative evaluation

CR CATEGORIES: 3.10, 3.69, 3.71, 3.72, 3.74

Introduction

HISTORICAL BACKGROUND. Shortly after research in automatic translation began, interest was aroused in the possibility of automatically abstracting documents. Emphasis was placed on the production of indicative abstracts (i.e. abstracts that allow a searcher to screen a body of literature to decide which documents deserve more detailed attention) rather than on the production of informative abstracts (i.e. abstracts that can serve as substitutes for the document).

Also, it was hypothesized that an extract of a document (i.e. a selection of "significant" sentences of a document) can serve as an abstract. This hypothesis concerning the substitutability of extracts for abstracts has been discussed in [1, 2, and 4]. All automatic abstracting methods to date have only extracted documents, i.e. the computer has selected sentences of the document and listed them in text order. Although it has been recognized for some time that this kind of automatic abstract might better be called an "automatic extract," "abstract" is often used as the generic term.

The original method of Luhn assigned weights to each sentence of the document

* Computer Science Center. The work reported here was initially conducted at Thompson-Ramo-Wooldridge, Inc. (now Bunker-Ramo Corporation) with the support of the Rome Air Development Center, Research and Technology Division, Air Force Systems Command, and was later continued at System Development Corporation under their Independent Research Program.

according to statistical criteria, in fact, a simple function of the number of high frequency words occurring in the sentence. Common words such as "the," "and," "at," and "are" were disregarded because of their very high frequency alone, and the remaining words were assigned frequency weights that provided sentence weights for measuring sentence significance. The extracts produced by this strictly statistical method were of sufficient quality to encourage further research [3, 6]. However, a purely statistical method of producing extracts was suspected of being inadequate, and hence other methods were sought [7].

SUMMARY OF PRESENT STUDY.   The objective of this study was twofold: first, an extracting system to produce indicative extracts, and second, a research methodology to handle new text and new extracting criteria efficiently. The purpose of the present paper is to make the results of this study more readily available.

The research methodology comprised a study of the abstracting behavior of humans, a general formulation of the abstracting problem and its relation to the problem of evaluation, a mathematical and logical study of the problem of assigning numerical weights to sentences, and a set of extracting experiments employing cyclic improvement.

The extracting system developed uses four basic methods to produce automatic extracts of technical documents approximately 4000 words in length with the IBM 7090–7094 (and has been reprogrammed for the UNIVAC 1103A and CDC 1604). The automatic extracts are believed to be of sufficiently high quality to be used in the screening of large collections of documents. The system has been parameterized to permit modification of both prestored and generated word lists, to readjust weights assigned to text characteristics, to permit selection from 15 combinations of the four basic methods of extracting, and to alter the length of an automatic extract.

Three different evaluation schemes were applied to the resulting automatic extracts. Comparison of the automatic extracts and corresponding "target" extracts of 40 documents, which had not been used in the developmental research, showed that a mean of 44 percent of the sentences were coselected. Also, the mean similarity rating, in terms of a subjective evaluation of content by information type, was 66 percent. These are to be compared with a mean of 25 percent coselected sentences and a mean of 34 percent similarity rating between target extracts and random extracts, respectively. Statistical comparison of the automatic and the corresponding target extracts for the documents used in the developmental phase showed a mean of 57 percent coselected sentences with a standard deviation of 15 percent. A sentence-by-sentence analysis of the corresponding automatic and target extracts of 20 of these documents resulted in a judgment that 84 percent of the computer-selected sentences could be classified as extract-worthy; i.e. they would be worthy of selection in an extract of unrestricted length.

The following sections of this paper treat the research methodology used in the study, the extracting system, and the outlook for further research.

Research Methodology

RESEARCH STEPS.   The work reported here relies on the detection and use of sentence "significance." Within sentences selected by humans in forming an extract,

H. P. EDMUNDSON

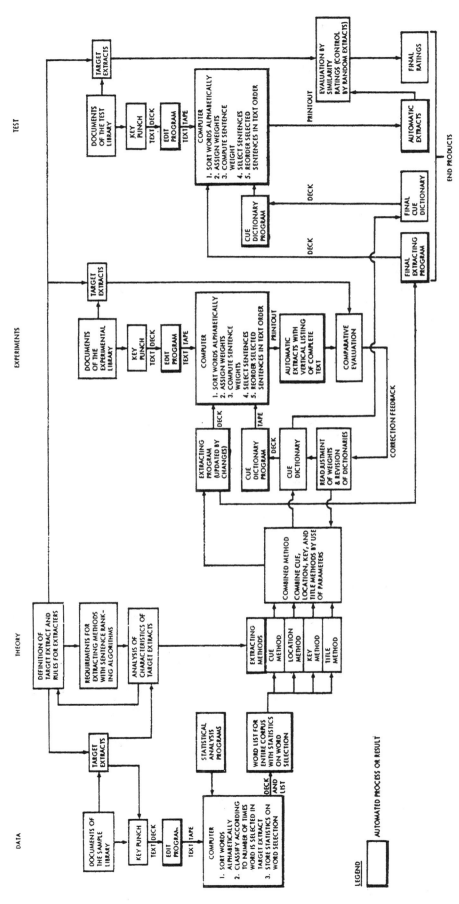

FIG. 1. Research methodology for automatic extracting study

there exist certain clues that, independent of subject content, tend to indicate that those sentences are significant. The goal was to replace the subjective notion of "significant" by an operational procedure. A methodology was sought whereby a computer could produce extracts as useful as conventionally created abstracts. The approach was to look for selection criteria among manually selected and rejected sentences.

The research steps, in chronological order, were:

(1) select a corpus of documents;

(2) study the characteristics—both in terms of content and machine-recognizability—of traditional manual abstracts of documents;

(3) specify the desired form and content of the "target" (manual) extracts;

(4) manually produce, for an experimental library of documents, target extracts that meet both the content and machine specifications;

(5) develop a system that assigns numerical weights to machine-recognizable characteristics;

(6) program a computer to produce automatic extracts;

(7) cyclically improve the program by comparing the automatic extracts and their target extracts; and

(8) evaluate the extracting system on a new group of documents not previously used in the experimental development.

The steps of the research methodology are shown in Figure 1.

SELECTION OF THE CORPUS. For the purpose of determining initial weights and parameters, preliminary statistical data (on common words, sentence length, and sentence position) were obtained from 200 documents in the fields of physical science, life science, information science, and the humanities; hereafter this collection is called the heterogeneous corpus.

For the extracting experiments a different corpus, consisting of 200 documents in chemistry, was used. These documents were contractor reports to various government agencies and ranged in length from 100 to 3900 words, with an average of 2500. The limitation on document length was imposed by the limited computer storage available for the text of a document under the present program. These technical reports, written by chemists, chemical engineers, and physicists, were highly formatted and terse, and contained equations and experimental data.

Since a fair evaluation of experimental results required that the system be tested on documents different from those used in developing it, the chemistry corpus was divided into an experimental library of documents to serve as the data base and for experimentation, and a test library of documents reserved for evaluation of the extracting program after experimentation had been completed.

TARGET EXTRACTS

Specification of Target Extracts. A set of instructions for human extractors was developed comprising the following specifications for the content and form of the target extracts, and the systematic procedures for composing them.

1. Sentences were selected only if they were eligible in terms of content. A sentence was called *eligible* if it contained information of at least one of the following six types:

Subject Matter. Information indicating the general subject area with which the author is principally concerned (i.e. *what?*).

H. P. EDMUNDSON

Purpose. Information indicating whether the author's principal intent is to offer original research findings, to survey or evaluate the work performed by others, to present a speculative or theoretical discussion, or to serve some other main purpose (i.e. *why?*).

Methods. Information indicating the methods used in conducting the research. Depending on the type of research, such statements may refer to experimental procedures, mathematical techniques, or other methods of scientific investigation (i.e. *how?*).

Conclusions or Findings. Information indicating the author's conclusions or the research results.

Generalizations or Implications. Information indicating the significance of the research and its bearing on broader technical problems or theory.

Recommendations or Suggestions. Information indicating recommended courses of action or suggested areas of future work.

2. Sentences were selected to minimize redundancy in the extract. A sequence of sentences was said to be *nonredundant* if their information content was not repeated by reiteration, paraphrasing, or direct implication.

3. Sentences were selected to maximize coherence. A sequence of sentences was said to be *coherent* if all crucial antecedents and referents were present, no semantic discontinuities were present, and the sequence of ideas progressed logically.

4. The number of sentences selected was predetermined by a rule. Even though 25 percent of the sentences of the document was used as the length parameter for this research, this is not proposed as the optimal figure because it depends both on the purpose the extract is to serve and on the length and nature of the document.

An example of a target extract appears in Figure 2.

PREPARATION OF TARGET EXTRACTS

Analysis Procedure. To systematize the manual preparation of target extracts by humans, an analysis sheet itemizing every sentence was completed for each document. Here the extractor recorded his judgment about the eligibility of the sentence, his findings on its dependency on other sentences (e.g. antecedents), and whether the sentence was selected for the target extract. To facilitate comparisons, columns were also provided to record sentence selections by the various automatic methods and by a random-selection procedure used to evaluate the comparison scores described below.

Composition Problems. Much of the target-extracting effort was devoted to locating duplications of information throughout the document. A typical chemistry document had a summary at the beginning, an orientation section, a methods section, a discussion section, and, frequently, a conclusion that rephrased the initial summary. Hence the same information often appeared in several places in a document. Occasionally, however, nearly the entire document comprised research conclusions. When a hierarchy, either of significance or of generality, could not be established, no abstract could logically be composed by extracting. In this case a description representation was appropriate. However, if the document did contain a description of itself, this description rarely amounted to 25 percent of the sentences; if it did not, then the present extracting rules did not yield a coherent extract. Furthermore, to select 25 percent of the sentences, it was occasionally necessary to select several less condensed sentences instead of an equivalent, but

PAR SENT

DOCUMENT NUMBER 6 1

ABSTRACT BASED ON HUMAN SELECTION

EVALUATION OF THE EFFECT OF DIMETHYLAMINE BORINE AND SEVERAL OTHER ADDITIVES ON COMBUSTION STABILITY CHARACTERISTICS OF VARIOUS HYDROCARBON TYPE FUELS IN PHILLIPS MICROBURNER (AD87730)

R. L. BRACE

PAR	SENT	
1	0	SUMMARY
2	1	AT THE REQUEST OF THE NAVY BUREAU OF AERONAUTICS, PHILLIPS PETROLEUM COMPANY UNDERTOOK THE EVALUATION OF DIMETHYLAMINE BORINE AS AN ADDITIVE FOR IMPROVING THE COMBUSTION CHARACTERISTICS OF AVIATION GAS TURBINE TYPE FUELS.
2	2	BECAUSE OF THE SAMLL AMOUNT (100 GRAMS) OF DIMETHYLAMINE BORINE RECEIVED FROM CALLERY CHEMICAL COMPANY, THIS EVALUATION HAS BEEN LIMITED TO THE MEASUREMENT OF ITS EFFECT ON THE FLASH-BACK CHARACTERISTICS OF THREE PURE HYDROCARBONS (TOLUENE, NORMAL HEPTANE AND BENZENE) IN THE PHILLIPS MICROBURNER.
2	3	DIMETHYLAMINE BORINE CONCENTRATIONS OF FROM 0.1 to 1.0 PER CENT BY WEIGHT WERE EVALUATED.
3	1	FOR COMPARATIVE PURPOSES TWO COMMON IGNITION ADDITIVES (AMYL NITRATE AND CUMENE HYDROPEROXIDE) WERE ALSO EVALUATED DURING THIS STUDY, AS WELL AS CONCENTRATIONS UP TO 20 PER CENT BY WEIGHT OF PROPYLENE OXIDE - A RELATIVELY HIGH FLAME VELOCITY FUEL.
3	2	PREVIOUS STUDIES IN PHILLIPS 2 INCH TURBOJET ENGINE TYPE COMBUSTOR HAD INDICATED THAT SUCH MATERIALS COULD SUBSTANTIALLY INCREASE THE MAXIMUM RATE OF HEAT RELEASE ATTAINABLE, ESPECIALLY WITH LOW PERFORMANCE FUELS SUCH AS THE ISO PARAFFIN TYPE HYDROCARBONS - PARTICULARLY WHEN OPERATING UNDER SEVERE CONDITIONS FOR COMBUSTION (I.E., HIGH AIR FLOW VELOCITY OR LOW COMBUSTION PRESSURE).
4	4	WITH RESPECT TO THE DIMETHYLAMINE BORINE, ITS EFFECT AS A FUEL ADDITIVE WAS NOTEWORTHY; 0.1 WEIGHT PER CENT IN TOLUENE BEING EQUIVALENT TO 20 PER CENT BY WEIGHT OF ADDED PROPYLENE OXIDE.
4	5	IN GENERAL, ADDITIVE CONCENTRATIONS OF ONE PER CENT BY WEIGHT IN THE SEVERAL PURE HYDROCARBONS WHICH NORMALLY DIFFERED QUITE WIDELY IN PERFORMANCE. PRODUCED UNIFORMLY SUPERIOR COMBUSTION STABILITY CHARACTERISTICS AS MEASURED USING THE PHILLIPS MICROBURNER.
5	0	I. INTRODUCTION
8	0	II. DESCRIPTION OF PHILLIPS MICROBURNER (MODEL 1A)
10	0	III. DESCRIPTION OF TEST APPARATUS
14	0	IV. DESCRIPTION OF TEST FUELS
15	2	THESE FUELS REPRESENT VARIATIONS IN CHEMICAL STRUCTURE WHICH WILL IN TURN PROVIDE INDICES OF BOTH GOOD AND POOR COMBUSTION STABILITY PERFORMANCE.
17	0	V. TEST PROCEDURE
21	0	VI. RESULTS
24	1	THE REGION OF STABLE OPERATION IS DEFINED AS THE STATE OF FLASH BACK-THE CONDITIONS OF COMBUSTION WHERE THE FLAME WOULD BECOME ANCHORED TO A FLAME HOLDER - AS IN STABLE GAS TURBINE OR RAM JET COMBUSTOR OPERATION - IF THE FLAME HOLDER WERE PROVIDED IN THE BURNER TUBE.
25	0	VII. DISCUSSION
26	2	THE ASSUMPTION IS MADE THAT THE GREATER THE ALLOWABLE BEAT INPUT RATE AT A GIVEN VELOCITY, THE GREATER THE DEGREE OF STABILITY.
31	3	ALL FOUR ADDITIVES INDICATED THEIR ADDITION TO BE SUBJECT TO THE EFFECT OF DEMINISHING RESULTS UPON FURTHER ADDITION - THAT IS, THEIR EFFECT WAS NOT ESSENTIALLY A BLENDING EFFECT.
32	1	MENTION SHOULD BE MADE OF THE FACT THAT DURING THE COMBUSTION OF THE DIMETHYLAMINE BORINE-HYDROCARBON FUEL BLENDS NO NOTICEABLE ODORS OR SMOKE WERE OBSERVED.
33	0	VIII. CONCLUSIONS
36	1	3. THE ADDITION OF ADDITIVE CONCENTRATIONS (UP TO 1 PER CENT) OF AMYL NITRATE, CUMENE HYDROPERIOXIDE, AND DIMETHYLAMINE BORINE ALL RESULTED IN IMPROVED STABILITY PERFORMANCE; THE GREATEST INCREASES WERE SHOWN WHEN BLENDED WITH A FUEL OF POOR PERFORMANCE CHARACTERISTICS - SUCH AS TOLUENE.
36	2	BENEFICIAL EFFECTS WERE APPRECIABLY LESS WHEN BLENDED WITH A FUEL OF GOOD PERFORMANCE CHARACTERISTICS - SUCH AS N-HEPTANE.
37	0	IX. RECOMMENDATIONS
38	1	BASED ON THE EVALUATION OF THE EFFECTS OF ADDITIVES ON THE FLASHBACK LIMITS OF THE ADDITIVE-FUEL BLENDS TESTED IN THE MICROBURNER (MODEL 1A) IT IS RECOMMENDED THAT DIMETHYLAMINE BORINE SHOULD BE FURTHER INVESTIGATED.
38	2	THIS FUTURE WORK SHOULD INCLUDE STUDY OF COMBUSTION STABILITY AND COMBUSTION EFFICIENCY EFFECTS IN THE PHILLIPS 2 INCH COMBUSTOR AND AN INVESTIGATION OF ITS INFLUENCE ON COMBUSTION CLEANLINESS.

Sic

FIG. 2. Target extract

more succinct, one. Although the 25 percent length parameter seemed workable for most documents, in some cases it was manifestly not appropriate.

An attempt was made to classify eligible sentences as to qualitative degree of "extract-worthiness" (a concept analogous to that of quantitative weightings). However, in practice it did not prove satisfactory for sentence selection since it was often impossible to determine if a sentence, seen only in the context of an extract, reported a well-known fact, a result of some previous experiment, or a conclusion of the document being extracted. Furthermore, a sentence was often anaphoric, i.e. depended on another one for its meaning (and there may even have been a series of such dependencies), requiring the selection of both even though the other sentence did not qualify in terms of content. Certain words or phrases such as "this," "therefore," and "since" frequently indicated this situation, and studying their occurrence seemed necessary to the refinement of the automatic method. The more an author used such words for reasons of structuring and style, the more difficult it was to extract sentences from context without destroying their function in the document.

In the composition of maximally coherent and meaningful target extracts, it was noticed that requirements of antecedents, deletions of text due to preediting, minimization of redundancy, and restrictions on the length parameter often took precedence over a sentence-by-sentence rating of extract-worthiness. In the evaluation step it was found that target extracts consistently differed from automatic extracts in precisely these aspects.

AUTOMATIC EXTRACTS

Guiding Principles for Automation. The following principles were devised to guide the development of automatic extracting methods so as to yield close approximations to target extracts:

1. Detect and use all content and format clues to the relative importance of sentences that were originally provided by the author, editor, and printer.

2. Employ mechanizable criteria of selection and rejection, i.e. a system of reward weights for desired sentences and penalty weights for undesired sentences.

3. Employ a system of parameters that can be varied to permit different specifications for extracts.

4. Employ a method that is a function of several linguistic factors (syntactic, semantic, statistical, locational, etc.).

Clearly, a computer can operate only on machine-recognizable characteristics of text (e.g. occurrence of certain words, position of a sentence in a paragraph, number of words in a sentence). A text characteristic was said to be *positively relevant* if it tended to be associated with sentences manually selected to comprise an extract, *negatively relevant* if it tended to be associated with unselected sentences, and *irrelevant* if it tended to be associated equally with selected and unselected sentences (see [5]). The task was to find relevant characteristics of the text and program the computer to recognize and weight them.

The Four Basic Methods. The automatic extracting system was based on assigning to text sentences numerical weights that were functions of the weights assigned to certain machine-recognizable characteristics or clues. For computational simplicity the sentence weights were taken as sums of the weights of these characteristics. The four basic methods (called Cue, Key, Title, and Location) to be discussed next used different sets of clues to the probable desirability of selecting a sentence for the automatic extract.

It was necessary to distinguish two types of word lists. A *dictionary* was regarded as a list of words with numerical weights that formed a fixed input to the automatic extracting system and was independent of the words in the particular document being extracted. A *glossary* was regarded as a list of words with numerical weights that formed a variable input to the automatic extracting system and was composed of words selected from the document being extracted.

1. *Cue Method.* In the Cue method the machine-recognizable clues are certain general characteristics of the corpus provided by the bodies of documents. The Cue method is based on the hypothesis that the probable relevance of a sentence is affected by the presence of pragmatic words such as "significant," "impossible," and "hardly." The Cue method uses the prestored Cue dictionary of selected words of the corpus. The Cue dictionary comprises three subdictionaries: Bonus words, that are positively relevant; Stigma words, that are negatively relevant; and Null words, that are irrelevant. The final Cue weight for each sentence is the sum of the Cue weights of its constituent words.

The Cue dictionary was compiled on the basis of statistical data and refined by linguistic criteria. Initial statistical data were obtained from 100 documents of the heterogeneous corpus for which target extracts had been prepared. A concordance program provided the following statistics for each word: frequency (number of occurrences in the corpus), dispersion (number of documents in which the word occurred), and selection ratio (ratio of number of occurrences in extractor-selected sentences to number of occurrences in all sentences of the corpus) (see [4]).

The following classes were then defined and listed by a computer program: Null candidates—dispersion greater than a chosen threshold and selection ratio between two chosen thresholds; Bonus candidates—selection ratio above the upper threshold; Stigma candidates—selection ratio below the lower threshold; and Residue—dispersion less than the threshold and selection ratio between the thresholds.

These categories were modified in three further steps. First, since most of the counterintuitive assignments occurred with low-frequency words, certain words were reclassified on this basis as Residue. Second, the statistics for 20 documents of the chemistry corpus were examined, and those additional words that exceeded a frequency threshold were also assigned, according to their selection ratio, to the Bonus, Stigma, and Null dictionaries. The final Cue dictionary contained 139 Null words, 783 Bonus words, and 73 Stigma words. The Null dictionary was created to list words excluded from the Key and Title glossaries, which are discussed next. Furthermore, it constituted a reservoir of common words that might, upon further research, be transferred to the Bonus or Stigma dictionaries.

Linguistic analysis of the experimental data revealed the following classes of Cue words: Null—ordinals, cardinals, the verb "to be," prepositions, pronouns, adjectives, verbal auxiliaries, articles, and coordinating conjunctions; Bonus—comparatives, superlatives, adverbs of conclusion, value terms, relative interrogatives, causality terms; Stigma—anaphoric expressions, belittling expressions, insignificant-detail expressions, hedging expressions; and Residue—positives, technical terms, and archaic terms.

2. *Key Method.* The principle (but not the algorithm) of the Key method is like the one first proposed by Luhn for creating automatic extracts (see [6]). Its

machine-recognizable clues are certain specific characteristics of the body of the given document. It is based on the hypothesis that high-frequency content words are positively relevant.

The Key method compiles a Key glossary for each document, ideally consisting of topic words statistically selected from the body of that document. The words comprising a Key glossary were selected by listing all words not in the Cue dictionary in order of decreasing frequency of occurrence in the document. The frequencies were cumulated, from the highest downward, to a given percent of the total number of word occurrences in the document. Non-Cue words with frequencies above this threshold were designated Key words and were assigned positive weights equal to their frequency of occurrence in the document. The final Key weight of a sentence is the sum of the Key weights of its constituent words.

Initially, Key words were defined as non-Cue words of the highest Cue-weighted sentences, and their Key weights were taken to be their frequency of occurrence in that set. In the final system, Key words were chosen from a given percent of the total number of words in the document, and their Key weights were taken to be their frequency of occurrence over all words in the document. It was felt that the change from a fixed threshold to a fractional threshold was an improvement because of increased coverage and flexibility. Moreover, both statistical and linguistic investigations have supported the shift from the narrower environment of high Cue-weighted sentences to the wider environment of all text words.

3. *Title Method.* In the Title method the machine-recognizable clues are certain specific characteristics of the skeleton of the document, i.e. title, headings, and format. The Title method is based on the hypothesis that an author conceives the title as circumscribing the subject matter of the document. Also, when the author partitions the body of the document into major sections he summarizes it by choosing appropriate headings. The hypothesis that words of the title and headings are positively relevant was statistically accepted at the 99 percent level of significance.

The Title method compiles, for each document, a Title glossary consisting of all non-Null words of the title, subtitle, and headings for that document. Words in the Title glossary are assigned positive weights. The final Title weight for each sentence is the sum of the Title weights of its constituent words.

The weights assigned to the words of a Title glossary were determined on the basis of their effect in the combined weighting scheme of the four methods. Content words of the title were given heavier weights than content words of the headings. However, the initial assignment of weights led to a difficulty in the ranking of all sentences of the document when the Title method was used, since one weight was an exact multiple of the other, and this caused many ties among sentence weights. To minimize the occurrence of ties, title words were assigned a weight relatively prime to that of heading words.

4. *Location Method.* In the Location method the machine-recognizable clues are certain general characteristics of the corpus provided by the skeletons of documents, i.e. headings and format. The Location method is based on the hypotheses that: (1) sentences occurring under certain headings are positively relevant; and (2) topic sentences tend to occur very early or very late in a document and its paragraphs. These location characteristics of sentences were tested for correlation with selection ratios, and statistically derived weights were assigned to reflect the

probable relevance of sentences according to their occurrence under certain headings and their position in a document and a paragraph.

The Location method uses the prestored Heading dictionary of selected words of the corpus that appear in headings of documents, e.g. "Introduction," "Purpose," "Conclusions." In addition to assigning positive weights provided by the Heading dictionary, the Location method also assigns positive weights to sentences according to their ordinal position in the text, i.e. in first and last paragraphs, and as first and last sentences of paragraphs. The final Location weight for each sentence is the sum of its Heading weight and its Ordinal weight.

To investigate the importance of headings for a sentence, all words occurring in the headings of 100 documents of the heterogeneous corpus and 20 documents of the chemistry corpus were listed, excluding prepositions, articles, and highly specific words. A set of words was common to both corpora, and a selection ratio was computed for each. Selection ratios were found to confirm the intuitive appraisal of heading-word importance. Weights proportional to the selection ratios were then assigned to each of these heading words, and the remaining heading words were assigned the same weights as their synonyms in that set. Deletions were made on the basis of low frequency and unrelatedness to the desired information types (i.e. subject, purpose, method, conclusion, generalization, recommendation). The resulting Heading dictionary contained 90 words.

To investigate the importance of sentence position—both within a paragraph and in the document as a whole—300 sentences were randomly picked from the heterogeneous corpus, and selection ratios computed. These data were used as the basis for the assignment of Ordinal weights to the positional characteristics of a sentence according to whether it occurred in the first paragraph, last paragraph, and as first sentence, or last sentence. Intermediate sentences and paragraphs were assigned zero weights. The final weights adopted reflected the gross behavior of the above selection ratios.

Rationale of the Basic Methods. Extracting clues may come from two structural sources: (1) the *body* (text) of the document; and (2) the *skeleton* (title, headings, format) of the document. Also, clues may come from two linguistic sources: (1) *general* characteristics of the corpus and language (e.g. value-judgment words); and (2) *specific* characteristics of the individual documents (e.g. high-frequency words).

The two structural sources and the two linguistic sources of clues yielded four opportunities to create basic methods of automatic extracting which were defined simply by the class of clues upon which they rely. When applied to word clues this classification yielded four distinct word lists. These distinctions and standardizations of terminology permitted the following convenient classification of the four methods and their corresponding word lists (see Figure 3).

EXPERIMENTAL CYCLES. Seventeen experiments were performed in the course of the research to verify the significance of the various extracting clues, to refine the Cue and Heading dictionaries, to adjust weights, to reprogram the four basic methods, to improve the output format, and to evaluate the extracting methods (singly and in all possible combinations).

In the final system the relative weights among the four basic methods were parameterized in terms of the linear function

$$a_1 C + a_2 K + a_3 T + a_4 L$$

H. P. EDMUNDSON

		Structural Sources of Clues:	
		Body of Document (Text)	Skeleton of Document (Title, Headings, Format)
Linguistic Sources of Clues:	General Characteristics of Corpus	CUE METHOD: Cue Dictionary (995 words) (Includes Bonus, Stigma, and Null subdictionaries)	LOCATION METHOD: Heading Dictionary (90 words) (Location method also uses ordinal weights)
	Specific Characteristics of Document	KEY METHOD: Key Glossary	TITLE METHOD: Title Glossary

FIG. 3. Rationale of the four basic methods

where a_1, a_2, a_3, and a_4 are the parameters (positive integers) for the Cue, Key, Title, and Location weights, respectively. Moreover the length parameter P was modified so that it can be adjusted to any integral percent of the number of sentences in a document. Thus by means of a single program card, the values of a_1, a_2, a_3, a_4, and P can be specified as desired. Also, the 7090–7094 system was modified to extract documents of 4000 words instead of 3000 words (as initially programmed).

SELECTION OF PREFERRED METHOD. The percent of the number of sentences coselected in both the automatic and the target extracts was computed for each of the extracting methods, separately and in combination. The mean percentages for the most interesting methods are shown in Figure 4, with the intervals encompassing the sample mean plus and minus one sample standard deviation. The corresponding percentages for the random extracts (i.e. a random selection of 25 percent of the sentences) and the automatic extracts are given for comparison. The Cue-Title-Location method is seen to have the highest mean coselection score, while the Key method in isolation is the lowest of the automatic methods.

On the basis of these data it was decided to omit the Key method as a component in the preferred extracting system. These data confirm the hypothesis set forth

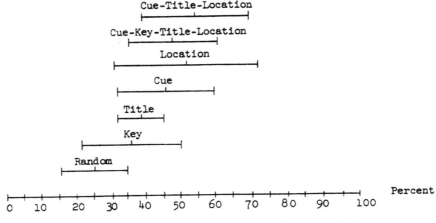

FIG. 4. Mean coselection scores of the methods

previously (see [4]) that Key words, although important for indexing, may not be as useful for extracting. This decision has important consequences for an extracting system since avoiding frequency-counting the entire text results in considerable simplification and shorter running time for the computer program.

EVALUATION OF PREFERRED METHOD

Studies of Evaluation. Two different studies of evaluation of the preferred method were conducted: (1) subjective similarity ratings by evaluators, with respect to each of the information types, of the automatic extracts versus the corresponding target extracts and random extracts of the same length; and (2) statistical error analysis in terms of the percent of extract-worthy sentences in the automatic extract computed as the sum of coselected sentences, plus sentences cointensional (i.e. conveying the same information) with sentences of the target extract, plus additional sentences judged to be extract-worthy. No attempt was made to evaluate the utility of the target extracts for the screening purposes that they were designed to serve, and no conclusions were drawn about the utility of the automatic extracts from the relative evaluation methods utilized in this study since that was the subject of another study.

Subjective Similarity Ratings. The first evaluation study involved a gross evaluation of the similarity of the automatic extracts to the corresponding target extracts for a group of documents that had not been used in the developmental phase. Automatic extracts generated by the Cue-Title-Location method and target extracts were prepared for a sample of 40 documents from the test library. Individual raters were asked to subjectively score the similarity between two pairs of extracts for each document: target and automatic; target and random. For each pair of extracts the similarity with respect to each of the six information types was considered in turn and reported on a five-point scale: no similarity, moderate similarity, considerable similarity, complete similarity, and not applicable.

Comparison between target and automatic extracts yielded a mean similarity rating of 66 percent (with 44 percent of the sentences coselected); while target and random extracts had a mean similarity rating of 34 percent (with 25 percent of the sentences coselected). For both, the sample standard deviation of the mean was 3 percent.

Statistical Error Analysis. The second evaluation study involved detailed comparison of extracts produced by the Cue-Title-Location method with the corresponding target extracts for 20 documents from the experimental library. Every sentence in a document can be classified uniquely by considering all combinations of the following properties: worthy to be in an extract of unrestricted length, in the target extract, in the automatic extract, and the negations of these properties. Eight classes result, of which two define the most significant types of statistical error, namely, type 1 error—sentence is worthy and in the target extract but contains information not in the automatic extract; and type 2 error—sentence is not worthy and is not in target extract but is in the automatic extract.

The 20 extracts comprised 311 sentences, of which 37 percent were classified as type 1 errors and 16 percent as type 2 errors. Of the computer-extracted sentences, 57 percent were identical with sentences in the target extracts, 10 percent were cointensional with other sentences in the target extracts, and 17 percent were judged to be extract-worthy. The sum for these three sets was 84 percent, a meas-

H. P. EDMUNDSON

ure of the percent of extract-worthy sentences. The 16 percent type 2 errors accounted for 100 percent of the computer-extracted sentences.

The identification of both meaning-similarity and extract-worthiness in running text was a highly subjective matter. Therefore this analysis represented careful and considered judgment. The sentences selected automatically, but judged not extract-worthy (type 2 errors), contained extraneous detail and represented "noise." They cluttered the extract and often interfered seriously with its coherence. The sentences resulting in type 1 errors represented information included in the target extract but not in the automatic extract. Their significance can be discovered only by studying the sentences in question.

The second study revealed the reasons for the apparent useful qualities of the automatic extracts. The number of coselected sentences showed only part of the actual correspondence between automatic and target extracts. When the number was expanded to include the automatically selected sentences cointensional with target extract sentences, the total roughly represented the degree to which the automatic process included the information in the target extract. The category of additional worthy sentences included some, but not all, eligible sentences that might be included in an extract of unrestricted length. It served as a reminder that for any document there are many possible abstracts differing in both length and content. This category and the preceding two comprised the total of extract-worthy sentences. Their average of 84 percent, even though uncorrected for redundancy in the automatic extract, appears to represent a promising achievement in the automation of the extracting process.

Extracting System

GENERAL CHARACTERISTICS. The cardinal feature of the extracting system is its flexibility. The system was parameterized, whenever possible, to allow easy modification of both the weights within a single extracting method and the relative weights of the methods in combination. This was accomplished by making it possible to modify both prestored dictionaries and program-generated glossaries, to readjust weights assigned to text characteristics, to permit the use of 15 combinations of the four basic methods of extracting, and to alter the length parameter that determines the length of the automatic extract. The operating system comprises two input programs: (1) Edit Program—creates the text tape used by the extracting program; and (2) Cue Dictionary Program—feeds Cue dictionary into extracting program. It also comprises four basic extracting programs: (1) Cue Routine—weights sentences according to match of text words with Cue dictionary; (2) Key Routine—weights sentences according to frequency of word occurrence; (3) Title Routine—weights sentences according to match of text words with title and heading words; and (4) Location Routine—weights sentences according to location in document and appearance under words of the Heading dictionary.

The IBM 7090 edit program has 1707 instructions and occupies 30K of core. The Cue dictionary program tape has 704 instructions and uses 23K of core. The extracting program has 2427 instructions and uses 32K of core. The flowchart of the extracting system is shown in Figure 5.

INPUT PROCEDURES

Preediting. The text must have a length of at most 4000 words and is manually

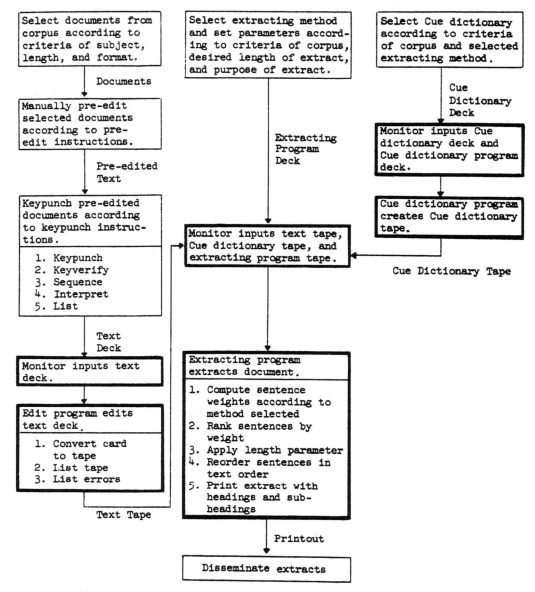

Note: Heavy boxes denote computer operations

FIG. 5. Extracting system

preedited according to preedit instructions, which cover the problems of formatting, graphics, special symbols, special alphabets, etc. Figure 6 shows a preedited document. The notations used are defined and discussed in [1].

Keypunching. The keypunch instructions are based on the preedit instructions and are subject to the conditions imposed by present input and output hardware. They contain rules and examples of sufficient generality to cover a wide variety of textual situations.

Edit Program. The edit program creates the text tape used by the extracting program. Text written in free format is punched on cards according to the keypunch instructions. The edit program interprets these cards, recognizing title, headings, author, paragraph boundaries, sentence boundaries, number of sentences in document, punctuation, capitalization, etc. The program also recognizes input errors, which are then printed together with a vertical listing of text described below.

H. P. EDMUNDSON

~~PHILLIPS PETROLEUM COMPANY - RESEARCH DIVISION - REPORT 5027-58R~~

~~SPECIAL REPORT~~

~~NAVY CONTRACT NOas 52-132-C, Amendment 7~~

~~A~~ EVALUATION OF THE EFFECT OF DIMETHYLAMINE BORINE AND SEVERAL OTHER ADDITIVES ON COMBUSTION STABILITY CHARACTERISTICS OF VARIOUS HYDROCARBON TYPE FUELS IN PHILLIPS MICROBURNER ~~4/A057730/4~~

~~* * * * *~~ ~~BY~~ R. L. Brace

- -
~~* * * *~~
△ △ △ ← —————————— S U M M A R Y ———————————————————

At the request of the Navy Bureau of Aeronautics, Phillips Petroleum Company undertook the evaluation of dimethylamine borine as an additive for improving the combustion characteristics of aviation gas turbine type fuels. Because of the small amount (100 grams) of dimethylamine borine received from Callery Chemical Company, this evaluation has been limited to the measurement of its effect on the flash-back characteristics of three pure hydrocarbons (toluene, normal heptane and benzene) in the Phillips Microburner. Dimethylamine borine concentrations of from 0.1 to 1.0 per cent by weight were evaluated.

For comparative purposes two common ignition additives (amyl nitrate and cumene hydroperoxide) were also evaluated during this study, as well as concentrations up to 20 per cent by weight of propylene oxide - a relatively high flame velocity fuel. Previous studies in Phillips 2 inch turbojet engine type combustor had indicated that such materials could substantially increase the maximum rate of heat release attainable, especially with low performance fuels such as the iso paraffin type hydrocarbons - particularly when operating under severe conditions for combustion (i.e., high air flow velocity or low combustion pressure).

The assumption has been made in this fuel evaluation that the greater the allowable heat input rate for a given velocity, the greater the degree of combustion stability. On this basis, the data indicate that all the additive materials tested caused an increase in stability performance; a fuel of relatively low performance such as toluene being benefited to a greater extent than a high performance fuel such as normal heptane. These data are in agreement with previous additive studies by Phillips. With respect to the dimethylamine borine, its effect as a fuel additive was noteworthy; 0.1 weight per cent in toluene being equivalent to 20 per cent by weight of added propylene oxide. In general, additive concentrations of one per cent by weight in the several pure hydrocarbons which normally differed quite widely in performance, produced uniformly superior combustion stability characteristics as measured using the Phillips Microburner.

~~* * * *~~
△ △ △ ← —————————— I.   INTRODUCTION

(#S) At the request of the Navy Bureau of Aeronautics the Jet Fuels Group has evaluated the effects of the addition of small amounts of dimethylamine borine ($(CH_3)_2NH:BH_3$) on the combustion stability performance of several hydrocarbon fuels. The dimethylamine borine was supplied to Phillips by the Callery Chemical Company.

Due to the small quantity of this material obtained the evaluation was conducted in the Phillips Microburner (Model 1A) which is a slightly modified version of the original Phillips Microburner (Model 1).

FIG. 6.   Preedited document (cont'd on next page)

Cue Dictionary Program.   The Cue dictionary program creates a Cue dictionary tape to be used by the extracting program when it is identifying Cue words and compiling the Key and Title glossaries. The input to the program consists of at most 1000 words and their weights; the words are punched one word per card and must be in alphabetical order. The output consists of a binary tape containing only one record, in which each entry takes four computer words. Certain input errors can be detected, and these, as well as a BCD listing of the Cue dictionary, are printed on an output tape.

PROCESSING STEPS
Cue Method:
1. Compare each word of text with Cue dictionary.

✻ ⋈ ✻✻
△△△△ ←——————— II. *A* DESCRIPTION OF PHILLIPS MICROBURNER (MODEL 1A)

The design of the original Phillips Microburner (Model 1) was discussed in
detail in Reference 1. The only significant change in burner detail was the
substitution of a #0 LeRoy Lettering Pen for the #3 LeRoy pen fuel nozzle in the
Model 1.   The details of the Model 1A are shown in Figure 1.

#50   #S3

✻ ⋈ ✻✻
△△△△ ←——————— III.   DESCRIPTION OF TEST APPARATUS

The fuel system on the Phillips Microburner (Model 1) was designed so as to
handle small quantities of highly corrosive substances. In the present evaluation
it was not necessary to consider the effect of corrosion, consequently a continuous
flow system providing greater flexibility and easier handling was incorporated which
requires only slightly more fuel per test than the original. This new system includes
a source of nitrogen gas, a surge tank, a pressurized fuel tank, a small capacity
Brooks Rotameter and a flow control valve.

The air heater circuit was modified so as to include a mercury relay and bi-
metallic thermoswitch thus providing automatic air temperature control.

The details of these modifications and of the test apparatus are shown in
schematic in Figure 2.

✻ ⋈ ✻✻
△△△△ ←——————— IV.   DESCRIPTION OF TEST FUELS

The chemical and physical properties of the hydrocarbon fuels tested are
summarized in Table I. These fuels represent variations in chemical structure
which will in turn provide indices of both good and poor combustion stability
performance.

The additives evaluated, dimethylamine borine, propylene oxide, amyl nitrate,
cumene hydroperoxide, were blended into the hydrocarbon fuel by weight in concentrations ranging from 0.1 to 20 per cent.

✻ ⋈ ✻✻
△△△△ ←——————— V.   TEST PROCEDURE

The conditions at which this study was made in the Microburner (model 1A) were: #T.

Air Pressure	20 psig
Inlet Air Temperature	300 ± 20 F
Fuel Pressure	30 psig
Fuel Flow x 10	3.85 to 6.82 pps
Air Flow x 10	3.77 to 6.69 pps

Once the air temperature was established the air flow was set at the desired
rate and the fuel turned on. Ignition of the then fuel-rich mixture was accomplished
by applying a lighted, portable propane torch to the top of the burner tube. The
fuel flow was then gradually decreased until the flame holding at the burner tube rim
flashed back into the tube. At the point of flashback the following were recorded:

←————————————————
Cold Air Temperature
Inlet Air Temperature
Air Rotameter Reading
Fuel Rotameter Reading

After checking the point at least once more the air flow was increased another
increment and the process repeated.

FIG. 6 (continued)

2. Tag all Bonus words with weight $b > 0$, all Stigma words with weight $s < 0$, all Null words with weight $n = 0$.

3. Compute Cue weight C of each sentence by summing its Cue word weights b, s, and n.

4. Rank all sentences in decreasing weight order.

5. Select sentences whose rank order is less than length parameter P percent of the number of sentences in the document.

6. Select all headings.

7. Merge selected sentences under their proper headings.

8. Output title, authors, and results of step 7.

H. P. EDMUNDSON

PAR SENT   DOCUMENT NUMBER   6 PAGE   1

EVALUATION OF THE EFFECT OF DIMETHYLAMINE BORINE AND SEVERAL OTHER ADDITIVES ON COMBUSTION STABILITY CHARACTERISTICS
OF VARIOUS HYDROCARBON TYPE FUELS IN PHILLIPS MICROBURNER (AD87730)
R. L. BRACE

ABSTRACT BASED ON CUE TITLE LOC. WTS.

1   0   SUMMARY

2   1   AT THE REQUEST OF THE NAVY BUREAU OF AERONAUTICS, PHILLIPS PETROLEUM COMPANY UNDERTOOK THE
          EVALUATION OF DIMETHYLAMINE BORINE AS AN ADDITIVE FOR IMPROVING THE COMBUSTION CHARACTERISTICS OF
          AVIATION GAS TURBINE TYPE FUELS.

2   2   BECAUSE OF THE SMALL AMOUNT (100 GRAMS) OF DIMETHYLAMINE BORINE RECEIVED FROM CALLERY CHEMICAL
          COMPANY, THIS EVALUATION HAS BEEN LIMITED TO THE MEASUREMENT OF ITS EFFECT ON THE FLASH-BACK
          CHARACTERISTICS OF THREE PURE HYDROCARBONS (TOLUENE, NORMAL HEPTANE AND BENZENE) IN THE PHILLIPS
          MICROBURNER.

3   2   PREVIOUS STUDIES IN PHILLIPS 2 INCH TURBOJET ENGINE TYPE COMBUSTOR HAD INDICATED THAT SUCH MATERIALS
          COULD SUBSTANTIALLY INCREASE THE MAXIMUM RATE OF HEAT RELEASE ATTAINABLE, ESPECIALLY WITH LOW
          PERFORMANCE FUELS SUCH AS THE ISO PARAFFIN TYPE HYDROCARBONS-PARTICULARLY WHEN OPERATING UNDER
          SEVERE CONDITIONS FOR COMBUSTION (I.E., HIGH AIR FLOW VELOCITY OR LOW COMBUSTION PRESSURE).

4   1   THE ASSUMPTION HAS BEEN MADE IN THIS FUEL EVALUATION THAT THE GREATER THE ALLOWABLE HEAT INPUT RATE
          FOR A GIVEN VELOCITY, THE GREATER THE DEGREE OF COMBUSTION STABILITY.

4   2   ON THIS BASIS, THE DATA INDICATE THAT ALL THE ADDITIVE MATERIALS TESTED CAUSED AN INCREASE IN
          STABILITY PERFORMANCE.. A FUEL OF RELATIVELY LOW PERFORMANCE SUCH AS TOLUENE BEING BENEFITED TO A
          GREATER EXTENT THAN A HIGH PERFORMANCE FUEL SUCH AS NORMAL HEPTANE.

4   5   IN GENERAL, ADDITIVE CONCENTRATIONS OF ONE PER CENT BY WEIGHT IN THE SEVERAL PURE HYDROCARBONS WHICH
          NORMALLY DIFFERED QUITE WIDELY IN PERFORMANCE, PRODUCED UNIFORMLY SUPERIOR COMBUSTION STABILITY
          CHARACTERISTICS AS MEASURED USING THE PHILLIPS MICROBURNER.

5   0   I. INTRODUCTION

6   1   AT THE REQUEST OF THE NAVY BUREAU OF AERONAUTICS THE JET FUELS GROUP HAS EVALUATED THE EFFECTS OF
          THE ADDITION OF SMALL AMOUNTS OF DIMETHYLAMINEBORIN -S ON THE COMBUSTION STABILITY PERFORMANCE OF
          SEVERAL HYDROCARBON FUELS.

7   1   DUE TO THE SMALL QUANTITY OF THIS MATERIAL OBTAINED THE EVALUATION WAS CONDUCTED IN THE PHILLIPS
          MICROBURNER (MODEL 1A) WHICH IS A SLIGHTLY MODIFIED VERSION OF THE ORIGINAL PHILLIPS MICROBURNER
          (MODEL 1).

8   0   II. DESCRIPTION OF PHILLIPS MICROBURNER (MODEL 1A)

New Methods in Automatic Extracting

10	0	III. DESCRIPTION OF TEST APPARATUS
14	0	IV. DESCRIPTION OF TEST FUELS
17	0	V. TEST PROCEDURE
21	0	VI. RESULTS
25	0	VII. DISCUSSION
29	1	PREVIOUS WORK CONDUCTED IN THE PHILLIPS 2 INCH COMBUSTOR (REF. 2) INDICATED THAT SOME ADDITIVES CAUSED A SIGNIFICANT INCREASE IN THE PERFORMANCE OF A LOW RATING FUEL WHILE THESE SAME ADDITIVES DID NOT SUBSTANTIALLY EFFECT THE HIGHER RATING FUELS.
31	3	ALL FOUR ADDITIVES INDICATED THEIR ADDITION TO BE SUBJECT TO THE EFFECT OF DEMINISHING RESULTS UPON FURTHER ADDITION—THAT IS, THEIR EFFECT WAS NOT ESSENTIALLY A BLENDING EFFECT.
33	0	VIII. CONCLUSIONS
34	1	1. THE ADDITION OF DIMETHYLAMINE BORINE IN CONCENTRATIONS OF ONE PER CENT BY WEIGHT TO JET FUEL TYPE HYDROCARBONS RESULTED IN A UNIFOMLY HIGH LEVEL OF COMBUSTION STABILITY PERFORMANCE AS MEASURED BY PHILLIPS MICROBURNER.
35	1	2. THE ADDITION OF RELATIVELY LARGE AMOUNTS OF PROPYLENE OXIDE TO TOLUENE WERE NECESSARY TO PROVIDE SIGNIFICANT IMPROVEMENT IN STABILITY PERFORMANCE AS INDICATED BY INCREASES IN ALLOWABLE HEAT INPUT RATES.
36	1	3. THE ADDITION OF ADDITIVE CONCENTRATIONS (UP TO 1 PER CENT) OF AMYL NITRATE, CUMENE HYDROPEROXIDE, AND DIMETHYLAMINE BORINE ALL RESULTED IN IMPROVED STABILITY PERFORMANCE.; THE GREATEST INCREASES WERE SHOWN WHEN BLENDED WITH A FUEL OF POOR PERFORMANCE CHARACTERISTICS—SUCH AS TOLUENE.
37	0	IX. RECOMMENDATIONS
38	1	BASED ON THE EVALUATION OF THE EFFECTS OF ADDITIVES ON THE FLASHBACK LIMITS OF THE ADDITIVE-FUEL BLENDS TESTED IN THE MICROBURNER (MODEL 1A) IT IS RECOMMENDED THAT DIMETHYLAMINE BORINE SHOULD BE FURTHER INVESTIGATED.
38	2	THIS FUTURE WORK SHOULD INCLUDE STUDY OF COMBUSTION STABILITY AND COMBUSTION EFFICIENCY EFFECTS IN THE PHILLIPS 2 INCH COMBUSTOR AND AN INVESTIGATION OF ITS INFLUENCE ON COMBUSTION CLEANLINESS.

FIG. 7. Automatic extract

H. P. EDMUNDSON

It is now beyond question that future automatic abstracting methods must take into account syntactic and semantic characteristics of the language and the text: they cannot rely simply upon gross statistical evidence.

It is believed that the research methodology outlined here has been, and will continue to be, fruitful. Future research should adhere to the principle of parameterization to gain flexibility and permit continuing improvement of abstracting methods. The present set of weights is subject to continuing experimentation to permit maximum specification of desired content of automatic extracts. Even now ways can be conceived to reduce both the number and size of experimental cycles with more powerful statistical and computational techniques.

It is highly desirable that the extracting system be modified to accommodate longer documents (in fact it has been reprogrammed for the UNIVAC 1103A to accommodate documents of approximately 40,000 words). To reduce operating time and costs, ways to make the programs more efficient should be investigated. Reprogramming can help, but the greatest need for improvement is in the method of inputting text. In this connection it is also important to devise ways of automatically capturing chemical and mathematical symbols in machine form. Clearly there are extracting clues that have not yet been exploited—in captions of figures and tables, in footnotes and references, and in larger linguistic structures such as phrases and clauses. Better ways must be sought to identify those specific characteristics of documents that are significant for automatic extracting (such as presence or lack of headings, technical or literary content, etc.) and to correlate these characteristics with some combination of extracting method, set of weights, and length parameter that will give better automatic extracts.

Further investigation of methods of evaluating automatic extracts is needed to increase their speed, simplicity, and discrimination. Future research should involve sharper statistical analysis of the two types of error with the purpose of modifying the program to minimize them. Study should be made to discover machine-recognizable clues to determine the proper length of an extract. The extent to which redundancy appears in automatic extracts and ways of minimizing it should be investigated. Linguistic clues to coherence should be identified and expressed in machine-recognizable form, perhaps in the form of a word-and-phrase dictionary indicating the need for selecting antecedent sentences. In summary, the main differences between manual and automatic extracts can now be described and procedures outlined to minimize them.

Although automatic extracts of the future may differ both in content and appearance from traditionally composed manual abstracts, these differences do not appear as insuperable barriers to their usefulness. In spite of the recognized problems it is now felt that automatic extracts can be defined, programmed, and produced in an operational system to supplement, and perhaps compete with, traditional ones.

ACKNOWLEDGMENTS. The author especially acknowledges the work of his colleagues Mr. J. L. Kuhns, who conducted mathematical and linguistic research; Dr. P. L. Garvin, who assisted in dictionary compilation; Mrs. L. Ertel and Mr. D. Dwiggins, who performed the programming; and Mrs. J. Brewer, who conducted the content analysis.

REFERENCES

1. Automatic abstracting. RADC-TDR-63-93, TRW Computer Div., Thompson-Ramo-Wooldridge, Inc., Canoga Park, Calif., Feb. 1963.

2. EDMUNDSON, H. P. Problems in automatic abstracting. *Comm. ACM 7*, 4 (Apr. 1964), 259–263.

3. EDMUNDSON, H. P., AND WYLLYS, R. E. Automatic abstracting and indexing—survey and recommendations. *Comm. ACM 4*, 5 (May 1961), 226–234.

4. Final report on the study for automatic abstracting. C107-1U12, Thompson-Ramo-Wooldridge, Inc., Canoga Park, Calif., Sept. 1961.

5. KUHNS, J. L. An application of logical probability to problems in automatic abstracting and information retrieval. Joint Man-Computer Indexing and Abstracting, Sess. 13, First Congress on the Information System Sciences, Nov. 1962.

6. LUHN, H. P. The automatic creation of literature abstracts. *IBM J. Res. Develop. 2*, 2 (1959), 159–165.

7. RATH, G. J., RESNICK, A., AND SAVAGE, T. R. Comparisons of four types of lexical indicators of content. *Amer. Docum. 12*, 2 (Apr. 1961), 126–130.

4

Automatic Abstracting Research at Chemical Abstracts Service†

J. J. POLLOCK* and A. ZAMORA

Chemical Abstracts Service, The Ohio State University, Columbus, Ohio 43210

Received July 17, 1975

This paper uses a modified version of the extraction algorithm of Rush, Salvador, and Zamora to describe current research at Chemical Abstracts Service into the automatic generation of abstracts from primary documents. The results suggest that: (a) some subject areas are inherently more amenable than others to automatic extraction; (b) tailoring the algorithm for application to a narrow subject area yields better results than attempting to apply it more generally. The scope and viability of both Rush–Salvador–Zamora algorithm and of automatic extracting in general are also discussed.

INTRODUCTION

Many attempts have been made to abstract original documents by computer but none has succeeded in producing abstracts approaching good manual abstracts in quality. Moreover, given the present state of linguistic theory, it does not seem likely that a program capable of producing abstracts of manual quality will be written in the near future. In spite of this, research into automatic abstracting is still attractive because of the following factors:

• Manual abstracting is expensive and time-consuming.

• Machine-readable journals will probably become more widely available in the near future due to the increasing use of computer-controlled composition in the printing industry. This will provide a relatively cheap and convenient data base for experimentation.

• Given the availability of machine-readable journals, automatic abstracting will be much cheaper and faster than manual abstracting.

• Automatic abstracting produces abstracts already in machine-readable form for later processing steps.

• While automatic abstracts may never be as good as manual abstracts, they may be good enough for practical purposes, especially with simple manual editing.

Research at Chemical Abstracts Service (CAS) on automatic abstracting differs from previous work in several ways. In the past, abstracting programs have usually been applied to very general data bases (e.g., novels, textbooks) or heterogeneous ones (e.g., articles from widely disparate magazines and journals). The original documents used in our work were all abstracted at CAS for *Chemical Abstracts* (CA) (Volume 77, Issues 25 and 26). Many are from the Pharmacodynamics section of CA (Section 1). We consider that this restriction of the data base to a well-defined subject area is important in principle, and that it is unrealistic to expect a single algorithm to be able to abstract documents on a wide range of subjects.

Another difference is that the present work is aimed at producing not just any kind of abstract, but a specific type which will conform to certain CAS standards.

The abstracting program used in this work is a modified version of the Rush–Salvador–Zamora Automatic Document Abstracting Method (ADAM).[1] The algorithm used is essentially the same, but the program has been greatly speeded up and tested on an extensive chemical data base.

ADAM—THE ABSTRACTING PROGRAM

Abstracts and Extracts. An *abstract* may be defined as

"an abbreviated, accurate representation of a document" while an *extract* may be said to consist of "one or more portions of a document selected to represent the whole."[2] Using these definitions, we would prefer *automatic extracting* to the traditional term of *automatic abstracting*, since virtually all automatic abstracting research has been confined to selecting sentences from the original document to form an extract. In the case of ADAM, this distinction is a little blurred since, although it does create an extract, editing is performed on the original sentences to produce somewhat different sentences. However, ADAM does not create new sentences, either de novo or by conjoining original sentences, as human abstractors do.

The Algorithm. Most automatic abstracting methods differ from ADAM in two important respects: they rely heavily on statistical criteria as a basis for sentence selection and rejection, and they are designed to *select* sentences for abstracts. In contrast, ADAM uses statistical data only peripherally and is designed for sentence *rejection* rather than selection.

In ADAM, sentence rejection and selection are based mainly on use of cue words (see Word Control List below), relevance of sentence to title, and frequency criteria. The last two are important conceptually as they allow the algorithm to adapt itself, to some extent, to each individual document. Coherence criteria are also used in sentence rejection and selection and in increasing the readability of the abstract.

Characteristics of ADAM Abstracts. ADAM was designed to produce *indicative* abstracts, i.e., abstracts which enable the reader to judge whether or not he needs to read the original document. These abstracts do not substitute for the original document.

ADAM abstracts have the following characteristics:

• Their size is typically 10–20% of that of the original documents (but no arbitrary cutoff is used).

• They use the terminology of the original document.

• They consist of character strings from the body of the text. No equations, footnotes, tables, graphs, figures, etc., are given.

• Preliminary remarks, negative results (unless these are the only results), methodologies of data gathering, explanations, examples, and opinions are excluded.

• Objectives, results, and conclusions are given.

THE WORD CONTROL LIST (WCL)

Format. The Word Control List (WCL) consists of an alphabetically ordered set of words and phrases (collectively referred to as *terms*) with two associated codes, one semantic and the other syntactic. The format of a WCL entry is

† Presented before the Division of Chemical Information, 169th National Meeting of the American Chemical Society, Philadelphia, Pa., April 8, 1975.

TERM*X*Y

where X is the semantic and Y the syntactic code. Both X and Y are single characters (defined below) and, for any term, one of the two may be undefined (i.e., left blank; see Table I). Multiword terms are found in the text if there are less than four nonterm words between term words. For example, the term *our work shows* would be found in *our brilliant and inventive work clearly shows*. At present, the WCL contains 777 terms.

The Semantic Codes and Sentence Rejection or Selection. The semantic code associated with a term indicates whether or not a sentence containing it is likely to be suitable for inclusion in an abstract. The semantic codes are implemented hierarchically if a sentence contains more than one WCL term [e.g., I overrides A (see Table II)].

Most of the semantic codes in the WCL are negative, i.e., designed to cause rejection of sentences concerned with background information, speculation, etc. For example, terms such as *previous work* and *not important* would have negative codes.

A few terms (e.g., *this study* and *present work*) do have positive codes, indicating that sentences containing them are probably suitable for inclusion in an abstract.

Intersentence reference may also cause rejection or selection of a sentence. If a rejected sentence refers to a previous sentence, this sentence would also be rejected and, similarly, a previously rejected sentence will be restored if an important sentence refers to it. For example, the second sentence below will cause the first one to be rejected.

Substance X and substance Y form solutions in liquid ammonia. It is well known that these solutions are blue.

Both sentences will be rejected because *known* has a negative semantic code and *these* indicates intersentence reference. (*It* does not indicate intersentence reference as it is closely followed by *that*.)

Table I.   Sample of the Word Control List (WCL)

NEXT SECTIONS*A	ON* *P
NO ACCURATE*A	ONCE*L
NO ATTEMPT*B	ONE CAN*A
NO* *Z	ONE OF*B
NOR* *Z	ONE SUBJECT*A
NOT ALWAYS*B	ONE*E
NOT BEEN*A	ONLY*E
NOT CLEAR*B	OPINION*A
NOT IMPORTANT*A	OR*H*
NOT ONLY*F*F	OTHER*E
NOT*L*Z	OTHERS*E
NOTED*A*V	OUR EXPERIMENTS*I
NOTEWORTHY*K	OUR INVESTIGATION*I
NOW BEEN*K	OUR OBSERVATIONS*I
NOW*B	OUR RESULTS*I
NOWADAYS*B	OUR STUDIES*I
NUMEROUS STUDIES*A	OUR WORK*I
O .*F*F	OUR*K*N
OBSCURE*A	OVER* *P
OBVIOUS*A	OVERT*B
OBVIOUSLY*A	P .*F*F
OF ABOUT*H	PARAGRAPH*A
OF COURSE*A	PARTICULAR*A
OF* *O	PAST*A
OFFER* *V	PER CENT*A
OFTEN*E	PERHAPS*A
ON THE OTHER HAND*B	PERMISSION*M
ON WHICH*B*P	PERMITTING*B

Table II. Semantic Codes Used in WCL

Code	Meaning	Example
M	Supernegative, automatically deletes sentence	Acknowledgment, appreciation
I	Very positive	Our work, reported here
A	Very negative	Previously, obvious
K	Positive	Noteworthy, postulate
B	Negative	However, i.e.
E	Intensifiers or determiners	Many, most, several
L	Introductory quantifiers	A, especially, once
C	Requires antecedent (intersentence reference)	This, these
H	Heads a modifying phrase	What, whose
F	Null term	Abbreviations
G	Assigned by program to indicate intersentence reference or title words	
J	Continuation of previously assigned semantic code	
D	Delete term	

Table III. Syntactic Codes Used in WCL

Code	Description	Code	Description
A	Article	O	OF
C	Conjunction	Q	TO
D	Delete this term	R	AS
F	Null term	V	Verb
J	Continuation of previously assigned code	W	Auxiliary verb
N	Pronoun	X	IS, ARE, WAS, WERE
P	Preposition	Z	Negatives

Words in the title of the original document also influence sentence rejection and selection. Before the body of the document is processed, its title is matched against the WCL and words in the title which are not found in the WCL are assigned a semantic code G. Sentences containing these words are retained in the absence of terms with negative semantic codes.

Syntactic Codes and Coherence. The syntactic codes (see Table III) are used to perform a partial syntactic analysis of each sentence. Theair main use is to classify commas so that contextual inferences may be applied. Commas are divided into four classes: numerical (e.g., in 123,456), clause (used to separate phrases), serial (which follow members of a series), and parenthetical (which delimit dependent clauses). If the second of a pair of commas delimiting a text string is followed by a verb or by *to*, the commas are parenthetical. If a series of one or more commas in a sentence is followed by a comma or conjunction which is not immediately preceded by a preposition or a verb, the commas are serial.

Parenthetical commas cause the text string they delimit to be deleted. Serial commas are masked to prevent confusion with clause commas during later processing but are unmasked for output. Introductory clauses are deleted if they contain a term with semantic code B, H, or L.

The deletion of parenthetical and introductory clauses is important in principle because it means the abstract will not consist of sentences taken verbatim from the original document.

Finally, before a sentence is accepted for the abstract, it is examined via the syntactic codes assigned during WCL-matching to see if it contains a verb; if it does not, it is rejected.

Frequency Criteria. Frequency criteria are employed in a restricted but theoretically important manner. The frequency of occurrence of a term in the original document determines whether the semantic code assigned a priori in the WCL will be accepted or modified. Terms with positive codes are given less positive codes if their occurrence per

Table IV.
Examples of Non-Substantive Introductory Phrases

Phrases Beginning With "in"	Phrases Ending With "that"
IN AGREEMENT WITH PREVIOUS WORK	IT APPEARS THAT
IN ALL OF THESE STUDIES	IT APPEARS, THEREFORE, THAT
IN ANY EVENT	IT HAS BEEN CONCLUDED THAT
IN CONCLUSION	IT HAS BEEN FOUND THAT
IN CONTRAST	IT HAS NOW BEEN FOUND THAT
IN SUMMARY	IT IS APPARENT THAT
IN OUR EXPERIMENTS	IT IS CLEAR THAT
IN OUR INVESTIGATIONS	IT IS CONCLUDED BY THE PRESENT
IN OUR WORK	INVESTIGATION THAT
IN THE PRESENT EXPERIMENT	IT IS CONCLUDED THAT
IN THE PRESENT EXPERIMENTS	IT IS EVIDENT THAT
IN THE PRESENT PAPER	IT IS FOUND THAT
IN THE PRESENT REPORT	IT IS INDICATED THAT
IN THE PRESENT STUDY	IT IS INTERESTING THAT
IN THE PRESENT WORK	IT IS POSSIBLE THAT
IN THIS EXPERIMENT	IT IS SHOWN THAT
IN THIS STUDY	IT IS SUGGESTED THAT
	IT IS THEREFORE, REASONABLE TO
Intersentential Reference Phrases	ASSUME THAT
	IT MAY BE CONCLUDED THAT
APPARENTLY	IT MAY THUS BE CONCLUDED THAT
AS A CONSEQUENCE	IT MAY BE NOTED THAT
AS CAN BE SEEN	IT SEEMS A REASONABLE CONCLUSION THAT
AS EXPECTED	IT WAS FOUND THAT
AS SHOWN IN THE PREVIOUS SECTION	IT WAS ALSO FOUND THAT
BASED ON THESE DATA	THE DATA PRESENTED IN THIS REPORT
CONCEIVABLY	DEMONSTRATE THAT
CONSEQUENTLY	THE DATA PRESENTED IN THIS REPORT
FIRST,	INDICATE THAT
FROM THESE RESULTS	THE DATA REPORTED IN THIS STUDY
HENCE	IMPLY THAT
HOWEVER	THE PURPOSE OF THIS REPORT IS TO
INDEED	DEMONSTRATE THAT
LAST,	THE PURPOSE OF THIS STUDY IS TO
ON THE OTHER HAND	DEMONSTRATE THAT
SECONDLY	THE PRESENT EXPERIMENTS SHOW THAT
THEREFORE	THE PRESENT RESULTS DEMONSTRATE
THUS	DIRECTLY THAT
TO THIS END	THE PRESENT STUDIES HAVE SHOWN THAT
UNFORTUNATELY	THE PRESENT STUDY HAS DEMONSTRATED
UNQUESTIONABLY	THAT
	THE PRESENT WORK INDICATES THAT
	THE PRESENT WORK SHOWS THAT

thousand words is greater than four, while negative codes are made less negative if it exceeds seven. These criteria tend to decrease positive codes and thus favor smaller abstracts.

The conceptual importance of the frequency criteria is that they adapt the WCL to each individual document. For example, in a document concerned with paper manufacture, the term _this paper_ has much less significance than it would in other contexts and its a priori (i.e., manually assigned) semantic code in the WCL would therefore be decreased. Similarly, in a paper on photographic chemistry, the term _negative_ has a special meaning and its semantic code would be changed.

Final Editing. As a final step, the abstract is automatically edited, in the ways indicated below, to delete certain nonsubstantive words and phrases which occur at the start of sentences and to abbreviate or replace certain words and phrases according to CAS standards.

Deletion of Nonsubstantive Introductory Words and Phrases from Sentences. Inspection of ADAM extracts revealed that author sentences often consist of an introductory word or phrase followed by a declarative sentence. (The preceding sentence is an example of this, _Inspection . . . that_ being the introductory phrase.) Such words and phrases are alien to the style of abstracts and can be removed without loss of information. These nonsubstantive words and phrases divide naturally into three groups: phrases ending in _that_, which are usually followed by a conclusion; phrases beginning with _In_, which often indicate the scope of the associated statement; and words or phrases signifying that the sentence in question is logically connected with a previous sentence. It is interesting to note that many phrases which are effective for sentence selection (e.g., _In our work_) should not appear in the final abstract as they no longer convey any useful information. (See Table IV for examples of the superfluous words and phrases.)

Abbreviation of Words or Phrases. Abbreviations are applied according to "Abbreviations and Symbols used in ACS Publications" (see Table V).

This includes not only the terms actually listed but also many verb, plural, and prefixed variants as well as words

ending in certain suffixes (e.g., ological, ographically).

Non-U.S. Spellings. Examples of spellings which differ from the U.S. practice include _sulph_ (which is changed to _sulf_ in _sulphone, sulphate,_ etc.) and _behaviour_ (which is replaced by _behavior_).

Replacing Chemical Compounds by Formulas. Replacing compound names with formulas can result in considerable space saving (e.g., substituting NaOAc for sodium acetate saves nine characters), but one must be careful to replace complete compounds. For example, changing nitrobenzene to $PhNO_2$ is good, but replacing trinitrobenzene with $triPhNO_2$ would be highly inappropriate.

THE DATA BASE

A machine-readable data base of 56 papers was created by keypunching original documents. The only essential rules for this keypunching are that each sentence must end in a period followed by two blanks, that blanks must not be inserted into words, and that there must be at least one blank between words.

The commonest subject area was pharmacodynamics, but the papers in other biochemical areas, physical chemistry, organic chemistry, polymer chemistry, inorganic chemistry, and analytical chemistry were also keypunched. The papers varied from short notes to long papers and had between 111 and 3217 words. Some papers were keypunched in full while other papers had sections giving methodological details (e.g., headed "Experimental" or "Methods") and were omitted. The reasons for this practice are described below.

RESULTS

Modification of the Data Base. ADAM is designed to produce indicative abstracts, which should not contain methodological details. Thus, one would not expect sections of papers connected with such details to be fruitful sources of good sentences for abstracts. Accordingly, ADAM was run on two versions of the first batches of papers to be keypunched: complete papers and papers with the sections containing experimental data omitted. The only portions omitted were those clearly headed "Experimental" or "Methods", which would be easily recognizable as such algorithmically in a machine-readable paper produced during computer-controlled composition.

The Experimental sections were found to contribute no useful sentences to the abstracts, and subsequent papers were keypunched without them. This effects considerable savings both in computer time and in keypunching.

Algorithm Performance: Quality of Abstracts. The difficulty of evaluating abstracts in a convenient and theoretically sound manner is discussed below. In our opinion, most of the abstracts produced by ADAM were functionally adequate. They were not as good as abstracts written by professional abstractors, but they contained enough information for the reader to be able to judge whether or not he needed to obtain the original document.

Subject Area, Document Structure, and Abstract Quality. ADAM produces better abstracts from some subject areas than others; the abstracts are affected by the composition of the WCL and the structure of the original documents.

The WCL was originally designed for general English text and later modified to optimize the abstracting of pharmacodynamic papers. Some specialization of vocabulary is necessary for each subject area, and WCL terms appropriate for one subject area may actually be detrimental in another. Thus the current WCL may favor pharmacodynamics at the expense of other topics, and it might be necessary to use different WCL's for each subject area.

ADAM works best with narrative-style documents.

Table V.

ABBREVIATIONS AND SYMBOLS USED IN ACS PUBLICATIONS

A   ampere
Å   angstrom unit
abs.   absolute
abstr.   abstract
Ac   acetyl (CH_3CO, not CH_3COO)
a.c.   alternating current
ACTH   adrenocorticotropin
addn.   addition
addnl.   additional(ly)
ADP   adenosine 5'-diphosphate
alc.   alcohol, alcoholic
aliph.   aliphatic
alk.   alkaline (not alkali)
alky.   alkalinity*
AMP   adenosine 5'-monophosphate
amt.   amount
amu   atomic mass unit
anal.   analysis*, analytical(ly)
anhyd.   anhydrous
AO   atomic orbital
app.   apparatus
approx.   approximate(ly)
approxn.   approximation
aq.   aqueous
arom.   aromatic
assoc.   associate
assocd.   associated
assocg.   associating
assocn.   association
at.   atomic (not atom)
atm   atmosphere (the unit)
atm.   atmosphere, atmospheric
ATP   adenosine 5'-triphosphate
ATPase   adenosinetriphosphatase
av.   average
b.   (followed by a figure denoting temperature) boils at, boiling at (similarly b_{13} at 13 mm pressure)
bcc   body centered cubic
BeV or GeV   billion electron volts
BOD   biochemical oxygen demand
μB   Bohr magneton
b.p.   boiling point
Btu   British thermal unit
Bu   butyl (normal)
Bz   benzoyl (C_6H_5CO, not $C_6H_5CH_2$)
c-   centi- (as a prefix, e.g., cm)
cal   calorie
calc.   calculate
calcd.   calculated
calcg.   calculating
calcn.   calculation
CD   circular dichroism
c.d.   current density
CDP   cytidine 5'-diphosphate
chem.   chemical(ly), chemistry
Ci   curie
clin.   clinical(ly)
CM-cellulose   carboxymethyl cellulose
CMP   cytidine 5'-monophosphate
CoA   coenzyme A
COD   chemical oxygen demand
coeff.   coefficient
com.   commercial(ly)
compd.   compound
compn.   composition
conc.   concentrate
concd.   concentrated
concg.   concentrating
concn.   concentration
cond.   conductivity*
const.   constant
contg.   containing
cor.   corrected
CP   chemically pure
crit.   critical
cryst.   crystalline (not crystallize)
crystd.   crystallized
crystg.   crystallizing

crystn.   crystallization
CTP   cytidine 5'-triphosphate
d-   deci-   (as a prefix, e.g., dl)
d.   density (d^{13}, density at 13° referred to water at 4°; d^{20}_{20} at 20° referred to water at the same temperature)
D   debye unit
d.c.   direct current
DEAE-cellulose   diethylaminoethyl cellulose
decomp.   decompose
decompd.   decomposed
decompg.   decomposing
decompn.   decomposition
degrdn.   degradation
deriv.   derivative
det.   determine
detd.   determined
detg.   determining
detn.   determination
diam.   diameter
dil.   dilute
dild.   diluted
dilg.   diluting
diln.   dilution
dissoc.   dissociate
dissocd.   dissociated
dissocg.   dissociating
dissocn.   dissociation
distd.   distilled
distg.   distilling
distn.   distillation
DMF   dimethylformamide
DNA   deoxyribonucleic acid
DNase   deoxyribonuclease
d.p.   degree of polymerization
dpm   disintegrations per minute
DPN   diphosphopyridine nucleotide (NAD)
DPNH   reduced DPN
DTA   differential thermal analysis
ED   effective dose
elec.   electric, electrical(ly)
emf.   electromotive force
emu   electromagnetic unit
en   ethylenediamine (used in Werner complexes only)
EPR   electron paramagnetic resonance
equil.   equilibrium(s)
equiv.   equivalent (the unit)
equiv.   equivalent
esp.   especially
ESR   electron spin resonance
est.   estimate
estd.   estimated
estg.   estimating
estn.   estimation
esu   electrostatic unit
Et   ethyl
eV   electron volt
evap.   evaporate
evapd.   evaporated
evapg.   evaporating
evapn.   evaporation
examd.   examined
examg.   examining
examn.   examination
expt.   experiment
exptl.   experimental(ly)
ext.   extract
extd.   extracted
extg.   extracting
extn.   extraction
F   farad
FAD   flavine adenine dinucleotide
fermn.   fermentation
fcc   face centered cubic
FMN   flavine mononucleotide
f.p.   freezing point
FSH   follicle-stimulating hormone
G   gauss

G-   giga-(10^9)
g   gram
(g)   gas, only as in $H_2O(g)$
g   gravitation constant
GDP   guanosine 5'-diphosphate
GMP   guanosine 5'-monophosphate
GTP   guanosine 5'-triphosphate
H   henry
ha   hectare
Hb   hemoglobin
hr   hour
Hz   hertz (cycles/sec)
ICSH   interstitial cell-stimulating hormone
ID   infective dose
IDP   inosine 5'-diphosphate
i.m.   intramuscular(ly)
IMP   inosine 5'-monophosphate
inorg.   inorganic
insol.   insoluble
i.p.   intraperitoneal(ly)
ir   infrared
irradn.   irradiation
ITP   inosine 5'-triphosphate
IU   International Unit
i.v.   intravenous(ly)
J   joule
k-   kilo- (as a prefix, e.g., kg)
l.   liter
(l)   liquid, only as in $NH_3(l)$
lab.   laboratory
LCAO   linear combination of atomic orbitals
LD   lethal dose
LH   luteinizing hormone
liq.   liquid
lm   lumen
lx   lux
m-   milli- (as a prefix, e.g., mm)
m   meter
m.   melts at, melting at
m molal
M-   mega- (10^6)
M molar
manuf.   manufacture
manufd.   manufactured
manufg.   manufacturing
math.   mathematical(ly)
max.   maximum(s)
Me   methyl (not metal)
mech.   mechanical(ly)
metab.   metabolism
min   minute (time)
min.   minimum(s)
misc.   miscellaneous
mixt.   mixture
MO   molecular orbital
mol.   molecule, molecular (not mole)
m.p.   melting point
μ micron; also micro- (as a prefix, e.g., μl)
MSH   melanocyte-stimulating hormone
Mx   maxwell
n-   nano- (10^{-9})
n refractive index (n^{20}_D for 20° and sodium D light)
N   newton
N normal (as applied to concn.)
NAD   nicotinamide adenine dinucleotide (DPN)
NADH   reduced NAD
NADP   nicotinamide adenine dinucleotide phosphate (TPN)
NADPH   reduced NADP
neg.   negative(ly)
NMN   nicotinamide mononucleotide
NMR   nuclear magnetic resonance
no.   number
NQR   nuclear quadrupole resonance
obsd.   observed
Oe   oersted
Ω ohm
ORD   optical rotatory dispersion
org.   organic
oxidn.   oxidation
P   poise
p-   pico- (10^{-12})
p.d.   potential difference
Ph   phenyl

phys.   physical(ly)
PMR   proton magnetic resonance
polymd.   polymerized
polymg.   polymerizing
polymn.   polymerization
pos.   positive(ly)
powd.   powdered
ppb   parts per billion
ppm   parts per million
ppt.   precipitate
pptd.   precipitated
pptg.   precipitating
pptn.   precipitation
Pr   propyl (normal)
prep.   prepare
prepd.   prepared
prepg.   preparing
prepn.   preparation
prodn.   production
psi   pounds per square inch
psia   pounds per square inch absolute
psig   pounds per square inch gage
purifn.   purification
py   pyridine (used in Werner complexes only)
qual.   qualitative(ly)
quant.   quantitative(ly)
R   roentgen
redn.   reduction
ref.   reference
rem   roentgen equivalent man
rep   roentgen equivalent physical
resp.   respective(ly)
RNA   ribonucleic acid
RNase   ribonuclease
rpm   revolutions per minute
RQ   respiratory quotient
(s)   solid, only as in $AgCl(s)$
sapon.   saponification
sapond.   saponified
sapong.   saponifying
sat.   saturate
satd.   saturated
satg.   saturating
satn.   saturation
s.c.   subcutaneous(ly)
SCE   saturated calomel electrode
SCF   self-consistent field
sec   second (time unit only)
sec secondary (with alkyl groups only)
sep.   separate(ly)
sepd.   separated
sepg.   separating
sepn.   separation
sol.   soluble
soln.   solution
soly.   solubility*
sp.   specific (used only to qualify physical constant)
sp. gr.   specific gravity
sr   steradian
St   stokes
std.   standard
sym.   symmetrical(ly)
T-   tera- (10^{12})
TEAE-cellulose   triethylaminoethyl cellulose
tech.   technical(ly)
temp.   temperature
$tert$ tertiary (with alkyl groups only)
theor.   theoretical(ly)
thermodn.   thermodynamic(s)
THF   tetrahydrofuran
titrn.   titration
TPN   triphosphopyridine nucleotide (NADP)
TPNH   reduced TPN
Tris   tris(hydroxymethyl)aminomethane
TSH   thyroid-stimulating hormone
UDP   uridine 5'-diphosphate
UMP   uridine 5'-monophosphate
USP   United States Pharmacopeia
UTP   uridine 5'-triphosphate
uv   ultraviolet
V   volt
vol.   volume (not volatile)
W   watt
wt.   weight

Plurals of noun abbreviations are formed by adding "s" to the singular abbreviation except when a single abbreviation is designated to show both the singular and plural forms and except for words marked * whose plurals are not abbreviated. Verb forms that require "s" are treated similarly. Words formed by adding prefixes to words normally abbreviated are also abbreviated, as microchem. for microchemical. Other well established abbreviations, as etc., i.e., e.g., and abbreviations for English units of weight and measure, are also used. Unit abbreviations signify both singular and plural forms. Words ending in -ology or -ological(ly) are abbreviated -ol., e.g., geol. for geology. Words ending in -ography or -ographic(al)(ly) are abbreviated -og., e.g. chromatog. for chromatographic.

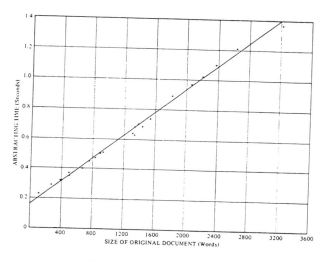

Figure 1. Program performance.

Many pharmacodynamic papers are written in this way; they begin with an introduction giving background information and stating the purpose of the work, follow this with "Methods" and "Results" sections, and end with a series of conclusions. This "linear" structure is well suited to the production of a coherent abstract as sentences are almost inevitably extracted in a logical narrative sequence. Other subject areas may be less linearly reported. For example, a physical chemistry paper may consist of a few measurements followed by a series of discussions, an organic chemistry paper may describe a number of syntheses, or an analytical paper may detail a recommended procedure. In these cases, there may be no sentences which adequately summarize the whole work. A human abstractor can summarize a discussion with a single sentence, but it is not feasible for a program to do this.

Also, some subject areas are more dependent on nontextual information than others. For example, the text of an organic chemistry paper may be incomprehensible without the accompanying structures and a physical chemistry document may be replete with complex equations without which the text makes little sense.

Program Speed. During our investigation of the execution speed of ADAM, we found that the time required to abstract each original document was proportional to the square (N^2) of the number (N) of words it contained. The first step of ADAM, in which the words of the original document were sorted alphabetically, initially used a sorting process in which the execution time was proportional to N^2. Since this initial sort was by far the most time-consuming part of the abstracting process, the initial sorting process was changed to one in which the execution time was dependent on $N \log N$. This caused a dramatic decrease in abstracting time; for example, the time required for the longest paper (3217 words) decreased from 23 to 1.4 sec, while the average amount of IBM 370/168 computer time per paper fell from 4.38 to 0.59 sec. The contribution of the sorting process to the total abstracting time now appears to be much smaller. This assumption is supported by Figure 1 which shows that the abstracting time required by a document is approximately proportional to the number of words in it. This virtually linear dependence on N makes the program attractive economically since processing large papers is no longer disproportionately expensive.

Abstract Size. On the average, ADAM abstracts contained 19% as many words as the original documents. This is longer than we would wish but still a very substantial reduction in size. In many cases, overlong abstracts could be significantly reduced in size by the removal of entire, inappropriate sentences. This would be a very simple manual editing task, not demanding intimate knowledge of the subject area.

The Problem of Abstract Evaluation. At first, this problem seems almost trivial. If it is possible to produce abstracts by computer, then surely it must be possible to determine how good they are? Moreover, without a reliable method of judging the quality of the abstracts, how can one modify the algorithm to produce better output? Here we would briefly like to review previous work on abstract evaluation and offer our own conclusions.

Methods for evaluating abstracts can be classified as intuitive, statistical, computational, and functional.

The *intuitive* method consists simply of human judgment of the abstract. It is the most popular method because of its simplicity, and it is widely used by automatic abstracting researchers and in training abstractors. It has the disadvantages of being inconsistent, time-consuming, and nonquantitative.

One important *statistical* method involves creating "ideal" extracts (composed of sentences chosen by professional abstractors) and correlating these statistically with the corresponding automatic extracts. The problem with this method lies in the assumption that there is a single ideal extract for each paper. In fact, there may be several good extracts for a given paper or none. It has also been shown experimentally[3-5] that each abstractor produces a different extract for a given paper, and that if an abstractor is given the same paper after a lapse of eight weeks, he will produce a substantially different abstract. In short, this method also relies heavily on human judgment and shares the defects of the intuitive method. It is also possible to statistically compare the vocabulary of the original document to that of the abstract to determine how representative the latter is. However, this tells little about how good the abstract is.

A *computational* method of evaluating abstracts would be extremely useful as it would almost certainly be very much faster and more convenient than manual methods. We investigated the possibility of evaluating abstracts by comparing the amounts of information in the original document and the abstract but were forced to conclude that this is not feasible. The main reason for this is that not enough is known about linguistics or the nature of information. For example, what is meant by the *information content* of a document? Does this mean only that information explicitly stated or does it include statements which follow logically from these? Is the amount of information in a document constant? It could be argued that it varied with the knowledge and intelligence of the reader. It could also be argued that an identical text passage written by different authors would have a different meaning in each case, varying with the assumptions of the writer. In order to evaluate abstracts meaningfully, it would be necessary to distinguish algorithmically between different kinds of information (new, old, trivial, important, etc.) and different levels of information (haloalkyl aryl ketones vs. bromodifluoropentyl naphthyl ketones). Should the above difficulties be overcome, then the problem of quantification arises. In what units should information be expressed and how would the numerical value of each piece be computed? Would the quantitative values depend on the type of information or the reader or author? It is not inconceivable that an algorithmic solution to these problems will eventually be developed, but we do not think it likely in the near future.

Various *functional* methods for evaluating abstracts have been tried in the past. Payne, Altman, and Munger[6,7] asked two groups of students to answer questions about a document after having read the document itself or its abstract. Resnick, Rath, and Savage[8,9] used a similar method to evaluate the usefulness of two types of abstracts compared to that of the complete text or just the title of documents. Abstracts have also been evaluated on the basis of index term content[10] and by their retrieval capabilities.[11]

For indicative abstracts, actual users of abstracts could be asked to read abstracts, decide if they needed the original document, read the original document, and review their decision. This would indicate whether or not the abstracts fulfilled their function and feedback might help to improve the abstracting process. Such a procedure would, of course, be slow and inconsistent.

Possibly the difficulty of automatic evaluation of abstracts is rooted in the same problems as automatic abstracting, and it may not be feasible to solve the one without the other.

CONCLUSIONS

- The quality of ADAM abstracts, while lower than that of good manual abstracts, is functionally adequate.
- ADAM requires, on the average, 0.6 sec of IBM 370/168 computer time per document.
- Since it is likely that more and more journals will become available in machine-readable form in the future, automatic abstracting is desirable because it is potentially much faster and cheaper than manual abstracting.
- Automatic extracting algorithms are most suited to documents with a linear, narrative structure and therefore are more successful with some subject areas than others.
- ADAM needs a specialized WCL for each subject area.
- ADAM abstracts can be improved by simple manual editing.
- It will not be possible to produce abstracts of manual quality by computer without a great breakthrough in linguistics, especially in the area of semantics.
- No theoretical basis now exists by which an abstract can be quantitatively evaluated by comparing its information content with that of the original document.

FUTURE WORK

Future work will include improving ADAM, possibly by modifying the algorithm to give greater weight to some sections of the original document than others (introducing location criteria), by applying it to a machine-readable journal, and by studying areas other than pharmacodynamics in depth to see how much specialization of the WCL is needed.

At present, the frequency thresholds at which the a priori semantic codes in the WCL are changed are the same for each term and are based on intuition. A statistical study of the vocabulary of each subject area will provide an individual frequency threshold for each term which will reflect more precisely its actual occurrence in text.

APPENDIX. ADAM ABSTRACTS

In the following examples, sentences shown in italics in the abstracts are those which we would expect a human editor to remove *in toto*; those which we consider essential are in boldface. In each example, the "experimental" section of the original document was not abstracted.

Structure-Toxicity Relationships of Substituted Phenothiazines.

Charles H. Nightingale, Melissa Tse, and Elliot I. Stupak CA-77-25-160007A

Phenothiazine hydrophobicity is related to pharmacol. response, i.e., the greater the hydrophobicity the greater the activity. Relatively complex pharmacol. effects were monitored but no attempt was made to elucidate the role of the absorptive process in modifying pharmacol. response. A relatively simple and inexpensive biol. test system can be utilized to correlate pharmacol. effect with the phys.-chem. properties of phenothiazines and to study the effect of the absorptive process in modifying such response. As stated by Zografi and Munshi, the phenothiazine mol. appears to be oriented at the interface with the ring toward the nonpolar phase and the alkylamino group directed toward the bulk aq. phase. Changes in hydrophobicity of the ring structure will, therefore, change surface activity significantly. Time of death detns. indicate that the greater the surface activity or partition coeff., the greater the toxicity. *A relationship exists between phenothiazine absorption and hydrophobicity as indicated by partitioning into dodecane.* Although a rank order correlation was also found between surface pressure and time of death for the 2-substituted derivs., a similar relationship could not be demonstrated for the 1-, 2-, and 3-chloro analogs. The goldfish test system is capable of discerning structure-toxicity relationships of substituted phenothiazines. Differences in the appearance of phenothiazine-induced toxicity depend upon the ability of the free drug to partition into the fish and this process can be correlated with dodecane partition coeffs. *One must use caution in extrapolating these results to tranquilizing activity in higher animals since inherent activity differences between the various phenothiazines were reported.*

COMMENT: The abstract is too long (23% of the original document) because too much background and trivial information is given. However, the main point of the paper (the use of the goldfish test system) is well emphasized (by being mentioned repeatedly) and the abstract faithfully reflects the content of the paper.

STATISTICS: Full original document = 1138 words.
ADAM abstract = 263 words.
Boldface abstract = 215 words.
CA abstract = 70 words.

Pseudoephedrine and the Dog's Eustachian Tube.
J. Edward Dempsey and Richard To. Jackson CA-77-25-160116K.

This study is an attempt to give an objective evaluation of the effectiveness on the dog's eustachian tube of two widely-used otolaryngic drugs-pseudoephedrine hydrochloride (sudafed) and triprolidine hydrochloride (actidil). *Merck, in 1893, obtained an isomeric alkaloid from the European E. vulgaris which he called pseudoephedrine. The pharmacol. properties of ephedrine and its isomers were largely established in the 1920's. Surprisingly, there are only a few studies of the effects of the ephedrine isomers on otolaryngic tissues-none on the eustachian tube. The four ephedrine isomers are d(-) ephedrine, l(+) ephedrine, d(-) pseudoephedrine and l(+) pseudoephedrine. Triprolidine is an antihistamine.* Two kinds of dose-response curves were obsd. We were unable to evoke a response with a single i.v. injection. *Our results are not as clear if the drug is given i.v.* In every instance tested in our expts., after complete tachyphylaxis to pseudoephedrine, repeated arterial administration 0.2 mg. of tyramine produced a normal series of responses. We found a drug, which is used daily, exhibiting tachyphylaxis. *We have seized on a particular datum as an indication.*

COMMENTS: The abstract contains a great deal of irrelevant information. Sentences which contain dates from 1959 onwards are usually rejected by ADAM but 1893 and 1920 are not in the WCL. Sentences like *Tripolidine is an antihistamine* illustrate the difficulty of distinguishing between different kinds of information. The statement is correct and contains a good deal of information per character but it is not suitable for an abstract because it is well-known to workers in the field. Sentences such as *Our results are not as clear if the drug is given i.v.* show the fallibility of relying on the surface patterns of language. The phrase *our results*, which usually occurs in important statements, is here attached to a trivial one.

STATISTICS: Full original document = 1596 words.
ADAM abstract = 174 words.
Boldface abstract = 90 words.
CA abstract = 54 words.

Plasma Levels and Absorption of Methaqualone after Oral Administration to Man.

Robert N. Morris, Gwendolyn A. Gunderson, Steven W. Babcock, and John F. Zaroslinski CA-77-25-160000T.

The present study was designed to det. human blood levels of methaqualone after oral administration of a com. prepn. of the drug, and to est. the rate and extent of absorption. The plasma elimination half-life detd. from the graph was 2.6 hr. The corresponding elimination rate const. was 0.267 hr. *The ratios obtained at each time point up to 3 hr are shown in the sixth column of table II.* 67% of the dose was absorbed within one hr and 99% in 2 hr. *Insufficient data for the absorptive phase of the curve presented in fig 2 are available to accurately est. the over-all rate const. for dissoln. and absorption.* The corresponding absorption half-time is 0.6 hr. *The value, K_a in this case represents the combined rate for dissoln. and absorption, insofar as the drug was administered orally in a solid dosage form. One subject was heavily sedated but did not sleep. The peak blood levels of these 3 were among the highest in the group.* The onset of the signs occurred between 15 and 40 min after drug. All subjects appeared alert and reported no symptoms of sedation after about 4 hr. Plasma levels indicated that 80 to 90% of the drug is cleared from the plasma within 8 hr. The plasma half-life of 2.6 hr agrees well with that estd. from the data reported by Berry. *Wide variations in plasma levels between individuals such as those noted in the present study were also reported by Berry, but he did not described the conditions in which the drug was given and reported plasma levels in only 3 patients receiving methaqualone alone.*

COMMENTS: This contains more than enough information for an indicative abstract but much of the data chosen is the same as that chosen by the CA abstractor. References are made to absent graphic data and some trivial information is given.

STATISTICS: Full original document = 1606 words.
ADAM abstract = 272 words.
Boldface abstract = 133 words.
CA abstract = 77 words.

Spectrophotometric Determination of Dimethyl Sulfoxide
Z. Dizdar, Z. Idjakovic. CA-77-26-172392K.

Working with aq. solns. of dimethyl sulfoxide(DMSO) has imposed the need for a quick and simple method for its quant. detn. *The method of potentiometric titrn. used for the detn. of the sulfoxide dissolved in Ac_2O, when the titrn. is performed with an Ac_2O or dioxan soln. of $HClO_4$, cannot be applied to such solns. either. The oxidn. methods fail in the presence of reducing agents, e.g., Me_2S which is often present in the sulfoxide.* As a result, a change should be expected in the position of the absorption spectra, which are shifted to longer wavelengths. *This medium effect has long been known.* Though the shapes of the spectra are not essentially modified by the change of the medium, the intensities of the bands are increased and red shifts obsd. in the presence of DMSO. As the best result was obtained with ammonium iron(III) sulfate the spectrophotometric detn. of mg quantities of DMSO in aq. solns. was developed with this salt as the reagent. DMSO is quant. recovered from the resin, which is in agreement with an earlier finding, and also proves the correctness of the method used for elimination of interfering cations. Sensitivity: the molar absorptivity is 3.1 mole-1 at 419 nm. The min. amt. detectable is 260 mug/cm^2.

COMMENTS: The abstract contains a great deal of trivial and background information. The useful information given is essentially the same as that chosen by the professional abstractor for CA.

STATISTICS: Full original document = 884 words.
ADAM abstract = 220 words.
Boldface abstract = 149 words.
CA abstract = 114 words.

Antispasmodics Derived from Aminopyrimidines.

P. K. Jesthi and M. K. Rout CA-77-25-160005Y.

The following types of compds. derived from various amino-pyrimidines have been prepd.: betadiethylacetamido, betaamino ethylamino, beta-diethylamino ethylamino-, morpholino ethylamino-, (5) piperidino ethylamino-. For prepg. the compds. of type (1) the corresponding amino-pyrimidines were condensed with $ClCH_2COCl$ and the resulting products were made to condense with Et_2NH under appropriate conditions. Altogether ten representative members of the different type of compds. prepd., in the present investigation have been screened for their antispasmodic and antihistaminic properties. The tests were performed on strips of guinea-pig ileum. Compd. no. 3 of table V was the most active antispasmodic and inhibited 50% of the spasm produced by std. dose acetylcholine in a dose of 162 mug./ml. Compd. no. 1 of table II was found to be most active anthihistaminic and inhibited 50% of the spasm produced by std. dose of histamine acid phosphate in a dose of 200 mug./ml.

COMMENTS: This abstract illustrates a characteristic difficulty in extracting synthetic organic text: the indispensability of the graphic material of the paper. For example, the reader cannot deduce the structure of compound no. 3 of Table V. In spite of this, the reader should receive an accurate impression of the paper and be able to decide whether or not he wants to read it.

STATISTICS: Full original document = 884 words.
ADAM abstract = 143 words.
CA abstract = 76 words.

Effects of Vasoactive Agents and Diuretics on Isolated Superfused Interlobar Renal Arteries. J. W. Strandhoy, R. Cronnelly, J. P. Long and H. E. Williamson. CA-77-25-160038M.

Little information is available concerning the actions of diuretics and other drugs on renal vascular smooth muscle, uncomplicated by reflex, hormonal or other extraneous influences. The purpose of this study therefore was to isolate a segment of the renal vascular tree for evaluation in vitro of direct actions of diuretics and other vasoactive agents. Two diuretics were evaluated for activity on the interlobar artery. No relaxant effects were obsd. with either agent. No change in base line tension was obsd. The isolated intralobar artery was found to contract in response to KCl and sympathetic nerve stimulation. No evidence was found to indicate that tension of larger renal arteries is decreased in response to furosemide. Superfusion of the tissue with hydrochlorothiazide was found to attenuate the contractile responses of norepinephrine. The highest doses of norepinephrine used were not antagonized sufficiently suggesting a competitive depression of reactivity. Hydrochlorothiazide was found to produce dose-related contractions of the interlobar strips. High doses were necessary. The interlobar arteries contribute to the renal vasoconstriction produce by norepinephrine and dopamine, but do not contribute to the renal vasodilation produced by furosemide or small doses of dopamine.

COMMENTS: Too much background, negative, and trivial information is given but the abstract still contains enough information for an indicative abstract.

STATISTICS: Full original document = 1502 words.
ADAM abstract = 199 words.
Boldface abstract = 165 words.
CA abstract = 83 words.

LITERATURE CITED

(1) Rush, J. E., Salvador, R., and Zamora, A., "Automatic Abstracting and Indexing. II. Production of Indicative Abstracts by Application of Contextual Inference and Syntactic Coherence Criteria," *J. Am. Soc. Inf. Sci.*, **22** (4), 260–74 (1971).

(2) Weil, B. H., "Standards for Writing Abstracts," *J. Am. Soc. Inf. Sci.*, **22** (4), 351–7 (1970).

(3) Rath, G. J., Resnick, A., and Savage, T. R., "The Formation of Abstracts by the Selection of Sentences. Part I. Sentence Selection by Men and Machines," *Am. Doc.*, **12** (2), 139–41 (1961).

(4) Resnick, A., "The Formation of Sentences by the Selection of Sentences. Part II. The Reliability of People in Selecting Sentences," *Am. Doc.*, **12** (2), 141–3 (1961).

(5) Resnick, A., and Savage, T. R., "The Consistency of Human Judgments of Relevance," *Am. Doc.*, **15** (2), 93–5 (1964).

(6) Payne, D., Altman, J., and Munger, S. J., "A Textual Abstracting Technique, Preliminary Development and Evaluation for Automatic Abstracting Evaluation," American Institute for Research, Pittsburgh, Pa., 1962 (AD 285 032).

(7) Payne, D., "Automatic Abstracting Evaluation Support," American Institute for Research, Pittsburgh, Pa., 1964 (AD 431 910U).

(8) Rath, G. J., Resnick, A., and Savage, T. R., "Comparisons of Four Types of Lexical Indicators of Content," *Am. Doc.*, **12** (2), 126–30 (1961).

(9) Resnick, A., "Relative Effectiveness of Document Titles and Abstracts for Determining Relevance of Documents," *Science*, **134** (3438), 1004–6 (1961).

(10) Caras, G. J., "Indexing from Abstracts of Documents," *J. Chem. Doc.*, **8** (1), 20–22 (1968).

(11) "Final Report on the Study for Automatic Abstracting," Thompson Ramo Wooldridge, Inc., Canoga Park, Calif., 1961 (PB 166 532).

Section 2

Corpus-based Approaches

Section 1 described the use of various features such as thematic features, title, cue phrase, and location in determining salience of information for summarization. An obvious issue here is determining the relative contribution of different features to any given text summarization problem. The answer to this question is likely to be dependent on the text genre; for example, take the Location feature. In newspaper stories, the leading text often contains a cogent summary (Brandow et al., Section 5); in TV news broadcasts, a preview segment may contain a summary of the news to come; in scientific text, the abstract and conclusion may offer useful summary information. One attraction of corpus-based approaches is that the importance of different text features for any given summarization problem may be determined by counting the occurrences of such features in text corpora. In particular, researchers have investigated whether an analysis of a corpus of human-generated summaries along with their corresponding full-text sources could be used to learn rules or techniques for automated summarization.

There are also other advantages to a corpus-based approach. In addition to its usefulness in building empirically-based language models, there are many summarization problems beyond evidence combination for which they can be very useful, including the construction of accurate models of the types of constructions which occur in summaries (cf. McKeown et al.'s paper in Section 4), and determining relationships between full-text and corresponding summaries. Finally, it allows researchers to share data sets, permitting comparisons of different techniques.

Of course, one might use a corpus to model particular components, without necessarily using a completely trainable approach. A common use of a corpus is in computing weights based on term frequency. The *tf.idf* measure, which is widely used in information retrieval (e.g., Spärck Jones 1972) as well as text summarization, is used to pick out terms that distinguish one document from others in the corpus. There are several different variants of this measure, of which one is:

$$w_{ij} = tf_{ij} * \log_2 \frac{N}{n}$$

Here, w_{ij} is the weight of term t_i in document d_j, tf_{ij} is the frequency of term t_i in document d_j, N is the number of documents in the corpus, and n is the number of documents in the corpus in which term t_i occurs.

The corpus-based approach faces a number of challenges, including:

- Creating and making available a suitable text corpus. This requires constructing a representative sample of the kinds of text one is interested in summarizing, obtaining permission to exploit and distribute the texts, designing an annotation scheme for use in summarization, etc.

- Ensuring that a suitable set of summaries is available. A corpus without summaries is somewhat less useful for summarization. In the case of scientific texts, abstracts are often available, but this may not be the case for other genres. The summaries may be supplied by an author, or by professional abstractors, or by judges asked to extract sentences. When not supplied by the author, considerable care has to be taken in terms of the criteria used to construct these summaries (see Section 5 for discussion of this). Further, author-supplied abstracts are often not as systematic as those constructed by professional abstractors, who are trained to follow certain prescriptive guidelines.

- Evaluating such approaches, in terms of accuracy on unseen test data, the amount of training material required, relative cost and efficacy compared to hand-engineered knowledge, and impact on some user task (Section 5 discusses evaluation issues in more detail)

- Extending these approaches to production of coherent extracts and abstracts

- Discovering new features for different genres, which can help discriminate summary-relevant information

- Using term-statistics based on concept-level term aggregation

- Combining the use of corpora with concept hierarchies, which make possible various kinds of generalization of use in summarization.

The papers in this section cover recent developments that offer interesting approaches to some of these challenges.

The first paper by Kupiec, Pedersen, and Chen (henceforth, KPC) represents a major advance in this area. The overall approach to learning using a KPC-approach is shown in Figure 1. Note that the training summaries are used only to label the full-text sentence vectors as positive or negative examples of summary-worthy sentences. (An alternative approach might be to analyze the training summaries as well.)

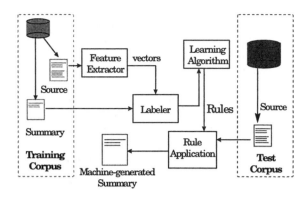

Figure1. Methodology for Machine Learning in KPC.

The corpus KPC use is a collection of 188 full-text/summary pairs, drawn from 21 different scientific collections. Each summary was written by a professional abstractor and was 3 sentences long on average. Their Bayesian classifier algorithm takes each test sentence and computes a probability that it should be included in a summary, based on the frequency of features in the full-text vectors and the vectors' labels (1 if it is to be included in a summary, 0 otherwise). The features used in these experiments are sentence length, presence of fixed cue phrases ("in summary", etc.), whether a sentence's location is paragraph-initial, paragraph-medial, or paragraph-final, presence of high-frequency content words, and presence of proper names.

Of course, human summaries don't necessarily lift sentences from the full-text. In addressing this, the authors describe various categories of matches, the simplest of which is a *direct* match, where the summary sentence and source sentence are identical or can be considered to have the same content. The overall performance on test documents was 42% recall of sentences in the summaries. As the summaries were lengthened, performance improved, peaking at 84% sentence recall at 25% of the full-text length. The authors did not, however, measure precision. (As the recall goes up, the number of false positives may be expected to go up; since the human summaries had only a fixed compression - about 3 sentences long on the average- most of the sentences extracted at 25% compression would not be in the summary and thus could be viewed as being false positives.) As with Edmundson's paper in Section 1, KPC found that location was the best individual feature; in their feature mix, location, cue phrase, and sentence length was the best combination.

The KPC work has stimulated a flurry of related research. In Section 3, Teufel and Moens extend the KPC approach to discourse segment identification, as a step towards the generation of abstracts. Also, Mani and Bloedorn (1998) have extended this model beyond Bayesian classifiers, using decision tree rules to train summarizers to generate

both generic and user-specific summarization rules for a corpus of articles with author-supplied abstracts, obtaining good results without the use of cue-phrases.

The next paper, by Myaeng and Jang, describes a variant of the KPC method applied to technical texts in Korean. They consider material in the Introduction and Conclusion sections alone, and manually tag each sentence in those sections as to whether it represents the background, a main theme, an explanation of the document structure, or a description of future work. They found that more than 96% of the summary sentences were main theme sentences. The sentences are also manually tagged as to whether they are present in a human-constructed summary. Their training method first uses a Bayesian classifier to determine whether a sentence belongs to a main theme, and then combines evidence from multiple Bayesian feature classifiers to determine whether a sentence belongs to a summary. Finally, a filter is applied to eliminate redundant sentences. They found that on their data, using a combination of cue words, sentence location, and presence of title words in a sentence led to the best results.

The third paper, by Aone, Okurowski, Gorlinsky, and Larsen, uses an approach to summarization similar to KPC. The authors go beyond that work, however, in showing that in using term-based statistics, different ways of aggregating terms can impact summarization performance. For example, in addition to counting morphologically variant forms of a word as occurrences of the same root term, one might aggregate synonym occurrences together as occurrences of the same concept. Also, one could identify proper names as terms, and treat name aliases (e.g., "IBM" for "International Business Machines") as occurrences of the same entity, thereby counting name references rather than mentions. The authors compare a sentence extraction algorithm based on weighting terms of these different types against human sentence extracts. They show that performance can be improved when place names and organization names are identified as terms, and when person names are filtered out.. They suggest the reason why person names need to be identified and then suppressed is that in the TREC collections (Harman and Voorhees 1996) they used to train and test their system, document topics are generally not person-focused.

The final paper in this section by Hovy and Lin describes a variety of different corpus-based techniques for summarization. They describe a three-part process: topic identification, corresponding to the analysis phase described in our Introduction, concept interpretation (corresponding to the transformation phase), and summary generation (corresponding to the synthesis phase). Topic identification aims at extracting the salient concepts in a document, with these salient concepts being used to weight sentences for extraction. The authors introduce a new method for identifying location-relevant information. By training on a corpus of documents with their associated topics provided in the form of keywords, their method yields a ranked list of sentence positions that tend to contain the most topic-related keywords. The system was trained on a 13,000 article corpus (Ziff-Davis) containing texts, abstracts, and keywords. The resulting Optimal Position Policy got encouraging results. They also describe the use of several feature combination algorithms.

Hovy and Lin's (somewhat preliminary) work on concept interpretation attempts to fuse together related concepts in the text to arrive at more general topics. They count frequencies in the text of concepts from the WordNet thesaurus (Miller 1995), using the thesaurus hierarchy to arrive at an appropriate generalization. These aggregation and generalization operations can be used to produce abstracts instead of just extracts. However, since many expected relationships were hard to find in WordNet, they exploit other corpus-based methods, involving text categorization (binning documents into existing categories) and text clustering (grouping documents into classes). The authors report on text categorization experiments where they trained on 30,000 texts from a Wall Street Journal corpus, where each article is labeled with one out of 32 possible topic labels (e.g., aerospace, banking, environment, telecommunications). For each such topic, the top 300 terms scored by a term-weighting metric were treated as topic signatures; the terms in a test documents can be matched against these signatures to determine the document topics. Future research will be required to determine the effectiveness of these methods in creating summaries.

Overall, these four papers present an interesting sample of current research in corpus-based text summarization. Of course, having a trainable sentence extractor in itself does not guarantee that the summaries are useful. For one thing, unless discourse coherence is used as a feature, the sentences extracted could be out of context, with dangling anaphors and gaps between them. In addition, comparison against an ideal summary does not necessarily mean that the summaries produced are effective in any task. Finally, questions remain open regarding the choice of different feature representations, and the extent to which corpus-based methods of the kind described here can be extended to later phases of the summarization task.

As an interdisciplinary application area, text summarization has traditionally relied on advances in information retrieval, information extraction, and natural language processing in general. The advances in corpus-based methods in these latter fields continue to grow, and we expect that developments in corpus-based approaches to semantics and natural language generation will further accelerate progress in text summarization.

References

Harman, D., and Voorhees, E.M. 1996. *The Fifth Text Retrieval Conference (TREC-5),* Technical Report, SP-500-238, National Institute of Standards and Technology, Gaithersburg, Maryland.

Mani, I., and Bloedorn, E. 1998. Machine Learning of Generic and User-Focused Summarization. In *Proceedings of the Fifteenth National Conference on Artificial Intelligence (AAAI'98),* Madison, Wisconsin, 821-826. Menlo Park, Calif.: AAAI Press.

Miller, G. 1995. WordNet: A Lexical Database for English. *Communications of the Association for Computing Machinery (CACM)* 38(1):39-41.

Paice, C., and Jones, P. 1993. The Identification of Important Concepts in Highly Structured Technical Papers. In *Proceedings of the Sixteenth Annual International ACM SIGIR Conference on Research and Development in Information Retrieval (ACM-SIGIR'93),* 69-78.

Spärck Jones, K. 1972. A Statistical Interpretation of Term Specificity and Its Application in Retrieval. *Journal of Documentation,* 28(1):11-20.

5

A Trainable Document Summarizer

Julian Kupiec, **Jan Pedersen** and **Francine Chen**

Xerox Palo Alto Research Center

3333 Coyote Hill Road, Palo Alto, CA 94304

{kupiec,pedersen,fchen}@parc.xerox.com

Abstract

- To summarize is to reduce in complexity, and hence in length, while retaining some of the essential qualities of the original.

- This paper focusses on document extracts, a particular kind of computed document summary.

- Document extracts consisting of roughly 20% of the original can be as informative as the full text of a document, which suggests that even shorter extracts may be useful indicative summaries.

- The trends in our results are in agreement with those of Edmundson who used a subjectively weighted combination of features as opposed to training the feature weights using a corpus.

- We have developed a trainable summarization program that is grounded in a sound statistical framework.

Keywords: summary sentence, original documents, summary pairs, training corpus, document extracts

1 Introduction

To summarize is to reduce in complexity, and hence in length, while retaining some of the essential qualities of the original. Titles, keywords, tables-of-contents and abstracts might all be considered as forms of summary, however a *document summary* conventionally refers to an abstract-like condensation of a full-text document. Traditionally, document summaries are provided by the author. This paper focusses on *document extracts*, a particular kind of computed document summary.

Abstracts are sometimes used as full document surrogates, for example as the input to text search systems, but they also speed access by providing an easily digested intermediate point between a document's title and its full text that is useful for rapid relevance assessment. It is this second interface-related use that is our motivation for automatic document summarization. The goal is to generate a concise document description that is more revealing than a title but short enough to be absorbed in a single glance. A traditional author-supplied indicative abstract clearly fulfills this objective, but it is hoped that other, more easily computed condensations may also serve.

Numerous researchers have addressed automatic document summarization (see [10] for an overview). The nominal task of generating a coherent narrative summarizing a document is currently considered too problematic since it encompasses discourse understanding, abstraction, and language generation [6]. Nonetheless, knowledge intensive methods have had some success in restricted domains [11, 5, 3, 13, 18]. For example, a filled template produced by a message understanding system can be thought of as a targetted document summary. A simpler, more generic approach avoids the central difficulties of natural language processing by redefining the task to be *summary by extraction* [7]. That is, the goal is to find a subset of the document that is indicative of its contents, typically by scoring sentences and presenting those with the best scores. These sorts of summaries are not guaranteed to have narrative coherence, yet may be useful for rapid relevance assessment.

Document extracts consisting of roughly 20% of the original can be as informative as the full text of a document [9], which suggests that even shorter extracts may be useful indicative summaries. However, other studies [12, 2] suggest that the optimal extract can be far from unique. Numerous heuristics have been proposed to guide the selection of document extracts [7, 4, 17, 14], yet no clear criterion has been proposed to choose among them. Existing evidence [4] suggests that combinations of individual heuristics have the best performance.

We approach extract selection as a statistical classification problem. Given a training set of documents with hand-selected document extracts, develop a classification function that estimates the probability a given sentence is included in an extract. New extracts can then be generated by ranking sentences according to this probability and selecting a user-specified number of the top scoring ones.

This framework provides a natural evaluation criterion: the classification success rate or *precision*. It also offers a direct method for finding an optimal combination of extraction selection heuristics, or features. However, it does require a training corpus of documents with labelled extracts, which can be expensive to obtain. We have acquired such a corpus from Engineering Information Co., a non-profit company providing abstracts of technical articles to online information services, which will serve as the basis for the experiments described here.

The following sections detail our approach, describe the training corpus, present evaluation results that rate our document summarization method at 42% average precision, and discuss some practical implementation issues.

Aerospace America	Manufacturing Engineering
American Laboratory	Metal Finishing
Civil Engineering	Modern Plastics
Chemical Engineering Education	Oil and Gas Journal
Concrete International	Pulp and Paper International
IEEE Communications Magazine	Robotics World
IEEE Control System	Scripta Metallurgica et Materiala
Journal of Cellular Plastics	Sensors
Journal of Material Science Letters	Water Engineering and Management
Japanese Railway Engineering	Wire Association International '93
Machine Design	

Table 1: Journals in Corpus

2   A Trainable Summarizer

Extracting summarizers typically compute a score for each sentence in a document and then select the highest scoring subset. The scoring criteria employed include participation in predefined semantic roles[11], rhetorical relations[8], inclusion of phrasal index terms[16], document-specific keyword frequencies[7], location heuristics[1], and the assessment of sentence similarity structure[17, 15]. Methods either assume the document exists in isolation, or in the context of a larger collection, which al lows term weights to depend on corpus statistics[14, 15].

The precise formulation of the scoring rule is heuristic and empirical in nature. However, if one were given a training corpus of documents with matched extracts, it would be natural to approach the problem as one of statistical classification. This would provide a principled method for selecting among potential features, or scoring criteria, and for choosing a weighted combination of these to produce an "optimal" scoring scheme — optimal in the sense of doing the best job possible of predicting the extraction selection performed by human judges given the features and the method of combination. To pursue this approach, we need to establish the set of potential features, the classification method, and a training corpus of document/extract pairs.

2.1   Features

Paice [10] groups sentence scoring features into seven categories. *Frequency-keyword* heuristics use the most common content words as indicators of the main themes in the document. Sentences containing these words are scored using functions of their frequency counts [4, 19]. The *title-keyword* heuristic assumes that important sentences contain content words that are present in the title and major headings of a document. *Location* heuristics assume that important sentences lie at the beginning and end of a document, in the first and last sentences of paragraphs [1, 4], and also immediately below section headings. *Indicator phrases* contain words that are likely to accompany indicative or informative summary material (e.g., "This report..."). A related heuristic involves *cue words*. These may include two sets of "bonus" and "stigma" words [4] which are positively and negatively correlated with summary sentences. Example bonus words are "greatest" and "significant". Stigma words are exemplified by "hardly" and "impossible".

Through experimentation we settled on the following feature set, which are all discrete in nature.

Sentence Length Cut-off Feature: Short sentences tend not to be included in summaries (section headings generally count as short sentences). Given a threshold (e.g., 5 words), the feature is true for all sentences longer than the threshold, and false otherwise.

Fixed-Phrase Feature: Sentences containing any of a list of fixed phrases, mostly two words long (e.g., "this letter...", "In conclusion..." etc.), or occurring immediately after a section heading containing a keyword such as "conclusions", "results", "summary", and "discussion" are more likely to be in summaries. This features is true for sentences that contain any of 26 indicator phrases, or that follow section heads that contain specific keywords.

Paragraph Feature: This discrete feature records information for the first ten paragraphs and last five paragraphs in a document. Sentences in a paragraph are distinguished according to whether they are paragraph-initial, paragraph-final (for paragraphs longer than one sentence) and paragraph-medial (in paragraphs greater than two sentences long).

Thematic Word Feature: The most frequent content words are defined as thematic words (ties for words with the same frequency are resolved on the basis of word length). A small number of thematic words is selected and each sentence is scored as a function of frequency. This feature is binary, depending on whether a sentence is present in the set of highest scoring sentences. Experiments were performed in which scaled sentence scores were used as pseudo-probabilities, however this gave inferior performance.

Uppercase Word Feature: Proper names are often important, as is explanatory text for acronyms e.g., "... by the ASTM (American Society for Testing and Materials)". This feature is computed similarly to the previous one, with the constraints that an uppercase thematic word is not sentence-initial and begins with a capital letter. Additionally, it must occur several times and must not be an abbreviated unit of measurement (e.g., F, C, Kg, etc.). Sentences in which such words appear first score twice as much as later occurrences.

2.2   Classifier

For each sentence s we compute the probability it will be included in a summary $\mathcal{S}$ given the k features $F_j; j = 1...k$, which can be expressed using Bayes' rule as follows:

$$P(s \in \mathcal{S}|F_1, F_2, \ldots F_k) = \frac{P(F_1, F_2, \ldots F_k|s \in \mathcal{S})P(s \in \mathcal{S})}{P(F_1, F_2, \ldots F_k)}$$

Assuming statistical independence of the features:

$$P(s \in \mathcal{S}|F_1, F_2, \ldots F_k) = \frac{\prod_{j=1}^{k} P(F_j|s \in \mathcal{S}) \, P(s \in \mathcal{S})}{\prod_{j=1}^{k} P(F_j)}$$

$P(s \in \mathcal{S})$ is a constant and $P(F_j|s \in \mathcal{S})$ and $P(F_j)$ can be estimated directly from the training set by counting occurrences. Note that since all the features are discrete, we can formulate this equation in terms of probabilities rather than likelihoods. This yields a simple Bayesian classification function that assigns for each *s* a score which can be used to select sentences for inclusion in a generated summary.

3 The Corpus

The training corpus provided by Engineering Information employed in our investigation contains documents without author-supplied abstracts. Abstracts were instead created by professional abstractors by reference to the original. There are 188 document/summary pairs, sampled from 21 publications in the scientific/technical domain (see Table 1). These summaries are mainly indicative, and their average length is three sentences. An example is shown in Figure 1.

Documents were received in the form of photocopies which required scanning and optical character recognition (OCR) to extract their text portions. This process introduced spelling errors and occasional omissions of text. The resulting text files were manually checked, and either rejected due to excessive OCR errors or cleaned-up. Errors and omissions still remain in the files after cleanup, however they are unlikely to affect results. Particular care was taken to ensure that the beginnings and ends of documents were correct, as most summary sentences are located at these places. The average number of sentences per document is 86 (a slightly conservative estimate due to the omissions). Each document was "normalized" so that the first line of each file contained the document title. Text describing author, address etc., between the title and the start of the document proper was removed, as was the bibliography. (Techniques for dealing with more typical text are described in Section 6). The corresponding original text for Figure 1 is shown in Figure 2.

The training strategy outlined in Section 2 assumes that we have document/extract pairs. However, we have in fact manual summary sentences that are "inspired" by particular sentences in the original documents. Thus the summarization task we are addressing is to extract the same set of sentences from a document that an expert might use to make summary text, either verbatim or with minor modification, preserving content.

3.1 Sentence Matching

To proceed with training, we need to obtain a correspondence between the manual summary sentences and sentences in the original document. Sentences from the original documents can be matched to those in the manual summaries in several ways. A *direct sentence match* occurs when a manual summary sentence could either be extracted verbatim from the original, or with minor modifications, preserving the content (as exemplified by Figures 1 and 2). When it is obvious that two or more sentences were used from the original to make a summary sentence, a *direct join* occurs. If it is either obvious or suspected that the expert constructed a summary sentence from a general reading (i.e. using no specific sentence from the original) the summary sentence is labelled *unmatchable*. Individual summary sentences may also be labelled *incomplete* in two situations. The first is when some overlap does exist between a summary sentence and one in the original, but the content of the original is not preserved in the summary sentence. The second is when the summary sentence includes a sentence from the original document, but also contains other information that is not covered by a direct join. Joins may themselves be labelled *incomplete* for the same reasons. Examples of these correspondences are shown in the Appendix. The correspondences were produced in two passes. In the first, an automatic alignment program was used to find the best one-to-one sentence match in the original documents for each summary

sentence. These were used as a starting point for the manual assignment of correspondences made in the second pass. Table 2 shows the distribution of the correspondences in the training corpus.

Direct Sentence Matches	451	79%
Direct Joins	19	3%
Unmatchable Sentences	50	9%
Incomplete Single Sentences	21	4%
Incomplete Joins	27	5%
Total Manual Summary sents	568	

Table 2: Distribution of Correspondences

The table indicates that 79% of the summary sentences have direct matches. The 19 direct joins consist of a total of 41 different sentences from original documents. For three summary sentences, the best matching "sentences" in the original appeared to be the corresponding document titles. Nine of the manual summary sentences appeared to contain section headings (e.g. in lists). In eight instances a sentence in the original document was split up to make several sentences in the manual summaries.

4 Evaluation

Since we had insufficient data to reserve a separate test corpus we used a cross-validation strategy for evaluation. Documents from a given journal were selected for testing one at a time; all other document/summary pairs were used for training. Results were summed over journals. Unmatchable and incomplete sentences were excluded from both training and testing, yielding a total of 498 unique sentences. We evaluate performance in two ways.

The first evaluation measure is stringent – the fraction of manual summary sentences that were faithfully reproduced by the summarizer program. It is thus limited by the drawbacks of text excerpting and the highest performance attainable is the sum of all direct sentence matches and all direct joins. Referring to Table 2 this is:

$$\frac{451 + 19}{568} = 83\%$$

A sentence produced by the summarizer is defined as correct here if:

1. It has a direct sentence match, and is present in the manual summary.

2. It is in the manual summary as part of a direct join, and all other members of the join have also been produced (thus all the information in the join is preserved).

For each test document, the trained summarizer produced the same number of sentences as were in the corresponding manual summary. Of the 568 sentences, 195 direct sentence matches and 6 direct joins were correctly identified, for a total of 201 correctly identified summary sentences. The summarizer thus replicates 35% of the information in the manual summaries. This assumes that only one "correct" summary exists for a document which is very unlikely to be the case. Indeed, it has been observed that subjects differ greatly when asked to select summary sentences [2]. In particular, Rath et al. [12] found that extracts selected by four different human judges had only 25% overlap, and for a given judge over time only 55% overlap.

The second evaluation measure is the fraction of the 498 matchable sentences that were correctly identified by the summarizer (it is

> The work undertaken examines the drawability of steel wire rod with respect to elements that are not intentionally added to steel. Only low carbon steels were selected for experimentation. During wire drawing, failure-inducing tensile forces are greatest at the center of the wire. This accounts for the classic appearance of ductile failure with the center of the wire failing in a ductile manner.

Figure 1: A Manual Summary

> **Paragraph 2:** The work undertaken examines the drawability of steel wire rod with respect to elements that are not intentionally added to steel. The effect of microstructure was not of interest to the investigation. For this reason, only low carbon steels were selected for experimentation.
>
> .....
>
> **Paragraph 4:** Once nucleated, these microvoids grow and coalesce, until the wire can no longer support the drawing load and a break occurs. During wiredrawing, failure-inducing tensile forces are greatest at the center of the wire. This accounts for the classic appearance of ductile failure with the center of the wire failing in a ductile manner, while the circumference fails last, and in shear.

Figure 2: Relevant Paragraphs from Original

thus theoretically possible to attain 100% correct). When the summarizer outputs the same number of sentences as in corresponding manual summaries, 211 out of 498 (42%) were correctly identified.

The second column in Table 3 shows the sentence-level performance for individual features. In cases where sentences have the same probability, they are ranked in document order. Thus, the sentence length cut-off feature, if used alone, returns the text at the beginning of a document, excluding the title and headings.

Feature	Individual Sents Correct	Cumulative Sents Correct
Paragraph	163 (33%)	163 (33%)
Fixed Phrases	145 (29%)	209 (42%)
Length Cut-off	121 (24%)	217 (44%)
Thematic Word	101 (20%)	209 (42%)
Uppercase Word	100 (20%)	211 (42%)

Table 3: Performance of Features

The third column in Table 3 shows how performance varies as features are successively combined together, in descending order of individual performance. The best combination is (paragraph + fixed-phrase + sentence-length). Addition of the frequency-keyword features (thematic and uppercase word features) results in a slight decrease in overall performance.

For a baseline, we compared the summarizer with the strategy of simply selecting sentences from the beginning of a document (how documents are typically displayed and read). This baseline was computed by considering the sentence length cut-off feature alone, which ranks sentences in reading order, excluding short fragments, such as section headings. When compared to the baseline (which can be read off the third row of Table 3; 121 sentences correct) using the full feature set improves performance by 74% (211 sentences correct).

Figure 3 shows the performance of the summarizer (using all features) as a function of summary size. When generating summaries that automatically select 25% of the sentences in the original documents, Edmundson cites a sentence-level performance of 44%. By analogy, 25% of the average document length (86 sentences) in

our corpus is about 20 sentences. Reference to the table indicates performance at 84%.

5 Discussion

The trends in our results are in agreement with those of Edmundson [4] who used a subjectively weighted combination of features as opposed to training the feature weights using a corpus. He also found that location-based heuristics gave best performance. His best combination of heuristics were based on location, title-keywords and cue words. Edmundson also experimented with a frequency-keyword heuristic, omitting it from his preferred selection on account of inferior performance.

Frequency-keyword features (i.e. the thematic word feature and uppercase feature) also gave poorest individual performance in our evaluation. The likely reason is that they select sentences more evenly throughout a text, but our corpus contains a lot of indicative material located at the beginnings and ends. We have however retained these features in our final system for several reasons. The first is robustness; many text genres do not contain any of the indicator-phrases that are common in the corpus we have used [1]. Secondly, as the number of sentences in a summary grows, more dispersed informative material tends to be included.

As described in Section 3.1, we first used an automatic alignment program to obtain correspondences, which were then manually checked and corrected. We also evaluated performance using the manually corrected correspondences, but training using only the correspondences produced by the alignment program. The performance was 216 sentences (43%) correct, suggesting that for corpora such ours, summarizers can be trained automatically from document/summary pairs without manual intervention.

6 Implementation Issues

Our goal is to provide a summarization program that is of general utility. This requires attention to several issues beyond the training of features and performance evaluation. The first concerns robustness (in this regard multiple features have already been discussed).

---

[1] When the fixed-phrase feature is omitted, performance drops from 211 sentences (42%) to 178 (36%)

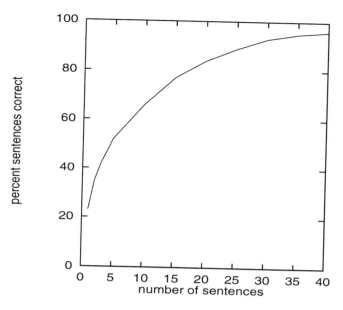

Figure 3: Performance vs. Summary Size

Key Phrases:

cold work	solute atmospheres
solute atoms	test piece
dislocation velocity	dynamic strain aging

Sentence Extracts:

- Drawability of low carbon steel wire

- The work undertaken examines the drawability of steel wire rod with respect to elements that are not intentionally added to steel.

- For this reason, only low carbon steels were selected for experimentation.

- During wiredrawing, failure-inducing tensile forces are greatest at the center of the wire.

- This accounts for the classic appearance of ductile failure with the center of the wire failing in a ductile manner, while the circumference fails last, and in shear.

Figure 4: Computed Summary

As mentioned earlier, documents in the corpus were edited so that the title appears first and the text of the document proper immediately follows. In practice, both the title (if present) and the beginning of the main body of text are often preceded by dates, addresses, names, and various other notations. It is advantageous to find the title, and the beginning of the main text (performance is sensitive to the beginning of the main text, by virtue of the paragraph feature). We therefore implemented another set of features specifically to find the start of the main text body, and to isolate a sentence that acts as a title, lying between the main text and beginning of the document. Briefly, these features include numbers, explicit sentence boundary marks, word case, and paragraph and sentence lengths. For example, uppercase or word-initial uppercase letters are often used in titles, and consecutive sentences ending with explicit punctuation are more likely to be in the main text body. Additionally, if an author-supplied abstract is present (identified by a heading containing the word *abstract*), then subsequent paragraphs are used directly as the summary and no feature-based extraction is attempted.

The second issue concerns presentation and other forms of summary information. The highest scoring sentences (including the likely title) are shown in reading order to the user in conjunction with the key phrases of the document (as illustrated in Figure 4). These key phrases must contain at least two adjacent words, are primarily noun phrases, and are presented in frequency order. They are computed based on a frequency analysis of word sequences in a document. To identify them, a stop list composed of articles, prepositions, common adverbs, and auxilary verbs is used to break the words in a sentence into phrases.

7 Conclusions

We have developed a trainable summarization program that is grounded in a sound statistical framework. For summaries that are 25% of the size of the average test document, it selects 84% of the sentences chosen by professionals. For smaller summary sizes an improvement of 74% was observed over simply presenting the beginning of a document. We have also described how extracts can be used with other information to create a summary useful of rapid relevance assessment while browsing.

8   Acknowledgments

We would like to thank Meg Withgott and John Tukey for their insights into this work. In particular, Meg Withgott was responsible for pioneering this work. We thank Austen Briggs for hand correcting the OCR data. We are also grateful to Dan Brotsky, Ken Feuerman, Sandy Garcia and Steve Putz for their help and for the implementation of the summarization program in the XSoft Visual Recall^{TM} product.

References

[1] P. B. Baxendale. Man-made index for technical literature – an experiment. *IBM J. Res. Develop.*, 2(4):354–361, 1958.

[2] F.R. Chen and M.M. Withgott. The use of emphasis to automatically summarize a spoken discourse. In *Proceedings of the IEEE Intl. Conf. on Acoust., Speech and Signal Proc.*, volume 1, pages 229–232, March 1992.

[3] G. DeJong. An overview of the FRUMP system. In W.G. Lehnert and M. H. Ringle, editors, *Strategies for Natural Language Parsing*, pages 149–176, 1982.

[4] H. P. Edmundson. New methods in automatic abstracting. *Journal of the ACM*, 16(2):264–285, April 1969.

[5] P.S. Jacobs and L. F. Rau. Scisor: Extracting information from on-line news. *Communications of the ACM*, 33(11):88–97, 1990.

[6] K. Sparck Jones. Discourse modelling for automatic summarising. Technical Report 29D, Computer Laboratory, University of Cambridge, 1993.

[7] H.P. Luhn. The automatic creation of literature abstracts. *IBM J. Res. Develop.*, 2:159–165, 1959.

[8] S. Miike, E. Itoh, K. Ono, and K. Sumita. A full-text retrieval system with a dynamic abstract generation function. In W. Bruce Croft and C.J. van Rijsbergen, editors, *Proceedings of Seventeenth Annual International ACM SIGIR Conference on Research and Development in Information Retrieval*, pages 152–161, July 1994.

[9] A. H. Morris, G. M. Kasper, and D. A. Adams. The effects and limitations of automated text condensing on reading comprehension performance. *Information Systems Research*, pages 17–35, March 1992.

[10] C. D. Paice. Constructing literature abstracts by computer: Techniques and prospects. *Information Processing and Management*, 26:171–186, 1990.

[11] C. D. Paice and P. A. Jones. The identification of important concepts in highly structured technical papers. In R. Korfhage, E. Rasmussen, and P. Willett, editors, *Proceedings of Sixteenth Annual International ACM SIGIR Conference on Research and Development in Information Retrieval*, pages 69–78. ACM Press, June 1993.

[12] G. J. Rath, A. Resnick, and T. R. Savage. The formation of abstracts by the selection of sentences. *American Documentation*, 12(2):139–143, April 1961.

[13] U. Reimer and U. Hahn. Text condensation as knowledge base abstraction. In *IEEE Conf. on AI Applications*, pages 338–344, 1988.

[14] G. Salton, J. Alan, and C. Buckley. Approaches to passage retrieval in full text information systems. In *Proceedings of SIGIR'93*, pages 49–58, June 1993.

[15] G. Salton, J. Allan, C. Buckley, and A. Singhal. Automatic analysis, theme generation, and summarization of machine-readable texts. *Science*, 264(3):1421–1426, June 1994.

[16] C. Schwarz. Content based text handling. *Information Processing & Management*, 26(2):219–226, 1990.

[17] E. F. Skorokhod'ko. Adaptive method of automatic abstracting and indexing. In *IFIP Congress, Ljubljana, Yugoslavia 71*, pages 1179–1182. North Holland, 1972.

[18] J. I. Tait. Generating summaries using a script-based language analyzer. In L. Steels and J.A. Campbell, editors, *Progress in Artificial Intelligence*, pages 312–318. Ellis Horwood, 1985.

[19] L. C. Tong and S. L. Tan. A statistical approach to automatic text extraction. *Asian Library Journal*.

9   Appendix

9.0.1   Direct Match

If a summary sentence is identical to a sentence in the original, or has essentially the same content, the match is defined as a direct match. An example match that is not exact but considered to convey the same content is shown below:

Manual: This paper identifies the desirable features of an ideal multisensor gas monitor and lists the different models currently available.

Original: The present part lists the desirable features and the different models of portable, multisensor gas monitors currently available.

9.0.2   Direct Join

If the content of the manual sentence is represented by two or more sentences in the original, the latter sentences are noted as joins. For example:

Manual: In California, Caltrans has a rolling pavement management program, with continuous collection of data with the aim of identifying roads that require more monitoring and repair.

Original (1): Rather than conducting biennial surveys, Caltrans now has a rolling pavement-management program, with data collected continuously.

Original (2): The idea is to pinpoint the roads that may need more or less monitoring and repair.

9.0.3   Incomplete Matches

A sentence in the original document is labelled as an incomplete match if it only partially covers the content of a manual summary sentence, or if a direct match is not clear. It can occur in the context of a single sentence or a join. The following exemplifies an incomplete single sentence match:

Manual: Intergranular fracture of polycrystalline Ni_3Al was studied at 77K.

Original: Before discussing the observed deformation and fracture behavior of polycrystalline Ni_3Al at 77K in terms of the kinetics of the proposed environmental embrittlement mechanism, we should ask whether the low temperature by itself significantly affects the brittleness of Ni_3Al.

6

Development and Evaluation of a Statistically-Based Document Summarization System

Sung Hyon Myaeng and Dong-Hyun Jang

Department of Computer Science
Chungnam National University
220 Gung-Dong, Yusong-Ku, Taejon, 305-764 KOREA

{shmyaeng, dhjang}@cs.chungnam.ac.kr

Abstract

This paper describes an automatic summarization approach that constructs a summary by extracting sentences that are likely to represent the main theme of a document. As a way of selecting summary sentences, the system uses model that takes into account lexical and statistical information obtained from a document corpus. As such, the system consists of two parts: the training part and the summarization part. The former processes sentences that have been manually tagged for summary sentences and extracts necessary statistical information of various kinds, and the latter uses the information to calculate the likelihood that a sentence is to be included in a summary. There are at least four unique aspects of this research. First of all, the system uses a text component identification model to categorize sentences into one of the text components. This allows us to eliminate parts of text that are not likely to contain summary sentences. Second, although our statistically-based model stems from an existing one developed for English texts, it applies the framework to individual features separately and computes the final score for each sentence by combining the pieces of evidence using the Dempster-Shafer combination rule. Third, not only were new features introduced but also all the features were tested for their efficacy in the summarization framework. Finally the system we developed is the first of this kind for Korean texts.

1. Introduction

With the growing popularity of the Internet and a variety of information services, obtaining the desired information is becoming a serious problem in this information age. In order to help users find useful information, search engines or information retrieval systems have been made available. When a system either retrieves information or finds the location of the requested information, however, it is not unusual that a large proportion of the result is not relevant to the query. That means, the user ends up spending a significant amount of time reading through details of documents that may or may not be relevant. This information overload problem has called for text summarization that provides helpful information for users to easily understand document contents without having to read the full text.

Along with a number of approaches that have emerged recently, we developed a summarization system whose current goal is to select a small number of most meaningful and representative sentences from a full document written in Korean. Our system is a statistically-based model that determines the degree to which individual sentences belong to a summary, by taking into account lexical and statistical information obtained from a training corpus. The main thrust of our approach is the use of thematic structures of documents in the summarization model, in conjunction with other features. The thematic structures, which are delineated with the same probabilistic framework, are used to decompose a document into a set of pieces or classify individual sentences into different thematic categories.

Another unique aspect of our work is that we investigated different ways to include various features in the model. Instead of blindly using all the features as part of a statistical classifier, we attempted to build a filter using each feature so that a sentence not possessing a particular feature is eliminated completely and not considered at all as a candidate summary sentence. In order to see the impact of individual features as well as the idea of employing filters, we ran a series of experiments with actual summarization tasks.

Our model is probabilistic in nature and similar to Kupiec's approach (Kupiec, Pedersen, and Chen 1995) that showed a reasonable level of performance with English texts. From the modeling perspective, however, our model differs form Kupiec's in that we apply the original statistical classifier idea to individual features, rather than the entire set of features, and combines the evidence from individual features using the Dempster-Shafer combination rule (Shafer 1976). The idea of using the text structure identification method, which employs the same probabilistic framework, is also new. While the model is applicable to any languages, we tested the model with Korean texts

Before we proceed further, it would be useful to have

some discussions about the specifics of the Korean language. There are 24 alphabets in Korean, 14 and 10 of which are consonants and vowels, respectively. One syllable is composed of two or three parts: the first being a consonant, the second a vowel, and the third an optional consonant. For instance, a syllable "공" (pronounced as *gohng*) is a combination of ㄱ, ㅗ, and ㅇ. A *morpheme* is the smallest unit that has a meaning, consisting of one or more syllables that make a complete sound. We define *lexeme* as one or more morphemes concatenated and clearly identified by a preceding and following white spaces and/or a punctuation symbol. Although a lexeme would be the same as a *word* in English, which appears in a dictionary, it may consist of a content-bearing word (or one or more free morphemes) and a bound morpheme that plays a grammatical role (e.g. case marker) in a sentence. In the following sentence, for example,

그는 공원에 갔다. (He went to the park.)
(*Guh-nun gohng-won-eh gatta*)

The first lexeme "그는" (Guh-nun) corresponds to *he* + <nominative case marker>, the second lexeme "공원에" to *park* + <locative case marker>, and the last lexeme "갔다" to the past form for *go* ("가다"). More details can be found in (Myaeng and Jang 1996).

In addition to the brief introduction to some terminology in the Korean language, we further explore some related works in the following section. Section 3 describes an overview of the current system we developed, which consists of the training process and actual summarization process. Sections 4 and 5 respectively provide the details of the two processes with theoretical justifications. In order to show the influences of the features and different ways of using them, we ran experiments. The results are discussed in the next section. We then conclude with some discussions and future works.

2. Related Work

A summarization system might be positioned on a spectrum between two approaches: one is based on sentence extraction or automatic abstracting, and the other is based on understanding of sentences and documents. The main thrust of the former approach is to select a few representative sentences from the source document, which are indicative of the contents, typically by scoring sentences and presenting those with the best scores with or without reordering. This task is well understood with the current technology, but the result may look unnatural because there is no guarantee that a list of representative sentences forms a coherent summary.

Previous research in this category typically makes use of some features that are indicative of good summary sentences. Examples are *cue words* often appearing in a summary sentence and the position of a sentence in a document. (Kupiec, Pedersen, and Chen 1995) developed a trainable summarization program using such features, which is grounded in a sound statistical framework. Given a training set of documents with hand-selected document extracts, he developed a classification function that estimates the probability that a given sentence is included in an extract. A summary can be generated by ranking sentences according to this probability and by subsequently selecting a user-specified number of the top ranked ones. Our system stems from this approach, but with further refinement on the model itself and features. Most notably, our system includes the notion of text structures and employs a new method for combining pieces of evidence from different feature sources.

Another research work belonging to the automatic abstracting approach is directly based on information retrieval techniques. Using statistics on word frequencies, a summarization system attempts to calculate the degree to which a word represents a document, applies the passage retrieval techniques so that paragraphs are related to each other, and extracts a summary paragraph based on the relationships (Abracos and Lopez 1997, Mitra, Singhal, and Buckley 1997).

The other extreme on the spectrum is based on text understanding and supposed to generate a more natural-looking summary. However, the task is not only difficult but also unreliable with the state-of-the-art natural language processing techniques. It is obvious that in order to generate a summary based on text understanding, there should be a meaning representation and a technique for generating a summary from the representation. Constructing a semantic representation of a document, in turn, requires semantic analysis and a knowledge representation technique (Jacobs and Rau 1988, McKeown and Radev 1995) as well as other lower level language processing techniques. In spite of the advantages, this approach suffers from the need to use domain knowledge. As a way to alleviate this problem, some research (Hovy and Lin 1997) attempts to make use of lexical databases such as WordNet (Miller et al. 1990) instead of a domain knowledge base.

A middle ground between the two extremes is the approach with a template (McKeown and Radev 1995, Paice and Jones 1993) that is created to contain all the necessary concepts to be included in a summary. Slots in a template are filled by analyzing a source document, and used to generate a summary. Templates can be designed directly by a domain expert or by learning the themes extracted from a training corpus. While slot-filling can be done with a relatively shallow processing of natural language text, this approach imposes a burden of creating a template for each subject area.

For example, Paice (Paice and Jones 1993) attempted to effectively combine the indexing and abstracting tasks for summarization purposes. His approach is applicable to highly structured empirical research papers, whose content can be organized using a semantic frame. During a scan of a source text, stylistic clues and constructs are used for extracting candidate fillers for the various slots in the frame. An actual concept name is chosen for each slot by comparing the various candidates and their weights. While this approach can be effective for a given domain, it requires a significant amount of manual work in developing semantic frames for new domains and are not very genealizable.

McKeown and Radev (McKeown and Radev 1995) developed a summary system that is capable of generating summaries of a series of news articles on the same event, highlighting changes over time. They showed how planning operators can be used to synthesize summary content from individual templates, each representing a single article. These planning operators are empirically based, coming from analysis of existing summaries, and allow for the generation of concise summaries. The framework allows for experimentation with different length summaries and for the combination of multiple, independent summary operators to produce more complex summaries. It should be noted that this work is based on templates that are generated from a document extraction system whose task is to process a document in a given domain and extract various facts that should enter the pre-constructed template.

Miike (Miike et al. 1994) developed a system that analyzes a document structure using only linguistic knowledge in a domain-independent way. In its text structure analysis, the system determines relations among paragraphs and sentences, based on linguistic clues such as connectives, anaphoric expressions, and idiomatic expressions. The system analyzes and stores the text structure in advance so that it can generate an abstract in real time by selecting sentences according to relative importance of rhetorical relations among the sentences.

3. Overview of the System

Our system summarizes a document by selecting sentences whose probability for inclusion in a summary is reasonably high. The probability value for each sentence is estimated based on occurrences of certain features that are likely to be found in a summary. The necessary statistical information about features is obtained from a training corpus. While our system takes an approach similar to an existing model developed for English text (Kupiec, Pedersen, and Chen 1995), it is unique in several aspects.

A probability value is separately computed from each feature, which is combined with other probability values computed from other features to produce the final value. Both positive and negative evidence is computed explicitly and combined later with the Dempster-Shafer's combination rule.

In addition to the cue words, keywords, and position features, we experimented with centrality, title resemblance, and text component features. Here the centrality measures the similarity between a sentence and the rest of the document in which it appears, and the title resemblance feature measures how similar a sentence is to the title of the document.

Since the text component feature effectively divides a document into several parts, it is used as a filter by which all the sentences except those belonging to the 'major content' component are eliminated. We also tested how effectively it can be used simply as one of the features in the probability calculation process.

Our system consists of two processes as shown in Figure.1: the training process and the summarization process. The former extracts necessary statistical information from a corpus where sentences belonging to a summary have been manually tagged, whereas the latter uses the information to calculate the likelihood that a sentence in a source document belongs to a summary.

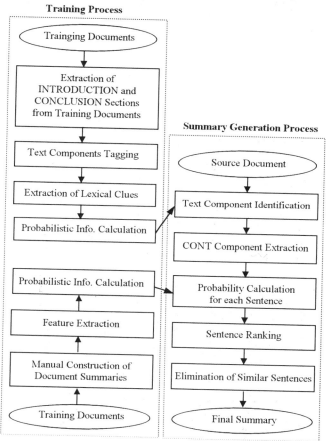

Figure. 1. Two Processes in Our System

The summarization process in turn can be divided into two parts: the first part identifies text structure components so that the later part can concentrate on the relevant components only. In other words, sentences in a not-so-important component can be filtered out in advance. The second part then considers only those individual sentences in the relevant components to calculate their values as a summary sentence. It should be noted that although the text component information can be used as an ordinary feature, we prefer the filtering mechanism because of the experimental results to be discussed in a later section.

The training process is divided into two parts as well: the first is related to the text component identification task, and the other is the task of actually selecting summary sentences. That is, the text component identification task can be considered as a task of categorizing each sentence into one of the given text components and is also based on the same probabilistic framework.

We observed that for the technical document database used for the current implementation, important summary sentences lie in the introduction and conclusion sections of a document. Furthermore, we realized that in the introduction and conclusion sections, a sentence belongs to one of the following text components: *background, main theme, explanation of the document structure, and future work*. After each sentence in training documents has been manually tagged with one of the text components, lexical clues are extracted from the sentences belonging to each of the components so that they can serve as an indicator for the particular component.

In order to provide the necessary statistical information required for computing the likelihood of each sentence to be part of a summary, sentences in the training corpus are tagged manually for their appropriateness to participate in a summary. More specifically, a summary for each training document is generated manually, and the statistical information for the features (i.e. cue words, position information) are extracted from this summary. It should be noted that in our approach, we consider the probability that a summary sentence does not include a certain feature as well as the probability that it does include the feature.

Once the statistical information is obtained in the training process, it is used by the summary process in calculating the probability of each sentence being included in the summary, which is calculated based on the degree to which each of the five features exist in the source sentence. The three features, content words, centrality, and similarity to the title, are independent of the training process and simply calculated for the source sentence. Five probabilities are then combined with the Dempster-Shafer theory to result in an overall belief indicating how strongly the sentence belongs to the summary.

As shown in the figure, the next step is to eliminate redundant sentences from the set of candidate sentences selected so far. This step is necessary because introduction and conclusion sections often contain similar sentences. The similarity value between two sentences is calculated as if the query-document similarity is calculated in a vector space model (Salton and McGill 1983).

4. Extraction of Summary Sentences

This section describes in detail the process that generates a summary by selecting sentences based on the statistical information acquired from the training process. Figure 2 shows individual steps. We assume that all the necessary

statistical information about the features has been calculated as described in the next section.

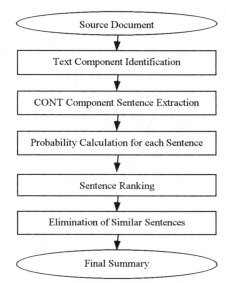

Figure 2. Summary Generation Process

4.1. Identification of Text Components

This process computes which text component category each sentence belongs to, so that sentences that are not likely to be included in a summary can be eliminated in advance. Advantages of this process include removal of noise occurring in full-text processing as well as some of the time-consuming processes for calculating probabilities. As mentioned above, text component information can be used as a feature, rather than as a filter.

The following formula, derived by applying Bayes' rule, is used to compute the probability that each sentence s will be included in a text component TC_i, $i=1..4$, representing *background, main theme, explanation of the document structure, and future works*, respectively:

$$P(TC_i \mid s) = \frac{P(s \mid TC_i)P(TC_i)}{P(s)} \approx \frac{\prod_{k=1}^{n} P(t_k \mid TC_i)P(TC_i)}{\prod_{k=1}^{n} P(t_k)}$$

(1)

Here $P(s|TC_i)$ is the probability that a summary sentence appears in a particular text component i. $P(TC_i)$ is the probability that the particular text component is observed, whereas $P(s)$ is the probability that a summary sentence is observed in the training corpus. Assuming that a sentence s consists of n words whose occurrences are independent of each other, the probabilities can be expressed as the product of other probabilities calculated for individual words t_k. For example, $P(t_k|TC_i)$ is the probability that a word t_k is observed in all the sentences belonging to the text component TC_i. Using the formula (1), we can automatically assign the best text component category to individual sentences, thereby making it possible to select those sentences belonging to the chosen text components determined to be useful for summarization. We found out that the *main theme* component is the most useful one; more than 96% of the human-selected summary sentences are included in the main theme component. In our experiments, therefore, we either filtered out those sentences not belonging to the particular text component or use as a feature the probability that a sentence belongs to the component.

4.2. Probability Calculation for a Feature

With the statistical information acquired from the training process and other values calculated directly from the source sentences, we can calculate the likelihood of each candidate sentence to become part of a summary. For each sentence s we compute the belief that it will be included in a summary by considering the contributions made by individual features.

Cue Word Probability: The most frequent words or phrases in the manually tagged summary sentences are defined as *cue words*. An occurrence of a cue word in a sentence is assumed to indicate that the sentence is likely to form a good summary since it is found in many summary sentences selected by human judges. Phrases like "the purpose of this article" and "suggests the procedure for" signal that a sentences containing them is theme-bearing ones. For each sentence s, we compute the probability that it will be included in a summary S given a cue word CW_i, which can be expressed using Bayes' rule as follows:

$$P(s \in S \mid CW_i) = \frac{P(CW_i \mid s \in S)P(s \in S)}{P(CW_i)}$$

(2)

Here $P(CW_i \mid s \in S)$ is the probability that a cue word appears in a summary sentence and calculated by counting the number of occurrences of the cue word in all the summary sentences in the training corpus. $P(s \in S)$ and $P(CW_i)$ are also calculated from the data in the training corpus as described in the following section.

Negative Word Probability: The most frequent words that are included in the non-summary sentences are defined as *negative words*. A phrase like "for example" belongs to this category and serves as negative evidence. Like the cue word features, we compute the probability that a sentence will *not* be included in a summary, given a negative word phrase NW_i.

$$P(s \notin S \mid NW_i) = \frac{P(NW_i \mid s \notin S)P(s \notin S)}{P(NW_i)}$$

(3)

This feature is the only one that is used exclusively for negative evidence; other features are used as both positive and negative evidence. The probabilities are calculated in the same way as in the case of the formula (2).

Position Feature: Sentences in a document are distinguished according to whether they are in the initial (for sentences within the first five), final (for sentences within the last five), or middle part. Since we consider only introduction and conclusion sections of a document for summarization, there are six different position values that can be assigned to individual sentences. Based on our observation, sentences in the final part of an introduction section or in the first part of a conclusion section are more likely to be included in a summary than those in other parts of the sections. The probability that a sentence appearing in one of the six regions is expressed as:

$$P(s \in S \mid P_i) = \frac{P(P_i \mid s \in S)P(s \in S)}{P(P_i)}$$

(4)

where $P(P_i \mid s \in S)$ and $P(P_i)$ are probabilities of observing a summary sentence in region i and of observing a summary sentence, respectively. The probability value of (4) for a sentence is determined by simply knowing in which region it appears, regardless of what it is composed of. Since a given sentence can have a single position, it will have only one probability value. We used 6 different values for i.

Theme Words: Content-bearing words or key words have played an important role in information retrieval since they can represent the content of a document reasonably well. Since it was intuitively appealing to consider only those sentences with strong keywords, we used this feature as evidence for a good summary sentence. The more important keywords are included in a sentence, the higher score it gets.

Centrality: It is natural to consider how central each sentence is with respect to the source document. The centrality value of a sentence can be calculated by comparing the vector representation[1] of the sentence and that of the document. In this work, we only consider the combination of the introduction and the conclusion sections of a document or its subset containing the sentences belonging to the main theme component, depending on whether text component feature is used as a filter or not. Although the way we calculate this aspect may not be the best one, we included this feature because of its intuitive value.

Resemblance to the Title: This feature is concerned about how similar a sentence is to the title of the source document. Since a document title is usually a good representation of what is in the document, it is in a sense a

---

1 A vector of a sentence or any unit of text can be constructed by taking all the key words and their relative weights as in the vector space model developed for information retrieval.

summary. With this feature, therefore, we measure the similarity between a source sentence and a given summary, which is calculated by the amount of overlap between the two in terms of the keywords.

4.3. Evidence Gathering

Since the length of a summary may vary depending on the user's purpose, it is best to rank sentences so that a designated number of the top sentences can be included in the final summary. For ranking, it is necessary to combine the probabilities calculated from the features as well as other values such as title resemblance. We use the Dempster-Shafer combination rule (Rich and Knight 1991) to calculate the belief that each sentence is included in a summary, by treating the probabilities and other values as evidence from different sources. In general, the notion of belief measures the strength of the evidence in favor of a set of propositions. It ranges from 0(indicating no evidence) to 1(denoting certainty) and measures not only the degree of belief in some propositions, but also the amount of information we have.

Using the Dempster-Shafer combination rule, we can obtain the degree of belief that a sentence is included in a summary. The idea is that with a new source of evidence, the overall degree of belief increases in a way to fill the gap between the current degree of belief and the maximum degree in proportion to the amount of new evidence (Jang and Myaeng 1997). While it is possible to apply a different formula for the purpose of combining the values, we opted for the Dempster-Shafer combination rule for its theoretical and intuitive justifications. Similarly we can also compute the degree of belief that a sentence does not belong to a summary. The difference between the positive belief and the negative belief becomes the final score for the sentence.

Although it is conceivable that different sources may have different weights in terms of their reliability or importance, we simply normalized the values obtained from the features so that they range from 0 to 1. In other words, we assumed that all the features have the same influence on the final belief value.

4.4. Elimination of Redundant Sentences

The final step in the summary sentence extraction process is to eliminate redundant sentences from the set of candidate sentences. This is necessary because authors often repeat the same idea using the same or similar sentences in both introduction and conclusion sections. Without this elimination process, not only does the summary look unnatural but also we may end up losing important summary sentences when the length of the summary is fixed.

For this purpose, we calculate the similarity value between all the pairs of the sentences selected by the above process. The similarity value is calculated as the vector similarity between two sentences represented as vectors. That is, the more common words in two sentences, the

more similar they are. If the similarity value of two sentences is greater than a threshold, we eliminate one whose rank based on the features is lower than that of the other. For the threshold value, we used 0.5 in the current implementation because it gave us the best performance in a preliminary study.

5. Training Process

As shown in Fig.3, the training process consists of two parts: one is for learning the degree to which one of the features exists in summary sentences, and the other is for learning what characteristics exist in different text components. The training data used is composed of 50 articles that were presented in the Korean Language Information Processing Conference.

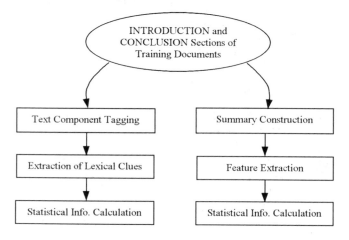

Figure. 3. Training Process

One branch of the training process is to learn the properties of each text component by observing what words or phrases occur with what frequency in the sentences belonging to the component. This corresponds to $P(t_k | TC_i)$ in the formula (1) in the previous section. For each word or phrase t_k, we compute the probability that it will be included in a text component TC_i, which can be expressed using Bayes' rule as follows:

$$P(TC_i | t_k) = \frac{P(t_k | TC_i)P(TC_i)}{P(t_k)}$$

(5)

Here $P(t_k | TC_i)$ is the probability that a term t_k is observed in a particular component i and calculated from the training corpus by counting how often that feature word occurs in all the sentences belonging to the component. $P(TC_i)$ is computed by counting how many sentences in the training corpus belongs to the component i whereas $P(t_k)$ is the relative frequency of the word in the collection. The other branch of the training process is to learn statistical information about sentences regarded as representing a good summary. We first identified important summary sentences from the training data manually, and extracted the necessary feature information. It is worth mentioning that for cue word and negative word features, the probability $P(CW_i| s \in S)$ in the formula (2) in the previous section is calculated by counting the number of occurrences of the cue words in all the summary sentences in the training corpus. $P(s \in S)$ in the same formula is computed as the ratio between the number of summary sentences and the total number of sentences in the corpus, whereas $P(CW_i)$ is the ratio between the number of occurrences of the cue word and the total number of words in the training corpus. Probabilities for negative words can be calculated in a similar way.

6. Evaluation

We evaluated our approach for two different aspects. One is the accuracy of the system in identifying the text components, and the other is the quality of the summaries generated by combinations of features. For the former, our interest was only in the *main theme* component although it was possible to evaluate how well other components are identified, since the primary goal of identifying text components was to help improving the summarization task.

6.1. Experimental Setting

In the experimental work, we asked three undergraduate and three graduate students:

- To categorize individual sentences into either the main theme class or *other* class since our interest was on the main theme component only, and
- To rank-order all the main theme sentences extracted from a single document for a summary.
- To eliminate redundancy of the extracted sentences by conducting pairwise comparisons and deleting one if a pair of sentences are sufficiently similar.

We used 30 documents in the test set, which are different from those used for training. Each document was reviewed by two judges, and the intersection of two sets of extracted sentences was used as the final "correct" summary generated by the humans. This was particularly important because evaluating the quality of a summary depends most critically on the requirement of the person reading a summary, and because it would not be easy to force human subjects to come up with an agreement for all the summarization tasks. The results were compared with the output generated by the system. For the text component identification task, the human subjects were asked to come up with a single result by consulting each other.

In order to evaluate the summarization function, each document was summarized by the system and by the human subjects. Each human subject was asked to select five best sentences, but because of the intersection

operation performed on two sets, the actual number became smaller sometimes. The system produced a ranked list of sentences because its task was to rank-order all the candidate sentences.

For precision and recall, we employed a method often used for evaluation of information retrieval results by treating the human-generated sentences as a set of relevant documents and the system-generated ranked list of sentences as a ranked list of retrieved documents. In other words, the summarization task was treated as a retrieval task. The combination of the summary results generated by the human subjects and the set of source documents was considered as a test collection from the information retrieval perspective.

6.2. Result for Text Component Identification Function

The set of sentences selected by the system was compared to another set selected by the human subjects. For this evaluation, we asked the subjects to come up with a single agreement. Out of 295 main-theme component sentences chosen by the group of the human subjects, 210 of them were also chosen by the system, resulting in 67% of recall and 40% of precision. The system selects a sentence as belonging to the main theme component if it is not more likely to belong to any of the other components. For the purpose of using text component identification as a filter, it is more important to achieve a high recall value than to have a high precision. This is because all the sentences chosen as belonging to the main theme component by the system are evaluated for their suitability as a summary sentence although too many false alarms will degrade the summarization function exactly in the same way the accurate filtering will improve it.

6.3. Results for Summarization

As discussed in Section 3, the current implementation exploits the text component identification function as a filter and all other features as providing evidence for inclusion or exclusion of a sentence in a summary. Here, however, we report the results of our experiments by which we tested what contribution each feature makes when used as a filter or as an evidence-providing device. The numbers are 11-point average precision values often used in IR evaluations. For the control case, we selected the first five sentences from the CONCLUSION section of a document. The 11-point average precision value for the control was 0.3682. It should be noted that this control gave the best performance when any five contiguous sentences were selected without using other information.

The results are summarized in Table 1 where the four columns show different filtering methods employed before the actual summarization. The numbers in parentheses indicate how much improvement was obtained against the control case mentioned above. We compared three different filtering methods with the case where no filtering was done.

Table 1. Comparisons among different Features and Filtering Methods

Features used	Filtering methods			
	No filtering	Filtering with text components	Filtering with keywords	Filtering with text components and keywords
All six features	0.3865 (+5)	0.3949 (+7)	0.3913 (+6)	0.3996 (+9)
Without cue word feature	0.3116	0.3203	0.3172	0.3259
Without position feature	0.3544	0.3572	0.3594	0.3594
Without text component feature	0.4007 (+9)	0.4167 (+13)	0.4228 (+15)	0.4228 (+15)
Without title resemblance feature	0.3439	0.3591	0.3487	0.3639
Without keyword feature	0.3976 (+8)	0.4033 (+10)	0.4022 (+9)	0.4075 (+11)
Without centrality feature	0.4318 (+17)	0.4337 (+18)	0.4365 (+19)	0.4389 (+19)
Title + Cue word + Position feature	0.4274 (+16)	0.4363 (+18)	0.4420 (+20)	0.4436 (+20)

"Filtering with keywords" means that sentences containing enough content words were fed into the summarization function whereas "Filtering with text components" means that sentences belonging to the main theme component were only subject to the summarization task.

The rows, on the other hand, indicate what features were used in the summarization task. For instance, "All six features" indicates that text components, cue words (and negative words), position, centrality, title resemblance, and keywords were all used. The row with "Without centrality feature" means all but the centrality feature were used.

Among the three filtering methods, the one using text components and keywords gave the best results, whereas the one using only text components gave the second best. Although the differences are consistent, the magnitude is not very significant. Greater differences were resulted from various combinations of the features. Among the cases with no filtering, the best result was obtained when all but the centrality features were. This indicates that inclusion of the centrality feature did not improve the result.

Moreover, we can conclude that the centrality, text component and keyword features are not good ones to include in the calculation model since the precision value was increased when each of them was included separately. In fact, the last row with "Title resemblance + cue words + position" shows the best result across all the cases regardless of what filtering methods were used.

This doesn't mean that text components and keywords are useless. On the contrary, they are useful when used as a filter. In fact, the best across all the cases was obtained when the text component and keyword features were together used as a filter and the three best features were used for ranking. It is our interpretation that keywords are important in selecting good candidates, but their existence does not necessary mean the sentence is a good summary sentence. The same seems to hold for the main theme component. We conjecture that a greater difference would have been resulted if the text component identification had been more accurate.

6.4. The Role of Text Components

In a separate experiment, we tested the role of the text component feature as a filter by considering only the cue word feature (together with the negative words) and the position feature in the sentence-ranking model. We compared the precision and recall values for two cases: one with the text component identification process included as a filter and the other without it. The experimental setup was identical to the previous one described in 6.3 except that only top five documents selected by the system participated in the evaluation, not all the ranked sentences, in measuring the recall and precision values.

Table 2. Evaluation Result with and without Text Components

# of sentences	Without Text Components		With Text Components	
	Precision	Recall	Precision (% change)	Recall (% change)
1	50.00	10.00	53.33 (+7)	14.55 (+46)
2	36.67	14.67	43.34 (+18)	21.37 (+46)
3	36.67	22.00	43.33 (+18)	35.46 (+61)
4	35.83	28.67	41.59 (+16)	45.00 (+57)
5	36.00	36.00	39.53 (+10)	53.19 (+48)

Table 2 shows precision and recall pairs for five cases where the number of sentences selected by the system varied. We can see the clear difference between the two cases both in terms of precision and recall. When five sentences were chosen by the system, for example, precision and recall values were increased by 10% and 48%, respectively, with text component information used as the filter. In other words, although the text component identification model was a rather simple one, it was good enough to serve as an effective filter for the summarization process.

6.5. Qualitative Analysis

We intellectually analyzed the features generated by the system to understand their semantic nature. Since all the lexems were automatically split into a set of morphemes as is the case in most natural language applications with Korean, it wasn't possible to identify phrases such as "in conclusion" in English. But we were able to observe that more than one third of the positive cue words were non-content words in the specific domain, such as "results", "article", "method", "analysis", and "research" (all in English translation), none of which appeared as negative words.

The system-generated summaries (a list of sentences) would be no match for human-generated, natural-looking summaries. Considering that the task was extraction of sentences, however, the sentences seemed to collectively represent the core meaning of the article reasonably well, albeit some obvious outliers. While less than 10% of the extracted sentences contain anaphora, most of them were not annoying because they referred to such things as "paper", "method", and "result", which were often mentioned in a previous sentence. This indicates that some demonstrative anaphora does not need to be resolved in sentence extraction tasks as long as they refer back to one of the important concepts that have been mentioned already in any of the previously selected sentences.

7. Conclusions

We developed a system that constructs a summary by extracting sentences that are likely to represent the main theme of a document. As a way of selecting summary sentences, the system uses a probabilistic model that takes into account lexical and statistical information obtained from a document corpus. There are at least four unique aspects of this research. First of all, the system uses a text component identification model to categorize individual sentences into different components of a text and eliminates parts of text that are not likely to contain summary sentences. Second, although the statistically-based model stems from an existing one developed for English texts, it applies the framework to individual features separately and computes the final score for each sentence by combining pieces of evidence from different sources (features) with the Dempster-Shafer combination rule. Third, not only were new features introduced but also all the features were tested to understand their role in the summarization framework. Finally, the system is the first of this kind for Korean texts.

We demonstrated the quality of the summarization system through some experiments and showed that a better result was obtained by using text component identification process. With the text component identification, not only could we save time required for calculating the necessary probabilities for the fruitless sentences, but also we obtained a higher precision and recall values. The overall performance of the summarization system was also encouraging in that the precision and recall values were higher than those obtained for English texts (Kupiec, Pedersen, and Chen 1995) using a similar approach although they are not directly comparable.

We obtained valuable results for usefulness of various features, too. It appeared that cue word, position, and title resemblance features were most useful when used as part of the sentence-ranking model. The text component and keyword features did not improve the performance when mixed with the other features, but were useful when used as a filter.

Since the research in this area is at its infant stage, there are many things to be investigated in the future. First, we need to have a better understanding about what constitutes a good summary so that we can exploit additional features of various kinds. Second, the recall value of 67% in recognizing text components should be considered as a baseline. A more sophisticated model would result in a higher level performance. Third, in order to provide a more natural-looking summary, we'll have to develop a system capable of reconstructing the summary by processing a variety of anaphoric expressions. Finally, although the underlying models are language-independent and generalizable to other domains, at least the text component identification part needs to be tuned for different text types. We will have to develop a methodology by which we can make the current approach more extensible.

References

Abracos, J., and Lopez, G. P. 1997. Statistical Methods for Retrieving Most Significant Paragraphs in Newspaper Articles. In *Proceedings of Workshop in Intelligent Scalable Summarization*, 51-57. Madrid, Spain, July.

Hovy, E., and Lin, C. Y. 1997. Automated Text Summarization in SUMMARIST. In *Proceedings of Workshop on Intelligent Scalable Summarization*, 18-24. Madrid, Spain, July.

Jacobs, P. S., and Rau, L. F. 1988. Natural Language Techniques for Intelligent Information Retrieval. In *Proceedings of the Eleventh Annual International ACM SIGIR Conference on Research and Development in Information Retrieval*, 85-99. Grenoble, France, June.

Jang, D. H., and Myaeng, S. H. 1997. Development of a Document Summarization System for Effective Information Services. In *Proceedings of RIAO '97 Conference*, 101-111. Montreal, Canada, June.

Kupiec, J., Pedersen, J., and Chen, F. 1995. A Trainable Document Summarizer. In *Proceedings of the Eighteenth Annual International ACM SIGIR Conference on Research and Development in Information Retrieval*, 68-

73. Seattle, Washington, July.

McKeown, K., and Radev, D. R. 1995. Generating Summaries of Multiple News Articles. In *Proceedings of Eighteenth Annual International ACM SIGIR Conference on Research and Development in Information Retrieval*, 74-82. Seattle, Washington, July.

Miike, S., Itoh, E., Ono, K., and Sumita, K. 1994. A Full-Text Retrieval System with a Dynamic Abstract Generation. In *Proceedings of Seventeenth Annual International ACM SIGIR Conference on Research and Development in Information Retrieval*, 152-161. Dublin, Ireland, July.

Miller, G., George, A., Beckwith, R., Fellbaum, C., Gross, D., and Miller, J. 1990. Introduction to WordNet: an On-line Lexical Database. *International Journal of Lexicography*, 3 (4): 235-312.

Mitra, M., Singhal, A., and Buckley, C. 1997. Automatic Text Summarization by Paragraph Extraction. In *Proceedings of Workshop in Intelligent Scalable Text Summarization*, 39-46. Madrid, Spain, July.

Myaeng, S. H., and Jang, D. H. 1996. On Language Dependency in Indexing. In *Proceedings of the Workshop on Information Retrieval with Oriental languages*, 17-23. Taejon, KOREA, June.

Paice, C. D., and Jones, P. A. 1993. The Identification of Important Concepts in Highly Structured Technical Papers. In *Proceedings Of Sixteenth Annual International ACM SIGIR Conference on Research and Development in Information Retrieval*, 69-78. Pittsburgh, PA, June-July.

Rich, E. and Knight, K. 1991. *Artificial Intelligence*, second edition: McGraw-Hill.

Salton, G and McGill, M. J. 1983. *Introduction to Modern Information Retrieval*: McGraw-Hill.

Shafer, G. 1976. *A Mathematical Theory of Evidence*: Princeton University Press.

7

A Trainable Summarizer with Knowledge Acquired from Robust NLP Techniques

Chinatsu Aone
James Gorlinsky
Bjornar Larsen
SRA International, Inc.
4300 Fair Lakes Court
Fairfax, VA 22033
{aonec, gorlinsk, laresenb}@sra.com

Mary Ellen Okurowski
Department of Defense
9800 Savage Road
Fort George G. Meade
MD 20755-6000
meokuro@afterlife.ncsc.mil

Abstract

We describe a trainable summarization system Dim-Sum which takes advantage of robust NLP technology such as information extraction, corpus-based statistical Natural Language Processing (NLP) techniques, and readily available on-line resources. The system attempts to compensate for the bottlenecks of traditional approaches by reshaping the single word counting unit, acquiring domain knowledge with the inclusion of corpus statistics, and approximating text structure through sources of discourse cohesion. We employ a batch feature combination technique and a trainable feature combination technique to identify potential contributing features. Evaluation results are reported on the best combination of features, the effect of data sources and training. We also describe the Dim-Sum multi-dimensional summary viewer.

1 Introduction

Summarization research and system development can be broadly characterized as frequency-based, knowledge-based or discourse-based. These categories correspond to a continuum of increasing understanding of a text and increasing complexity in text processing.

Earliest attempts at summarization (Luhn 1958; Edmundson 1969; Rush, Salvador, & Zamora 1971) essentially relied on lexical and locational information within the text, i.e., frequency of words or key terms, their proximity, and location within the text. More recent adaptations of this approach have employed an automated method to combine these types of feature sets through classification techniques (Kupiec, Pedersen, & Chen 1995) or have drawn upon traditional information retrieval indexing methods to incorporate knowledge of a text corpus (Brandow, Mitze, & Rau 1995). To a large extent, these types of shallow approaches are ignorant of domain knowledge and the text macrostructure. They create summaries by extracting sentences from the original document.

Knowledge-based approaches generally depend on rich domain knowledge sources to interpret the conceptual structure of the text. Systems like TOPIC (Reimer & Hahn 1988), SUSY (Fum, Guida, & Tasso 1985) or SCISORS (Rau, Jacobs, & Zernik 1989) parse texts in a particular domain and create conceptual representations for the generation of text summaries. These types of knowledge-based systems apply knowledge of the domain to characterize specific conceptual knowledge of a text. Paice and Jones (Paice & Jones 1993) provides a good example of the role of this conceptual information and Riloff (Riloff 1995) gives a method for automatically identifying relevant concepts highly correlated with a category of interest. Because these systems create a rich conceptual representation, there are multiple ways in which a text summary may be created. For example, SUMMONS (McKeown & Radev 1995) generates a text summary from such a template representation, while (Maybury 1995) describes multiple methods for selecting events and presenting event summaries. Knowledge-based approaches are usually very knowledge-intensive and domain-specific.

Discourse-based approaches are grounded in theories of text cohesion and coherence and vary considerably in how much they push the limits of text understanding and the complexity as well as automation of that processing. Motivated by the lack of cohesion and coherence in extracts produced by frequency-based approaches, much of the work typifying discourse-based approaches focuses on linguistic processing of the text to identify the best cohesive sentence candidates (Paice 1990; Johnson et al. 1993) or the best sentence candidates for representing the rhetorical structure of the text (Miike et al. 1994). Both approaches involve parsing the text and analyzing discourse relations to select sentences for extraction.

Frequency-based approaches (Brandow, Mitze, & Rau 1995) may incorporate heuristics to handle readability-related issues and knowledge-based approaches systematically may perform discourse processing in analyzing and condensing the text, but in a broad classification schema it is the discourse-based approaches that tend to focus on the text macrostructure and surface clues to that structure. An exception is work by Mani and Bloedorn (Mani & Bloedorn 1997) in which domain and text-structure information is captured by exploiting differences and similarities of lexical and phrasal conceptual sources within a document. At the far end of the continuum lies work by

Jones (Jones 1993; 1995) in describing a manual method for source text representation based on linguistic, domain and communicative information. From the NLP technology point of view, discourse theory is the least understood among sub-fields of linguistics.

Our work addresses challenges encountered in these previous approaches by applying robust and proven NLP techniques such as corpus-based statistical NLP, robust information extraction, and readily-available on-line NLP resources. We follow the common paradigm of summarizing by extracting sentences, but create a new model with a linguistically motivated and automatically derived set of features for weighing sentence worthiness. We redefine the concept of word, add domain knowledge through corpus statistics, and approximate discourse knowledge through cohesive techniques. So that our system is trainable to user requirements, we determine experimentally which set of features best mirror human generated summary extracts. With the best conceptual feature set capturing *signature terms*, we then add conventional positional information and train the system using a Bayesian model. We demonstrate the positive effect of training and the mixed effect of different sources upon summarization quality. Our ultimate goal is to make our summarization system scalable and portable by learning how to summarize from a set of easily extractable text features.

2 System Description

Our summarization system DimSum consists of the Summarization Server and the Summarization Client. The Server extracts features (the Feature Extractor) from a document using various robust NLP techniques, described in Section 3, and combines these features (the Feature Combiner) to produce sentence extracts as summaries, as described in Section 4. The feature combination rules are learned automatically from human-annotated summaries using batch and trainable techniques. The Java-based Client, which will be discussed in Section 5, provides a graphical user interface (GUI) for the end user to customize the summarization preferences and see multiple views of generated summaries.

3 Extracting Summarization Features

In this section, we describe how we apply robust NLP technology to extract different linguistic features for calculating sentence worthiness. Our goal is to add more linguistic knowledge to frequency-based approaches by re-shaping the single word counting unit, to acquire domain knowledge by using external corpus statistics in the calculation and to approximate text structure by enhancing the text statistics with sources of discourse cohesion.

3.1 Going Beyond a Word

Frequency-based summarization systems typically use a single word string as a unit for counting frequencies. While such a method is very robust, it ignores

```
{potato tortilla corn chocolate bagle} chips
{computer pentium intel microprocessor memory} chips
{wood oak plastic} chips
bargaining chips
blue chips
mr. chips
```

Table 1: Collocations with "chips"

the semantic content of words and their potential membership in multi-word phrases. For example, it does not distinguish between "bill" in "Bill Clinton" and "bill" in "reform bill". This may introduce noise in frequency counting as the same strings are treated uniformly no matter how the context may have disambiguated the sense or regardless of membership in multi-word phrases. In DimSum, we use both text statistics (term frequency, or *tf*) and corpus statistics (inverse document frequency, or *idf*) (Salton & McGill 1983; Brandow, Mitze, & Rau 1995) to derive *signature words* as one of the summarization features. If single words were the sole basis of counting for our summarization application, noise would be introduced both in term frequency and inverse document frequency.

However, recent advances in statistical NLP and information extraction make it possible to utilize features which go beyond the single word level. Our approach is to extract multi-word phrases automatically with high accuracy and use them as the basic unit in the summarization process to calculate term and corpus statistics.

First, just as word association methods have proven effective in lexical analysis, e.g. (Church & Hanks 1990), we are exploring whether frequently occurring collocational information can improve on simple word-based approaches. We have pre-processed about 800 MB of LA times/Washington Post newspaper articles using a POS tagger (Brill 1993) and derived two-word noun collocations using mutual information. The result included, for example, various "chips" phrases as shown in Table 1. The word "chips" occurred 1143 times in this corpus, and the table shows that this word is semantically very ambiguous. In word associations, it can refer to food, computer components, abstract concepts, etc. By incorporating these collocations, we can disambiguate different meanings of "chips."

Second, as the recent Message Understanding Conference (MUC-6) showed (ARPA 1995), the accuracy and robustness of name extraction has reached a mature level, equaling the level of human performance in accuracy (mid-90%) and exceeding human speed by many thousands of times. We employed SRA's NameTag^{TM} (Krupka 1995) to tag the aforementioned corpus with names of people, entities, and places, and derived a baseline database for *tf*idf* calculation. In the database, we not only treated multi-word names (e.g., "Bill Clinton") as single tokens but also disambiguated the semantic types of names so that, for instance, the company "Ford" is treated separately from President

"Ford". Our approach is thus different from (Kupiec, Pedersen, & Chen 1995) where only capitalization information was used to identify and group various types of proper names. And it is also different from Mani and Bloedorn (Mani & Bloedorn 1997) in that the tagger is applied to both the external domain corpus and the text targeted for summarization.

3.2 Acquiring Knowledge of the Domain

In knowledge-based summarization approaches, the biggest challenge is to acquire enough domain knowledge to create conceptual representations for a text. Though summarization from conceptual representation has many advantages (as discussed in Section 1), extracting such representations constrains a system to domain dependency and requires rich manually built knowledge sources.

We took an automatic and robust approach where we acquire *some* domain knowledge from a large corpus and incorporate that knowledge as summarization features in the system. We incorporated corpus knowledge in three ways, that is, by using a large corpus baseline database to calculate *idf* values for selecting signature words, by deriving collocations statistically from a large corpus, and by creating a word association index derived from a large corpus (Jing & Croft 1994).

With this method, the system can automatically adapt to each distinct domain, like newspapers vs. legal documents without manually developing domain knowledge. Domain knowledge is embraced in *signature words*, which indicate key concepts of a given document, in *collocation phrases*, which provide contextually richer key concepts than isolated single-word key concepts (e.g. "appropriations bill," "omnibus bill," "brady bill," "reconciliation bill," "crime bill," "stopgap bill,", etc.), and in their *associated words*, which are clusters of domain related terms (e.g., "Bayer" and "aspirin," "Columbia River" and "gorge," "Dead Sea" and "scrolls").

While this corpus-based approach requires a corpus to create a baseline database, in contrast to an approach which relies only on term frequency in a single document, it is a straightforward one-time task to be done for each domain. As shown in Section 4, the benefit of having corpus statistics over text statistics outweighs this extra work.

3.3 Recognizing Sources of Discourse Cohesion

Past research (Paice 1990) has described the negative impact on abstract quality of failing to perform some type of discourse processing. Since discourse structure is difficult to automatically acquire with high accuracy and robustness, heuristic techniques are often employed in summarization systems to suppress sentences with interdependent cohesive markers.

However, there are several shallower but robust methods we can employ now to account for relations in the discourse by identifying some of the cohesive mechanisms that link a sentence with what has gone before. Namely, we exploit two types of cohesive devices described in Halliday and Hasan (Halliday & Hasan 1976): reference and lexical cohesion through reiteration of name aliases, synonyms and morphological variation. Identifying these relationships allows us to more accurately account for term frequency and, in turn, to be more likely to extract related sentences.

When the same entity enters the discourse repeatedly, cohesion is maintained through continuity of reference. Typically, subsequent references to the full names of persons or organizations are often aliases or abbreviated variants. Thus, identifying both the full names and aliases as coreferent provides a way to show which sentences are inter-related as shown below.

The **Institutional Revolutionary Party,** *or* **PRI,** *capped its landmark assembly to reform itself with a flourish of pomp and promises* ··· *Among the measures coming out of the assembly's fiercest public debate, in which party members rose up against their leadership Saturday night, are new requirements for future* **PRI** *presidential candidates, qualifications that neither Zedillo nor any of Mexico's previous four presidents would have met.*

We used the NameTag name extraction tool discussed in the previous section to link name aliases within a document such as "Albright" to "Madeleine Albright," "U.S." to "United States," and "IBM" for "International Business Machine". Not only is term frequency count more accurate given "IBM" and "International Business Machines" counted as two occurrences of the same term, but also the more accurate term weighting will affect selection for sentence extraction.

General term counting accounts for simple repetition of the same lexical item, but we also collapse the reiteration of synonyms and morphological variants. When the topic of an article is developed, synonymous words often appear as variants in the text. In the example below, for instance, "pictures" and "images" are used interchangeably.

A new medical **imaging** *technique may someday be able to detect lung cancer and diseases of the brain earlier than conventional methods, according to doctors at the State University of New York, Stony Brook, and Princeton University.* ··· *If doctors want to take* **pictures** *of the lungs, he noted, they have to use X-ray machines, exposing their patients to doses of radiation in the process.* ··· *The new technique uses an anesthetic, xenon gas, instead of water to create* **images** *of the body.*

We used WordNet (Miller *et al.* 1990) to identify potential synonyms for signature terms in the text and then search for these candidates within the texts. This allows us to increase the signature term count by incorporating synonym counts. We hypothesize that if a synonym of a signature term exists in the article, the term has been disambiguated by the context of the article and the *correct* synonym, not a synonym of the term in a different sense, is likely to co-occur in the same document. For example, other synonyms of the word "image" from WordNet include "icon," "persona," "prototype" and so forth, but none of these inappropriate synonyms appeared in the example article above.

Reiteration through morphological variants is another source of semantic relations within the text. These variants are often used to refer to the same concept throughout a document. A term frequency count includes the word count plus its morphological variants. In the above example, morphologically linked "imaging" and "images" help to establish continuity of topic and thus contribute to a single term frequency count that helps DimSum preserve cohesive ties.

One can easily see the cumulative effect of exploiting the above-mentioned cohesive features. Since our approach relies on term frequency, we want to accurately capture some of the lexical "glue" of the text and avoid handling related lexical items as disparate, unrelated terms.

4 Combining Summarization Features

We experimented with combining summarization features in two stages. In the first batch stage, we experimented to identify what features are most effective for signature words. In the second stage, we took the best combination of features determined by the first stage and used it as the baseline performance for the system without training. Then, we trained over these "best" signature word features, along with conventional length and positional information, to determine which Bayesian training features are most useful in rendering useful summaries. We also experimented with the effect of training and different corpora types.

4.1 Batch Feature Combiner

4.1.1 Method In DimSum, sentences are selected for a summary based upon a score calculated from the different combinations of signature word features and their expansion with the discourse features of aliases, synonyms, and morphological variants. To obtain the best combination of features for sentence extraction, we experimented extensively. This allowed us to judge empirically which features actually produce the closest match to the human summaries. With our first method, the DimSum summarizer exploits our flexible definition of signature words and sources of domain and discourse knowledge in the texts through:

- the creation of multiple baseline databases corresponding to multiple definitions of signature words
- the application of the discourse features in multiple-term frequency calculation methods.

The summarizer allows us to experiment with both how we count and what we count for both inverse document frequency and term frequency values. Because different baseline databases can affect *idf* values, we examined the effect on summarization of multiple baseline databases based upon multiple definitions of the signature words. Similarly, the discourse features, i.e., synonyms, morphological variants, or name aliases, for signature words, can affect *tf* values. Since these discourse features boost the term frequency score within a text when they are treated as variants of signature words, we also examined their impact upon summarization.

From our possible signature word definitions and discourse features, we selected a subset (i.e., names, synonyms, and name aliasing), identified *tf**idf calculation variations, and experimented with a range of possible parameter combinations:

- Using and/or suppressing any and all of the following:
  - NameTag derived types: persons, places and entities
  - NameTag derived aliases for the above types
  - WordNet derived synonyms for adjectives, adverbs, nouns and verbs
- Using variations on the *tf**idf calculation
  - Altering the method in which *tf* is calculated
  - Altering the method in which *idf* is calculated
  - Altering the method in which *tf**idf is normalized

In DimSum, sentences are selected for a summary based upon sentence scores. Every token in a document is assigned a score based on its *tf**idf value. The token score is used, in turn, to calculate the score of each sentence in the document. The score of a sentence is calculated as the average of the scores of the tokens contained in that sentence.

After every sentence is assigned a score, the top n highest scoring sentences are chosen as a summary of the content of the document. Currently, the DimSum system chooses the number of sentences equal to a power k (between zero and one) of the total number of sentences. Thus, the system can vary the length of a summary according to k. For instance, if 0.5 is chosen as the power, and the document consists of 100 sentences, the output summary would contain 10 sentences. This scheme has an advantage over choosing a given percentage of document size as it yields more information for longer documents while keeping summary size manageable. The results of this method provide the baseline summary performance (i.e., without any training).

4.1.2 Evaluation Over 135,000 combinations of the above parameters were performed using 70 texts from L.A. Times/Washington Post. We evaluated the summary results against the human-generated extracts for these 70 texts in terms of F-Measures. As the results in Table 2 indicate, the presence of all the features, except for person names, produces the best summaries.

The good effect of leaving person names out is one of our most significant findings resulting from the application of the NameTag information extraction technol-

Entity Name	Place Name	Person Name	Alias	Synonym	F-Measure
+	+	-	+	+	41.3
+	+	-	-	+	40.7
+	+	-	+	-	40.4
+	+	-	-	-	39.6
-	-	-	-	+	39.5
-	-	-	-	-	39.0
+	+	+	-	-	37.4
+	+	+	+	+	37.4
+	+	+	+	-	37.2
+	+	+	-	+	36.7

Table 2: Results for Different Feature Combinations

ogy, which identifies multi-word expressions and semantically types them. Withholding NameTag-identified person names from the feature combination algorithm (but still using the other features) considerably improved performance, in contrast to results in which persons were included (first row versus eighth row in Table 2). The most probable reason for this is that personal names usually have high *idf* values, but they are generally not good indicators of topics of articles which we used for evaluation. For instance, names of reporters and spokespersons do not make good keywords. Even when names of people are associated with certain key events, documents are not usually *about* these people. Thus, personal names are very misleading in terms of signature word identification. This finding supported our view that a different type of counting unit can lead to more effective summarization.

Moreover, we also discovered that our methodology of experimenting with different feature combinations could also lead us to uncover how a single feature might mask another. Not only did the identification and subsequent removal of person names from the score of a sentence increased the test corpus F-measure by up to five points, but their removal also increased the effectiveness of WordNet synonyms. The high scoring person names no longer mask out the contribution of synonyms. Thus, paradoxically WordNet appears to be effective only when used in conjunction with name recognition, where we actually use the recognition to suppress the contribution of names and reveal the contribution of synonyms.

Because we had tagged the corpus with part of speech, we were also able to judge differences in their contribution to scoring. We determined that deriving synonyms for adverbs and adjectives contributes little in contrast to synonym expansion for nouns and verbs. Moreover, the expansion of nouns and verbs together contributes more than when expanded individually. We offer this finding as another illustration of the value of redefining the concept of word in counting. By preprocessing with part of speech information and by experimenting with feature combinations, we are better able to select how to calculate word values.

Finally, experimenting with methods in which *tf*idf*

is normalized, we verified that taking *tf*idf* scores of each word outperformed the solely *idf*-based calculation, and the latter in turn outperformed the solely *tf*-based score calculation.

Our experimentation clearly revealed that even with a flexible definition of word, not all words contribute equally to selection of sentences for extraction. Moreover, we learned that, given current NLP techniques and on-line resources, researchers can re-define word units and can more effectively weigh word contributions to extraction through automatic techniques. In the next section, we will show how this more robust counting mechanism can be further enhanced with training on multiple corpora types for more conventionally acknowledged features.

4.2 Trainable Feature Combiner

4.2.1 Method With our second method, we developed a trainable feature combiner using Bayes' rule. Having defined the best feature combination for high *tf*idf* signature words in a sentence, we tested the inclusion of commonly acknowledged positional and length information similar to work of (Kupiec, Pedersen, & Chen 1995). DimSum probabilistically learns to combine extracted features from manually extracted summaries from multiple corpus types. We chose the following features for summarization:

- short sentence length (less than 5 words)
- inclusion of high *tf*idf* signature words in a sentence
- sentence position in a document (1st, 2nd, 3rd or 4th quarter)
- sentence position in a paragraph

Inclusion in the high *tf*idf* signature word set was determined by the batch feature combiner discussed above. Possible values of the paragraph feature are initial, final, and middle sentences in a paragraph. Final requires at least two sentences per paragraph, and middle at least three. This is identical to how (Kupiec, Pedersen, & Chen 1995) used this feature, except that we do not discount paragraphs past the first ten and not in the last five (that is, we do this for all paragraphs). Since the newspaper texts in our study are shorter than the journal articles Xerox used, we consider all paragraphs.

Unlike Kupiec *et al.*'s experiment, we did not use the *cue word* feature, though it was most effective in their experiment. We did observe that the manual sentence extracts tended to contain cue word-like repetitions, but the newspaper data contained few of the type characterizing the scientific journals used in their experiment.

We score our machine generated extracts against a test set of manually annotated extracts after training on a development set. Research (Rath, Resnick, & Savage 1961; Edmundson 1969; Mitra, Singhal, & Buckley 1997; Marcu 1997) has clearly shown that human reliability in summarizing is low. To handle this problem, as well as the resultant difficulty of evaluation, a number of approaches have been applied by several researchers, including ranking of sentences (Rath, Resnick, & Savage 1961), maximizing user agreement (Mitra, Singhal, & Buckley 1997; Nomoto & Matsumoto 1997; Marcu 1997), identifying correspondences between machine and human summaries (Kupiec, Pedersen, & Chen 1995), or correlating conceptual correspondence between extract and original sentences (Paice & Jones 1993).

In contrast, we took a simple approach which trains for a user. We acknowledge user variation and aim to tailor the output for individual user preferences. Therefore, we train the system with a modest amount of data manually extracted by users. Moreover, the user can actually change, through the DimSum GUI, his or her preferences as to not only the summary length but also the use of various features such as synonyms, names, etc.

4.2.2 Evaluation We performed two different rounds of experiments, the first with newspaper sets and the second with a broader set from the TREC 5 collection. We were interested in gauging how much training could improve summary scores because of our ultimate goal of a training for individual user needs. We were also interested in assessing the impact of corpus type since our approach is dependent on an external corpus baseline database. In both rounds we experimented with different feature sets and data sources and with the effects of training.

In the first round, we found that the effects of training in certain instances increased system scores by as much as 10% F-Measure or greater. The best results were obtained using an 'ltn' *tf*idf* metric with WordNet synonyms enabled, NameTag person-tags suppressed but all other tags active, and a 0.6 sentence selection factor engaged. Table 3 summarizes the results of using subsets of the available features for the feature combiner on the 70 texts from L.A. Times/Washington Post (latwp-dev1). It is evident that positional information is the most valuable, while the sentence length feature introduces the most noise. High scoring signature word sentences are also very useful, especially in conjunction with the positional information and the paragraph fea-

ture.

The reader should note that the text sets used in this experiment (i.e., latwp-dev1) is the same set upon which we trained the system so one would expect decent performance. However, we also tested the system on other text sets, 50 texts from L.A. Times/Washington Post (latwp-test1) and 50 texts from Philadelphia Inquirer (pi-test1) from different time frames upon which we did not train. Note the results in Table 4 are just as significant as above in each case even when the news sources differ.[1]

These results suggest that similar news sources with different time frames can provide corpus statistics for different corpora. Note additionally that each test result using the trainable combiner is better than the lead summaries. We believe that these experiments show the likelihood of successful tailorization for individual users given the features above alone.

DimSum relies on external corpus statistics to capture domain knowledge. In the second round of experiments, we attempted to assess the impact of different corpora by using 100 training and 100 test texts for each of five sources from the the TREC 5 corpora (i.e., Associated Press, Congressional Records, Federal Registry, Financial Times, Wall Street Journal). Each corpus was trained and tested on a baseline database specifically created for that corpus. Results on the test are shown in Table 5. The discrepancy in results among data sources suggests that summarization may not be equally viable for all data types. DimSum performed well on Associated Press and Wall Street Journal, taking advantage of all the training features. However, the system found it more difficult to summarize Congressional Record and Federal Registry texts. The human annotator who extracted summaries from these two sources also found it more difficult or sometimes almost impossible to summarize texts from these sources.

Qualitatively, examples of summaries with and without training are shown in Figure 1.

5 Multi-dimensional Summary Views

The DimSum Summarization Client provides a summary of a document in multiple dimensions through a graphical user interface (GUI) to suit different users' needs. In contrast to a static view of a document, the system brings the contributing linguistic and other resources to the desktop and the user chooses the view he wants. As shown in Figure 2, the GUI is divided into the List Box on the left and the Text Viewer on the right.

When a user asks for a summary of a text, extracted summary sentences are highlighted in the Text Viewer. The user can also choose to see only the summary sentences in the Viewer through the SUMMARY ONLY option. The user can dynamically control a percentage of sentences for a summary. In addition, the Client can

---

[1]The F-measure of the latwp-dev1 set without training, 41.3, is the baseline performance.

F-Measure	Precision	Recall	Length	High Score	Position	Paragraph
24.6	22.6	27.1	-	-	-	+
24.6	22.6	27.1	+	-	-	+
39.2	36.0	43.1	+	-	-	-
39.7	36.4	43.6	-	-	-	-
39.7	36.4	43.6	-	+	-	-
39.7	36.4	43.6	+	+	-	-
39.7	36.4	43.6	-	+	-	+
39.7	36.4	43.6	+	+	-	+
43.8	40.2	48.2	-	-	+	-
45.1	41.4	49.5	-	-	+	
45.5	41.8	50.0	+	-	+	+
45.7	42.0	50.2	+	-	+	-
46.6	42.7	51.1	-	+	+	-
46.6	42.7	51.1	+	+	+	-
48.4	44.4	53.2	-	+	+	
49.9	45.8	54.8	+	+	+	+

Table 3: Results of Using Different Training Features

Text Set	Uses Training	F-Measure	Precision	Recall	Lead Sum.
latwp-dev1	NO	41.3	32.3	57.3	
latwp-dev1	YES	49.9	45.1	55.8	48.2
latwp-test1	NO	31.9	26.0	41.1	
latwp-test1	YES	44.6	35.3	60.6	42.0
pi-test1	NO	40.5	37.4	44.1	
pi-test1	YES	49.7	46.0	54.2	47.7

Table 4: Results on Different Test Sets with or without Training

Text Set	F-M	Precision	Recall	Sentence Selection	Short	High Score	In Section	Paragraph
ap-test1	52.2	52.2	52.3	0.56	NO	YES	YES	YES
cr-test1	35.1	34.2	36.1	0.69	YES	YES	YES	YES
fr-test1	39.1	32.7	48.6	0.68	YES	YES	YES	YES
ft-test1	45.8	40.1	53.3	0.69	NO	NO	YES	NO
wsj-test1	53.6	51.4	56.0	0.66	YES	YES	YES	YES

Table 5: Results of Summaries for Different Corpora

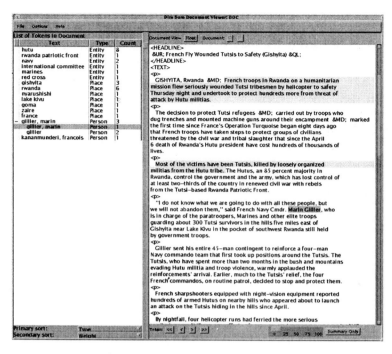

Figure 2: Name Mode Summary

With Training

French troops in Rwanda on a humanitarian mission flew seriously wounded Tutsi tribesmen by helicopter to safety Thursday night and undertook to protect hundreds more from threat of attack by Hutu militias. Most of the victims have been Tutsis, killed by loosely organized militias from the Hutu tribe.

Without Training

Most of the victims have been Tutsis, killed by loosely organized militias from the Hutu tribe. "I do not know what we are going to do with all these people, but we will not abandon them," said French Navy Cmdr. Martin Gillier, who is in charge of the paratroopers, Marines and other elite troops guarding about 300 Tutsi survivors in the hills five miles east of Gishyita near Lake Kivu in the pocket of southwest Rwanda still held by government troops.

Figure 1: Summaries with and without Training

automatically color-code top keywords in different colors for different types (i.e., person, entity, place and other) for quick and easy browsing.

In the List Box, the user can explore two different summary views of a text. First, the user can choose the "Name Mode," and all the names of people, entities, and places which were recognized by the name extraction tool are sorted and displayed in the List Box (cf. Figure 2). The user can also select a subset of name types (e.g., only person and entity, but not place) to display. Aliases of a name are indented and listed under their full names.

In the "Keyword Mode," the top keywords, or signature words, (including names) are displayed in the List Box. Analogous to the name aliases, for each keyword its synonyms and morphological variants, if they exist, are indented and listed below it (cf. Figure 3). The user can choose the score threshold or percentage to vary the number of keywords for display.

In both modes, the names and signature words in the List Box can be sorted alphabetically, by frequency, or by the *tf*idf* score. Clicking on a term in the List Box also causes the first occurrence of the term to be highlighted in the Text Viewer. From there, the user can use the FIRST, PREVIOUS, NEXT, or LAST button at the bottom of the GUI to track the other occurrences of the term, including its aliases, synonyms, and morphological variants. This provides the user with a way to track themes of the text interactively.

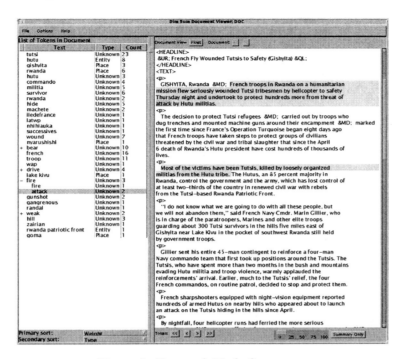

Figure 3: Keyword Mode Summary

6 Summary

Our work with the DimSum system advances the field of summarization through identification of linguistically motivated but automatically derived sources of information, inclusion of corpus statistics, application of information extraction, morphological pre-processing, and on-line WordNet for text cohesion, as well as experimentation with automated training over different corpus types.

In future work, we would like to improve output coherence by adding discourse information (Marcu 1997) and applying text segmentation algorithms (Richmond, Smith, & Amitay 1997; Beeferman, Berger, & Lafferty 1997). We also would like to increase performance scores by examining the effect of different machine learning algorithms given our diverse set of features and would like to assess how variation in machine-generated summarization output actually affects the utility of the summaries by conducting task-based evaluation.

References

Advanced Research Projects Agency (ARPA). 1995. *Proceedings of Sixth Message Understanding Conference (MUC-6)*, San Francisco, California: Morgan Kaufmann Publishers, Inc.

Beeferman, D.; Berger, A.; and Lafferty, J. 1997. Text Segmentation Using Exponential Models. In *Proceedings of the Second Conference on Empirical Methods in Natural Language Processing (EMNLP-2)*. Somerset, New Jersey: Association for Computational Linguistics.

Brandow, R.; Mitze, K.; and Rau, L. 1995. Automatic condensation of electronic publications by sentence selection. *Information Processing and Management* 31:675–685.

Brill, E. 1993. *A Corpus-based Approach to Language Learning.* Ph.D. Dissertation, University of Pennsylvania.

Church, K., and Hanks, P. 1990. Word Association Norms, Mutual Information, and Lexicography. *Computational Linguistics* 16(1).

Edmundson, H. P. 1969. New methods in automatic abstracting. *Journal of the Association for Computing Machinery* 16(2):264–228.

Fum, D.; Guida, G.; and Tasso, C. 1985. Evaluating importance: A step towards text summarization. In *International Joint Conference on Artificial Intelligence (IJCAI)*, 840–844. Los Altos, California: Morgan Kaufmann Publishers, Inc.

Halliday, M. A. K., and Hasan, R. 1976. *Cohesions in English.* London: Longman.

Jing, Y., and Croft, B. 1994. *An Association Thesaurus for Information Retrieval.* Technical Report 94-17. Center for Intelligent Information Retrieval, University of Massachusetts.

Johnson, F. C.; Paice, C. D.; Black, W. J.; and Neal, A. P. 1993. The application of linguistic processing to automatic abstract generation. *Journal of Documentation and Text Management* 1(3):215–241.

Jones, K. S. 1993. What might be in a summary? In Knorz, G.; Krause, J.; and Womser-Hacker, C., eds.,

Information Retrieval '93: Von der Modellierung zur Anwendung, 9–26.

Jones, K. S. 1995. Discourse modeling for automatic summaries. In Hajicova, E.; Cervenka, M.; Leska, O.; and Sgall, P., eds., *Prague Linguistic Circle Papers*, volume 1, 201–227.

Krupka, G. 1995. SRA: Description of the SRA System as Used for MUC-6. In *Proceedings of Sixth Message Understanding Conference (MUC-6)*. San Francisco, California: Morgan Kaufmann Publishers, Inc.

Kupiec, J.; Pedersen, J.; and Chen, F. 1995. A trainable document summarizer. In *Proceedings of the 18th Annual International SIGIR Conference on Research and Development in Information Retrieval*, 68–73.

Luhn, H. P. 1958. The automatic creation of literature abstracts. In *IBM Journal of Research Development*, volume 2, 159–165.

Mani, I., and Bloedorn, E. 1997. Multi-document Summarization by Graph Search and Matching. In *Proceedings of Fourteenth National Conference on Artifical Intelligence (AAAI-97)*. Cambridge, Massachusetts: MIT Press.

Marcu, D. 1997. From Discourse Structures to Text Summaries. In *Proceedings of Intelligent Scalable Text Summarization Workshop, Association for Computational Linguistics (ACL)*, 82–88. Somerset, New Jersey: Association for Computational Linguistics.

Maybury, M. T. 1995. Automated event summarization techniques. In Endres-Niggemeyer, B.; Hobbs, J.; and Jones, K. S., eds., *Summarizing Text for Intelligent Communication*, 101–149.

McKeown, K., and Radev, D. 1995. Generating summaries of multiple news articles. In *Proceedings of the 18th Annual International SIGIR Conference on Research and Development in Information*, 74–78.

Miike, S.; Itho, E.; Ono, K.; and Sumita, K. 1994. A full text retrieval system with a dynamic abstract generation function. In *Proceedings of 17th Annual International ACM SIGIR Conference on Research and Development in Information Retrieval*, 152–161.

Miller, G.; Beckwith, R.; Fellbaum, C.; Gross, D.; and Miller, K. 1990. Five papers on WordNet. Technical Report CSL Report 43, Cognitive Science Laboratory, Princeton University.

Mitra, M.; Singhal, A.; and Buckley, C. 1997. An Automatic Text Summarization and Text Extraction. In *Proceedings of Intelligent Scalable Text Summarization Workshop, Association for Computational Linguistics (ACL)*, 39–46.

Nomoto, T., and Matsumoto, Y. 1997. Data reliability and its effects on automatic abstraction. In *Proceedings of the Fifth Workshop on Very Large Corpora*.

Paice, C., and Jones, P. 1993. The identification of important concepts in highly structured technical papers. In *Proceedings of the 16th Annual International ACM SIGIR Conference of Research and Development in Information Retrieval*, 69–78. New York, New York: Association for Computing Machinery.

Paice, C. 1990. Constructing literature abstracts by computer: Techniques and prospects. *Information Processing and Management* 26(1):171–186.

Rath, G.; Resnick, A.; and Savage, T. R. 1961. The formation of abstracts by the selection of sentences. *American Documentation* 12(2):139–143.

Rau, L. F.; Jacobs, P. S.; and Zernik, U. 1989. Information extraction and text summarization using linguistic knowledge acquisition. *Information Processing and Management* 25(4):419–428.

Reimer, U., and Hahn, U. 1988. Text condensation as knowledge base abstraction. In *Proceedings of the 4th Conference on Artificial Intelligence Applications (CAIA)*, 338–344.

Richmond, K.; Smith, A.; and Amitay, E. 1997. Detecting Subject Boundaries within Text: a Language Independent Approach. In *Proceedings of the Second Conference on Empirical Methods in Natural Language Processing (EMNLP-2)*. Somerset, New Jersey: Association for Computational Linguistics.

Riloff, E. 1995. A corpus-based approach to domain-specific text summarization. In Endres-Niggemeyer, B.; Hobbs, J.; and Jones, K. S., eds., *Summarizing Text for Intelligent Communication*, 69–84.

Rush, J. E.; Salvador, R.; and Zamora, A. 1971. Automatic abstracting and indexing: Production of indicative abstracts by application of contextual inference and syntactic criteria. *Journal of the American Society for Information Science* 22(4):260–274.

Salton, G., and McGill, M., eds. 1983. *Introduction to Modern Information Retrieval*. New York, New York: McGraw-Hill Book Co.

8

Automated Text Summarization in SUMMARIST

Eduard Hovy and Chin-Yew Lin

Information Sciences Institute
of the University of Southern California
4676 Admiralty Way
Marina del Rey, CA 90292-6695
U.S.A.
Tel: +1-310-822-1511
Fax: +1-310-823-6714
Email: {hovy,cyl}@isi.edu

Abstract

SUMMARIST is an attempt to create a robust automated text summarization system, based on the 'equation': *summarization = topic identification + interpretation + generation*. Each of these stages contains several independent modules, many of them trained on large corpora of text. We describe the system's architecture and provide details of some of its modules.

1. Introduction

1.1 Extract, Abstract, or Something Else?

The task of a text summarizer is to produce a synopsis of any document (or set of documents) submitted to it. The level of sophistication of a synopsis can vary from a simple list of isolated keywords that indicate the major content of the document(s), through a list of independent single sentences that together express the major content, to a coherent, fully planned and generated text that compresses the document(s). The more sophisticated a synopsis, the more effort it generally takes to produce.

Several existing systems, including some Web browsers, claim to perform summarization. However, a cursory analysis of their output shows that their summaries are simply portions of the text, produced verbatim. While there is nothing wrong with such *extracts*, per se, the word 'summary' usually connotes something more, involving the fusion of various concepts of the text into a smaller number of concepts, to form an *abstract*. We define extracts as consisting wholly of portions extracted verbatim from the original (they may be single words or whole passages) and abstracts as consisting of novel phrasings describing the content of the original (which might be paraphrases or fully synthesized text). Generally, producing an abstract requires stages of topic fusion and text generation not needed for extracts.

In addition to extracts and abstracts, summaries may differ in several other ways. Some of the major types of summary that have been identified include indicative (keywords indicating topics) vs. informative (content-laden); generic (author's perspective) vs. query-oriented (user-specific); background vs. just-the-news; single-document vs. multi-document; neutral vs. evaluative. A full understanding of the major dimensions of variation, and the types of reasoning required to produce each of them, is still a matter of investigation. This makes the study of automated text summarization an exciting area in which to work.

1.2 SUMMARIST

Over the past two years we have been developing the text summarization system SUMMARIST. Our goal is to investigate the nature of text summarization, using SUMMARIST both as a research tool and as an engine to produce summaries for people upon demand. In order to maintain functionality while we experiment with new aspects, and since not all kinds of summary require the same processing steps, we have adopted a very open, modular design.

In this paper, we describe the architecture of SUMMARIST and provide details on the evaluated results of two of its component modules. Since it is still under development, not all the modules of SUMMARIST are at the same level of completeness. We describe the states of various modules in Sections 3.2, 3.3, and 3.4.

The goal of SUMMARIST is to provide both extracts and abstracts for arbitrary English and other-language text. SUMMARIST combines robust NLP processing (using IR and statistical techniques) with symbolic world knowledge (embodied in the concept thesaurus WordNet, dictionaries, and similar resources) to overcome the problems endemic to either approach alone. These problems arise because existing robust NLP methods tend to operate at the word level, and hence miss concept-level generalizations (which are provided by symbolic world knowledge), while on the other hand symbolic knowledge is too difficult to acquire in large enough scale to provide adequate coverage and robustness. For high-quality yet robust summarization, both aspects are needed.

To produce abstract-type summaries, the core process is a step of interpretation. In this step, two or more topics are fused together to form a third, more general, one. (We define *topic* as a particular subject that we write about or discuss.). This step must occur in the middle of the summarization procedure: First, an initial stage of topic identification and extraction is required to find the central topics in the input text; finally, to produce the summary, a concluding stage of sentence generation is needed. Thus SUMMARIST is based on the following 'equation':

$$summarization = topic\ identification + interpretation + generation$$

This breakdown is motivated as follows:

1. Identification: The goal is to filter the input to retain only the most important, central, topics. For generality we assume that a text can have many (sub)-topics, and that the topic extraction process can be parameterized in at least two ways: first, to include more or fewer topics to produce longer or shorter summaries, and second, to include only topics relating to the user's expressed interests. Typically, topic identification can be achieved using various complementary techniques, including those based on stereotypical text structure, cue words, high-frequency indicator phrases, and discourse structure. We describe these in Section 3.2.

2. Interpretation: Once the desired central topics have been identified, they can simply be output, to form an extract. In human summaries, however, a process of interpretation is usually performed to achieve further compaction. In one study, (Marcu 98) counted how many clauses had to be extracted from a text in order to fully contain all the material included in a human abstract of that text. Working with a newspaper corpus of 10 texts and 14 judges, he found a compression factor of 2.76—in this genre, extracts are almost three times as long (counting words) as their corresponding abstracts! Results of this kind indicate the need for summarization systems to further process extracted material: to remove redundancies, rephrase sentences to pack material more densely, and, importantly, to merge or fuse related topics into more 'general' ones. The various types of fusion are not yet known, but they include at least simple concept generalization (*he ate pears, apples, and bananas → he ate fruit*) and script identification (*he sat down, read the menu, ordered, ate, and left → he visited the restaurant*). See Section 3.3.

3. Generation: The goal is to reformulate the extracted and fused material into a coherent, densely phrased, new text. If this stage is skipped, the output is a verbatim quotation of some portion(s) of the input, and is not likely to be high-quality text (although this might be sufficient for the application). The modules implemented or planned for SUMMARIST are described in Section 3.4.

2. Related Work: A Summary of Methods

2.1 Older Approaches

Automated summarization is not a new idea. However, the techniques tried during the 1950's and 60's were characterized by their simplicity of processing, since at that time neither large corpora of text, nor sophisticated NLP modules, nor powerful computers with large memory existed. Pioneering work (Luhn 59; Edmundson 68) studied the following techniques:

- *Position in the text:* Sentences in privileged locations (first paragraph, or immediately following section headings "Introduction", "Purpose", "Conclusions", etc.) contain the topic(s).
- *Lexical cues:* The presence of words such as *significant*, *hardly*, *impossible* signals topic sentences.
- *Location:* First (and last) sentences of each paragraph contain topic information.

Although each of these approaches has some utility, they depend very much on the particular format and style of writing. The strategy of taking the first paragraph, for example, works only in the newspaper and news magazine genres, and not always then either. No automatic techniques were developed for determining optimal positions, relevant cues, etc.

2.2 Traditional Semantic NLP Approaches

Compared to the complex processing people perform when summarizing (see for example (Endres-Niggemeyer 97)), automated summarization techniques are likely to remain mere approximations for a long time yet. True summarizing requires the understanding and interpretation of the text into a new synthesis, at different levels of abstraction. Semantics-based Artificial Intelligence (AI) techniques developed in the 1970's and early 80's promised to provide the necessary reasoning capabilities.

Lehnert's work on Plot Units (Lehnert 83) is an interesting historical example. Plot Units represent high-level interpersonal interactions such as *denied-request, give-up, success-born-of-adversity*. By representing the series of interactions of protagonists in a story as a connected network of Plot Units, and by simply counting the number of interconnections from each Plot Unit to its neighbors, Lehnert could capture the centrality of each action to the story. She was able to generate a summary of stories represented as chains of Plot Units to any level of detail, simply by leaving out more or fewer of the peripheral Units. Unfortunately, Lehnert did not succeed in developing a parser powerful enough to parse stories into Plot Units in more than a toy domain.

Plot Units are a rather abstract representation scheme. More recent approaches instead use frames or templates that house the most pertinent aspects of stereotypical situations and objects (Mauldin 91; Rau 91). As outlined in (McKeown and Radev 95), such templates form an obvious basis from which to generate summaries. Once you know what kind of information you want in a summary, you can specify a template for it, and then you simply need a powerful enough parser/analyzer to identify and extract the appropriate pieces of information from the text.

The recent TIPSTER funding program in the USA has

supported the development of analyzers that perform information extraction from real-world newspaper texts in circumscribed topic domains such as terrorism. Using a variety of methods, these systems pinpoint and extract the types of information that have been prespecified to be interesting. TIPSTER/MUC systems such as FASTUS (Hobbs 92), GE-CMU (Jacobs 90), CIRCUS (Lehnert 91), and others are great achievements.

If the goal is to provide a detailed analysis, according to a predefined template, of the content of a text in a circumscribed but still fairly large domain, then systems of this ilk are the best available in the world today. But if one wants a system that can reflect what appears in the text and not just what the analyst has predefined to be of interest, then this approach is not adequate. A fixed-output template system is by its definition limited to the contents of the template, and it can never exceed this boundary. One is forced to turn to less semantic, more robust techniques.

2.3 IR Approaches

One place to turn for robust text processing techniques is Information Retrieval (IR). Active since the 1950's, IR researchers have spent a great deal of effort in developing methods of locating texts based on their characteristics, categorizing texts into predefined classes, and searching for incisive characterizations of the contents of texts (Salton 88; Rijsbergen 79; Paice 90).

Scaling down one's perspective from a large text collection to a single text (i.e., a collection of words and phrases), topic identification for extracts can be seen as a localized IR task. Can the IR techniques that pinpoint the significant passages in a collection of texts operate successfully when working on a single text? The question is still open, though recent research, and a majority of systems (see the other chapters of this book), seem to indicate that they can, at least to some extent.

The pure IR approach does have limitations, however. IR researchers have tended to eschew symbolic representations; anything deeper than the word level has often been viewed with suspicion. This attitude is both the strength and the weakness of IR. It is a strength, because it frees IR researchers from the seductive call of some magical powerful internal representation that will solve all the problems easily; it is a weakness, because it prevents researchers from employing reasoning at the non-word level. Unfortunately, abstract-type summaries require analysis and interpretation at levels deeper than the word level. This is mostly due to step 2 of the 'equation' above: without topic reinterpretation / fusion these systems can do no more than word counting and word recombination. Unless they have recourse to significant, large repositories of world knowledge, word-level systems can never know that the sequence *enter + order + wait + eat + pay + leave* can be summarized as *restaurant-visit*.

Although word-level techniques have been well developed and applied in many practical cases, they have

been criticized in several respects (Mauldin 91; Riloff 94; Hull 94) for the following reasons:

- *Synonymy:* One concept can be expressed by different words. For example, *cycle* and *bicycle* can both refer to some kind of vehicle (Hudson 95).
- *Polysemy:* One word can have several meanings. For example, *cycle* could mean *life cycle* or *bicycle*.
- *Phrases:* A phrase may have meaning different from the words in it. For example, an *alleged murderer* is not a *murderer*.
- *Term Dependency:* Terms are not totally independent of each other (as with synonymy).

Synonymy, polysemy, phrases, and term dependency problems all relate to semantics. A natural question is: why not use existing, pre-compiled, semantic knowledge sources as approximations to world knowledge, to help perform the interpretation step? Online dictionaries, thesauri, and wordlists are increasingly available. Using a thesaurus, one can identify synonyms. Using a sense disambiguation algorithm (e.g., Yarowsky 92), one can select the correct sense of a polysemous word. Using a syntactic parser, one can extract phrase segments and use them as terms (Lewis 92). Latent semantic indexing (Deerwester et al. 90; Hull 94) has been used to remedy the term dependency problem. All these efforts are attempts to bridge the gap between word form and word meaning. Following this trend, there is increasing interest in integrating shallow semantic processing and word-based statistical techniques to improve the performance of automatic text categorization systems (Liddy 94; Riloff 94).

Our approach with SUMMARIST is to employ IR techniques as far as they can take us, and then to augment them with symbolic/semantic and statistical methods. For example, SUMMARIST performs not only word counting (an IR technique for determining central topics), but also *concept counting* (using WordNet and similar resources) so that it can operate on a level 'deeper' than surface lexis. At this time, the interpretation stage in SUMMARIST is still rudimentary; most attention has been placed on the development of the topic identification modules. It therefore currently resembles other IR-based summarization systems such as DimSum (Aone et al. 97). Later, SUMMARIST will perform topic fusion at this deeper, non-lexical level, a step impossible to perform with pure IR techniques. SUMMARIST embodies one variant of knowledge-rich, assisted summarization, in which the requisite topic fusion/interpretation knowledge is acquired by statistical NLP with the help of online semantic and lexical resources.

3. The Structure of SUMMARIST

For each of the three steps of the above 'equation', SUMMARIST uses a mixture of symbolic world knowledge (from WordNet and similar resources) and statistical or IR-based techniques. Each stage employs several different, complementary, methods. To date, we

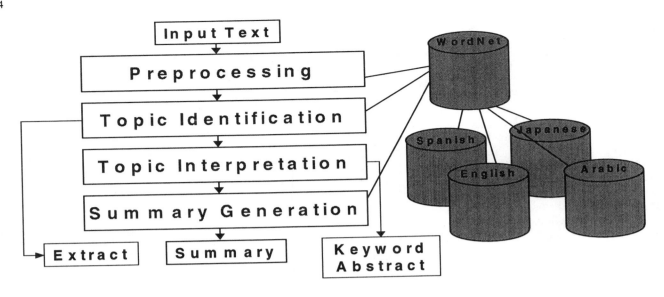

Figure 1. Architecture of SUMMARIST

have developed some methods for each stage of processing, and are busy developing additional methods and linking them into a single system. In the next sections we describe some methods from each stage. The overall architecture is shown in Figure 1.

Within each stage, each module is designed to operate independently (though some modules use the results of other modules). During the preprocessing stage, each word of the input document is written on a separate line of the processing file. Every module inspects the file and adds information to the relevant word(s), usually in the form of some numerical value or rating. At any time during processing, one can inspect the file and see which modules have run and how they have rated and/or augmented each portion of the input text. At the end of each stage, an integrator module combines the scores using a combination function and adds the resulting overall scores and/or values into the processing file. An example of SUMMARIST's extract production is provided in Section 4.

3.1 Preprocessing

The system's architecture most easily supports extensions with new modules when all input texts are converted into a standardized internal format. Before summarization starts, several preprocessing modules are activated. Each module either performs certain preprocessing tasks (such as tokenization) or attaches additional features (such as part-of-speech tags) to the input texts. These modules are:

- **tokenizer:** reads English texts and outputs tokenized texts.
- **part-of-speech tagger:** reads tokenized texts and outputs part-of-speech tagged texts. This tagger is based on Brill's part-of-speech tagger (Brill 93).
- **converter:** converts tagged texts into SUMMARIST

internal representation.

- **morpher:** finds all root forms of each input token, using a modification of WordNet's (Miller et al. 90) demorphing program.
- **phraser:** finds collocations (multi-word phrases), as recorded in WordNet.
- **token frequency counter:** counts the occurrence of each token in an input text.
- **tf.idf weight calculator:** calculates the *tf.idf* weight (Salton 88) for each input token, and ranks the tokens according to this weight.
- **query relevance calculator:** to produce query-sensitive summaries, this module records with each sentence the number of (demorphed) content words in the user's query that also appear in that sentence.

The results of these modules are shown in Section 4.

3.2 Topic Identification

Several techniques for topic identification have been reported in the literature, including methods based on Position (Luhn 58, Edmundson 69), Cue Phrases (Baxendale 58), word frequency, and Discourse Segmentation (Marcu 97). SUMMARIST will eventually contain modules that employ each of these methods. To date, modules for position, various types of word frequency, and cue phrases have been implemented, and a module based discourse structure is under construction. When each module has rated each sentence, a combination function implemented in the Topic Id Integration Module combines their scores to produce the overall ranking. The Topic Identification stage then returns the top-ranked $n\%$ of sentences as its final result.

3.2.1 Position Module

As first described by (Luhn 59; Edmundson 68), this method exploits the fact that in some genres, regularities of discourse structure and/or methods of exposition mean

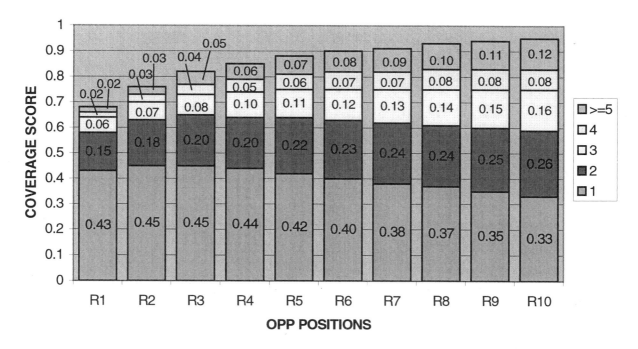

Figure 2. Coverage scores for top ten OPP sentence positions, window sizes 1 to 5.

that certain sentence positions tend to carry important topics. In (Lin and Hovy 97), we generalize their results with a method for automatically identifying the sentence positions most likely to yield good summary sentences. We define the *Optimal Position Policy* (OPP) as a list that indicates in what ordinal positions in the text high-topic-bearing sentences occur. We developed scoring metrics and normalization techniques for the automatic training of new OPPs, given a collection of genre-related texts with abstracts. To our knowledge, this work is the first systematic study and evaluation of the Position method.

For the Ziff-Davis corpus (13,000 newspaper articles announcing computer products) we have found that the OPP is

[T1, P2S1, P3S1, P4S1, P1S1, P2S2, {P3S2, P4S2, P5S1, P1S2}, P6S1, ...]

i.e., the title (T1) is the most likely to bear topics, followed by the first sentence of paragraph 2, the first sentence of paragraph 3, etc. (Paragraph 1 is invariably a teaser sentence in this corpus.) In contrast, for the *Wall Street Journal,* the OPP is

[T1, P1S1, P1S2, ...]

Evaluation: We evaluated the OPP method in various ways. In one of them, *coverage* is the fraction of the (human-supplied) keywords that are included verbatim in the sentences selected under the policy. (A random selection policy would extract sentences with a random distribution of topics; a good position policy would extract rich topic-bearing sentences.) We measured the effectiveness of an OPP by taking cumulatively more of

its sentences: first just the title, then the title plus P2S1, and so on. In order to determine the effect of multi-word key phrases, we matched using windows of increasing size, from 1 word to 5 words. The resulting coverage scores are shown in Figure 2, by window size. Summing together the multi-word contributions (window sizes 1 to 5) in the top ten sentence positions (R10), the columns reach 95% over an extract of 10 sentences (approx. 15% of a typical Ziff-Davis text): an encouraging result

3.2.2 Cue Phrases

Phrases such as "in summary", "in conclusion", and superlatives such as "the best", "the most important" can be good indicators of important content (Edmundson 69). Cue phrases are usually genre dependent. For example, "Abstract" and "in conclusion" are more likely to occur in scientific literature than in newspaper articles.

In one experiment, we manually compiled a list of cue phrases from a training corpus of paragraphs that themselves were summaries of texts. In this corpus, sentences containing phrases such as "this paper", "this article", "this document", and "we conclude" fairly reliably reflected the major content of the paragraphs. This indicated to us the possibility of summarizing a summary. Figure 3 contains an example, with sentences containing cue phrases underlined.

During processing, the Cue Phrase Module recognizes the occurrence of cue phrases and 'rewards' each word in the sentence containing the phrase with an appropriate score (constant per cue phrase).

In another experiment, we examined methods to automatically generate cue phrases (Liu and Hovy 98). By comparing the ratios (w_s/w_t) of occurrences of words in

Projections of levels of radioactive fallout from a nuclear war are sensitive to assumptions about the structure of the nuclear stockpiles as well as the assumed scenarios for a nuclear war. Recent arms control proposals would change these parameters. This paper examines the implications of the proposed (Intermediate-range Nuclear Forces) INF treaty and (Strategic Arms Reduction Treaty) START on fallout projections from a major nuclear war. We conclude that the INF reductions are likely to have negligible effects on estimates of global and local fallout, whereas the START reductions could result in reductions in estimates of local fallout that range from significant to dramatic, depending upon the nature of the reduced strategic forces. Should a major war occur, projections of total fatalities from direct effects of blast, thermal radiation, and fallout, and the phenomenon known as nuclear winter, would not be significantly affected by INF and START initiatives as now drafted. 14 refs.

Figure 3. Highlighted summary, generated by SUMMARIST using cue phrases.

summaries (w_s) and in the corresponding texts (w_t), we extracted the words showing the highest increase in occurrence density between text and associated abstract. We then searched for frequent concatenations of such privileged words into phrases. While we found no useful phrases in a corpus of 1,000 newspaper articles, we found the following in 87 articles on Computational Linguistics:

w_s/w_t phrase

11.500 multilingual natural language
8.500   paper presents the
7.500   paper gives
6.000   paper presents
6.000   now present
5.199   this paper presents
4.555   paper describes
2.510   this paper

A more comprehensive study of the automated gathering of cue phrases is reported in (Teufel and Moens 97).

3.2.3 Concept Signatures for Topic Identification

A Concept Signature is a topic word (the *head*) together with a list of associated (*keyword weight*) pairs. Concept signatures represent concepts using word co-occurrence patterns. The idea is based on a simple observation: when some concept plays an important role in a text, a related set of words occurs fairly predictably. This idea is used in IR systems to achieve query term expansion.

We describe in Section 3.3.2 how we automatically build Concept Signatures and plan to use them for topic interpretation. It is, however, also possible to use concept signatures for topic identification. In one experiment, we created a Signature for each of five groups of 200 documents, drawn from five domains. When performing topic identification for a document, the Topic Id Signature Module assigned to each occurrence of a Signature keyword that keyword's weight. Each sentence received a Signature score equal to the total of all Signature words contained in it, normalized by its length. This score indicates the relevance of the sentence to the signature topic. Examples appear in Section 4.

3.2.4 Topic Identification Integration Module

Each separate topic identification module assigns its score to each sentence. How should the various scores be combined for the best result?

Various approaches have been tried. Most of them employ some sort of combination function, in which coefficients assign various weights to the individual scores, which are then summed. (Kupiec et al. 95) and

(Aone et al. 97) employ the Expectation Maximization algorithm to derive coefficients for their systems.

Initially, SUMMARIST contained a linear combination function, in which the coefficients were determined by manual experimentation. The results of this function were not optimal, as found in the formal TIPSTER/SUMMAC evaluation of various summarization systems (Firmin Hand and Sundheim 98). In subsequent work, we tested two automated methods of creating a better combination function. First, we used the C4.5 (Quinlan 86) to build a decision tree automatically in the standard manner. As training data, we used a portion of the results of the TIPSTER/SUMMAC summarization evaluation dry run, annotated to indicate the relevance and popularity of each sentence (Baldwin 98). The algorithm generated a tree of 1,611 nodes, of which the top (most informative) questions pertain to the query signature, term frequency, overlap with title, and OPP. Compared with the manually built function, the decision tree is considerably better. SUMMARIST now scores 58.07% (Recall and Precision) on an unseen test set of 82 dry-run texts in a 5-way cross-validation run. (On the same data, the system used to score 33.02%.) We also implemented a 6-node perceptron. Training it on the same data produced results within 1% of the decision tree.

3.3 Topic Interpretation (Concept Fusion)

The second step in the summarization process is that of topic interpretation. In this step, two or more extracted topics are 'fused' into one (or more) unifying concept(s). Topic fusion can be as simple as part-whole construction, as when *wheel*, *chain*, *pedal*, *saddle*, *light*, *frame*, and *handlebars* fuse together to *bicycle*. Generally, though, it is more complex, ranging from direct concept/word clustering as used in IR for query expansion (Paice 90) to script-based inference such as *drive in + pay + fill tank + close tank → gasoline fill up* (Schank and Abelson 77).

Fusing topics into one or more characterizing concepts is the most difficult step of automated text summarization. The reason is that fusion requires knowledge about the world that is seldom included in the text explicitly. Consider the following example:

> John and Bill wanted money. They bought ski-masks and guns and stole an old car from a neighbor. Wearing their ski-masks and waving their guns, the two entered the bank, and within minutes left the bank with several bags of $100 bills. They drove away happy, throwing away the ski-

masks and guns in a trash can. They were never caught.

Word counting would indicate that the story is about ski-masks and guns, both of which are mentioned more than any other content word. Clearly, however, the story is about a robbery, and any summary of it must mention this fact. Some process of interpreting the individual words as part of some encompassing concept is required.

A variety of methods can be employed. All of them associate a set of concepts (the *indicators*) with a characteristic generalization (the *fuser* or *head*). The challenge is to develop methods that work reliably and to construct a large enough collection of indicator-fuser sets to achieve effective topic reduction.

SUMMARIST's topic interpretation methods currently include *Concept Wavefront* (Lin 95) and *Concept Signature* (Lin and Hovy 98).

3.3.1 Concept Counting and the Wavefront

To identify the topics of texts, IR researchers make the assumption that the more a word is used in a text, the more important it is in that text. But although word frequency counting operates robustly across different domains without relying on stereotypical text structure or semantic models, they cannot handle synonyms, pronominalization, or other forms of coreferentiality, and they miss conceptual generalizations:

John bought some vegetables, fruit, bread, and milk. → *John bought some groceries.*

Using a concept generalization taxonomy, we have developed a method to recognize that *vegetables*, *fruit*, etc., can be summarized as *groceries*. We count *concepts* instead of words, and generalize them using WordNet (Miller et al. 90) (though we could have used any machine-readable thesaurus) for inter-concept links. In the limit case, when WordNet does not contain concepts for the words in the text, this technique defaults to word counting.

The idea is simple. We count the number of occurrences of each content word in the text, and assign that number to the word's associated concept in WordNet. We then propagate all these weights upward, assigning to each node the sum of its weight plus all its childrens' weights. Next, we proceed back down, deciding at each node whether to stop or to continue downward. We stop when the node is an appropriate generalization of its children; that is, when its weight derives so equally from two or more of its children that no child is the clear majority contributor to its weight. This algorithm picks the most specific generalization of a set of concepts as their fuser.

In fact, one can find layers of fuser concepts. As described in (Lin 95), we locate the most appropriate generalizations by finding concepts on the *interesting wavefront*, a set of nodes representing concepts that each generalize a set of approximately equally strongly represented subconcepts (ones that have no obvious dominant subconcept to specialize to). To find the wavefront, we define a concept's *weight* to be the sum of the frequency of occurrence of the concept C plus the weights of all its subconcepts. We then define the

concept frequency ratio between a concept and its subconcepts:

$$R = \frac{MAX(sum\,of\,all\,children\,of\,C)}{SUM(sum\,of\,all\,children\,of\,C)}$$

R is a way to identify the degree of summarization informativeness. We use this ratio to find interesting concepts in a hierarchical concept taxonomy. Starting from the top of the hierarchy, we proceed downward along each child branch whenever the branch ratio is greater than or equal to a cutoff value R_b, and stopping at that node otherwise. The resulting set of nodes we call the interesting wavefront. We can start another exploration of interesting concepts downward from this interesting wavefront, resulting in a second, lower, wavefront, and so on. By repeating this process until we reach the leaf concepts of the hierarchy, we can derive a set of interesting wavefronts. From the interesting wavefronts, we choose the most general one below a certain depth D to ensure a good balance of generality and specificity. For WordNet, we found $D=6$, by experimentation.

Evaluation: We selected 26 articles about new computer products from *BusinessWeek* (1993–94) of average 750 words each. For each text we extracted the eight sentences containing the most interesting concepts using the wavefront technique, and comparing them to the contents of a professional's abstracts of these 26 texts from an online service. We developed several weighting and scoring variations and tried various ratio and depth parameter settings for the algorithm. We also implemented a random sentence selection algorithm as a baseline comparison.

The average recall (R) and precision (P) values over the three scoring variations were $R=0.32$ and $P=0.35$, when the system produces extracts of 8 sentences. In comparison, the random selection method had $R=0.18$ and $P=0.22$ precision in the same experimental setting. While these R and P values are not tremendous, they show that semantic knowledge—even as limited as that in WordNet—does enable improvements over traditional IR word-based techniques. However, the limitations of WordNet are serious drawbacks: there is no domain-specific knowledge, for example to relate *customer*, *waiter*, *cashier*, *food*, and *menu* together with *restaurant*. We thus developed a second technique of concept interpretation, using topic signatures.

3.3.2 Interpretation using Topic Signatures

Can one automatically find a set of related words that can collectively be fused into a single word appropriate for summarization? To test this idea we developed the Topic Signature method (Lin 97; Lin and Hovy 98). We define a signature to be a *head* together with a list of (*keyword score*) pairs, where each score provides the relative strength of association of its keyword.

To construct signatures automatically, we used a set of 30,000 texts from the 1987 *Wall Street Journal* (WSJ) corpus. The paper's editors have classified each text into one of 32 classes—AROspace, BNKing, ENVironment,

RANK	ARO	BNK	ENV	TEL
1	contract	bank	epa	at&t
2	air_force	thrift	waste	network
3	aircraft	banking	environmental	fcc
4	navy	loan	water	cbs
5	army	mr.	ozone	cable
6	space	deposit	state	bell
7	missile	board	incinerator	long-distance
8	equipment	fslic	agency	telephone
9	mcdonnell	fed	clean	telecomm.
10	northrop	institution	landfill	mci
11	nasa	federal	hazardous	mr.
12	pentagon	fdic	acid_rain	doctrine
13	defense	volcker	standard	service
14	receive	henkel	federal	news
15	boeing	banker	lake	turner

Figure 4. Portions of the signatures of several concepts.

TELecommunications, etc. We counted the occurrences of each content word (canonicalized morphologically to remove plurals, etc.), in the texts of each class, relative to the number of times they occur in the whole corpus, using the standard *tf.idf* method. We then selected the top-scoring 300 terms for each category and created a signature with the category name as its head. The top terms of four example signatures are shown in Figure 4. It is quite easy to determine the identity of the signature head just by inspecting the top few signature indicators. SUMMARIST will use signatures for summary creation as follows. After the topic identification stage identifies a set of important topics, the topic signature interpretation module will identify from its library of signatures the one(s) most fully subsuming the topic words, and these signatures' heads will then be used as the summarizing fuser concepts. Matching the identified topic terms against all signature indicators involves several problems, including taking into account the relative frequencies of occurrence and resolving matches with multiple signatures, and specifying thresholds of acceptability. Since this work has not yet been completed, the ultimate effectiveness of this method remains unknown.

Evaluation. We needed to evaluate the quality of the signatures formed by our algorithm. Recognizing the similarity of signature recognition to document categorization, we evaluated the effectiveness of each signature by seeing how well it served as a selection criterion on texts. As data we used a set of 2,204 previously unseen WSJ news articles from 1988.

For each test text, we created a single-text 'document signature' using the same *tf.idf* measure as before, and then matched this document signature against the category signatures. The closest match provided the class into which the text was categorized. We tested several matching functions, including a simple *binary* match (count 1 if a term match occurs; 0 otherwise); *curve-fit* match (minimize the difference in occurrence frequency

of each term between document and concept signatures), and *cosine* match (minimize the cosine angle in the hyperspace formed when each signature is viewed as a vector and each word frequency specifies the distance along the dimension for that word). These matching functions all provided approximately the same results. The values for Recall and Precision ($R=0.7566$ and $P=0.6931$) are encouraging and compare well with recent IR results (TREC 95). Current experiments are investigating the use of contexts smaller than a full text to create more accurate signatures.

3.3.3 Clustering Tool
Extending the above-mentioned concept signature work will require the creation of signatures for hundreds, and eventually thousands, of different topics, as needed for robust summarization. An important step is obviously the grouping of documents about the same or similar topics before signatures can be trained. For this reason, we have implemented a variety of standard clustering techniques (CLINK, SLINK, Median, Ward's Method; see (Rasmussen 92)) in a Clustering Tool, and are adding more recent, faster, clustering methods based on sparse matrix reordering (Berry et al. 96). In addition, we have recently embarked on a large-scale signature building enterprise.

In order to build accurate signatures, we had to ensure that the document sets are pure; i.e., that they do not contain too much unrelated material. Therefore, we tested document set purification using clustering in the following experiment. We used a set of 1000 documents, pre-compiled from five domains, extracted from three sources (*Wall Street Journal*, *Associated Press*, and *Federal Register*) by the TIPSTER Summarization Evaluation committee (Firmin Hand 97). After mixing the documents, we used the Clustering Tool to regenerate the five clusters. Precision of the results varied from over 99% to about 70%, depending on method, with CLINK (Defays 77) giving the best performance. Using the

Cluster 1		Cluster 2		Cluster 3	
bush	8.16	inmate	12.28	south	19.51
navy	7.00	prison	10.50	africa	9.69
defense	6.85	prisoner	4.08	congress	8.36
stealth	6.28	jail	3.67	black	7.39
house	5.67	county	3.63	african	7.14
bomber	5.11	sunday	2.89	white	4.60
program	4.96	correction	2.78	apartheid	3.62
missile	4.80	riot	2.35	sanction	3.16
billion	4.29	guard	2.27	de	2.98
plane	4.23	cell	2.26	anti-apartheid	2.97
air	3.95	court	2.16	bush	2.84
propose	3.93	department	2.13	leader	2.80
company	3.92	hold	2.01	political	2.65
fighter	3.70	federal	2.00	party	2.60
include	3.68	serve	1.98	government	2.52

Figure 5. Three concept signatures produced from automatically generated clusters.

above-mentioned signature training module, we then produced concept signatures for each cluster. The top-scoring elements of three of these signatures are shown in Figure 5. They seem to separate very clearly into distinct semantic domains.

3.4 Summary Generation

The final step in the summarization process is the generation of a summary. A range of possibilities occurs here, from simple word or phrase printing to sophisticated sentence planning and surface-form realization. SUMMARIST will eventually contain three generation modules, associated as appropriate with the various levels needed for various applications.

Extraction: For extract-type summaries, no generation is required. The terms or sentences selected by the Topic Identification stage can simply be reproduced. Despite the likely incoherence of the result, it may contain enough information to support humans performing tasks such as document routing. This output mode is currently used in SUMMARIST.

Topic lists: Sometimes no summary is really needed; a simple list of the summarizing topics is enough. SUMMARIST can simply print the extracted keywords or interpreted fuser concepts, sorted in decreasing importance.

Phrase concatenation: SUMMARIST will include a rudimentary generator that composes noun phrase-sized and clause-sized units into simple sentences. It will follow links from the fuser concepts through the words that support them in the input text, and from those sentences gather related noun phrases and clauses.

Full sentence planning and generation: SUMMARIST will employ the sentence planner being built at ISI in collaboration with the HealthDoc project from the University of Waterloo (Hovy and Wanner 96), together with a sentence generator, such as Penman (Penman 88, Matthiessen and Bateman 91), FUF (Elhadad 92), or NITROGEN (Knight and Hatzivassiloglou 95). Producing

well-formed, fluent, summaries is not a trivial generation task, as shown by (McKeown and Radev 95): a considerable amount of planning is required to achieve dense packing of content. The input will be a list of the fuser concepts and their most closely related topics, as identified by SUMMARIST's topic identification stage.

4. An Example Extract Summary

Figure 6 shows a portion of SUMMARIST's internal preamble for text AP880212-0009. It includes a document number (*docno*); the title of the document (*title*); the modules that have processed the document (*module*); the words contained in the user's query (*query_signature*; the signature term | its weight. Terms are listed in descending weight order. The same format is used for *tf, tfidf, sig* and *opp* keywords); term frequency keywords (*tf_keywords*); *tf.idf* keywords (*tfidf_keywords*); the OPP rule used (*opp_rule*; p: the paragraph rule, with vertical bars separating paragraph number and rank. Title is indicated as paragraph 0); and OPP keywords (*opp_keywords*); the top three most similar topic signatures (*signature*, the first number is the topic/cluster number and the second one is the similarity of this signature to the document); signature keywords (*sig_keywords*). Note that keywords selected by term frequency, *tf.idf*, signature, and OPP are different. Figure 7 shows the content portion of the internal format of text AP880212-0009. Each line contains one word of the text followed by its attribute list. The attributes are [*pno*, paragraph number], [*sno*, sentence number], [*pos*, part-of-speech tag], [*cwd*, common word (true or false)], [*ttl*, word appears in title (true or false)], [*mph*, root form], [*wnc*, the file identifer(s) of the WordNet file(s) containing this word], [*frq*, word frequency count], [*tfidf*, tf.idf weight], [*opp*, OPP weight (global, local)], [*sig*, signature weights of the top three most pertinent signatures], [*qry*, word in user query (true or false)]. Figure 9 shows the original full text of document AP880212-0009, and Figure 8 the generic summary of it.

```
<*docno=AP880212-0009>
<*title="90 Soldiers Arrested After Coup Attempt In Tribal Homeland. ">
<*module=PREITTLIMPHICATITFIDFIOPPISIGIQRY>
<*query_signature=black,13.406|blacks,13.406|africa,12.737|south,12.737|anc,5.855|challenge,5.855|domination,5.855|greatest,5.855|w
hite,5.855|political,5.272|african,5.162|apartheid,5.162|majority,5.162|effort,5.118|efforts,5.118|minority,4.756|armed,4.469|congress,3.9
09|form,3.552|personnel,3.457|change,3.370|national,2.859|economic,2.764|military,2.720|interest,2.677|activities,2.559|activity,2.559|st
ate,2.094|states,2.094|government,2.005>
<*tf_keywords=south,13.000|homeland,11.000|african,8.000|africa,7.000|bophuthatswana,7.000|mangope,7.000|soldier,7.000|coup,6.00
0|minister,5.000|arrest,4.000>
<*tfidf_keywords=bophuthatswana,43.453|mangope,43.453|homeland,37.446|coup,25.570|soldier,16.729|south,13.895|malebanemetsin
g,13.801|mmabatho,13.801|rathebe,13.801|african,12.622>
<*opp_rule=p:0,1|1,2|2,4|3,4 s:-,->
<*opp_keywords=homeland,42.667|south,37.917|coup,26.083|african,26.000|soldier,23.583|mangope,20.667|bophuthatswana,20.167|a
frica,19.667|attempt,14.333|tribal,14.333>
<*signature=110,0.269|138,0.184|151,0.137|->
<*sig_keywords=africa,9.074|anc,8.636|south,8.465|black,6.857|african,6.429|apartheid,3.390|botha,2.832|political,2.521|government,2.
448|national,2.397|police,2.208|leaders,2.019|congress,1.981|party,1.779|organization,1.729|leader,1.706|group,1.552|pretoria,1.513|co
untry,1.295|homeland,1.243|majority,1.243>
```

Figure 6. Preamble of text AP880212-0009.

```
About    <pno=1 sno=1 pos=IN cwd=1 ttl=0 mph=- wnc=- frq=0 tfidf=0 opp=-,- sig=-,-|-,-|-,-|-,- qry=->
90    <pno=1 sno=1 pos=CD cwd=1 ttl=1 mph=- wnc=- frq=0 tfidf=0 opp=-,- sig=-,-|-,-|-,-|-,- qry=->
soldiers    <pno=1 sno=1 pos=NNS cwd=0 ttl=1 mph=soldier wnc=18,5 frq=7 tfidf=16.729 opp=23.583,4.500 sig=-,-|53,1.530|-,-|-,- qry=->
have <pno=1 sno=1 pos=VBP cwd=1 ttl=0 mph=- wnc=- frq=0 tfidf=0 opp=-,- sig=-,-|-,-|-,-|-,- qry=->
been <pno=1 sno=1 pos=VBN cwd=1 ttl=0 mph=- wnc=- frq=0 tfidf=0 opp=-,- sig=-,-|-,-|-,-|-,- qry=->
arrested<pno=1 sno=1 pos=VBN cwd=0 ttl=1 mph=arrest wnc=35,33,38 frq=4 tfidf=9.064 opp=13.000,4.500 sig=166,0.555|-,-
|121,0.564|-,- qry=->
and    <pno=1 sno=1 pos=CC cwd=1 ttl=0 mph=- wnc=- frq=0 tfidf=0 opp=-,- sig=-,-|-,-|-,-|-,- qry=->
face    <pno=1 sno=1 pos=VB cwd=0 ttl=0 mph=- wnc=32,33,42,38,35 frq=1 tfidf=1.783 opp=4.500,4.500 sig=-,-|-,-|-,-|-,- qry=->
possible <pno=1 sno=1 pos=JJ cwd=1 ttl=0 mph=- wnc=- frq=0 tfidf=0 opp=-,- sig=-,-|-,-|-,-|-,- qry=->
death    <pno=1    sno=1    pos=NN    cwd=0    ttl=0    mph=-    wnc=11,19,28,18,26,4    frq=2    tfidf=3.554    opp=7.333,4.500
sig=273,0.426|64,1.350|149,0.497|-,- qry=->
...
```

Figure 7. Word-attribute list of text AP880212-0009, produced by SUMMARIST.

```
<DOC>
<DOCNO>AP880212-0009</DOCNO>
<TITLE>90 Soldiers Arrested After Coup Attempt In Tribal Homeland.</TITLE>
<TEXT>
About 90 soldiers have been arrested and face possible death sentences stemming from a coup attempt in Bophu-thatswana , leaders
of the tribal homeland said Friday .
Rebel soldiers staged the takeover bid Wednesday , detaining homeland President Lucas Mangope and several top Cabinet officials
for 15 hours before South African soldiers and police rushed to the homeland , rescuing the leaders and restoring them to power .
Bophuthatswana , which has a population of 1.7 million spread over seven separate land blocks , is one of 10 tribal homelands in
South Africa .
Hennie Riekert , the homeland 's defense minister , said South African troops were to remain in Bophuthatswana but
will not become a " permanent presence ."
</TEXT>
</DOC>
```

Figure 8. Generic summary produced by SUMMARIST.

```
<DOCNO> AP880212-0009 </DOCNO>

<HEAD>90 Soldiers Arrested After Coup Attempt In Tribal Homeland</HEAD>

<DATELINE>MMABATHO, South Africa (AP) </DATELINE>

<TEXT>
```

About 90 soldiers have been arrested and face possible death sentences stemming from a coup attempt in Bophuthatswana, leaders of the tribal homeland said Friday.

Rebel soldiers staged the takeover bid Wednesday, detaining homeland President Lucas Mangope and several top Cabinet officials for 15 hours before South African soldiers and police rushed to the homeland, rescuing the leaders and restoring them to power.

At least three soldiers and two civilians died in the uprising.

Bophuthatswana's Minister of Justice G. Godfrey Mothibe told a news conference that those arrested have been charged with high treason and if convicted could be sentenced to death. He said the accused were to appear in court Monday.

All those arrested in the coup attempt have been described as young troops, the most senior being a warrant officer.

During the coup rebel soldiers installed as head of state Rocky Malebane-Metsing, leader of the opposition Progressive Peoples Party. Malebane-Metsing escaped capture and his whereabouts remained unknown, officials said. Several unsubstantiated reports said he fled to nearby Botswana.

Warrant Officer M.T.F. Phiri, described by Mangope as one of the coup leaders, was arrested Friday in Mmabatho, capital of the nominally independent homeland, officials said.

Bophuthatswana, which has a population of 1.7 million spread over seven separate land blocks, is one of 10 tribal homelands in South Africa. About half of South Africa's 26 million blacks live in the homelands, none of which are recognized internationally.

Hennie Riekert, the homeland's defense minister, said South African troops were to remain in Bophuthatswana but will not become a "permanent presence."

Bophuthatswana's Foreign Minister Solomon Rathebe defended South Africa's intervention.

"The fact that ... the South African government (was invited) to assist in this drama is not anything new nor peculiar to Bophuthatswana," Rathebe said. "But why South Africa, one might ask? Because she is the only country with whom Bophuthatswana enjoys diplomatic relations and has formal agreements."

Mangope described the mutual defense treaty between the homeland and South Africa as "similar to the NATO agreement," referring to the Atlantic military alliance. He did not elaborate.

Asked about the causes of the coup, Mangope said, "We granted people freedom perhaps ... to the extent of planning a thing like this."

The uprising began around 2 a.m. Wednesday when rebel soldiers took Mangope and his top ministers from their homes to the national sports stadium.

On Wednesday evening, South African soldiers and police stormed the stadium, rescuing Mangope and his Cabinet.

South African President P.W. Botha and three of his Cabinet ministers flew to Mmabatho late Wednesday and met with Mangope, the homeland's only president since it was declared independent in 1977.

The South African government has said, without producing evidence, that the outlawed African National Congress may be linked to the coup.

The ANC, based in Lusaka, Zambia, dismissed the claims and said South Africa's actions showed that it maintains tight control over the homeland governments. The group seeks to topple the Pretoria government.

The African National Congress and other anti-government organizations consider the homelands part of an apartheid system designed to fragment the black majority and deny them political rights in South Africa.

```
</TEXT>
```

Figure 9. Full text AP890417-0617.

5. Conclusion

As outlined in Section 1, extract summaries require only the stage of topic identification. Accordingly, most of our early efforts have been devoted to the preprocessing and topic identification stages. At this time, we plan to include into the topic identification stage only one new module. The Discourse Structure module, on which work is currently well underway (Marcu 98), will form the heart of the topic identification stage. By determining the importance of each clause within the overall discourse structure, this module will contribute directly to the scores of individual sentences. In addition, this module will also provide the interclause discourse relations (relations signaled by cue phrases such as "but", "although", "in order to") required by the generation stage to produce coherent text. Thus the current internal representation scheme of SUMMARIST, a linear sequence of sentences, will be changed into a discourse tree of the kind used in (Marcu 97).

We are beginning to address the subsequent stages of summarization as well. By including modules to perform topic interpretation and summary generation, SUMMARIST will also be able to produce abstract summaries. In order to perform concept interpretation, SUMMARIST requires a rather more elaborated concept taxonomy than it currently has. Work is underway to extend the SENSUS ontology (Knight and Luk 94; Hovy 98) by including other ontologies' contents and by parsing dictionary entries. In addition, in order to perform signature-based concept interpretation, SUMMARIST requires a large library of topic signatures. Work is also underway to acquire such a library using text searches on the web.

Automated summarization is simultaneously an old topic—work on it dates from the 1950's—and a new topic—it is so difficult that interesting headway can be made for many years to come. We are excited about the possibilities offered by the combination of semantic and statistical techniques in what is surely one of the most complex tasks of all natural language processing!

Acknowledgments

We thank Benjamin Liberman for his implementation of the Clustering Tool and Sara Shelton for her enthusiastic support, comments, and suggestions.

References

Aone, C., M.E. Okurowski, J. Gorlinsky, B. Larsen. 1997. A Scalable Summarization System using Robust NLP. *Proceedings of the Workshop on Intelligent Scalable Text Summarization*, 66–73. ACL/EACL Conference, Madrid, Spain.

Baldwin, B. 1998. Reworking of TIPSTER/SUMMAC Dry Run Evaluation Results. University of Pennsylvania.

Baxendale, P.B. 1958. Machine-Made Index for Technical Literature—An Experiment. *IBM Journal* (October) 354–361.

Berry, M.W., B. Hendrickson, and P. Raghavan. 1996. Sparse Matrix Reordering Schemes for Browsing Hypertext. *Lectures in Applied Mathematics* 32: 99–123.

Brill, E. 1993. A Corpus-Based Approach to Language Learning. Ph.D. diss., University of Pennsylvania.

Deerwester, S., S.T. Dumais, T.K. Landauer, G.W. Furnas, and R.A. Harshman. 1990. Indexing by latent semantic analysis. *Journal of the American Society for Information Science* 41(6): 391–407.

Defays, D. 1977. An Efficient Algorithm for a Complete Link Method. *Computer Journal* 20, 346–366.

Edmundson, H.P. 1968. New Methods in Automatic Extraction. *Journal of the ACM* 16(2), 264–285.

Elhadad, M. 1992. Using Argumentation to Control Lexical Choice: A Functional Unification-Based Approach. Ph.D. diss, Columbia University.

Endres-Niggemeyer, B. 1997. SimSum: Simulation of Summatizing. In *Proceedings of the Workshop on Intelligent Scalable Summarization* at the ACL/EACL Conference, 89–96. Madrid, Spain.

Firmin Hand, T. 1997. A Proposal for Task-Based Evaluation of Text Summarization Systems. In *Proceedings of the Workshop on Intelligent Scalable Summarization, a*t the ACL/EACL Conference, 31–38. Madrid, Spain.

Firmin Hand, T. and B. Sundheim. 1998. TIPSTER-SUMMAC Summarization Evaluation. *Proceedings of the TIPSTER Text Phase III Workshop*. Washington.

Hobbs, J.R., D. Appelt, M. Tyson, J. Baer, and D. Israel. 1992. Description of the FASTUS System used for MUC-4. In *Proceedings of the Fourth Message Understanding Conference (MUC-4)*, 268–275. McLean, VA.

Hovy, E.H. and L. Wanner. 1996. Managing Sentence Planning Requirements. In *Proceedings of the Workshop on Gaps and Bridges in NL Planning and Generation*, 53–58. ECAI Conference. Budapest, Hungary.

Hovy, E.H. 1998. Combining and Standardizing Large-Scale, Practical Ontologies for Machine Translation and Other Uses. In *Proceedings of the First International Conference on Language Resources and Evaluation (LREC)*, 535–542. Granada, Spain.

Hudson, R. 1995. *Word Meaning*. London, England: Routledge.

Hull, D.A. 1994. Information Retrieval Using Statistical Classification. Ph.D. diss., Stanford University.

Jacobs, P.S. and L.F. Rau. 1990. SCISOR: Extracting Information from On-Line News. *Communications of the ACM* 33(11): 88–97.

Knight, K. and S.K. Luk. 1994. Building a Large-Scale Knowledge Base for Machine Translation. *Proceedings of the Conference of the American Association of Artificial Intelligence* (AAAI-94), 773–778. Seattle, WA.

Knight, K. and V. Hatzivassiloglou. 1995. Two-Level Many-Paths Generation. In *Proceedings of the Thirty-third Conference of the Association of Computational*

Linguistics (ACL-95), 252–260. Boston, MA.

Kupiec, J., J. Pedersen, and F. Chen. 1995. A Trainable Document Summarizer. In *Proceedings of the Eighteenth Annual International ACM Conference on Research and Development in Information Retrieval* (SIGIR), 68–73. Seattle, WA.

Lehnert, W.G. 1983. Narrative complexity based on summarization algorithms. In *Proceedings of the Eighth International Joint Conference of Artificial Intelligence (IJCAI-83)*, 713–716. Karlsruhe, Germany.

Lehnert, W.G. 1991. *Symbolic/Subsymbolic Sentence Analysis: Exploiting the Best of Two Worlds*, vol. 1, 135–164. Norwood, NJ: Ablex.

Lewis, D.D. 1992. An evaluation of phrasal and clustered representations of a text categorization task. In *Proceedings of the Fifteenth Annual International ACM Conference on Research and Development in Information Retrieval* (SIGIR), 37–50. New York, NY.

Liddy, E., W. Paik, and E.S. Yu. 1994. Text Categorization for Multiple Users Based on Semantic Features from a Machine-Readable Dictionary. *ACM Transactions on Information Systems*, vol. 12: 278–295.

Lin, C-Y. 1995. Topic Identification by Concept Generalization. In *Proceedings of the Thirty-third Conference of the Association of Computational Linguistics (ACL-95)*, 308–310. Boston, MA.

Lin, C-Y. 1997. Robust Automated Topic Identification. Ph.D. diss., University of Southern California.

Lin, C-Y. and E.H. Hovy. 1997. Identifying Topics by Position. In *Proceedings of the Applied Natural Language Processing Conference (ANLP-97)*, 283–290. Washington.

Lin, C-Y. and E.H. Hovy. 1998. Automatic Text Categorization: A Concept-Based Approach. In prep.

Liu, H. and E.H. Hovy. 1998. Automated Learning of Cue Phrases for Text Summarization. In prep.

Luhn, H.P. 1959. The Automatic Creation of Literature Abstracts. *IBM Journal of Research and Development*, 159–165.

Marcu, D. 1997. The Rhetorical Parsing, Summarization, and Generation of Natural Language Texts. Ph.D. diss. University of Toronto.

Marcu, D. 1998. *The Automatic Construction of Large-scale Corpora for Summarization Research*. Forthcoming.

Matthiessen, C.M.I.M. and J.A. Bateman. 1991. *Text Generation and Systemic-Functional Linguistics*. London, England: Pinter.

Mauldin, M.L. 1991. *Conceptual Information Retrieval— A Case Study in Adaptive Partial Parsing*. Boston, MA: Kluwer Academic Publishers.

McKeown, K.R. and D.R. Radev. 1995. Generating Summaries of Multiple News Articles. In *Proceedings of the Eighteenth Annual International ACM Conference on Research and Development in Information Retrieval* (SIGIR), 74–82. Seattle, WA.

Miller, G., R. Beckwith, C. Fellbaum, D. Gross, and K. Miller. 1990. Five papers on WordNet. CSL Report 43, Cognitive Science Laboratory, Princeton University.

Paice, C.D. 1990. Constructing Literature Abstracts by Computer: Techniques and Prospects. *Information Processing and Management* 26(1): 171–186.

The Penman Primer, User Guide, and Reference Manual. 1988. Unpublished documentation, Information Sciences Institute, University of Southern California.

Quinlan, J.R. 1986. Induction of Decision Trees. *Machine Learning* 81–106.

Rasmussen, E. 1992. Clustering Algorithms. In W.B. Frakes and R. Baeza-Yates (eds.), *Information Retrieval: Data Structures and Algorithms*, 419–441. Upper Saddle River, NJ: Prentice-Hall.

Rau, L.S. and P.S. Jacobs. 1991. Creating Segmented Databases from Free Text for Text Retrieval. In *Proceedings of the Fourteenth Annual International ACM Conference on Research and Development in Information Retrieval* (SIGIR), 337–346. New York, NY.

Van Rijsbergen, C.J. 1979. *Information Retrieval* (2nd edition). London, England: Butterworths.

Riloff, E. and W.G. Lehnert. 1994. Information Extraction as a Basis for High-Precision Text Classification. *ACM Transactions on Information Systems*, vol. 12: 296–333.

Salton, G. 1988. *Automatic Text Processing*. Reading, MA: Addison-Wesley.

Salton, G., J. Allen, C. Buckley, and A. Singhal. 1994. Automatic Analysis, Theme Generation, and Summarization of Machine-Readable Texts. *Science* 264: 1421–1426.

Schank, R.C. and R.P. Abelson. 1977. *Scripts, Plans, Goals, and Understanding*. Hillsdale, NJ: Lawrence

Erlbaum Associates.

Teufel, S. and M. Moens. 1997. Sentence Extraction as a Classification Task. In *Proceedings of the Workshop on Intelligent Scalable Summarization.* ACL/EACL Conference, 58–65. Madrid, Spain.

TREC. Harman, D. (ed). 1995. *Proceedings of the TREC Conference.*

Yarowsky, D. 1992. Word sense disambiguation using statistical models of Roget's categories trained on large corpora. In *Proceedings of the Fourteenth International Conference on Computational Linguistics (COLING-92),* 454–460. Nantes, France.

Section 3

Exploiting Discourse Structure

Discourse structure presents an interesting frontier for summarization. Discourse models are likely to be useful because (as discussed in the Introduction to this book) it appears to play an important role in the strategies used by human abstractors and in the structure of their abstracts. In other words, an abstract is not just a collection of sentences, each of which represents some salient information in the document. Rather, it has a (possibly tight) internal organization, which reflects the need to have the abstract be coherent, and (especially for scientific text) to represent some of the argumentation used in the source.

One way of classifying discourse models used in text summarization is in terms of the linguistic distinction between cohesion and coherence (Halliday and Hasan 1996). Text cohesion involves relations between words or referring expressions, which determine how tightly connected the text is. The relations involved include linguistic devices such as anaphora, ellipsis, conjunction and lexical relations such as reiteration, synonym, and hypernymy (e.g., *dog* is-a-kind-of *animal*).

Models based on coherence (Mann and Thompson 1988, vanDijk 1988), on the other hand, represent the overall structure of a multi-sentence text in terms of macro-level relations between sentences or clauses (though in some accounts, the elementary text units may be smaller than a clause). For example, the cue phrase "in order to," one could argue, expresses some sort of purpose relation between clauses; likewise clauses linked by "although" express some sort of contrast relation. These relations determine the overall argumentative structure of the text, which are responsible for making the text *cohere*.

In the first paper in this section, Boguraev and Kennedy explore the use of cohesion in terms of anaphoric relations to yield phrasal summaries. They address the issue of term aggregation and normalization at the level of discourse entities referred to by anaphoric expressions. (Thus, their work is related to other approaches to term aggregation addressed in Sections 1 and 2; see also Barzilay and Elhadad's paper below.) They use this method as a way of reducing the set of summary phrases. For anaphora resolution, they use robust parsing and heuristics for ranking candidate antecedents based on local features (they call this a "local salience" measure) and claim 75% accuracy of the results.

To produce summaries, the authors segment text using a variant of the TextTiling approach of Hearst (1997), which is a segmentation method relying on similarity between blocks of text based on vocabulary overlap. For every referent in the text, they construct a global "discourse salience" measure based on local salience and frequency calculations; they then identify the most globally salient entities in the segment as "topic stamps." (Note that this fine-grained approach to arriving at a form of topic characterization can be contrasted with Hovy and Lin's corpus-based approach to topic signatures in Section 2). To form a summary, the coreferential phrases associated with topic stamps are listed, based on salience scores, along with some information from the surrounding context; this presentation format is referred to as a "capsule overview."

In the second paper, Barzilay and Elhadad produce a summary of a source text by exploiting "lexical chains," namely, sequences of related terms grouped together by text cohesion relationships of repetition, synonymy, hypernymy, antonymy, and holonymy (part-of relations, e.g., *body* is-a-part-of *arm*), with the latter 4 relations being derived from the WordNet thesaurus (Miller 1995). By grouping together words into lexical chains, they suggest a reader might get a better identification of the topic of a text than simply picking the most frequent words in the text. In some cases, they argue, a chain of low-frequency words representing the same salient concept may be more indicative of a topic than high- frequency words. Their paper thus addresses the problem of term aggregation and normalization (addressed in different ways in the papers in Section 1 and 2) in terms of cohesion relationships between terms.

The basic problem in computing chains using WordNet is the high degree of polysemy of words in WordNet, resulting in many possible chains being formed. The authors choose the best chain for a text based on the number and weight of different relations in the chain. The nodes in the chains stand for terms which can be nouns as well as noun compounds (found using a shallow parser). Chains are built in a two-stage process: first, chains are built for individual text segments found using TextTiling; then, the chains from different segments are merged whenever they contain a common term with the same sense. Chains are scored such that a "strong" chain will include many occurrences of members of the chain and will be homogeneous. Sentences are then extracted from chains based on a variety of heuristics.

The authors point out that their method has some limitations (e.g., no way to control the length and level of detail of the summary, the presence of dangling anaphors, inability to select constituents smaller than a sentence). Nevertheless, in an intrinsic evaluation against an ideal summary constructed by humans, they found their system outperformed commercial summarizers.

The remaining papers address the use of text coherence models in summarization. In his paper, Marcu uses a rhetorical parser for unrestricted text that exploits cue-phrases to build rhetorical structure theory (RST) trees out of clauses in the text. (For another approach to parsing rhetorical structure which factors in more syntactic knowledge, see Corston-Oliver (1998)). Marcu's formalization of the structure of RST trees allows one to compute salience of clauses based on the tree structure, and this forms the basis of a summarization program. RST theory (Mann and Thompson 1988) distinguishes between a nucleus node (which represents information which is more essential to the writer's purpose) and a satellite node. Assuming that nuclei are more salient than satellites, salience of information can be determined based on tree depth. Each parent node identifies its nuclear children as salient, and this identification continues recursively down the tree. The salience scores can then be used to extract corresponding sentences or clauses to form summaries.

Marcu describes an experiment with 5 short *Scientific American* texts that shows a strong positive correlation between the nuclei of the RST tree for a text and what subjects believe are the most important units of text. As others have done in this book, Marcu compares the performance of his automatic discourse-based summarization system with Microsoft's AutoSummarize as a baseline. With performance on these texts being in the high 60% precision and recall, his automated system compares favorably with the baseline, which performs in the range of 40% precision and recall. A summarizer based on rhetorical trees constructed by a human performed the best of all, with 78% precision and 67% recall.

The paper by Strzalkowski et al. describes a summarization tool which offers both generic as well as topic-related summaries. Their summarization algorithm is passage- rather than sentence-based, where a passage corresponds either to a paragraph or to a fixed-size block of text (the latter is especially useful for transcripts of spoken discourse). The algorithm treats summarization as a problem of passage ranking given a query, where the "query" is constructed out of the user's query if any, terms in the title, and frequently occurring terms in the text.

In many systems, the problem of dealing with out-of-context extracts is addressed in a post-processing "repair" step. However, this can result in loss of compression, due to introduction of extraneous material; further, since the "core" summary is already committed to, recovery of compression is often difficult at such a late stage. In contrast, Strzalkowski et al. treat the selection of contextual information as intrinsic to the summarization process. In particular, they motivate this with reference to a simple rhetorical model of the discourse structure of news story summaries, based on a *Background* component and a *What-is-the-News* component.

Every passage is tested to see if it requires a background passage by the presence of anaphors in the first six words of the referential passage, and the presence of cue phrases in those passages (the cue phrases are often removed if they occur at the beginning of the passage). Background passages are usually identified by selecting the immediately previous passage. Both main and background passages are then scored based on overlap with terms in the query, with a penalty for passages which are long in comparison to the desired length, and with a bonus given to passages near the beginning of the text, to passages containing noun phrases in their initial segments, and (for informative summaries) to passages containing proper names or numerical amounts (the latter aimed at extracting more factual data). Groups of passages are then merged into new passages, with the merging being extended to include any needed background passages. The passages are then re-scored, with a penalty for passages which contain elided material. The merge-and-score steps are repeated until there is no further change in the top-scoring passage over two iterations.

In discussing evaluation results, the authors include experiments using their topic-related summaries as candidate "paste-in" passages for query expansion in information retrieval. They found that having a human expand queries by selecting from just among these summaries was just as accurate as having the human make the selection from the entire text, showing the effectiveness of summarization in this task.

The paper by Teufel and Moens extends the work of Kupiec et al. (KPC) in Section 2 to address the discourse structure of abstracts. Like Strzalkowski et al., they exploit the idea of a rhetorical structure for summaries, in part as a means of more fine-grained control over compression. In the KPC approach, sentences in the full-text are labeled as extract-worthy based on alignment with a professionally-authored abstract; these sentences constitute the "ideal" summary for the document. Teufel and Moens use a corpus of computational linguistics articles which have author-supplied abstracts. Since fewer of the abstract sentences align with the source sentences than in KPC (31% compared to 79%), they augment the ideal summary with additional source sentences labeled by a human. In addition, they label each sentence in the ideal summary with a list of rhetorical roles covered by that sentence, drawn from a set of seven possible roles: *Background, Topic/Aboutness, Related Work, Purpose/Problem, Solution/Method, Result,* and *Conclusion/Claim.*

Teufel and Moens break down the summarization task into two stages: extraction of sentences, and identification of rhetorical roles for each extracted sentence. Both stages use Bayesian classifiers modeled on KPC's approach. In evaluations of sentence extraction performance at 4.4% compression, the Indicator Quality feature (presence of cue phrases with manually assigned scores, similar to the Word Control List in Pollock et al.'s paper in Section 1) led to the best performance (54.4% precision), and collectively, the combination of Indicator Quality, Location, Sentence

Length, Title, Header (presence of section header keywords), and Thematic Word were best (66% precision). In comparison, a leading text baseline achieved only 28% precision. These results compare favorably with results obtained in other applications of the KPC method (e.g., the papers in Section 2).

For rhetorical role identification, the best performance of a single feature was 56.3% precision, with collective performance at 64.2% precision, compared to a baseline (where the most frequent rhetorical role of *Solution/Method* was used) of 40.1% precision. The most common error in rhetorical role identification was distinguishing between *Purpose/Problem* and *Solution/Method* (the most common rhetorical roles); these were difficult to distinguish by humans as well.

In summary, techniques that aim to recover the discourse structure associated with the source text and exploit these to provide more effective summary's show promise in adding value to our repertoire of extraction and abstraction techniques. The underlying methods assemble discourse structure representations based on primitive units either at the level of word, phrase, clause, sentence, paragraph, or "passage," and questions remain as to which level is most appropriate in a summarization task for any given phase of the summarization process. Such methods could benefit considerably from further development of empirically-grounded theoretical models of discourse, as well as increased use of corpora with discourse annotations to provide additional data for discourse modeling. An important question which arises is how applicable these methods are to various genres of text. As our general understanding of discourse improves (e.g., increasing focus on robust anaphora resolution and topic detection and tracking), we might expect the performance of these systems to improve considerably without incurring substantial costs in terms of knowledge engineering or scalability.

References

Corston-Oliver, S. 1998. Beyond String Matching and Cue Phrases: Improving Efficiency and Coverage in Discourse Analysis. *Working Notes of the AAAI Spring Symposium on Intelligent Text Summarization*, Spring 1998, Technical Report, AAAI, 1998, pp.~9-15.

Halliday, M. and Hasan, R 1996. *Cohesion in Text.* Longmans, London.

Hearst, M. 1997. TextTiling: Segmenting Text into Multi-Paragraph Subtopic Passages. *Computational Linguistics* 23(1):33-64.

Mann, W.C. and Thompson, S. A. 1988. Rhetorical Structure Theory: Towards a Functional Theory of Text Organization, *Text*, 8(3):243-281.

Miller, G. 1995. WordNet: A Lexical Database for English. *Communications of the Association for Computing Machinery (CACM)* 38(1):39-41.

vanDijk, T.A. 1988. *News as Discourse.* Lawrence Erlbaum, Hillsdale, NJ.

9

Salience-Based Content Characterisation of Text Documents

Branimir Boguraev
IBM T.J. Watson Research Center
P.O. Box 704, Yorktown Heights, NY 10598
bkb@watson.ibm.com

Christopher Kennedy
Department of Linguistics, Northwestern University
2016 Sheridan Road, Evanston, IL 60208
kennedy@ling.nwu.edu

Abstract

Summarisation is poised to become a generally accepted solution to the larger problem of content analysis. We offer an alternative perspective on this problem, by tackling the complementary task of content characterisation; our motivation for doing so is to avoid some of the fundamental shortcomings of summarisation technologies today. Traditionally, the document summarisation task has been tackled either as a natural language processing problem, with an instantiated meaning template being rendered into coherent prose, or as a passage extraction problem, where certain fragments (typically sentences) of the source document are deemed to be highly representative of its content, and thus delivered as meaningful "approximations" of it. Balancing the conflicting requirements of depth and accuracy of a summary, on the one hand, and document and domain independence, on the other, has proven a very hard problem. This paper describes a novel approach to content characterisation of text documents. It is domain- and genre-independent, by virtue of not requiring an in-depth analysis of the full meaning. At the same time, it remains closer to the core meaning by choosing a different granularity of its representations (phrasal expressions rather than sentences or paragraphs), by exploiting a notion of discourse contiguity and coherence for the purposes of uniform coverage and context maintenance, and by utilising a strong linguistic notion of salience, as a more appropriate and representative measure of a document's "aboutness".

1 Introduction

As the volume of document-based information online continues growing, so does the need for *any* kind of document abstraction mechanism. Consequently, summarisation has become one of the hottest topics in applied natural language processing, and some summarisation technologies are rapidly gaining deployment in real world situations.

1.1 Document summarisation and content characterisation

The wide acceptance of the term "summarisation" does not reflect the fact that several constraints apply to the commonly shared notion of a document "summary". First, summaries are assumed to be, in essence, small documents (smaller, in any case, than the originals). A summary thus may vary in size, over a range from a single sentence to one or more paragraphs, but there is always the expectation that it will be delivered to its intended users in the form of coherently readable prose. To a large extent, the shared (and for the most part unspoken) intuition is that summaries are to documents very much what abstracts are to full-length articles. This reflects another pervasive assumption: namely that there is a canonical, definitive (or at least optimal) summary for any document. As a result, work on summarisation technologies tends to proceed outside of any strong considerations of the operational environments where users may seek to deploy summarisation. Indirectly, this tendency reinforces the summary-as-an-abstract view which underlies most examples of the document summarisation paradigm today.

Largely, such observations are attributable to the globally pervasive fact that all of the current work in the field is carried out without reference to any theory of summarisation. We share cognitive intuitions about what a summarisation technology might strive to develop as operational machinery, but there is no grounding of such technology in a framework which has something concrete to say about what it is that defines a summary, nor how such a summary should be related to its full document source. For instance, agreement on the need for relevance measures for summarisation still leaves open the questions of how relevance ought to be computed, what units it should be computed over, and how it best might drive a generation process which tries to weave a coherent statement about the relevant highlights of a document. Currently, summarisation work is very much about the whole package, and hardly at all about individual pieces which underlie the construction of summaries.

Only recently have these views been challenged. The TIPSTER/SUMMAC evaluation conference (Def 1998) defined *several* different uses for summarisation, thus taking the first step to acknowledging that different information management tasks are likely to require different kinds of summary, even from the same document. While the conference itself still focused on seeking one particular type of summary as a baseline, in general, the community is becoming much more attuned to the fact that there is no such thing as a 'canonical' summary for a document; see e.g. (Sparck Jones 1997). However, there is much less discussion about the genre characteristics of the different summary types themselves.

There have been some implicit references to summary types departing from the notion of a small, coherent document. Library cataloging services, for instance, effectively utilise summaries in the form of key index terms; technical documents of average-to-large size can be 'abstracted' by using a mix between table of contents and back-of-the-book index; cross-language 'gisting' using undiscriminating phrasal spotting can convey something of the content of a document to determine whether it should be fully translated or not (Endres-Niggemeyer 1998), (Resnik 1997). However, such work tends to be regarded as peripheral to mainstream summarisation research which focuses, primarily, on deriving document-like document abstractions.

This paper reports on some work which departs from the mainstream view, while still seeking to address the general problem of conveying to a user the gist of a document. Instead of focusing on summarisation, in its accepted sense, we define the problem to be that of characterising the essential content of a document. Again, in the absence of a strong theory, we appeal to intuitions concerning the relationship between the distributional prominence of linguistic expressions, computed as a function of their occurrence in a text, and the topical prominence of the objects and events they refer to. We seek to characterise a document's content by identifying a (relatively) brief enumeration of those expressions that refer to the most prominent, or most *salient* objects and events mentioned in the discourse.

These are similar intuitions to those shared by the summarisation community; the differences in our position lie in what we consider to be the linguistic units that should be targeted for the purpose of content abstraction, how we determine a measure of the relative prominence—or salience—of these units, how this measure is used to derive a document abstraction, and how the resulting abstractions are presented to users. The question of optimal presentation of our document abstractions for best use is outside of the scope of this paper; (Boguraev *et al.* 1998) discusses an experiment in situating our document abstraction technology in the context of supporting dynamic, on-line news skimming. Before we present details of our approach, and highlight the differences between content characterisation and document summarisation, we briefly outline the main characteristics of current approaches to summarisation.

1.2   Approaches to document summarisation

The majority of techniques for summarisation, as applied to average-length documents, fall within two broad categories: those that rely on template instantiation and those that rely on passage extraction. Work in the former framework traces its roots to some pioneering research by DeJong (1982) and Tait (1983); more recently, the DARPA-sponsored TIPSTER programme (Adv 1993b)—and, in particular, the message understanding conferences MUC: e.g. (Def 1992) and (Adv 1993a)—have provided fertile ground for such work, by placing the emphasis of document analysis to the identification and extraction of certain core entities and facts in a document, which are packaged together in a template. There are shared intuitions among researchers that generation of smooth prose from this template would yield a summary of the document's core content; recent work, most notably by McKeown and colleagues, cf. (McKeown & Radev 1995), focuses on making these intuitions more concrete.

While providing a rich context for research in generation, this framework requires an analysis front end capable of instantiating a template to a suitable level of detail. Given the current state of the art in text analysis in general, and of semantic and discourse processing in particular, work on template-driven, knowledge-based summarisation to date is hardly domain- or genre-independent (see Sparck Jones 1993a, 1993b for discussion of the depth of understanding required for constructing true summaries).

The alternative framework—passage extraction—largely escapes this constraint, by viewing the task as one of identifying certain segments of text (typically sentences) which, by some metric, are deemed to be the most representative of the document's content. The technique dates back at least to the 50's (Luhn 1958), but it is relatively recently that these ideas have been filtered through research with strongly pragmatic constraints, for instance: what kinds of documents are optimally suited for being "abstracted" in such a way (e.g. Preston & Williams 1994; Brandow, Mitze, & Rau 1995); how to derive more representative scoring functions, e.g. for complex documents, such as multi-topic ones (Salton *et al.* 1996), or where training from professionally prepared abstracts is possible (Kupiec, Pedersen, & Chen 1995); what heuristics might be developed for improving readability and coherence of "narratives" made up of discontiguous source document chunks (Paice 1990); or with optimal presentations of such passage extracts, aimed at retaining some sense of larger and/or global context (Mahesh 1997).

The cost of avoiding the requirement for a language-aware front end is the complete lack of intelligence—or even context-awareness—at the back end: the validity, and utility, of sentence- or paragraph-sized extracts as representations for the document content is still an open question (see, for instance, Rau, 1988, and more recently, AAAI 1998). This question is becoming more urgent, especially with the recent wave of commercial products announcing built-in "summarisation" (by extraction) features (Caruso 1997).[1] Nonetheless, progressively more sophisticated techniques are being deployed in attempts to improve the quality of sentence-based summaries, by seeking to mediate the passage selection process with, for instance, strong notions of topicality (Hovy & Lin 1997), lexical chains (Barzilay & Elhadad 1997), and discourse structure (Marcu 1997), (Reimer & Hahn 1997).

---

[1] Also at: `http://www.nytimes.com/library/cyber/digicom/012797digicom.html`.

1.3 Capsule overviews

The approach we take in this work, while addressing a slightly different problem to that of strict summarisation, can be construed as striving for the best of both worlds. We use linguistically-intensive techniques to identify those phrasal units across the entire span of the document that best function as representative highlights of the document's content. The set of such phrasal units, which we refer to as *topic stamps*, presented in ways which both retain local and reflect global context, is what we call a *capsule overview* of the document.

A capsule overview is not a conventional summary, in that it does not attempt to convey document content as a sequence of sentences. It is, however, a semi-formal (normalised) representation of the document, derived after a process of data reduction over the original text. Indeed, by adopting finer granularity of representation (below that of sentence), we consciously trade in "readability" (or narrative coherence) for tracking of detail. In particular, we seek to characterise a document's content in a way which is representative of the full flow of the narrative; this contrasts with passage extraction methods, which typically highlight only certain fragments (an unavoidable consequence of the compromises necessary when the passages are sentence-sized). While we acknowledge that a list of topic stamps by itself is lacking in many respects as a coherent summary, we will argue that such a list is nevertheless highly representative of what a document is about, and, when combined with contextual cues associated with the topic stamps as they appear in the text, provides the basis for a useful, and informative, abstraction of document content.

Still, a capsule overview is—by design—not intended to be read the same way in which a document, or an abstract, would be. This paper focuses on the linguistic processes underlying the automatic identification and extraction of topic stamps and their organisation within capsule overviews. As already mentioned, the issues of the right presentation metaphor and operational environment(s) for use of topic stamps-based capsule overview are the subject of a different discussion; see, for instance, (Boguraev *et al.* 1998).

As this sugests, a capsule overview is not a fully instantiated meaning template. A primary consideration in our work is that content characterisation methods apply to any document source or type. This emphasis on *domain independence* translates into a processing model which stops short of a fully instantiated semantic representation. Similarly, the requirement for efficient, and scalable, technology necessitates operating from a shallow syntactic base; thus our procedures are designed to circumvent the need for a comprehensive parsing engine. Not having to rely upon a parsing component to deliver in-depth, full, syntactic analysis of text makes it possible to generate capsule overviews for a variety of documents, up to and including real data from unfamiliar domains or novel genres.

In its most basic respects, then, a capsule overview is composed of a list of the linguistic expressions referring to the most prominent objects mentioned in the discourse—the topic stamps—and a specification of the relational contexts (e.g. verb phrases, minimal clauses) in which these expressions appear. The intuitions underlying our approach can be illustrated with the following news article:[2]

> PRIEST IS CHARGED WITH POPE ATTACK
>
> *A Spanish Priest* was charged here today with attempting to murder the Pope. *Juan Fernandez Krohn*, aged 32, was arrested after *a man armed with a bayonet* approached the Pope while he was saying prayers at Fatima on Wednesday night.
>
> According to the police, *Fernandez* told the investigators today that *he* trained for the past six months for the assault. *He* was alleged to have claimed the Pope 'looked furious' on hearing *the priest's* criticism of his handling of the church's affairs. If found guilty, *the Spaniard* faces a prison sentence of 15–20 years.

There are a number of reasons why the title, *'Priest Is Charged with Pope Attack'*, is a highly representative abstraction of the content of the passage. It encapsulates the essence of what the story is about: there are two actors, identified by their most prominent characteristics; one of them has been attacked by the other; the perpetrator has been charged; there is an implication of malice to the act. The title brings the complete set of salient facts together, in a thoughtfully composed statement, designed to be brief yet informative. Whether a present day natural language analysis program can derive—without being primed of a domain and genre—the information required to generate such a summary is arguable. (This is assuming, of course, that generation techniques could, in their own right, do the planning and delivery of such a concise and information-packed message.) However, part of the task of delivering accurate content characterisation is being able to identify the components of this abstraction (e.g., *'priest'*, *'pope attack'*, *'charged with'*). It is from these components that, eventually, a message template would begin to be constructed.

It is also precisely these components, viewed as phrasal units with certain discourse properties, that a capsule overview should present as a characterisation of the content of a text document. Abstracting from the technicalities of automatic document analysis, the difference between a summary and a capsule overview thus could be informally illustrated by the difference between a summary-like statement, such as *'A Spanish priest is charged after an unsuccessful murder attempt on the Pope'*, and an enumeration of the salient document highlights of the document, such as:

---

[2]Adapted from an example of S. Nirenburg; italics are ours, and are explained in Section 4.1 below.

A SPANISH PRIEST *was charged*
attempting to murder the POPE
HE *trained for the assult*
POPE *furious on hearing* PRIEST'S *criticisms*

Our strategy therefore is to mine a document for the phrasal units that are most representative of its content, as well as the relational expressions they are associated with, with the goal of establishing the kind of content characterisation exemplified here. The goal of this paper is to describe a procedure that implements this selective mining of a document for its most representative—its most *salient*—phrases, which we refer to as *salience based content characterisation*.

The remainder of this paper is organised as follows. Given the importance we assign to phrasal analysis, we outline in Section 2 and Section 3 the starting point for this work: research on terminology identification and the extension of this technology to non-technical domains. In particular, we focus on the problems that base-line terminology identification encounters when applied to open-ended range of text documents, and outline a set of extensions required for adapting it to the goal of core content identification. These boil down to formalising and implementing an operational, computable notion of salience which can be used to impose an ordering on phrasal units according to the topical prominence of the objects they refer to; this is discussed in Section 4. Section 5 illustrates the processes involved in topic identification and construction of capsule overviews by example. We close by positioning this work within the space of summarisation techniques.

2   Technical terminology: strengths and limitations

The identification and extraction of technical terminology is, arguably, one of the better understood and most robust NLP technologies within the current state of the art of phrasal analysis. What is particularly interesting for us is the fact that the linguistic properties of technical terms support the definition of computational procedures for term identification that maintain their quality regardless of document domain and type. What is even more interesting is that there is strong empirical evidence in support of the intuition that, in technical prose at least, terminological noun phrases are topical (Justeson & Katz 1995).

Since topic stamps as defined above are just phrasal units with certain discourse properties (they are topically prominent within contiguous discourse segments), we can define the task of content characterisation as one of identifying phrasal units that have lexico-syntactic properties similar to those of technical terms and discourse properties that signify their status as most prominent. In Section 4, we show how salience is computable as a function of the grammatical distribution of the phrase. Before moving to this discussion, however, we address the issues that arise when termi-

nology identification is applied to the content characterisation task.

One of the best defined procedures for technical terminology identification is the TERMS algorithm developed by Justeson & Katz (1995), which focuses on multi-word noun phrases occurring in continuous texts. A study of the linguistic properties of these constituents—preferred phrase structures, behaviour towards lexicalisation, contraction patterns, and certain discourse properties—leads to the formulation of a robust and domain-independent algorithm for term identification. Justeson and Katz's TERMS algorithm accomplishes high levels of coverage, it can be implemented within a range of underlying NLP technologies (e.g.: morphologically enhanced lexical look-up, Justeson & Katz, 1995; part-of-speech tagging, Dagan & Church, 1995; or syntactic parsing, McCord 1990), and it has strong cross-linguistic application (see, for instance, (Bourigault 1992)). Most importantly for our purposes, the algorithm is particularly useful for generating a "first cut" towards a broad characterisation of the content of the document.

Conventional uses of technical terminology are most commonly identified with text indexing, computational lexicology, and machine-assisted translation. Less common is the use of technical terms as a representation of the topical content of a document. This is to a large extent an artifact of the accepted view—at least in an information retrieval context—which stipulates that terms of interest are the ones that *distinguish* documents from each other. Almost by definition, these are not necessarily the terms which are representative of the "aboutness" of a document, as the expressions that provide important information about a document's content often do not distinguish that document from other texts within the same domain.

Still, is is clear that a program like TERMS is a good starting point for distilling representative lists. For example, (Justeson & Katz 1995, appendix) presents several term sets that clearly identify the technical domain to which the documents they originate in belong: *'stochastic neural net'*, *'joint distribution'*, *'feature vector'*, *'covariance matrix'*, *'training algorithm'*, and so forth, accurately characterise a document as belonging to the statistical pattern classification domain; *'word sense'*, *'lexical knowledge'*, *'lexical ambiguity resolution'*, *'word meaning'*, *'semantic interpretation'*, *'syntactic realization'*, and so forth assign, equally reliably, a document to the lexical semantics domain.

However, although such lists are representative, their size can easily become overwhelming. Conventionally, volume is controlled by promoting terms with higher frequencies. This is a very weak metric for our purposes, however, as it does not scale down well for texts that are smaller than typical instances of technical prose or scientific articles—such as news stories, press releases, or web pages. More generally, without the closed nature of technical domains and documentation, it is not clear that sets of term-like phrases derived from arbitrary texts can provide the same level of informativeness as term sets derived from technical documents. Certainly, we cannot even talk of "technical terms" in the narrower sense assumed by the TERMS algorithm. This raises the following question: can the notion of technical term be appropriately extended, so that it applies not just to scientific prose, but to an open-ended set of document types and genres? In other words, can a set of phrases derived in this way provide a representational base which enables rapid, compact, and accurate appreciation of the information contained in an arbitrarily chosen document? We believe that the answer to this question is "yes", and in the following sections, we present an overview of how term identification can be augmented and extended for the purpose of content characterisation.

3 Extended phrasal analysis and anaphora resolution

The questions raised at the end of the previous section concern the wider applicability of linguistic processing targeted at term identification. Three problems arise when "vanilla" term sets are considered as the basis for a content characterisation task.

3.1 Terms as content indicators

The first is, broadly construed, a problem of undergeneration. For a set of phrases to be truly representative of document content, it must provide an exhaustive description of the entities discussed in the text. That is, it must contain not just those expressions which satisfy the strict phrasal definition of "technical term", but rather every expression which mentions a participant in the events described in the text. Such broad coverage is precisely *not* the goal of canonical term identification, which extracts only those expressions that have a suitably rich amount of descriptive content (compound nominals and nominals plus modifiers), ignoring e.g. pronouns and reduced descriptions. Phrasal analysis must therefore be extended to include (at least) all the nominal expressions in a text.

Extending phrasal analysis in this way, however, exacerbates a problem already noted: a full listing of all the terms that occur in a text, even when attention is restricted to technical terms in the strict sense, is typically too large to be usefully presented as a representation of a document's content. Thus the second problem when using term sets as a basis for content characterisation is one of overgeneration: presentation of a list of phrases whose size rapidly leads to information overload. A system that extracts phrases on the basis of relaxed canonical terminology constraints, without recourse to domain or genre restrictions that might help to limit the size of the term set (a constraint imposed by the goal of constructing a system that works on arbitrary texts), will typically generate a term set far larger than a user can absorb. What is needed, then, is some means of establishing referential links be-

tween phrases, therby reducing a large phrase set to just those that *uniquely* identify the participants in the discourse.

The final problem is one of differentiation. While lists of terms such as the ones presented above (Justeson & Katz 1995, appendix) might be topical for the particular source document in which they occur, other documents within the same domain are likely to yield similar, overlapping sets of terms. (This is precisely the reason why technical term sets are not necessarily readily usable for document retrieval.) The result is that two documents containing the same or similar terms could be incorrectly classified as "about the same thing", when in fact they focus on completely different subtopics within a shared domain. In order to resolve this problem, it is necessary to differentiate term sets not only according to their membership, but also according to the relative representativeness (of document content) of the terms they contain.

Although we approach these three problems in different ways, the solutions are related, and it is this inter-relation that provide the basis for constructing capsule overviews from phrasal analysis. The mechanisms involved in the construction of capsule overviews from a term set—in effect, the solution to the problem of differentiation—are described in Section 4. In the remainder of this section, we focus on the modifications and extensions to traditional term identification technology that are needed in order to use term sets as sources for content characterisation in the first place. These modifications solve the first of the two problems listed above.

3.2 Term sets and coreference classes

The problem of undergeneration is resolved by implementing a suitable generalisation—and relaxation—of the notion of a term, so that identification and extraction of phrasal units involves a procedure essentially like TERMS (Justeson & Katz 1995), but results in an exhaustive listing of all of the nominal expressions in the text. This is accomplished by running a phrasal grammar over text that has been analyzed by the LINGSOFT supertagger (Karlsson *et al.*, 1995), which provides information about the part of speech, number, gender, and grammatical function (as well as other features) of tokens in a text. The phrasal grammar targets expressions that consist of a head noun preceded by some number (possibly zero) of pre-nominal modifiers (nouns or adjectives). As a result, it extracts not just the complex nominals that meet the formal definition of technical terms, but reduced descriptions and pronouns as well. Phrasal analysis yields the set of all nominal expressions occurring in the text, which we refer to as an *extended phrase set*.

In order to eliminate the problem of overgeneration, it is necessary to reduce the extended phrase set to a smaller set of expressions which uniquely identify the objects referred to in the text, hereafter a *referent set*. We make the simplifying assumption that every phrase identified by extended phrasal analysis constitutes a "mention" of a participant in the discourse (see Mani & MacMillan, 1996, for discussion of the notion of mention in the context of proper name interpretation); in order to construct a referent set, it is necessary to determine which expressions constitute mentions of the same referent.

Coreference is established largely through the application of an anaphora resolution procedure that is based on the algorithm developed by Lappin & Leass (1994). The fundamental difference between our algorithm (described in detail in Kennedy & Boguraev 1996a, 1996b) and the one developed by Lappin and Leass is that it is designed to provide a reliable interpretation from a considerably shallower linguistic analysis of the input.[3] This constraint is imposed by the type of analysis we are working with—the shallow analysis provided by LINGSOFT and the set of terms constructed from it, structured only according to precedence relations, not hierarchical relations—which is dictated by our goal of extending content characterisation to arbitrary types of text documents.

The basic approach to anaphora resolution, however, is the same. The interpretation procedure involves moving through the text sentence by sentence and analysing the nominal expressions in each sentence from left to right (expressions identified by the phrasal grammar are marked both for overall position in the text and for the sentence in which they occur). There are two possible outcomes of this examination. Either an expression is identified as a mention of a new participant in the discourse, or it is taken to refer to a previously mentioned referent—i.e., it either introduces a new referent or is identified as coreferential with some other expression in the text.

Coreference is determined by a three step procedure. First, a set of candidate antecedents is collected, which includes all nominals within a local segment of discourse. Second, those expressions with which an anaphoric expression cannot possibly corefer, by virtue of morphological mismatch or syntactic restrictions , are eliminated from consideration.[4] Finally, the remaining candidates are ranked according to their relative *salience* in the discourse (see below), and the most salient candidate is selected as the antedecent for the anaphor. (In the event that a coreference link cannot be established to some other expression, the nominal is taken to introduce a new referent.) Linguistic expressions that are identified as coreferential are grouped into equivalence classes, or *coreference classes*, and each coreference class is taken to represent a unique referent

in the discourse. For any text, the set of such coreference classes constitutes its reference set.

A crucial component of this anaphora resolution procedure is the computation of a salience measure for terms that are identified as candidate andecedents for an anaphoric expression. This measure, which we refer to as *local salience*, is straightforwardly determined as a function of how a candidate satisfies a set of grammatical, syntactic, and contextual parameters, or "salience factors" (this term is borrowed from Lappin & Leass 1994). Individual salience factors are associated with numerical values, as shown below.[5]

SENT(*term*) = 100 iff *term* is in the current sentence
CNTX(*term*) = 50 iff *term* is in the current discourse segment
SUBJ(*term*) = 80 iff *term* is a subject
EXST(*term*) = 70 iff *term* is in an existential construction
POSS(*term*) = 65 iff *term* is a possessive
ACC(*term*) = 50 iff *term* is a direct object
DAT(*term*) = 40 iff *term* is an indirect object
OBLQ(*term*) = 30 iff *term* is the complement of a preposition
HEAD(*term*) = 80 iff *term* is not contained in another phrase
ARG(*term*) = 50 iff *term* is not contained in an adjunct

The local salience of a candidate is the sum of the values of the salience vfactors that are satisfied by some member of the coreference class to which the candidate belongs; values may be satisfied at most once by each member of the class.

The most important aspect of this characterisation of local salience for our purposes is that the numerical values associated with the salience factors correspond to a relational structure that is directly computable on the basis of grammatical information about particular terms. This relational structure in turn provides the basis for ordering candidate antecedents according to their relative salience in some local segment of discourse, and (by hypothesis) their likelihood as antecedents for a pronoun.[6]

The overall success of anaphora resolution procedures built on top of such a measure (Lappin & Leass 1994 report 85% accuracy; our system, built on top of a shallower linguistic analysis, runs at 75% accuracy: see Kennedy & Boguraev, 1996a) provides evidence of its usefulness in the domain of anaphora resolution.

A much broader consequence of this approach to anaphora resolution, and one of particular relevance to the task at hand, is that it introduces both a working definition of salience and a mechanism for determining the salience of particular linguistic expressions

---

[3] The Lappin-Leass algorithm works from the analysis provided by the McCord Slot Grammar parser (McCord 1990); our algorithm achieves comparable results on the basis of the LINGSOFT analysis (Karlsson *et al.* 1995); see (Kennedy & Boguraev 1996a) for a comparison.

[4] For discussion of how syntactic relations are inferred on the basis of a shallow linguistic analysis, see (Kennedy & Boguraev 1996a).

[5] Our salience factors mirror those used by Lappin and Leass, with the exception of POSS, which is sensitve to possessive expressions, and CNTX, which is sensitive to the discourse segment in which a candidate appears (see Section 4 below).

[6] The relational structure imposed by the values of the salience factors listed here is justified both linguistically, as a reflection of the functional hierarchy (Keenan & Comrie 1977), as well as by experimental results (Lappin & Leass 1994).

based on straightforwardly computable grammatical properties of terms. In the next section, we show how this measure can be extended for the purpose of salience-based content characterisation.

4 Salience-based content characterisation

Anaphora resolution solves a number of the problems that arise when term identification technology is extended to work on arbitrary texts. First, it reduces the total list of terms identified by extended phrasal analysis to just those that uniquely identify objects in the discourse. Second, it establishes crucial connections between text expressions that refer to the same entities. This latter result is particularly important, as it provides a means of "tracking" occurrences of prominent expressions throughout the discourse; see (Kennedy & Boguraev 1996b) for discussion of this point.

4.1 Topic stamps

The data reduction arising from distilling the extended phrase set down to a smaller referent set is still not enough, however. In order to further reduce the referent set to a compact, coherent, and easily absorbed listing of just those expressions which identify the most important objects in the text (i.e., in order to solve the third problem discussed above, that of differentiation), some additional structure must be imposed upon its members. One way to accomplish this is to rank the members of a referent set according to the relative prominence or importance in the discourse of the entities to which they refer—in other words, to order a term set according to the *salience* of its members.

Salience is a measure of the relative prominence of objects in discourse: objects at the centre of discussion have a high degree of salience; objects at the periphery have a correspondingly lower degree of salience. The hypothesis underlying salience-based content characterisation is that even though two related documents may instantiate the same term sets, if the documents are about different things, then the relative salience of the terms in the two documents should differ. If the relative salience of the members of a referent set can be determined, then, an ordering can be imposed which, in connection with an appropriate choice of threshold value, permits the reduction of the entire referent set to only those expressions that identify the most prominent participants in the discourse.

The reduced set of terms, in combination with information about local context at various levels of granularity (verb phrase, minimal clause, sentence, etc.) may then be folded into an appropriate presentation metaphor and displayed as a characterisation of a document's content. Crucially, this type of analysis satisfies the important requirements of usability mentioned in Section 1.3: it is concise, it is coherent, and it does not introduce the cognitive overload associated with a full-scale term set. In a more general sense, this strategy for scaling up the phrasal analysis provided by

standard term identification technology has at its core the utilisation of a crucial feature of discourse structure: the prominence, over some segment of text, of particular referents—something that is missing from the traditional technology for 'bare' terminology identification.

Clearly, what is necessary to implement this type of approach to content characterisation is a means of computing the relative salience of the participants in a discourse as a function of the terms that refer to them. The hypothesis underlying the anaphora resolution procedure discussed in the previous section is that a measure of local salience, which reflects the prominence of an expression in some local segment of discourse, can be determined on the basis of the frequency of use and grammatical distribution of expressions in a text. Our proposal is that the same principles can be applied to determine a more global level of salience, which reflects the prominence of expressions across the entire discourse.

An important feature of local salience is that it is variable: the salience of a referent decreases and increases according to the frequency with which it is mentioned (by subsequent anaphoric expressions). When an anaphoric link is established, the anaphor is added to the equivalence class to which its antecedent belongs, and the salience of the class is boosted accordingly. If a referent ceases to be mentioned in the text, however, its local salience is incrementally decreased. This approach works well for the purpose of anaphora resolution, because it provides a realistic representation of the antecedent space for an anaphor by ensuring that only those referents that have mentions within a local domain have increased prominence. However, the goal of salience-based content characterisation differs from that of anaphora resolution in an important respect. In order to determine which linguistic expressions should be presented as broadly representative of the content of a document, it is necessary to generate a picture of the prominence of referents across the entire discourse, not just within a local domain.

For illustration of the intuition underlying this idea, consider the news article discussed in Section 1.3. Intuitively, the reason why 'priest' is the primary element of the title is that there are no less than eight references to the same actor in the body of the story (marked by italics in the example); moreover, these references occur in prominent syntactic positions: five are subjects of main clauses, two are subjects of embedded clauses, and one is a possessive. Similarly, the reason why 'Pope attack' is the secondary object of the title is that a constituent of the compound, 'Pope', also receives multiple mentions (five), although these references tend to occur in less prominent positions (two are direct objects).

In order to generate the broader picture of discourse structure needed to inform the selection of certain expressions as most salient, and therefore most representative of content, we introduce an elaboration of the local salience computation described above that uses the same conditions to calculate a non-decreasing, global salience value for every referent in the text. This non-decreasing salience measure, which we refer to as *discourse salience*, reflects the distributional properties of a referent as the text story unfolds. In conjunction with the "tracking" of referents made available by anaphora resolution, discourse salience provides the basis for a coherent representation of discourse structure that indicates the topical prominence of specific terms in isolated segments of text. Most importantly, discourse salience provides exactly the information that is needed to impose the type of importance-based ranking of referents discussed above, which in turn provides the basis for the construction of capsule overviews out of referent sets (which are derived from terms sets, as discussed in Section 3.2). Specifically, by associating every referent with a discourse salience value, we can identify the topic stamps for a segment of text S as the n highest ranked objects in S, where n is a scalable value.

4.2 Discourse segments

The notion "segment of text" plays an extremely important role in the content characterisation task, as it provides the basic units around which a capsule overview for a document is constructed. Again, the example from Section 1.3 provides a useful illustration of the important issues. The reason that the title of this passage works as an overview of its content is because the text itself is fairly short. As a text increases in length, the "completeness" of a short description as a characterisation of content deteriorates. If the intention is to use concise descriptions consisting of one or two salient phrases—i.e., topic stamps—along with information about the local context in which they appear as the primary information-bearing units for a capsule overview, then it follows that texts longer than a few paragraphs must be broken down into smaller units or "segments".

In order to solve this problem, we recast a document as a set of *discourse segments*, which correspond to topically coherent, contiguous sections of text. The approach to segmentation we adopt implements a similarity-based algorithm along the lines of the one developed by (Hearst 1994), which identifies discourse segments text using a lexical similarity measure. By calculating the discourse salience of referents with respect to the results of discourse segmentation, each segment can be associated with a listing of those expressions that are most salient within the segment, i.e., each segment can be assigned a set of topic stamps. The result of these calculations, the set of segment-topic stamp pairs, ordered according to linear sequencing of the segments in the text, is the data structure on the basis of which the capsule overview for the entire document is constructed. In this way, the problem of content characterisation of a large text is reduced to the problem of finding topic stamps for each discourse segment.

4.3 Capsule overviews

To summarize, the approach to content characterisation that we have outlined here involves defining a suitable selection procedure, operating over a larger set of phrasal units than that generated by a typical term identification algorithm (including not only all terms, but term-like phrases, as well as their variants, reduced forms, and anaphoric references), with the following properties. First, it reduces this set to a list of expressions that uniquely refer to objects in the discourse (the referent set). Second, it makes informed choices about the degree to which each phrase is representative of the text as a whole. Finally, it presents its output in a form which retains contextual information for each phrase. The key to normalising the content of a document to a small set of distinguished, and discriminating, phrasal units is being able to establish a containment hierarchy of phrases (term-relational context-clause-sentence-paragraph-and so forth; this would eventually be exploited for capsule overview presentation at different levels of granularity), and being able to make refined judgements concerning the degree of importance of each unit, within some segment of text.

In simple terms, the goal is to filter a term set in such a way that those expressions which are identified as most salient are presented as representative of document content. This process of "salience-based content characterisation" builds on and extends the notion of salience that forms a crucial component of the anaphora resolution procedure developed by (Lappin & Leass 1994). Moreover, it presupposes very little in the way of linguistic processing, working solely on the basis of the shallow analysis provided by the LING-SOFT tagger. It thus meets the desired requirement of domain independence, permitting extension of the technology to a wide range of texts, without regard to genre, style, or source. The following diagram provides a schematic illustration of the primary components of the content characterisation procedure.

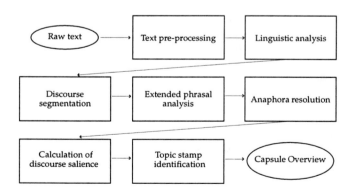

5 Example

We illustrate the procedure by highlighting certain aspects of a capsule overview of a recent *Forbes* article

(Hutheesing 1996). The document is of medium-to-large size (approximately four pages in print), and focuses on the strategy of Gilbert Amelio (former CEO of Apple Computer) concerning a new operating system for the Macintosh. Too long to quote here in full, the following passage from the beginning of the article contains the first, second and third segments, as identified by the discourse segmentation component described in Section 4.2, cf. (Hearst 1994); in the example below, segment boundaries are marked by extra vertical space).

"ONE DAY, everything Bill Gates has sold you up to now, whether it's Windows 95 or Windows 97, will become obsolete," declares Gilbert Amelio, the boss at Apple Computer. "Gates is vulnerable at that point. And we want to make sure we're ready to come forward with a superior answer."

Bill Gates vulnerable? Apple would swoop in and take Microsoft's customers? Ridiculous! Impossible! In the last fiscal year, Apple lost $816 million; Microsoft made $2.2 billion. Microsoft has a market value thirty times that of Apple.

Outlandish and grandiose as Amelio's idea sounds, it makes sense for Apple to think in such big, bold terms. Apple is in a position where standing pat almost certainly means slow death.

It's a bit like a patient with a probably terminal disease deciding to take a chance on an untested but promising new drug. A bold strategy is the least risky strategy. As things stand, customers and outside software developers alike are deserting the company. Apple needs something dramatic to persuade them to stay aboard. A radical redesign of the desktop computer might do the trick. If they think the redesign has merit, they may feel compelled to get on the bandwagon lest it leave them behind.

Lots of "ifs," but you can't accuse Amelio of lacking vision. Today's desktop machines, he says, are ill-equipped to handle the coming power of the Internet. Tomorrow's machines must accommodate rivers of data, multimedia and multitasking (juggling several tasks simultaneously).

We're past the point of upgrading, he says. Time to scrap your operating system and start over. The operating system is the software that controls how your computer's parts (memory, disk drives, screen) interact with applications like games and Web browsers. Once you've done that, buy new applications to go with the reengineered operating system.

Amelio, 53, brings a lot of credibility to this task. His resume includes both a rescue of National Semiconductor from near-bankruptcy and 16 patents, including one for coinventing the charge-coupled device.

But where is Amelio going to get this new operating system? From Be, Inc., in Menlo Park, Calif., a half-hour's drive from Apple's Cupertino headquarters, a hot little company founded by ex-Apple visionary Jean-Louis Gassee. Its BeOS, now undergoing clinical trials, is that radical redesign in operating systems that Amelio is talking about. Married to hardware from Apple and Apple cloners, the BeOS just might be a credible competitor to Microsoft's Windows, which runs on IBM-compatible hardware.

The capsule overview was automatically generated by a fully implemented, and operational, system, which incorporates all of the processing components identified above. The relevant sections of the overview (for the three segments of the passage quoted) are listed below. We ignore here the issue of the right presentation metaphor for topic stamps (but see Boguraev *et al.*, 1998). The listing of topic stamps in context shown below provides the core data out of which a capsule overview is constructed; such a listing is not the most effective and informative presentation of the data, and should be regarded as indicative of the data structure underlying the overview.

1 APPLE; MICROSOFT

APPLE *would swoop in and take* MICROSOFT'S *customers?*
APPLE *lost $816 million;*
MICROSOFT *made $2.2 billion.*

MICROSOFT *has a market value thirty times that of* APPLE
it makes sense for APPLE
APPLE *is in a position*
APPLE *needs something dramatic*

2 DESKTOP MACHINES; OPERATING SYSTEM

Today's DESKTOP MACHINES, *he [Gilbert Amelio] says*
Tomorrow's MACHINES *must accommodate rivers of data*
Time to scrap your OPERATING SYSTEM *and start over*
The OPERATING SYSTEM *is the software that controls*
to go with the REENGINEERED OPERATING SYSTEM

3 GILBERT AMELIO; NEW OPERATING SYSTEM

AMELIO, *53, brings a lot of credibility to this task*
HIS *[Gilbert Amelio] resumé includes*
where is AMELIO *going to get this* NEW OPERATING SYSTEM?
radical redesign in OPERATING SYSTEMS *that* AMELIO *is talking about*

The division of this passage into segments, and the segment-based assignment of topic stamps, exemplifies a capsule overview's "tracking" of the underlying coherence of a story. The discourse segmentation component recognizes shifts in topic—in this example, the shift from discussing the relation between Apple and Microsoft to some remarks on the future of desktop computing to a summary of Amelio's background and plans for Apple's operating system. Layered on top of segmentation are the topic stamps themselves, in their relational contexts, at a phrasal level of granularity.

The first segment sets up the discussion by positioning Apple opposite Microsoft in the marketplace and focusing on their major products, the operating systems. The topic stamps identified for this segment, APPLE and MICROSOFT, together with their local contexts, are both indicative of the introductory character of the opening paragraphs and highly representative of the gist of the first segment. Note that the apparent uninformativeness of some relational contexts, for example, '... APPLE *is in a position* ...', does not pose a serious problem. An adjustment of the granularity—at capsule overview presentation time—reveals the larger context in which the topic stamp occurs (e.g., a sentence), which in turn inherits the high topicality ranking of its anchor: 'APPLE *is in a position where standing pat almost certainly means slow death.*'

For the second segment of the sample, OPERATING SYSTEM and DESKTOP MACHINES have been identified as representative. The set of topic stamps and contexts illustrated provides an encapsulated snapshot of the segment, which introduces Amelio's views on coming challenges for desktop machines and the general concept of an operating system. Again, even if some of these are somewhat under-specified, more detail is easily available by a change in granularity, which reveals the definitional nature of the even larger context '*The* OPERATING SYSTEM *is the software that controls how your computer's parts...*'

The third segment of the passage exemplified above is associated with the stamps GILBERT AMELIO and NEW OPERATING SYSTEM. The reasons, and linguistic rationale, for the selection of these particular noun phrases as topical are essentially identical to the intuition behind *'priest'* and *'Pope attack'* being the central topics of the example in Section 1.3. The computational justification for the choices lies in the extremely high values of salience, resulting from taking into account a number of factors: co-referentiality between *'Amelio'* and *'Gilbert Amelio'*, co-referentiality between *'Amelio'* and *'His'*, syntactic prominence of *'Amelio'* (as a subject) promoting topical status higher than for instance *'Apple'* (which appears in adjunct positions), high overall frequency (four, counting the anaphor, as opposed to three for *'Apple'*—even if the two get the same number of text occurrences in the segment)—and boost in global salience measures, due to "priming" effects of both referents for *'Gilbert Amelio'* and *'operating system'* in the prior discourse of the two preceding segments. Even if we are unable to generate a single phrase summary in the form of, say, *'Amelio seeks a new operating system'*, the overview for the closing segment comes close; arguably, it is even better than *any* single phrase summary.

As the discussion of this example illustrates, a capsule overview is derived by a process which facilitates partial understanding of the text by the user. The final set of topic stamps is designed to be representative of the core of the document content. It is *compact*, as it is a significantly cut-down version of the full list of identified terms. It is highly *informative*, as the terms included in it are the most prominent ones in the document. It is *representative* of the whole document, as a separate topic tracking module effectively maintains a record of where and how referents occur in the entire span of the text. As the topics are, by definition, the primary content-bearing entities in a document, they offer *accurate* approximation of what that document is about.

6   Related and future work

Our framework clearly attempts to balance the conflicting requirements of the two primary approaches to the document summarisation task. By design, we target *any* text type, document genre, and domain of discourse, and thus compromise by forgoing in-depth analysis of the full meaning of the document. On the other hand, because our content characterisation procedure presents extracted elements in the contexts in which they appear in a text, it provides a less ambiguous abstraction of the core meaning of the text than the traditional passage extraction algorithms, which offer certain sentence- or paragraph-sized passages deemed indicative of content by means of similarity scoring metrics.

By choosing a phrasal—rather than sentence- or paragraph-based—granularity of representation, we can obtain a more refined view into highly relevant fragments of the source; this also offers a finer-grained control for adjusting the level of detail in capsule overviews. Exploiting a notion of discourse contiguity

and coherence for the purposes of full source coverage and continuous context maintenance ensures that the entire text of the document is uniformly represented in the overview. Finally, by utilising a strong linguistic notion of salience, the procedure can build a richer representation of the discourse objects, and exploit this for informed decisions about their prominence, importance, and ultimately topicality. These are notable characteristics of our notion of capsule overviews—to the extent that the focused and rich semantic information they encapsulate is sufficiently indicative of content to offset the (initial) unfamiliarity in dealing with phrasal-, rather than sentence-based, fragments.

At present, salience calculations are driven from contextual analysis and syntactic considerations focusing on discourse objects and their behaviour in the text.[7] Given the power of our phrasal grammars, however, it is conceivable to extend the framework to identify, explicitly represent, and similarly rank, higher order expressions (e.g. events, or properties of objects). This may not ultimately change the appearance of a capsule overview; however, it will allow for even more informed judgements about relevance of discourse entities. More importantly, it is a necessary step towards developing more sophisticated discourse processing techniques (such as those discussed in Sparck Jones, 1993b), which are ultimately essential for the automatic construction of true summaries.

Currently, we analyse individual documents; unlike (McKeown & Radev 1995), there is no notion of calculating salience across the boundaries of more than one document—even if we were to know in advance that they are somehow related. However, we are experimenting with using topic stamps as representation and navigation "labels" in a multi-document space; we thus plan to fold in awareness of document boundaries (as an extension to tracking the effects of discourse segment boundaries within a single document).

The approach presented here can be construed, in some sense, as a type of passage extraction, it is however considerably less exposed to problems like pronouns out of context, or discontinuous sentences presented as contiguous passages; cf. (Paice 1990). This is a direct consequence of the fact that we employ anaphora resolution to construct a discourse model with explicit representation of objects, and use syntactic criteria to extract coherent phrasal units. For the same reason, topic stamps are quantifiably adequate content abstractions: see (Kennedy & Boguraev 1996a), and Section 3.2 above, for evaluation of the anaphora resolution algorithm. Following deployment of capsule overviews in an environment designed to facilitate rapid on-line skimming of news stories (Houde, Bellamy, & Leahy 1998), we are also in the process of

---

[7]Issues arising from differences in the semantic types of phrases—e.g. definite vs. indefinite descriptions—are currently ignored; the extent to which these might impact a procedure like ours is an open question.

designing a user study to determine the utility, from usability point of view, of capsule overviews as defined here.

Recent work in summarisation has begun to focus more closely on the utility of document fragments with granularity below that of a sentence. For example, (McKeown & Radev 1995) pro-actively seek, and use to great leverage, certain cue phrases which denote specific rhetorical and/or inter-document relationships. (Mahesh 1997) uses phrases as "sentence surrogates", in a process called sentence simplification; his rationale is that with hypertext, a phrase can be used as a place-holder for the complete sentence, and/or is a more conveniently manipulated, compared to a sentence. Even in passage extraction work, notions of multi-word expressions have found use as one of several features driving a statistical classifer scoring sentences for inclusion in a sentence-based summary (Kupiec, Pedersen, & Chen 1995). In all of these examples, the use of a phrase is somewhat peripheral to the fundamental assumptions of the particular approach; more to the point, it is a different kind of object that the summary is composed from (a template, in the case of McKeown & Radev 1995), or that the underlying machinery is seeking to identify (sentences, in the case of Mahesh 1997, and Kupiec, Pedersen, & Chen 1995). In contrast, our adoption of phrasal expressions as the atomic building blocks for capsule overviews is central to the design; it drives the entire analysis process, and is the underpinning for our discourse representation.

References

AAAI 1998 Spring Symposium Series. 1998. *Intelligent Text Summarization (Working Papers)*, Stanford, California.

Advanced Research Projects Agency. 1993a. *Fifth Message Understanding Conference (MUC-5)*, Baltimore, Maryland: Software and Intelligent Systems Technology Office.

Advanced Research Projects Agency. 1993b. *Tipster Text Program: Phase I*, Fredericksburg, Virginia.

Barzilay, R., and Elhadad, M. 1997. Using lexical chains for text summarization. In *Proceedings of ACL'97 Workshop on Intelligent, Scalable Text Summarisation*, 10–17.

Boguraev, B.; Wong, Y. Y.; Kennedy, C.; Bellamy, R.; Brawer, S.; and Swartz, J. 1998. Dynamic presentation of document content for rapid on-line browsing. In *AAAI Spring Symposium on Intelligent Text Summarization (Working Papers)*, 118–128.

Bourigault, D. 1992. Surface grammatical analysis for the extraction of terminological noun phrases. In *15th International Conference on Computational Linguistics*.

Brandow, R.; Mitze, K.; and Rau, L. 1995. Automatic condensation of electronic publications by sentence selection. *Information Processing and Management* 31(5):675–685.

Caruso, D. 1997. New software summarizes documents. The New York Times.

Dagan, I., and Church, K. 1995. Termight: identifying and translating technical terminology. In *4th Conference on Applied Natural Language Processing*.

Defense Advanced Research Projects Agency. 1992. *Fourth Message Understanding Conference (MUC-4)*, McLean, Virginia: Software and Intelligent Systems Technology Office.

Defense Advanced Research Project Agency. 1998. TIPSTER/SUMMAC *Summarization Analysis; Tipster Phase III 18-Month Meeting*, NIST, Fairfax, Virginia.

DeJong, G. 1982. An overview of the FRUMP system. In Lehnert, W., and Ringle, M., eds., *Strategies for Natural Language Parsing*. Hillsdale, NJ: Lawrence Erlbaum Associates. 149–176.

Endres-Niggemeyer, B. 1998. A grounded theory approach to expert summarizing. In *Proceedings of AAAI Spring Symposium on Intelligent Text Summarization (Working Papers)*, 140–142.

Hearst, M. 1994. Multi-paragraph segmentation of expository text. In *32nd Annual Meeting of the Association for Computational Linguistics*.

Houde, S.; Bellamy, R.; and Leahy, L. 1998. In search of design principles for tools and practices to support communication within a learning community. *SIGCHI Bulletin* 30(2).

Hovy, E., and Lin, C. Y. 1997. Automated text summarization in SUMMARIST. In *Proceedings of ACL'97 Workshop on Intelligent, Scalable Text Summarisation*, 18–24.

Hutheesing, N. 1996. Gilbert Amelio's grand scheme to rescue Apple. Forbes Magazine.

Justeson, J. S., and Katz, S. M. 1995. Technical terminology: some linguistic properties and an algorithm for identification in text. *Natural Language Engineering* 1(1):9–27.

Karlsson, F.; Voutilainen, A.; Heikkilä, J.; and Antilla, A. 1995. *Constraint grammar: A language-independent system for parsing free text*. Berlin/New York: Mouton de Gruyter.

Keenan, E., and Comrie, B. 1977. Noun phrase accessibility and universal grammar. *Linguistic Inquiry* 8:62–100.

Kennedy, C., and Boguraev, B. 1996a. Anaphora for everyone: Pronominal anaphora resolution without a parser. In *Proceedings of COLING-96 (16th International Conference on Computational Linguistics)*.

Kennedy, C., and Boguraev, B. 1996b. Anaphora in a wider context: Tracking discourse referents. In Wahlster, W., ed., *Proceedings of ECAI-96 (12th European Conference on Artificial Intelligence)*. Budapest, Hungary: John Wiley and Sons, Ltd, London/New York.

Kupiec, J.; Pedersen, J.; and Chen, F. 1995. A trainable document summarizer. In *Proceedings of the 18th An-*

nual International ACM SIGIR Conference on Research and Development in Information Retrieval, 68–73.

Lappin, S., and Leass, H. 1994. An algorithm for pronominal anaphora resolution. *Computational Linguistics* 20(4):535–561.

Luhn, H. 1958. The automatic creation of literature abstracts. *IBM Journal of Research and Development* 2:159–165.

Mahesh, K. 1997. Hypertext summary extraction for fast document browsing. In *Proceedings of AAAI Spring Symposium on Natural Language Processing for the World Wide Web*, 95–104.

Mani, I., and MacMillan, T. 1996. Identifying unknown proper names in newswire text. In Boguraev, B., and Pustejovsky, J., eds., *Corpus Processing for Lexical Acquisition*. Cambridge, Mass: MIT Press. 41–59.

Marcu, D. 1997. From discourse structures to text summaries. In *Proceedings of ACL'97 Workshop on Intelligent, Scalable Text Summarisation*, 82–88.

McCord, M. M. 1990. Slot grammar: a system for simpler construction of practical natural language grammars. In Studer, R., ed., *Natural language and logic: international scientific symposium*, Lecture Notes in Computer Science. Berlin: Springer Verlag. 118–145.

McKeown, K., and Radev, D. 1995. Generating summaries of multiple news articles. In *Proceedings of the 18th Annual International ACM SIGIR Conference on Research and Development in Information Retrieval*, 74–82.

Paice, C. D. 1990. Constructing literature abstracts by computer: techniques and prospects. *Information Processing and Management* 26:171–186.

Preston, K., and Williams, S. 1994. Managing the information overload: new automatic summarization tools are good news for the hard-pressed executive. Physics in Business.

Rau, L. 1988. Conceptual information extraction and retrieval from natural language input. In *Proceedings of RIAO-88, Conference on User-oriented Content-Based Text and Image Handling*, 424–437.

Reimer, U., and Hahn, U. 1997. A formal model of text summarization based on condensation operators of a terminological logic. In *Proceedings of ACL'97 Workshop on Intelligent, Scalable Text Summarisation*.

Resnik, P. 1997. Evaluating multilingual gisting of web pages. In *AAAI Spring Symposium on Natural Language Processing and the World-Wide Web (Working Papers)*.

Salton, G.; Singhal, A.; Buckley, C.; and Mitra, M. 1996. Automatic text decomposition using text segments and text themes. In *Seventh ACM Conference on Hypertext*.

Sparck Jones, K. 1993a. Discourse modelling for automatic text summarising. Technical Report 290, University of Cambridge Computer Laboratory, Cambridge, England.

Sparck Jones, K. 1993b. What might be in a summary? In Knorz; Krause; and Womser-Hacker., eds., *Information Retrieval 93: Von der Modellierung zur Anwendung*, 9–26.

Sparck Jones, K. 1997. Summarising: Where are we now? Where should we go? In *Keynote address to ACL'97 Workshop on Intelligent, Scalable Text Summarisation*.

Tait, J. 1983. *Automatic summarising of English texts*. Ph.D. Dissertation, University of Cambridge Computer Laboratory, Cambridge, England. Technical Report 47.

10

Using Lexical Chains for Text Summarization

Regina Barzilay and **Michael Elhadad**
Mathematics and Computer Science Dept.
Ben Gurion University in the Negev
Beer-Sheva, 84105 Israel
{regina, elhadad}@cs.bgu.ac.il

Abstract

We investigate one technique to produce a summary of an original text without requiring its full semantic interpretation, but instead relying on a model of the topic progression in the text derived from lexical chains. We present a new algorithm to compute lexical chains in a text, merging several robust knowledge sources: the WordNet thesaurus, a part-of-speech tagger, shallow parser for the identification of nominal groups, and a segmentation algorithm. Summarization proceeds in four steps: the original text is segmented, lexical chains are constructed, *strong* chains are identified and *significant* sentences are extracted.

We present in this paper empirical results on the identification of strong chains and of significant sentences. Preliminary results indicate that quality indicative summaries are produced. Pending problems are identified. Plans to address these short-comings are briefly presented.

1 Introduction

Summarization is the process of condensing a source text into a shorter version preserving its information content. It can serve several goals — from survey analysis of a scientific field to quick indicative notes on the general topic of a text. Producing a quality informative summary of an arbitrary text remains a challenge which requires full understanding of the text. Indicative summaries, which can be used to quickly decide whether a text is worth reading, are naturally easier to produce. In this paper we investigate a method for the production of such indicative summaries from arbitrary text.

Sparck Jones (Jones 1993) describes summarization as a two-step process:

1. Building from the source text a source representation;

2. Summary generation — forming a summary representation from the source representation built in the first step and synthesizing the output summary text.

Within this framework, the relevant question is what information has to be included in the source representation in order to create a summary. There are three types of source text information: linguistic, domain and communicative. Each of these text aspects can be chosen as a basis for source representation.

Summaries can be built on a deep semantic analysis of the source text. For example, in (McKeown & Radev 1995), McKeown and Radev investigate ways to produce a coherent summary of several texts describing the same event, when a full semantic representation of the source texts is available (in their case, they use MUC-style systems to interpret the source texts). This type of source abstraction is the most expressive, but very domain dependent and hard to compute.

On the other hand, summaries can be built from a shallow linguistic analysis of the text:

1. For example, early summarization systems (Luhn 1958) directly exploit word distribution in the source, based on the intuition that the most frequent words represent the most important concepts of the text.

   This representation abstracts the source text into a frequency table.

2. Another method also based on linguistic information is the *cue phrase method*, which uses meta-linguistic markers (for example, *"in conclusion"*, *"the paper describes"*) to select important phrases (Edmunson 1969). The cue phrase method is based on the assumption that such phrases provide a "rhetorical" context for identifying important sentences.

   The source abstraction in this case is a set of cue phrases and the sentences that contain them.

3. The *location method* relies on the following intuition — headings, sentences in the beginning and end of the text, text formatted in bold, contain important information to the summary (Hovy & Lin 1997; Edmunson 1969).

All the techniques presented above are easily computed and rely on shallow formal clues found in the text. As reported in (Paice 1990), location and cue phrases produce better results than the word frequency method, and can be accurately computed. Recently, (Kupiec, Pedersen, & Chen 1995), (Teufel & Moens 1997) use learning in order to combine several shallow heuristics (cue phrase, location, sentence length, word frequency and title), using a corpus of research papers with manually produced abstracts.

The most severe limitation of location and cue phrases abstraction is their dependence on the text genre: the number of rhetorical markers changes critically from "Scientific American" articles to political articles. Ono et al. (Ono, Sumita, & Miike 1994) reports large differences in accuracy when building a discourse representation from technical tutorial texts and from newspaper texts. Techniques relying on formal clues can be seen as high risk gamble: either you win it all, or you lose all.

Methods that rely more on content do not suffer from this brittleness. The method we present belongs to a family of of techniques that rely on word distribution and lexical links among them to approximate content in a more robust form.

For example, word frequency is a good indicator for words that represent important concepts — this is true with most texts, independently of their style. A frequency table, however, is too simplistic as a source representation. It abstracts the source text into the union of its words without considering any connection among them. Adding information about word relations could significantly increase source abstraction quality. As a trivial illustration of the limitations of frequency information, consider the following two sequences:

1. "*Dr.Kenny has invented an anesthetic machine. This device controls the rate at which an anesthetic is pumped into the blood.*"

2. "*Dr.Kenny has invented an anesthetic machine. The doctor spent two years on this research.*"

"*Dr.Kenny*" appears once in both sequences and so does "*machine*". But sequence 1 is about the *machine*, and sequence 2 is about the "*doctor*". This example indicates that if the source representation does not supply information about semantically related terms, one cannot capture the "aboutness" of the text, and therefore the summary will not capture the main point of the original text.

The notion of cohesion, introduced in Halliday and Hasan (Halliday & Hasan 1976) captures part of the intuition. Cohesion is a device for "sticking together" different parts of the text. Cohesion is achieved through the use of semantically related terms, co-reference, ellipsis and conjunctions.

Boguraev and Kennedy (Boguraev & Kennedy 1997) present a noun-phrase extraction method that relies on the identification of co-reference chains as an approximation of the cohesive links in the source text.

Among the different cohesion-building devices, the most easily identifiable and the most frequent type is, however, lexical cohesion (as discussed in (Hoey 1991)). Lexical cohesion is created by using semantically related words. Halliday and Hasan classified lexical cohesion into reiteration category and collocation category. Reiteration can be achieved by repetition, synonyms and hyponyms. Collocation relations specify the relation between words that tend to co-occur in the same

lexical contexts (e.g., "*She works as a* **teacher** *in the* **school**").

Collocation relations are more problematic for identification than reiteration, but both of these categories are identifiable on the surface of the text. Lexical cohesion occurs not only between two terms, but among sequences of related words — called *lexical chains* (Morris & Hirst 1991). Lexical chains provide a representation of the lexical cohesive structure of the text. Lexical chains have also been used for information retrieval (Stairmand 1996) and for correction of malapropisms (Hirst & St-Onge 1998 to appear). In this paper, we investigate how lexical chains can be used as a source representation for summarization.

Obviously, a more comprehensive identification of all possible cohesion-building elements would only strengthen the source text abstraction. We focus in this work on only one form of cohesion (lexical cohesion), other forms (co-reference and collocations) would enrich the potential for more precise text extraction methods.

Another important dimension of the linguistic structure of a source text is captured under the related notion of *coherence*. Coherence defines the macro-level semantic structure of a connected discourse, while cohesion creates connectedness in a non-structural manner. Coherence is represented in terms of coherence relations between text segments, such as *elaboration, cause* and *explanation*. Some researchers, *e.g.*, (Ono, Sumita, & Miike 1994) and (Marcu 1997), use discourse structure (encoded using RST (Mann & Thompson 1988)) as a source representation for summarization. Discourse representation can be used to prune a hierarchical tree of discourse segments and keep only the nucleus of the discourse. In contrast to lexical cohesion, however, coherence is difficult to identify without complete understanding of the text and complex inferences. Consider the following example from (Jerry 1978): "*John can open the safe. He knows the combination.*"

Morris and Hirst (Morris & Hirst 1991) show that the relation between these two sentences can be interpreted as *elaboration* or as *explanation*, depending on context, knowledge and beliefs. As a consequence, methods that attempt to approximate discourse structure based on discourse markers only, can produce an imprecise discourse structure abstraction, and also suffer from the brittleness of the formal methods indicated above.

There is a close connection between discourse structure and cohesion. Related words tend to co-occur within a discourse unit of the text. So cohesion is one of the surface indicators of discourse structure and lexical chains can be used to identify it. Other indicators can be used to identify discourse structure as well (connectives, paragraph markers, tense shifts). Here again, merging discourse structure approaches with lexical cohesion techniques should lead to further improvement of the source text abstraction.

In this paper, we investigate the use of lexical chains as a model of the source text for the purpose of producing a summary. As already explained, other aspects of the source text need to be integrated in the text representation to produce quality summaries (discourse structure, other forms of cohesion, domain knowledge); but we want to investigate empirically how far one can go by exploiting mainly lexical chains. In the rest of the paper we first present our algorithm for lexical chain construction (Section 2). We then present empirical results on the identification of strong chains among the possible candidates produced by our algorithm (Section 3), and describe how lexical chains are used to identify significant sentences within the source text and eventually produce a summary. Finally, we present preliminary evaluation of the results obtained by our method (Section 4).

2 Algorithm for Chain Computing

One of the chief advantages of lexical cohesion is that it is an easily recognizable relation, enabling lexical chain computation. The first computational model for lexical chains was presented in the work of Morris and Hirst (Morris & Hirst 1991). They define lexical cohesion relations in terms of categories, index entries and pointers in Roget's Thesaurus. Morris and Hirst evaluated that their relatedness criterion covered over 90% of the intuitive lexical relations. Chains are created by taking a new text word and finding a related chain for it according to relatedness criteria. Morris and Hirst introduce the notions of "activated chain" and "chain returns", to take into account the distance between occurrences of related words. They also analyze factors contributing to the strength of a chain — repetition, density and length. Morris and Hirst did not implement their algorithm, because there was no machine-readable version of Roget's Thesaurus at that time.

One of the drawbacks of their approach was that they did not require the same word to appear with the same sense in its different occurrences for it to belong to a chain. For semantically ambiguous words, this can lead to confusions (e.g., mixing two senses of *table* as a piece of furniture or an array). Note that choosing the appropriate chain for a word is equivalent to disambiguating this word in context, which is a well-known difficult problem in text understanding.

More recently, two algorithms for the calculation of lexical chains have been presented in (Hirst & St-Onge 1998 to appear) and (Stairmand 1996). Both of these algorithms use the WordNet lexical database for determining relatedness of the words (Miller *et al.* 1990). Senses in the WordNet database are represented relationally by synonym sets ('synsets') — which are the sets of all the words sharing a common sense. For example two senses of "*computer*" are represented as: {calculator, reckoner, figurer, estimator, computer} (*i.e.*, a person who computes) and {computer, data processor, electronic computer, information processing system}. WordNet contains more than 118,000 different word forms. Words of the same category are linked through semantic relations like synonymy and hyponymy.

Polysemous words appear in more than one synsets (for example, *computer* occurs in two synsets). Approximately 17% of the words in WordNet are polysemous. But, as noted by Stairmand, this figure is very misleading: "a significant proportion of WordNet nouns are Latin labels for biological entities, which by their nature are monosemous and our experience with the news-report texts we have processed is that approximately half of the nouns encountered are polysemous." (Stairmand 1996).

Generally, a procedure for constructing lexical chains follows three steps:

1. Select a set of candidate words;

2. For each candidate word, find an appropriate chain relying on a relatedness criterion among members of the chains;

3. If it is found, insert the word in the chain and update it accordingly.

An example of such a procedure is represented by Hirst and St-Onge (henceforth, H&S). In the preprocessing step, all words that appear as a noun entry in WordNet are chosen. Relatedness of words is determined in terms of the distance between their occurrences and the shape of the path connecting them in the WordNet thesaurus. Three kinds of relations are defined: extra-strong (between a word and its repetition), strong (between two words connected by a WordNet relation) and medium-strong when the link between the synsets of the words is longer than one (only paths satisfying certain restrictions are accepted as valid connections).

The maximum distance between related words depends on the kind of relation: for extra-strong relations, there is not limit in distance, for strong relations, it is limited to a window of seven sentences; and for medium-strong relations, it is within three sentences back.

To find a chain in which to insert a given candidate word, extra-strong relations are preferred to strong-relations and both of them are preferred to medium-strong relations. If a chain is found, then the candidate word is inserted with the appropriate sense, and the senses of the other words in the receiving chain are updated, so that every word connected to the new word in the chain relates to its selected senses only. If no chain is found, then a new chain is created and the candidate word is inserted with all its possible senses in WordNet.

The greedy disambiguation strategy implemented in this algorithm has some limitations illustrated by the following example:

Mr. *Kenny is the* **person** *that invented an anesthetic* **machine** *which uses* **micro-computers** *to control the rate at which an anesthetic is pumped into the blood. Such* **machines** *are nothing new. But his* **device** *uses two* **micro-computers** *to achieve much closer monitoring of the* **pump** *feeding the anesthetic into the patient.*

According to H&S's algorithm, the chain for the word *"Mr."* is first created [lex "Mr.", sense {mister, Mr.}]. *"Mr."* belongs only to one synset, so it is disambiguated from the beginning. The word *"person"* is related to this chain in the sense *"a human being"* by a medium-strong relation, so the chain now contains two entries:
[lex "Mr.", sense {mister, Mr.}]
[lex "person", sense {person, individual, someone, man, mortal, human, soul}].
When the algorithm processes the word *"machine"*, it relates it to this chain, because *"machine"* in the first WordNet sense (*"an efficient person"*) is a holonym of *"person"* in the chosen sense. In other words, *"machine"* and *"person"* are related by a strong relation. In this case, *"machine"* is disambiguated in the wrong way, even though after this first occurrence of *"machine"*, there is strong evidence supporting the selection of its more common sense: *"micro-computer"*, *"device"* and *"pump"* all point to its correct sense in this context — *"any mechanical or electrical device that performs or assists in the performance"*.

This example indicates that disambiguation cannot be a greedy decision. In order to choose the right sense of the word the 'whole picture' of chain distribution in the text must be considered. We propose to develop a chaining model according to all possible alternatives of word senses and then choose the best one among them.

Let us illustrate this method on the above example. First, a node for the word *"Mr."* is created [lex "Mr.", sense {mister, Mr.}]. The next candidate word is *"person"*. It has two senses: *"human being"* (*person* − 1) and *"grammatical category of pronouns and verb forms"* (*person* − 2). The choice of sense for *"person"* splits the chain world into two different interpretations as shown in Figure 1.

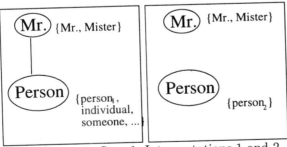

Figure 1: Step 1, Interpretations 1 and 2

We define a *component* as a list of interpretations that are exclusive of each other. Component words influence each other in the selection of their respective senses.

The next candidate word *"anesthetic"* is not related to any word in the first component, so we create a new component for it with a single interpretation.

The word *"machine"* has 5 senses *machine*$_1$ to *machine*$_5$. In its first sense, *"an efficient person"*, it is related to the senses *"person"* and *"Mr."*. It therefore influences the selection of their senses, thus *"machine"*

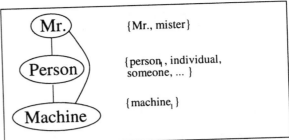

Figure 2: Step 2, Interpretation 1

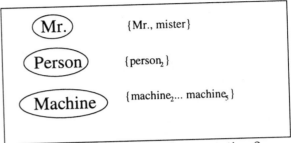

Figure 3: Step 2, Interpretation 2

has to be inserted in the first component. After its insertion the picture of the first component becomes the one shown in Figures 2 to 5.

But if we continue the process and insert the words *"micro-computer"*, *"device"* and *"pump"*, the number of alternatives greatly increases. The strongest interpretations are given in Figures 6 and 7.

Under the assumption that the text is *cohesive*, we define the best interpretation as the one with the most connections (edges in the graph). In this case, the second interpretation at the end of Step 3 is selected, which predicts the right sense for *"machine"*. We define the score of an interpretation as the sum of its chain scores. A chain score is determined by the number and weight of the relations between chain members. Experimentally, we fixed the weight of reiteration and synonym to 10, of antonym to 7, and of hyperonym and holonym to 4. Our algorithm computes all possible interpretations, maintaining each one without self contradiction. When the number of possible interpretations is larger

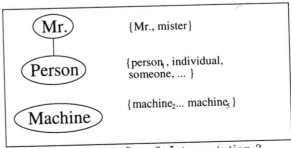

Figure 4: Step 2, Interpretation 3

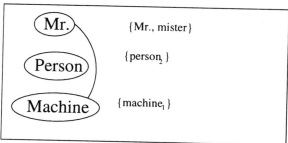

Figure 5: Step 2, Interpretation 4

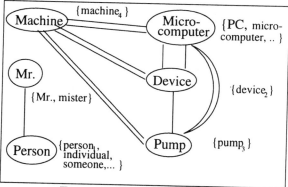

Figure 7: Step 3, Interpretation 2

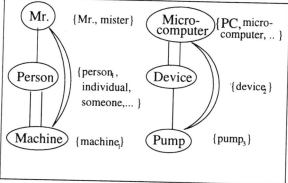

Figure 6: Step 3, Interpretation 1

than a certain threshold, we prune the weak interpretations according to this criteria, this is to prevent exponential growth of memory usage. In the end, we select from each component the strongest interpretation.

In summary, our algorithm differs from H&S's algorithm in that it introduces, in addition to the relatedness criterion for membership to a chain, a nongreedy disambiguation heuristic to select the appropriate senses of chain members.

The two algorithms differ in two other major aspects: the criterion for the selection of candidate words and the operational definition of a text unit.

We choose as candidate words simple nouns and noun compounds. As mentioned above, nouns are the main contributors to the "aboutness" of a text, and noun synsets dominate in WordNet. Both (Stairmand 1996) and H&S rely only on nouns as candidate words. In our algorithm, we rely on the results of Brill's part-of-speech tagging algorithm to identify nouns (Brill 1992), while H&S do not go through this step and only select tokens that happen to occur as nouns in WordNet. Using WordNet to identify nouns can lead to erroneous situations where a word that is used as a verb will be identified as a noun, e.g., "walk".

In addition, we extend the set of candidate words to include *noun compounds*. We first empirically evaluated the importance of noun compounds by taking into account the noun compounds explicitly present in WordNet (some 50,000 entries in WordNet are noun compounds such as "sea level" or collocations such as "dig-

ital computer"). However, English includes a productive system of noun compounds, and in each domain, new noun-compounds and collocations not present in WordNet play a major role.

We addressed the issue, by using a shallow parser (developed by Ido Dagan's team at Bar-Ilan University) to identify noun-compounds using a simple characterization of noun sequences. This has two major benefits: (1) it identifies important concepts in the domain (for example, in a text on "quantum computing", the main token was the noun compound "quantum computing" which was not present in WordNet); (2) it eliminates words that occur as modifiers as possible candidates for chain membership. For example, when "quantum computing" is selected as a single unit, the word "quantum" is not selected. This is beneficial because in this example, the text was not about "quantum", but more about computers. When a noun compound is selected, the relatedness criterion in WordNet is used by considering its head noun only. Thus, "quantum computer" is related to "machine" as a "computer".

The second difference in our algorithm lies in the operational definition we give to the notion of text unit. We use as text units the segments obtained from Hearst's algorithm of text segmentation (Hearst 1994). We build chains in every segment according to relatedness criteria, and in a second stage, we merge chains from the different segments using much stronger criteria for connectedness only: two chains are merged across a segment boundary only if they contain a common word with the same sense. Our intra-segment relatedness criterion is less strict: members of the same synsets are related, a node and its offspring in the hyperonym graph are related, siblings in the hyperonym graph are related only if the length of the path is less than a threshold.

The relation between text segmentation and lexical chains is delicate, since they are both derived from partially common sources of knowledge: lexical distribution and repetitions. In fact, lexical chains could serve as a basis for an algorithm for segmentation. We have found empirically, however, that Hearst's algorithm behaves well on the type of texts we checked and that it provides a solid basis for the construction of lexical chains.

3 Building Summaries Using Lexical Chains

We now investigate how lexical chains can serve as a source representation of the original text to build a summary. The next question is how to build a summary representation from this source representation.

The most prevalent discourse topic will play an important role in the summary. We first present the intuition why lexical chains are a good indicator of the central topic of a text. Given an appropriate measure of strength, we show that picking the concepts represented by strong lexical chains gives a better indication of the central topic of a text than simply picking the most frequent words in the text (which forms the zero-hypothesis).

For example, we show in Appendix A a sample text about Bayesian Network technology. There, the concept of network is denoted by the words *"network"* with 6 occurrences, *"net"* with 2, and *"system"* with 4. But the summary representation has to reflect that all these words represent the **same** concept. Otherwise, the summary generation stage would extract information separately for each term. The chain representation approach avoids completely this problem, because all these terms occur in the same chain, which reflects that they represent the same concept.

An additional argument for the chain representation as opposed to a simple word frequency model is the case when a single concept is represented by a number of words, each with relatively low frequency. In the same Bayesian Network sample text, the concept of *"information"* is denoted by the words *"information"* (3), *"datum"* (2), *"knowledge"* (3), *"concept"* (1) and *"model"* 1. In this text, *"information"* is a more important concept than *"computer"* which occurs 4 times. Because the *"information"* chain combines the number of occurrences of all its members, it can overcome the weight of the single word *"computer"*.

Scoring Chains

In order to use lexical chains as outlined above, one must first identify the strongest chains among all those that are produced by our algorithm. As is frequent in summarization, there is no formal way to evaluate chain strength (as there is no formal method to evaluate the quality of a summary). We therefore rely on an empirical methodology. We have developed an environment to compute and graphically visualize lexical chains to evaluate experimentally how they capture the main topics of the texts. Figure 8 shows how lexical chains are visualized to help human testers evaluate their importance.

We have collected data for a set of 30 random texts extracted from popular magazines (from "The Economist" and "Scientific American"), all of them

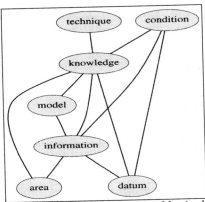

Figure 8: Visual representation of lexical chains

are popular science genre. For each text, we manually ranked chains in terms of relevance to the main topics. We then computed different formal measures on the chains, including: chain length, distribution in the text, text span covered by the chain, density, graph topology (diameter of the graph of the words) and number of repetitions. The results on our data set indicate that only the following parameters are good predictors of the strength of a chain:

Length: The number of occurrences of members of the chain.

Homogeneity index: 1 - the number of distinct occurrences divided by the length.

We designed a score function for chains as:
$$Score(Chain) = Length * HomogeneityIndex$$
When ranking chains according to their score, we evaluated that strong chains are those which satisfy our "Strength Criterion":
$$Score(Chain) > Average(Scores) + 2 * StandardDeviation(Scores)$$

These are preliminary results but they are strikingly confirmed by our experience on the 30 texts we analyzed extensively. We have experimented with different normalization methods for the score function, but they do not seem to improve the results. We plan to extend the empirical analysis in the future and to use formal learning methods to determine a good scoring function.

The average number of strong chains selected by this selection method was 5 for texts of 1055 words on average (474 words minimum, 3198 words maximum), when 32 chains were originally generated on average. The strongest chains of the sample text are presented in Appendix B.

Extracting Significant Sentences

Once strong chains have been selected, the next step of the summarization algorithm is to extract full sentences from the original text based on chain distribution.

We investigated three alternatives for this step:

Heuristic 1 For each chain in the summary representation choose the sentence that contains the first appearance of a chain member in the text.

This heuristic produced the following summary for the text shown in Appendix:

> When Microsoft Senior Vice President Steve Ballmer first heard his company was planning to make a huge investment in an Internet service offering movie reviews and local entertainment information in major cities across the nation, he went to Chairman Bill Gates with his concerns. Microsoft's competitive advantage, he responded, was its expertise in Bayesian networks. Bayesian networks are complex diagrams that organize the body of knowledge in any given area by mapping out cause — and — effect relationships among key variables and encoding them with numbers that represent the extent to which one variable is likely to affect another.
>
> Programmed into computers, these systems can automatically generate optimal predictions or decisions even when key pieces of information are missing.
>
> When Microsoft in 1993 hired Eric Horvitz, David Heckerman and Jack Breese, pioneers in the development of Bayesian systems, colleagues in the field were surprised.

The problem with this approach is that all words in a chain reflect the same concept, but to a different extent. For example, in the AI chain, (Appendix B, Chain 3) the token "*technology*" is related to the concept "*AI*", but the word "*field*" is more suitable to represent the main topic "*AI*" in the context of the text. That is, not all chain members are good representatives of the topic (even though they all contribute to its meaning).

We therefore defined a criterion to evaluate the appropriateness of a chain member to represent its chain based on its frequency of occurrence in the chain. We found experimentally that such words, call them *representative* words, have a frequency in the chain no less than the average word frequency in the chain. For example, in the third chain the representative words are "*field*" and "*AI*".

Heuristic 2 We therefore defined a second heuristic based on the notion of representative words: For each chain in the summary representation, choose the sentence that contains the first appearance of a representative chain member in the text.

In this special case this heuristic gives the same result as the first one.

Heuristic 3 Often, the same topic is discussed in a number of places in the text, so its chain is distributed across the whole text. Still, in some text unit, this global topic is the central topic (focus) of the segment. We try to identify this unit and extract sentences related to the topic from this segment (or successive segments) only.

We characterize this text unit as a cluster of successive segments with high density of chain members. Our third heuristic is based on this approach.

For each chain, find the text unit where the chain is highly concentrated. Extract the sentence with the first chain appearance in this central unit. Concentration is computed as the number of chain members occurrences in a segment divided by the number of nouns in the segment. A chain has high concentration if its concentration is the maximum of all chains. A cluster is a group of successive segments such that every segment contains chain members.

Note that in all these three techniques only one sentence is extracted for each chain (regardless of its strength).

For most texts we tested, the first and second techniques produce the same results, but when they are different, the output of the second technique is better. Generally, the second technique produces the best summary. We checked these methods on our 30 texts data set. Surprisingly, the third heuristic, which intuition predicts as the most sophisticated, gives the least indicative results. This may be due to several factors: our criteria for 'centrality' or 'clustering' may be insufficient or, more likely, the problem seems to be related to the interaction with text structure. The third heuristic tends to extract sentences from the middle of the text and to extract several sentences from distant places in the text for a single chain. The complete results of our experiments are available on-line at http://www.cs.bgu.ac.il/research/projects/summarization-test/.

4   Evaluation of the Method

Description of the Experiment

Most evaluations of summarization systems use an intrinsic method (Edmunson 1969; Paice 1990; Kupiec, Pedersen, & Chen 1995; Marcu 1997; Salton *et al.* 1997; Ono, Sumita, & Miike 1994). The typical approach is to create an "ideal" summary, either written by professional abstractors or by merging summaries provided by multiple human subjects using methods such as majority opinion, union, or intersection. The output of the summarizers is then compared with the "ideal" summary. Precision and recall are used to measure the quality of the summary.

We designed a similar experiment to evaluate the summaries obtained by the lexical-chain based technique with an ideal summary constructed by human subjects. We also compared the summaries with those obtained by the Microsoft Summarizer available in Word97.

To study agreement among human subjects, 40 documents were selected; for each document, 10 summaries were constructed by 5 human subjects using sentence extraction. Each subject constructed 2 summaries of a document: one at 10% length and the other at 20%[1]. For convenience, percent of length was computed in terms of number of sentences.

In addition to these 10 human-constructed summaries, we built 10% and 20% summaries using our system and Microsoft's summarizer (embedded in Word). The documents were selected from the TREC collection (Harman 1994). They are news articles on computers, terrorism, hypnosis and nuclear treaties. The average length of the articles is 30 sentences. Human subjects are graduate students in the Department of Computer Science at Columbia University, Cornell University, and Beer-Sheva University in Israel.

Agreement Among Human Subjects

We measured agreement among human subjects using *percent agreement*, a metric defined by (Gale, Church, & Yarowsky 1992) for the sense disambiguation task, but also used in other applications such as discourse segmentation (Passonneau & Litman 1993; Hearst 1994). Percent agreement is the ratio of observed agreements with the majority opinion to possible agreements with the majority opinion. For our experiments, agreement among 3 or more subjects is a majority opinion. The total possible agreements with the majority opinion is the number of human subjects times the number of sentences in a document. Observed agreement is equal to the number of times that a subject's decision agrees with the majority opinion, including both the decision to extract the sentence and not to extract the sentence. The results are shown in Table 1.

Length	Avg. Agreement	Max	Min
10%	96%	100%	87%
20%	90%	100%	83%

Table 1: Agreement among 5 human subjects for 40 documents.

The percent agreement in our experiment is surprisingly high compared to results presented by other researchers. (Marcu 1997) found percent agreement of 13 judges over 5 texts from Scientific American is 71%. (Rath, Resnick, & Savage 1961) found that extracts selected by four different human judges had only 25% overlap. (Salton *et al.* 1997) found that the most important 20% paragraphs extracted by 2 subjects have only 46% overlap. The two most probable reasons for this high percent agreement are the style of the TREC articles and our restriction on uniform length.

Statistical Significance

Using the same methodology as in (Passonneau & Litman 1993; Hearst 1994; Marcu 1997), we applied

[1]According to (Jing *et al.* 1998) ideal summary based evaluation is extremely sensitive to the required summary length. Therefore, we use an evaluation of 10% and 20% summaries in order to decrease the bias of the length factor.

	Microsoft		Lexical Chain	
	Prec	Recall	Prec	Recall
10%	33	37	61	67
20%	32	39	47	64

Table 2: Evaluation of summarization programs.

Cochran's test to our data. For our application, Cochran's test evaluates the null hypothesis that the total number of human subjects extracting the same sentence is randomly distributed. Our results show that the agreement among subjects is highly significant. That is, the probability that human subjects extract the same sentence is much higher than would be expected by chance. For all 40 documents, the probability is very low: $p < 10^{-6}$.

Systems Comparison

The "ideal" summary was constructed by taking the majority opinion of five human summaries at the same length, the precision and recall were used as similarity measures. The results are shown in Table 2.

This data demonstrates a notable improvement above a commercially available summarizer both in precision and in recall. Results are significantly better for the 10%-length summaries than for the 20%. These results indicate the strong potential of lexical chains as a knowledge source for sentence extraction. As discussed in the introduction, we expect that combining lexical chains with additional knowledge sources will improve the precision and recall of the system.

More extensive evaluation results, both intrinsic and task-based are provided in (Jing *et al.* 1998) and (Barzilay 1997).

5 Limitations and Future Work

We have identified the following main problems with our method:

- Sentence granularity: all our methods extract whole sentences as single units. This has several drawbacks: long sentences have significantly higher likelihood to be selected, they also include many constituents which would not have been selected on their own merit. The alternative is extremely costly: it involves some parsing of the sentences, the extraction of only the central constituents from the source text and the regeneration of a summary text using text generation techniques.

- Extracted sentences contain anaphora links to the rest of the text. This has been investigated and observed by (Paice 1990). Several heuristics have been proposed in the literature to address this problem (Paice 1990), (Paice & Husk 1991). The strongest seems to be to include together with the extracted sentence the one immediately preceding it. Unfortunately, when we select the first sentence in a segment, the preceding sentence does not belong to the paragraph and its insertion has a detrimental effect on the overall coherence of the summary. A preferable solution would be to replace anaphora with their referent, but again this is an extremely costly solution.

- Our method does not provide any way to control the length and level of detail of the summary. In all of the methods, we extract one sentence for each chain. The number of strong chains remains small (around 5 or 6 for the texts we have tested, regardless of their length), and the remaining chains would introduce too much noise to be of interest in adding details. The best solution seems to be to extract more material for the strongest chains.

The method presented in this paper is obviously partial in that it only considers lexical chains as a source representation, and ignores any other clues that could be gathered from the text. Still, we have achieved results of a quality superior to that of summarizers usually employed in commercial systems such as search systems on the World Wide Web on the texts we investigated.

Acknowledgments

This work has been supported by grants from the Israeli Ministry of Science and the Israeli-US Binational Scientific Foundation. We are grateful to Ido Dagan for his help and for providing us with a shallow parser developed at Bar Ilan University. We also want to thank Yaakov Choueka, Hong-Yan Jing, Dragomir Radev, Graeme Hirst and Kathleen McKeown for their assistance and comments on earlier drafts of this paper.

A   Bayesian Networks Text

When Microsoft Senior Vice President Steve Ballmer first heard his company was planning to make a huge investment in an Internet service offering movie reviews and local entertainment information in major cities across the nation, he went to Chairman Bill Gates with his concerns.

After all, Ballmer has billions of dollars of his own money in Microsoft stock, and entertainment isn't exactly the company's strong point.

But Gates dismissed such reservations. Microsoft's competitive advantage, he responded, was its expertise in Bayesian networks.

Asked recently when computers would finally begin to understand human speech, Gates began discussing the critical role of "Bayesian" systems.

Ask any other software executive about anything Bayesian and you're liable to get a blank stare.

Is Gates onto something? Is this alien-sounding technology Microsoft's new secret weapon?

Bayesian networks are complex diagrams that organize the body of knowledge in any given area by mapping out cause-and-effect relationships among key variables and encoding them with numbers that represent the extent to which one variable is likely to affect another.

Programmed into computers, these systems can automatically generate optimal predictions or decisions even when key pieces of information are missing.

When Microsoft in 1993 hired Eric Horvitz, David Heckerman and Jack Breese, pioneers in the development of Bayesian systems, colleagues in the field were surprised. The field was still an obscure, largely academic enterprise.

Today the field is still obscure. But scratch the surface of a range of new Microsoft products and you're likely to find Bayesian networks embedded in the software. And Bayesian nets are being built into models that are used to predict oil and stock prices, control the space shuttle and diagnose disease.

Artificial intelligence (AI) experts, who saw their field discredited in the early 1980s after promising a wave of "thinking" computers that they ultimately couldn't produce, believe widening acceptance of the Bayesian approach could herald a renaissance in the field.

Bayesian nets provide "an overarching graphical framework" that brings together diverse elements of AI and increases the range of its likely application to the real world, says Michael Jordon, professor of brain and cognitive science at the Massachusetts Institute of Technology.

Microsoft is unquestionably the most aggressive in exploiting the new approach. The company offers a free Web service that helps customers diagnose printing problems with their computers and recommends the quickest way to resolve them. Another Web service helps parents diagnose their children's health problems.

The latest version of Microsoft Office software uses the technology to offer a user help based on past experience, how the mouse is being moved and what task is being done.

"If his actions show he is distracted, he is likely to need help," Horvitz says. "If he's been working on a chart, chances are he needs help formatting the chart".

"Gates likes to talk about how computers are now deaf, dumb, blind and clueless. The Bayesian stuff helps deal with the clueless part," says Daniel T. Ling, director of Microsoft's research division and a former IBM scientist.

Horvitz and his two Microsoft colleagues, who were then classmates at Stanford University, began building Bayesian networks to help diagnose the condition of patients without turning to surgery.

The approach was efficient, says Horvitz, because you could combine historical data, which had been meticulously gathered, with the less precise but more intuitive knowledge of experts on how things work to get the optimal answer given the information available at a given time.

Horvitz, who with two colleagues founded Knowledge Industries to develop tools for developing Bayesian systems, says he and the others left the company to join Microsoft in part because they wanted to see their theoretical work more broadly applied. Although the company did important work for the National Aeronautics and Space Administration and on medical diagnostics, Horvitz says, "It's not like your grandmother will use it".

Microsoft's activities in the field are now helping to build a groundswell of support for Bayesian ideas.

People look up to Microsoft," says Pearl, who wrote one of the key early texts on Bayesian networks in 1988 and has become an unofficial spokesman for the field. "They've given a boost to the whole area".

Microsoft is working on techniques that will enable the Bayesian networks to "learn" or update themselves automatically based on new knowledge, a task that is currently cumbersome.

The company is also working on using Bayesian techniques to improve upon popular AI approaches such as "data mining" and "collaborative filtering" that help draw out relevant pieces of information from massive databases. The latter will be used by Microsoft in its new online entertainment service to help people identify the kind of restaurants or entertainment they are most likely to enjoy.

B Bayesian Network Text: the Strongest Chains

The Criterion is 3.58, here are the five strong chains:

CHAIN 1: Score = 14.0
    microsoft: 10 concern: 1 company: 6
    entertainment-service: 1 enterprise: 1
    massachusetts-institute: 1
CHAIN 2: Score = 9.0
    bayesian-system: 2 system: 2 bayesian-net: 2
    network: 1 bayesian-network: 5 weapon: 1
CHAIN 3: Score = 7.0
    ai: 2 artificial-intelligence: 1
    field: 7 technology: 1 science: 1
CHAIN 4: Score = 6.0
    technique: 1 bayesian-technique: 1 condition: 1
    datum: 2 model: 1 information: 3 area: 1
    knowledge: 3
CHAIN 5: Score = 3.0
    computer: 4

References

Barzilay, R. 1997. Lexical chains for summarization. Master's thesis, Ben-Gurion University, Beer-Sheva, Israel.

Boguraev, B., and Kennedy, C. 1997. Salience-based content characterisation of text documents. In *ACL/EACL-97 Workshop on Intelligent Scalable Text Summarization*, 2–9. Madrid: Association for Computational Linguistics and the European Chapter of the Association for Computational Linguistics.

Brill, E. 1992. A simple rule-based part-of-speech tagger. In *Proceedings of the Third Conference on Applied Computational Linguistics*. Trento, Italy: Association for Computational Linguistics.

Edmunson, H. 1969. New methods in automatic extracting. *Journal of the ACM* 16(2):264–285.

Gale, W.; Church, K.; and Yarowsky, D. 1992. Estimating upper and lower bounds on the performance of word-sense disambiguation programs. In *Proceedings of the 30th Annual Meeting of the Association for Computational Linguistics (ACL-92)*, 249–256. University of Delaware, Newark, Delaware: Association for Computational Linguistics.

Halliday, M., and Hasan, R. 1976. *Cohesion in English*. London: Longman.

Harman, D. 1994. An overview of the third text retrieval conference. In *TREC Proceedings*. Gaithesburg, MD: National Institute of Standards and Technology.

Hearst, M. 1994. Multi-paragraph segmentation of expository text. In *Proceedings of the 32th Annual Meeting of the Association for Computational Linguistics*,

9–16. Las Cruces, New Mexico: Association for Computational Linguistics.

Hirst, G., and St-Onge, D. 1998 [to appear]. Lexical chains as representation of context for the detection and correction of malapropisms. In Fellbaum, C., ed., *WordNet: An Electronic Lexical Database and Some of its Applications*. Cambridge, MA: The MIT Press.

Hoey, M. 1991. *Patterns of Lexis in Text*. Oxford: Oxford University Press.

Hovy, E., and Lin, C. 1997. Automated text summarization in summarist. In *ACL/EACL-97 Workshop on Intelligent Scalable Text Summarization*, 18–24. Madrid: Association for Computational Linguistics and the European Chapter of the Association for Computational Linguistics.

Jerry, H. 1978. Coherence and coreference. Technical Report Technical note 168, SRI International.

Jing, H.; Barzilay, R.; McKeown, K.; and Elhadad, M. 1998. Summarization evaluation methods: Experiments and analysis. In *Proceedings of AAAI-98 Symposium*. Stanford University, Stanford, California: American Association for Artificial Intelligence.

Jones, K. S. 1993. What might be in a summary? In Knorz, G.; Krause, J.; and Womser-Hacker, C., eds., *Information Retrieval '93: von der modellierung zur anwendung*. Konstanz: Universitatsverlag Konstanz. 9–26.

Kupiec, J.; Pedersen, J.; and Chen, F. 1995. A trainable document summarizer. In *Proceedings, 18th Annual International ACM SIGIR Conference on Research and Development in Information Retrieval*, 68–73. Seattle, Washington: Special Interest Group on Information Retrieval.

Luhn, H. 1958. The automatic creation of literature abstracts. *IBM Journal of Research and Development* 2(2).

Mann, W., and Thompson, S. 1988. Rhetorical structure theory: Toward a functional theory of organization. *Text* 8(3):243–281.

Marcu, D. 1997. From discourse structures to text summaries. In *ACL/EACL-97 Workshop on Intelligent Scalable Text Summarization*, 82–88. Madrid: Association for Computational Linguistics and the European Chapter of the Association for Computational Linguistics.

McKeown, K., and Radev, D. 1995. Generating summaries of multiple news articles. In *Proceedings, 18th Annual International ACM SIGIR Conference on Research and Development in Information Retrieval*, 74–82. Seattle, Washington: Special Interest Group on Information Retrieval.

Miller, G.; Beckwith, R.; Fellbaum, C.; Gross, D.; and Miller, K. 1990. Introduction to WordNet: An on-line lexical database. *International Journal of Lexicography (special issue)* 3(4):235–245.

Morris, J., and Hirst, G. 1991. Lexical cohesion computed by thesaural relations as an indicator of the structure of text. *Computational Linguistics* 17(1):21–43.

Ono, K.; Sumita, K.; and Miike, S. 1994. Abstract generation based on rhetorical structure extraction. In *Proceedings of the 15th International Conference on Computational Linguistics (COLING-94)*, volume 1, 344–348. Kyoto, Japan: Association for Computational Linguistics.

Paice, C., and Husk, G. 1991. Towards the automatic recognition of anaphoric features in english text: The impersonal pronoun "it". *Computer Speech and Language* 2:109–132.

Paice, C. 1990. Constructing literature abstracts by computer: Techniques and prospects. *Information Processing and Management* 26(1):171–186.

Passonneau, R., and Litman, D. 1993. Intention-based segmentation: Human reliability and correlation with linguistic cues. In *Proceedings of the 31th Annual Meeting of the Association for Computational Linguistics (ACL-93)*, 148–155. Ohio: Association for Computational Linguistics.

Rath, G.; Resnick, A.; and Savage, R. 1961. The formation of abstracts by the selection of sentences: Part 1: Sentence selection by men and machines. *American Documentation* 12(2):139–141.

Salton, G.; Singhal, A.; Mitra, M.; and Buckley, C. 1997. Automatic text structuring and summarization. *Information Processing and Management* 33(2):193–208.

Stairmand, M. 1996. *A Computational Analysis of Lexical Cohesion with Applications in Information Retrieval*. Ph.D. Dissertation, Center for Computational Linguistics UMIST, Manchester.

Teufel, S., and Moens, M. 1997. Sentence extraction as a classification task. In *ACL/EACL-97 Workshop on Intelligent Scalable Text Summarization*, 58–65. Madrid: Association for Computational Linguistics and the European Chapter of the Association for Computational Linguistics.

11

Discourse trees are good indicators of importance in text

Daniel Marcu
Information Sciences Institute
University of Southern California
4676 Admiralty Way
Marina del Rey, CA 90292-6695
`marcu@isi.edu`

Abstract

Researchers in computational linguistics have long speculated that the nuclei of the rhetorical structure tree of a text form an adequate "summary" of the text for which that tree was built. However, to my knowledge, there has been no experiment to confirm how valid this speculation really is.

In this paper, I describe a psycholinguistic experiment that shows that the concepts of discourse structure and nuclearity *can* be used effectively in text summarization. More precisely, I show that there is a strong correlation between the nuclei of the discourse structure of a text and what readers perceive to be the most important units in that text. In addition, I propose and evaluate the quality of an automatic, discourse-based summarization system that implements the methods that were validated by the psycholinguistic experiment. The evaluation indicates that although the system does not match yet the results that would be obtained if discourse trees had been built manually, it still significantly outperforms both a baseline algorithm and Microsoft's Office97 summarizer.

1 Motivation

Traditionally, previous approaches to automatic text summarization have assumed that the salient parts of a text can be determined by applying one or more of the following assumptions:

- important sentences in a text contain words that are used frequently (Luhn 1958; Edmundson 1968);

- important sentences contain words that are used in the title and section headings (Edmundson 1968);

- important sentences are located at the beginning or end of paragraphs (Baxendale 1958);

- important sentences are located at positions in a text that are genre dependent, and these positions can be determined automatically, through training techniques (Kupiec, Pedersen, & Chen 1995; Lin & Hovy 1997; Teufel & Moens 1997);

- important sentences use *bonus words* such as "greatest" and "significant" or *indicator phrases* such as "the main aim of this paper" and "the

purpose of this article", while unimportant sentences use *stigma words* such as "hardly" and "impossible" (Edmundson 1968; Rush, Salvador, & Zamora 1971; Kupiec, Pedersen, & Chen 1995; Teufel & Moens 1997);

- important sentences and concepts are the highest connected entities in elaborate semantic structures (Skorochodko 1971; Hoey 1991; Lin 1995; Barzilay & Elhadad 1997; Mani & Bloedorn 1997);

- important and unimportant sentences are derivable from a discourse representation of the text (Sparck Jones 1993b; Ono, Sumita, & Miike 1994).

In determining the words that occur most frequently in a text or the sentences that use words that occur in the headings of sections, computers are accurate tools. Therefore, in testing the validity of using these indicators for determining the most important units in a text, it is adequate to compare the direct output of a summarization program that implements the assumption(s) under scrutiny with a human-made summary or to use human subjects to assess the quality of the generated summaries or their usefulness for carrying out specific tasks. However, in determining the concepts that are semantically related or the discourse structure of a text, computers are no longer so accurate; rather, they are highly dependent on the coverage of the linguistic resources that they use and the quality of the algorithms that they implement. Although it is plausible that elaborate cohesion- and coherence-based structures can be used effectively in summarization, I believe that we should distinguish between the adequacy for summarization of a method that we choose to implement and the adequacy of a particular implementation of that method.

Hence, the position that I advocate in this paper is that, in order to build high-quality summarization programs, we need to evaluate not only a representative set of automatically generated outputs (a highly difficult problem by itself), but also the adequacy of the assumptions that these programs use. That way, we are able to distinguish the problems that arise from a particular implementation from those that arise from the underlying theoretical framework and explore new

Relation name:	EVIDENCE
Constraints on N:	The reader R might not believe the information that is conveyed by the nucleus N to a degree satisfactory to the writer W.
Constraints on S:	The reader believes the information that is conveyed by the satellite S or will find it credible.
Constraints on N + S combination:	R's comprehending S increases R's belief of N.
The effect:	R's belief of N is increased.
Locus of the effect:	N.
Example:	[The truth is that the pressure to smoke in junior high is greater than it will be any other time of one's life:[1]] [we know that $3,000$ teens start smoking each day.[2]]

Figure 1: The definition of the EVIDENCE relation in Rhetorical Structure Theory [Mann and Thompson, 1988].

---

ways to improve each.

To this end, I first review briefly the Rhetorical Structure Theory (Mann & Thompson 1988) and the *rhetorical parsing algorithm* proposed by Marcu (1997a), which takes as input an unrestricted text and derives its discourse structure (see (Marcu 1997b) for details). I then show how one can use discourse structures in order to assign to each textual unit an importance score and to determine the most important units of the corresponding text. In section 3, I describe a psycholinguistic experiment that shows that the mapping between discourse structures and importance scores *can* be used effectively for determining the most important units in a text. More precisely, I show that there is a strong correlation between the nuclei of a discourse structure of a text and what readers perceive to be the most important units in a text. I end the paper with an evaluation of an implemented summarization system that uses the discourse structures derived by the rhetorical parser (Marcu 1997a) and with a broader analysis of the summarization and evaluation methodologies that I employed.

2 From discourse structures to text summaries

A short review of Rhetorical Structure Theory

Driven mostly by research in natural language generation, Rhetorical Structure Theory (RST) (Mann & Thompson 1988) has become one of the most popular discourse theories of the last decade. Central to the theory is the notion of *rhetorical relation*, which is a relation that holds between two non-overlapping text spans called NUCLEUS and SATELLITE. (There are a few exceptions to this rule: some relations, such as CONTRAST, are multinuclear.) The distinction between nuclei and satellites comes from the empirical observation that the nucleus expresses what is more essential to the writer's purpose than the satellite; and that the nucleus of a rhetorical relation is comprehensible independent of the satellite, but not vice versa.

Text coherence in RST is assumed to arise from a

set of constraints and an overall effect that are associated with each relation. The constraints operate on the nucleus, on the satellite, and on the combination of nucleus and satellite. For example, an EVIDENCE relation (see figure 1) holds between the nucleus (labelled as 1 in the example) and the satellite (labelled as 2 in the example), because the nucleus presents some information that the writer believes to be insufficiently supported to be accepted by the reader; the satellite presents some information that is thought to be believed by the reader or that is credible to her; and the comprehension of the satellite increases the reader's belief in the nucleus. The effect of the relation is that the reader's belief in the information presented in the nucleus is increased. Rhetorical relations can be assembled into rhetorical structure trees (RS-trees) by recursively applying individual relations to spans that range in size from one clause-like unit to the whole text.

Recent developments in computational linguistics have created the means for deriving the rhetorical structure of unrestricted texts. For example, when the text shown in (1), below, is given as input to the *rhetorical parsing algorithm* that is discussed in detail in (Marcu 1997a; 1997b), it is broken into ten elementary units (those surrounded by square brackets), and two parenthetical units (those surrounded by curly brackets).[1] The rhetorical parsing algorithm uses the cue phrases shown in italics in (1) in order to hypothesize rhetorical relations among the elementary units. Eventually, the algorithm derives the rhetorical structure tree shown in figure 2.

(1) [*With* its distant orbit {— 50 percent farther from the sun than Earth —[P1]} and slim atmospheric blanket,[1]] [Mars experiences frigid weather conditions.[2]] [Surface temperatures typically average about −60 degrees Celsius (−76 degrees Fahrenheit) at the equator and can dip to −123 degrees C near the poles.[3]] [Only the midday sun at tropical latitudes is warm enough to thaw ice

---

[1]Parenthetical units are related only to the elementary units that they belong to; their deletion does not affect the coherence of the text.

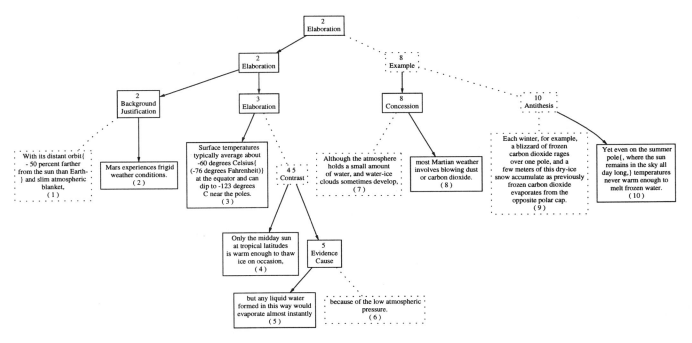

Figure 2: The discourse tree for text (1) that is built by the rhetorical parsing algorithm.

on occasion,[4] [*but* any liquid water formed in this way would evaporate almost instantly[5]] [*because* of the low atmospheric pressure.[6]]

[*Although* the atmosphere holds a small amount of water, and water-ice clouds sometimes develop,[7]] [most Martian weather involves blowing dust or carbon dioxide.[8]] [Each winter, *for example,* a blizzard of frozen carbon dioxide rages over one pole, and a few meters of this dry-ice snow accumulate as previously frozen carbon dioxide evaporates from the opposite polar cap.[9]] [*Yet* even on the summer pole, {*where* the sun remains in the sky all day long,[P10]} temperatures never warm enough to melt frozen water.[10]]

This discourse structure obeys the constraints put forth by Mann and Thompson (1988) and Marcu (1996). It is a binary tree whose leaves are the elementary textual units in (1). Each node in the tree plays either the role of nucleus or satellite. In figure 2, nuclei are represented by solid boxes, while satellites are represented by dotted boxes. The internal nodes of the discourse structure are labelled with names of rhetorical relations: for example, according to figure 2, a rhetorical relation of CONCESSION holds between units 7 and 8; and a rhetorical relation of ELABORATION holds between the text span that contains units [1–2] and the text span that contains units [3–6]. In addition to the names of rhetorical relations, each internal node has a *promotion set* that is given by the *salient* or *promotion* units of that node. The salient units are the most important units in the corresponding text span. They are determined in a bottom-up fashion, as follows: The salient unit of

a leaf is the leaf itself; the salient units of an internal node are given by the union of the salient units of its immediate nuclear children. For example, the node that spans units [4–6] has salient units 4 and 5 because the immediate children of the node labelled with relation CONTRAST are both nuclei, which have promotion units 4 and 5 respectively; the root node, which spans units [1–10] has 2 as its salient unit because only the node that corresponds to span [1–6] is a nucleus, whose salient unit is 2. In figure 2, parent nodes are linked to subordinated nuclei by solid arrows; parent nodes are linked to subordinated satellites by dotted lines.[2]

From discourse structures to importance scores

Researchers in computational linguistics have long speculated that the nuclei of a rhetorical structure tree, such as that shown in figure 2, constitute an adequate summarization of the text for which that tree was built (Mann & Thompson 1988; Matthiessen & Thompson 1988; Hobbs 1993; Polanyi 1993; Sparck Jones 1993a; 1993b). As we have discussed in the previous subsection, the elementary units in the promotion set of a node of a tree structure, which depend on the nuclear statuses of its immediate children, denote the most important units of the textual span that is dominated by that node. A simple inspection of the structure in figure 2, for example, allows us to determine that

[2]For a first-order formalization of the mathematical properties of the discourse structure shown in figure 2, see (Marcu 1996; 1997b).

Unit	1	$P1$	2	3	4	5	6	7	8	9	10	$P10$
Score	3	2	6	4	3	3	1	3	5	3	4	2

Table 1: The importance scores of the textual units in text (1).

unit 2 is the most important textual unit in text (1) because it is the only promotion unit associated with the root node. Similarly, we can determine that unit 3 is the most important unit of span [3–6] and that units 4 and 5 are the most important units of span [4–6].

A more general way of exploiting the ideas of nuclearity, discourse structure, and promotion units that are associated with a discourse tree is from the perspective of text summarization. If we repeatedly apply the concept of salience to each of the nodes of a discourse structure, we can induce a partial ordering on the importance of all the units of a text. The intuition behind this approach is that the textual units that are in the promotion sets of the top nodes of a discourse tree are more important than the units that are salient in the nodes found at the bottom. A very simple way to induce such an ordering is by computing a score for each elementary unit of a text on the basis of the depth in the tree structure of the node where the unit occurs first as a promotion unit. The larger the score of a unit, the more important that unit is considered to be in a text. Formula (2), below, provides a recursive definition for computing the importance score $s(u, D, d)$ of a unit u in a discourse structure D that has depth d.

$$(2) \quad s(u, D, d) = \begin{cases} 0 & \text{if } D \text{ is NIL,} \\ d & \text{if } u \in prom(D), \\ d-1 & \text{if } u \in paren(D), \\ max(s(u, \\ \qquad C(D), \\ \qquad d-1)) & \text{otherwise.} \end{cases}$$

The formula assumes that the discourse structure is a tree and that the functions $prom(D)$, $paren(D)$, and $C(D)$ return the promotion set, parenthetical units, and the child subtrees of each node respectively. If a unit is among the promotion set of a node, its score is given by the current value of d. If a unit is among the parenthetical units of a node, which can happen only in the case of a leaf node, the score assigned to that unit is $d - 1$ because the parenthetical unit can be represented as a direct child of the elementary unit to which is related. For example, when we apply formula (2) to the tree in figure 2, which has depth 6, we obtain the scores in table 1 for each of the elementary and parenthetical units of text (1). Because unit 2 is among the promotion units of the root, it gets a score of 6. Unit 3 is among the promotion units of a node found two levels below the root, so it gets a score of 4. Unit 6 is among the promotion units of a leaf found 5 levels below the root, so it gets a score of 1. Unit $P1$ is a parenthetical unit of elementary unit 1, so its score is

$s(1, D, 6) - 1 = 3 - 1 = 2$ because the elementary unit to which it belongs is found 3 levels below the root.

If we consider now the importance scores that are induced on the textual units by the discourse structure and formula (2), we can see that they correspond to a partial ordering on the importance of these units in a text. This ordering enables the construction of text summaries with various degrees of granularity: for example, the partial ordering shown in (3) was induced on the textual units of text (1) by the discourse structure in figure 2 and formula (2).

(3)　　$2 > 8 > 3, 10 > 1, 4, 5, 7, 9 > P1, P10 > 6$

If we are interested in generating a very short summary of text (1), we can create a text with only one unit, which is unit 2. A longer summary can contain units 2 and 8; a longer one, units 2, 8, 3, and 10; and so on.

A discourse-based summarizer

Given that we can use the rhetorical parser described by Marcu (1997a; 1997b) to build the discourse structure of any text and that we can use formula (2) to determine the partial ordering that is consistent with the idea that the nuclei of a discourse structure constitute a good summary of a text, it is trivial now to implement a summarization program.

The summarization algorithm in figure 3 takes two arguments: a text and a number p between 1 and 100. It first uses the rhetorical parsing algorithm in order to determine the discourse structure of the text given as input. It then applies formula (2) and determines a partial ordering on the elementary and parenthetical units of the text. It then uses the partial ordering in order to select the $p\%$ most important textual units of the text.

The idea that I emphasized in the introductory section was that if we would take now the most important $p\%$ textual units and ascertain their suitability for a text summary, we would evaluate only the quality of one particular implementation of the discourse-based summarization algorithm. However, since this algorithm constructs trees that are not always correct (Marcu 1997a), such an evaluation would not assess the appropriateness of the discourse-based method for text summarization. In order to distinguish between the quality of the method and the quality of the implementation, I designed a psycholinguistic experiment that shows that the *theoretical concepts* of discourse structure and nuclearity *can* be used effectively for determining the most important units in a text. Once the suitability of using discourse structures for text summarization is established (see section 3), I turn back to the evaluation of

---

Input: A text T
  A number p, such that $1 \leq p \leq 100$.
Output: The most important $p\%$ of the elementary units of T.

1.   I.   Determine the discourse structure DS of T by means of the rhetorical
2.   parsing algorithm (Marcu 1997a; 1997b).
3.   II.   Determine a partial ordering on the elementary and parenthetical
4.   units of DS by means of formula (2).
5.   III.   Select the first $p\%$ units of the ordering.

Figure 3: The discourse-based summarization algorithm

---

the algorithm and discuss its strengths and weaknesses. As will become apparent in section 4, although the implementation does not generate summaries of the quality predicted by the evaluation of the method, it still significantly outperforms both a baseline algorithm and Microsoft's Office97 summarizer.

3   From discourse structure to text summaries — an empirical view

Materials and methods of the experiment

We know from the results reported in the psychological literature on summarization (Johnson 1970; Chou Hare & Borchardt 1984; Sherrard 1989) that there exists a certain degree of disagreement between readers with respect to the importance that they assign to various textual units and that the disagreement is dependent on the quality of the text and the comprehension and summarization skills of the readers (Winograd 1984). In an attempt to produce an adequate reference set of data, I selected for my experiment five short texts from *Scientific American* that I considered to be well-written. The texts ranged in size from 161 to 725 words. The shortest text was that shown in (1).

Because my intention was to evaluate the adequacy for summarizing text not only of a particular implementation but also of discourse-based methods in general, I first determined manually the minimal textual units of each text. Overall, I broke the five texts into 160 textual units with the shortest text being broken into 18 textual units, and the longest into 70. Each textual unit was enclosed within square brackets and numbered. For example, when the text on Mars was manually broken into elementary units, I obtained not 10 units, as in the case when the rhetorical parsing algorithm was applied (see text (1)), but 18. The text whose minimal units were obtained manually is given in (4), below.

(4)   [With its distant orbit[1]] [— 50 percent farther from the sun than Earth —[2]] [and slim atmospheric blanket,[3]] [Mars experiences frigid weather conditions.[4]] [Surface temperatures typically average about −60 degrees Celsius (−76 degrees Fahrenheit) at the equator[5]] [and can dip to −123 degrees C near the poles.[6]] [Only the midday sun at tropical latitudes is warm enough to thaw ice

on occasion,[7]] [but any liquid water formed in this way would evaporate almost instantly[8]] [because of the low atmospheric pressure.[9]]

[Although the atmosphere holds a small amount of water,[10]] [and water-ice clouds sometimes develop,[11]] [most Martian weather involves blowing dust or carbon dioxide.[12]] [Each winter, for example, a blizzard of frozen carbon dioxide rages over one pole,[13]] [and a few meters of this dry-ice snow accumulate[14]] [as previously frozen carbon dioxide evaporates from the opposite polar cap.[15]] [Yet even on the summer pole,[16]] [where the sun remains in the sky all day long,[17]] [temperatures never warm enough to melt frozen water.[18]]

I followed Johnson's (1970) and Garner's (1982) strategy and asked 13 independent judges to rate each textual unit according to its importance to a potential summary. The judges used a three-point scale and assigned a score of 2 to the units that they believed to be very important and should appear in a concise summary, 1 to those they considered moderately important, which should appear in a long summary, and 0 to those they considered unimportant, which should not appear in any summary. The judges were instructed that there were no right or wrong answers and no upper or lower bounds with respect to the number of textual units that they should select as being important or moderately important. The judges were all graduate students in computer science; I assumed that they had developed adequate comprehension and summarization skills on their own, so no training session was carried out. Table 2 presents the scores that were assigned by each judge to the units in text (4).

The same texts were also given to two computational linguistics analysts with solid knowledge of Rhetorical Structure Theory. The analysts were asked to build one rhetorical structure tree (RS-tree) for each text. I took then the RS-trees built by the analysts and associated with each node in a tree its salient units. I then computed for each textual unit a score, by applying formula (2). Table 2 also presents the scores that were derived from the RS-trees that were built by each analyst for text (4) and the scores that were derived from

Unit	Judges													Analysts		Program
	1	2	3	4	5	6	7	8	9	10	11	12	13	1	2	
1	0	2	2	2	0	0	0	0	0	0	0	0	0	3	3	3
2	0	0	0	0	0	0	0	0	0	0	0	0	1	1	0	2
3	0	2	0	2	0	0	0	0	0	0	0	0	1	3	2	3
4	2	1	2	2	2	2	2	2	2	2	2	2	2	6	5	6
5	1	1	0	1	1	1	0	1	2	1	0	2	2	4	3	4
6	0	1	0	1	1	1	0	1	1	1	0	2	2	4	3	4
7	0	2	1	0	0	0	1	1	1	0	0	0	0	4	3	3
8	0	1	0	0	0	0	0	0	0	0	0	0	0	4	3	3
9	0	0	2	0	0	0	0	0	0	0	1	0	1	1	0	1
10	0	2	2	2	0	0	2	0	0	0	0	0	0	3	4	3
11	0	0	0	2	0	0	0	1	0	0	0	0	1	3	4	3
12	2	2	2	2	2	2	2	2	2	0	1	2	2	5	4	5
13	1	1	0	0	0	1	0	1	0	0	0	2	0	3	3	3
14	1	0	0	0	0	1	1	0	0	0	0	2	0	3	3	3
15	0	0	0	0	0	1	0	0	0	0	0	1	0	2	3	3
16	0	1	1	0	1	0	0	0	2	0	0	1	0	4	3	4
17	0	1	0	0	0	0	0	0	1	0	0	1	0	2	1	2
18	2	1	1	0	1	0	1	0	2	0	1	1	2	4	3	4

Table 2: The scores assigned by the judges, analysts, and the discourse-based summarizer to the textual units in text (4).

Text	T.1	T.2	T.3	T.4	T.5	Overall
All units	72.64	73.23	69.23	69.89	70.08	70.67
Very important units	88.46	63.07	64.83	63.73	67.30	65.66
Less important units	51.28	73.07	53.84	46.15	–	58.04
Unimportant units	75.14	82.51	73.07	72.85	71.25	73.86

Table 3: Percent agreement with the majority opinion.

the discourse tree that was built by the discourse-based summarizer.

Usually, the granularity of the trees that are built by the rhetorical parser is coarser than the granularity of those that are built manually. The last column in table 2 reflects this: all the units that were determined manually and that overlapped an elementary unit determined by the rhetorical parser were assigned the same score. For example, units 1 and 3 in text (4) correspond to unit 1 in text (1). Because the score of unit 1 in the discourse structure that is built by the rhetorical parser is 3, both units 1 and 3 in text (4) are assigned the score 3.

Agreement among judges

Overall agreement among judges. I measured the agreement of the judges with one another, by means of the notion of *percent agreement* that was defined by Gale (1992) and used extensively in discourse segmentation studies (Passonneau & Litman 1993; Hearst 1997). Percent agreement reflects the ratio of observed to possible agreements with the majority opinion. The percent agreements computed for each of the five texts and each level of importance are given in table 3. The agree-

ments among judges for my experiment seem to follow the same pattern as those described by other researchers in summarization (Johnson 1970). That is, the judges are quite consistent with respect to what they perceive as being very important and unimportant, but less consistent with respect to what they perceive as being less important. In contrast with the agreement observed among judges, the percentage agreements computed for 1000 importance assignments that were randomly generated for the same texts followed a normal distribution with $\mu = 47.31, \sigma = 0.04$. These results suggest that the agreement among judges is significant.

Agreement among judges with respect to the importance of each textual unit. I considered a textual unit to be labelled consistently if a simple majority of the judges (≥ 7) assigned the same score to that unit. Overall, the judges labelled consistently 140 of the 160 textual units (87%). In contrast, a set of 1000 randomly generated importance scores showed agreement, on average, for only 50 of the 160 textual units (31%), $\sigma = 0.05$.

The judges consistently labelled 36 of the units as very important, 8 as less important, and 96 as unimportant. They were inconsistent with respect

Text T.1	Text T.2	Text T.3	Text T.4	Text T.5	Overall
0.645	0.676	0.960	0.772	0.772	0.798

Table 4: The Spearman correlation coefficients between the ranks assigned to each textual unit on the basis of the RS-trees built by the two analysts.

to 20 textual units. For example, for text (4), the judges consistently labelled units 4 and 12 as very important, units 5 and 6 as less important, units 1, 2, 3, 7, 8, 9, 10, 11, 13, 14, 15, 17 as unimportant, and were inconsistent in labeling unit 18. If we compute percent agreement figures only for the textual units for which at least 7 judges agreed, we get 69% for the units considered very important, 63% for those considered less important, and 77% for those considered unimportant. The overall percent agreement in this case is 75%.

Statistical significance. It has often been emphasized that agreement figures of the kinds computed above could be misleading (Krippendorff 1980; Passonneau & Litman 1993). Since the "true" set of important textual units cannot be independently known, we cannot compute how valid the importance assignments of the judges were. Moreover, although the agreement figures that would occur by chance offer a strong indication that our data are reliable, they do not provide a precise measurement of reliability.

To compute a reliability figure, I followed the same methodology as Passonneau and Litman (1993) and Hearst (1997) and applied Cochran's Q summary statistics to the data (Cochran 1950). Cochran's test assumes that a set of judges make binary decisions with respect to a dataset. The null hypothesis is that the number of judges that take the same decision is randomly distributed. Since Cochran's test is appropriate only for binary judgments and since my main goal was to determine a reliability figure for the agreement among judges with respect to what they believe to be important, I evaluated two versions of the data that reflected only one importance level. In the first version I considered as being important the judgments with a score of 2 and unimportant the judgments with a score of 0 and 1. In the second version, I considered as being important the judgments with a score of 2 and 1 and unimportant the judgments with a score of 0. Essentially, I mapped the judgment matrices of each of the five texts into matrices whose elements ranged over only two values: 0 and 1. After these modifications were made, I computed for each version and each text the Cochran Q statistics, which approximates the χ^2 distribution with $N - 1$ degrees of freedom, where N is the number of elements in the dataset. In all cases I obtained probabilities that were very low: $p < 10^{-6}$. This means that the agreement among judges was extremely significant.

Although the probability was very low for both versions, it was lower for the first version of the modified data than for the second. This means that it is more reliable to consider as important only the units that were assigned a score of 2 by a majority of the judges.

As I have already mentioned, my ultimate goal was to determine whether there exists a correlation between the units that judges find important and the units that have nuclear status in the rhetorical structure trees of the same texts. Since the percentage agreement for the units that were considered very important was higher than the percentage agreement for the units that were considered less important, and since the Cochran's significance computed for the first version of the modified data was higher that the one computed for the second, I decided to consider the set of 36 textual units labelled by a majority of judges with 2 as a reliable reference set of importance units for the five texts. For example, units 4 and 12 from text (4) belong to this reference set.

Agreement between analysts

Once I determined the set of textual units that the judges believed to be important, I needed to determine the agreement between the analysts who built the discourse trees for the five texts. Because I did not know the distribution of the importance scores derived from the discourse trees, I computed the correlation between the analysts by applying Spearman's correlation coefficient on the scores associated to each textual unit. I interpreted these scores as ranks on a scale that measures the importance of the units in a text.

The Spearman rank correlation coefficient is an alternative to the usual correlation coefficient. It is based on the ranks of the data, and not on the data itself, and so is resistant to outliers. The null hypothesis tested by the Spearman coefficient is that two variables are independent of each other, against the alternative hypothesis that the rank of a variable is correlated with the rank of another variable. The value of the statistics ranges from -1, indicating that high ranks of one variable occur with low ranks of the other variable, through 0, indicating no correlation between the variables, to $+1$, indicating that high ranks of one variable occur with high ranks of the other variable.

The Spearman correlation coefficient between the ranks assigned for each textual unit on the bases of the RS-trees built by the two analysts was high for each of the five texts. It ranged from 0.645, for text T.1, to 0.960, for text T.3 at the $p < 0.0001$ level of significance. The Spearman correlation coefficient between the ranks assigned to the textual units of all five texts was 0.798, at the $p < 0.0001$ level of significance (see

Text	No. of units that were considered important by judges	First Analyst		Recall	Precision
		No. of units that were labelled as important on the basis of the RS-tree built by the analyst	No. of units that were correctly labelled as important on the basis of the RS-tree built by the analyst		
T.1	2	2	2	100.00	100.00
T.2	9	6	5	55.55	83.33
T.3	7	5	4	57.14	80.00
T.4	12	10	6	50.00	60.00
T.5	6	7	3	50.00	42.85
All	36	30	20	55.55	66.66

Table 5: Summarization results obtained by using the text structures built by the first analyst — the clause-like unit case.

Text	No. of units that were considered important by judges	Second Analyst		Recall	Precision
		No. of units that were labelled as important on the basis of the RS-tree built by the analyst	No. of units that were correctly labelled as important on the basis of the RS-tree built by the analyst		
T.1	2	1	1	50.00	50.00
T.2	9	8	6	66.66	75.00
T.3	7	5	4	57.14	80.00
T.4	12	7	5	41.66	71.42
T.5	6	9	4	66.66	44.44
All	36	30	20	55.55	66.66

Table 6: Summarization results obtained by using the text structures built by the second analyst — the clause-like unit case.

table 4).

Agreement between the analysts and the judges with respect to the most important textual units

In order to determine whether there exists any correspondence between what readers believe to be important and the nuclei of the RS-trees, I selected, from each of the five texts, the set of textual units that were labelled as "very important" by a majority of the judges. For example, for text (4), I selected units 4 and 12, i.e., 11% of the units. Overall, the judges selected 36 units as being very important, which is approximately 22% of the units in all the texts. The percentages of important units for the five texts were 11, 36, 35, 17, and 22 respectively.

I took the maximal scores computed for each textual unit from the RS-trees built by each analyst and selected a percentage of units that matched the percentage of important units selected by the judges. In the cases in which there were ties, I selected a percentage of units that was closest to the one computed for the judges. For example, I selected units 4 and 12, which represented the most important 11% of the units that were induced by formula (2) on the RS-tree built by the first analyst. However, I selected only unit 4, which represented 6% of the most important units that were induced on the RS-tree built by the second analyst, because units 10, 11, and 12 have the same score (see table 2). If I had selected units 10, 11 and 12 as well, I would have ended up selecting 22% of the units in text (4), which is farther from 11 than 6. Hence, I determined for each text the set of important units as labelled by judges and as derived from the RS-trees of those texts.

I calculated for each text the recall and precision of the important units derived from the RS-trees, with respect to the units labelled important by the judges. The overall recall and precision was the same for both analysts: 55.55% recall and 66.66% precision. In contrast, the average recall and precision for the same percentages of units selected randomly 1000 times from the same five texts were both 25.7%, $\sigma = 0.059$. Tables 5 and 6 show the recall and precision figures for each an-

Text	No. of units that were considered important by judges	First Analyst		Recall	Precision
		No. of units that were labelled as important on the basis of the RS-tree built by the analyst	No. of units that were correctly labelled as important on the basis of the RS-tree built by the analyst		
T.1	7	7	7	100.00	100.00
T.2	12	12	12	100.00	100.00
T.3	10	9	8	80.00	88.88
T.4	18	11	8	44.44	72.72
T.5	11	10	5	45.45	50.00
All	58	49	40	68.96	81.63

Table 7: Summarization results obtained by using the text structures built by the first analyst — the sentence case.

Text	No. of units that were considered important by judges	Second Analyst		Recall	Precision
		No. of units that were labelled as important on the basis of the RS-tree built by the analyst	No. of units that were correctly labelled as important on the basis of the RS-tree built by the analyst		
T.1	7	7	7	100.00	100.00
T.2	12	11	9	75.00	81.81
T.3	10	9	8	80.00	88.88
T.4	18	11	6	33.33	54.54
T.5	11	13	8	72.72	61.53
All	58	51	38	65.51	74.50

Table 8: Summarization results obtained by using the text structures built by the second analyst — the sentence case.

alyst and each of the five texts.

In summarizing text, it is often useful to consider not only clause-like units, but full sentences. To account for this, I considered as important all the textual units that pertained to a sentence that was characterized by at least one important textual unit. For example, I labelled as important textual units 1 to 4 in text (4), because they make up a full sentence and because unit 4 was labelled as important. For the adjusted data, I determined again the percentages of important units for the five texts and I recalculated the recall and precision for both analysts: the recall was 68.96% and 65.51% and the precision 81.63% and 74.50% respectively. Tables 7 and 8 show the sentence-related recall and precision figures for each analyst and each of the five texts.

In contrast with the results in tables 7 and 8, the average recall and precision for the same percentages of units selected randomly 1000 times from the same five texts were 38.4%, $\sigma = 0.048$. These results confirm that there exists a strong correlation between the nuclei of the RS-trees that pertain to a text and what readers perceive as being important in that text. Given

the values of recall and precision that I obtained, it is plausible that an adequate computational treatment of discourse theories would provide most of what is needed for selecting accurately the important units in a text. However, the results also suggest that the discourse theory that was employed here is not enough by itself if one wants to strive for perfection.

The above results not only provide strong evidence that discourse theories can be used effectively for text summarization, but also suggest strategies that an automatic summarizer might follow. For example, the Spearman correlation coefficient between the judges and the first analyst, the one who did not follow the paragraph structure, was lower than that between the judges and the second analyst. This might suggest that human judges are inclined to use the paragraph breaks as valuable sources of information when they interpret discourse. If the aim of a summarization program is to mimic human behavior, it would then seem adequate for the program to take advantage of the paragraph structure of the texts that it analyzes.

Text	No. of units that were considered important by judges	Discourse-based Summarizer			
		No. of units that were labelled as important on the basis of the tree built by the rhetorical parser	No. of units that were correctly labelled as important on the basis of the tree built by the rhetorical parser	Recall	Precision
T.1	2	2	2	100.00	100.00
T.2	9	8	5	55.55	62.50
T.3	7	8	3	42.85	37.50
T.4	12	14	6	50.00	42.85
T.5	6	6	3	50.00	50.00
All	36	38	19	52.77	50.00

Table 9: Summarization results obtained by using the text structures built by the rhetorical parser — the clause-like unit case.

Text	No. of units that were considered important by judges	Discourse-based Summarizer			
		No. of units that were labelled as important on the basis of the tree built by the rhetorical parser	No. of units that were correctly labelled as important on the basis of the tree built by the rhetorical parser	Recall	Precision
T.1	7	7	7	100.00	100.00
T.2	12	14	12	100.00	85.71
T.3	10	9	6	60.00	66.66
T.4	18	20	10	55.55	50.00
T.5	11	6	5	45.45	83.33
All	58	56	38	65.51	67.85

Table 10: Summarization results obtained by using the text structures built by the rhetorical parser — the sentence case.

4 An evaluation of the discourse-based summarization program

Agreement between the results of the summarization program and the judges with respect to the most important textual units

To evaluate the summarization program, I followed the same method as in section 4. That is, I used the importance scores assigned by formula (2) to the units of the discourse trees built by the rhetorical parser in order to compute statistics similar to those discussed in conjunction with the manual analyses. Tables 9 and 10 summarize the results.

When the program selected only the textual units with the highest scores, in percentages that were equal to those of the judges, the recall was 52.77% and the precision was 50%. When the program selected the full sentences that were associated with the most important units, in percentages that were equal to those of the judges, the recall was 65.51% and the precision 67.85%. Tables 9 and 10 show recall and precision results for each of the five texts that were summarized. The lower recall and precision scores associated with clause-like units seem to be caused primarily by the difference in granularity with respect to the way the texts were broken into subunits: the program does not recover all minimal textual units, and as a consequence, its assignment of importance scores is coarser. When full sentences are considered, the judges and the program work at the same level of granularity, and as a consequence, the summarization results improve.

Comparison with other work

I am not aware of any other discourse-based summarization program for English. However, Ono et al. (1994) discuss a summarization program for Japanese that uses a discourse parser built by Sumita (1992) and that constructs trees whose minimal textual units are sentences. Due to the differences between English and

Text	No. of units considered important by judges	Microsoft Office97 Summarizer			
		No. of units identified	No. of units identified correctly	Recall	Precision
T.1	2	3	1	50.00	33.33
T.2	9	10	5	55.55	50.00
T.3	7	9	3	42.85	33.33
T.4	12	11	1	8.33	9.09
T.5	6	6	0	0.00	0.00
All	36	39	10	27.77	25.64

Table 11: Recall and precision figures obtained with the Microsoft Office97 summarizer — the clause-like unit case.

Text	No. of units considered important by judges	Microsoft Office97 Summarizer			
		No. of units identified	No. of units identified correctly	Recall	Precision
T.1	7	8	3	42.85	37.50
T.2	12	12	5	41.66	41.66
T.3	10	11	8	80.00	72.72
T.4	18	20	3	16.66	15.00
T.5	11	11	5	45.45	45.45
All	58	62	24	41.37	38.70

Table 12: Recall and precision figures obtained with the Microsoft Office97 summarizer — the sentence case.

Japanese, it was impossible to compare Ono's summarizer with ours. Fundamental differences concerning the assumptions that underlie Ono's work and the work described here are discussed at length in (Marcu 1997b; 1998b).

I was able to obtain one other program that summarizes English text — the program included in the Microsoft Office97 package. I ran the Microsoft summarization program on the five texts from *Scientific American* and selected the same percentages of textual units as those considered important by the judges. When I selected percentages of text that corresponded only to the clause-like units considered important by the judges, the Microsoft program recalled 27.77% of the units, with a precision of 25.64%. When I selected percentages of text that corresponded to sentences considered important by the judges, the Microsoft program recalled 41.37% of the units, with a precision of 38.70%. Tables 11 and 12 show the recall and precision figures for each of the five texts.

In order to provide a better understanding of the results in this section, I also considered a baseline algorithm that randomly selects from a text a number of units that matches the number of units that were considered important in that text by the human judges. Tables 13 and 14 show recall and precision results for the baseline, Microsoft Office97, and discourse-based summarizers, as well as the results that would have

been obtained if we had applied the score function (2) on the discourse trees that were built manually. In tables 13 and 14, I use the term "Analyst-based Summarizer" as a name for a summarizer that identifies important units on the basis of discourse trees that are manually built. The recall and precision figures associated with the baseline algorithm that selects textual units randomly represent averages of 1000 runs. The recall and precision results associated with the "Analyst-based Summarizer" in tables 13 and 14 are averages of the results shown in tables 5 and 6, and 7 and 8 respectively.

Discussion

Discussion of the summarization methodology. Throughout this paper, I used words such as "summary" and "to summarize" in a very narrow way, which often equated summarization with the process of selecting the most important units in a text. Obviously, selecting the salient units is only part of the problem that a sophisticated summarization system needs to solve, because the information encoded in the selected units must be eventually mapped into coherent abstracts. From this perspective, the experiment described here showed only that discourse structures can be reliably used to *extract* salient textual units at a level that is comparable to that of humans. However, the experiment did not show that these units are actually useful

Text	Baseline Summarizer	Microsoft Summarizer		Discourse-based Summarizer		Analyst-based Summarizer	
	Recall & Prec.	Recall	Prec.	Recall	Prec.	Recall	Prec.
T.1	12.05	50.00	33.33	100.00	100.00	75.00	75.00
T.2	38.01	55.55	50.00	55.55	62.50	61.11	78.57
T.3	36.20	42.85	33.33	42.85	37.50	57.14	57.14
T.4	18.32	8.33	9.09	50.00	42.85	45.83	64.70
T.5	23.06	0.00	0.00	50.00	50.00	58.33	43.75
All	25.7	27.77	25.64	52.77	50.00	55.55	66.66

Table 13: Recall and precision figures obtained with the baseline, Microsoft Office97, discourse-based, and analyst-based summarizers — the clause-like unit case.

Text	Baseline Summarizer	Microsoft Summarizer		Discourse-based Summarizer		Analyst-based Summarizer	
	Recall & Prec.	Recall	Prec.	Recall	Prec.	Recall	Prec.
T.1	40.12	42.85	37.50	100.00	100.00	100.00	100.00
T.2	50.02	41.66	41.66	100.00	85.71	87.50	91.30
T.3	52.12	80.00	72.72	60.00	66.66	80.00	88.88
T.4	26.91	16.66	15.00	55.55	50.00	38.88	63.63
T.5	42.31	45.45	45.45	45.45	83.83	59.09	56.52
All	38.40	41.37	38.70	65.51	67.85	67.24	78.00

Table 14: Recall and precision figures obtained with the baseline, Microsoft Office97, discourse-based, and analyst-based summarizers — the sentence case.

to create *abstracts* of document content.

The simplest way to make use of a set of textual units that are extracted according to any salience-based method is to catenate them in their order of occurrence in the original text. When I applied this procedure to the texts used in this experiment, I found that the resulting extracts read well — after all, the discourse-based summarizer selects nuclei, which represent what is most essential for the writer's purpose and which can be understood independent of their satellites. Yet, I have not carried out any readability evaluation. Although it is plausible that the extracts resulted from catenating the units that are identified as salient by a discourse structurer read better than extracts resulted from catenating units identified using lexically-based, position-based, or other heuristics, a discourse-based summarizer still needs to solve the problem of dangling references: in some cases, the selected units use anaphoric expressions to referents that were not selected. It is likely that by exploiting the relationship between discourse structure and anaphora (Fox 1987), one can provide an elegant solution to this problem. Also, by taking advantage of the rhetorical relations that hold between the selected units, which are implicitly represented in the discourse structure of a text, one is in a good position to investigate ways of mapping the selected units into coherent abstracts. Dealing with these issues is, however, beyond the scope of this paper.

The results presented here confirm the suitability of using discourse structures for summarizing texts from the *Scientific American* genre. In (Marcu 1998a), I show that the same techniques can be applied successfully for summarizing texts from the newspaper genre as well and provide a methodology for integrating the discourse-based approach to summarization with position-, title-, and semantic-similarity-based approaches.

In spite of the promising results, in some cases, the recall and precision figures obtained with the discourse-based summarizer are still far from 100%. I believe that there are two possible explanations for this: either the rhetorical parser does not construct adequate discourse trees; or the mapping from discourse structures to importance scores is too simplistic. Examining the influence of these factors on summarization requires, however, more sophisticated experiments (see Marcu (1998b) for a discussion).

Discussion of the evaluation methodology. Most of the current summarization systems have focused only on the task of extracting the salient units of a text (usually sentences or paragraphs). Although the evaluation methodology that I employed in this paper is adequate for assessing the quality of such systems, it cannot be probably used at a very large scale because it assumes the existence of a large corpus of texts whose units were manually annotated for salience. Also, it is not very clear whether this methodology can be applied in the case in which the selected units are smaller than clauses, i.e., they are, for example, concepts, noun compounds, and verbal phrases (see Boguraev and Kennedy (1997) for an approach to summarization that outputs such constructs). A prerequisite for applying the same evaluation methodology in such a case is that human judges can agree on the important concepts of a text. To my knowledge, no experiments have been carried out to investigate this. If the agreement between humans proves to be low, a different evaluation methodology will have to be sought.

5 Conclusions

I described the first experiment that shows that the concepts of rhetorical analysis and nuclearity can be used effectively for summarizing texts. The experiment suggests that discourse-based methods can account for determining the most important units in a text with a recall and precision as high as 70%. I showed how the concepts of rhetorical analysis and nuclearity can be treated algorithmically and I compared recall and precision figures of a summarization program that implements these concepts with recall and precision figures that pertain to a baseline algorithm and to a commercial system, the Microsoft Office97 summarizer. The discourse-based summarization program that I propose outperforms both the baseline and the commercial summarizer. Since the results of the discourse-based summarizer do not match yet the recall and precision figures that pertain to the manual discourse analyses, it is likely that improvements of the rhetorical parser algorithm and more sophisticated mappings from discourse structures to importance scores will result in better performance of subsequent implementations.

Acknowledgements. I am grateful to Graeme Hirst for the invaluable help he gave me during every stage of this work and to Marilyn Mantei, David Mitchell, Kevin Schlueter, and Melanie Baljko for their advice on experimental design and statistics. I am also grateful to Marzena Makuta for her help with the RST analyses and to my colleagues and friends who volunteered to act as judges in the experiments described here.

This research was conducted while I was at the University of Toronto, and was supported by the Natural Sciences and Engineering Research Council of Canada.

References

Barzilay, R., and Elhadad, M. 1997. Using lexical chains for text summarization. In *Proceedings of the ACL'97/EACL'97 Workshop on Intelligent Scalable Text Summarization*, 10–17.

Baxendale, P. 1958. Machine-made index for technical literature — an experiment. *IBM Journal of Research and Development* 2:354–361.

Boguraev, B., and Kennedy, C. 1997. Salience-based content characterisation of text documents. In *Proceedings of the ACL'97/EACL'97 Workshop on Intelligent Scalable Text Summarization*, 2–9.

Chou Hare, V., and Borchardt, K. 1984. Direct instruction of summarization skills. *Reading Research Quarterly* 20(1):62–78.

Cochran, W. 1950. The comparison of percentages in matched samples. *Biometrika* 37:256–266.

Edmundson, H. 1968. New methods in automatic extracting. *Journal of the Association for Computing Machinery* 16(2):264–285.

Fox, B. 1987. *Discourse Structure and Anaphora*. Cambridge Studies in Linguistics; 48. Cambridge University Press.

Gale, W.; Church, K.; and Yarowsky, D. 1992. Estimating upper and lower bounds on the performance of word-sense disambiguation programs. In *Proceedings of the 30th Annual Meeting of the Association for Computational Linguistics (ACL-92)*, 249–256.

Garner, R. 1982. Efficient text summarization: costs and benefits. *Journal of Educational Research* 75:275–279.

Hearst, M. 1997. TextTiling: Segmenting text into multi-paragraph subtopic passages. *Computational Linguistics* 23(1):33–64.

Hobbs, J. 1993. Summaries from structure. In *Working Notes of the Dagstuhl Seminar on Summarizing Text for Intelligent Communication*.

Hoey, M. 1991. *Patterns of Lexis in Text*. Oxford University Press.

Johnson, R. 1970. Recall of prose as a function of structural importance of linguistic units. *Journal of Verbal Learning and Verbal Behaviour* 9:12–20.

Krippendorff, K. 1980. *Content analysis: An Introduction to its Methodology*. Beverly Hills, CA: Sage Publications.

Kupiec, J.; Pedersen, J.; and Chen, F. 1995. A trainable document summarizer. In *Proceedings of the 18th ACM/SIGIR Annual Conference on Research and Development in Information Retrieval*, 68–73.

Lin, C., and Hovy, E. 1997. Identifying topics by position. In *Proceedings of the Fifth Conference on Applied Natural Language Processing (ANLP-97)*, 283–290.

Lin, C. 1995. Knowledge-based automatic topic identification. In *Proceedings of the 33rd Annual Meeting of the Association for Computational Linguistics (ACL-95)*, 308–310.

Luhn, H. 1958. The automatic creation of literature abstracts. *IBM Journal of Research and Development* 2(2):159–165.

Mani, I., and Bloedorn, E. 1997. Multi-document summarization by graph search and matching. In *Proceedings of the Fourteenth National Conference on Artificial Intelligence (AAAI-97)*, 622–628.

Mann, W., and Thompson, S. 1988. Rhetorical structure theory: Toward a functional theory of text organization. *Text* 8(3):243–281.

Marcu, D. 1996. Building up rhetorical structure trees. In *Proceedings of the Thirteenth National Conference on Artificial Intelligence (AAAI–96)*, volume 2, 1069–1074.

Marcu, D. 1997a. The rhetorical parsing of natural language texts. In *Proceedings of the 35th Annual Meeting of the Association for Computational Linguistics (ACL–97)*, 96–103.

Marcu, D. 1997b. *The rhetorical parsing, summarization, and generation of natural language texts*. Ph.D. Dissertation, Department of Computer Science, University of Toronto.

Marcu, D. 1998a. Improving summarization through rhetorical parsing tuning. In preparation.

Marcu, D. 1998b. To build text summaries of high quality, nuclearity is not sufficient. In *Working Notes of the AAAI–98 Spring Symposium on Intelligent Text Summarization*, 1–8.

Matthiessen, C., and Thompson, S. 1988. The structure of discourse and 'subordination'. In Haiman, J., and Thompson, S., eds., *Clause combining in grammar and discourse*, volume 18 of *Typological Studies in Language*. John Benjamins Publishing Company. 275–329.

Ono, K.; Sumita, K.; and Miike, S. 1994. Abstract generation based on rhetorical structure extraction. In *Proceedings of the International Conference on Computational Linguistics (Coling–94)*, 344–348.

Passonneau, R., and Litman, D. 1993. Intention-based segmentation: human reliability and correlation with linguistic cues. In *Proceedings of the 31st Annual Meeting of the Association for Computational Linguistics (ACL–93)*, 148–155.

Polanyi, L. 1993. Linguistic dimensions of text summarization. In *Working Notes of the Dagstuhl Seminar on Summarizing Text for Intelligent Communication*.

Rush, J.; Salvador, R.; and Zamora, A. 1971. Automatic abstracting and indexing. Production of indicative abstracts by application of contextual inference and syntactic coherence criteria. *Journal of American Society for Information Sciences* 22(4):260–274.

Sherrard, C. 1989. Teaching students to summarize: Applying textlinguistics. *System* 17(1).

Skorochodko, E. 1971. Adaptive method of automatic abstracting and indexing. In *Information Processing*, volume 2, 1179–1182. North-Holland Publishing Company.

Sparck Jones, K. 1993a. Summarising: analytic framework, key component, experimental method. In *Working Notes of the Dagstuhl Seminar on Summarizing Text for Intelligent Communication*.

Sparck Jones, K. 1993b. What might be in a summary? In *Information Retrieval 93: Von der Modellierung zur Anwendung*, 9–26.

Sumita, K.; Ono, K.; Chino, T.; Ukita, T.; and Amano, S. 1992. A discourse structure analyzer for Japanese text. In *Proceedings of the International Conference on Fifth Generation Computer Systems*, volume 2, 1133–1140.

Teufel, S., and Moens, M. 1997. Sentence extraction as a classification task. In *Proceedings of the ACL'97/EACL'97 Workshop on Intelligent Scalable Text Summarization*, 58–65.

Winograd, P. 1984. Strategic difficulties in summarizing texts. *Reading Research Quaterly* 19(4):404–425.

12

A Robust Practical Text Summarizer

Tomek Strzalkowski, Gees Stein, Jin Wang, and **Bowden Wise**
GE Corporate Research & Development
1 Research Circle
Niskayuna, NY 12309, USA

Abstract

We present an automated method of generating human-readable summaries from a variety of text documents including newspaper articles, business reports, government documents, even broadcast news transcripts. Our approach exploits an empirical observation that much of the written text display certain regularities of organization and style, which we call the Discourse Macro Structure (DMS). A summary is therefore created to reflect the components of a given DMS. In order to produce a coherent and readable summary we select continuous, well-formed passages from the source document and assemble them into a mini-document within a DMS template. In this paper we describe an automated summarizer that can generate both short indicative abstracts, useful for quick scanning of a list of documents, as well as longer informative digests that can serve as surrogates for the full text. The summarizer can assist the users of an information retrieval system in assessing the quality of the results returned from a search, preparing reports and memos for their customers, and even building more effective search queries.

Introduction

Perhaps the most difficult problem in designing an automatic text summarization is to define what a summary is, and how to tell a summary from a non-summary, or a good summary from a bad one. The answer depends in part upon who the summary is intended for, and in part upon what it is meant to achieve, which in large measure precludes any objective evaluation. For most of us, a summary is a brief synopsis of the content of a larger document, an abstract recounting the main points while suppressing most details. One purpose of having a summary is to quickly learn some facts, and decide what you want to do with the entire story. Therefore, one important evaluation criterion is the tradeoff between the degree of compression afforded by the summary, which may result in a decreased accuracy of information, and the time required to review that information. This interpretation is particularly useful, though it isn't the only one acceptable, in summarizing news and other report-like documents. It is also well suited for evaluating the usefulness of summarization in context of an information retrieval system, where the user needs to rapidly and efficiently review the documents returned from search for an indication of relevance and, possibly, to see which aspect of relevance is present.

Our early inspiration, and a benchmark, have been the Quick Read Summaries, posted daily off the front page of New York Times on-line edition (http://www.nytimes.com). These summaries, produced manually by NYT staff, are assembled out of passages, sentences, and sometimes sentence fragments taken from the main article with very few, if any, editorial adjustments. The effect is a collection of perfectly coherent tidbits of news: the who, the what, and when, but perhaps not why. Indeed, these summaries leave out most of the details, and cannot serve as surrogates for the full article. Yet, they allow the reader to learn some basic facts, and then to choose which stories to open.

This kind of summarization, where appropriate passages are extracted from the original text, is very efficient, and arguably effective, because it doesn't require generation of any new text, and thus lowers the risk of misinterpretation. It is also relatively easier to automate, because we only need to identify the suitable passages among the other text, a task that can be accomplished via shallow NLP and statistical techniques. Nonetheless, there are a number of serious problems to overcome before an acceptable quality summarizer can be built. For one, quantitative methods alone are generally too weak to deal adequately with the complexities of natural language text. For example, one popular approach to automated abstract generation has been to select key sentences from the original text using statistical and linguistic cues, perform some cosmetic adjustments in order to restore cohesiveness, and then output the result as a single passage, e.g., (Luhn 1958) (Paice 1990) (Brandow, Mitze, & Rau 1995) (Kupiec, Pedersen, & Chen 1995). The main advantage of this approach is that it can be applied to almost any kind of text. The main problem is that it hardly ever produces an intelligible summary: the resulting passage often lacks coherence, is hard to understand, sometimes misleading, and may be just plain incomprehensible. In fact, some studies show (cf. (Brandow, Mitze, & Rau 1995)) that simply selecting the first paragraph from a document tends to produce better summaries than a sentence-based algorithm.

A far more difficult, but arguably more "human-like" method to summarize text (with the possible exception of editorial staff of some well-known dailies) is to comprehend it in its entirety, and then write a summary "in your own words." What this amounts to, computationally, is a full linguistic analysis to extract key text components from which a summary could be built. One previously explored approach, e.g., (Ono, Sumita, & Miike 1994) (McKeown & Radev 1995), was to extract discourse structure elements and then generate the summary within this structure. In another approach, e.g., (DeJong 1982) (Lehnert 1981) pre-defined summary templates were filled with text elements obtained using information extraction techniques. Marcu (Marcu 1997a) uses rhetorical structure analysis to guide the selection of text segments for the summary; similarly Teufel and Moens (Teufel & Moens 1997) analyze argumentative structure of discourse to extract appropriate sentences. While these approaches can produce very good results, they are yet to be demonstrated in a practical system applied to a reasonable size domain. The main difficulty is the lack of an efficient and reliable method of computing the required discourse structure.

The approach we adopted in our work falls somewhere between these two extremes, although philosophically we are closer to NYT cut-and-paste editors. We overcome the shortcomings of sentence-based summarization by working on paragraph level instead. Paragraphs are generally self-contained units, more so than single sentences, and their relationships with the surrounding text are somewhat easier to trace. This notion has been explored by Cornell's group (Salton *et al.* 1994) to design a summarizer that traces inter-paragraph relationships and selects the "best connected" paragraphs for the summary. Like in Cornell's system, our summaries are made up of paragraphs taken out of the original text. In addition, in order to obtain more

coherent summaries, we impose some fundamental discourse constraints on the generation process, but avoid a full discourse analysis.

We would like to note at this point that the summarization algorithm, as described in detail later in this chapter, does not explicitly depend on nor indeed require the input text that is pre-segmented into paragraphs. In general, any length passages can be used, although this choice will impact the complexity of the solution. Lifting well-defined paragraphs from a document and then recombining them into a summary is relatively more straightforward than recombining other text units. In some situations there may be little choice, however. For example, summarizing documents with long, elaborate paragraphs, such as transcripts of Congressional proceedings, may be best done at the sentence level; for texts where there is no structure at all, as in a closed-captioned stream in broadcast television, fixed word-count passages can be used. We will return to this point later when we present the full summarization algorithm.

It has been observed, eg., (Rino & Scott 1994), (Weissberg & Buker 1990), that certain types of texts, such as news articles, technical reports, research papers, etc., conform to a set of style and organization constraints, called the Discourse Macro Structure (DMS) which help the author to achieve a desired communication effect. News reports, for example, tend to be built hierarchically out of components which fall roughly into one of the two categories: the what's-the-news category, and the optional background category. The background, if present, supplies the context necessary to understand the central story, or to make a follow up story self-contained. This organization is often reflected in the summary, as illustrated in the example below from NYT 10/15/97, where the highlighted portion provides the background for the main news:

SPIES JUST WOULDN'T COME IN FROM COLD WAR, FILES SHOW

Terry Squillacote was a Pentagon lawyer who hated her job. Kurt Stand was a union leader with an aging beatnik's slouch. Jim Clark was a lonely private investigator. [A 200-page affidavit filed last week by] the Federal Bureau of Investigation says the three were out-of-work spies for East Germany. And after that state withered away, it says, they desperately reached out for anyone who might want them as secret agents.

In this example, the two passages are non-consecutive paragraphs in the original text; the string in the square brackets at the opening of the second passage has been omitted in the summary. Here the human summarizer's actions appear relatively straightforward, and it would not be difficult to propose an algorithmic method to do the same. This may go as follows:

1. Choose a DMS template for the summary; e.g., Background+News.

2. Select appropriate passages from the original text and fill the DMS template.

3. Assemble the summary in the desired order; delete extraneous words.

It is worth noting here that the background-context passage is critical for understanding of this summary, but as such provides essentially no relevant information except for the names of the people involved. Incidentally, this is precisely the information required to make the summary self-contained, if for no other reason than to supply the antecedents to the anaphors in the main passage (*the three, they*).

There is another important feature of news-like texts which the above algorithm exploits, albeit indirectly, and that is their hierarchical organization. In other words, we are expecting to find a few passages in Step 2 that would make an acceptable summary, rather than a scattering of information bits, as one may expect in a novel. Moreover, if such a set of summary passages exist, and if any of them require background or context information to go along with it, the latter may be expected to be nearby, most likely in an adjoining paragraph. We can therefore simplify the above algorithm by adding that the Background and News passages are preferably consecutive paragraphs. This modification reduces Step 3 to mere cosmetics.[1]

At this point we may want to pause again and note that the summarization algorithm is not specifically tailored to work with news-like documents, and we can, in principle, summarize any type of text. However, we have thus far made no attempt to handle any more elaborate DMSs than the simple hierarchical background+news template. Therefore, while we may be able to obtain a summary of a scientific paper, or even a novel, it is unlikely to be useful for the purpose such summaries are usually generated, unless appropriate DMS models are in place.

---

[1]Obviously, this would not work for the NYT summary above since the two passages are not consecutive in the original document, and to get them would require a coreference tracking system. However, picking up a background passage adjacent to the main news passage would very likely produce a good summary as well.

It is, of course, no coincidence that we have selected to implement a news summarizer as an initial instantiation of our approach. Routing, retrieval and delivery of news and other factual documents is a commercially important application area (e.g., news on demand, market intelligence), and accurate summaries help users to digest and re-use information more rapidly thus increasing their productivity.

Our program has been tested on a variety of news-like documents, including Associated Press news-wire messages, articles from the New York Times, The Wall Street Journal, Financial Times, San Jose Mercury, as well as documents from the Federal Register, and the Congressional Record. The summarizer is domain independent, and it can be easily adapted to most European languages. It is also very robust: we used it to derive summaries of thousands of documents returned by an information retrieval system.

The summarizer can work in two modes: generic and topical. In the generic mode, it simply summarizes the main points of the original document. In the topical mode, it takes a user supplied statement of interest, a topic, and derives a summary related to this topic. A topical summary is thus usually different than the generic summary of the same document. The summarizer can produce both indicative and informative summaries. An indicative summary, typically 5-10% of the original text, is when there is just enough material retained from the original document to indicate its content. An informative summary, on the other hand, typically 20-30% of the text, retains all the relevant facts that a user may need from the original document, that is, it serves as a condensed surrogate, a digest.

Thus far there has been only one systematic multi-site evaluation of summarization approaches conducted, in early 1998, organized by U.S. DARPA[2] in the tradition of Message Understanding Conferences (MUC) (DAR 1993) and Text Retrieval Conferences (TREC) (Harman 1997a), which have proven successful in stimulating research in their respective areas: information extraction and information retrieval. The summarization evaluation focused on content representativeness of indicative summaries and comprehensiveness of informative summaries. Other factors affecting the quality of summaries, such as brevity, readability, and usefulness were evaluated indirectly, as parameters of the main scores.

The indicative summaries were scored for relevance to pre-selected topics and compared to the classification of respective full documents. In this

---

[2](The U.S.) Defense Advanced Research Projects Agency

evaluation, a summary was considered successful if it preserved the original document's relevance or non-relevance to a topic. Moreover, the recall and precision scores were normalized by the length of the summary (in words) relative to the length of the original document, as well as by the clock time taken by the evaluators to reach their topic relevance decisions. The first normalization measured the degree of content compression provided by the summaries, while the second normalization was intended to gauge their readability. The results showed a strong correlation between these two measures, which may indicate that readability was in fact equated with meaningfulness, that is, hard to read summaries were quickly judged non-relevant.

The informative summaries were scored for their ability to provide answers to *who, what, when, how,* etc. questions about the topics. These questions were unknown to the developers, so systems could not directly extract facts to satisfy them. Again, scores were normalized for summary length, but no time normalization was used. This evaluation was done on a significantly smaller scale than for the indicative summaries, simply because scoring for question answering was more time consuming for the human judges than categorization decisions. This evaluation could probably be recast as categorization problem, if we only assumed that the questions in the test were the topics, and that a summary needs to be relevant to multiple topics.

Early results from these evaluations indicate that the summaries generated using our DMS method offer an excellent tradeoff between time/length and accuracy. Our summaries tend to be shorter and contain less extraneous material than those obtained using different methods. This is further confirmed by the favorable responses we received from the users.

A separate experimental study[3] was conducted to find out how the summaries would be judged independently of their task-based purpose. A random subset of 30 texts along with their corresponding summaries, were selected from among those supplied by all evaluation participants in the categorization task. Four human assessors were asked to score summaries giving each either a 'pass' or a 'fail', and specifying the main problem for the failed summaries. The main result of this exercise was that the summaries considered acceptable for the categorization task were generally not good enough for these assessors, as they seemed to expect more from a summary than what it takes to successfully cat-

egorize a document. Specifically, as many as 50% to 75% of summaries were found lacking either because of missing some important details, or containing superfluous text, or because of overall incoherence. While we are unclear about the significance of this result, it seems to underscore the fact that summaries created for one purpose may not be useful or even acceptable for another. Clearly, the summaries generated by our present system will not satisfy everyone, nonetheless we believe they represent a solid, if modest, advance in the state of the art.

In the following sections we describe the details of the summarizer design and then discuss its possible uses in an information retrieval system.

Discourse macro structure of a text

Empirical studies show that certain types of texts conform to relatively simple macro discourse structures. (Rino & Scott 1994), for instance, has shown that both physics papers and abstracts align closely with the *Introduction-Methodology-Results-Discussion-Conclusion* macro structure. It is likely that other scientific and technical texts will also conform to this or similar structure, since this is exactly the structure suggested in technical writing guidebooks, e.g. (Weissberg & Buker 1990). One observation to make here is that a proper summary or an abstract should reflect the DMS of the original document. On the other hand, we need to note that a summary can be given a different DMS, and this choice would reflect our interpretation of the original text. A scientific paper, for example, can be treated as a piece of news, and serve as a basis of an un-scientific summary.

Clearly, different types of text will display different macro structures. For news-like texts, this structure appears quite simple: *Background+What-Is-The-News*. The *Background* section covers previous events and supplies the context necessary to understand the main story. The *Background* section is optional: when the background is a common knowledge or is implied in the main news section, it can, and usually is omitted. The *What-Is-The-News* section covers the new developments and the new facts that make the news. Both sections, which do not have to occupy continuous regions of text, can be identified by a number of features, such as content words, verb tense, proper names, etc.

We make no claims that this macro-structure is the only one possible, nor that it accounts for a majority of news-like summaries. To establish this we would need to conduct further empirical studies. A tentative examination of various news articles and their abstracts appears to support our hypothesis.

---

[3]This study has been organized by Mike Chrzanowski, one of the coordinators of the summarization evaluation workshop.

Furthermore, this simple DMS is quite effective in producing usable summaries for nearly any type of text, which only underscores the fact that news-style organization of information is very efficient. Therefore, in designing our summarizer we selected the news DMS to be the implicit default organization, a set of assumptions underlying the summarization process. We also believe that the news DMS subsumes other, more elaborate summary structures, thus making news-style summarization the most basic one. In fact, the argument structure of a typical news piece appears predominantly linear and localized, which definitely helps faster comprehension and digestion of information, a primary goal of commercial news services. In order to construct specialized summarizers, e.g., for scientific or legal texts where the argument structure tends to be more complex, one can build on top of the current summarizer, simply by supplying a mechanism to deal with richer DMSs.

Extracting text for a summary

Each component of a summary DMS needs to be instantiated by one or more passages extracted from the original text. These can be paragraphs, paragraph parts, sentences, or even sentence fragments. The selection of sub-sentential elements normally requires advanced information extraction techniques (DAR 1993) (DAR 1996) or statistical learning methods (Strzalkowski & Wang 1996), and could substantially increase the complexity of a summarizer. At present, our summarizer works at the paragraph level and builds the summary out of either the whole paragraphs, or continuous proper subpassages, which are simply the paragraphs with some front or back material deleted.

As we noted before, paragraph-level summarization has various merits, e.g., versus sentence-based approaches, but it can also be problematic at times. For example, what to do if one needs to summarize a document with very long paragraphs? Or with no paragraphs at all? Or, for that matter, with no structure whatsoever, not even punctuations?

A well thought out paragraph structure organizes information within a text and can be exploited for summarization. Paragraphs are reasonably self-contained, they usually address a single thought or issue, and their connections with other parts of text are relatively straightforward, most of the time. In many texts, including transcripts of spoken discourse, there may be no paragraph structure, and if an automated speech recognition is used, there could be no sentences boundaries either. When paragraph breaks cannot be detected at expected intervals, content-based segmentation techniques may be applicable, e.g., Hearst's Text-Tiling (Hearst 1997).

On the other hand, we may argue that essentially any length *segments* of text can be used so long as one could figure out a way to reconnect them into paragraph-like passages even if their boundaries were somewhat off. This is actually not unlike dealing with the texts with very fine grained paragraphs, as is often the case with news-wire articles. For such texts, in order to obtain an appropriate level of chunking, some paragraphs need to be reconnected into longer passages. This may be achieved by tracking co-references and other text cohesiveness devices, and their choice will depend upon the initial segmentation we work up from.

Once the segmentation question is settled, the next task is to select the passages from which we can build our summary. Clearly, different sets of criteria will apply depending upon which element of the summary DMS we are trying to fill. Since our focus in this paper is on news summarization, we will only consider the news DMS.

Selecting the main news sections

In this section we consider several criteria (or metrics) that can be used in selecting passages for the News segment of the summary DMS. Many of these criteria were used in one or another form by other researchers but this is probably the first time all of them are being used in concert. The list below is not meant to be exhaustive, and not all of the items discussed are utilized in the current summarizer, while others have evolved substantially based on initial evaluation results. Moreover, some of these metrics are more "practical" than others, e.g., the use of text collection statistics for term weighting may limit usability of a summarizer to situations where such statistics are available or can be computed. In designing our summarizer we tried to avoid reliance on such "external" knowledge sources so that the system could be as generally applicable and as robust as possible.

The following list discusses the passage selection criteria in general. Further implementation details will be given in the next section where we present the final summarization algorithm. The general strategy is to compute a score for each passage, using a combination of partial scores associated with each metric. This may look like the following:

$$score(passage) = \frac{1}{F(|l - t|)} \bullet \sum_h w_h \bullet S_h$$

where S_h is a partial score calculated using metric h; w_h is the weight reflecting how effective this metric is in general; l is the length of the segment, t is a target length of the summary, and F is a normalization function.

In the end, all passages, as well as their combinations of two, three, etc., will be ranked and the highest ranking passage or group becomes the summary.

PASSAGE SELECTION CRITERIA:

1. Words and phrases frequently occurring in a text are likely to be indicative of content, especially if such words or phrases do not occur often elsewhere. A weighted frequency score, akin of *tf*idf* can be used to derive term weights, and subsequently passage scores. Here, *idf* stands for the inverted document frequency of a term with respect to some representative control collection.[4] Note that this requires knowledge of statistical distribution of words and phrases within a larger body of like texts, e.g., a sizable collection of recent news articles. These statistics generally do not carry well from domain to domain or even from one time period to next.[5] Therefore, the use of collection-level information should be limited to information retrieval applications, where documents retrieved from a large text database need to be summarized for presentation to the user. Collection statistics are not used in the present version of our summarizer.

2. Title of a text is often strongly related to its content. Therefore, words and phrases from the title are considered as important indicators of content concentration within a document. Of course stopwords can and should be removed. This criterion works quite well for news, again thanks to their factual, focused style. Titles are less useful for summarizing complex, multi-threaded documents, such as scientific papers, and may be right off misleading for certain kinds of commentaries or editorials. While there may be no obvious way to tell a factual title from an anecdotal one, this is not necessarily a problem if other passage selection criteria are used at the same time. In general, we believe using the title rarely hurts, and often is all you really need.

3. Noun phrases occurring in the opening sentences of multiple paragraphs, or those used in the subject phrases or even as the first non-trivial phrase in multiple sentences, tend to refer to entities that are central to text content. Passages containing such phrases will receive additional scores for each occurrence. Note that multiple occurrences of the same term should not have a strong impact on the score lest we risk including redundant material, especially when a group of paragraphs is evaluated. This criterion complements the title-based scoring, and enables the summarizer to deal robustly with anectotal titles.

4. Words and phrases occurring in only some paragraphs are weighted more highly than those scattered across the entire document, because such terms are more likely to be discriminators of summary passages. This scoring makes sense only if applied to terms already considered as strong content indicators (cf. steps 1-3 above). Therefore, in addition to other scores, all terms in a passage (except for the common stopwords, such as articles, prepositions, pronouns, etc.) are weight-ranked by a passage-level formula *tfp*ipf*, where *tfp* is the term's frequency within a paragraph, and *ipf* is an inverted passage frequency. The *ipf* score is best interpreted as N/pf, where pf is the number of passages containing the term and N is the total number of passages within the document.[6] This criterion is not currently implemented in our summarizer.

5. Paragraphs that are closer to the beginning of a news report tend to be more content-loaded than those towards the end. This ordering may be reversed in editorial-like texts. Therefore, the position of each passage carries an additional score. We may note here that position scoring is appropriate in generic summarization, but arguably not in topic-based summarization, where themes which are not necessarily central to the original text need to be summarized. In generic summarization this score is set up so that the summary-worthiness of paragraphs is decreasing as we read deeper into the text. In many cases, a summarizer does not need to look beyond the first 6-7 paragraphs. In the initial version of our summarizer, this criterion produced a score supplement that was used to break ties if more than one contender summary emerged at the top of the passage ranking list. In the subsequent versions, it

---

[4] *tf* is term frequency within a document.

[5] The temporal aspect of this external corpus is very important in dealing with news documents. To give an example: a term *OJ Simpson* relatively rare in today's news, was commonplace a year ago, which made it a rather poor content discriminator.

[6] We need to keep in mind that passages could be single paragraphs, multiple paragraphs, or some other combinations.

has been replaced by a score supplement for summaries containing either the first or the second paragraph of a document. This way, the summarizer naturally defaults to the opening segment of a document if no other information is available to guide the passage selection.

6. Proper names of people, places, organizations, etc., various acronyms, numerical amounts, etc. are likely to refer to factual data that can improve the informativeness of a summary. At present we add score supplements to passages containing names or numbers, if the summary is requested to be an informative digest (approx. 30% of the original).

7. Certain cue phrases explicitly suggest that what follows is in fact a summary or the main point of an article. Passages containing such cues should therefore be preferred for selection. Examples of summary cue phrases include: "In summary", "To sum up", "The point is", etc. In general, such heuristics are of little use, except in summarizing editorials or commentaries, where the usual top-down flow of arguments is frequently reversed. They are not at present implemented in our summarizer.

Looking at the above points, particularly 1 through 4, it is easy to see that the process of passage selection is closely resembling query-based document retrieval. The "documents" here are the passages (paragraphs), and the "query" is a set of words and phrases collected from the title and from across the document. This analogy, while not entirely accurate, is nonetheless a useful one since other proven IR techniques may be applicable to summarization. Specifically, automatic query expansion techniques discussed later in this chapter may benefit the passage search process. We are currently experimenting with such options.

Selecting the background section

The background section supplies information that makes the summary self-contained. A passage selected from a document may have significant links, both explicit and implicit, to the surrounding context, which if severed are likely to render the passage uncomprehensible, or even misleading. For example, the following passage would make a rather poor summary: we have no idea *what* happened, which is clearly indicated by outgoing anaphoric links (*this, the action*). And who is *Redman*? Is this important to know what he says?

> "Once again this demonstrates the substantial influence Iran holds over terrorist kidnapers," Redman said, adding that it is not yet clear what prompted Iran to take the action it did.

Adding a background paragraph improves things substantially. We still don't know much about Redman, but we get a far more informative summary. Note that both outgoing anaphors are now covered.

> Both the French and Iranian governments acknowledged the Iranian role in the release of the three French hostages, Jean-Paul Kauffmann, Marcel Carton and Marcel Fontaine.

> "Once again this demonstrates the substantial influence Iran holds over terrorist kidnapers," Redman said, adding that it is not yet clear what prompted Iran to take the action it did.

So when do we need a background/context passage? Below we list some criteria that we have considered.

BACKGROUND PASSAGE CRITERIA:

1. One indication that background information may be needed is the presence of significant outgoing references, such as anaphors. For example, when the main content-bearing passage selected for the summary begins with, say, "*He* also said that..." or "In the report released Monday, FBI said that *the three* were ...", or "Once again *this* demonstrates ...", we may need to supply an extra passage to anchor the anaphors. In order to minimize the possibility of confusion with a local (intra-passage) anaphor, we require that a pronoun or a definite noun phrase occur within first N (=6) words of the referring passage. This very simplistic strategy can be improved by providing a limited structural analysis of the first sentence to delineate leading prepositional phrases, appositives, and also to exclude from consideration certain constructs such as definites with defining subordinates.

2. Another way to deal with dangling references is to resolve them, for instance by replacing the pronoun with the name, e.g., "President Clinton". This is acceptable only if there is no other background information required from the anchoring passage. Indeed, one disadvantage of adding a background passage is that except for supplying antecedents to anaphors, it may add nothing useful to the summary, while obviously increasing its length. We may also combine criteria 1 and 2, allowing more passages to qualify as a background,

thus gaining flexibility to select the right combination. At this time, our summarizer does no explicit co-reference resolution.

3. Partial names, particularly last names of people, create an effect similar to anaphors, and therefore require an anchoring passage where the name is fully defined or otherwise introduced. An exception should be made for well-known and universally recognizable names, although its unclear how this can be achieved without some knowledge source, at least a corpus of like documents.

4. Passages may also be connected via rhetorical and other discourse relations. Some of these relations are made explicit by the use of cohesive markers such as conjunctions and adverbials (e.g., *Furthermore, As a result, But, Also*), and disregarding them may render the summary unreadable or unacceptable the same way unresolved anaphors can. If a full discourse analysis is an unpalatable option, we can resort, again, to supplying a background/context passage. Here, the risk of selecting a wrong passage is somewhat greater than with anaphors, although not for news-like texts, thanks to their predominantly linear argument structure. In our summarizer we cover a few overt cohesive links and treat them at par with anaphors.

5. An easy way to deal with cohesive links is to simply get rid of them. If your summary begins with *But, And, ...* or contains *also, therefore, ...* within the first few words, just remove them, adjust the uppercase accordingly, and the summary is bound to improve. It may in fact be perfect. We use this little trick regularly in our summarizer.

6. Once we know that a background passage is needed to complete a summary, how do we go about finding it? In most cases the immediately preceding passage/paragraph is selected. In other cases, dates and verb tenses may help to identify background information. Specifically, a tense shift from present to past, or the use of certain temporal adverbs, e.g., "now", "before", "used to", etc., often indicate the changing temporal perspective in the narrative.

7. Arguably, the proper way to supply the context is to follow the rhetorical structure of a discourse, e.g., (Marcu 1997b). This is conditioned upon one's ability to compute the latter efficiently and accurately. While people can do these things really well (cf. NYT summaries), computer's performance still leaves much to be desired, so for practical reasons we are better off without, at least for now.

8. Experiments performed at Cornell (Salton *et al.* 1994) showed that passages within a long document display varying degrees of interconnection in terms of shared vocabulary, which includes the choice of words and word forms. They noticed that background information sections tend to stand out as a relatively isolated cluster. This metric is not implemented in the current version of the summarizer, but it may be required for processing structurally complex documents, such as editorials or patent applications.

Generating the summary

The process of assembling DMS components into a summary depends upon the complexity of the discourse structure itself. For news or even for scientific texts, it may be just a matter of concatenating components together with a little of "cohesiveness glue", which may include deleting some obstructing sentences, expanding acronyms, adjusting verb forms, etc. In a highly specialized domain (e.g., court rulings) the final assembly may be guided by a very detailed pattern or a script that conforms to specific style and content requirements.

Below we present a 10-step algorithm for generating summaries of news-like texts. This is the algorithm underlying our current summarizer. The reader may notice that there is no explicit provision for dealing with DMS structures here. Indeed, the basic Background+News summary pattern has been tightly integrated into the passage selection and weighting process. This obviously streamlines the summarization process, but it also reflects the notion that news-style summarization is in many ways basic and subsumes other more complex summarization requirements.

THE GENERALIZED SUMMARIZATION ALGORITHM

s0: Segment text into passages. Use any available handles, including indentation, SGML, empty lines, sentence ends, etc. If no paragraph or sentence structure is available, use approximately equal size chunks.

s1: Build a paragraph-search query out of the content words, phrases and other terms found in the title, a user-supplied topic description (if available), as well as the terms occurring frequently in the text.

s2: Reconnect adjacent passages that display strong cohesiveness by one-way *background links*, using handles such as outgoing anaphors and other backward references. A background link from passage $N+1$ to passage N means that if passage $N+1$ is selected for a summary, passage N must also be selected. Link consecutive passages until all references are covered.

s3: Score all passages, including the linked groups with respect to the paragraph-search query. Assign a point for each co-occurring term. The goal is to maximize the overlap, so multiple occurrences of the same term do not increase the score.

s4: Normalize passage scores by their length, taking into account the desired target length of the summary. The goal is to keep summary length as close to the target length as possible. The weighting formula is designed so that small deviations from the target length are acceptable, but large deviations will rapidly decrease the passage score. The exact formulation of this scheme depends upon the desired tradeoff between summary length and content. The following is the basic formula for scoring passage P of length l against the passage-search query Q and the target summary length of t, as used in current version of our summarizer:

$$NormScore(P,Q) = \frac{RawScore(P,Q)}{\sqrt{\frac{|l-t|}{t} + 1}}$$

where:

$$RawScore(P,Q) = \sum_{q \in Q} weight(q,P) + prem(P)$$

with sum over unique content terms q, and

$$weight(q,P) = \begin{cases} 1 & \text{if } q \in P \\ 0 & \text{otherwise} \end{cases}$$

with $prem(P)$ as a cummulative non-content based score premium (cf s7).

s5: Discard all passages with length in excess of 1.5 times the target length. This reduces the number of passage combinations the summarizer has to consider, thus improving its efficiency. The decision whether to use this condition depends upon our tolerance to length variability. In extreme cases, to prevent obtaining empty summaries, the summarizer will default to the first paragraph of the original text.

s6: Combine passages into groups of 2 or more based on their content, composition and length. The goal is to maximize the score, while keeping the length as close to the target length as possible. Any combination of passages is allowed, including non-consecutive passages, although the original ordering of passages is retained. If a passage attached to another through a background link is included into a group, the other passage must also be included, and this rule is applied recursively. We need to note that the background links work only one way: a passage which is a background for another passage, may stand on its own if selected into a candidate summary.

s7: Recalculate scores for all newly created groups. This is necessary, and cannot be obtained as a sum of scores because of possible term repetitions. Again, discard any passage groups longer than 1.5 times the target length. Add premium scores to groups based on the inverse degree of text discontinuity measured as a total amount of elided text material between the passages within a group. Add other premiums as applicable.

s8: Rank passage groups by score. All groups become candidate summaries.

s9: Repeat steps s6 through s8 until there is no change in top-scoring passage group through 2 consecutive iterations. Select the top scoring passage or passage group as the final summary.

Implementation and evaluation

The summarizer has been implemented in C++ with a Java interface as a demonstration system, primarily for news summarization. At this time it can run in both batch and interactive modes under Solaris, and it can also be accessed via Web using a Java compatible browser. A version of the summarizer has been integrated into an application called Query Expansion Tool that allows for interactive expansion of search queries in an Information Retrieval system.

Figure 1 shows the interface to the interactive version of the summarizer, called the SummarizerTool. The interface allows the user to set a few critical parameters of the summarization process:

1. Generic vs Topical summary: to obtain a topical summary, the user can type a topic description into appropriate window and push the *Use the Topic* button.

2. Indicative vs. Informative summary: at this time the distinction reflects SUMMAC evaluation categories: classification (IR) vs. question-answering (QA).

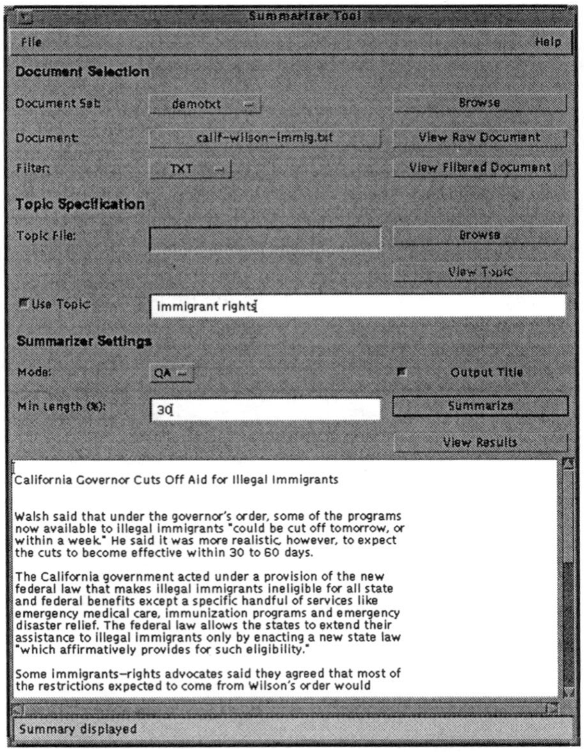

Figure 1: SummarizerTool interface

3. Select desired length of the summary: this is specified as a percentage of the length of the original text.

In general we are quite pleased with the summarizer performance. This is also reflected by the results of the summarization evaluation conference conducted earlier this year (Firmin & Sundheim 1998), where our summarizer was consistently ranked among the top systems. We participated in all three evaluation categories, which included two classes of indicative summaries (generic and topical), and a category of informative summaries. As we explained earlier, the indicative summaries were judged for source compression and the ability to preserve the critical portion of the content. The informative summaries, on the other hand, were primarily judged for their "completeness" of coverage of a topic: who, where, when, etc. Informative summaries were generated using the same general algorithm with two modifications. First, the expected summary length was set at 30% of the original, following an observation by the conference organizers while evaluating human generated summaries. Second, since the completeness of an informative summary was judged on the basis of its containing satisfactory answers to questions which were not part

of the topic specification, we added extra scores to passages containing possible answers: proper names (who, where) and numerics (when, how much). Finally, we note that the test data used for evaluation, while generally of news-like genre, varied greatly in content, style and the subject matter, therefore domain-independence was critical.

In the remainder of this section we present several summaries that illustrate both the robustness and limitations of the current algorithm.

The first example is a generic indicative 5% summary generated from an article appearing in the New York Times on-line edition, followed by a 10% summary of the same article.[7] Please note how the summarizer ranks the passages within the available space. For an easy reference, paragraphs are numbered in the order they appear in the original text.

TITLE: Mrs. Clinton Says U.S. Needs 'Ways That Value Families'
SUMMARY TYPE: indicative
TARGET LENGTH: 5%
TOPIC: none

(6) The United States, Mrs. Clinton said, must become "a nation that doesn't just talk about family values but acts in ways that values families."

SUMMARY TYPE: indicative
TARGET LENGTH: 10%
TOPIC: none

(1) CHICAGO – Stern and focused, planted behind the lectern, eschewing any attempt to top Elizabeth Hanford Dole in the charm sweepstakes, Hillary Rodham Clinton stuck to her guns on Tuesday night at the Democratic convention, playing the teacher and not the television personality in her much-anticipated appearance before the delegates gathered to renominate her husband.

(6) The United States, Mrs. Clinton said, must become "a nation that doesn't just talk about family values but acts in ways that values families."

The second example shows a longer summary of another NYT article. The reader may note that the three consecutive paragraphs are tied together by the anaphoric background links, as highlighted in text.

TITLE: Jury Awards $5.5 Million in ABC Case
SUMMARY TYPE: indicative
TARGET LENGTH: 15%
TOPIC: none

(1) Federal jury in Greensboro, N.C., on Wednesday awarded a supermarket chain more than $5.5 million in punitive damages from ABC and two of its employees in a closely watched media case that focused on the propriety of widely used television news techniques like hidden cameras and undercover reporters.

---

[7]Original texts can be found in the appendix.

(2) Last month, *the same panel* ordered ABC to pay $1,400 in actual damages to the chain, Food Lion, after finding that network producers had trespassed and committed fraud when researching a "Primetime Live" segment in 1992 that accused the company of selling spoiled meat.

(3) *The case* has attracted broad attention in media and legal circles because it is a leading example of a new trend in lawsuits against networks and television news magazines. Although Food Lion officials disputed the accuracy of the ABC report, they did not sue for libel. Rather, they accused ABC of fraud because it used techniques like having producers submit fake resumes to get jobs in the meat department of company stores, and then used hidden cameras to film there.

The above summary can be compared with a topical summary of the same article. First we may note that both summaries are disjoint. We also note also that the first paragraph of the topical summary has a dangling anaphor (*the segment*) which has been missed by the summarizer because it appears too late in the sentence. This problem could be fixed if we considered the phrase structure rather than words when calculating the offset for the anaphor.

SUMMARY TYPE: indicative
TARGET LENGTH: 15%
TOPIC: Hidden cameras used in news reporting

(4) Roone Arledge, the president of ABC News, defended the methods used to report the segment and said ABC would appeal the verdict.

(5) "*They* could never contest the truth" of the broadcast, Arledge said. "These people were doing awful things in these stores."

(6) Wednesday's verdict was only the second time punitive damages had been meted out by a jury in a hidden-camera case. It was the first time punitive damages had been awarded against producers of such a segment, said Neville L. Johnson, a lawyer in Los Angeles who has filed numerous hidden-camera cases against the major networks.

(7) Many journalists argue that hidden cameras and other undercover reporting techniques have long been necessary tools for exposing vital issues of public policy and health. But many media experts say television producers have overused them in recent years in a push to create splashy shows and bolster ratings. The jurors, those experts added, may have been lashing out at what they perceived as undisciplined and overly aggressive news organizations.

Finally, we show what was intended as an informative summary of yet another NYT article. This summary is significantly longer than others, and, we may note, is somewhat rough on the edges. For example, the last paragraph is somewhat disconnected from the others, and the anaphor in the second to last paragraph (*the offer*) is left dangling.[8]

TITLE: U.S. Buyer of Russian Uranium Said to Put Profits Before Security
SUMMARY TYPE: informative
TARGET LENGTH: 25%
TOPIC: nuclear nonproliferation

---

[8]In spite of the number mismatch, this anaphor is likely assumed to refer to the *repeated requests* in the first paragraph, which is reasonably accurate, by chance.

(1) In a postscript to the Cold War, the American government-owned corporation that is charged with reselling much of Russia's military stockpile of uranium as civilian nuclear reactor fuel turned down repeated requests this year to buy material sufficient to build 400 Hiroshima-size bombs.

(2) The incident raises the question of whether the corporation, the U.S. Enrichment Corp., put its own financial interest ahead of the national-security goal of preventing weapons-grade uranium from falling into the hands of terrorists or rogue states.

(7) The corporation has thus far taken delivery from Russia of reactor fuel derived from 13 tons of bomb-grade uranium. "The nonproliferation objectives of the agreement are being achieved," a spokesman for the Enrichment Corp. said.

(8) But since the beginning of the program, skeptics have questioned the wisdom of designating the Enrichment Corp. as Washington's "executive agent" in managing the deal with Russia's Ministry of Atomic Energy, or MINATOM.

(19) Domenici, chairman of the energy subcommittee of the Senate Appropriations Committee, which is shepherding the privatization plan through Congress, was never informed of the offer by the administration. After learning of the rebuff to the Russians, he wrote to Curtis asking that the Enrichment Corp. "be immediately replaced as executive agent" and warning that "under no circumstances should the sale of the USEC proceed until this matter is resolved." Once Domenici entered the fray, the administration changed its tune.

(20) Curtis sent a letter to Domenici stating that all the problems blocking acceptance of the extra six tons had been solved. People close to the administration said that the Enrichment Corp. has now been advised to buy the full 18-ton shipment in 1997. Moreover, Curtis quickly convened a new committee to monitor the Enrichment Corp. for signs of foot-dragging.

Applications in Information Retrieval

Information retrieval (IR) is a task of selecting documents from a database in response to a user's query, and ranking these documents according to relevance. Document summarization has various applications in information retrieval: from content-indicative quick-read summaries supplied along with the titles returned from search, to informative summaries providing digests of requested information, to cross-document summaries correlating aspects of relevant information and organizing the search results for the user. Anyone who has ever tried a web search engine would probably appreciate the difference between having good summaries of the returned documents and having no summaries, or for that matter, having useless or misleading summaries. Unfortunately, the latter is too often the case. The summarizer described in the preceding sections goes some way to change that, we hope, but many challenges still remain, including summarization of non-news documents, multi-modal documents (such as web pages), and groups of documents covering one or more topics. We are actively pursuing research into these problems.

In this section we would like to discuss briefly a different, perhaps unorthodox use of summarization in information retrieval, that is, as a helper application in building effective information need statements for an automated document search system. The premise is quite simple: use the initial user's statement of information need to sample the database for documents, summarize the returned documents topically, then add selected summaries to the initial statement to make it richer and more specific. For expository purposes we make a distinction here between the user's statement, or *topic*, usually an English phrase, sentence, or a short paragraph, and the *search query*, which is the search system internal representation of the topic, usually a list of weighted terms that correspond to the words used in the topic though not necessarily in any straightforward way.

Building effective topic descriptions

We have been experimenting with both manual and automatic techniques of topic expansion, under the assumption that an appropriately expanded topic would translate into a more effective search query than the original user-supplied statement would, *independently of any particular search strategy used*. This approach differs from most query modification techniques used in IR because it attempts to reformulate the user initial statement rather than the search system's internal representation of it, as relevance feedback techniques do.[9] Our goal has been to devise a method for topic expansion such that: (1) the performance of any system using the expanded topics would be significantly better than when the same system is run using unexpanded topics, and (2) the expansion method, originally manual or human-assisted, could be eventually automated so as to become transparent to a non-expert user. Note that the first of the above requirements effectively calls for a free text, but highly precise and exhaustive description of user's information need, something that an average user may not be willing or able to do.

One way to view topic expansion is to make the topics resemble more closely the documents they are expected to retrieve. This may include their content as well as composition, style, language type, etc. If the topic were to resemble a "typical" relevant document, then everything about this topic would become valid search criteria: words, collocations, phrases, various relationships, etc. Unfortunately, user search statements rarely are this specific,

instead they are likely to be statements specifying semantic criteria of relevance. This means that except for the semantic or conceptual resemblance (which we cannot model very well as yet) much of the appearance of the topic (which we can model reasonably well) may be, and often is, quite misleading for search purposes.

In our early experiments, topics were expanded by pasting in entire sentences, paragraphs, and other passages directly from the sample retrieved documents. Those were the manually selected passages that captured some important aspect of relevance, the very material that appeared to make a text relevant to the topic. In order to make this process efficient, we first performed a search with the original, un-expanded topics, and then used top 10 or 20 returned documents for expansion. These sampled documents were not judged for relevancy, nor assumed relevant; instead, they were scanned for passages that could be added to the topic. In fact, the presence of such expansion text in otherwise non-relevant documents underscored the inherent limitations of distribution-based term reweighting used in relevance feedback.

These initial experiments indicated that topics expanded manually following certain prescribed guidelines are improving retrieval performance (precision and recall) by as much as 40% or more. This appeared to be the case also for other systems: we asked other groups participating in TREC[10] to run search using our expanded topics, and they reported similar improvements. The biggest problem was the manual effort required to create these expanded topics.

Using the summarizer for topic expansion

In the next round of experiments we used our summarizer to obtain the material for expansion. We derived topical summaries of top-ranked documents returned from search, and have the summaries reviewed by the users via a Query Expansion Tool (QET) interface. If a summary appeared relevant and moreover captured some previously unseen aspect of relevant information, then the user had an option to paste it into the topic, thus increasing the chances of a more successful subsequent search. Note that it wasn't important for the summary selection if the original documents were themselves rel-

---

[9]Relevance feedback techniques are generally less effective than the expansion method proposed here because they rely heavily on relevance information which is normally unavailable or inaccurate. For further details the reader is referred to (Strzalkowski *et al.* 1997), (Strzalkowski *et al.* 1998), (Strzalkowski, Wang, & Wise 1998)

[10]TREC stands for Text Retrieval Conference organized annually by U.S. National Institute of Standards and Technology to evaluate progress in information retrieval research. For more information the reader is referred to (Harman 1997a).

evant, although they usually were.

A preliminary examination of the outcomes of this new series of experiments[11] indicate that this mode of expansion is at least as effective as the purely manual expansion which requires a user to read entire documents in order to select passages for expansion. This is a very good news, since we appear to be a step closer to an automatic expansion. The human-decision factor has been reduced to an accept/reject decision for expanding the topic with a summary.

As an example, we show below a partially expanded Topic 304.

< top >

< num > Number: 304

< title > Endangered Species (Mammals)

< desc > Description:

Compile a list of mammals that are considered to be endangered, identify their habitat and, if possible, specify what threatens them.

< narr > Narrative:

Any document identifying a mammal as endangered is relevant. Statements of authorities disputing the endangered status would also be relevant. A document containing information on habitat and populations of a mammal identified elsewhere as endangered would also be relevant even if the document at hand did not identify the species as endangered. Generalized statements about endangered species without reference to specific mammals would not be relevant.

< expd > Expanded:

The Service is responsible for eight species of marine mammals under the jurisdiction of the Department of the Interior, as assigned by the Marine Mammal Protection Act of 1972. These species are polar bear, sea and marine otters, walrus, manatees (three species) and dugong. The report reviews the Service's marine mammal-related activities during the report period. Administrative actions discussed include appropriations, marine mammals in Alaska, endangered and threatened marine mammal species, law enforcement activities, scientific research and public display permits, certificates of registration, research, Outer Continental Shelf environmental studies and international activities.

The U.S. Fish and Wildlife Service had classified the primate as a "threatened" species, but officials said that more protection was needed in view of recent studies documenting a drastic decline in the populations of wild chimps in Africa.

The Endangered Species Act was passed in 1973 and has been used to provide protection to the bald eagle and grizzly bear, among other animals.

Under the law, a designation of a threatened species means it is likely to become extinct without protection, whereas extinction is viewed as a certainty for an endangered species.

The bear on California's state flag should remind us of what we have done to some of our species. It is a grizzly. And it is extinct in California and in most other states where it once roamed. Hundreds of other mammals, birds, reptiles and other animals have been lost in the inexorable drive to cut down our forests, fill in our wetlands and destroy millions of acres of other plant and animal habitats.

< /top >

---

[11] The results referred to here are from TREC-6 evaluation completed in November 1997 (Harman 1997b).

Table 1: Precision improvement for expanded topics

topics:	TD	TDN	TDNE	TDE	TDE
PREC.	base	base	auto	auto	manu
11pt. avg	0.1077	0.1524	0.1796	0.1809	0.2672
%change		+41.5	+66.7	+67.9	+148.0
@10 docs	0.2420	0.3280	0.3780	0.3680	0.5060
%change		+35.5	+56.2	+52.1	+109.1
@30 docs	0.1947	0.2540	0.2753	0.2780	0.3887
%change		+30.0	+41.4	+42.8	+99.6
@100 doc	0.1274	0.1684	0.1670	0.1684	0.2480
%change		+32.9	+31.1	+32.9	+94.7

Table 1 compares the performance of the Cornell's SMART system (version 11) on different formulation of the same 50 topics. The basic topics, numbered 301 through 350, and including the fields TITLE, DESCRIPTION, and NARRATIVE were used in official TREC-6 evaluations (Strzalkowski *et al.* 1997). The two automatic baseline runs were obtained using different combinations of fields: *full topics*, using all three fields (TDN), and *short topics*, using only the first two fields (TD). We may note that there is a pronounced difference in performance between these two baselines, because the NARRATIVE field is often (though not always) serving the similar purpose as topic expansion, that is, to supply some specific facts on what the relevant material may look like. The narrative field is one of the special features of TREC topics which supports accurate human assessment of relevance, and as such is unlikely to be found elsewhere.

Columns denoted TDE and TDNE show selected runs for the expanded topics. The two TDE runs compare fully automatic expansion process against the semi-manual one, where human users select the summaries to be used for topic expansion. The automatic run is obtained by taking all the summaries which cover at least 80% of the content words found in the topic title. We may note that while the automatic expansion is clearly having a positive effect, there is also a lot of room for improvement.

It is also interesting to compare the performance of expanded topics when they are obtained from the short topics (TDE) rather than the full topics (TDNE). There are two factors to consider here. First, the exclusion of the narrative field makes the initial topics (and subsequently, the queries derived from them) less effective, thus potentially affecting the expansion process because of fewer relevant documents available to the summarizer. Second, the expanded topics lacking the narrative text may themselves be less effective. Nonetheless, we found that the expanded TD topics are no worse, in fact slightly better than the expanded full topics.

CONCLUSIONS

We have developed a method to derive quick-read summaries from news-like texts using a number of shallow NLP techniques and simple quantitative methods. In our approach, a summary is assembled out of passages extracted from the original text, based on a pre-determined Background-News discourse template. The result is a very efficient, robust, and portable summarizer that can be applied to a variety of tasks. These include brief indicative summaries, both generic and topical, as well as longer informative digests. Our method has been shown to produce summaries that offer an excellent tradeoff between text reduction and content preservation, as indicated by the results of the government-sponsored formal evaluation.

The present version of the summarizer can handle most written texts with well-defined paragraph structure. While the algorithm is primarily tuned to newspaper-like articles, we believe it can produce news-style summaries for other factual texts, as long as their rhetorical structures are reasonably linear, and no prescribed stylistic organization is expected. For such cases a more advanced discourse analysis will be required along with more elaborate DMS templates.

We used the summarizer to build effective search topics for an information retrieval system. This has been demonstrated to produce dramatic performance improvements in TREC evaluations. We believe that this topic expansion approach will also prove useful in searching very large databases where obtaining a full index may be impractical or impossible, and accurate sampling will become critical.

Our future development plans will focus on improving the quality of the summaries by implementing additional passage scoring functions. Further plans include handling more complex DMS's, and adaptation of the summarizer to texts other than news, as well as to texts written in foreign languages. We plan further experiments with topic expansion with the goal of achieving a full automation of the process while retaining the performance gains.

Acknowledgements

We thank the anonymous reviewers for their thoughtful comments and suggestions which helped to make this into a more effective article. This chapter is based upon work supported in part by the Defense Advanced Research Projects Agency under Tipster Phase-3 Contract 97-F157200-000 through the Office of Research and Development.

References

Brandow, R.; Mitze, K.; and Rau, L. 1995. Automatic condensation of electronic publications by sentence selection. *Information Processing and Management* 31(5):675–686.

DARPA. 1993. *Proceedings of the 5th Message Understanding Conference*, San Francisco, CA: Morgan Kaufman Publishers.

DARPA. 1996. *Tipster Text Phase 2: 24 month Conference*, Morgan-Kaufmann.

DeJong, G. G. 1982. An overview of the frump system. In Lehnert, W., and Ringle, M., eds., *Strategies for Natural Language Processing*. Lawrence Erlbaum, Hillsdale, NJ.

Firmin, T., and Sundheim, B. 1998. Tipster/summac evaluation analysis. In *Tipster Phase III 18-month Workshop*.

Harman, D., ed. 1997a. *The 5th Text Retrieval Conference (TREC-5)*, number 500–253. National Institute of Standards and Technology.

Harman, D., ed. 1997b. *Proceedings of the 6th Text Retrieval Conference (TREC-6)*. National Institute of Standards and Technology.

Hearst, M. 1997. Texttiling: Segmenting text into multi-paragraph subtopic passages. *Computational Linguistics* 23(1):33–64.

Kupiec, J.; Pedersen, J.; and Chen, F. 1995. A trainable document summarizer. In *Conference of the ACM Special Interes Group on Information Retrieval (SIGIR)*, 68–73.

Lehnert, W. 1981. Plots units and narrative summarization. *Cognitive Science* 4:293–331.

Luhn, H. 1958. The automatic creation of literature abstracts. *IBM Journal* 159–165.

Marcu, D. 1997a. From discourse structures to text summaries. In *Proceedings of the ACL Workshop on Intelligent, Scallable Text Summarization*, 82–88.

Marcu, D. 1997b. The rhetorical parsing of natural language texts. In *Proceedings of 35th Annual Meetings of the ACL*, 96–103.

McKeown, K., and Radev, D. 1995. Generating summaries of multiple news articles. In *Proceedings of the 8th Annual ACM SIGIR Conference on R&D in IR*.

Ono, K.; Sumita, K.; and Miike, S. 1994. Abstract generation based on rhetorical structure extraction. In *Proceedings of the International Con-*

ference on Computational Linguisitcs (COLING-94), 344–348.

Paice, C. 1990. Constructing literature abstracts by computer: techniques and prospects. *Information Processing and Management* 26(1):171–186.

Rino, L., and Scott, D. 1994. Content selection in summary generation. In *Third International Conference on the Cognitive Science of Natural Language Processing*.

Salton, G.; Allan, J.; Buckley, C.; and Singhal, A. 1994. Automatic analysis, theme generation, and summarization of machine readable texts. *Science* 264:1412–1426.

Strzalkowski, T., and Wang, J. 1996. A self-learning universal concept spotter. In *Proceedings of the 17th International Conference on Computational Linguistics (COLING-96)*, 931–936.

Strzalkowski, T.; Guthrie, L.; Karlgren, J.; Leistensnider, J.; Lin, F.; Perez-Carballo, J.; Straszheim, T.; Wang, J.; and Wilding, J. 1997. Natural language information retrieval: Trec-5 report. In *The 5th Text Retrieval Conference (TREC-5)*. National Institute of Standards and Technology.

Strzalkowski, T.; Lin, F.; Perez-Carballo, J.; and Wang, J. 1998. Natural language information retrieval: Trec-6 report. In *The 6th Text Retrieval Conference (TREC-6)*. National Institute of Standards and Technology.

Strzalkowski, T.; Wang, J.; and Wise, B. 1998. Summarization-based query expansion in information retrieval. In *Proceedings of the joint conference on Computational Linguistics, Coling-ACL*.

Teufel, S., and Moens, M. 1997. Sentence extraction as classification task. In *Proceedings of the ACL Workshop on Intelligent, Scallable Text Summarization*.

Weissberg, R., and Buker, S. 1990. *Writing up Research: Experimental Research Report Writing for Student of English*. Prentice Hall, Inc.

APPENDIX: Original Documents

The full text of documents used to produce example summaries discussed in this chapter. We number the paragraphs for an easy reference.

(0) MRS. CLINTON SAYS U.S. NEEDS 'WAYS THAT VALUE FAMILIES'

(1) CHICAGO – Stern and focused, planted behind the lectern, eschewing any attempt to top Elizabeth Hanford Dole in the charm sweepstakes, Hillary Rodham Clinton stuck to her guns on Tuesday night at the Democratic convention, playing the teacher and not the television personality in her much-anticipated appearance before the delegates gathered to renominate her husband.

(2) She told a joke or two after the crowd at the United Center gave her a four-minute ovation. A friend, she joshed, had suggested she cut her hair short, die it orange and change her name to Hillary Rodman Clinton, after the exotic defensive specialist of the Chicago Bulls, the arena's main tenants.

(3) But that was the last note of levity. Mrs. Clinton said she wished she could sit at a kitchen table – "just us" – and talk to the nation around it, but she sounded more as if she were teaching a class or perhaps making a speech, a rather pointedly political speech, to the national PTA.

(4) "Right now," she said, eyes levelled at the prime-time television audience beyond the camera, unsmiling, "in our biggest cities and our smallest towns, there are boys and girls being tucked gently into bed, and there are boys and girls who have no one to call mom or dad, and no place to call home."

(5) She never mentioned the Republicans or their nominee, Bob Dole. She did not even allude to Mrs. Dole, who caused a minor sensation at the Republican convention in San Diego by strolling, Oprah-like, among the delegates. But she picked up several of the rhetorical grenades Dole and his backers had lobbed in her direction and threw them back, with equal velocity.

(6) The United States, Mrs. Clinton said, must become "a nation that doesn't just talk about family values but acts in ways that values families."

(7) And she insisted, Dole to the contrary notwithstanding, that it does "take a village" – the phrase comes from the title of her latest book – to rear a child. Dole had suggested that a family was enough, and he had attacked the teachers' union, but Mrs. Clinton said that teachers, clergy, friends and others helped.

(8) She also omitted any mention of the welfare bill signed by President Clinton, which many critics have contended puts millions of the nations poorest children at risk. Among those critics is Marian Wright Edelman of the Children's Defense Fund, on whose board Mrs. Clinton once served.

(9) Dressed in a light blue suit with the collar turned up, wearing four strands of small pearls, Mrs. Clinton looked every inch the professional woman she is. The Democrats in the hall loved her, though most applauded rather than cheered at her punch lines, and she generated less heat than Jesse Jackson and Mario Cuomo, a pair of fiery old liberals who preceded her to the podium.

(10) Arguably, it was her most important public appearance since she joined her husband on national television early in 1992 to help him defuse accusations of infidelity that threatened to derail his presidential campaign.

(11) On Tuesday night, there were no echoes of that controversy and others that followed it. Mrs. Clinton noted pointedly that she and her husband would soon observe their 21st wedding anniversary, and she said that for them, "family has been the center of our lives."

(12) "Bill was with me when Chelsea was born," she said, painting a cozy picture of longtime family togetherness at odds with detailed accounts of tensions in their marriage over many years. "In the delivery room. In my hospital room. And when we brought our baby daughter home."

(13) To some, it seemed an effort to eradicate that earlier image, the "stand-by-your-man" wife of the interview with Steve Kroft of "60 Minutes."

(14) Ranging over family-related issues from health care to family leave to education to flex-time, she lauded the man to whom she referred alternately as "Bill," "the president" and – in the style of her heroine, Eleanor Roosevelt – "my husband."

(15) If she did not describe her husband's modesty, as did Mrs. Dole, she hailed him as a man "who believes not only in the strength of his own family, but of the American family, who believes not only in the promise of each of us as individuals, but in out promise together as a nation."

(16) Like almost every other speaker in the 1996 campaign, she sought to define "what this election is all about." Her answer: It is about the administration's efforts to insure that young women like Chelsea "will face fewer obstacles and more possibilities."

(17) Long before the first lady mounted the podium on Tuesday night, the questions were posed on the front pages of newspapers and on television newscasts across the country: Would she match Mrs. Dole? Should she try? If so, how?

(18) There is no evidence to suggest that either Mrs. Clinton or Mrs. Dole will have a significant impact on their husbands' fortunes at the polls. But after a period of relative popularity Mrs. Clinton has emerged in the last two years as such a divisive figure that her every step is scrutinized.

(19) Sen. Christopher Dodd of Connecticut, the general chairman of the Democratic Party, said in an interview on Tuesday morning that "by a small margin" Mrs. Clinton was now liked by more Americans than disliked her. In the latest New York Times/CBS News Poll, the balance tips slightly in the other direction (35 percent favorable, 37 percent unfavorable, 19 percent undecided).

(20) In any event, Dodd said, there was clearly a need for Mrs. Clinton to "round off the edges" of her somewhat abrasive public image. Her mission on Tuesday night, he said, was to show herself "much more as a human being" than as the supremely well-informed, statistics-spouting automaton who drew a standing ovation from the American Medical Association several years ago.

---

(0) Jury Awards $5.5 Million in ABC Case

(1) Federal jury in Greensboro, N.C., on Wednesday awarded a supermarket chain more than $5.5 million in punitive damages from ABC and two of its employees in a closely watched media case that focused on the propriety of widely used television news techniques like hidden cameras and undercover reporters.

(2) Last month, the same panel ordered ABC to pay $1,400 in actual damages to the chain, Food Lion, after finding that network producers had trespassed and committed fraud when researching a "Primetime Live" segment in 1992 that accused the company of selling spoiled meat.

(3) The case has attracted broad attention in media and legal circles because it is a leading example of a new trend in lawsuits against networks and television news magazines. Although Food Lion officials disputed the accuracy of the ABC report, they did not sue for libel. Rather, they accused ABC of fraud because it used techniques like having producers submit fake resumes to get jobs in the meat department of company stores, and then used hidden cameras to film there.

(4) Roone Arledge, the president of ABC News, defended the methods used to report the segment and said ABC would appeal the verdict.

(5) "They could never contest the truth" of the broadcast, Arledge said. "These people were doing awful things in these stores."

(6) Wednesday's verdict was only the second time punitive damages had been meted out by a jury in a hidden-camera case. It was the first time punitive damages had been awarded against producers of such a segment, said Neville L. Johnson, a lawyer in Los Angeles who has filed numerous hidden-camera cases against the major networks.

(7) Many journalists argue that hidden cameras and other undercover reporting techniques have long been necessary tools for exposing vital issues of public policy and health. But many media experts say television producers have overused them in recent years in a push to create splashy shows and bolster ratings. The jurors, those experts added, may have been lashing out at what they perceived as undisciplined and overly aggressive news organizations.

(8) "The irony of the Food Lion case is that those pursuing a noble journalistic goal are being punished for the excessive and trivial use of hidden cameras," said Tom Rosenstiel, director of the Project for Excellence in Journalism, a media ethics initiative in Washington supported by the Pew Charitable Trust.

(9) Officials of all major television networks said in recent interviews that they had tightened guidelines for when producers can use hidden cameras and deception to report a program. But Rosenstiel and other experts said they believed that further checks may appear, particularly at stations lacking the financial resources of a network to fight a costly legal battle.

(10) "This verdict has the potential to chill important investigative reporting and to prompt news organizations to back off," said Bob Steele, director of the ethics program at the Poynter Institute, a program for journalists in St. Petersburg, Fla.

(11) The 12-member jury never viewed the "Primetime Live" segment at issue but was told by Judge N. Carlton Tilley Jr., who presided over the case, to treat it as accurate. The panel, which deliberated for six days, deadlocked twice before agreeing on Wednesday's award. Punitive damages reflect a jury's decision that a defendant should be punished for its conduct, and are intended to deter such behavior in the future.

(12) In its decision, the jury ordered Capital Cities/ABC Inc. to pay $4 million and ABC Inc. to pay $1.5 million to Food Lion, a subsidiary of Etablissements Delhaize Freres et Cie "Le Lion" SA of Belgium, which operates 1,100 stores in 14 states. Richard Kaplan, "Primetime Live" executive producer at the time of the broadcast, was ordered to pay $35,000 in punitive damages, and Ira Rosen, the senior producer of the program, was told to pay $10,750.

(13) Several members of the jury said in interviews Wednesday that although they supported investigative reporting, they took issue with ABC's methods. In particular, they pointed to the use by network producers of false resumes to gain jobs in Food Lion stores in South Carolina and North Carolina.

(14) "I don't have anything against undercover investigations," said Carla Jackson, a receptionist from Winston-Salem, N.C. "I like them. But if you are going to do them, just do them legal."

(15) Several jurors also blamed ABC's legal department for failing to oversee the activities of the segment's producers properly and said they did not see the $5.5 million award against the network as onerous.

(16) "In my opinion, this was a slap on the wrist," said Tony Kinton, a brewery worker from Reidsville, N.C. "I had problems even giving punitive damages, but I think that somebody needs to call it to their attention. You know, that they have to go about gathering the news in a different way."

(17) In their deliberations, the jurors considered punitive damages against the network ranging from $1 to $1 billion, one juror said.

(18) Tom Smith, president and chief executive of Food Lion, said the company was pleased with all of the jury's verdicts in the case. "This case is not about money," Smith said. "We believe that this jury has said that ABC must be held accountable when it breaks laws that everyone else is expected to obey."

(19) Arledge, the ABC executive, said that the network never approved the use of undercover reporting lightly and that those connected with the Food Lion segment had believed their actions were lawful. He called the panel's decision "ridiculous" and said Food Lion's lawyers had diverted jurors' attention.

(20) "Their lawyers managed to fight a battle that really had nothing to do with the essence of the story," he said.

(21) In the 1992 "Primetime Live" segment, the network accused Food Lion of selling spoiled meat, tainted fish and rotten produce. The company started litigation against the network even before the segment was broadcast, and its stock plummeted once the segment appeared.

(22) Neal Shapiro, the executive producer of NBC "Dateline," a news magazine that also uses concealed cameras, said he was disturbed by Wednesday's verdict but added that his program would not change its policies because of it.

(23) The verdict, however, may well bring more plaintiffs into the courtroom. Johnson, the lawyer in Los Angeles, said recently that he had eight active hidden-camera cases against ABC, NBC and CBS. But now, he said, there could be more.

(24) "I think this is going to open the floodgates to the extent that networks still have the guts to produce hidden-camera stories where impersonation is used," he said.

---

(0) U.S. BUYER OF RUSSIAN URANIUM SAID TO PUT PROFITS BEFORE SECURITY

(1) In a postscript to the Cold War, the American government-owned corporation charged with reselling much of Russia's military stockpile of uranium as civilian nuclear reactor fuel turned down repeated requests this year to buy material sufficient to build 400 Hiroshima-size bombs.

(2) The incident raises the question of whether the corporation, the U.S. Enrichment Corp., put its own financial interest ahead of the national-security goal of preventing weapons-grade uranium from falling into the hands of terrorists or rogue states.

(3) "I am convinced that the USEC is acting directly contrary to the national-security interests of the United States," Sen. Pete Domenici, a New Mexico Republican and an important congressional figure in the swords-to-plowshares program, wrote to deputy secretary of Energy Charles Curtis in a letter dated July 31.

(4) Under a deal negotiated by the Bush administration and signed by the Clinton administration in 1993, Russia agreed to sell 500 tons of bomb-grade uranium from dismantled warheads – 40 percent of its stockpile – after the uranium had been blended with natural uranium to make it suitable for reactor fuel. This fuel would then be resold to electric utilities, competing with the substance that the Enrichment Corp. itself makes from American uranium.

(5) Moreover, handling the Russian fuel would make considerably less money for the Enrichment Corp. than it could make from its own processing operations. And because utilities can use only so much nuclear fuel, the demand for the corporation's American uranium would shrink proportionally with the added supply. Thus, from a purely commercial perspective, it behooves the corporation to limit its purchases of Russian uranium.

(6) The controversy is all the more important now because the Enrichment Corp. is scheduled to be sold to private investors as early as this winter.

(7) The corporation has thus far taken delivery from Russia of reactor fuel derived from 13 tons of bomb-grade uranium. "The nonproliferation objectives of the agreement are being achieved," a spokesman for the Enrichment Corp. said.

(8) But since the beginning of the program, skeptics have questioned the wisdom of designating the Enrichment Corp. as Washington's "executive agent" in managing the deal with Russia's Ministry of Atomic Energy, or MINATOM.

(9) On the one hand, the government corporation, created in 1992 to operate the Energy Department's gigantic uranium enrichment plants in Kentucky and Ohio, is experienced in both producing and marketing nuclear fuel. On the other, the Enrichment Corp. directly competes with MINATOM as a supplier.

(10) The more of the highly enriched uranium that MINATOM extracts from weapons and exports in blended form as reactor fuel, the less need there will be for American uranium in the world market, and the lower the price the Enrichment Corp. can expect to receive from its own processing services.

(11) Furthermore, the incentive to maximize profits at the expense of other goals would appear to become stronger as the privatization nears.

(12) "It seems absurd to designate an agent that must constantly be policed," argued Richard Falkenrath, director of the Center for Science and International Affairs at the Kennedy School of Government at Harvard University.

(13) Curtis acknowledged this "natural tension between the Enrichment Corp.'s commercial interest and its capacity to serve the more fundamental national-security interest," but he defended the corporation's performance to date. That is where the question arises about the extra uranium that was refused.

(14) Documents made available to The New York Times show that in January of this year, Russian officials first asked the Enrichment Corp. to accept blended-down fuel from 18 metric tons of weapons-grade uranium in 1997 rather than the previously agreed 12 tons. Timely payment for the extra delivery, the Russians said, would permit them to complete the job of dismantling all the weapons that had been removed from Ukraine.

(15) The Enrichment Corp. did not accept the offer. At a meeting early last month, it countered with the idea of advancing MINATOM money instead. According to a senior government official, who insisted on anonymity, the administration was aware of the offer from the beginning and counseled the Enrichment Corp. to refuse shipment of the extra six tons. Washington was not convinced that Russia could prepare deliveries on the accelerated schedule, the official said, nor did it have the means of verifying that the material would come from dismantled bombs or existing stockpiles rather than from new production.

(16) The White House also feared, the official said, that the Russian wish to accelerate shipments would upset negotiations in Congress to privatize the Enrichment Corp.

(17) But other people are skeptical that the administration was indeed informed – or if it was, that administration officials fully understood the implications of what they were told. Moreover, these people questioned the validity of the reasons that were given for the rejection. There was no foreign-policy reason to refuse the shipments outright, they suggest, when the agreement could have been made conditional on settling verification issues. And those issues were resolved quickly when Russia agreed to inspections of the conversion plants.

(18) Moreover, while the relevant legislation on privatization of the Enrichment Corp. was passed only in April 1996, the terms were completed in November 1995, two months before the Russian offer.

(19) Domenici, chairman of the energy subcommittee of the Senate Appropriations Committee, which is shepherding the privatization plan through Congress, was never informed of the offer by the administration. After learning of the rebuff to the Russians, he wrote to Curtis asking that the Enrichment Corp. "be immediately replaced as executive agent" and warning that "under no circumstances should the sale of the USEC proceed until this matter is resolved." Once Domenici entered the fray, the administration changed its tune.

(20) Curtis sent a letter to Domenici stating that all the problems blocking acceptance of the extra six tons had been solved. People close to the administration said that the Enrichment Corp. has now been advised to buy the full 18-ton shipment in 1997. Moreover, Curtis quickly convened a new committee to monitor the Enrichment Corp. for signs of foot-dragging.

(21) But Thomas Neff, a physicist and nuclear policy specialist at MIT who came up with the original idea of buying the uranium from Russia, said that the Enrichment Corp., once privatized, would still have strong financial incentives to stall deliveries and to pay as little as possible. Such policies would reduce the money available to the cash-starved Russian enterprises that must prevent the uranium from finding its way into unauthorized bombs.

(22) A spokesman for the Enrichment Corp. said, however, that the corporation would not stall deliveries, out of concern that the government might retaliate by stripping the corporation of its authority to handle all Russian imports.

(23) Both the White House and congressional Republicans apparently remain committed to selling the Enrichment Corp., a transaction that would raise upwards of $1.3 billion.

(24) But the government is not committed to maintaining the Enrichment Corp. as the executive agent for the Russian agreement. "We are considering appointing multiple agents," Curtis said.

(25) Neff of MIT argues for a clean break, designating the Energy Department as executive agent. The Russians, under this arrangement, would be encouraged to export as much of the converted bomb material as possible, at a price set by an auction.

(26) "In this way the U.S. could carry out its obligations under the original government-to-government agreement," he said, "and USEC could privatize without having to worry about the government forcing it to sacrifice profits in the name of nonproliferation."

13

Argumentative classification of extracted sentences as a first step towards flexible abstracting

Simone Teufel and Marc Moens
HCRC Language Technology Group
University of Edinburgh
2 Buccleuch Place
Edinburgh EH8 9LW, UK
S.Teufel@ed.ac.uk   M.Moens@ed.ac.uk

Abstract

Knowledge about the rhetorical structure of a text is useful for automatic abstraction. We are interested in the automatic extraction of rhetorical units from the source text, units such as PROBLEM STATEMENT, CONCLUSIONS and RESULTS. We want to use such extracts to generate high-compression abstracts of scientific articles. In this paper, we present an extension of Kupiec, Pedersen and Chen's (1995) methodology for trainable statistical sentence extraction. Our extension additionally classifies the extracted sentences according to their rhetorical role.

1 Introduction

1.1 Flexible abstracting

Until recently, the world of research publications was heavily paper-oriented. Journals, dissertations and other publications were available only in paper form. To keep researchers informed of publications in their area of interest, secondary publishers produced journals with abstracts of research material. The main role of these abstracts was to act as a *decision* tool: on the basis of the abstract a researcher could decide whether the source text was worth a visit to the library or a letter to the author requesting a copy of the full article.

For reasons of consistency (and copyright) these abstracts often were not the abstracts produced by the original authors, but by professional abstractors, and written according to agreed guidelines and recommendations (Borko & Chatman 1963). These guidelines suggest that such abstracts should be aimed at the "partially informed reader"—someone who knows enough about the field to understand the basic methodology and general goals of the paper but does not necessarily have enough of an overview of previous work to assess where a certain article is situated in the field or how articles are related to each other (Kircz 1991). For a novice reader, such an abstract would be too terse; for experienced researchers the abstract would provide unnecessary detail. In addition, because the abstract is a pointer to an article not immediately available, the abstract has to be self-contained: the reader should be able to grasp the main goals and achievements of the full article without needing the source text for clarification.

Over the past few years this picture has changed dramatically. Research articles are now increasingly being made available on-line. Indeed, the goal of automated summarization presupposes that the full article is available in machine-readable form. As a result, abstracts will have different or additional functions from the ones they used to have.

A typical scenario might be one where a user receives a large quantity of machine-readable articles, for example in reply to a search query, from a database of scientific articles or from the Internet. In such a context, abstracts can still be used as a decision tool, to help the user decide which articles to look at first. But in this context abstracts could also be used as a *navigation* tool, helping users find their way through the retrieved document collection. When abstracts are generated as needed, rather than stored in a fixed form, they could show how certain articles are related to other articles in logical and chronological respect, e.g. they could summarize similarities between articles, indicating which of the retrieved articles share the same research questions or methodologies. This type of navigation within a set of papers can support users in making a more informed decision on how well a paper fits their information needs.

Abstracts also don't need to be self-contained anymore. They can contain pointers (e.g. in the form of hyperlinks) to certain passages in the full article. And they can be "embedded" in the source text, highlighting in context the most relevant sentences, as has been demonstrated with commercial products such as Microsoft's "AutoSummarize" feature in Word97.

Abstracts can thus play an important role for the non-linear reading of textual material—the process whereby readers efficiently take in the content of a text by jumping in seemingly arbitrary fashion from conclusion to table of contents, section headers, captions, etc. Nonlinear reading is typical for scientists (Pinelli, Cordle, & Vondran 1984, Bazerman 1988); it serves to efficiently build a model of the text's structure as well as to extract the main concepts of the paper. However, O'Hara and Sellen (1997) have shown that non-linear reading is something people only do well with paper: the physical properties of paper allow readers to quickly scan the document and jump back and forth without losing their place in the document. On-line display mechanisms do not as yet have such facilities. Embedded or otherwise contextualized abstracts can facilitate this process of nonlinear reading by revealing the text's logical and semantic organization.

The old type of abstract was a fixed, long-lived, stand-alone text, targeted at one particular type of user. The new type of abstract is more dynamic and user-responsive, generated automatically when needed and thus less long-lived. Even though such abstracts will be of a lower quality when compared to human-crafted abstracts, we predict that they will be of more use in many situations. It is the flexible automatic generation of such abstracts which we see as our long-term goal.

1.2   Our approach

We would like to develop a summarization system which is not tied to a particular scientific *domain*. The processing robustness needed for this, as well as the speed with which we would like to be able to deliver abstracts, suggests that a deep semantic analysis of the source text is not a viable option.

Many robust summarization systems have opted for statistical sentence extraction: systems have been designed which extract "important" sentences from a text, where the importance of the sentence is inferred from low-level properties which can be more or less objectively calculated. Over the years there have been many suggestions as to which low-level features can help determine the importance of a sentence in the context of a source text, such as stochastic measurements for the significance of key words in the sentence (Luhn 1958), its location in the source text (Baxendale 1958, Edmundson 1969), connections with other sentences (Skorochod'ko 1972, Salton *et al.* 1994), and the presence of cue or indicator phrases (Paice 1981) or of title words (Edmundson 1969). The result of this process is an *extract*, i.e. a collection of sentences selected verbatim from the text.

These extracts are then used as the abstract of the text. But this has a number of disadvantages. For one thing, they are just a collection of sentences, possibly difficult to interpret because of phenomena like unresolved anaphora and unexpected topic shifts. Postprocessing of the extracts can remove some of these shortcomings, e.g. by not using sentences in the extract which contain obviously anaphoric expressions or by including surrounding sentences into the extract which are likely to resolve the anaphora (Johnson *et al.* 1993). Of course, this may lead to extracts which are too long, or it might mean losing sentences which are crucial to the content of the source text, thereby reducing the value of the resulting extract.

But even if—after postprocessing—each individual sentence might be interpretable in isolation, that still does not mean that the extract as a whole will be easy to understand. Assuming that the text is coherent, people will try to fill in the semantics gaps between potentially unconnected sentences. In the act of doing so, they may introduce inappropriate semantics links and get the wrong idea about the content of the source text.

Another problem is that sentence extraction does not work very well for high compression summarization. Typical sentence extraction programs compress to about 10 or 15% of the original—for example, reducing a short newspaper article to a few sentences. Even if these sentences do not form a coherent text, that does not matter much: the extract is short enough to still make sense. But we are interested in summarizing longer texts, such as journal articles. Simple sentence extraction methods will reduce a 20-page article to a 2-page collection of unconnected sentences, a document surrogate which is not adequate as an abstract. Reducing the extract further to obtain a real abstract is difficult.

The reason for this difficulty is that once the abstract-worthy sentences have been extracted, the logical and rhetorical organization of the text is lost, and it becomes difficult to make sensible decisions on how to reduce the text further. To overcome this problem, we want to select abstract-worthy material from the source text, whilst at the same time keeping information about the overall rhetorical structure of the source text and of the role of each of the extract sentences in that rhetorical structure.

However, the full rhetorical structure of a paper (and the logical structure of the research it reports) is a very complex structure, and is difficult to model automatically. Although Marcu (1997) presents an approach for the automated rhetorical analysis of texts, these texts are considerably shorter than the ones we are interested in summarizing. Rather than attempting a full rhetorical analysis of the source text, we wanted to extract just enough rhetorical information so as to be able to determine the rhetorical contribution of all and only the abstract-worthy sentences, without modeling domain knowledge or performing domain-sensitive reasoning. We make use of meta-comments in the text, phrases like *"we have presented a method for"*, and *"however, to our knowledge there is no"* which signal rhetorical status.

The abstract we envisage is construed as an argumentative template, where the slots represent certain argumentative or rhetorical roles, such as GOAL, ACHIEVEMENT, BACKGROUND, METHOD, etc. Abstracting means analysing the argumentative structure of the source text and identifying textual extracts which constitute appropriate fillers for the template. For each slot in the template (i.e. each rhetorical role) the system identifies a number of plausible fillers (i.e. text excerpts), with different levels of confidence. We call this collection of meaningful sentences *together* with information about their rhetorical role in the full article a *rhetorically annotated extract*.

Our idea of an abstract is thus more related to the *structured abstracts* which have become prevalent in the medical domain in the past decade (Broer 1971, Ad Hoc Working Group For Critical Appraisal Of The Medical Literature 1987, Rennie & Glass 1991). Hartley, Sydes, & Blurton (1996) and Hartley & Sydes (1997) show in user studies that these abstracts are easier to read and more efficient for information assessment than traditional summaries.

In a further step (the generation of the real abstract), some of this information can be added or suppressed, in order to allow abstracts of varying length to be generated. For example, the amount of BACKGROUND information supplied in the abstract can be varied depending on whether users have been identified as novices or experienced readers. Rhetorical roles for which only low-probability evidence was found in the source document can be pruned until an abstract of the required length is reached.

Two questions arise from this approach. The first question is how the building blocks of the abstract template, i.e. the rhetorical roles, should be defined. This is a particular problem for our approach because very little is known about what our new type of abstract should look like. Most of the information on good abstracts deals with the world of paper, not with the use of on-line research publications. That means that we cannot take existing guidelines on how to produce balanced, informative, concise abstracts at face value; we will need to fall back on a different set of intuitions as to what constitutes a good abstract. To answer this question, we take research on the argumentative structure of research articles and their abstracts as our starting point. This will be discussed in section 2.

The second question is how a system can be trained to find suitable fillers in a source text to complete such a template. In section 3 we report on our experiments to train a system to automatically detect meaningful sentences in the source text together with their rhetorical role.

2 The argumentative structure of research articles and their abstracts

2.1 Rhetorical divisions in research articles

Scholarly articles serve the process of communicating scientific information. The communicative function of a scientific research article is thus very well-defined: to present and refer to the results of specific research (Salager-Meyer 1992). In some scientific domains research follows predictable patterns of methodology and also of presentation. A rigid, highly structured building plan for research articles has evolved as a result, where rhetorical divisions are clearly marked in section headers (Kintsch & van Dijk 1978). Prototypical rhetorical divisions include *Introduction, Purpose, Experimental Design, Results, Discussion*, and *Conclusions*. This is very efficient: researchers in psycholinguistics, for example, know with great accuracy where in any given article to find the information on the number of participants in an experiment.

The papers in our corpus do not show this pattern. This has undoubtedly to do with the fact that our corpus consists of articles in computational linguistics and cognitive science. The papers draw from many sub-disciplines, and most papers in our collection cannot be uniquely classified by sub-discipline, because they report on truly interdisciplinary research coming from different sub-disciplines. As a rough estimate, about 45% of the articles in our collection are predominantly technical in style, describing implementations (i.e. engineering solutions); about 25% report on research in theoretical linguistics, with an argumentative tenet; the remaining 30% are empirical (psycholinguistic or psychological experiments or corpus studies). As a result, we found a heterogeneous mixture of methodologies and traditions of presentation, with fewer prototypical rhetorical divisions than expected. Even though most of our articles have an introduction and conclusions (sometimes occurring under headers with different names), and almost all of them cite previous work, the presentation of the problem and the methodology/solution are idiosyncratic to the domain and personal writing style. Figure 1 shows the headers with the highest frequency for 123 examined papers—surprisingly few of them correspond to prototypical rhetorical divisions; the rest contain content specific terminology.

Freq.	Header
104	Introduction
56	Conclusion
27	Conclusions
21	Acknowledgments
15	Discussion
14	Results
11	Experimental Results
8	Related Work
8	Implementation
8	Evaluation
7	Example
7	Background

Figure 1: Headers with highest frequency from our collection

Apart from not being easily identified in our corpus, distinctions as expressed in rhetorical divisions are also too coarse for our purposes, namely to analyze scientific articles with respect to document structure, in a way which is flexible enough to cover the variety found in our corpus. A rhetorical division like *Introduction* can contain a problem statement, a motivation, a description of previous relevant work, and other such units. These smaller units are the ones that we are interested in, units which Swales (1981) calls *moves*, where a move is defined as "a semantic unit related to the writer's purpose".

2.2 Author intentions and argumentation in research articles

Swales (1990) claims that the main communicative goal of an author, far from the unbiased reporting of research, is to convince readers of the validity and importance of the work, in order to have the paper reviewed positively and thus published. Argumentation is used to show that the presented research was a contribution to science: that the solution proposed in the paper either solves a *new* problem, or, if a *known* problem is addressed, that the presented solution is better than that proposed by other researchers.

Swales analyzed several hundred introduction sections of scientific research papers from two data collections: research articles in the physical sciences and a mixture of research articles from several science and engineering fields. This analysis led to his CARS model ("Create a Research Space") which is schematically depicted in Figure 2; the right hand side of the figure shows examples from our corpus. This model describes prototypical rhetorical building plans of introductions, based on the rhetorical moves that authors typically employ to fulfill the communicative goal of writing a paper. One such rhetorical move is to motivate the need for the research presented (Move 2), which can be done in different ways, e.g. by pointing out a weakness of a previous approach (Move 2A/B) or by explicitly stating the research question (Move 2C). Note that context plays an important role for the classification of a sentence in Swales' system: the example sentence for Move 2D (which characterizes the work actually reported in the article) would constitute a different move if it had appeared towards the end of the article, or under the heading *Future Work*.

Inspection of introduction sections in our corpus showed that the steps defined by Swales' CARS model describe the argumentation phenomena at the right level of abstraction for our purposes; the author's typical intentions, expressed as predictable textual moves, seem to generalize well to the domain of computational linguistics and cognitive science.

We also observed a wide range of meta-comments in our corpus (the underlined phrases in the right hand side of Figure 2). The source of our collection being an unmoderated medium, writing style in the articles varies from formal to quite informal. About a third of the articles were not written (or subsequently edited) by native speakers of English. Also, meta-comments need not be unambiguous with respect to the rhetorical move they signal. Nevertheless, we claim that overall, they are still good enough indicators of rhetorical status to be extremely useful in a practical, shallow kind of discourse analysis.

2.3 Argumentative structure of abstracts

Although we argued that guidelines for abstracts cannot be taken at face value when designing a high-level framework for on-line abstracts, there is ample information in the literature which can be used to inform decisions about a desirable argumentative structure for abstracts.

As is the case with the communicative function of the whole paper, the communicative function of an abstract is one of a narrow range of things: it can be an indicative abstract, reporting the topic of the full article, or an informative abstract, reporting the topic of the source article as well as its main findings and conclusions (Cremmins 1996, Rowley 1982). As in the case of research articles, the communicative function of abstracts has led to common expectations of their rhetorical building blocks, such as *General Background, Specific Problem* tackled by full article, *Main Results, Recommendations*, etc. Buxton & Meadows (1978) provide a comparative survey of the contents of abstracts in the physics domain. They studied which rhetorical section in the source text (*Introduction–Method–Result–Discussion*) corresponds to the information in the abstracts and found, for example, that abstracts tend not to report material from the *Method* section. There is similar research on medical abstracts (Salager-Meyer 1992) and sociological and humanities abstracts (Milas-Bracovic 1987).

There is a consensus about the content units of informative abstracts for such articles in the experimental sciences—the majority of information in the descriptive and prescriptive abstracting literature seems to have concentrated on experimental sciences. Most authors agree that informative abstracts should mention the following four information units (American National Standards Institute, Inc. 1979, International Organisation for Standardisation 1976, Day 1995, Rowley 1982, Cremmins 1996):

1. the PURPOSE or PROBLEM of the full article,
2. the SCOPE or METHODOLOGY,
3. the RESULTS,
4. and CONCLUSIONS or RECOMMENDATIONS

In line with these recommendations, Manning (1990) argues that informative abstracts are not a miniature version of the full article in the sense of offering "a paraphrase of every rhetorical section" of the source article.

There is more disagreement about "peripheral" content units, such as BACKGROUND, INCIDENTAL FINDINGS, FUTURE WORK, RELATED WORK, and DATA. Of particular interest to us is the content unit BACKGROUND. According to Alley (1996), BACKGROUND is a useful content unit in an abstract if it is restricted to being the first sentence of the abstract. Other authors (Rowley 1982, Cremmins 1996) recommend not to include any background information at all. We believe that background information is potentially important,

MOVE 1: ESTABLISHING A TERRITORY

1.1	**Claiming centrality**	• *The last decade has seen a growing interest in the application of machine learning to different kinds of linguistic domains* ...
1.2	**Making topic generalizations** (background knowledge) OR (description of phenomena)	• *The traditional approach has been to plot isoglosses, delineating regions where the same word is used for the same concept.* • *In the Japanese language, the causative and the change of voice are realized by agglutinations of those auxiliary verbs at the tail of current verbs.*
1.3	**Reviewing previous research**	• *Brown et al. (1992) suggest a class-based n-gram model in which words with similar cooccurrence distributions are clustered in word classes.*

MOVE 2: ESTABLISHING A NICHE

2A	**Counter-claiming**	• *However, we argue that such formalisms offer little help to computational linguists in practice.*
or 2B	**Indicating a gap**	• ...*no formal framework has been proposed, to our knowledge, to regulate the interaction between regular and exceptional grammatical resources.*
or 2C	**Question-Raising**	• *Can the restrictive power of a single constraint be estimated in a reliable way to allow an effective scheduling procedure being devised?*
or 2D	**Continuing a tradition**	• *The remaining issue is to find a way of better accounting for unsymmetrical accommodation.*

MOVE 3: OCCUPYING A NICHE

3.1A	**Outlining purpose**	• *The aim of this paper is to examine the role that training plays in the tagging process* ...
or 3.1B	**Announcing present research**	• *In this paper, we argue that instead of applying the arbitration process to the discourse level, it should be applied to...*
3.2	**Announcing principle findings**	• *In our corpus study, we found that three types of utterances (prompts, repetitions and summaries) were consistently used to signal control shifts....*
3.3	**Indicating article structure**	• *This paper is organized as follows: We begin in Section [CREF] by examining the distribution of possessive pronouns...*

Figure 2: Swales' (1990) CARS model with illustrative examples from our corpus

especially for self-contained abstracts and for abstracts for novice readers.

There is similar disagreement over the content unit RELATED WORK. Cremmins (1996) states that it should not be included in an abstract unless the studies are replications or evaluations of earlier work. However, depending on the information need, previous work might actually have been central to the original information need of the user. Therefore, we want to preserve the possibility of including it in our modular abstract.

For the experiments reported in this paper, we chose the four generally accepted categories, but we had to redefine each class slightly in order to achieve higher domain-independence.

For example, we use the label SOLUTION/METHOD instead of METHODOLOGY/SCOPE: unlike in purely experimental research, where methodologies are long-lived research tools that are agreed upon in the field and do not change often, the range of possible methodologies in computational linguistics is vast, and a new, short-lived methodology might be invented just for the given problem-solving task, in which case the label "solution" seems more appropriate.

We added the two controversial roles RELATED WORK and BACKGROUND. And we added the role TOPIC, as the name of the research area or of the most general problem in the field. Thus, we ended up with the seven argumentative units listed in Figure 3.

Note that the labels of our annotation scheme can be naturally defined by rhetorical moves, such as the

RHETORICAL ROLE	
BACKGROUND	BACK
TOPIC/ABOUTNESS	TOPI
RELATED WORK	RWRK
PURPOSE/PROBLEM	PU/PR
SOLUTION/METHOD	SOLU
RESULT	RESU
CONCLUSION/CLAIM	CO/CL

Figure 3: Rhetorical roles in our annotation scheme

ones in Swales' CARS model. For example, Move 1.1 ("claiming centrality") provides good fillers for the TOPIC slot, whereas PROBLEM, i.e. the specific problem of the paper, is very likely to be found in Move 2A–D ("indicating a gap").

Our annotation scheme forms the basis of the manual and automatic classification which is reported in the next section.

3 Our experiment

3.1 Previous work

(Kupiec, Pedersen, & Chen 1995) introduce the notion of corpus-based abstracting: they recast the problem of sentence extraction as statistical classification. More specifically, they use supervised learning to automatically adjust feature weights with a Naive Bayesian classifier, combining the features (heuristics) mentioned in the literature. They used a corpus of research articles and corresponding summaries. The new idea in Kupiec et al.'s work is how they defined their *gold standards*. Gold standards are the class of sentences that, by definition, constitute the correct set of answers, usually defined by an expert in the field. The gold standard has to be defined independently and before the experiment. In Kupiec et al.'s work, the gold standard sentences are defined as the set of sentences in the source text that "align" with a sentence in the summary—i.e. sentences that show sufficient semantic and syntactic similarity with a summary sentence. The underlying reason is that a sentence in the source text is abstract-worthy if professional abstractors used it or parts of it when producing their summary. In Kupiec et al.'s corpus of 188 engineering articles with summaries written by professional abstractors, 79% of sentences in the summary also occurred in the source text with at most minor modifications.

Kupiec et al. then try to determine the characteristic properties of abstract-worthy sentences according to a number of features, viz. presence of particular cue phrases, location in the text, sentence length, occurrence of thematic words, and occurrence of proper names. Each document sentence receives a score for each of the features, resulting in an estimate for the sentence's probability to also occur in the summary. This probability is calculated for each feature value as a combination of the probability of the feature-value pair occurring in a sentence which is in the summary (successful case) and the probability that the feature-value pair occurs unconditionally.

Evaluation of the training relies on cross-validation: the model is trained on a training set of documents, leaving all documents from one journal out at a time (the current test set). The model is then used to extract candidate sentences from all documents of the test set. Evaluation measures co-selection between the extracted sentences and the gold standard sentences in precision (number of sentences extracted correctly over total number of sentences selected) and recall (number of sentences extracted correctly over total number of gold standard sentences). Since from any given test text as many sentences are selected as there are gold standard sentences, numerical values for precision and recall are the same. The precision/recall values of the individual heuristics range between 20–33%; the highest cumulative result (44%) was achieved using paragraph, fixed phrases (indicators) and sentence length features.

3.2 Abstracting as stepwise classification

We decided to perform the automatic generation of rhetorically annotated extracts by a process of repeated classification, borrowing the classification methodology from Kupiec et al. The basic procedure for the sentence extraction and classification experiment is the following:

Step one: Extraction of abstract-worthy sentences. We try to separate sentences which carry *any* rhetorical roles (grey set of sentences in Figure 4) from irrelevant sentences, which are by far the larger part of the text (white set of sentences in Figure 4). The output of this step is called the *intermediate extract*. Errors in this task will lead to the inclusion of irrelevant material in the extracts (false positives), or the exclusion of relevant material from the extracts (false negatives).

Step two: Identification of the correct rhetorical role. Once good sentence candidates have been identified, we classify them according to one of the seven rhetorical roles (in Figure 4, this corresponds to the subclassification of the grey sentences). The output of this step is called a *rhetorically annotated extract*.

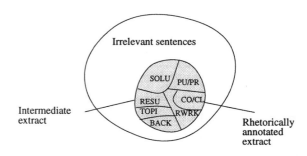

Figure 4: Abstracting as classification

We decided to split the task because we suspected that different heuristics would be more useful for the different tasks—a two-step process allows for the separation of these distinctions into two training processes.

Also, another motivation for the separation of the tasks stems from the fact that indicator phrases don't have to be unambiguous with respect to their argumentative status. For example, the phrase *"in this paper, we have"* is a very good overall relevance indicator, and it is quite likely that a sentence or paragraph starting with it will carry important global-level information. However, without an analysis of the following verb, we cannot be sure about the argumentative status of the extract. The sentence could continue with *". . . used machine learning techniques for . . . "*, in which case we have a solution instance; just as well, the sentence could be a conclusion (*". . . argued that . . . "*) or a problem statement (*". . . attacked the hard problem of . . . "*). Thus, the phrase *"in this paper we will"* is very useful for step one, but not useful for step two.

3.3 Corpus

Our corpus is a collection of 201 articles and their author-written summaries from different areas of computational linguistics and cognitive science, drawn from the computation and language archive (`http://xxx.lanl.gov/cmp-lg`). We assume that most of the articles had been accepted for publication in conference proceedings, although we have not verified this in each case. The documents were converted from LaTeX source into HTML in order to extract raw text and minimal structure automatically, then transformed into SGML format and manually corrected. We used all documents dated between 04/94 and 05/96 which we could semi-automatically retrieve with our conversion pipeline and which contained no less than 2,000 and no more than 10,000 words. The resulting corpus contains 568,000 word tokens; the average length of the documents is 187 sentences, the average length of the original summaries 4.7 sentences. In each text we marked up the following structural information: title, summary, headings, paragraph structure and sentences. We also removed tables, equations, figures, captions, references and cross references and replaced them by place holders (e.g. the symbol [REF] marks the place where a reference was cited in the text; [EQN] marks the place of equations).

We randomly divided our corpus into a training and test set of 123 documents which were further analyzed and annotated, and a remaining set of 78 documents which remain unseen. Only the first set was used for the experiments described here.

3.4 Annotation of gold standards

In line with Kupiec *et al.*'s method, we tried to use the summaries in our corpus for training and evaluation. However, the summaries of our articles were written by the authors themselves, and it is commonly assumed that author summaries are of a lower quality when compared to summaries by professional abstractors.

We first tested to which degree the authors' summaries reused sentences from the body of the document. In order to establish alignment between summary and document sentences, we used a semi-automatic method, assisted by a simple surface similarity measure which computed the longest common subsequence of non-stop-list words. Final alignment was decided by a human judge, where the criterion was similarity of semantic contents of the compared sentences. The following sentence pair illustrates a *direct match*:

Summary: In understanding a reference, an agent determines his confidence in its adequacy as a means of identifying the referent.

Document: An agent understands a reference once he is confident in the adequacy of its (inferred) plan as a means of identifying the referent.

Unlike Kupiec *et al.*'s professional annotators, our authors had not reused document sentences to a large degree—we had a low 31% alignment rate as compared to Kupiec *et al.*'s 79%.

In addition to this, the authors had obviously not used a prototypical scheme to write their summaries, in contrast to professional abstractors surveyed by Liddy (1991). When we inspected the rhetorical contents of the sentences in the author summaries by applying our annotation scheme to them, we found that argumentative structure varied widely, even though most summaries are understandable and many are well-written. Some summaries are extremely short, and many of them are not self-contained, and would thus be difficult to understand for the partially informed reader. This again confirms the claim that author summaries are less systematically constructed than summaries by professional abstractors.

Because of the low alignment and the heterogeneous rhetorical structure of the summaries, we decided not to use them directly for annotation and evaluation. Annotation of the training corpus had to proceed in the following three steps:

1. Alignment of summary and document sentences (semi-automatic);

2. Additional annotation of further relevant sentences (manual);

3. Annotation of the argumentative status of these sentences (manual).

A human judge annotated additional abstract-worthy sentences in the source text. We gave no restrictions as to how many additional sentences were to be selected. After this process, our texts had two gold standards of different origin: gold standard A, consisting of aligned sentences; and gold standard B, consisting of sentences selected by the human judge, 948 sentences in total.

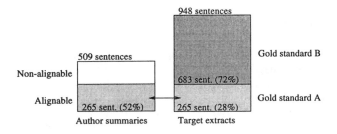

Figure 5: Composition of gold standards with respect to origin

Figure 5 shows the composition of gold standards: there are 2.5 times as many gold standard B sentences as there are gold standard A sentences. The alignment rate in our training and test set of 123 documents, which consists of the best-aligned documents, is 52% (the alignment rate of 31% refers to all 201 documents). With respect to compression (i.e. ratio of gold standard sentences to document sentences), our combined gold standards achieve 4.4% (as compared to Kupiec et al.'s 3.0% compression). Gold standard A had a compression of 1.2%, gold standard B 3.2%.

The second annotation step consisted of manually determining the argumentative roles for the abstract-worthy sentences (as defined in step one) for each article in the training set.

The following sentence with its rhetorical label illustrates this type of mark-up:

> Repeating the argument of Section 2, we conclude that a construction grammar that encodes the formal language [EQN] is at least an order of magnitude more compact than any lexicalized grammar that encodes this language.   CONCLUSION/CLAIM

Difficulties encountered during annotation often concerned the status of a statement in the line of the argument, when the status was dependent on the context. For example, a weakness of the authors' solution might be classified as a limitation or as a local problem, depending on whether that problem will be solved later on in the given article. In cases of true ambiguity between two roles, we allowed for multiple annotation.

Another difficulty had to do with the fact that we annotated entire sentences: often, one sentence covers more than one role, as the following sentence illustrates:

> We also examined how utterance type related to topic shift and found that few interruptions introduced a new topic.   PURPOSE/PROBLEM AND
>   CONCLUSION/CLAIM

Figure 6 shows the composition of the gold standard sentences with respect to rhetorical roles. SOLUTION and PROBLEM are the most common rhetorical roles with about one third each of the judgements, the other roles sharing the last third. The least common role was RESULT.

There were 1172 instances of rhetorical roles in our 948 gold standard sentences. 232 sentences (24%) con-

tained multiple mark-up (either ambiguous or concatenative). Figure 7 shows the distribution of *multiple* markup over the rhetorical roles, which is about proportional, except for a low involvement of BACKGROUND in multiple markup and a proportionally higher one for RELATED WORK and PROBLEM. We believe this is partly due to conceptual difficulties and partly due to concatenative markup: BACKGROUND sentences tend to contain nothing but background information, whereas the information units for PROBLEM statements and RELATED WORK tend to be smaller.

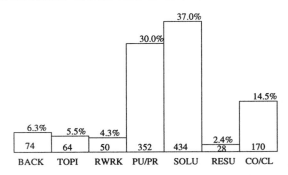

Figure 6: Composition of gold standard sentences with respect to rhetorical roles set

Rhetorical role	Multiple annotation	
BACKGROUND	16	(21%)
TOPIC/ABOUTNESS	25	(39%)
RELATED WORK	24	(48%)
PURPOSE/PROBLEM	168	(47%)
SOLUTION/METHOD	167	(38%)
RESULT	11	(39%)
CONCLUSION/CLAIM	64	(37%)

Figure 7: Percentages of judgements involving multiple annotation for the respective rhetorical roles

3.5   Heuristics Pool

We employed 7 heuristics in the two tasks: 4 of the heuristics used by Kupiec et al. (Indicator Quality Feature, Relative Location Feature, Sentence Length Feature and Thematic Word Feature), and 3 additional ones (Indicator Rhetorics Feature, Title Feature and Header Type Feature).

Indicator Quality Feature: The Indicator Quality Feature identifies meta-comments in a text, as opposed to subject matter. We use a list consisting of 1728 indicator phrases or formulaic expressions, such as communicative verbs and phrases related to argumentation and research activities. Our indicator phrase list was manually created by a cycle of inspection of extracted sentences and addition of indicator phrases to the list.

Figure 8 shows an extract from the indicator list; the first group of indicator phrases is centered around the concept *"argue"*, the second group uses the global indicator *"in this article"*, the third is centered around the concept *"attempt"*.

The largest part of these phrases is positive, but the last entry in Figure 8 illustrates a negative indicator phrase, typically occurring in the rhetorical division *Acknowledgements* (which is of no interest to content selection).

Indicator Phrase	Quality Score
we argued	2
we have argued	1
we have argued that	1
we will argue	1
what I have argued is	1
what we have argued is	1
This article	3
in this article	3
is an attempt to	1
I attempt to	2
I have attempted	2
I have attempted to	2
our work attempts	2
the present paper is an attempt	2
this paper is an attempt to	2
supported by grant	-1

Figure 8: An extract from the indicator list

Using the strings directly as values in a feature would result in a sparse distribution, and thus in an over-fitted feature, i.e. a feature that works well for the training data but not for different, but similar kinds of data. Thus, we classified the strings according to different criteria. For the Indicator Quality Feature, indicator phrases were manually classified into 5 quality classes according to their occurrence frequencies within the target extract sentences (cf. the column 'Quality Score' in Figure 8). The scores mirror the likelihood of a sentence containing the given indicator phrase to be included in the summary on a 5-valued scale from 'very likely to be included in a summary' to 'very unlikely'. For example, the likelihood of the phrase *"we argued"* to appear in the summary is higher than the likelihood of variations of this string in other tenses, a fact that is mirrored by its higher score of +2.

Indicator Rhetorics Feature: This feature tries to model the semantics (rhetorical contribution) of the phrases. Each indicator phrase was manually classified into one of 16 classes. Classes correspond to the 7 rhetorical roles (BACK, TOPI, RWRK, PU/PR, SOLU, RESU, CO/CL), and 8 confusion classes, viz. SOLU–PU/PR, SOLU–CO/CL, PU/PR–CO/CL, PU/PR–RWRK, PU/PR–BACK, CO/CL–RWRK, CO/CL–RESU, BACK–RWRK plus the value ZERO for phrases that do not predict a specific rhetor-

ical role. The first group of phrases in Figure 8 (*"argue"*), for example, was classified as a most likely indicator of the rhetorical class CONCLUSION/CLAIM, and the third group (*"attempt"*) was classified as an indicator of PURPOSE/PROBLEM, whereas the second and fourth groups received the value ZERO.

Relative Location Feature: This feature distinguishes peripheral sentences in the document and within each paragraph, assuming a hierarchical organization of documents and paragraphs. The algorithm is sensitive to prototypical headings (e.g. *Introduction*); if such headings cannot be found, it uses a fixed range of paragraphs (first 7 and last 3 paragraphs). Document final and initial areas receive different values, but paragraph initial and final sentences are collapsed into one group.

Sentence Length Feature: All sentences under a certain length (current threshold: 15 tokens including punctuation) receive a 0 score, all sentences above the threshold a 1 score.

Thematic Word Feature: This feature is a variation of the "Term-frequency times inverse document frequency" (tf.idf) feature, a document specific keyword weighing method which is commonly used in Information Retrieval (Salton & McGill 1983). It tries to identify key words that are characteristic for the contents of the document, viz. those of a medium range frequency relative to the overall collection. The 10 top-scoring words according to the tf.idf method are chosen as thematic words; sentence scores are then computed as a weighted count of thematic words in a sentence, meaned by sentence length. The 40 top-rated sentences obtain score 1, all others 0.

Title Feature: Words occurring in the title are good candidates for document specific concepts. The Title Feature score of a sentence is the mean frequency of title word occurrences (excluding stop-list words). The 18 top-scoring sentences receive the value 1, all other sentences 0. We also experimented with taking words occurring in all headings into account (these words were scored according to the tf.idf method) but received better results for title words only.

Header Type Feature: The rhetorical division that a sentence appears in can be a good indication of its rhetorical status. The Header Type Feature uses a list of prototypical header key words like *discussion, introduction, concluding remarks, conclusions*. Each sentence is assigned one of 15 values, depending on the header it appears under. Headers are classified as one of 14 prototypical groups if they contain one or more of the header key words (or a morphological variant of it); otherwise (i.e. if they contain only domain-specific strings) they are classified as 'non-prototypical'.

3.6 Classifiers

As in Kupiec *et al.*'s (1995) experiment, each document sentence receives scores for each of the features, resulting in an estimate for the sentence's probability to also occur in the summary. This probability is calculated for each feature value as a combination of the probability of the feature-value pair occurring in a sentence which is in the summary (successful case) and the probability that the feature-value pair occurs unconditionally.

Kupiec *et al.*'s estimation for the probability that a given sentence is contained in the summary is:

$$P(s \in E | F_1, \ldots, F_k) \approx \frac{P(s \in E) \prod_{j=1}^{k} P(F_j | s \in E)}{\prod_{j=1}^{k} P(F_j)}$$

where

$P(s \in E | F_1, \ldots, F_k)$: Probability that sentence s in the source text is included in the intermediate extract E, given its feature values;

$P(s \in E)$: compression rate (constant);

$P(F_j | s \in E)$: probability of feature-value pair occurring in a sentence which is in the extract;

$P(F_j)$: probability that the feature-value pair occurs unconditionally;

k: number of feature-value pairs;

F_j: j-th feature-value pair.

For the second step, the probability that a certain sentence from the new base set (the intermediate extract) is associated with a rhetorical role is calculated analogously as follows:

$$P(e \in R_i | F_1, \ldots, F_k) \approx \frac{P(e \in R_i) \prod_{j=1}^{k} P(F_j | e \in R_i)}{\prod_{j=1}^{k} P(F_j)}$$

where

$P(e \in R_i | F_1, \ldots, F_k)$: Probability that sentence e in the intermediate extract is assigned the rhetorical role R_i, given its feature values;

$P(e \in R_i)$: probability of role R_i in extract (unconditional of feature values);

$P(F_j | e \in R_i)$: probability of feature-value pair occurring in an extract sentence which has rhetorical role R_i;

$P(F_j)$: probability that the feature-value pair occurs unconditionally in the extract;

k: number of feature-value pairs;

F_j: j-th feature-value pair.

Assuming statistical independence of the features, $P(F_j)$ (for the two different base sets), $P(F_j | s \in E)$ and $P(F_j | e \in R_i)$ can be estimated from the corpus for each F_j and each R_i. The second step returns a vector of probabilities for each sentence in a document (cf. Figure 9), with each cell in the vector corresponding to a rhetorical role. For each sentence, the role with the highest probability is chosen (cf. grey boxes).

0.9e-9	0.1e-9	0.2e-9	0.6e-10	0.3e-9	0.7e-10	0.9e-10	0
BACK	TOPI	RWRK	PU/PR	SOLU	RESU	CO/CL	

0.3e-12	0.9e-14	0.3e-14	0.6e-13	0.1e-17	0.7e-14	0.9e-12	1
BACK	TOPI	RWRK	PU/PR	SOLU	RESU	CO/CL	

0.6e-14	0.4e-10	0.9e-11	0.5e-10	0.3e-7	0.7e-8	0.1e-10	2
BACK	TOPI	RWRK	PU/PR	SOLU	RESU	CO/CL	

· · ·

0.4e-8	0.9e-10	0.3e-9	0.5e-10	0.6e-8	0.7e-9	0.1e-10	235
BACK	TOPI	RWRK	PU/PR	SOLU	RESU	CO/CL	

Figure 9: Probability vectors for document sentences No. 0, 1, 2 and 235

3.7 Evaluation

The evaluation we report here is based on co-selection between the gold standard sentences (i.e. target extracts) and the automatic results. This kind of evaluation is useful in a corpus-based approach like ours to fine-tune the single heuristics, but in our opinion final evaluation should not be based on co-selection with target extracts. Co-selection measures might give a distorted picture of the quality of an extract, because there might be many good abstracts/extracts, but a comparison with a target can only ever measure how well it approximates *one* of these. Real evaluation should be task-based, i.e. measure how well a certain document surrogate supports a human in fulfilling a certain task.

In our experiments, co-selection measures were used as follows: for extraction, co-selection reports how many of the extracted sentences had independently been identified as relevant sentences by the human annotator. For classification, co-selection reports how often the rhetorical roles identified by the algorithm were indeed the roles the human annotator had assigned. The numerical results reported for classification refer to the intermediate extract as a base set (i.e. those sentences that have been correctly identified in the first step). Cross-validation is used: the model is trained on a training set of documents, leaving a single document out at a time (the current test document). We did not have an indication as to subject matter like Kupiec *et al.* did (by journal name), so we chose to use all other documents but the single test document for training. After training, the model is used to extract candidate sentences from the test document, and co-selection values are measured.

Numerical values in the tables always give precision and recall rates as percentages. Due to the setup of the experiment (there are always as many sentences chosen as there are gold standards), precision and recall values are identical for extraction and for the *overall* results of classification. However, it is possible that precision and recall values for the classification of a *specific* rhetorical role differ. This is because it is possible that the algorithm overestimates the frequency of one role X at the expense of another role Y, in which case the recall of X would increase, but the precision of X would decrease. For multiply-annotated gold standard sentences, a correct classification was scored when the algorithm identified *one* of the ambiguous roles correctly.

As a baseline for the first task we chose sentences from the beginning of the source text, which constituted a recall and precision of 28.0%. This "from-top" baseline is a more conservative baseline than random order: it is more difficult to beat, as prototypical document structure places a high percentage of relevant information in the beginning.

The baseline for the second task (classification) is computed by classifying each sentence as the most frequent role (SOLUTION); it stands at an amazing 40.1% which means that this task is statistically much easier than extraction.

3.8 Results

3.8.1 Extraction

Extraction	Indiv.	Cumul.
Indicator Quality Feature	54.4	54.4
Relative Location Feature	41.0	63.9
Sentence Length Feature	28.9	65.6
Title Feature	21.6	65.6
Header Type Feature	39.6	65.3
Thematic Word Feature	16.2	66.0
Indicator Rhetorics Feature	44.0	65.6
Baseline	28.0	

Figure 10: Impact of individual heuristics on extraction

Figure 10 summarizes the contribution of the features, individually and cumulatively. Precision and recall values for the features vary between 16.2% (Thematic Word Feature) and 54.4% (Indicator Quality Feature). The most successful combination of the 7 available heuristics at 66.0% actually excludes the Indicator Rhetorics Feature—including it would decrease the results slightly (by 0.4%). The fact that a subset of all heuristics achieves a better result than all heuristics taken together means that the combination of heuristics in our implementation is non-monotonic. Non-monotonicity would be an unfortunate property in a real world setting where there are no gold standards available, and where we have to rely on the fact that *each* heuristic in the pool contributes positively to the results. However, in the supervised experiments described here co-selection measures are used to fine-tune the heuristics, in order to identify weaknesses of features (or features that should be removed from the pool completely).

Also note that even such weak features as the Title Feature and Thematic Word Feature with precision and recall lower than the baseline can still contribute positively to the results, whereas the relatively strong Indicator Rhetorics Feature does not. This does not

mean that the Indicator Rhetorics Feature is not a good feature, but only that it is not completely independent from the more successful features, contrary to assumption (in this case, it is probably very similar to the Indicator Quality Feature). Thus, how helpful a heuristic will be in combination with others cannot be judged from its individual performance alone, but also from its similarity to the other heuristics.

Overall, these results reconfirm the usefulness of Kupiec *et al.*'s method of heuristic combination. The method increases precision for the best feature by around 20%.

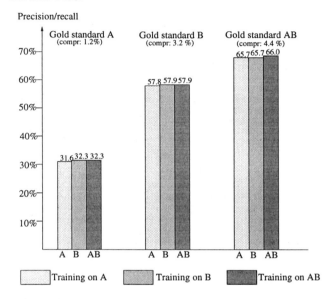

Figure 11: Influence of training material/gold standards

In order to see how the different origins of our gold standards contribute to the results, we trained three models (cf. Figure 11): one by training only on gold standard A sentences (light grey), one by training only on gold standards B (medium grey), and the third by training on both kinds of gold standards (dark grey). We then used the 3 models for 3 different tasks—first trying to identify A gold standards, then B gold standards and then both. Due to the higher compression of the task, extraction in the first task is statistically more difficult, which accounts for the much lower precision and recall values when compared to the other tasks. If we compare the values *within* extraction tasks, where the only difference is in *training*, the results show a surprising consistency: the distribution of heuristics values was almost identical between gold standards, no matter which gold standards we had trained our model on. The practical conclusion from this experiment is that we can get intermediate extracts of a similar quality (if we were to be content with these as end results) by training only on the relatively cheaply attainable gold standard A (alignment), rather than using the labor-intensive gold standard B (human judgement).

3.8.2 Classification

Classification	Indiv.	Cumul.
Indicator Rhetorics Feature	56.3	56.3
Relative Location Feature	46.5	63.8
Title Feature	40.0	64.2
Indicator Quality Feature	45.9	63.8
Sentence Length Feature	39.7	61.6
Thematic Word Feature	16.2	61.5
Header Type Feature	39.6	57.2
Baseline		40.1

Figure 12: Impact of individual heuristics on classification

Figure 12 summarizes the contribution of the individual features for classification, taken individually and cumulatively. Precision and recall values for the features vary between 16.2% (Thematic Word Feature) and 56.3% (Indicator Rhetorics Feature). The most successful combination consisted of Indicator Rhetorics Feature, Relative Location Feature and Title Feature (with a combined precision/recall value of 64.2%). The combination is non-monotonic to a higher degree than in the extraction task: addition of the other 4 heuristics steadily decreased precision and recall to 57.2%.

Where does the system make errors? The confusion matrix in Figure 13 shows the distribution of machine and human classifications for the different roles (best heuristic combination), where the columns in the table refer to the roles assigned by our algorithm ("Machine") and the rows denote roles assigned in the gold standard sentences ("Human"). For example, out of the 227 SOLUTION gold standard sentences that the human judge identified, the system found 170 correctly; it misclassified 41 as PROBLEM and the remaining 16 as CONCLUSION. The grey boxes along the diagonal show the absolute numbers of successful machine classifications per role; also, precision and recall values of the automatic classification are given for each rhetorical role.

It is obvious that the system significantly underestimates low-frequency roles—there are only very few RELATED WORK and RESULT roles assigned by the system, and none at all for TOPIC. In comparison, the estimation of the frequency of the higher frequency roles is quite adequate.

The confusion matrix illustrates that our system often misclassifies PROBLEMS as SOLUTIONS (38 times) and SOLUTIONS as PROBLEMS (41 times). But these roles are often co-classified by the human judge, as Figure 14 shows: 113 out of the 434 SOLUTION instances and the 352 PROBLEM instances were co-classifications "PROBLEM and/or SOLUTION". Apart from ambiguities between PROBLEM and SOLUTION, there were also many misclassifications including these roles and CONCLUSION (cf. the hatched boxes in Figure 14). These were exactly the ones where our algorithm had a high percentage of misclassifications (cf. the hatched boxes in Figure 13), which implies that the low performance

MACHINE

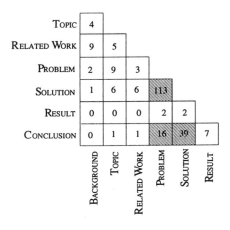

HUMAN	BACKGROUND	TOPIC	RELATED WORK	PROBLEM	SOLUTION	RESULT	CONCLUSION	Total	Recall
BACKGROUND	48			2	3			53	0.91
TOPIC	8	0	1	28	5		2	44	0.00
RELATED WORK	5		0	9	4			18	0.00
PROBLEM	2		2	137	38		10	189	0.72
SOLUTION				41	170		16	227	0.75
RESULT				2	5	3	4	14	0.21
CONCLUSION	1			13	32	1	62	109	0.57
Total	65	0	3	232	257	4	94	654	0.64

Precision 0.75 0.00 0.00 0.59 0.66 0.75 0.65 0.64

Figure 13: Confusion matrix for argumentative classification by roles (machine)

	BACKGROUND	TOPIC	RELATED WORK	PROBLEM	SOLUTION	RESULT
TOPIC	4					
RELATED WORK	9	5				
PROBLEM	2	9	3			
SOLUTION	1	6	6	113		
RESULT	0	0	0	2	2	
CONCLUSION	0	1	1	16	39	7

Figure 14: Number of sentences involved in multiple markup (gold standards)

of the system must be partly attributed to the inherent difficulty of the task. The distinction between these roles is conceptually difficult: conclusions are often statements *about* properties of the solution or *about* phenomena in the world (which are annotated as problems); problems and solutions co-occur often in the same sentence, and sometimes it is difficult to distinguish between a research goal and its solution, i.e. to find out if the sentence describes a goal in itself or a research step towards the main goal. This decision is particularly hard where the status of the sentence is not linguistically marked. In that case, only inference on the argumentation in the article as a whole might help a human judge disambiguate, a possibility obviously not open to our system.

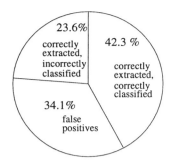

Figure 15: Overall results

Overall results for both tasks of the experiment (extraction and classification) are shown in Figure 15. At our high compression of 4.4%, 42.3% of all gold-standard sentences have been both correctly extracted and classified. This number includes the cases where one of several ambiguous roles has been identified correctly. A further 23.6% of the presented sentences can be counted as almost correct; they have been correctly extracted but have been assigned the wrong rhetorical role. 34.1% of all sentences are false positives, i.e. they should not have been extracted at all because the human annotator had not marked them.

Figure 16 shows a typical example of a rhetorically annotated extract. It is the output of our system after processing the first article in our collection, cmp_lg-9404003. Examples for correctly extracted and classified sentences are sentences 0 and 4, and also sentences 235, 236 and 238 (where one role was correctly identified). Correctly extracted, but incorrectly classified, are sentences 2 and 7. In our example, the only false positive is sentence 8.

The example also shows just how difficult rhetorical classification is. Consider sentence 7—a point could be made for the system's classification as well as for the human classification. Is "redefinition of synchronous TAG derivation" the Topic of the paper, or is it the Solution? Or is the Problem "How can synchronous TAG derivation be redefined?" One of these possibilities had to be chosen by objective criteria, which are documented in the coding manual for the annotation task.

4 Discussion

We find the results encouraging: with shallow processing, in a high-compression task, our algorithm finds 66% of all marked-up gold standard sentences in our training text and subsequently associates the right role for 64% of the correctly extracted sentences. Even though these results are only measurements of co-selection, they support our hypothesis that argumentative document structure can be approximated by low-level properties of the sentence. We see our prototype as a shallow document structure analyzer, specially designed for scientific text and geared towards the kinds of meta-

		MACHINE	HUMAN
0	The formalism of synchronous tree-adjoining grammars [REF], a variant of standard tree-adjoining grammars (TAG), was intended to allow the use of TAGs for language transduction in addition to language specification.	BACK	BACK
2	This paper concerns the formal definitions underlying synchronous tree-adjoining grammars.	SOLU	TOPI
4	This sort of rewriting definition of derivation is problematic for several reasons.	PROB	PROB
7	In this paper, we describe how synchronous TAG derivation can be redefined so as to eliminate these problems.	PROB	SOLU TOPIC
8	The redefinition relies on an independent redefinition of the notion of tree-adjoining derivation [REF] that was motivated completely independently of worries about the generative capacity of synchronous TAGs, but which happens to solve this problem in an elegant manner.	PROB	—
235	We have introduced a simple, natural definition of synchronous tree-adjoining derivation, based on isomorphisms between standard tree-adjoining derivations, that avoids the expressivity and implementability problems of the original rewriting definition.	SOLU	SOLU PROB
236	The decrease in expressivity, which would otherwise make the method unusable, is offset by the incorporation of an alternative definition of standard tree-adjoining derivation, previously proposed for completely separate reasons, that allows for multiple adjunctions at a single node in an elementary tree.	PROB	SOLU PROB
238	Nonetheless, some remaining problematic cases call for yet more flexibility in the definition; the isomorphism requirement may have to be relaxed.	SOLU	SOLU RWRK

Figure 16: Example of a rhetorically annotated extract, with gold standard judgement ("Human")

summaries claims are stated boldly without explanations or comments, whereas in the full article a sentence conveying the same information tends to be formulated much more tentatively and with a higher level of reserve. Thus, it is unlikely that we will be able to use sentences extracted from the body of the text without change. The main problem is that sentences are too large a unit for rhetorical annotation and extraction, as became apparent during the human annotation phase: ideally, one would like to annotate and extract a unit that corresponds to a proposition, i.e. a clause. However, due to problems of ambiguity between sentential and phrasal coordination (and subordination), it is difficult to find clauses automatically with low-level tools like tokenizers. For now, we have to content ourselves with sentences as our selection unit for purely practical reasons. The sentence-based approach put forward here achieves good results, which might be improved later by a more sophisticated unit identification.

One of the main motivations behind our definition of rhetorical roles found in scientific articles is that this classification is intuitive to humans. This could be relevant for the procedure of how gold standards for training are gained. Typically, when human annotation is used to define gold standards for sentence extraction (Zechner 1995, Marcu 1997), the instructions to the annotators are vague and phrased in terms of importance ("annotate important sentences"). Due to the subjectivity and task dependence of the term 'important', such instructions usually result in individually varying annotations. If our claim that our annotation scheme defines relevance criteria in a more objective way is true, a definition of importance in terms of these rhetorical roles should make the task of annotating gold standards easier.

An experiment is currently underway to substantiate this claim. We have written a coding manual, i.e. an operational description of how the rhetorical roles are to be annotated, based on Swales' rhetorical moves, indicator phrases, and context. In the experiment, we compare the inter-annotator reliability of annotators who have read the annotation guidelines to that of two control groups: a second group who has been instructed to mark instances of the seven rhetorical roles without any further instructions, and a third group which had only been instructed to annotate important sentences. If our definitions of the rhetorical roles can be conveyed to other humans operationally, group 1 will have the highest inter-annotator reliability. If they are intuitive, group 2 will annotate similarly to group 1. Inter-annotator reliability should be higher in either group 1 or 2 than in group 3.

The usability of gold standards gained in an annotation based on our rhetorical roles will have to be established in an independent, task-based evaluation.

5   Related Work

(Paice 1981) was probably the first attempt at implementing an extraction mechanism for physics articles that relied on pattern-matching operations, based on indicator phrases. Indicator phrases have been frequently used since then (Johnson et al. 1993). Paice & Jones (1993) made the method more flexible by supplying a finite state grammar for indicator phrases specific to the agriculture domain. However, we are the first to explicitly use the rhetorical status of indicator phrase for extraction and rhetorical classification.

There is a similar notion of cue phrases, typically used in discourse analysis, which is closely related to our notion of indicator phrases. Cohen (1987) defines cue words as all words and phrases used by the speaker to directly indicate the structure of the argument to the hearer. Cue phrases are typically short and come from a closed-class vocabulary (e.g. adverbials or sentence connectives (Litman 1996)). As a result, the linguistic realization of the cue phrases between different authors tends to be invariant. Our indicator phrases, on the other hand, are longer and more variable; because they depend on the individual writing style, they are more difficult to identify automatically.

Rhetorical Structure Theory (RST) defines local rhetorical relations between sentences and clauses (Mann & Thompson 1987), in order to build up a fixed rhetorically annotated tree structure through a complete rhetorical analysis of the text. There are automatic procedures for recognizing RST relations, either heuristically (Miike et al. 1994, Sumita et al. 1992) or by full rhetorical parse (Marcu 1997).

There are some analogies between these approaches and the analysis proposed in this paper, even though they are not obvious. We, too, believe that the main discourse structure of a paper is a hierarchical, rhetorically annotated tree structure. The branches are annotated differently, but one could argue that our rhetorical roles are text-type specific realizations of RST relations.

We believe that the upper parts of the tree are more important for abstracting than the lower level parts. Unlike RST, we are not concerned with rhetorical relations between each sentence or clause, but we concentrate on the higher levels of the tree, what we call global rhetorical relations: relations of content units with respect to the content of the whole article. We use indicator phrases which mark global rhetorical moves, rather than those that mark rhetorical relations between sentences or clauses.

As a result, we can perform a robust rhetorical analysis without the need for a full analysis. Our two-step approach ensures that we find global fillers for this flat tree structure with a reasonably high confidence level, at the cost of some detail in the lower areas of the tree. Indeed, the annotation scheme described in this chapter only allows us to build rhetorical trees which are one level deep.

Of course the representation of the text's structure

linguistic, argumentative constructs typically found in this text type.

However, our approach crucially depends on the quality of the indicator list. As our indicator list is hand-crafted, (i.e. gained during the reading and annotation of the 123 papers in our training corpus), as opposed to automatically acquired, one might be suspicious of its performance—it might be over-fitted to the data, i.e. too dependent on phrases that occur only rarely rather than relying on generic phrases. As a result, it might not generalize well to other documents from the same source. The first question is thus how robust the indicator list is to different data of the same source.

In order to test the robustness of the list, we need *unseen* data, i.e. documents which were not taken into account when building the system or its knowledge sources, but for which gold standard judgements exist. As the process of annotation and indicator phrase addition happened simultaneously in our experiment, we do not have gold standards for the unseen part of our corpus. But we can simulate 'unseen' data as follows. We compare versions of our indicator phrase list before and after the annotation process for the last third of our training set (42 documents). Before the annotation process for that third, the indicator phrase list already contained 1501 indicator phrases; the annotation process for the last third only contributed another 262 phrases. When using the indicator list before the annotation process, the last third of the training data is practically treated as unseen: only indicator phrases are used that already occurred in the first two thirds of our training corpus. We report results only for the Indicator Features, because the performance of the other heuristics would not change by the analysis of more data. The results (Figure 17) show that there is only a minor decrease in performance if the first list is used (left column). This means that the indicator list, even though hand-crafted, is robust and general enough for our purposes; it generalizes reasonably well to texts of a similar kind, viz. research articles in computational linguistics of around 6 to 20 pages in length.

Another question is how well the list of phrases we collected might scale up to other domains. We make no claims about other *text types*, e.g. newspaper articles on scientific topics, or articles in *Scientific American*; our method depends on the explicitness of meta-linguistic information of scientific research articles which is not necessarily present in other text types.

We are interested in different domains, however, because we believe that the definition of rhetorical roles in our annotation scheme are generic rhetorical steps in scientific research papers. We are now planning to move to articles in the medical domain, in order to validate this hypothesis. With our corpus already consisting of articles from different sub-domains of computational linguistics, we are confident that performance should be similar in different domains as long as we have the right indicator phrases available. In the light of these considerations, the main challenge is to make the indicator

Extraction		
	Last 42 files treated as	
Heuristics used	seen	unseen
Indicator Quality Feature	57.62	54.32
Indicator Rhetorics Feature	47.76	44.48
Indicator Quality, Title, Sentence Length, and Header Type Features	68.36	64.78
Baseline	25.67	

Classification		
	Last 42 files treated as	
Heuristics used	seen	unseen
Indicator Quality Feature	50.21	49.36
Indicator Rhetorics Feature	56.47	55.79
Indicator Rhetorics, Relative Location and Title Features	61.37	60.26
Baseline	45.26	

Figure 17: Difference between seen and unseen data

features more adaptive to new text. What is needed is a method for the automatic and reliable acquisition of indicator phrases from corpus data, so that indicators get recognized even if the linguistic expression found is not identical, but only similar to one of the examples in the list.

We have run some preliminary experiments in indicator list acquisition. We used a simple method: using the gold standard sentences as a base, we compiled frequency lists of strings of different length occurring under each rhetorical role. Because subject matter specific strings get automatically cancelled out during this procedure, we ended up with a proto-list of around 500 very frequently occurring indicator phrases. In the extraction/classification experiment, this list performed about 30% below our hand-crafted list, a drop in performance which we believe to be mostly due to the fact that the new list is very short compared to the manually created list. On the positive side, the automatically created list is very unlikely to be over-fitted to our data. Further research could aim at improving this baseline by taking more sophisticated criteria like statistical interaction between the words in phrases into account, and by using different similarity measures to cluster similar phrases together.

In our approach, the rhetorically annotated extracts are collections of *sentences*. Although sentences are a natural choice of information unit when the collection of sentences is itself the abstract, there are several reasons why sentences are *not* the ideal information units for the approach we take. One problem is that as sentences are rhetorically connected to previous ones, they might not mean the same thing in isolation. They certainly don't look the same: Salager (1992), who analyzed summaries in the medical domain for the use of hedging and their rhetorical structure, found that in as a flat tree is a simplification. In principle, our annotation scheme could be extended to include these lower-level relations (e.g. the subproblem relationship between two problems), with intersegment relations holding at each level (e.g. the problem-solution relationship between a given problem and a solution when more than one problem is mentioned). This more detailed analysis may prove useful for the construction of longer and even more modular abstracts. But we believe that many of the local rhetorical relations between sentences and clauses are not immediately important for robust high-compression abstracting.

Our use of meta-linguistic information makes our approach different from methods which aim at representing the *contents* of the text. Lexical cohesion methods (Barzilay & Elahad 1997), like statistical, keyword based methods, model main document concepts shallowly by using presumably content-specific lexical items observed in the text. Our method, in contrast, employs structural heuristics alone and uses *everything else* in the text but the content-specific lexical items.

Having said this, we can very well envisage our method cooperating with a complementary module that is based on an analysis of content rather than form. In a larger summarizing system, information from both types of module could flow together, in order to fulfill the tasks needed for generating abstracts from rhetorically annotated extracts: finding duplicate fillers, deciding on the best candidates for a filler, and resolving conflicts between fillers.

6   Conclusion

Robust, high-compression abstracting can be improved greatly if the discourse structure of the text is taken into account. We have argued that rhetorical classification of extracted material is a useful subtask for the production of a new kind of abstract that can be tailored in length and focus to users' expertise and specific information needs.

Our goal is to recognize abstract-worthy sentences with respect to global rhetorical structure, and to perform a subsequent classification of these sentences into a set of predefined rhetorical roles. We have presented a robust method which uses supervised learning techniques to deduce rhetorical roles from lower-level properties of sentences. This is technically feasible, because restrictions with respect to the task of the reader on the one hand, and knowledge about the typical argumentation of the writers on the other hand, can be exploited.

The results are encouraging; our algorithm determines 66% of all marked-up gold standards sentences in our training text and subsequently associates the right role for 64% of the correctly extracted sentences.

7   Acknowledgements

Data collection of our corpus took place collaboratively with Byron Georgantopolous. The first author is supported by an EPSRC studentship.

References

Ad Hoc Working Group For Critical Appraisal Of The Medical Literature. 1987. A proposal for more informative abstracts of clinical articles. *Annals of Internal Medicine.*

Alley, M. 1996. *The craft of scientific writing.* Englewood Cliffs, N.J.: Prentice-Hall.

American National Standards Institute, Inc. 1979. American national standard for writing abstracts. American National Standards Institute, Inc., New York. ANSI Z39.14.1979.

Barzilay, R., and Elahad, M. 1997. Using lexical chains for text summarization. In Mani, I., and Maybury, M. T., eds., *Proceedings of the ACL/EACL-97 workshop on Intelligent Scalable Text Summarization.* Association for Computational Linguistics.

Baxendale, P. B. 1958. Man-made index for technical literature – an experiment. *IBM journal on research and development* 2(4):354–361.

Bazerman, C. 1988. *Shaping writing knowledge.* Madison: University of Wisconsin Press.

Borko, H., and Chatman, S. 1963. Criteria for acceptable abstracts: a survey of abstractors' instructions. *American Documentation* 14(2):149–160.

Broer, J. W. 1971. Abstracts in block diagram form. *IEEE Transactions on Engineering Writing and Speech* 14(2):64–67. ISA, 72-1626.

Buxton, A. B., and Meadows, A. J. 1978. Categorization of the information in experimental papers and their author abstracts. *Journal of Research in Communication Studies* 1:161–182.

Cohen, R. 1987. Analyzing the structure of argumentative discourse. *Computational Linguistics* 13:11–24.

Cremmins, E. T. 1996. *The art of abstracting.* Information Resources Press.

Day, R. A. 1995. *How to write and publish a scientific paper.* Cambridge: Cambridge University Press.

Edmundson, H. P. 1969. New methods in automatic extracting. *Journal of the Association for Computing Machinery* 16(2):264–285.

Hartley, J., and Sydes, M. 1997. Are structured abstracts easier to read than traditional ones? *Journal of Research in Reading* 20(2):122–136.

Hartley, J.; Sydes, M.; and Blurton, A. 1996. Obtaining information accurately and quickly: are structured abstracts more efficient? *Journal of Information Science* 22(5):349–356.

International Organisation for Standardisation. 1976. Documentation – Abstracts for publication and documentation. International Organisation for Standardisation ISO 214-1976.

Johnson, F. C.; Paice, C. D.; Black, W. J.; and Neal, A. P. 1993. The application of linguistic processing to automatic abstract generation. *Journal of Document and Text Management* 1(3):215–42.

Kintsch, W., and van Dijk, T. A. 1978. Toward a model of text comprehension and production. *Psychological Review* 85(5):363–394.

Kircz, J. G. 1991. The rhetorical structure of scientific articles: the case for argumentational analysis in information retrieval. *Journal of Documentation* 47(4):354–372.

Kupiec, J.; Pedersen, J. O.; and Chen, F. 1995. A trainable document summarizer. In *Proceedings of the 18th ACM-SIGIR Conference, Association for Computing Machinery, Special Interest Group Information Retrieval*, 68–73.

Liddy, E. D. 1991. The discourse-level structure of empirical abstracts: an exploratory study. *Information Processing and Management* 27(1):55–81.

Litman, D. J. 1996. Cue phrase classification using machine learning. *Journal of Artificial Intelligence Research* 5:53–94.

Luhn, H. P. 1958. The automatic creation of literature abstracts. *IBM Journal of Research and Development* 2(2):159–165.

Mann, W. C., and Thompson, S. A. 1987. Rhetorical structure theory: A theory of text organisation. Technical report, Information Sciences Institute, U of South California. ISI/RS-87-190.

Manning, A. 1990. Abstracts in relation to larger and smaller discourse structures. *Journal of Technical Writing and Communication* 20(4):369–390.

Marcu, D. 1997. *The rhetorical parsing, summarization, and generation of natural language texts*. Ph.D. Dissertation, University of Toronto.

Miike, S.; Itoh, E.; Ono, K.; and Sumita, K. 1994. A full-text retrieval system with a dynamic abstract generation function. In *Proceedings of the 17th ACM-SIGIR Conference, Association for Computing Machinery, Special Interest Group Information Retrieval*, 152–163.

Milas-Bracovic, M. 1987. The structure of scientific papers and their author abstracts. *Informatologia Yugoslavica* 19(1-2):51–67.

O'Hara, K., and Sellen, A. 1997. A comparison of reading paper and on-line documents. In *Proceedings of CHI-97, Special Interest Group on Computer & Human Interaction*.

Paice, C. D., and Jones, A. P. 1993. The identification of important concepts in highly structured technical papers. In *Proceedings of the Sixteenth Annual International ACM-SIGIR conference on research and development in IR, Association for Computing Machinery, Special Interest Group Information Retrieval*.

Paice, C. D. 1981. The automatic generation of literary abstracts: an approach based on the identification of self-indicating phrases. In Oddy, R. N.; Robertson, S. E.; van Rijsbergen, C. J.; and Williams, P. W., eds., *Information Retrieval Research*. London: Butterworth. 172–191.

Pinelli, T. E.; Cordle, V. M.; and Vondran, R. F. 1984. The function of report components in the screening and reading of technical reports. *Journal of Technical Writing and Communication* 14(2):87–94.

Rennie, D., and Glass, R. M. 1991. Structuring abstracts to make them more informative. *Journal of the American Medical Association* 266(1).

Rowley, J. 1982. *Abstracting and indexing*. London: Bingley.

Salager-Meyer, F. 1992. A text-type and move analysis study of verb tense and modality distributions in medical English abstracts. *English for Specific Purposes* 11:93–113.

Salton, G., and McGill, M. J. 1983. *Introduction to Modern Information Retrieval*. Tokyo: McGraw-Hill.

Salton, G.; Allan, J.; Buckley, C.; and Singhal, A. 1994. Automatic analysis, theme generation, and summarisation of machine readable texts. *Science* 264:1421–1426.

Skorochod'ko, E. F. 1972. Adaptive method of automatic abstracting and indexing. In *Information Processing 71*, volume 2. North Holland Publishing company. 1179–1182.

Sumita, K.; Ono, K.; Chino, T.; Ukita, T.; and Amaro, S. 1992. A discourse structure analyzer for japanese text. In *Proceedings of the International Conference on Fifth Generation Computer Systems*.

Swales, J. 1981. Aspects of article introductions. Aston ESP Research Project No. 1. Technical report, The University of Aston, Birmingham, U.K.

Swales, J. 1990. *Genre analysis: English in academic and research settings*. Cambridge University Press.

Zechner, K. 1995. Automatic text abstracting by selecting relevant passages. Master's thesis, Centre for Cognitive Science, University of Edinburgh.

Section 4

Knowledge-rich Approaches

Whereas previous sections have considered summarization of text documents, emphasizing analysis and selection of natural language text, in this section we turn our attention toward the final two processes in the tri-partite model of analysis, transformation, and synthesis that was discussed in the beginning of this book. Unlike previous sections, papers herein focus primarily on structured information (e.g., data and knowledge bases, that may in some cases have been produced by processing input texts) as the starting point for summarization. Whereas this frees the summarizer from addressing the linguistic complexities and variability of the input, an attendant consequence is that structure normally present in the input source (e.g., lexical cohesion, document structure, rhetorical structure) is not available to be exploited during processing. This implies a need for measures of salience and relevance that are dependent upon the knowledge source. It also implies that addressing coherence, cohesion, and fluency becomes the entire responsibility of the generator.

The first article by Lehnert nicely bridges the gap between previous sections on text analysis and the subsequent articles on later summarization phases in this section. Lehnert points out that it is estimated that in narrative texts, the ratio of inferred propositions to those explicitly stated is approximately 8:1 (Graesser, 1981). This highlights the centrality of semantic representations for stories that humans exploit in making inferences, creating causal chains and integrating new information into knowledge structures. This also suggests that for modeling the discourse structure of narratives, the relatively knowledge-poor models of discourse discussed in Section 3 will not be sufficient.

Focusing on narrative texts, Lehnert proposes a summarization strategy that builds upon prior research by DeJong (1979). DeJong's FRUMP system analyzed UPI (United Press International) stories in 50 domains using top-down, domain-specific, non-varying, script-based extraction. For example, a summary of an earthquake report would always state when and where it occurred, the Richter level, and the number of killed or injured. Of course this expectation-based processing could not deal with unexpected information that does not conform to a script (Schank and Abelson, 1977).

In contrast to this top-down approach of instantiating pre-stored schemas, Lehnert presents an approach in which higher-level (plot) structures are constructed bottom-up. Lehnert builds on three general, primary affect states (Schank and Abelson, 1977): positive event, negative event, and mental state (with neutral affect). She describes links among these. For example, links from negative events to mental states include motivation (causations), actualization (intentions), termination, or equivalence. 15 legal pairwise configurations of affect states with these links result in "plot-units," building blocks for more complex configurations. For example, the plot unit "success" is a mental state linked to a positive event by actualization, whereas "failure" is a mental state linked to a negative event by actualization.

Her partially implemented frame-based system builds specific plot units from affect states. For example, if two mental states are encountered, a daemon checks if a subgoal, mutual exclusion, or equivalence relationship exists to construct a primitive plot unit, from which more complex plot units can be derived. A recognized subgoal might predict the occurrence of nested subgoals, a request, a threat, a kind act, or a malicious act, thus constructing a hierarchical structure of plot units. Summarization can then proceed on plot-units as abstract units of narrative.

An evaluation of 10 human subjects' summary performance suggested that 1. plot-unit analysis was central to paraphrase production, 2. a number of plot units were implicit (via inference) in the human created summary, and 3. certain units were "pivotal" in driving inferences about other units. Lehnert defines pivotal units by analyzing plot unit graph connectivity. She describes a summarization process that includes identifying top-level plot units, deriving a plot-unit graph structure, identifying the pivotal unit, generating a baseline summary and augmenting this with information from plot units related to the pivotal unit. This final integration of new information in the base-line summary is accomplished by either adding a new clause or further refining existing references in the baseline summary. This kind of revisionist strategy is addressed in McKeown et al.'s subsequent article in this section in a richer and more fully implemented manner.

Lehnert's work leaves open as many questions as it answers, e.g., How sufficient are the current plot-units for what range of narrative? What is a minimally sufficient summary? How will the technique perform on real-world texts? Nevertheless, it provides an impressive analysis and potential foundation for a general strategy for narrative summary.

The next paper by Hahn and Reimer considers summarization as an operator-based transformation that takes output from a natural language analyzer and creates conceptually more abstract condensed knowledge structures. In particular, the authors propose a formal model of text summarization that is embedded in a classification-based model of terminological reasoning, thus integrating the text summarization process into the formal reasoning system underlying the knowledge representation language. The authors illustrate their TOPIC system implemented in their model in the domain of information technology reviews and legal reports. They describe a three-step process to summarization: first, a repertoire of salience operators are applied to paragraphs, second, topic descriptions are determined and aggregated over paragraphs as appropriate, and third, generalization operators are applied across the topic descriptions to create a hierarchical text graph. Salience operators in step one determine what are salient concepts, properties, and relationships in the text via frequency measures and inferences on entities in the source text. Topic descriptions (collections of concepts, properties, relations) are then computed and related across paragraphs. Using an interactive text graph navigation aid, a user is able to traverse the resulting text graph, varying the detail of the summaries.

The remaining papers focus on the synthesis phase of summarization. The article by McKeown, Robin, and Kukich describes techniques for opportunistically packing information into sentences using linguistic constructions. The resulting expressions attempt to convey maximal information in minimal space through elimination operations such as deleting repetitions, and aggregation operations such as conjoining similar content. Motivated by corpus analysis of human summaries from two domains, their approach to summary generation distinguishes between essential and optional content, using revision strategies to fold information into the same sentence using linguistic devices such as words that convey multiple facts, noun and verb modifiers, conjunction and ellipsis, and abridged references. Using a common lexicalizer and syntactic generation module (FUF/SURGE) together with a domain specific lexical chooser, the authors explored two summary systems, STREAK, which generates basketball game summaries, and PLANDOC, which summarizes network planning activity.

While both generate summaries in an opportunistic manner, STREAK uses a revision approach (editing a draft of essential facts) whereas PLANDOC uses discourse planning, looking ahead to perform repetition, deletion and conjunction operations. For example, instead of reporting *Jay Humphries scored 24 points. He came in as a reserve*, a noun phrase modification rule is invoked in STREAK to create the resulting more economical expression *Reservist Jay Humphries scored 24 points*. In a different kind of operation, PLANDOC compresses messages by searching for common actions and associated features, sorting these, and using conjunction together with ellipsis to generate a concise summary. In both of these systems, control is exercised to avoid generating overly complex or ambiguous output. In STREAK, imposing a maximum word length of 45 and allowing a maximum of 10 levels of syntactic embedding controls sentence complexity. In contrast,

PLANDOC blocks conjoin (aggregation) operations when a threshold is exceeded.

Interestingly, in their approach the distinction between information that must be present versus that which may be present is treated as being domain-dependent. (In other papers in this section, by Maybury and by Hahn and Reimer, we see the use of both domain specific and domain independent measures, e.g., frequency analysis, as heuristics for determining importance). The authors conclude by emphasizing the practicality of summary generation and the opportunity to leverage advances in information extraction to generate summaries from text, a topic also addressed by Maybury's paper in this section and McKeown and Radev's paper in Section 6.

In the final paper, Maybury describes SumGen, a user-focused and generic summarizer applied to a complex military simulation and to a knowledge base of information extracted from news sources. The paper describes techniques for event selection, condensation (including aggregation and generalization) and presentation, essentially arguing that combining these techniques result in more effective and efficient summaries that any single technique alone.

While domain-specific techniques are used for some selection operations, SumGen is principally based on statistical measures used to determine significance of events in the simulation or knowledge base. Another important contributor to the summary process are two classes of condensation operations that are performed, aggregation and generalization. For example, a tripartite focus model of time, space, and topic is used to generate more compact event expressions using such devices as temporal and spatial adverbials (e.g., "five minutes later"). Aggregation operations (e.g., find all events with equivalent event types or participants) similarly might result in more compact conjunctive and adverbial expressions (e.g., "Site-A and Site-D simultaneously fired a missile at ..."). In contrast, generalization operations (which the author refers to as "abstraction") replace a more specific action or set of actions with a more general one, such as stating "Mission OCA101 flew an ingress route" as opposed to reporting each individual leg of the air route the mission aircraft flew. The author shows how rhetorical structure can be exploited during synthesis to determine what content to include or exclude. (This can be compared with the use of rhetorical structure by Marcu in Section 3, where it helps identify key content to extract during text summarization). Both the battle simulator and business news summarizer were evaluated with 22 subjects by assessing information extraction performance on both source (long) and summary (short) texts. SumGen was shown to reduce average sentence length by approximately 15%, document length by 70%, and time to perform information extraction by 58%.

As a whole, the papers in this section underscore the practicality, importance, and at the same time potential complexity of producing summaries from structured data. Collectively, they address a range of domains, including basketball, network planning, technical and business news, and battlefield simulation. Related work on the FOG (Bourbeau et al. 1990) marine weather forecast generation system is illustrative of both the operational readiness of summary generation (FOG is in daily use) as well as the importance of multilingual generation (French and English). In Section 6, McKeown and Radev demonstrate how synthesis techniques can be used effectively for summarizing multiple articles about terrorist incidents.

The techniques described in this section illustrate the hybrid application of statistical analysis and domain specific techniques. In these systems, condensation operations occur during all phases of the summarization process. The complementarity of these papers suggests our understanding can advance through a combination of analysis of human-produced summaries, formal modeling and computational implementation of transformation and synthesis processes, and task-based summary evaluation. Also identified is the opportunity for the transfer of techniques between summarization analysis and synthesis.

Finally, these papers uncover many remaining unexplored issues. These include the need for more comprehensive corpus analysis of conceptual and linguistic summarization operations, the formalization of the range of condensation operations, the evaluation of approaches, and the move toward more general purpose, domain independent techniques. A key technical challenge will be the effective integration and reuse of previous and future results in information extraction, text planning, and linguistic realization to maximize progress. A methodological challenge is to understand the generality and replicability of results of experiments involving specific source genres, domains, users and tasks.

References

Bourbeau, L., Carcagno, D., Goldberg, E., Kittredge, R. & Polguere, A. 1990. Bilingual generation of weather forecasts in an operations environment. *Proceedings of the 13th International Conference on Computational Linguistics (COLING-90)*, Vol. 1, pp. 90-92, Helsinki, Finland, 1990.

Graesser, A. C. 1981. *Prose Comprehension beyond the Word*. New York: Springer-Verlag.

DeJong, G. F. 1979. *Skimming stories in real time: An experiment in integrated understanding* (Dept of CS Report Number 156). Yale University, New Haven.

Schank and Abelson, 1977. *Scripts, Plans, Goals and Understanding*. Hillsdale, N. J.: Lawrence Erlbaum Associates.

14

Plot Units: A Narrative Summarization Strategy

Wendy G. Lehnert
Yale University

INTRODUCTION

When a person reads a narrative story, an internal representation for that story is constructed in memory. One way that we can examine the contents of this memory representation is by asking the reader simple questions about the story. Typical question-answering behavior will reveal evidence for numerous inferences, causal chain constructions, and the predictive integration of information into instantiated knowledge structures (Dyer & Lehnert, 1980; Graesser, Robertson, & Anderson, 1981; Lehnert, 1978). The complexity of an internal memory representation is reflected in part by the number of propositions that are present in memory, but not explicitly present in the original source text. For narrative texts, the ratio of inferred propositions to explicitly stated propositions is estimated to be about 8:1 (Graesser, 1981). Although some of these inferences may be reconstructed only as needed for answering a question, we are still faced with the standard search space problems that characterize most problem areas in artificial intelligence. How can large memory representations be effectively accessed and searched by efficient retrieval heuristics? What are the organizational structures of memory that underlie internal representations for text? And finally, what sorts of human memory phenomena can be examined in an effort to shed light on issues of memory organization?

Even though question answering provides us with a method for examining the contents of a memory representation, the task of question answering does not readily yield a more global picture of the memory representation as a whole. We can only guess at how the various pieces fit together within a single structure. If we are interested in the structure of narrative memory representations, the summarization task is a rich (and largely untapped) source of enlightening phenomena. When a reader is asked to summarize a story, vast amounts of information within the memory representation are selectively ignored in order to produce a distilled version of the original narrative. This process of simplification relies on a global structuring of memory that allows search procedures to concentrate on central elements of the story while ignoring peripheral details. We intuitively expect that some global or "macro" structure is holding memory together, but a precise formulation of this structure is much more elusive.

One popular approach to the summary problem involves the notion of a story grammar (Rumelhart, 1977, Simmons & Correira, 1979; Thorndyke, 1977). Although many different story grammars have been proposed, the general idea is to anticipate structural devices that are common to all stories. For example, Rumelhart points out that a number of short narratives fall into what he calls the "EPISODE" schema. The EPISODE schema about protagonist "P" consists of:

1. EVENT "E" CAUSES "P" TO DESIRE GOAL "G"
2. "P" TRIES TO GET "G" UNTIL OUTCOME "O" OCCURS

Each of the relational terms in this schema (CAUSE, DESIRE, and TRY) refer in turn to other schema that will likewise be instantiated by particular variables within a given story. The EPISODE schema provides a root node for a hierarchical tree structure that will expand to arbitrary depth as the schemata on each level are instantiated and expanded in a recursive manner.

Story grammars have been criticized on many levels (Black & Wilensky, 1979), but the most basic limitation of a story grammar derives from an unaviodable feature of all purely top-down processors: A top-down processor cannot integrate input that does not conform to its expectations. A hierarchical story grammar simply cannot be general enough to capture large variations in plot structures.

People, on the other hand, can process stories and create memory representations for texts even if they have never seen another story with a similar plot structure. As with most information-processing tasks, we must expect the optimal system to work bottom-up at first, until it knows enough to go top-down (Riesbeck & Schank, 1976). In this chapter, we present a system for text analysis and memory organization that is essentially bottom-up. Using this system, plot structures are built by examining relationships between memory structures called plot units; there is no effort to instantiate any anticipated plot schemata. We begin by describing the primitive elements that are used to construct plot units.

AFFECT-STATE PATTERNS

In the system about to be proposed, emotional reactions and states of affect are central to the notion of a plot or story structure. The structure of a narrative text is

14. PLOT UNITS: NARRATIVE SUMMARIZATION

a configuration of plot units, and each plot unit is itself a configuration of smaller entities called "affect states." Affect states do not attempt to describe complex emotional reactions or states of desire in the detail that inference mechanisms would require; they merely mark gross distinctions between "positive" events, "negative" events, and mental events of null or neutral emotionality. A number of researchers have seriously tackled the problem of affect (deRivera, 1977; Roseman, 1979), and it is hoped that our notion of a plot unit will naturally dovetail with these more sophisticated representational systems. But for the moment, it suffices for us to see just how far these very gross differentiations can carry us in our quest for summarization algorithms.

The notation we use for plot units utilizes abbreviations for three affect states:

+ (Positive Event)   Events that please
− (Negative Event)   Events that displease
M (Mental State)   Mental states (with neutral affect)

Each of these affect states occurs with respect to a single character, and events involving multiple characters require multiple affect states. For example, if John marries Mary, the event is presumably positive for John and Mary, whereas Mary's father (who cannot stand John) experiences a negative event.

As a story progresses, a linear map of chronologically ordered affect states is created for each character in the story. When we examined a number of affect-state maps from a variety of stories, general patterns were found to emerge. These patterns lead us to the notion of a plot unit. To see how this works, consider the affect map for John in the following story:

When John tried to start his car this morning, it wouldn't turn over. He asked his neighbor Paul for help. Paul did something to the carburetor and got it going. John thanked Paul and drove to work.

The affect analysis for John consists of three affect states:

−   the car won't start
M   John wants to get it started
+   Paul gets it started

To make causality explicit, we connect appropriate pairs of affect states with pairwise causal links. John's three affect states are connected by three different link types. An aversive event *motivated* John to get his car started, John *actualized* this desire by getting Paul to start the car, and Paul's assistance *terminated* the original difficulty. This pattern represents an affect configuration (or plot unit) that is extremely pervasive in narrative texts: *resolution of a problem by intentional means*.

Now suppose we extend our analysis to include the affect states of Paul:

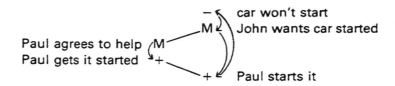

The diagonal links signify causalities of affect across characters. When Paul agrees to help, he is assuming John's state of desire; now Paul wants to get the car started too. This configuration of embedded achievement across characters signals an *honored request*. When this configuration is followed by its symmetrical counterpart, we have an instance of an *exchange*. Favors (voluntary services) are often exchanged, and the idea of a loan is a special case of exchanged services:

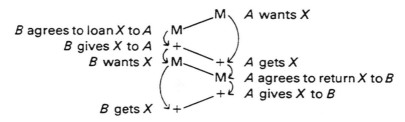

If we were missing the last two positive events in this structure, we would understand that *A* is obligated to *B;* it would be up to *A* to complete the symmetry of the configuration. A *trade* is also a special case of an exchange, where the two transactions occur simultaneously:

$$
\begin{array}{ll}
A \text{ wants } X & B \text{ wants } Y \\
A \text{ wants } B \text{ to have } Y & B \text{ wants } A \text{ to have } X \\
A \text{ gives } Y \text{ to } B & B \text{ gives } X \text{ to } A \\
A \text{ gets } X & B \text{ gets } Y
\end{array}
$$

A number of standard affect configurations arise in this manner that allow us to recognize narrative structures and build plot structures from affect states. But before we can identify standard configurations, we must present a system of causal links to join pairs of affect states.

CAUSAL LINKS

A link that runs from a negative event to a mental state describes motivation, whereas a link running from a mental state to a positive event describes actualization. To make these and other distinctions explicit, we use a system of four link types: MOTIVATION (m), ACTUALIZATION (a). TERMINATION (t), and EQUIVALENCE (e). Motivation links describe causalities behind mental states and actualization links describe intentionalities behind events. The termination link is used not when an event per se is terminated, but when the affective impact

14. PLOT UNITS: NARRATIVE SUMMARIZATION

TABLE 14.1
Causal Syntax

	M M	M +	M −	+ M	− M	+ −	− +	+ +	− −
m	*			*	*				
a		*	*						
t	*					*	*	*	*
e	*					*	*	*	*

of that event is surplanted or displaced. For example, a second marriage may "terminate" a prior divorce in this sense if it nullifies the emotional reactions to that divorce. Equivalent events and states are linked when multiple perspectives of a single affect state can be separated. The use of these links is hopefully clarified by some examples given in the next section. But first we describe the syntax of these four links.

Each link describes an oriented arc between two affect states: m-links and a-links point forward in time, whereas t-links and e-links point backward in time. With three affect states and four link types, there are 36 possible pairwise configurations if we consider all the possible combinations. But in fact, only 15 of these will occur when we observe some syntactic constraints on the use of causal links. To summarize these constraints, the Table 14.1 illustrates which combinations occur by marking legal configurations with an "*."

The constraints can be described as follows:

m-links must point to a mental state.
a-links must point from a mental state to an event.
t-links and e-links must point:
    (1) from a mental state to a mental state, or
    (2) from an event to an event.

These links have been given an orientation for intuitive convenience rather than notational necessity. For m-links and a-links, the pointer moves from a temporal antecedent to its consequent. With t-links, the pointer goes from a subsequent event to the prior event it terminates. E-links are used to identify redundant state descriptions that appear at different times. The backward orientation of e-links is therefore arbitrary.

PRIMITIVE PLOT UNITS

Our 15 legal pairwise configurations act as the building blocks for more complex configurations. We refer to them as the "primitive plot units," and each is specified by name:

MOTIVATION	SUCCESS	FAILURE
$\begin{matrix} M \\ M \end{matrix} \rangle m$	$\begin{matrix} M \\ + \end{matrix} \rangle a$	$\begin{matrix} M \\ - \end{matrix} \rangle a$
CHANGE OF MIND	**LOSS**	**MIXED BLESSING**
$\begin{matrix} M \\ M \end{matrix} \rangle t$	$\begin{matrix} + \\ - \end{matrix} \rangle t$	$\begin{matrix} + \\ - \end{matrix} \rangle e$
PERSEVERANCE	**RESOLUTION**	**HIDDEN BLESSING**
$\begin{matrix} M \\ M \end{matrix} \rangle e$	$\begin{matrix} - \\ + \end{matrix} \rangle t$	$\begin{matrix} - \\ + \end{matrix} \rangle e$
ENABLEMENT	**NEGATIVE TRADE-OFF**	**COMPLEX POSITIVE EVENT**
$\begin{matrix} + \\ M \end{matrix} \rangle m$	$\begin{matrix} - \\ \end{matrix} \rangle t$	$\begin{matrix} + \\ + \end{matrix} \rangle e$
PROBLEM	**POSITIVE TRADE-OFF**	**COMPLEX NEGATIVE EVENT**
$\begin{matrix} - \\ M \end{matrix} \rangle m$	$\begin{matrix} + \\ + \end{matrix} \rangle t$	$\begin{matrix} - \\ \end{matrix} \rangle e$

Sometimes a primitive plot unit will appear without other interceding affect states. This occurs more commonly with the units "problem," "enablement," and "motivation." Other primitive plot units tend to be broken up by interceding affect states. For example, it may take months (with lots of interceding emotional reactions) to find out that a job promotion is now leading to an ulcer. This would be an example of a mixed blessing, a good thing turned sour.

EXAMPLES OF PRIMITIVE PLOT UNITS

PROBLEM:
You get fired and need a job.
You bounce a check and need to deposit funds.
Your dog dies and you long for companionship.

SUCCESS:
You ask for a raise and you get it.
You fix a flat tire.
You need a car so you steal one.

FAILURE:
Your proposal of marriage is declined.
You can't find your wallet.
You can't get a bank loan.

RESOLUTION:
Your broken radio starts working again.
They catch the theif who has your wallet.
You fix a flat tire after a blow out.

LOSS:
Your big income tax refund is a mistake.
The woman you love leaves you.
The car you just bought is totaled.

14. PLOT UNITS: NARRATIVE SUMMARIZATION

POSITIVE TRADE-OFF: You buy a new Toyota and then inherit a Porsche.
You take a day off and then realize it's a holiday.
You get a raise and then win the Irish Sweepstakes.

NEGATIVE TRADE-OFF: You get fired so you don't have to take a lousy job assignment.
Your car blows up so you don't have to make the next insurance payment.
You lose the election so you don't have to placate demanding voters

PERSEVERANCE: You want to get married (again).
You reapply to Yale after being rejected.
You want to ski again after a bad skiing accident.

HIDDEN BLESSING: You get audited and they owe you.
You sprain an ankle and win damages.
Your mother dies and you inherit a million.

MIXED BLESSING: You buy a car and it turns out to be a lemon.
You fall in love and become insanely jealous.
Your book is reviewed but they hate it.

CHANGE OF MIND: You apply to Harvard and then go to Yale.
You want to buy a car but decide against it.
You want to see a movie until a friend pans it.

MOTIVATION: You need advice so you decide to ask a friend.
You want to buy a car so you apply for a loan.
You want to reach a client so you call him.

ENABLEMENT: You decide to celebrate after a raise.
You receive a book and decide to read it.
You get a loan and have to pay it back.

COMPLEX POSITIVE: A gift is indicative of close friendship.
Your raise signifies recognition.
You win respect by getting a Rolls Royce.

COMPLEX NEGATIVE: You lose $100 when your wallet is stolen.
You break an arm in a car accident.
Your house burns down and you aren't covered.

These primitive plot units serve as building blocks for more complicated plot configurations. They do not, by themselves, provide us with all of the recognition abilities we need. We now expand beyond our set of primitive units in order to describe more complicated situations.

COMPLEX PLOT UNITS

Using the 15 primitive plot units, we can build larger plot units to represent general plot configurations. For example, the string (− M +) of three affect states is used by three different plot units that are distinguished only by the causal links involved:

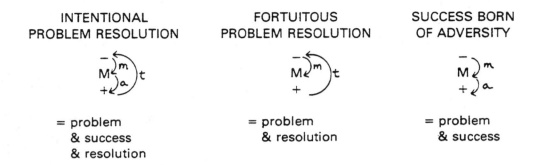

INTENTIONAL PROBLEM RESOLUTION	FORTUITOUS PROBLEM RESOLUTION	SUCCESS BORN OF ADVERSITY
= problem & success & resolution	= problem & resolution	= problem & success

These are examples of complex plot units that are commonly found in narrative texts. Other closely related plot units include:

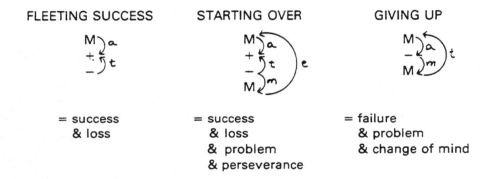

FLEETING SUCCESS	STARTING OVER	GIVING UP
= success & loss	= success & loss & problem & perseverance	= failure & problem & change of mind

Many complex plot units can be transformed into different units by way of a minor variation:

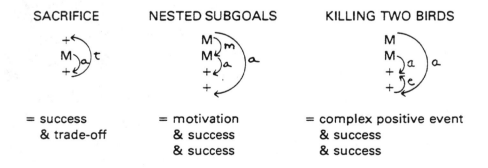

SACRIFICE	NESTED SUBGOALS	KILLING TWO BIRDS
= success & trade-off	= motivation & success & success	= complex positive event & success & success

Thus far, we have concentrated on plot units that describe configurations within a single character. A large number of complex plot units involve multiple charac-

14. PLOT UNITS: NARRATIVE SUMMARIZATION

ters. Plot units with more than one character require crosscharacter causal links. These are represented by diagonal segments between affect states, where the higher affect state precedes the lower affect state in time. Even though we found it useful to distinguish four types of intracharacter links in building the primitive plot units, we do not need to distinguish crosscharacter links. Crosscharacter links can occur between any pair of affect states, and their interpretation relies on the following conventions:

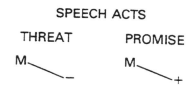

RESULTING MENTAL STATES

REQUEST   ENABLEMENT   MOTIVATION

These configurations describe the initiation of a goal state as a direct response to another character's situation. All of the resulting mental states are initiated by free choice. In the case of "M/M," the resulting mental state occurs in response to a request. This resulting mental state may assume the desires of the initiator, or it may oppose them. The request configuration does not commit us to any assumptions about the contents of the two mental states or how their contents are related. In the cases of "+/M" and "−/M," we have mental states enabled or motivated by vicarious events. For example, a desire to celebrate is normally enabled by a positive event, whereas a desire to help out is typically motivated by a negative state.

SPEECH ACTS

THREAT   PROMISE

These two configurations describe communications that result in positive and negative affect states. The antecedent in either case is a mental state describing the intentions of that character. These two configurations often appear in tandem when an agreement is acheived by coercion—that is, a promise is motivated by a threat.

SHARED EVENTS   MIXED EVENTS

Shared events are shared in the sense that two characters are affected by them in a similar manner. The same event is experienced by both people as either a positive event or a negative event. Mixed events are just the opposite. Here the same event is experienced differently by both people: One is affected positively, and one negatively.

These nine crosscharacter configurations can now be used to build complex plot units involving two characters. Some of the most common configurations involving two characters are those that describe cooperative agreements and behavior. In the simplest case, a request is made and the respondent behaves either cooperatively or not:

HONORED REQUEST   DENIED REQUEST   BUNGLED REQUEST

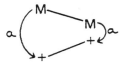 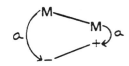 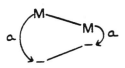

In our story about John's car we had an instance of an honored request. John asked Paul for help and Paul got the car started for John. In this situation, the second character assumes the mental goal state of the first character. Paul wanted to get the car started too. When a request is denied, we should assume different mental states. If Paul tells John that he's too busy, we should not assume that Paul wanted to get John's car started.

A slightly different situation arises when the speech act of a threat is invoked instead of a request:

EFFECTIVE COERCION   INEFFECTIVE COERCION   BUNGLED COERCION

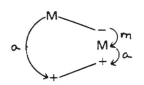 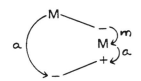 

In these situations the respondent is confronted with a problem situation that can be resolved with either cooperative behavior or a challenging denial. These situations are very common, and in some cases it is appropriate to represent them in greater detail. For example, what if Paul agrees to help John get his car started, but then fails to do so? In some stories, the extraction of an agreement receives enough attention to warrant its own affect analysis:

PROMISED REQUEST HONORED   PROMISED REQUEST BUNGLED

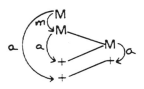 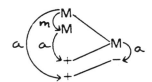

14. PLOT UNITS: NARRATIVE SUMMARIZATION

When John asks Paul to help, he has set up a subgoal for getting help. If Paul agrees to help, Paul satisfies John's subgoal by making a promise. If Paul then succeeds in helping John, the top-level goal is achieved as well. But if Paul fails, his actions amount to nothing more than good intentions that were bungled. The plot units for an honored request and a promised request that is honored are very similar. When a request is honored, we have a request and shared success. When a request is promised and then honored, we have nested subgoals, a request, a promise, and shared success. These are identical except for details about the agreement as an interaction that is separate from the service performed. This more detailed level of description is necessary when we try to represent "good intentions" that fail in response to a request or threat.

If we examine the notion of a threat at this level of detail we can see the difference between a threat that is agreed to and successful versus a threat that is sincerely agreed to but unsuccessful anyway. (These are elaborations on effective coercion and bungled coercion.)

COERCED AGREEMENT HONORED

COERCED AGREEMENT BUNGLED

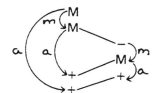
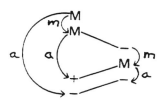

In both of these cases, the respondent intends to go along with the threat. When the threat succeeds, it is because the respondent succeeds. When the threat fails, it is because the respondent fails. In both cases, the respondent promises to cooperate. A slightly different situation arises when the respondent promises to cooperate but intentionally fails to come through:

DOUBLE-CROSS

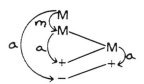

In a double-cross, the respondent deceptively agrees to go along, and then intentionally does something to foil the other's goal. This unit contains subgoals, a request, a promise, and a mixed event of success and failure. We could also represent a double-cross in response to coercion if the request were replaced with a threat:

COERCED DOUBLE-CROSS

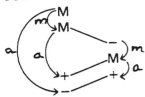

This coerced version of a double-cross is somewhat more self-contained than the plain double-cross because it is motivated by a coercive act. We can see symmetry in the negative consequences to both characters. In addition to cooperative and uncooperative responses, people often interact in unsolicited ways:

UNSOLICITED HELP

In this case the problem state is completely assumed by an intervening character who is motivated by the initial problem state to initiate his or her own assistance. If Paul had noticed John's problem and volunteered his services, we would have had a case of unsolicited help.

Any of the preceding plot units for cooperative behavior can be embedded in a problem resolution. For example, a problem resolution via a successful threat would look like:

PROBLEM RESOLUTION BY EFFECTIVE COERCION

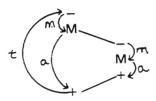

In addition to the various ways in which one character can react to another's desires, there are also a number of standard plot configurations that describe situations of reciprocation. When cooperative behavior is reciprocated, we arrive at plot units for obligation, exchange, and trades:

OBLIGATION   SERIAL EXCHANGE   SIMULTANEOUS EXCHANGE

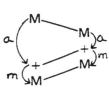

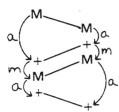
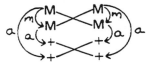

14. PLOT UNITS: NARRATIVE SUMMARIZATION

Notice that the unit for a serial exchange (of requests) is very similar to the unit for a simultaneous exchange (or trade). In a serial exchange, the requests are satisfied one after another, whereas in a simultaneous exchange, requests are handled in parallel. The same affect states and link configurations occur in both units; only the temporal sequencing of the affect states is different.

Another variation on exchanged requests occurs when the respondent agrees to honor the initial request pending a conditional request of his or her own. Paul could have agreed to fix John's car if John would first give him a beer. Then we would have two requests with one being conditional on the completion of the other:

REQUEST HONORED WITH CONDITIONAL REQUEST   REQUEST HONORED WITH CONDITIONAL PROMISE

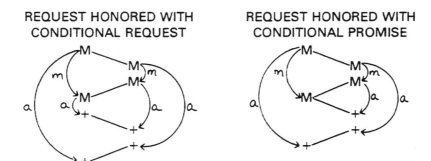

Of course, John may only promise to give Paul a beer. In this case, the request is met with a conditional promise. Although we expect John to honor his promise, he may not. If he does not, we will find the pattern for a double-cross.

Many plot units are recognized by predictive processing off of primitive plot units. For example, whenever a promise unit is encountered, we must activate expectations for success resulting in a positive shared event, or success resulting in a positive mixed event. That is, a primitive unit for a promise always sets up expectations for the complex units describing an honored promise or a reneged promise.

HONORED PROMISE   RENEGED PROMISE

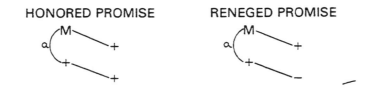

Promises and cooperative behavior are not the only plot units that rely on shared and mixed events. Other complex plot units include:

MALICIOUS ACT   KIND ACT   COMPETITION

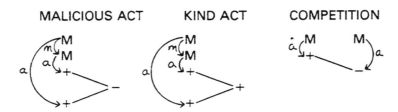

And finally, a number of plot units involve variable affect states:

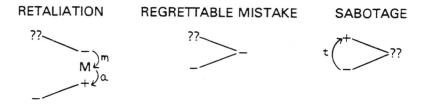

RETALIATION   REGRETTABLE MISTAKE   SABOTAGE

The unspecified affect state here signifies a "wild card" for the purposes of pattern recognition. Any affect state will match an unspecified state.

This section has attempted to show how complex units can be constructed to provide infinite variations of plot structures. For example, a kind act with a resulting trade-off will amount to an act of self-sacrifice, whereas a fortuitous problem resolution with a trade-off will merely signify an undesirable side effect. It would be pointless to try to enumerate at this time all of the possible combinations that are useful for plot recognition, although the question of what constitutes a valid unit is very interesting in its own right. From a psychological viewpoint, we might expect different people to operate with different sets of plot units. This could account for at least some of the individual differences that appear in summarization data, and might further provide an interesting basis for developmental theories of reading comprehension.

SUMMARIZATION

By recognizing plot units, we can achieve a high-level analysis of activities and interactions within a narrative. We should expect to find evidence for this "chunking" of information in paraphrase and summarization behavior. To see how this works, consider the following narrative:

> John was thrilled when Mary accepted his engagement ring. But when he found out about her father's illegal mail-order business, he felt torn between his love for Mary and his responsibility as a police officer. When John finally arrested the old man, Mary called off the engagement.

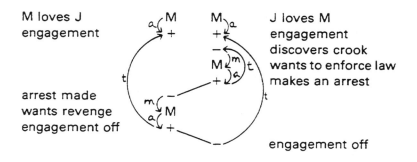

M loves J
engagement

arrest made
wants revenge
engagement off

J loves M
engagement
discovers crook
wants to enforce law
makes an arrest

engagement off

14. PLOT UNITS: NARRATIVE SUMMARIZATION

The affect analysis for John and Mary reveal configurations of a trade-off from retaliation on the part of Mary, and a problem resolution leading to loss for John.[1] Ideally, one might expect good summaries to convey each of these four plot units (trade-off, retaliation, problem resolution, and loss). A stronger claim about summaries would argue that any summary that does not convey all four plot units is an unacceptable summary:

> "When John arrested Mary's father, she interfered with his wedding."
> (no trade-off for Mary)
> "When John arrested an old crook, Mary called off their engagement."
> (no retaliation for Mary)
> "When Mary's father was arrested, she called off their engagement."
> (no problem resolution for John)
> "When John arrested Mary's father, she called off her engagement."
> (no loss for John)

But a summary that includes all four plot units provides an accurate description of the story:

> "When John arrested Mary's father, she called off their engagement."
> (all units present)

Of course "inclusion" here means inclusion by inference as well as by explicit mention. We must infer that there is a causality between John's act and Mary's act in order to understand retaliation, but this inference had to be made with the original narrative as well.

Ultimately, an affect analysis in terms of plot units should allow us to predict the sorts of summaries that human subjects will produce. But initially, we must study actual summary behavior in order to develop a process model that converts plot-unit configurations into narrative summaries. Consider the following story:

> John and Bill were competing for the same job promotion at IBM. John got the promotion and Bill decided to leave IBM to start his own consulting firm, COM-SYS. Within three years COMSYS was flourishing. By that time John had become dissatisfied with IBM so he asked Bill for a job. Bill spitefully turned him down.

Here we have a competitive situation between John and Bill in which John wins. Bill's failure turns into success out of adversity, and then he retaliates against John for his initial failure. John sets the stage for Bill's retaliation by asking Bill for a job. John consequently experiences a failure when Bill uses this opportunity to get revenge by denying John's request. The plot units here are (1) competition

---

[1] We ignore the initial success units for reasons that are explained in the section *Summary Generation*.

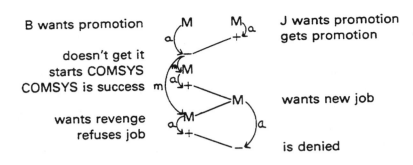

that subsumes (2) John's success and (3) Bill's failure; (4) success born of failure; (5) retaliation; and (6) a denied request that subsumes (7) John's request and (8) Bill's denial. To see how these units are integrated into summaries of the story, we look at 10 summaries provided by experimental subjects. The subjects were asked to read the story. and were then instructed to summarize the story in one sentence. The summaries that appear here are verbatim responses, except for some name corrections (subjects frequently reversed Bill and John).

SUMMARIZATION BEHAVIOR

1. John, Bill compete for a job which John wins, causing Bill to quit the company and start his own firm (COMSYS), which leads to Bill's spiteful rejection of John's request for a job some years later at Bill's successful company.

2. Bill was spiteful when John asked him for a job, because they had once competed for the same job at IBM.

3. John and Bill were both competing for a job at IBM which John got so Bill started his own business and later had the opportunity to turn John down when John wanted a job.

4. John got promoted by IBM, so Bill, his friend, started his own business which soon flourished and when John came asking for a job, Bill spitefully turned him down.

5. Bill and John worked for IBM, and were friends until 3 years later Bill turned John down when he asked for a job.

6. Bill turned John down for a job because John had beat him out of a promotion when they both worked for IBM.

7. Bill started his own business COMSYS after losing out to John for a job at IBM and later out of spite refused to give John a job when John was dissatisfied with his old one.

8. Bill, who lost a job promotion to his competitor John, establishes a lucrative consulting firm of his own, and rejects John's request for a job later on.

9. John beat out Bill for a promotion at IBM whereupon Bill decided to leave and form his own company, COMSYS, which was flourishing within 3

14. PLOT UNITS: NARRATIVE SUMMARIZATION

years, and which John turned to for a job when he was fed up at IBM which he did not get due to Bill's spite.

10. John was promoted at IBM instead of Bill, so when Bill left IBM to start his own firm and the business flourished, he turned John down when the latter, dissatisfied at IBM, applied to Bill for a job.

In analyzing these summaries for the presence of plot units, we find that a number of units are present only in an implicit manner. For example, numbers 1, 2, 4, 7, and 9 explicitly refer to "spite" and therefore make explicit reference to the retaliation unit. Summaries 3, 6, 8, and 10 are constructed with suggestive causal ties, and the presence of retaliation is only implicitly present. These implicit cases can be contrasted with 5 in which there is no basis for a retaliation unit whatsoever. When retaliation is implicit, it is conveyed by the causal constructions of clause formation. Other plot units may be implicitly present by conceptual entailment. For example, in 3, 6, and 7, the request (for a job) is implicit from the verb phrase "to turn down," because this expression describes a denied request. In all of the other summaries, John's request is explicit. In Table 14.2 we have marked with an "IMP" those plot units that are implicit in the text.

Other plot units are implicitly present by processes of inference. For example, in 2, the explicit presence of retaliation and competition force us to infer that John won and Bill lost. The patterns of competition and retaliation would not overlap at a negative event if Bill got the job. Without this overlap, we would say that it just does not make sence for Bill to get the job and then feel spiteful about it. This inference is a "role-binding inference," driven by the retaliation unit.

"X is spiteful towards Y" sets us up for:
1. a causal antecedent: Y causes a [−] for X, and
2. a causal consequent: X causes a [−] for Y.

Because competitive resolution entails the configuration needed by 1, we can

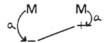

establish who is the winner and who is loser by a role-binding inference (IF X is spiteful towards Y, X is the loser and Y is the winner). So we can say that Bill's failure and John's success are present by implicit inference in summary 2. The presence of denial is also supplied by the retaliation unit in which the structure for a negative mixed event is encoded.

If we analyze these summaries for the presence of our eight plot units, we get the distribution shown in Table 14.2.

TABLE 14.2
Plot Unit Distributions

	COMP[a]	BS[a]	RET[a]	DR[a]	BF[a]	JS[a]	JR[a]	JF[a]
1	X	X	X	X	X	X	X	X
2	X		X	IMP	IMP	IMP	X	IMP
3	X	X	IMP	X	X	X	IMP	X
4		X	X	X		X	X	X
5				X			X	X
6	X		IMP	X	X	X	IMP	X
7	X	X	X	X	X	X	IMP	X
8	X	X	IMP	X	X	X	X	X
9	X	X	X	IMP	X	X	X	X
10	X	X	IMP	X	X	X	X	X

[a]competition (COMP); retaliation (RET); Bill's success (BS); John's success (JS); Bill's failure (BF); denied request (DR); John's failure (JF); John's request (JR).

We could postulate a rough qualitative ranking of the summaries based on the number of plot units present. It is the case that most (six) of the summaries reference all eight plot units, and the summary containing the least (three) plot units is arguably the worst summary.

This distribution suggests that plot-unit analysis is central to paraphrase production. Summary 5 with three plot units does seem to be the poorest summary, whereas the others (albeit stylistically different) are more on par in terms of their content.

To confirm our intuitions, we asked 12 more subjects to read the original story and then rate the 10 summaries on a scale of 1 to 7. We instructed these subjects to concentrate on the conceptual content of the summaries rather than the syntactic structure or writing style. A graph of the mean ratings is given in Fig. 14.2.

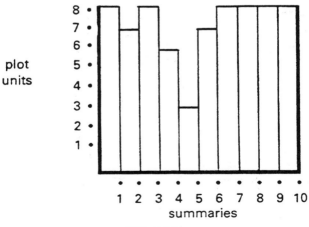

FIG. 14.1.

14.   PLOT UNITS: NARRATIVE SUMMARIZATION

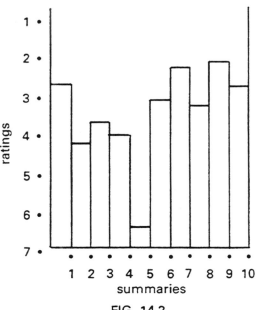

FIG. 14.2.

Using a Newman Keuls test for making multiple comparisons of means, we found that summary 5 was clearly the worst, with a mean rating that was significantly different from all others ($p < .01$). Summaries 2 and 4 were significantly worse than summaries 7 and 9 ($p < .05$), and the remaining summaries 1, 3, 6, 7, 8, 9, and 10 were statistically indistinguishable. Given the small number of subjects, these results are quite encouraging, especially because we made no attempt to control for summary length or syntactic complexity.

When we analyze summaries such as these, looking for evidence of plot-unit occurrences in either explicit expressions or implicit inference, we begin to see that some units are "pivotal" in driving inferences about other units. The identification of pivotal units is very important in the actual process of summarization. We return to this idea later, when we outline the process model for summarization.

To see how summaries are built from plot configurations, we can look at these 10 summaries in terms of their clause constructions. In the following abstractions, we have abbreviated all clauses that describe plot units and identified them accordingly. What remains is a structural backbone for the sentences generated:

1. [COMP] which [JS, FB] causing [BS] which leads to [RET, DR, JF] of [JR].
2. [RET] when [JR,] because [COMP]. (infer JS, BF, DR, JF)
3. [COMP] which [JS, BF] so [BS] and later had the opportunity to [DR, JF]. (implicit JR, RET)
4. [JS] so [BS] and when [JR], [DR, RET, JF].
5. [DR, JF] when [JR].
6. [DR, JF] because [COMP, JS, BF]. (implicit JR, RET)

7. [BS] after [COMP, JS, BF] and later [DR, RET, JF]. (implicit JR)
8. Bill, who [COMP, JS, BF], [BS] and [DR, JF, JR] later on. (implicit RET)
9. [COMP, BF, JS] whereupon [BS] and which [JR] which [JF] due to [RET]. (infer DR)
10. [COMP, BF, JS] so when [BS], [DR, JF] when [JR]. (implicit RET)

These skeletons reveal natural "clumps" of information. For example, Bill's failure and John's success are naturally tied to their competition. This follows from the fact that competition entails units for success and failure. If Bill's success is mentioned at all, it occurs in isolation of other units. and always follows the COMP-JS-BF clump (when their order is inverted in 7, the connective makes their relationship explicit). John's failure and his denied request tend to appear together, and can be easily combined with retaliation when retaliation is made explicit. The choice of specific connectors appears to be determined by retaliation, because the causality connecting other plot units serves to convey retaliation implicitly. The interplay between global factors (like retaliation) and more local entities (like John's job request) can be handled in a variety of ways. Some constructions are stylistically more pleasing than others, and the use of implicit and inferential information seems central to the more successful strategies.

NARRATIVE COHESION

It is possible to assess the cohesiveness of a narrative by analyzing its connectivity across plot units. For example, in the COMSYS story, we have a totally coherent text: John's success causes Bill's failure and this motivates Bill to become successful on his own. Bill then exploits an opportunity to retaliate against John by causing John to fail in his job hunting. The causal chain is not quite linear, but it is completely connected:

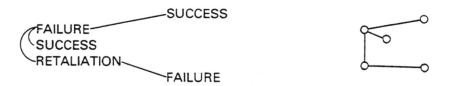

Suppose the last sentence of the COMSYS story was:

"Bill gave John a key position in his company."

Then we would have a slightly different set of plot units:

14. PLOT UNITS: NARRATIVE SUMMARIZATION

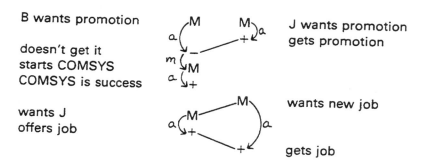

Now we no longer have retaliation. Instead, we have Bill honoring a request by John, which yields John another success. The story is no less plausible, but its cohesiveness is lessened; now there is no connectivity between the first three and the last two plot units. Bill's success enables him to help John, but there is no affect-oriented connection to unify the story.

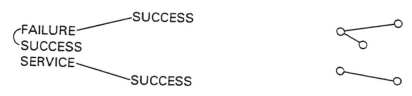

We would tend to say that Bill gave John a good job in spite of the fact that John won the promotion Bill wanted. We are more surprised to see Bill act magnanimously; a retaliation seems more likely. But this expectation is not founded on any knowledge of Bill's personality or attitude towards John. We have no such information to help us predict Bill's behavior. It is instead a general expectation for narrative unity. We have a preference for cohesive narratives, and retaliation allows us to tie everything together. If Bill offers John the job, we cannot establish total connectivity across all plot units.

This type of expectation derives from our knowledge about narratives rather than our knowledge about the world in general. It is a weak expectation in the sense that it can be easily overridden by specific knowledge. For example, if we knew that Bill was in the habit of "turning the other cheek." then we would not expect retaliation.

It could be argued that any expectation for retaliation in the COMSYS story is really an expectation about an eye for an eye rather than narrative unity. Bill was John's rival and Bill will want to get even. This level of expectation relates to the symmetry of a story. A story is weakly cohesive if it has a symmetry in its crosscharacter affect causalities. Retaliation is a plot unit that completes the symmetry of aversive causalities. When Bill refuses John the job, we have both strong cohesion (total connectivity across plot units) and weak cohesion (symmetry in the crosscharacter affect links). But when Bill offers John a good job, we have neither strong nor weak cohesion.

When a narrative embodies total symmetry, we detect this immediately and remember it is a salient feature of the story. For example, consider "The Gift of the Magi," by O'Henry. This is a story about a young couple who want to buy each other Christmas presents. They are both very poor. Della has long beautiful hair, and Jim has a prized pocket watch. To get money for the presents, Della sells her hair and Jim sells his pocket watch. Then she buys him a gold chain for his watch, and he buys her an expensive ornament for her hair. When they find out what they have done, they are consoled by the love behind each other's sacrifices.

This story exhibits an extreme symmetry:

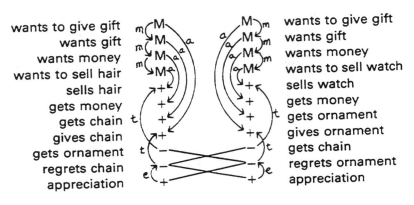

This configuration involves (1) nested subgoals and (2) achievement (in getting and giving the gifts); (3) loss (in no longer having the things they sold); (4) another loss (in no longer having pleasure from the act of giving); (5) regrettable mistakes (the bad gifts); and (6) hidden blessings (in realizing what the gifts signify). Not only is there complete symmetry across both characters, but there are ironic causalities across the plot units. For example, the sense of loss does not occur until the top-level goals are achieved (when the gifts are exchanged). At the same time, this loss is also the basis for a hidden blessing at the end of the story when they realize how the gifts signify their unselfish love for each other.

Symmetries of this sort can be heavily exploited in long-term memory representations. For example, a long-term recall of this story might include the fact that (1) Della sold her hair to buy Jim a gift; and (2) Jim bought Della an ornament for her hair. If these facts are augmented by knowledge of symmetry, a subject might then remember that (3) Jim sold X in order to buy the ornament; and (4) Della's gift to Jim was no longer appropriate after he sold X. If (3) and (4) were remembered by symmetric reconstruction, the actual identity of X and Della's gift might be forgotten.

Narrative cohesion is an important factor for effective memory retention: Cohesive texts (as defined by connectivity across plot units) should be remembered with greater accuracy than noncohesive texts. Although this claim is not central to the problem of text summarization, we can expect the two problems to

14. PLOT UNITS: NARRATIVE SUMMARIZATION

be strongly related. But before we can proceed with either problem, we must become a bit more rigorous about the notion of connectivity across plot units.

CONNECTIVITY DEFINED

This section develops the terminology necessary for a precise statement of our process model. As humans, we can look at graphic affect representations for narratives, and perceive rough degrees of connectivity within those representations. But a computational model that relies on connectivity will have to manipulate a precise formulation of connectivity. So we must now resort to a few dry definitions. Once we have a suitably precise terminology, the actual process model will follow with relative ease.

In all that follows, let A and B be plot units:

DEFINITION: A is *related* to B if and only if A and B share a common affect state (for convenience, we assume $A \neq B$).

DEFINITION: A is *connected* to B if and only if one of the following conditions hold:

1. $A = B$.
2. A is related to B.
3. There is a sequence of intervening plot units $U_1, \ldots, U_n$ such that A is related to U_1, U_i is related to U_{i+1}, and U_n is related to B.

DEFINITION: A *family* around A is the set of plot units that are related to A. The family around A is designated as $F(A)$.

DEFINITION: A *cluster* around A is the set of plot units that are connected to A.

In all that follows, let F be a family and K be a cluster:

DEFINITION: A *entails* B if and only if all affect states contained in B are also contained in A (we may say that A entails B or that B is entailed by A).

DEFINITION: Let A be a plot unit contained in K. A is a *top-level plot unit* in K if and only if A is not entailed by any other plot units contained in K.

DEFINITION: *The size of K is the number of top-level plot units contained in K. The size of K is designated as $o(K)$.*

DEFINITION: F is a *maximal family* in K if and only if F is a family contained in K and $o(F) :\geqslant o(G)$ for all families G contained in K.

DEFINITION: A is a *pivotal unit* in K if and only if the family around A is a maximal family in K.

DEFINITION: *K* is a *simple cluster* if and only if *K* has one pivotal unit.

DEFINITION: We define a distance metric on *K* as follows:
1. $d(A,B) = O$ iff $A = B$.
2. $d(A,B) = 1$ iff A is related to B.
3. $d(A,B) = k$ iff $U_1, \ldots, U_{k-1}$ is the shortest sequence of *plot units connecting A and B*.

DEFINITION: The *span* of *K* is defined as the $\max\{d(A,B) \mid A \text{ and } B \text{ are units in } K\}$.

DEFINITION: Let *K* be a simple cluster. The *depth of K* is defined as the $\max\{d(A,B) \mid A \text{ is the pivotal unit, } B \text{ is a unit in } K\}$.

These definitions describe simple graph structures that can be readily recognized in pictoral representations. We will look at three examples of plot-unit graphs, but first, a few observations:

[1.] Maximal families may contain more than one pivotal unit. It is therefore possible to have a cluster with a unique maximal family that is not a simple cluster.

[2.] The definition for relatedness describes the simplest condition possible. We may later need to refine this to distinguish units that share *n* affect states (*n* = 1, 2, 3, and so on) and units whose shared affect states have certain properties of connectivity in terms of the affect links between them.

[3.] The notion of a top-level unit is relative to the specification of some set of plot units. This allows us to examine the effect that different set specifications have on summarization behavior. For example, if we did not include a unit for a denied request, the top-level units for that configuration would drop down to the request, success, and positive mixed event. Various set specifications might be a key to individual differences in summary behavior.

[4.] More entailment between plot units results in simpler graph structures.

[5.] Larger units (in terms of affect states) are likely to result in greater connectivity as well as simpler graph structures.

The best way to get a sense of all this is to play with some concrete examples of the definitions in action. Consider the story of John's broken engagement:

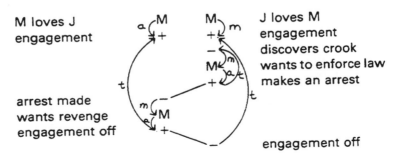

14.   PLOT UNITS: NARRATIVE SUMMARIZATION

There are six to-level plot units:

Mary's success	[MS]
John's success	[JS]
Mary's trade-off	[TO]
Mary's retaliation	[RET]
John's resolution	[RES]
John's loss	[JL]

The families for these units can be represented with a connectivity graph:

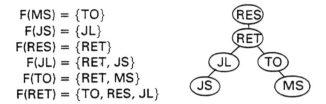

$$F(MS) = \{TO\}$$
$$F(JS) = \{JL\}$$
$$F(RES) = \{RET\}$$
$$F(JL) = \{RET, JS\}$$
$$F(TO) = \{RET, MS\}$$
$$F(RET) = \{TO, RES, JL\}$$

There is only one maximal family and one pivotal unit (RET). This makes the cluster of six units a simple cluster. It has a depth of two and a span of four. Now consider the COMSYS story:

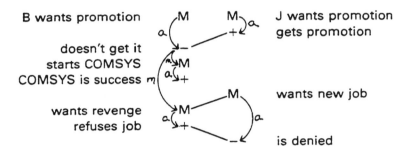

B wants promotion		J wants promotion
		gets promotion
doesn't get it		
starts COMSYS		
COMSYS is success		
		wants new job
wants revenge		
refuses job		
		is denied

There are four top-level plot units:

success born of failure	[SBF]
competition	[COM]
retaliation	[RET]
request denied	[RD]

The connectivity graph for these families is:

$$F(RD) = \{RET\}$$
$$F(COM) = \{RET, SBF\}$$
$$F(SBF) = \{COM, RET\}$$
$$F(RET) = \{COM, RD, SBF\}$$

There is only one maximal family and one pivotal unit (RET). This yields a simple cluster with a depth of one and a span of two.

Both of the previous stories result in fairly simple affect connectivity. For our last example, we look at "The Gift of the Magi":

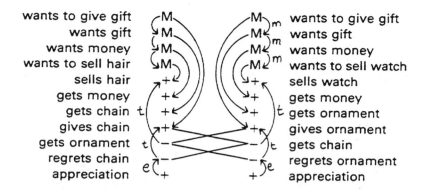

Now we have 10 top-level plot units. Because of the symmetry of the story, we see the same units appearing for both the husband and the wife. These are prefaced with "w" and "w" to signify which is which.

[HN]	nested subgoals	[WN]
[HM]	regrettable mistake	[WM]
[HL1]	loss of object	[WL1]
[HL2]	loss of achievement	[WL2]
[HB]	hidden blessing	[WB]

The connectivity graph for these looks like:

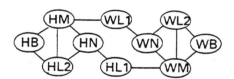

There are two maximal families, $F(HM)$ and $F(WM)$, with pivotal units HM and WM. Because this is not a simple cluster, the depth of the cluster is not defined. The span is five.

SUMMARY GENERATION

Once the connectivity of the plot units has been established, we can drive a process of summary generation based on affect analysis. The generation of summaries for arbitrary narratives requires an extensive process model that can handle various classes of plot-unit configurations. For example, the summary process for a simple cluster has to be different from the summary process for a cluster with multiple pivotal units.

We do not attempt to present the complete solution here. But we can discuss

14. PLOT UNITS: NARRATIVE SUMMARIZATION

the solution for a simple case in order to illustrate the techniques needed for the general case. We therefore outline the process model for summaries of simple clusters, and then discuss methods for extending this solution to arbitrary clusters.

Summarization of Simple Clusters

The algorithm for generating summaries of simple clusters is a five-step process:

STEP 1. Find all top-level plot units in K.
STEP 2. Derive the plot-unit graph structure.
STEP 3. Identify the pivotal unit, P.
STEP 4. Generate a base-line summary (S) from a frame for P.
STEP 5. Augment S with information from plot units related to P.

Steps 1, 2, and 3 are simple manipulations based on the definitions in the section summarization.[2] Steps 4 and 5 require some explanation.

Plot-Unit Generational Frames.   All plot units are associated with generational frames that designate how the plot unit can be expressed in natural language. For example, a frame for the "competition unit" might look like:

X and Y both [M], but Y [+].

where X, Y, M, and + are slots in the affect configuration:

This frame would give us summaries like, "Fred and Hank both loved Mary, but Hank married her." Or, "Bill and John both wanted the same job at IBM, but John got it." Although this is a general frame that can be applied to any situation of competition, this very general frame may be overridden by knowledge-specific frames that are dependent on the specific instantiations of the affect states. For example, when the competition is for a job promotion, we can say "*Y* was promoted over *X* at IBM," and this will convey the entire competion unit as well. This knowledge-specific frame can be invoked whenever the concept of a promotion appears in the parallel mental states by a scheme of double indices on competition and promotion. The specification and selection of knowledge-specific generational frams is a major problem for the production of smooth summaries.

---

[2]Step 3 involves summing the rows and columns of an adjacency matrix.

Integrating Related Units.   Once a generational frame is chosen for the pivotal unit, we transform the resulting base-line summary into a final summary by integrating any additional information from plot units related to the pivotal unit. By delimiting our integration to those units that are directly related to the pivotal unit, we essentially delete from our summary any information that is more peripheral to the heart of the cluster. The effectiveness of this cut-off heuristic is open to further investigation. Perhaps the cut-off boundary should be a function of cluster depth and/or span.

The actual integration of new information into the base-line summary can be handled in roughly two ways: (1) the addition of a new clause; or (2) the further refinement of existing references in the base-line summary. To see how these two techniques work, we consider the COMSYS and broken-engagement stories.

Both of these stories have retaliation as their pivotal units.

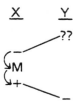

We use a general frame for retaliation in our base-line summaries:

"Because Y's [?] caused a [−] for X, X (later) [+]ed to cause a [−] for Y."

This frame allows us to build base-line summaries for both stories:

"Because John prevented Bill from getting a job at IBM, Bill later prevented John from getting a job."

"Because John did something bad to Mary's father, she prevented his engagement."

Notice that both of these summaries already convey the plot units for John's failure, Bill's failure, and John's loss. This is because the specification of a negative event that is part of a failure or loss unit automatically communicates the notion of that failure or loss.

The base-line summary for the COMSYS story must now be augmented by the units for competition, success born of failure, and a denied request. Competition and the denied request are integrated by a further specification of existing references. Success born of failure requries a new clause:

S:

"Because John prevented Bill from getting a job at IBM, Bill later prevented John from getting a job."

14. PLOT UNITS: NARRATIVE SUMMARIZATION

S + competition:

"Because John was promoted over Bill at IBM, Bill later prevented John from getting a job."

S + competition + success born of failure:

"Because John was promoted over Bill at IBM, Bill started his own company, and later prevented John from getting a job."

S + competition + success born of failure + denied request:

"Because John was promoted over Bill at IBM, Bill started his own company, and later refused to give John a job when he asked for one."

The base-line summary for the broken-engagement story must be augmented with the units for the problem resolution and the trade-off. Both of these units are integrated by further specification of existing references.

S:

"Because John did something bad to Mary's father, she prevented his engagement."

S + problem resolution:

"Because John arrested Mary's father, she prevented his engagement."

S + problem resolution + trade-off:

"Because John arrested Mary's father, she called off their engagement."

Even though this algorithm specifies the general structure of the summarization process, there are a number of problem areas that require extensive work:

1. Plot-unit generational frames must be specified for both simple and complex plot units.
2. Knowledge-specific generational frames must be designed for those concepts that lend themselves to special verbs or constructions.
3. A selection process for the best generational frame must be designed.
4. The integration of additional information into the base-line summary must be described in detail for both further specifications and clause additions.
5. The interplay between 3 and 4 must be studied.

In addition to these fundamental problems within the process model, we must also examine the problems of summarization for clusters of more than one pivotal unit, and stories of more than one cluster.

Summarization of Arbitrary Clusters

It may be the case that stories involving more than one cluster cannot be easily reduced to a one-sentence summary. For example, when a story has a single cluster, but that cluster has more than one pivotal unit. it may be difficult to derive a one-sentence summary. These hypotheses can be tested by examining a number of stories. For now, we look at "The Gift of the Magi" to get a sense of what the difficulties are.

Recall that there were 10 top-level plot units for this story:

[HN]	nested goals	[WN]
[HM]	regrettable mistake	[WM]
[HL1]	loss of object	[WL1]
[HL2]	loss of achievement	[WL2]
[HB]	hidden blessing	[WB]

"Loss of object" refers to the sense of loss experienced in no longer having his watch (or her hair). "Loss of achievement" refers to the sense of loss experienced in giving a gift that turns out to be a mistake (they can no longer feel good about the gifts they gave). The first sense of loss occurs as soon as the gifts are exchanged: They each realize that the gift they received in inappropriate. The second sense of loss comes with the regrettable mistake: They each realize that the gift they gave in inappropriate. The connectivity graph reveals that there are two pivotal units:

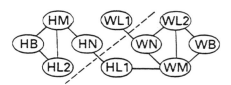

HM and WM yield maximal families, and the units for nested goals (WN and HN) and loss of objects (WL1 and HL1) are "boundary units" in the sense that they are related to units from both maximal families. Before we discuss possible algorithms, let us look at a sample summary:

> A woman sold her long locks of hair so she could buy her husband a watch chain for Christmas. But when she gave him the chain, she found out that he had sold his watch so he could buy her a comb for her hair. Initially they regretted their expensive gifts, but then they realized how much love was signified in the sacrifices made.

14. PLOT UNITS: NARRATIVE SUMMARIZATION

This summary assumes the wife's point of view for the first two sentences. Because of the symmetry in this story, it is natural to infer plot units concerning the husband as information becomes available. Let us take another look at this summary, this time identifying plot units as they are conveyed. Plot units in parentheses are inferred by shifting the perspective:

> A woman sold her long locks of hair so she could buy her husband a watch chain for Christmas [WN]. But when she gave him the chain, she found out that he had sold his watch [WL2,(HL1)] so he could buy her a comb for her hair [HN.WL1,(HL2)]. Initially they regretted their expensive gifts [WM,HM], but then they realized how much love was signified in the sacrifices made [WB,HB].

The boundary units seem to be conveyed first, whereas the two units with the largest span occur at the very end. If this story is representative, it suggests that summaries should start with units that bound maximal families, and then proceed to those units that are more isolated later. In fact, we would have an acceptable summary if we deleted the last sentence altogether.

Whereas pivotal units are central for stories with simple clusters, clusters with more than one maximal family are organized around the boundaries between those families. This summary started off with WN, a boundary unit from F[WM]. The other boundary unit from F[WM] is HL1. Can we build a summary starting with HL1? Try this one:

> When Jim received a watch chain from Della for Christmas, he explained that he had sold his watch [HL1,(WL2)]. He sold his watch so he could buy Della a comb for her hair [HN], but he didn't know that she had sold her hair [HL2,(WL1)] in order to buy him the watch chain [WN].

In the first summary, HL1 follows from WL2 by inference. In the second summary, WL2 follows from HL1 by inference. Similarly, in the first summary, HL2 follows from WL1 by inference, and in the second summary, WL1 follows from HL2. Because these pairs of plot units are inferentially dependent on each other, we should not allow them to distract us from the actual flow of control that is at work here. To see the pattern emerge, let us identify the HL1-WL2 pair as X and the HL2-WL1 pair as Y. The order of presentation for plot units in the first summary is:

$$WN - X - HN - Y$$

The order of presentation in the second summary is:

$$X - HN - Y - WN$$

These presentations differ by a simple rotation of one unit. We could change the perspectives on these two summaries to get:

$$HN - Y - WN - X$$

$$Y - WN - X - HN$$

which gives us all four rotations. There are 20 more possible arrangements, and it is possible to generate summaries that correspond to all the permutations. So any random ordering of the four boundary units will provide a good summary. Can we get a decent summary out of anything less than these four units? Consider:

> Della had sold her long locks of hair to buy her husband a watch chain [WN], and he sold his watch to buy her a comb for her hair [HN].

This summary is based on two boundary plot units of maximal connectivity:

$$o(F[WN]) = o(F[HN]) = 3 > 2 = o(F[WL1]) = o(F[HL1]).$$

Perhaps minimal summaries can always be derived from maximally connected boundary units. To answer this question and others like it, we have to study the affect analyses for a number of narratives. How often do clusters arise with two or more maximal families? Can stories with multiple clusters be reduced to single-sentence summaries? Does the algorithm outlined in the preceding section work for all simple clusters? How does symmetry affect the process of summarization? These questions can only be resolved by testing proposed algorithms on a variety of narratives.

RECOGNIZING PLOT UNITS

Thus far we have explained how plot units can be used to generate summaries, but we have not explained where the plot units come from in the first place. Although the intuitive notion of plot units may be attractive, this is a useless notion for a process model unless we can specify the processes that will analyze text and produce plot units as output.

The first step in the derivation of plot units is the derivation of affect states. We cannot possibly identify a plot unit unless its component states are available to us first. The identification of an affect state is actually a fairly straightforward process, if we can assume the computational power of a predictive knowledge-based story understander. Using the knowledge structures outlined in Schank and Abelson (1977), we can recognize affect states in terms of fairly fundamental taxonomies:

MENTAL STATE (M)

1. Initiatine an A, D, E or I-goal.
2. Missing an enabling condition.

14. PLOT UNITS: NARRATIVE SUMMARIZATION

3. Needing a goal subsumption state.
4. Suspension or absence of a positive interpersonal theme
5. A plan is intended.

POSITIVE EVENT (+)

1. Achieving an A, D, E, or I-goal.
2. Obtaining a necessary enabling condition.
3. Achieving a goal subsumption state.
4. Initiating or resuming a positive interpersonal theme.
5. Intended plan succeeds.
6. Getting news about (+: 1-5) for some person you care about.
7. Getting news about (−: 1-7) for some person you dislike or hate.
8. Getting news about (M: 1-5) for some person you dislike or hate.

NEGATIVE EVENT (−)

1. A, D, E, or I-goal is thwarted.
2. P or C-goal is initiated.
3. Script interference is encountered.
4. Initiation or intensification of a negative interpersonal theme.
5. Intended plan fails.
6. Termination of a positive interpersonal theme.
7. Losing a necessary enabling condition.
8. Getting news about (−: 1-7) for some person you care about.
9. Getting news about (M: 1-5) for some person you care about.
10. Getting news about (÷: 1-5) for some person you dislike or hate.

A discussion of this terminology would take us far afield from our central concerns, but the interested reader can find ample discussion of these references in Schank and Abelson (1977). Recognition for these entities has been implemented in a number of knowledge-based systems, including SAM (Cullingford, 1978), PAM (Wilensky, 1978), and BORIS (Dyer & Lehnert, 1980; Lehnert, Dyer, Johnson, Yang, & Harley, 1981).

Once the three primary affect states are recognized, we can implement a predictive system of demons to build specific plot units. For example, the appearance of a mental state should construct a demon that can be activated by:

1. Another mental state (a possible m-, t-, or e-link).
2. A positive event (a possible a-link).
3. A negative event (a possible a-link).

If another mental state is encountered, the demon should check to see if there is a subgoal relationship (m-link), mutual exclusion (t-link), or equivalence (e-link) at work. If one of these can be verified, we have identified a primitive plot unit.

As soon as a primitive plot unit is identified, demons for complex plot units are constructed. For example, a subgoal unit should predict the possible occurrence of nested subgoals, a request, a threat, a kind act, or a malicious act. In this way, a hierarchical structure of predictions that looks for successively complicated plot units as information appears to support those possibilities can be implemented.

The verification of specific affect links relies on specific instantiations behind each affect state. There is no way of knowing whether or not two mental states should be joined by a motivation link unless we can establish a subgoal relationship between them. This subgoal relationship is naturally dependent on the specific content of each mental state. But these checks do not ask for anything that a standard inference mechanism would not need to know anyway. The information needed for these verifications should already be present in the system for inference purposes that are independent of plot-unit recognition. So we are essentially constructing these units as a side effect of existing processes. We do not need to propose additional knowledge structures to build plot units. They will fall out quite naturally from other memory manipulations with a minimal amount of extra processing.

CONCLUSIONS

It appears that a high-level analysis for narratives can be derived from configurations of three primary affect states. These configurations consist of primitive and complex plot units whose overlapping structures allow us to measure the connectivity and symmetry of character interactions. Once the plot units in a story have been properly identified, they provide us with a framework for text summarization.

Relatively little progress has been made on the problem of text summarization due to the complexities of natural-language processing. The work of Kintsch has approached the problem by organizing textual propositions into hierarchical tree structures and extracting summaries from nodes near the top of the tree. Although this approach has been supported by many psychology experiments (Kintsch, 1974; Kintsch & Keenan, 1973; Kintsch & VanDijk. 1975; Kintsch & VanDijek, 1978), little has been done to explain exactly how Kintsch's propositions are recognized in source texts. Text-processing techniques must be tested with computational models before the validity of the hierarchical tree approach can be fully examined.

Of course, a full natural-language implementation is a nontrivial undertaking and we cannot say that the plot-unit approach has been fully implemented either. But plot units have been designed with the recognition problem in mind, and are

14. PLOT UNITS: NARRATIVE SUMMARIZATION

largely constrained by existing techniques in natural-language processing. Thus far, the only program to attempt a total implementation (from a variety of input texts to output summaries) is the FRUMP system (DeJong, 1979). FRUMP analyzes UPI stories in about 50 domains and provides summaries based on a top-down script-based extraction of relevant information in those domains. The set of summaries driven by a single knowledge domain do not exhibit much variation, because those summaries are all based on a priori set of scriptal expectations about that domain. For example, an earthquake story will be sum-marized in terms of (1) when and where it occurred; (2) what the Richter scale registered; and (3) how many people were killed or injured. All earthquake summaries will describe those three components when they are available. This style of summarixation is completely top-down, being driven by specific expecta-tions. FRUMP cannot deal with unexpected information and its summaries will reflect total ignorance of anything unexpected, even if the unexpected informa-tion is critically important. In this respect FRUMP is similar to the story-grammar approach to text analysis (Rumelhart, 1975, 1977; Thorndyke, 1977).

Rumelhart uses summarization data to illustrate how various levels of detail coincide with expansions to a particular level within the tree structure. A level-0 summary is based on the root node alone. A level-1 summary is based on the first level of expansion from the root, a level-2 summary is based on the second level of expansion, and so forth. Thorndyke's data analysis also substantiates story grammars in a similar manner. Even though summarization data do appear to support story grammars. the Rumelhart and Thorndyke analyses were not de-signed to tease apart competing hypotheses about summarization behavior. In a recent experiment comparing specific story-grammar predictions to specific plot-unit predictions, summarization data appears to verify plot-unit analyses over story grammars (Lehnert, Black, & Reiser, 1981).

Aside from any experimental evidence, the problem with story grammars simply boils down to an overwhelming limitation of all top-down processors: A story grammar cannot characterize input that does not conform to its expecta-tions. Just as FRUMP cannot deal with input outside of its knowledge domains, a story grammar would be of no help when confronted with a story whose plot was not a priori anticipated by the grammar. To what extent does ''The Gift of the Magi'' conform to a story schema? A hierarchical story grammar cannot be general enough to capture large variations in plot structures. Yet this does not mean that knowledge of narrative structure cannot be operating predictively at the time of understanding. Such predictions can be valid processing techniques, but most of these predictions can be treated as artifacts of other knowledge structures. For example, the symmetry arguments for strong and weak cohesion in the section *Narrative Cohesion* were naturally integrated in terms of plot unit and affect state predictions.

There is infinite variation in the number of plots that are possible, and people can understand a story with a new plot line whether they have seen a similar plot before or not. This suggests that plot recognition must be based on bottom-up processing rather than a top-down analysis. We can attain the flexible recognition capabilities of a bottom-up analysis scheme by constructing configurations of primitive and complex plot units. Most of the information needed to recognize affect states has already been incorporated in predictive knowledge-based systems (Schank & Riesbeck, 1981) to drive various inference mechanisms, and the additional processing needed to link affect states together into plot units is in many cases already being handled by existing systems.

Because affect states are based on information about plans, goals, and themes, affect analysis will not be applicable to stories that do not contain information along these lines. We will not be able to handle descriptions of sunsets or burnt steaks or waking up in the morning. Of course, it is not clear that people can comfortably summarize stories that center on perceptual descriptions either, so this limitation is not a cause for concern. It would not be difficult to generate a summary that said, ''This is a story describing a sunset.'' A human could easily be reduced to such a synopsis as well.

On a related note, we should point out that plot-unit analyses are also inappropriate for expository texts. In view of the evidence that expository texts are structured by hierarchical trees, the applicability of plot units (or lack of it) to a given text might provide us with a criterion for distinguishing expository text from narratives. For example, the ''Circle Island'' story (Thorndyke, 1977) cannot be analyzed with plot units and would therefore be classified as expository text rather than narrative text.

In this chapter we have stressed the relevance of affect analysis for the task of narrative summarization. There are also other applications to explore with plot units. For example, a high-level analysis of a story is probably used as an index into long-term memory. Such an index would determine when the story can be remembered and under what conditions information from the story can be accessed (Schank, this volume). We have evidence that plot units contribute to the ability to recognize similarities across stories. In a recent experiment, 36 subjects were instructed to group 36 stories according to their plot similarities. A cluster analysis of the data shows that plot-unit structures predict the resulting groups very effectively (Reiser, Lehnert, & Black, 1981). Plot units may also have a place in generational tasks. Although processes of generation and understanding differ by much more than a procedural inverse (Meehan. 1976), it might be the case that stories are generated from initial affect configurations as the starting point.

Although all of these other areas are potentially relevant to plot units, the task of narrative summarization has the advantage of providing a relatively clean I/O problem. We can give stories (input) to human subjects and ask them to produce summaries (output). These data are initially valuable in the design of a summarization process, and they will eventually allow us to test resulting programs for their psychological validity. If the process model becomes sufficiently sophisti-

14. PLOT UNITS: NARRATIVE SUMMARIZATION

cated, it would be appropriate to study individual differences across subjects. Perhaps it would even be possible to analyze a subject's summarization behavior on a few key texts, and then predict subsequent summarization behavior on completely different texts. For the moment, however, our job is to design a system that can generate reasonable summaries for a variety of narrative texts. This chapter has attempted to show how such a goal may be realized in the near future.

ACKNOWLEDGMENTS

The author is indebted to Roger Schank, Chris Riesbeck, Jim Meehan, Art Graesser, Haj Ross, and Marty Ringle for their extensive and helpful comments on various drafts of this chapter. This work was supported in part by the Advanced Research Projects Agency under contract N00014-75-C-1111 and in part by the National Science Foundation under contract IST7918463.

REFERENCES

Black, J. B., & Wilensky, R. (1979) An evaluation of story grammars. *Cognitive Science, 3*(No. 3), 213-230.

Cullingford, R. E. (1978) *Script application: Computer understanding of newspaper stories* (Department of Computer Science Research Report #116). Yale University, New Haven.

DeJong, G. F. (1979) Skimming stories in real time: An experiment in integrated understanding (Department of Computer Science Research Report #156). Yale University, New Haven.

deRivera. J. (1977) A structural theory of the emotions. *Psychological issues,* (Monograph No. 40). New York: International Universities Press.

Dyer, M., & Lehnert, W. (1980) *Memory organization and search processes for narratives* (Department of Computer Science Research Report #175). Yale University, New Haven.

Graesser, A. (1981) *Prose comprehension beyond the word.* New York: Springer-Verlag.

Graesser, A. C., Robertson. S. P., & Anderson, P. A. (1981) Incorporating inferences in narrative representations: A study of how and why. *Cognitive Psychology. 13*(No. 1), 1-26.

Kintsch, W. (1974) *The representation of meaning in memory.* Hillsdale, N.J.: Lawrence Erlbaum Associates.

Kintsch, W., & Keenan, J. (1973) Reading rate and retention as a function of the number of propositions in the base structure of sentences. *Cognitive Psychology, 5,* 257-274.

Kintsch. W., & vanDijk. T. (1975) Recalling and summarizing stories. *Language, 40,* 98-116.

Kintsch, W., & vanDijk, T. (1978) Toward a model of text comprehension and production. *Psychological Review, 85,* 363-394.

Lehnert, W. G. (1978) *The process of question answering.* Hillsdale, N.J.: Lawrence Erlbaum Associates.

Lehnert, W., Black, J., & Reiser, B. (1981) *Summarizing narratives.* 7th International Joint Conference on Artificial Intelligence. Vancouver, British Columbia.

Lehnert, W. G., Dyer, M. G., Johnson, P. N., Yang, C. J., & Harley, S. (1981) *BORIS—An experiment in in-depth understanding of narratives* (Research Rep. #188). Department of Computer Science, Yale University. New Haven.

Meehan, J. R. (1976) *The metanovel: Writing stories by computer* (Department of Computer Science Research Report #74). Yale University, New Haven.

Reiser, B. R., Lehnert, W. G., & Black, J. B. (1981) *Recognizing thematic units in narratives.* Third Annual Conference of the Cognitive Science Society, Berkeley, California.

Riesbeck and Schank (1976) "Comprehension by Computer: Expectation-Based Analysis of Sentences in Context." Department of Computer Science Research Report #78 Yale University.

Roseman, I. (1979) *Cognitive aspects of emotion and emotional behavior.* 87th Annual Convention of the American Psychological Association, New York.

Rumelhart, D. E. (1975) Notes on a schema for Stories. In D. G. Bobrow & A. M. Collins (Eds.), *Representation and understanding.* New York: Academic Press.

Rumelhart, D. E. (1977) Understanding and summarizing brief stories. In D. Laberge & S. Samuels (Eds.), *Basic processing in reading, perception, and comprehension.* Hillsdale, N.J.: Lawrence Erlbaum Associates

Schank, R. C., & Abelson, R. P. (1977) *Scripts plans goals and understanding.* Hillsdale, N.J.: Lawrence Erlbaum Associates.

Schank, R., & Riesbeck, C. (1981) *Inside computer understanding.* Hillsdale, N.J.: Lawrence Erlbaum Associates.

Simmons, R. F., & Correira, A. (1979) Rule forms for verse, sentences and story trees. In N. Findler (Ed.), *Associative networks—representation and use of knowledge by computers.* New York: Academic Press.

Thorndyke, P. W. (1977) Cognitive structures in comprehension and memory of narrative discourse. *Cognitive Psychology, 9,* 77–110.

Wilensky, R. (1978) *Understanding goal-based stories* (Department of Computer Science Research Report #140). Yale University, New Haven.

15

Knowledge-Based Text Summarization: Salience and Generalization Operators for Knowledge Base Abstraction

Udo Hahn
Freiburg University
Computational Linguistics Group
D–79085 Freiburg, Germany
hahn@coling.uni-freiburg.de

Ulrich Reimer
Swiss Life
Information Systems Research Group
CH–8022 Zürich, Switzerland
ulrich.reimer@swisslife.ch

Abstract

We present an approach to text summarization that is entirely rooted in a formal model of terminological knowledge representation. Text summarization is considered an operator-based transformation process by which knowledge representation structures, as generated by a natural language text understanding system, are mapped into conceptually more abstract, condensed knowledge structures forming a text summary at the representational level. The methodological framework we propose offers a variety of parameters on which scalable text summarization can be based.

1 Introduction

From its very beginning, the development of text understanding systems has been intimately tied to the field of knowledge representation and reasoning methods (Schank 1982). This close relationship was justified by the observation that any adequate form of text understanding not only requires grammatical knowledge about the particular language the text is written in, but also has to incorporate prior knowledge about the domain the text deals with. Thus, the inferencing capabilities of knowledge representation languages are taken to be crucial for functionally adequate text understanding systems. In order to assess the adequacy of the inferences being made and that of the representation structures resulting from the text understanding process, several capabilities were considered indicative of the systems' language understanding potential, e.g., the ability to answer questions correctly about the contents of the text, to provide reasonable paraphrases (either within one or across several languages) or – to summarize a given text at various levels of informational abstraction.

Out of this tradition, a series of knowledge-based text summarization systems was being developed, the vast majority of which rooted in Schankian-type *Conceptual Dependency (CD)* representations (e.g., (Cullingford 1978; Lehnert 1981; DeJong 1982; Dyer 1983; Tait 1985; Alterman 1986)). The summarization operations these first-generation systems provide were usually built upon more complex representation facilities which made use of basic CD structures, such as scripts, memory organization packages (MOPs) or thematic abstraction units (TAUs). CD representations, however, lack any serious formal foundation. As a matter of fact, these higher-level representations inherit the formal underspecification of CD representations. Moreover, they are only used as data structures to which informal heuristics are applied in order to determine the salient topics from the text representation structures for the purpose of summarization. Only Lehnert's graph-theoretically based summarization criteria within the plot units framework (Lehnert 1981) provide an exception to this general observation.

A second generation of summarization systems then adopted a more mature knowledge representation approach, based on the already established methodological framework of hybrid, classification-based knowledge representation languages (cf. (Woods & Schmolze 1992) for a survey). These principles have been incorporated in summarization systems such as SUSY (Fum, Guida, & Tasso 1985), SCISOR (Rau, Jacobs, & Zernik 1989), and TOPIC (Reimer & Hahn 1988). But even in these frameworks no attempt was made to properly integrate the text summarization process into the underlying knowledge representation language.

This is where our interest comes in. We propose a formal model of text summarization that is entirely embedded in the framework of a terminological logic. Text summarization is considered a *formally guided* transformation process on knowledge representation structures, the so-called text knowledge base, as derived by a natural language text parser. The transformations involved share the formal rigor of the underlying knowledge representation model, as corresponding summarization operators build on that model. Thus, our work describes a methodologically coherent, representation-theory-based approach to text summarization that has been lacking in the literature so far (for a survey cf. (Hutchins 1987)).

Basing our summarization model on the transformation of knowledge structures offers a wide variety of parameters to realize *scalable* summarization pro-

$$\begin{aligned}
\langle terminology\rangle &::= \langle conc\text{-}intro\rangle^* \\
\langle conc\text{-}intro\rangle &::= \langle conc\text{-}name\rangle \leq \langle c\text{-}expr\rangle \mid \langle conc\text{-}name\rangle \doteq \langle c\text{-}expr\rangle \\
\langle c\text{-}expr\rangle &::= (\textbf{and } \langle c\text{-}expr\rangle^+) \mid \langle conc\text{-}name\rangle \mid \\
& \quad (\textbf{all-p } \langle prop\text{-}name\rangle \langle prop\text{-}range\rangle^+) \mid \\
& \quad (\textbf{all-r } \langle rel\text{-}name\rangle \langle conc\text{-}name\rangle^+) \mid \\
& \quad (\textbf{exist-v } \langle prop\text{-}name\rangle \langle value\rangle) \mid \\
& \quad (\textbf{exist-c } \langle rel\text{-}name\rangle \langle conc\text{-}name\rangle) \mid \\
& \quad (\textbf{at-least } \langle rel\text{-}prop\text{-}name\rangle \langle pos\text{-}integer\rangle) \mid \\
& \quad (\textbf{at-most } \langle rel\text{-}prop\text{-}name\rangle \langle pos\text{-}integer\rangle) \\
\langle rel\text{-}prop\text{-}name\rangle &::= \langle rel\text{-}name\rangle \mid \langle prop\text{-}name\rangle \\
\langle rel\text{-}name\rangle &::= \langle identifier\rangle \\
\langle prop\text{-}name\rangle &::= \langle identifier\rangle \\
\langle prop\text{-}range\rangle &::= \langle int\text{-}range\rangle \mid \langle string\text{-}range\rangle \\
\langle int\text{-}range\rangle &::= \langle interval\rangle^+ \\
\langle interval\rangle &::= [\,\langle integer\rangle \langle unit\rangle, \langle integer\rangle \langle unit\rangle\,] \\
\langle unit\rangle &::= \langle identifier\rangle \\
\langle value\rangle &::= \langle integer\rangle \langle unit\rangle \mid \langle string\rangle \\
\langle string\text{-}range\rangle &::= \langle string\rangle^+ \mid * \\
\langle conc\text{-}name\rangle &::= \langle identifier\rangle \mid \textbf{thing} \\
\langle pos\text{-}integer\rangle &::= 1 \mid 2 \mid 3 \ldots \\
\langle integer\rangle &::= 0 \mid \text{-}1 \mid 1 \mid \text{-}2 \mid 2 \ldots
\end{aligned}$$

Figure 1: Syntax of the Terminological Logic $\mathcal{TL}$

cesses. This claim will be exemplified by the introduction of text graphs, the representational correlate of a summary. This proposal contrasts, in particular, with those approaches to text summarization which almost entirely rely upon built-in features of frame and script-based representations and, consequently, provide rather simple reduction heuristics in order to produce text summaries (e.g., (DeJong 1982; Young & Hayes 1985)). The formal model we present has been implemented and tested in TOPIC (Hahn & Reimer 1984; 1986; Reimer & Hahn 1988), a text summarization system which processes expository texts in the domain of information technology product reviews, as well as various kinds of texts dealing with legal issues (company regulations, advisory texts, etc.).

This paper is organized as follows. In Section 2 we lay down a description of the syntax and semantics of the terminological logic which serves as the formal backbone for the specification of salience operators on (text) knowledge bases. In order to illustrate how text knowledge is derived from the domain knowledge, in Section 3 we briefly outline the functionality of TOPIC's text parser and deal with the criteria according to which text knowledge bases are generated. The formal model of text summarization is then described in detail in Section 4.

2   The Terminological Knowledge Representation Model

In the following, we describe the terminological logic on which our summarization model is based. Section 2.1 considers the terminological component which goes

well with the most common features of related terminological languages (cf. (Woods & Schmolze 1992)). Section 2.2 deals with appropriate extensions for representing text-specific knowledge. These are particularly adapted to the needs of text summarization, as they include representation constructs which account for the frequency of reference to concepts and conceptual relations.

2.1   The Basic Terminological Component: Representing Domain Knowledge

Unlike many concept description languages, the particular terminological logic $\mathcal{TL}$ we introduce here (cf. (Reimer 1985; Reimer *et al.* 1995) for a deeper account) distinguishes between two kinds of relations, namely properties and conceptual relationships. A *property* denotes a relation between individuals and string or integer values. A *conceptual relationship* denotes a relation between two individuals. $\mathcal{TL}$ provides constructs to formulate necessary (and possibly sufficient) conditions on the properties and conceptual relationships every individual in the extension of a concept is required to have.

The syntax of $\mathcal{TL}$ is given in Figure 1. The operators $\leq$ and $\doteq$ introduce new concepts by associating a concept name with an expression for the concept definition. While the operator $\leq$ states necessary conditions for an individual to belong to the extension of the concept being defined, the operator $\doteq$ introduces necessary and sufficient conditions (cf. the semantics given in Figure 2). Every constructor in Figure 1 can be used to define a concept. The **all-p** constructor in-

$$\varepsilon[c] \subseteq \varepsilon[c\text{-}expr] \quad , \quad \text{if} \quad c \overset{.}{\leq} c\text{-}expr$$

$$\varepsilon[c] = \varepsilon[c\text{-}expr] \quad , \quad \text{if} \quad c \overset{.}{=} c\text{-}expr$$

$$\varepsilon[(\textbf{and } c_1 \ldots c_n)] = \bigcap_{i=1}^{n} \varepsilon[c_i]$$

$$\varepsilon[(\textbf{all-p } prop \; r_1 \ldots r_n)] = \{x \in D \mid \|\{y \in D \mid \langle x,y \rangle \in \varepsilon[prop]\}\| = 1 \; \wedge$$
$$\forall y : (\langle x,y \rangle \in \varepsilon[prop] \Rightarrow y \in (\varepsilon[r_1] \cup \ldots \cup \varepsilon[r_n]))\}$$

$$\varepsilon[(\textbf{all-r } rel \; c_1 \ldots c_n)] = \{x \in D \mid \forall y : (\langle x,y \rangle \in \varepsilon[rel] \Rightarrow y \in (\varepsilon[c_1] \cup \ldots \cup \varepsilon[c_n]))\}$$

$$\varepsilon[(\textbf{exist-v } prop \; v)] = \{x \in D \mid \langle x, \varepsilon[v] \rangle \in \varepsilon[prop]\}$$

$$\varepsilon[(\textbf{exist-c } rel \; c)] = \{x \in D \mid \exists y \in \varepsilon[c] : \langle x,y \rangle \in \varepsilon[rel]\}$$

$$\varepsilon[(\textbf{at-least } rel\text{-}prop \; n)] = \{x \in D \mid \|\{y \in D : \langle x,y \rangle \in \varepsilon[rel\text{-}prop]\}\| \geq n\}$$

$$\varepsilon[(\textbf{at-most } rel\text{-}prop \; n)] = \{x \in D \mid \|\{y \in D : \langle x,y \rangle \in \varepsilon[rel\text{-}prop]\}\| \leq n\}$$

$$\varepsilon[\textbf{thing}] = D$$

$$\varepsilon[*] = PV$$

Figure 2: Model-Theoretic Semantics of $\mathcal{TL}$

troduces the class of individuals all of which have a certain property (whose value may vary from individual to individual). For example, (**all-p** *price* [200 \$,5000 \$]) denotes the class of individuals that have a property called 'price' with a value ranging between \$200 and \$5,000. An individual can only have one value for each of its properties (cf. Figure 2). The **all-r** constructor introduces the class of individuals that all participate in a certain kind of relationship to individuals belonging only to those concepts given in the constructor. For example, (**all-r** *equipped-with OperatingSystem ApplicationSoftware*) denotes the class of individuals that are in a relationship called 'equipped-with' only to individuals of the concept 'OperatingSystem' or of the concept 'ApplicationSoftware'. The distinction between the constructs **all-p** and **all-r** is uncommon for most terminological logics (Woods & Schmolze 1992), because primitive types like string and integer are usually considered concepts, too. As we will see in Section 4, the inferences underlying the text summarization process exploit exactly this distinction between properties and relationships.

The **exist-v** constructor introduces the class of individuals that all have a certain property value. For example, (**exist-v** *weight 6.5lbs.*) denotes the class of individuals that have a property called 'weight' with the value '6.5lbs.'. The **exist-c** constructor defines the class of individuals that have a conceptual relationship to at least one individual of a specific concept. For example, (**exist-c** *has-part Cpu*) denotes the class of individuals that are in a relationship called 'has-part' to at least one individual of the class 'Cpu'. Finally, the **at-least** (**at-most**) constructor introduces the class of individuals that have either a relation or a property that is to be instantiated at least (at most) n times. For instance, (**at-most** *manufactured-by* 1) denotes the class of individuals that have the property 'manufactured-by' that can only be instantiated with one single value. Using the **and** constructor several concept descriptions can be combined into one.

The model-theoretic semantics of the terminologi-

cal language $\mathcal{TL}$ is depicted in Figure 2. It specifies the properties of an interpretation function ε which maps concept descriptions to subsets of a domain of individuals D. Moreover, ε maps conceptual relationships and properties to subsets of $D \times D$ and $D \times PV$, respectively, where PV is the set of all property values. A feature specific to the terminological logic $\mathcal{TL}$ is the fact that the (**all-p** p v) construct implies the construct (**at-least** p 1). This seems to be more natural than to allow individuals without a value for a property (in contrast to relations to other individuals which may indeed not always exist).

The model-theoretic semantics not only determines the meaning of an expression in $\mathcal{TL}$ but, as a side effect, allows one to find out whether a concept description is inconsistent, i.e., whether its extension is necessarily empty. We have operationalized various consistency criteria by providing integrity constraints that impose context-sensitive restrictions on the syntactic form of a concept description. Integrity checking ensures that these restrictions are never violated. The constraints were not included in the syntax definition, firstly, because they are context-sensitive and would thus extremely complicate the syntax, and secondly, because those constraints can only be formulated when a semantics has already been supplied.

Figure 3 contains some of the constraints with which $\mathcal{TL}$ has been equipped in order to rule out illegal concept definitions. Each of them specifies a syntactic structure that is to be considered illegal. Constraints (IC1) and (IC2) express that a property or a relation may not be defined twice with different value ranges – or, phrased differently, for a property or a relation with a given value range no other range may be defined. Constraints (IC3) and (IC4) say that whenever a certain property or a relationship to a certain kind of individual is claimed it must conform with the value range given. These constraints also contribute to the parser's capability to determine correct property and relation assignments.

(IC1) $(\textbf{and} \cdots (\textbf{all-p}\ p_1\ p\text{-}range_1) \cdots (\textbf{all-p}\ p_2\ p\text{-}range_2) \cdots)$ with $p_1 = p_2$

(IC2) $(\textbf{and} \cdots (\textbf{all-r}\ r_1\ r\text{-}range_1) \cdots (\textbf{all-r}\ r_2\ r\text{-}range_2) \cdots)$ with $r_1 = r_2$

(IC3) $(\textbf{and} \cdots (\textbf{all-p}\ p\ p\text{-}range) \cdots (\textbf{exist-v}\ p\ v) \cdots)$ where $v \notin \varepsilon[p\text{-}range]$

(IC4) $(\textbf{and} \cdots (\textbf{all-r}\ r\ r\text{-}range) \cdots (\textbf{exist-c}\ r\ c) \cdots)$ where $\varepsilon[c] \not\subseteq \varepsilon[r\text{-}range]$

(Note that requiring $\varepsilon[c] \cap \varepsilon[r\text{-}range] \neq \emptyset$ instead would be much less restrictive and still semantically valid but the required integrity check would be far too expensive.)

Figure 3: Various Constraints for the Identification of Illegal Concept Definitions in $\mathcal{TL}$

$$
\begin{aligned}
\langle tconc\text{-}intro \rangle \quad &::= \quad \langle conc\text{-}name \rangle \overset{.}{\leq}_T (\textbf{and}\ \langle conc\text{-}name \rangle\ \langle tc\text{-}expr \rangle^+) \\
\langle tc\text{-}expr \rangle \quad &::= \quad (\textbf{exist-v}\ \langle prop\text{-}name \rangle\ \langle value \rangle\ \langle flag \rangle)\ | \\
&\qquad (\textbf{exist-c}\ \langle rel\text{-}name \rangle\ \langle conc\text{-}name \rangle\ \langle flag \rangle)\ | \\
&\qquad (\textbf{ccount}\ \langle aweight \rangle)\ | \\
&\qquad (\textbf{pcount}\ \langle prop\text{-}name \rangle\ \langle aweight \rangle)\ | \\
&\qquad (\textbf{rcount}\ \langle rel\text{-}name \rangle\ \langle conc\text{-}name \rangle\ \langle aweight \rangle)\ | \\
&\qquad (\textbf{at-least}\ \langle rel\text{-}prop\text{-}name \rangle\ \langle pos\text{-}integer \rangle)\ | \\
&\qquad (\textbf{at-most}\ \langle rel\text{-}prop\text{-}name \rangle\ \langle pos\text{-}integer \rangle) \\
\langle aweight \rangle \quad &::= \quad 0\ |\ 1\ |\ 2 \ldots \\
\langle flag \rangle \quad &::= \quad ON\ |\ OFF
\end{aligned}
$$

Figure 4: Additional Constructs for Representing Text Knowledge in $\mathcal{TL}_T$ on the Basis of $\mathcal{TL}$

2.2   The Extended Terminological Component: Representing Text Knowledge

So far, we have been dealing with a terminological language by which knowledge about a particular domain can be expressed conveniently. In this section, we turn to representational constructs by which the knowledge contained in a text can be represented and distinguished from that which, in general, holds for a particular domain. In the course of text analysis, the parser extends this domain knowledge incrementally by properties and relations concerning already known concepts, as well as by features associated with new concept definitions. In order to distinguish between prior domain knowledge and newly acquired text knowledge we extend the basic terminological language $\mathcal{TL}$ with the constructs specified in Figure 4 – these constitute the syntax of the extended language $\mathcal{TL}_T$. The operator $\leq_T$ indicates a concept originating from the text analysis. Only a limited number of constructs can be used for such a concept definition – they correspond to the kinds of knowledge the parser may extract from a text:

- A new concept can only be acquired when the text makes a reference to a superordinate concept already known in the domain knowledge. Thus, the concept expression on the right-hand side of the $\leq_T$ construct must comprise a reference to a superordinate concept, as expressed by the syntax. Example: A new product is introduced in a text, and it is said that it is a colour printer.

- Properties of a new concept can be acquired (**exist-v**). Example: TOPIC learns the weight of

a notebook.

- Relationships to other concepts can be acquired (**exist-c**) in case the relationship range is already defined by a corresponding **all-r** construct. Example: Knowing already (via an **all-r** construct) that a notebook may have various built-in devices, TOPIC learns about a CD-ROM drive being present for a specific kind of notebook.

- Sometimes, even cardinality restrictions can be acquired (**at-least**, **at-most**). Example: A two-processor machine has at least and at most two cpu processors.

We do not allow the text parser to modify an existing concept in the domain knowledge. If a text being parsed contains a proposition which refers to a concept already known in the domain knowledge, a subordinate of this concept is created in the text knowledge, which is then augmented according to the new knowledge acquired from the text[1]. The text-knowledge-specific versions of the **exist-v** and **exist-c** constructs have an additional argument which serves as a flag that is set whenever one of these constructs is added to a concept description (i.e., when the associated property or relationship has been acquired). The text summarization component of TOPIC makes use of this flag in order to determine those facts which have been elicited since a certain reference point (where all flags were set to "OFF").

Besides acquiring new domain knowledge from a text, the parser performs certain book-keeping activi-

---

[1]The text parser detects if a text passage says that a concept does *not* have a certain property and in this case does not generate facts in the knowledge base.

$$\varepsilon[c] \subseteq \varepsilon[\text{tc-expr}] \quad , \quad \text{if} \quad c \leq_T \text{tc-expr}$$
$$\varepsilon[(\textbf{ccount } i)] = D$$
$$\varepsilon[(\textbf{pcount } prop \; i)] = D$$
$$\varepsilon[(\textbf{rcount } rel \; c \; i)] = D$$
$$\varepsilon[(\textbf{exist-v } prop \; v \; f)] = \varepsilon[(\textbf{exist-v } prop \; v)]$$
$$\varepsilon[(\textbf{exist-c } rel \; c \; f)] = \varepsilon[(\textbf{exist-c } rel \; c)]$$

Figure 5: Model-Theoretic Semantics of $\mathcal{TL}_T$

ties in order to record how often a concept, a property of a concept, or a relationship to another concept is explicitly mentioned or implicitly referred to in the text. For this purpose, we provide the constructs **ccount**, **pcount**, and **rcount** for concept descriptions, respectively. These constructs belong to the text knowledge level and can become part of concept descriptions derived from the text, as well as of concepts of the domain knowledge. The **ccount** (**pcount**) construct indicates how often (a property of) a concept has been mentioned, whereas (**rcount** *rel conc aweight*) indicates how often the relationship *rel* to a concept *conc* has been referred to. We call the numbers introduced by the count operators *activation weights*. An (**rcount** *rel conc aweight*) construct can only occur as part of a text concept description when it also contains a construct (**all-r** *rel* $c_1 \ldots c_n$) where *conc* is subsumed by one of the c_i. If this is not the case, **rcount** would refer to a concept being related via a relationship *rel* which is not in the range of this relationship – thus, the **rcount** statement would not make any sense. An analogous argument holds for the **pcount** and (**all-p**) constructs. Since none of the count constructs (and the flags) make an assertion about the meaning of the concepts involved, they have no influence on the concepts' extension (cf. Figure 5).

3 Text Parsing: Transforming Texts into Text Knowledge Representation Structures

In this section, we first consider the basic procedures which map a linear text into text knowledge representation structures and then generalize the basic functionality of a natural language parser required for building up text knowledge representation structures that can be summarized upon. Since we deal with original magazine articles and legal texts, the parser of the TOPIC system must pay its tribute to the requirements of "real-world" text processing. It provides a type of functionality usually referred to as *partial parsing*. This implies a shallow form of text understanding that deepens to the extent with which linguistic and conceptual specifications are made available. The system is based on the principles of expectation-based, conceptual parsing, thus guaranteeing an inherent degree of robustness. Its coverage for the analysis of German language test reports and product announce-

ments in the domain of information technology encompasses nominal compounds, noun phrases (including complex forms of adjectival, nominal and prepositional phrases), assertional sentences (including active/passive paraphrases, simple varieties of relative clauses and coordinations, etc.), text cohesion phenomena such as nominal and pronominal forms of anaphora and textual ellipsis (Hahn 1989), as well as the recognition of coherence relations in terms of thematic progression patterns (Hahn 1990). We are currently considering to port the parser of the SYNDIKATE system for text knowledge acquisition (Hahn & Schnattinger 1997) to the TOPIC system. This parser is linguistically more sophisticated and builds on a fully lexicalized, head-oriented dependency grammar (Bröker *et al.* 1997).

We shall not go here into the details of grammar encoding and parsing mechanisms, but concentrate instead on the output produced by the parser. According to the principles of conceptual parsing no intermediate linguistic descriptions are built up. So parsing proceeds in terms of the *direct creation of knowledge representation structures*. TOPIC's parsing machinery thus produces readings that constitute a continuous stream of update operations on the emerging text knowledge base. The basic repertoire from which these readings are formed consists of the following primitive operations:

(1) *Incrementation of activation weights* of either a concept (**ccount**), a property (**pcount**), or a relationship (**rcount**).

The motivation behind the incremental modification of concept, property, and relationship weights is to reflect the ongoing reference to particular entities in the knowledge base. The underlying hypothesis (which is also common wisdom in the information retrieval community) is that the more frequently an item is referred to, the more important it is for summarization purposes. References to a knowledge base entity are very often distinct from a plain mention of the literal surface form of the corresponding lexical item as evidenced, e.g., in the cases of pronominal and nominal anaphors, textual ellipses, as well as thematic progression patterns (Hahn 1989). Therefore, the text parser's service of keeping track of references is an indispensable functionality at the text level of analysis, ensuring that also implicit mention is accounted for. Activation weights get a bigger increment when the associated lexical item occurs at a prominent place in the text, e.g. in the title, the abstract, or in a heading.

(2) *Assignment of property values* to concepts (**exist-v**) or *creation of a relationship* to some concept (**exist-c**).

The motivation behind the assignment operation is to mirror the continuous knowledge increment the text knowledge base faces in the course of incremental text

Domain Knowledge:

$$\text{Notebook} \;\dot{\leq}\; (\textbf{and} \quad (\textbf{all-r } \text{manufactured-by Manufacturer})$$

(**exist-c** has-part Cpu) (**exist-c** has-part RAM1)

(**exist-c** has-part HardDisk1)

(**all-p** weight [1lb.,15lbs.])

(**all-p** price [200$, 5000$])

(**all-r** equipped-with OperatingSystem ApplicationSoftware))

RAM1 $\dot{\leq}$ (**and** (**all-p** size [8MB, 64MB]) ...)

HardDisk1 $\dot{\leq}$ (**and** (**all-p** size [500MB, 4GB]) ...)

Figure 6: Fragment of the Domain Knowledge Required to Parse the Sample Text

Text Knowledge (1):

Notebooster $\dot{\leq}_T$ (**and** *Notebook* (**ccount** 2)

(**exist-c** manufactured-by LeadingEdgeTech *ON*)

(**rcount** manufactured-by LeadingEdgeTech 1)

(**exist-c** has-part Cpu *OFF*) (**exist-c** has-part RAM1 *OFF*)

(**exist-c** has-part HardDisk1 *OFF*)

(**all-p** weight [1lb.,15lbs.])

(**all-p** price [200$, 5000$])

(**all-r** equipped-with OperatingSystem ApplicationSoftware))

RAM1 $\dot{\leq}$ (**and** (**all-p** size [8MB, 64MB]) ...)

HardDisk1 $\dot{\leq}$ (**and** (**all-p** size [500MB, 4GB]) ...)

Figure 7: Text Knowledge Structures Resulting from Parsing the First Phrase of the Sample Text

understanding. Note also that any assignment operation implies an appropriate weight update, i.e., the addition of an **exist-v** expression also fuels the incrementation of the activation weights of the corresponding concept and property, while adding an **exist-c** expression implies to increment the weights of the concept and relationship being referred to. It is exactly this kind of functionality we require a parser to contribute in order to deliver text knowledge representation structures that can then be submitted to text summarization.

In order to illustrate the working of those principles we briefly sketch a text understanding process based on these premises. We start by introducing a sample text fragment and discuss the step-wise construction of text representation structures.

Sample Text:

> "*LeadingEdgeTech's Notebooster* is a state-of-the-art *notebook* that *weighs 9.5lbs. It* runs on a *Pentium*, has *NT4.0*, and comes with *32 MB of RAM*. At *$2,800* it can be considered a good buy, although some may possibly find its *weight* too heavy."

This text refers to the concept NOTEBOOK which is defined in the domain knowledge (cf. Figure 6). When processing the sample text the following intermediate parsing steps will be traced, all of them making heavy use of the structures and constraints illustrated in Figure 6:

1. Parsing the phrase "*LeadingEdgeTech's Notebooster is a state-of-the-art notebook* ..." leads to the initialization of the domain knowledge structures given in Figure 6 in terms of text knowledge structures (Figure 7, changes are underlined).

2. Continuing with the first sentence, we proceed with the relative clause "*...that weighs 9.5lbs.*". This leads to the update of the text knowledge structures shown in Figure 8 (the (**all-p** weight ...) construct is omitted in the following, as the actual weight is known by now).

3. When processing the second sentence "*It runs on a Pentium, has NT4.0, and comes with 32MB of RAM.*" one should keep in mind that the pronominal anaphor *it* will be resolved to NOTEBOOSTER (cf. (Hahn 1989) for the corresponding text parsing procedures), thus incrementing its activation weight by one activation unit. Furthermore, any additional reference to one of its attributes (its CPU, operating system, and RAM) will also lead to activation weight increments – not only for its attributes being referred to, but also for NOTEBOOSTER itself. These considerations are reflected in Figure 9.

4. The third sentence of the sample text "*At $2,800 it can be considered a good buy, although some may possibly find its weight too heavy.*" leads to the final result in terms of the generation of text knowledge representation structures in Figure 10.

The text parser is currently designed to cope with textual phenomena as they occur in expository texts

Text Knowledge (2):

Notebooster $\dot{\leq}_T$ (**and** *Notebook* (**ccount** <u>3</u>)
                  (**exist-c** manufactured-by LeadingEdgeTech *ON*)
                  (**rcount** manufactured-by LeadingEdgeTech 1)
                  (**exist-c** has-part Cpu *OFF*) (**exist-c** has-part RAM1 *OFF*)
                  (**exist-c** has-part HardDisk1 *OFF*)
                  (**exist-v** <u>weight</u> <u>9.5lbs.</u> <u>*ON*</u>) (**pcount** <u>weight</u> <u>1</u>))
                  (**all-p** price [200\$, 5000\$])
                  (**all-r** equipped-with OperatingSystem ApplicationSoftware))
       RAM1 $\dot{\leq}$ (**and** (**all-p** size [8MB, 64MB]) ...)
   HardDisk1 $\dot{\leq}$ (**and** (**all-p** size [500MB, 4GB]) ...)

Figure 8: Text Knowledge Structures Resulting from Parsing the Entire First Sentence of the Sample Text

Text Knowledge (3):

Notebooster $\dot{\leq}_T$ (**and** *Notebook* (**ccount** <u>7</u>)
                  (**exist-c** manufactured-by LeadingEdgeTech *ON*)
                  (**rcount** manufactured-by LeadingEdgeTech 1)
                  (**exist-c** <u>has-part</u> <u>Pentium</u> <u>*ON*</u>) (**rcount** <u>has-part</u> <u>Pentium</u> <u>1</u>)
                  (**exist-c** <u>has-part</u> <u>RAM1-1</u> <u>*ON*</u>) (**rcount** <u>has-part</u> <u>RAM1-1</u> <u>1</u>)
                  (**exist-c** has-part HardDisk1 *OFF*)
                  (**exist-v** weight 9.5lbs. *ON*) (**pcount** weight 1))
                  (**all-p** price [200\$, 5000\$])
                  (**exist-c** <u>equipped-with</u> <u>NT4.0</u> <u>*ON*</u>) (**rcount** <u>equipped-with</u> <u>NT4.0</u> <u>1</u>))
    <u>RAM1-1</u> $\dot{\leq}_T$ (**and** *RAM1* (**ccount** <u>1</u>)
                (**exist-v** <u>size</u> <u>32MB</u> <u>*ON*</u>) (**pcount** <u>size</u> <u>1</u>))
   HardDisk1 $\dot{\leq}$ (**and** (**all-p** size [500MB, 4GB]) ...)

Figure 9: Text Knowledge Structures Resulting from Parsing the Second Sentence of the Sample Text

Text Knowledge (4):

Notebooster $\dot{\leq}_T$ (**and** *Notebook* (**ccount** <u>11</u>)
                  (**exist-c** manufactured-by LeadingEdgeTech *ON*)
                  (**rcount** manufactured-by LeadingEdgeTech 1)
                  (**exist-c** has-part Pentium *ON*) (**rcount** has-part Pentium 1)
                  (**exist-c** has-part RAM1-1 *ON*) (**rcount** has-part RAM1-1 1)
                  (**exist-c** has-part HardDisk1 *OFF*)
                  (**exist-v** weight 9.5lbs. *ON*) (**pcount** weight <u>2</u>))
                  (**exist-v** <u>price</u> <u>2800 \$</u> <u>*ON*</u>) (**pcount** <u>price</u> <u>1</u>))
                  (**exist-c** equipped-with NT4.0 *ON*) (**rcount** equipped-with NT4.0 1))
    RAM1-1 $\dot{\leq}_T$ (**and** *RAM1* (**ccount** 1)
                (**exist-v** size 32MB *ON*) (**pcount** size 1))
   HardDisk1 $\dot{\leq}$ (**and** (**all-p** size [500MB, 4GB]) ...)

Figure 10: Text Knowledge Structures Resulting from Parsing the Third Sentence of the Sample Text

(independently of the domain). Moving to a completely different sort of text, like political texts or narratives, would certainly make adaptations necessary.

4 Summarizing Text Knowledge

The text summarization process examines the text knowledge base generated by the parser to determine certain distributions of activation weights, patterns of property and relationship assignments to concept descriptions, and particular connectivity patterns of active concepts in the concept hierarchy. They constitute the basis for the construction of thematic descriptions as the result of text summarization. Only the most significant (hereafter called *salient*) concepts, relationships and properties are considered parts of such topic descriptions.

TOPIC might parse the complete text and then start the condensation at its very end. This would, however, result in a serious loss of the organizational structure a text implicitly exhibits through the way its topics are elaborated (Hahn 1990). On the other hand, determining topic descriptions during text parsing after every single update in the text knowledge base would cause an unnecessary and rather expensive computational overhead. As a compromise, we have chosen to start the summarization process only in certain well-defined intervals. Actually, this conforms quite well with the observation that in the sublanguage domain of expository texts topic shifts occur predominantly (but not necessarily) at paragraph boundaries. Therefore, text summarization is started at the end of every paragraph so that thematic overlaps as well as topic shifts and topic breaks between adjacent paragraphs can be detected and the extension of a topic be exactly delimited. So, we end up with a three-step summarization procedure: First, determine the salient concepts, relationships and properties of a single paragraph by applying the repertoire of *salience operators* as discussed in Section 4.1. Second, derive a topic description from these salient items for the paragraph and determine its extension, which might range over several consecutive paragraphs (cf. Section 4.2). Finally, combine the entire collection of paragraph-level topic descriptions of a single text by employing various *generalization operators*. The result is a hierarchical *text graph* (cf. Section 4.3), which constitutes a text summary at the representational level. Thus, text summarization can be considered an *abstraction process on (text) knowledge bases* employing salience and generalization as fundamental abstraction principles. Figure 11 gives an overall description of that abstraction process.

4.1   Salience Operators

We apply several operators to text knowledge bases to determine which concepts, properties, and relationships play a dominant role in the corresponding texts and should therefore become part of their topic description. All of these operators are grounded in the semantics of the terminological logic $\mathcal{TL}$ and its extension $\mathcal{TL}_T$. Some of the operators make additional use of cut-off values which are heuristically motivated and have been evaluated empirically (cf. (Hahn & Reimer 1984) for the experimental set-up). Informal characterizations of these operators have already been given in (Hahn & Reimer 1986) and (Reimer & Hahn 1988). The criteria we formulate make use of definitions of sets and functions, all listed in Table 1.

Salient Concepts:
There are several criteria to determine salient concepts. The most simple, less "knowledgeable" criterion considers all those concepts salient whose activation weight exceeds the average activation weight of all

```
i := 1;
topic-descr_i := ∅;
at the end of every paragraph do
begin
    determine salient concepts,
        salient relationships,
        salient properties,
        and related salient concepts;        Sec.4.1
    combine them to a paragraph-level
        topic description t̄;                 Sec.4.2
    if t̄ is included in the current topic
            description topic-descr_i
        or topic-descr_i is included in t̄ then
        topic-descr_i := topic-descr_i ∪ t̄
    otherwise
    begin
        i := i + 1;
        topic-descr_i := t̄;
    end
    reset all activation weights (except for
        the current focus) and flags;
end

T := { topic-descr_1, ..., topic-descr_i };   Sec.4.3
at the end of the text do
begin
    for every two distinct topic descriptions
            t, t' from T do
        generate all topic descriptions that
            generalize t as well as t' and add
            them to T;
    unless no generalized topic description
                not already in T can be generated
end
```

Figure 11: The Overall Text Summarization Algorithm

active concepts.[2] This is a numerical criterion which simply exploits the activation weights assembled in the course of the text parsing process.

(SC1): c is a salient concept iff

$$ccount(c) > \frac{\sum_{c_i \in AC} ccount(c_i)}{\|AC\|}$$

A second criterion renders a concept salient, if the total sum of references made to its properties and to its relationships to other concepts is greater than the average sum for all other active concepts. This criterion may render a concept salient even if its activation weight is not strong enough to fulfill criterion (SC1). (SC2) exploits the structure of the aggregation hierarchy inherent to terminological logics and evaluates it by the associated activation weights.

---

[2]Throughout the paper, we call a concept c an active one, if $ccount(c) > 0$ (cf. Table 1).

$$ccount(c) = n \Leftrightarrow c \overset{.}{\leq} (\textbf{and} \ldots (\textbf{ccount } n) \ldots) \text{ or } c \leq_T (\textbf{and} \ldots (\textbf{ccount } n) \ldots)$$

$$rpcount(c, rp) = \begin{cases} \sum\limits_{c' \in C} rcount(c, rp, c'), & \text{if } rp \in R \\ pcount(c, rp), & \text{if } rp \in P \end{cases}$$

$$rcount(c, rel, c') = \begin{cases} n, & \text{if } c \overset{.}{\leq} (\textbf{and} \ldots (\textbf{rcount } rel \ c' \ n) \ldots) \\ n, & \text{if } c \leq_T (\textbf{and} \ldots (\textbf{rcount } rel \ c' \ n) \ldots) \\ 0, & \text{else} \end{cases}$$

$$pcount(c, prop) = \begin{cases} n, & \text{if } c \overset{.}{\leq} (\textbf{and} \ldots (\textbf{pcount } prop \ n) \ldots) \\ n, & \text{if } c \leq_T (\textbf{and} \ldots (\textbf{pcount } prop \ n) \ldots) \\ 0, & \text{else} \end{cases}$$

$$rpactive(c, rp) = \begin{cases} 1, & \text{if } rpcount(c, rp) > 0 \\ 0, & \text{else} \end{cases}$$

$$existcount(c, rp) = \begin{cases} \sum\limits_{c' \in C} existc(c, rp, c'), & \text{if } rp \in R \\ \sum\limits_{v \in V} existv(c, rp, v), & \text{if } rp \in P \end{cases}$$

$$existc(c, rel, c') = \begin{cases} 1, & \text{if } c \leq_T (\textbf{and} \ldots (\textbf{exist-c } rel \ c' \ ON) \ldots) \\ 0, & \text{else} \end{cases}$$

$$existv(c, prop, v) = \begin{cases} 1, & \text{if } c \leq_T (\textbf{and} \ldots (\textbf{exist-v } prop \ v \ ON) \ldots) \\ 0, & \text{else} \end{cases}$$

$$is\text{-}a(c_1, c_2) \Leftrightarrow c_1 \overset{.}{\leq} c_2 \vee c_1 \leq_T c_2 \vee c_1 \overset{.}{\leq} (\textbf{and} \ldots c_2 \ldots) \vee c_1 \leq_T (\textbf{and} \ldots c_2 \ldots)$$

$$C = \{c \mid c \overset{.}{\leq} c\text{-}expr \text{ or } c \leq_T c\text{-}expr \text{ is part of the knowledge base}\}$$

$$AC = \{c \mid c \in C \wedge ccount(c) > 0\} \text{ , the set of active concepts (the ones referred to in the text)}$$

$$V = \text{the set of all property values occurring in the knowledge base}$$

$$P = \text{the set of all properties occurring in the knowledge base}$$

$$R = \text{the set of all relationships occurring in the knowledge base}$$

Table 1: Auxiliary Set and Function Definitions for Salience Computation

(SC2): c is a salient concept iff

$$\sum_{rp_i \in R \cup P} rpcount(c, rp_i) > \frac{\sum\limits_{c_i \in AC} \sum\limits_{rp_j \in R \cup P} rpcount(c_i, rp_j)}{\|AC\|}$$

A third criterion checks whether properties of a concept or relationships to other concepts have been mentioned more often than on the average. While (SC2) checks for the total number of references made to *any* property or relationship, (SC3) is concerned with the number of *different* properties and relationships that have been mentioned.

(SC3): c is a salient concept iff

$$\sum_{rp_i \in R \cup P} rpactive(c, rp_i) > \frac{\sum\limits_{c_i \in AC} \sum\limits_{rp_j \in R \cup P} rpactive(c_i, rp_j)}{\|AC\|}$$

The following two criteria exploit the inherent specialization structure of the concept hierarchy together with activation criteria. (SC4) determines an active concept c as being salient *iff* a significant amount of subordinates of c are active, too. Note that if superordinates of the currently considered concept c also fulfil the criterion they are included in the set of dominant concepts as well. However, the chance for such a superordinate to exist is quite low, because they are likely to be *inactive*.

(SC4): c is a salient concept iff
$$ccount(c) > 0 \wedge \|\{c' \mid is\text{-}a(c', c)\} \cap AC\| \geq \frac{\|\{c' \mid is\text{-}a(c', c)\}\|}{\|\{c' \mid is\text{-}a(c', c)\} \cap AC\|}$$

(SC5) is similar to (SC4), but it marks all non-active (!) concepts as being salient which are related to a significant number of active subordinates. Thus, concepts can be included in the topic description which have never been mentioned explicitly in a text. (SC5) only yields the most specific concepts, i.e., it excludes concepts for which the main criterion is fulfilled, but which are superordinate to another concept that also fulfills the criterion.

(SC5): c is a salient concept iff

$$\|\{c' \mid is\text{-}a(c',c)\} \cap AC\| \geq 3 \quad \text{and}$$
$$ccount(c) = 0 \wedge c \in CAND \wedge \neg \exists c' \in CAND : is\text{-}a(c',c)$$

where

$$CAND = \{c \mid \|\{c' \mid is\text{-}a(c',c)\} \cap AC\| \geq$$
$$0.25 \cdot \|\{c' \mid is\text{-}a(c',c)\}\| \}$$

(SC5) has a more stringent cut-off criterion than (SC4). This is necessary because it makes non-active concepts salient; accordingly, one has to be careful not to include irrelevant concepts. Therefore, (SC5) requires a quarter of all subordinates (in our experiments, at least 3) to be active, while (SC4) has a relative cut-off value (the cut-off values have been determined empirically). Both criteria, (SC4) and (SC5), demonstrate quite convincingly the philosophy underlying the construction of the salience operators we propose, namely the combination of structural patterns based on the representation formalism and heuristically motivated cut-off values (an exception being (SC1) which is purely numerical).

Salient Relationships and Salient Properties:

Just as certain concepts may have been dealt with more extensively in a text than others, certain features of a concept definition may have been focused on to a higher degree than other features of the same concept. We check for such features by using the following criteria (refer again to Table 1 for definitions of the sets and functions being used).

Criterion (SR1) checks whether there have been more references to a particular relationship or property rp of a salient concept c than is the average case for other relationships and properties of that concept. This is mainly (but not purely, due to its implicit reference to conceptual relations) a numerical criterion.

(SR1): A relationship or property rp of a salient concept c is considered salient in the context of c iff $\sum_{rp_i \in R \cup P} rpactive(c, rp_i) \geq 3$ (i.e., c has at least three active relationships or properties) and the following criterion holds:

$$rpcount(c, rp) > \frac{\sum_{rp_j \in R \cup P} rpcount(c, rp_j)}{\sum_{rp_j \in R \cup P} rpactive(c, rp_j)}$$

The second criterion (SR2) is more sensitive to the aggregation hierarchy. It is only applied to a concept c that was newly acquired during text parsing and renders a relationship (or property) rp salient iff the number of concepts (or property values) to which c has

newly been related via rp is greater than is the average case for all the relationships (or properties) in c.

(SR2): A relationship or property rp of a salient concept c is considered salient in the context of c iff $\sum_{rp_i \in R \cup P} rpactive(c, rp_i) \geq 3$ and the following holds:

$$existcount(c, rp) > \frac{\sum_{rp_j \in R \cup P} existcount(c, rp_j)}{\sum_{rp_j \in R \cup P} rpactive(c, rp_j)}$$

(SR1) and (SR2) are evaluated for salient concepts only, because we are not interested in salient features of concepts that are irrelevant for a topic description.

Related Salient Concepts:

We may even extend our perspective and determine concepts that are strongly related to a salient concept and consider them as salient, too. Thus, according to the criterion (SRC1), a concept c' is considered a *related salient concept* of a salient concept c if there is a relationship rel from c to c' such that the sum of the activation weights of all relationships of type rel from c to c' or to subordinates of c' is greater than the average activation weight of all active relationships for c. Additionally, the associated relationship rel becomes a *salient relationship* of c. This criterion illustrates again how conditions concerning concept aggregation and concept subsumption can reasonably be combined with numerical conditions.

(SRC1): A relationship rel between a salient concept c and some concept c' is considered salient and c' is considered a related salient concept iff $\sum_{rel_i \in R} rpactive(c, rel_i) \geq 3$ and the following criterion holds:

$$\sum_{\{c_i \mid c_i = c' \vee is\text{-}a(c_i, c')\}} rcount(c, rel, c_i) >$$
$$\frac{\sum_{rel_j \in R} rpcount(c, rel_j)}{\sum_{rel_j \in R} rpactive(c, rel_j)}$$

All the salience criteria above have a computational complexity that grows linearly with the number of concepts and the number of properties and relationships per concept. A very important side effect of applying the salience criteria is that errors of the text parser (e.g., due to missing domain knowledge or an encountered text coherence phenomenon not known by the parser) are abstracted away because a faulty entry in the text knowledge is only occasional and does not make it to become a salient feature. This makes TOPIC very robust.

Recently, Lin (Lin 1995) provided a similar perspective on using semantic generalization relations for the computation of concept salience but his approach does not take relationships and properties of concepts in account, as criteria (SC2), (SC3), (SR1), (SR2), and (SRC1) do. In general, the basic generalization capability of the salience criteria we provide resembles the information reduction that can be achieved using macro rules (van Dijk 1980). These are based on logical entailment relations and, hence, as far as qualitative criteria are concerned, they are formally even more flexible and expressive than our approach which refers to taxonomic generalization only. However, their notion of salience does not incorporate quantitative data such as the frequency of mention. Only few proposals have been made to realize macro rules in implemented systems (e.g. (Correira 1980)). The criteria we propose, (SC4), (SC5) and (SRC1) in particular, also incorporate some notion of graph connectivity that has previously been considered by Lehnert (Lehnert 1981) for text summarization purposes. However, plot unit connectivity is a formal property that is not sensitive to particular conceptual relation types such as *is-a* or complementary aggregation relations.

The basic ideas underlying the summarization approach in (Boguraev & Kennedy 1997) can also be compared to those in TOPIC. Like TOPIC, the approach is based on the notion of salience of the objects in discourse. The greater the salience of an object the clearer it should become part of the summary. The objects that will actually go into a summary are determined by a threshold value. The main difference between TOPIC and Boguraev and Kennedy's approach is that their criteria are much more closely tied to the syntactical structure of the sentences and to the structure of the text, and thus give less room for more sophisticated criteria, like connectivity along an aggregation hierarchy. TOPIC's salience criteria have no reference to such surface structures – but, of course, take them implicitly into account because the representation structures they operate upon reflect those surface phenomena.

4.2 Paragraph-Level Topic Descriptions

The salience operators introduced above are applied at the end of every paragraph to the text knowledge base which results from parsing that paragraph. They yield a set of salient concepts, relationships, properties, and related salient concepts. Accordingly, let (c) denote a salient concept c, let $(c : rp)$ denote a salient relationship or property rp of concept c, and let $(c : r : c')$ denote a related salient concept c' for concept c with respect to the relationship r. In the next step, these raw salience data have to be combined to form a composite topic description for that paragraph. As overlaps or even entirely redundant representations may have been assembled, a combination of single salience data is performed according to the following rules:

- A salient concept (c) which is already covered by a salient relationship or property $(c : rp)$ or a related salient concept $(c : r : c')$ is removed.

$$td \dot{\cup} \{(c)\} = \begin{cases} td \text{ , if } \exists r \in R : (c : r) \in td \\ \qquad \vee \exists r \in R, c' \in C : \\ \qquad\qquad (c : r : c') \in td \\ td \cup \{(c)\} \text{ , else} \end{cases}$$

$$td \dot{\cup} \{(c : r)\} = \begin{cases} td \text{ , if } \exists c' \in C : (c : r : c') \in td \\ td \cup \{(c : r)\} \setminus \{(c)\} \text{ , else} \end{cases}$$

$$td \dot{\cup} \{(c : r : c')\} = td \cup \{(c : r : c')\} \setminus \{(c), (c : r)\}$$

$$td \dot{\cup} td' = \bigcup_{e \in td \cup td'} \{e\}$$

Table 2: The Operator $\dot{\cup}$ for Combining Topic Descriptions

- A salient relationship $(c : r)$ already covered by a related salient concept $(c : r : c')$ is removed.

Expressed more formally using the operator $\dot{\cup}$ defined in Table 2 (in this definition, the operator "$\setminus$" stands for the set complement operator):

Let S be the set of salient entities (i.e., salient concepts, relationships, properties, and related salient concepts) to be combined. The resulting topic description td of a single paragraph is then given by

$$td = \bigcup_{e \in S} \{e\}$$

After having determined the topic description td of the currently considered paragraph a check is made whether this paragraph deals with the same topic(s) as the immediately preceding paragraph(s). If this is the case, the topic description td of the current paragraph is added to the topic description of the preceding paragraph(s), otherwise a new current topic description is created and set to td. Formally (cf. Table 2, once again):

Let td be the topic description of the current paragraph and td_i be the topic description of one or more paragraphs immediately preceding td, then

td_i is set to $td_i \dot{\cup} td$ if td_i and td both deal with the same topic, i.e., if $td_i \dot{\cup} td = td_i \vee td_i \dot{\cup} td = td$

otherwise, td_i is not modified and td_{i+1} is set to td

For example, the following two topic descriptions of adjacent paragraphs

$td_i = \{(\text{Notebooster} : \text{has-part} : 486\text{SL}), (\text{Notepad})\}$
and $td = \{(\text{Notebooster} : \text{has-part})\}$

are combined into one due to the condition $td_i \dot{\cup} td = td_i$.

Analyzing a text in this way yields a set of consecutive topic descriptions $td_1, \ldots, td_n$, each one characterizing the topic of one or more adjacent paragraphs.

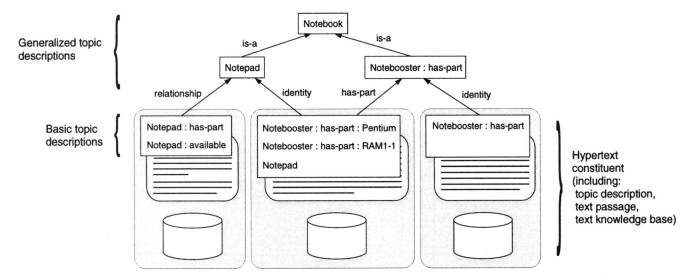

Figure 12: An Illustrative Fragment of a Text Graph (redundant is-a relations are omitted)

Since our text parsing device provides for only partial understanding, and text summarization intentionally abstracts from possibly relevant single facts and details, we associate with every topic description td_i its corresponding original text passage, as well as the new concepts and their properties and relationships acquired from it. We call the resulting composite structure a *hypertext constituent* that consists of

- a topic description that gives an indication of what the text passage making up that particular hypertext constituent is *about* (essential for *summaries*),

- a link to the associated text passage in the *full-text* data base (essential for *passage retrieval*),

- the text knowledge base which characterizes the *original* result of text parsing (essential for accessing *specific facts* acquired through text analysis).

4.3 The Text Graph: A Text Summary at the Representational Level

The topic descriptions, as discussed so far, are the summaries of all the thematically coherent passages of a text. From here we can go even farther and derive more generic conceptual descriptions in terms of a hierarchy of more and more general topic descriptions, the combination of which forms a *text graph*. The construction of a text graph proceeds from the examination of every pair of basic topic descriptions and takes their commonalities to generate more generic thematic abstractions. Exhaustively applying this procedure (also taking the newly generated topic abstractions into consideration) results in a text graph as an abstraction hierarchy of topic descriptions. The most specific descriptions (they correspond to the basic text constituents) form the leaf nodes of the text graph;

the generalized topic descriptions constitute its non-leaf nodes. Their hierarchical organization yields different levels of granularity of text summarization (see Figure 12) and, thus, realize our notion of *scalability* of text summaries.

Through a text graph a text appears divided into a variable number of thematically coherent units at different levels of conceptual specifity. Thus, a text need not be retrieved as a whole but only those of its passages which correspond to a certain topic. This is especially of value when large text knowledge bases and text data bases containing very long texts are queried. The inherent generalization property of text graphs sets them apart from recent approaches which determine thematically annotated, though entirely "flat", text segmentations by lexical co-occurrence characteristics and statistically determined similarities of the lexical items encountered (Hearst & Plaunt 1993). It is also an improvement over more sophisticated lexical chaining procedures based on lexical cohesion characteristics which integrate thesaural information about the lexical items involved (Morris & Hirst 1991). When querying a text knowledge base a user can choose from the text graph those nodes which best fit his or her current information needs – the root nodes offer the most abstract and most compact characterization of the associated text knowledge as a whole (since a text graph is poly-hierarchic it may have more than one root). By descending a text graph, more and more specific topic descriptions are encountered until the most specific ones, finally, allow access to the facts acquired from the text, or to original text passages of the source text. Increasing the specificity of a topic description by descending the text graph increases the number of text passages with different topics. Thus, the user executes control into how many thematically distinct text passages a text is split up by browsing up or down the text graph using TOPOGRAPHIC, an interactive graphical interface for navigating TOPIC's text graphs and text knowledge bases (Thiel & Hammwöhner 1987).

It is exactly this emergent generalization property of text graphs that we consider the source of our scalability arguments. Very brief summaries, only intended to capture the main topics of the text, can be generated from the upper level of the text graph. Continuously deepening the traversal level of the text graph provides access to more and more specific information. Our procedure thus not only has the potential for supplying summaries at the *indicative* level but at the *informative* level as well, although the parsing and summarization procedures would need several extensions for handling more specialized discourse structures, like argumentation patterns, to produce full-fledged informative summaries (cf. (Borko & Bernier 1975) for the distinction between indicative and informative abstracting).

Instead of directly delivering natural language summaries, TOPIC deliberately aims at producing summaries in the form of knowledge representation structures. This opens up a broad variety of opportunities – generating natural language summaries being only one possibility[3]. Among the services that become feasible with summaries as representation structures are:

- The topic descriptions are a much more detailed content representation compared to what *document retrieval* systems typically make use of (often they operate directly on the textual form). Thus, basing document retrieval on TOPIC's topic descriptions will cause an increase of precision and recall.

- The same argumentation applies to *document delivery* according to people's interest profiles. The representation of an interest profile uses the same formalism as the topic descriptions of TOPIC so that it becomes quite easy to match both.

- For the purpose of building *organizational memories* (Stein 1995; Reimer 1998) textual knowledge has to be integrated with other textual knowledge as well as with knowledge in a more formalized format. That knowledge integration can only be achieved if a formal representation of all the texts is available.

When applied to topic descriptions, the following *generalization operators* determine fundamental abstraction relations between a text graph node n and an associated, more generic node n' (n and n' being either basic topic descriptions or already generalized ones). The text graph depicted in Figure 12 illustrates some of the underlying abstraction relations (we here assume a slightly more extended text fragment than the one

---

[3] In fact, it is quite straightforward to produce natural language text from the topic descriptions by utilizing predefined textual patterns for each kind of topic description pattern (Sonnenberger 1988).

we used for illustrating the text parsing process). The computational complexity of text graph construction is quadratic with the number of nodes in the graph (all pairs have to be checked).

- $tg\text{-}abstract(\text{is-a}, n, n')$ holds iff for some c, c', c'', and r:
  $n = \{(c)\}$ or $n = \{(c : r)\}$ or $n = \{(c : r : c'')\}$ and $n' = \{(c')\}$ and $is\text{-}a(c, c')$.

- $tg\text{-}abstract(\text{identity}, n, n')$ holds iff $n \supseteq n'$ and $n' = \{e\}$ for some e of the form (c), $(c : r)$, or $(c : r : c'')$.

- $tg\text{-}abstract(\text{property}, n, n')$ holds iff for some property p and some concept c:
  $n \supseteq \{(c : p)\}$ and $n' = \{(c)\}$.

- $tg\text{-}abstract(\text{relationship}, n, n')$ holds iff for some relationship r and some c:
  $n \supseteq \{(c : r)\}$ and $n' = \{(c)\}$.

- $tg\text{-}abstract(r, n, n')$ holds iff for some c, c':
  $n \supseteq \{(c : r : c')\}$ and $n' = \{(c : r)\}$.

5 Related Work

The field of text summarization is characterized by a *"clash of civilizations"*. From the point of view of natural language understanding proper (Schank 1982) it is considered a heavily knowledge-based task requiring a substantial knowledge background. Any knowledge-based system then faces the problem to provide a reasonable amount of linguistic and domain knowledge in order to escape from the continuously raised blames of brittleness and critical comments on their status as mere toy systems. Systems close to that paradigm, in the meantime, have matured and either provide robust parsing devices for the natural language processing part and/or learning capabilities to automatically acquire major portions of linguistic and world knowledge (Soderland *et al.* 1997; Hahn & Schnattinger 1997).

In the field of information retrieval, however, the corresponding task of automatic abstracting has been considered from its very beginning (Luhn 1958; Edmundson 1969) a problem that can be dealt with by surface-level pattern matching techniques and domain-independent as well as language-independent statistical methods. Given a statistical approach and a set of methods that were originally developed for lexical selection tasks such as automatic indexing or classification, automatic summarization always boils down to a sentence extraction problem, *viz.* determining the most salient sentences based on surface-level indicators. A constant problem with any extraction approach to text summarization (including those based on linguistic considerations, as discussed below) concerns the lack of cohesiveness in the resulting extract. This led advocates of that methodology to suggest paragraphs instead of sentences as a more appropriate basic unit of extraction (Salton *et al.* 1994). Recently, this statistically-based work has been extended from a machine learning perspective. The sentence extraction task is then viewed as a learning problem for properly adjusting selection heuristics based on lexical frequency (tf-idf), the occurrence of clue words or positional indicators using classifier systems (Kupiec, Pedersen, & Chen 1995; Teufel & Moens 1997). The training data required by the classifiers must be supplied by humans, either professional abstractors (Kupiec, Pedersen, & Chen 1995) or the authors themselves (Teufel & Moens 1997).

Alternatively, as a side effect of the empirical move of natural language processing and the emergence of natural language engineering technology, several approaches to automatic summarizing have been proposed that use primarily linguistic knowledge. The most promising among them are based on the concept of lexical cohesion (Halliday & Hasan 1976). The extension of lexically cohesive text segments is determined on the basis of lexical chaining (Morris & Hirst 1991). The computation of lexical chains incorporates generalization as well as semantic relatedness criteria that are checked by looking up online lexical resources such as WordNet (Fellbaum 1998). Each chain is then scored according to some measure of strength or salience, and those with the highest degree of strength are selected for inclusion in an extract (Barzilay & Elhadad 1997). In this way, complex conceptual reasoning is replaced by the exploitation of basic semantic relations in large-scale lexical repositories. Statistical criteria often complement linguistic ones for capturing the notion of salience (cf. the SUMMARIST system (Hovy & Lin 1997)). One prototypical system for this hybrid approach is DimSum (Aone et al. 1997), which combines linguistic methodology such as morphological and collocational analysis, robust parsing, and text structure recognition with statistical relevance scoring.

Another, more text-structurally rooted approach builds on the recognition of coherence relations in texts and their use for determining relevant sentences in texts. Miike et al. (Miike et al. 1994), e.g., employ a standard linguistic sentence processing approach augmented by a text structure analyzer that recognizes RST-style (Mann & Thompson 1988) rhetorical patterns in full texts using a variety of lexical clues. Given such a text structure representation, sentence selection proceeds by salience factors attributed to single RST relations and their propagation through the text structure graph. Still, this selection procedure is not capable to prevent the extraction of informationally redundant or referentially dubious or even referentially invalid sentences, e.g., ones with dangling anaphors for which no antecedent is available. Hence, cohesion streamlining remains a topic of future work (Ono, Sumita, & Miike 1994), though inherent limitations to provide cohesive summaries from large sets of extracted sentences are discussed at length by Paice (Paice 1990) (some "repair strategies" are discussed in Johnson et al. (Johnson et al. 1993)). The integration

of RST relations into the text summarization process has only recently been considered in more depth by Marcu (Marcu 1997) who bases his work on a dedicated rhetorical text parser.

When text summarization is considered a knowledge-based process, the vast majority of text understanding systems remain in the sphere of baroque and sometimes even idiosyncratic representation approaches (cf., e.g. MOPs and TAUs as used by Dyer (Dyer 1983)). The most striking common feature is the unclear formal status of the underlying representation devices. Consider as examples the model of story grammars (Rumelhart 1975) and the debate on their methodological status proper (Black & Wilensky 1979), or the model of micro and macro propositions which, though based on the formal notion of semantic entailment, was never fully elaborated and stayed at the level of sketchy remarks about the criteria going into concrete macro rules (van Dijk 1980). Plot units (Lehnert & Loiselle 1989) provide some graph-theoretical background for the summarization task (Lehnert 1981), but inherit their unclear semantics from the CD-style framework to which they adhere. As it stands, none of these approaches provides a convincing formal foundation for summarization. This underspecification of representation mechanisms not only affects the inferencing processes on which text understanding is based, but extends also to the principles guiding those operations on knowledge structures which are required for text summarization.

The proponents of terminological representation systems in the text summarization field get a well-established, model-theoretic semantics for free. Unfortunately, they often tend to make only sketchy remarks concerning the underlying condensation procedures, as with SCISOR (Rau, Jacobs, & Zernik 1989), or they take refuge to formally unconstrained add-ons such as batteries of production rules in the SUSY system (Fum, Guida, & Tasso 1985). We also adhere to the knowledge-based, terminological paradigm of abstracting but diverge from the studies just mentioned in that we propose to treat text understanding and summarization within a single, formally homogeneous framework which considers abstracting as a transformation of knowledge representation structures provided by the text parser. Moreover, and most important, this model allows for a *staged* provision of information in summaries based on conceptual criteria (as illustrated by the discussion of text graphs).

6 Conclusions, Experiences, Outlook

We have introduced an approach to text summarization which is rooted in the formal semantics of the underlying terminological representation system. In this approach, text summarization is an operator-based transformation process on knowledge representation structures that have been derived by the text understanding system. The computational complexity of all the operators is linear with the size of the knowledge base, while text graph construction is quadratic with the size of the text graph. Thus, text summarization in TOPIC is highly tractable and scales up for large domain knowledge bases.

Currently, the summarization process considers only activity and connectivity patterns in the text knowledge base. We intend to include additional criteria and plan, in particular, to exploit text coherence patterns for summarization (cf. (Hahn 1990; Hahn & Strube 1997) for texttheoretical models and related proposals to build on text coherence structure by (Alterman 1986) and (Marcu 1997)).

The implementation of the summarization system TOPIC and its associated text understander have proved functional for expository texts in the domain of information technology as well as for texts from the legal and business domains. Our experience with building the knowledge base needed for running TOPIC on texts from a new domain shows that it is sufficient to provide between 50 and 100 concept definitions with about 4 properties or relationships per concept on the average. This gives already quite acceptable topic descriptions. The more concepts are defined and the more properties and relationships are given for them, the more detailed are the generated topic descriptions. Thus it cannot be said how much domain knowledge TOPIC needs to become operable. This is totally gradual and depends on the required detail of the summaries as well as how broad and complex the domain is to which the texts belong. This also means that TOPIC does not have a particular problem with incomplete knowledge: What is not given in the domain knowledge cannot be recognized in a text (with the exception of TOPIC's learning capabilities). Sometimes, this may cause understanding errors of the parser (just as with human readers lacking certain background knowledge), but to our experience such errors have very rarely an influence on the topic descriptions generated because the summarization process abstracts from the knowledge structures produced by the parser and only preserves what is salient therein. Consequently, parsing errors are just abstracted away, making TOPIC a very robust system.

TOPIC does not directly generate natural language output. We claim that this is one of TOPIC's main strengths since this allows it to be used for other tasks than summarization as well, like document retrieval, information filtering, integrating textual knowledge with other kinds of knowledge. All those aspects become highly relevant in the context of organizational memories. Therefore, utilizing TOPIC in such a context is very rewarding, not only because it provides much needed functionality, but also because a drawback of TOPIC vanishes, namely its requiring domain knowledge to become operative. This is because an organizational memory must comprise that kind of domain knowledge anyway so that it does not need to be built up only to make TOPIC running.

Future extensions of TOPIC will concentrate on two issues. The first one is directed at moving TOPIC from a single to a multi-document summarizer (cf. also (McKeown & Radev 1995; Mani & Bloedorn 1997)). Second, we may then consider an application of TOPIC for web retrieval. According to a given interest profile possibly relevant texts will, in a first step, be retrieved from the web via a common search engine. The texts will then be analyzed by TOPIC to find out if they are really relevant according to the user's interest profile in order to provide a concise summary of the retrieved subset of relevant documents using the multi-document summarization facilities just mentioned.

References

Alterman, R. 1986. Summarization in the small. In Sharkey, N., ed., *Advances in Cognitive Science 1*. Chichester: Ellis Horwood. 72–93.

Aone, C.; Okurowski, M. E.; Gorlinsky, J.; and Larsen, B. 1997. A scalable summarization system using robust NLP. In Mani, I., and Maybury, M., eds., *Proceedings of the ACL'97/EACL'97 Workshop on "Intelligent Scalable Text Summarization"*, 18–24. Madrid, Spain, July 11, 1997. Association for Computational Linguistics (ACL).

Barzilay, R., and Elhadad, M. 1997. Using lexical chains for text summarization. In Mani, I., and Maybury, M., eds., *Proceedings of the ACL'97/EACL'97 Workshop on "Intelligent Scalable Text Summarization"*, 10–17. Madrid, Spain, July 11, 1997. Association for Computational Linguistics (ACL).

Black, J. B., and Wilensky, R. 1979. An evaluation of story grammars. *Cognitive Science* 3(3):213–229.

Boguraev, B., and Kennedy, C. 1997. Salience-based content characterisation of text documents. In Mani, I., and Maybury, M., eds., *Proceedings of the ACL'97/EACL'97 Workshop on "Intelligent Scalable Text Summarization"*. Madrid, Spain, July 11, 1997. Association for Computational Linguistics (ACL).

Borko, H., and Bernier, C. L., eds. 1975. *Abstracting Concepts and Methods*. New York: Academic Press.

Bröker, N.; Strube, M.; Schacht, S.; and Hahn, U. 1997. Coarse-grained parallelism in natural language understanding: parsing as message passing. In Jones, D., and Somers, H., eds., *New Methods in Language Processing*. London: UCL Press. 301–317.

Correira, A. 1980. Computing story trees. *American Journal of Computational Linguistics* 6(3-4):135–149.

Cullingford, R. E. 1978. *Script Application: Computer Understanding of Newspaper Stories*. Ph.D. Dissertation, New Haven, CT: Yale University, Department of Computer Science. Research Report, 116.

DeJong, G. 1982. An overview of the FRUMP system. In Lehnert, W., and Ringle, M. H., eds., *Strategies for*

Natural Language Processing. Hillsdale, NJ: Lawrence Erlbaum. 149–176.

Dyer, M. G. 1983. *In-Depth Understanding: A Computer Model of Integrated Processing for Narrative Comprehension*. Cambridge, MA: MIT Press.

Edmundson, H. 1969. New methods in automatic extracting. *Journal of the Association for Computing Machinery* 16(2):264–285.

Fellbaum, C., ed. 1998. *WordNet: An Electronic Lexical Database*. Cambridge, MA: MIT Press.

Fum, D.; Guida, G.; and Tasso, C. 1985. Evaluating importance: a step towards text summarization. In *IJCAI'85 – Proceedings of the 9th International Joint Conference on Artificial Intelligence. Vol. 2*, 840–844. Los Angeles, Cal., 18-23 August 1985. Los Altos, CA: W. Kaufmann.

Hahn, U., and Reimer, U. 1984. Computing text constituency: an algorithmic approach to the generation of text graphs. In van Rijsbergen, C., ed., *Research and Development in Information Retrieval. Proceedings of the 3rd Joint BCS and ACM Symposium*. Cambridge, England, 2-6 July, 1984. Cambridge: Cambridge University Press. 343–368. [A longer version which contains technical details of the evaluation is available as technical report *"Bericht TOPIC 8/84"* from the University of Constance, Department of Information Science].

Hahn, U., and Reimer, U. 1986. Semantic parsing and summarizing of technical texts in the TOPIC system. In Kuhlen, R., ed., *Informationslinguistik. Theoretische, experimentelle, curriculare und prognostische Aspekte einer informationswissenschaftlichen Teildisziplin*. Tübingen: M. Niemeyer. 153–193. [This is an abbreviated version of *"The TOPIC Project: Text-Oriented Procedures for Information Management and Condensation of Expository Texts. Final Report."*; it is available as technical report *"Bericht TOPIC 17/85"* from the University of Constance, Department of Information Science].

Hahn, U., and Schnattinger, K. 1997. A qualitative growth model for real-world text knowledge bases. In *Proceedings of the RIAO'97 Conference: Computer-Assisted Information Searching on Internet*, 578–597. Montreal, Quebec, Canada, 25-27 June 1997. Centre de Hautes Etudes Internationales d'Informatique Documentaires (CID).

Hahn, U., and Strube, M. 1997. Centering in-the-large: computing referential discourse segments. In *Proceedings of the 35th Annual Meeting of the Association for Computational Linguistics & 8th Conference of the European Chapter of the Association for Computational Linguistics – ACL'97/EACL'97*, 104–111. Madrid, Spain, July 7-12, 1997. San Francisco, CA: Morgan Kaufmann.

Hahn, U. 1989. Making understanders out of parsers: semantically driven parsing as a key concept for realistic text understanding applications. *International Journal of Intelligent Systems* 4(3):345–393.

Hahn, U. 1990. Topic parsing: accounting for text macro structures in full-text analysis. *Information Processing & Management* 26(1):135–170.

Halliday, M., and Hasan, R. 1976. *Cohesion in English*. London: Longman.

Hearst, M. A., and Plaunt, C. 1993. Subtopic structuring for full-length document access. In *SIGIR '93 – Proceedings of the 16th Annual International ACM SIGIR Conference on Research and Development in Information Retrieval*, 59–68. Pittsburgh, PA, USA, June 27-July 1, 1993. New York, NY: Association for Computing Machinery (ACM).

Hovy, E., and Lin, C. Y. 1997. Automated text summarization in SUMMARIST. In Mani, I., and Maybury, M., eds., *Proceedings of the ACL'97/EACL'97 Workshop on "Intelligent Scalable Text Summarization"*, 66–73. Madrid, Spain, July 11, 1997. Association for Computational Linguistics (ACL).

Hutchins, J. W. 1987. Summarization: some problems and methods. In Jones, K., ed., *Informatics 9. Proceedings of a Conference Held by the Aslib Coordinate Indexing Group. Meaning: the Frontier of Informatics*. Cambridge, England, 26-27 March 1987. London: Aslib. 151–173.

Johnson, F.; Paice, C.; Black, W.; and Neal, A. 1993. The application of linguistic processing to automatic abstract generation. *Journal of Document and Text Management* 1(3):215–241.

Kupiec, J.; Pedersen, J.; and Chen, F. 1995. A trainable document summarizer. In Fox, E.; Ingwersen, P.; and Fidel, R., eds., *SIGIR'95 – Proceedings of the 18th Annual International ACM SIGIR Conference on Research and Development in Information Retrieval*, 68–73. Seattle, Washington, USA, July 9-13, 1995. New York, NY: Association for Computing Machinery (ACM).

Lehnert, W., and Loiselle, C. L. 1989. An introduction to plot units. In Waltz, D., ed., *Semantic Structures. Advances in Natural Language Processing*. Hillsdale, NJ: Lawrence Erlbaum. 125–165.

Lehnert, W. 1981. Plot units and narrative summarization. *Cognitive Science* 5:293–331.

Lin, C.-Y. 1995. Knowledge-based automatic topic identification. In *Proceedings of the 33rd Annual Meeting of the Association for Computational Linguistics*, 308–310. Cambridge, Mass., USA, 26-30 June 1995. Association for Computational Linguistics (ACL).

Luhn, H. P. 1958. The automatic creation of literature abstracts. *IBM Journal of Research and Development* 2(2):159–165.

Mani, I., and Bloedorn, E. 1997. Multi-document summarization by graph search and matching. In

AAAI'97/IAAI'97 – Proceedings of the 14th National Conference on Artificial Intelligence & 9th Innovative Applications of Artificial Intelligence Conference, 622–628. Providence, R.I., July 27-31, 1997. Menlo Park, CA: AAAI Press; Cambridge, MA: MIT Press.

Mann, W. C., and Thompson, S. A. 1988. Rhetorical structure theory: toward a functional theory of text organization. *Text* 8(3):243–281.

Marcu, D. 1997. From discourse structures to text summaries. In Mani, I., and Maybury, M., eds., *Proceedings of the ACL'97/EACL'97 Workshop on "Intelligent Scalable Text Summarization"*, 82–88. Madrid, Spain, July 11, 1997. Association for Computational Linguistics (ACL).

McKeown, K., and Radev, D. R. 1995. Generating summaries of multiple news articles. In Fox, E.; Ingwersen, P.; and Fidel, R., eds., *SIGIR'95 – Proceedings of the 18th Annual International ACM SIGIR Conference on Research and Development in Information Retrieval*, 74–82. Seattle, Washington, USA, July 9-13, 1995. New York, NY: Association for Computing Machinery (ACM).

Miike, S.; Itoh, E.; Ono, K.; and Sumita, K. 1994. A full-text retrieval system with a dynamic abstract generation function. In Croft, W. B., and van Rijsbergen, C., eds., *SIGIR'94 – Proceedings of the 17th Annual International ACM-SIGIR Conference on Research and Development in Information Retrieval*, 152–161. Dublin, Ireland, 3-6 July 1994. London: Springer.

Morris, J., and Hirst, G. 1991. Lexical cohesion computed by thesaural relations as an indicator of the structure of text. *Computational Linguistics* 17(1):21–48.

Ono, K.; Sumita, K.; and Miike, S. 1994. Abstract generation based on rhetorical structure extraction. In *COLING'94 – Proceedings of the 15th International Conference on Computational Linguistics. Vol. 1*, 343–345, 347–348. Kyoto, Japan, August 5-9, 1994.

Paice, C. D. 1990. Constructing literature abstracts by computer: techniques and prospects. *Information Processing & Management* 26(1):171–186.

Rau, L. F.; Jacobs, P. S.; and Zernik, U. 1989. Information extraction and text summarization using linguistic knowledge acquisition. *Information Processing & Management* 25(4):419–428.

Reimer, U., and Hahn, U. 1988. Text condensation as knowledge base abstraction. In *Proceedings of the 4th Conference on Artificial Intelligence Applications – CAIA '88*, 338–344. San Diego, Cal., March 14-18, 1988. Washington, D.C.: Computer Society Press of the IEEE.

Reimer, U.; Lippuner, P.; Norrie, M.; and Rys, M. 1995. Terminological reasoning by query evaluation: A formal mapping of a terminological logic to an object data model. In Ellis, G.; Levinson, R.; Fall, A.; and Dahl, V., eds., *Proceedings of the International KRUSE Symposium: Knowledge Retrieval, Use, and Storage for Efficiency*, 49–53. University of California at Santa Cruz, Cal., August 11-13, 1995.

Reimer, U. 1985. A representation construct for roles. *Data & Knowledge Engineering* 1(3):233–251.

Reimer, U. 1998. Knowledge integration for building organizational memories. In Gaines, B., and Musen, M., eds., *KAW'98 - Proc. 11th Banff Knowledge Acquisition for Knowledge-Based Systems Workshop*, KM–6–1 – KM–6–20. http://ksi.cpsc.ucalgary.ca/KAW/KAW98/... ...KAW98Proc.html.

Rumelhart, D. E. 1975. Notes on a schema for stories. In Bobrow, D., and Collins, A., eds., *Representation and Understanding. Studies in Cognitive Science*. New York: Academic Press. 211–236.

Salton, G.; Allan, J.; Buckley, C.; and Singhal, A. 1994. Automatic analysis, theme generation, and summarization of machine-readable texts. *Science* 264(3, June):1421–1426.

Schank, R. C. 1982. Representing meaning: An artificial intelligence perspective. In Allen, S., ed., *Text Processing. Proceedings of the Nobel Symposium*. Stockholm: Almqvist & Wiksell. 25–63.

Soderland, S.; Fisher, D.; Aseltine, J.; and Lehnert, W. 1997. CRYSTAL: Inducing a conceptual dictionary. In *IJCAI'95 – Proceedings of the 14th International Joint Conference on Artificial Intelligence. Vol. 2*, 1314–1319. Montreal, Quebec, Canada, August 19-25, 1995. San Mateo, CA: Morgan Kaufmann.

Sonnenberger, G. 1988. Flexible Generierung von natürlichsprachigen Abstracts aus Textrepräsentationsstrukturen. In Trost, H., ed., *4. Österreichische Artificial-Intelligence-Tagung. Wiener Workshop – Wissensbasierte Sprachverarbeitung*, 72–82. Berlin: Springer.

Stein, E. 1995. Organizational memory: Review of concepts and recommendations for management. *International Journal of Information Management* 15(2):17–32.

Tait, J. I. 1985. Generating summaries using a script-based language analyser. In Steels, L., and Campbell, J., eds., *Progress in Artificial Intelligence*. Chichester: Ellis Horwood. 312–318.

Teufel, S., and Moens, M. 1997. Sentence extraction as a classification task. In Mani, I., and Maybury, M., eds., *Proceedings of the ACL'97/EACL'97 Workshop on "Intelligent Scalable Text Summarization"*, 58–65. Madrid, Spain, July 11, 1997. Association for Computational Linguistics (ACL).

Thiel, U., and Hammwöhner, R. 1987. Informational zooming: an interaction model for the graphical access to text knowledge bases. In Yu, C., and van Rijsbergen, C., eds., *SIGIR '87 – Proceedings of the 10th Annual International ACMSIGIR Conference on*

Research and Development in Information Retrieval, 49–53. New Orleans, Louisiana, USA, June 3-5, 1987. New York, NY: Association for Computing Machinery (ACM).

van Dijk, T. A. 1980. *Macrostructures: an Interdisciplinary Study of Global Structures in Discourse, Interaction and Cognition.* Hillsdale, NJ: Lawrence Erlbaum.

Woods, W. A., and Schmolze, J. G. 1992. The KL-ONE family. *Computers & Mathematics with Applications* 23:133–177.

Young, S. R., and Hayes, P. J. 1985. Automatic classification and summarization of banking telexes. In *Proceedings of the 2nd Conference on Artificial Intelligence Applications: The Engineering of Knowledge-Based Systems,* 402–408. Miami Beach, FL, December 11-13, 1985. Washington, D.C.: Computer Society Press of the IEEE.

16

GENERATING CONCISE NATURAL LANGUAGE SUMMARIES

KATHLEEN McKEOWN,[1] JACQUES ROBIN[1] and KAREN KUKICH[2]

[1] Department of Computer Science, 450 Computer Science Building, Columbia University, New York, NY 10027, U.S.A. and [2] Bell Communication Research, Morristown, N.J., U.S.A.

Abstract—Summaries typically convey maximal information in minimal space. In this paper, we describe an approach to summary generation that opportunistically folds information from multiple facts into a single sentence using concise linguistic constructions. Unlike previous work in generation, how information gets added into a summary depends in part on constraints from how the text is worded so far. This approach allows the construction of concise summaries, containing complex sentences that pack in information. The resulting summary sentences are, in fact, longer than sentences generated by previous systems. We describe two applications we have developed using this approach, one of which produces summaries of basketball games (STREAK) while the other (PLANDOC) produces summaries of telephone network planning activity; both systems summarize input data as opposed to full text. The applications implement opportunistic summary generation using complementary approaches. STREAK uses revision, creating a draft of essential facts and then using revision rules constrained by the draft wording to add in additional facts as the text allows. PLANDOC uses discourse planning, looking ahead in its text plan to group together facts which can be expressed concisely using conjunction and deleting repetitions. In this paper, we describe the problems for summary generation, the two domains, the linguistic constructions that the systems use to convey information concisely and the textual constraints that determine what information gets included.

1. INTRODUCTION

Summarization is a task that seems to require solutions in both natural language interpretation and generation. Summarizing an article, for example, involves interpretation of the article to identify the most important facts conveyed and generation to produce a paragraph that conveys those facts concisely. This need for simultaneous solutions in two subareas has made automated text summarization an elusive goal. In fact, full text summarization using natural language interpretation and generation in unrestricted domains is very much an open research problem, although there are some systems that use statistical or language analysis techniques to select representative sentences from the input text to serve as a summary (Rau, 1987; Cox, 1993; Paice, 1990).

Contrary to this view, we have identified several summarization tasks involving generation only. We are working in two domains, summarization of sports events (Robin & McKeown, 1993; Robin, 1993) and automated documentation of telephone planning engineer activities (Kukich *et al.*, 1993). In the first of these domains, input is a set of box scores for a basketball game and the task for the system is to summarize the highlights of the game, underscoring their significance in the light of previous games. Output is a short summary such as the lead sentences found in newspaper sport reports. In the second domain, the system must produce a report documenting how an engineer investigated what new technology is needed in a telephone route to meet demand through use of a sophisticated software planning system, LEIS-PLAN.* Input to the generation system is a trace of user interaction with PLAN and output is a 1–2 page report, including a paragraph summary of PLAN's solution, a summary of refinements that an engineer made to the system solution, and a closing paragraph summarizing the engineer's final

---

* LEIS is a registered trademark of Bell Communications Research, Piscataway, N.J.

proposed plan. Since input to summary generation in both domains is data as opposed to full text, this has allowed us to focus on the problem of generating summaries as opposed to extracting information from text.

Problems for summary generation are quite distinct from the generic task of language generation. Summaries must convey maximal information in a minimal amount of space. This requires selecting linguistic structures that can convey information concisely. This means the use of complex sentence structure, including multiple modifiers of a noun or verb, conjunction (e.g. "*and*"), and ellipsis (i.e. deletion of repetitions across conjoined phrases). It also means the selection of words that can convey multiple aspects of the information to be communicated. Our analysis of example summaries in both domains supports these summarization needs (Robin & McKeown, 1993; Kukich *et al.*, 1993). In fact, we found that sentences in sports summaries range from 21 to 46 words in length, much longer and more complex than sentences generated by any previous generation system. Furthermore, our analysis shows that some information is opportunistically added into the summary, as the words and syntactic structure already used allow. These observations suggest the need for modifications to a typical language generation approach (e.g. McKeown, 1985a; Hovy, 1988; McDonald, 1983; Kukich, 1983) in order to produce summaries.

We characterize problems for summary generation as falling into two separate classes, *conceptual summarization*, or determining what information should be included in a summary, and *linguistic summarization*, the task of determining how to convey as much information as possible in a short amount of text. In this paper, our focus is on linguistic summarization, although, as we shall show, linguistic constraints often determine when information is included or omitted from a summary. Our systems take as input information which must be included, as well as information which potentially can be included in the summary. We characterize linguistic summarization as centering around the following issues:

- How to use syntactic and lexical devices to convey information concisely.
- Given the choice of a particular word or syntactic structure, how does this constrain (or allow) the attachment of additional information.
- How to fold multiple pieces of information into a single linguistic construction.

Our approach to summary generation is revision based, opportunistically adding in new information that can be folded into the summary text generated so far. A draft is first generated from information that must be included. Additional, potentially interesting, information is added when specific lexical, syntactic and semantic constraints match the draft text. Thus, the summary content is determined by linguistic constraints, as well as the usual conceptual constraints, an approach unique to our work. This revision based approach allows the generation of the complex, information rich sentences found in summaries. In this paper, we detail different linguistic constraints and constructions that can be used to concisely add information into a text, showing the computational rules our systems used to implement these constructions. In particular, we show how the following four constructions allow information from multiple facts in the input to be folded into the same sentence, avoiding repetition of similar information across sentences and resulting in a concise text:

(1) single word conveys multiple information
(2) modifiers of nouns or verbs
(3) conjunction and ellipsis
(4) abridged references.

We describe the implementation of opportunistic summary generation in both STREAK and PLANDOC, showing how they use these constraints and constructions. While STREAK and PLANDOC both opportunistically revise the summary, they use different, but complementary, techniques. STREAK uses a set of revisions rules, constructing a draft of the essential input facts; i.e. those that absolutely must appear in the summary. Constraints from draft wording determine how additional information is added to the text often changing the original wording. PLANDOC uses a discourse planning approach, looking beyond input for the current sentence in its content plan, using syntactic constraints from the current sentence to select information appearing ahead in the plan that can be folded in. It thus reorganizes the content plan, changing the order in which information will appear in the text. By selecting information that was originally planned to appear further ahead in the summary, it can often be collapsed into the current sentence, avoiding repetition and producing a much less verbose text.

In the following sections, we first describe traditional approaches to language generation which stand in contrast to the approach we claim is needed for summary generation. We then describe each application domain, showing both how summaries can be generated from structured data and the complex sentences that are required. From here, we turn to a discussion of linguistic summarization, describing our techniques for conveying maximal information in minimal space. We detail specific syntactic and lexical constructions from our domains that are used to convey information concisely, showing how wording constraints determine how information is opportunistically added to a summary. While conceptual summarization is not the primary focus of our work, we briefly describe how it can be carried out in the two application domains, pointing to places where decisions about whether information should be included are left open for linguistic summarization to resolve. We close by describing related work in the language generation field and our current directions in summarization.

2. TRADITIONAL LANGUAGE GENERATION APPROACHES

Traditionally, language generation systems are divided into two modules, a content planner and a surface sentence generator. It is the task of the content planner to determine what information should be communicated in the text, while the surface sentence generator takes the conceptual representation of text content produced by the planner and realizes it in natural language. This latter task involves determining the overall sentence structure for each input proposition, selecting the words, and ordering the words in a sentence by building syntactic structure and enforcing syntactic constraints between constituents (e.g. ensuring that the subject and main verb agree in person and number). While some researchers have argued about the kind of interaction that should occur between these two modules (e.g. Danlos, 1986; Appelt, 1985; Hovy, 1985; Suthers, 1991; Rubinoff, 1988), there seems to be general agreement that some division between the two modules is needed as evidenced by the large number of systems that have taken this approach (McKeown, 1985a; McCoy, 1986; Paris, 1987; Meteer et al., 1987; Maybury, 1990; Moore & Paris, 1989; Kukich, 1983; Elhadad, 1993a; Reiter, 1991; Dale, 1992; Wahlster et al., 1989; McKeown & Swartout, 1987; Mann, 1983; Jacobs, 1985; Feiner & McKeown, 1991).

A content planner uses conceptual information and reasoning strategies to select information from an underlying knowledge source and to determine its overall organization in the text. Many systems use some form of rhetorical knowledge in this task, whether embodied in schemas (McKeown, 1985a; Paris, 1987; McKeown et al., 1990; Rambow & Korelsky, 1992), rhetorical structure theory (Hovy, 1991; Moore & Paris, 1989; Wahlster et al., 1989), or plans (Dale, 1992; Suthers, 1991). Other forms of knowledge used in this task include information about the user's goals and background (Paris, 1987; Wahlster et al., 1989; Wolz et al., 1989; Elhadad, 1993a), knowledge about information communicated in previous discourse (Zukerman & Pearl, 1986; McKeown et al., 1990) and domain knowledge (Rambow & Korelsky, 1992). While some researchers have shown that determining wording of a text can also influence what information gets included (Appelt, 1985; McKeown et al., 1993; Danlos, 1986; Kukich, 1983), usually this has been shown to happen at specific points in generation and is implemented by allowing backtracking across the two modules. Thus, the issue of how linguistic form influences what gets said has generally not been given much attention.

Typically, the content planner selects information in proposition size chunks which each get realized in English as a sentence. A list of these propositions, or facts, are passed to the surface sentence generator which generates a sentence for each fact. To do so, the sentence generator must decide on the overall sentence structure, choosing for example whether to generate a question or declarative sentence, selecting a main verb and mapping elements in the fact to verb arguments. It also selects words for each verb argument and finally, builds a syntactic tree for the sentence, and enforcing syntactic constraints, produces the words in linear order. There are a few exceptions to this approach. Some systems choose words after the syntactic tree has been constructed (Matthiessen, 1991), while others choose words and build the tree simultaneously (Kukich, 1983; Hovy, 1985; Jacobs, 1985). While in most, a fact selected by the content planner will appear in the text as a separate sentence, in limited circumstances systems are able to combine a few, consecutive facts within a single sentence in specific situations. This is usually done only locally and in a domain specific way.

3. THE DOMAINS

In this section we describe the main characteristics of the two domains. In each, we describe input to the system showing how it is readily available from a non-text source, provide a system overview, and describe the state of system implementation. In both domains, we used an analysis of naturally occurring reports on which to base the generation system. These analyses revealed the textual techniques which can be used to convey information succinctly and they suggested a strategy for producing the complex sentences required.

Quick development of both systems was possible because of the existence of robust language generation tools for the surface sentence generator. Both systems use the FUF/SURGE package (Elhadad, 1993a, b) developed at Columbia for the lexicalizer and syntactic generation modules. FUF is a programming language based on functional unification (Kay, 1979) and SURGE is a large systemic grammar of English that was developed for FUF. The FUF/SURGE package handles the generation of individual sentences once the overall sentence structure has been determined and open class words chosen. It was used for this task in STREAK and PLANDOC as well as many other generation systems developed at Columbia University and elsewhere as well. FUF is used for the task of lexicalization, providing a language and interpreter in which to write a lexical chooser. However, the actual lexical chooser, encoding constraints on word choice and selecting overall sentence form, had to be developed separately for both domains.

3.1. Generation of summaries of quantitative data

Summarization of quantitative data raises several challenges for language generation systems. First, sentences in such reports are very complex (e.g. in newswire basketball game summaries the lead sentence ranges from 21 to 46 words in length). Second, while the essential facts consistently appear in *fixed* locations across reports (e.g. game results are always conveyed in the lead sentence), other potentially interesting facts *float*, appearing anywhere in a report and at different depths within a given sentence. Floating facts appear to be opportunistically placed where the form of the surrounding text allows. They vary significantly both in the form that is used to convey the same type of fact and in where they are placed in a report; the same fact type can appear anywhere from beginning to end of report. Examples 1–3 below show how the form can vary; sentences 2 and 3 result from adding the same background information to sentence 1: i.e. information that the player is only a reserve. Each example uses different syntactic categories at distinct structural levels.

1. Draft sentence: *"Hartford, CT—Jay Humphries scored 24 points Friday night as the Utah Jazz defeated the Boston Celtics 98–94."*
2. Add a noun modifier: *"Hartford, CT—**Reserve** Jay Humphries scored 24 points Friday night as the Utah Jazz defeated the Boston Celtics 98–94."*
3. Add a prepositional phrase to modify clause: *"Hartford, CT—Jay Humphries scored 24 points **off the bench** Friday night as the Utah Jazz defeated the Boston Celtics 98–94."*
4. Use new main clause, embedding old clause: *"Hartford, CT—Jay Humphries **came off the bench to** score 24 points Friday night as the Utah Jazz defeated the Boston Celtics 98–94."*

Although optional in any given sentence, floating facts cannot be ignored. In our domain, they account for over 40% of lead sentence content, with information conveying the historical

---

Sentence S0 of the simplest type:
Chicago -- Michael Jordan scored 30 points Saturday night and the Chicago Bulls defeated the Cleveland Cavaliers 108 92.

More complex sentence S1 with one more fact than S0 in the first clause:
*Minneapolis -- Pooh Richardson scored **a career high** 35 points Saturday night and the Minnesota Timberwolves beat the Golden State Warriors 121 113.*

Even more complex sentence S2 with one more fact than S1 in the second clause:
*Houston (UPI) -- Buck Johnson scored a season high 26 points Thursday night and the Houston Rockets routed the Orlando Magic 119 95 **for their sixth straight win.***

Fig. 1. Paired corpora sentences showing revisions.

significance of facts *only* conveyed as floating structures. Earlier report generators (Kukich, 1983; Bourbeau *et al.*, 1990), however, could not include historical information precisely because of the fact that it floats.

To determine how floating facts can be incorporated in a draft, we analyzed a corpus of basketball reports,* pairing sentences that differ semantically by a single floating fact and identifying the minimal syntactic transformation between them. Figure 1 shows an example of how this analysis was done. We started from the simplest sentences in the corpus, those containing only fixed information (i.e. location, teams, game result, score, date, and most significant player statistic). Sentence S0 is an example of such a sentence. Then we looked in the corpus for sentences that contain one more fact than S0 but otherwise follow the same syntactic structure. This is the case for S1, which is just like S0, except that it also explains what makes the reported player statistic significant. From this pair of sentences, we learn that such background facts can be slipped into a report by way of a noun phrase modifier (**boldfaced** in S1). We then proceeded to search for sentences with one more fact than S1. S2 is an example; it differs from S1 only in that it relates the game result to the winner's previous results. From this pair of sentences, we learn that this type of information can be added opportunistically by attaching a *"for"* prepositional phrase (**boldfaced**) to the second clause of the conjunction. We repeated this pairwise analysis starting with each distinct basic sentence structure and ending with the most complex sentence found.

The result is a set of *revision* tools, specifying precise semantic and syntactic constraints on (1) where a particular type of floating fact can be added in a draft and (2) what linguistic constructs can be used for the addition. Note that the actual words and syntactic structure of the draft, in addition to the semantic information it conveys, can determine when new information gets added in. These revision tools are directly used as rules in the underlying implementation. In Section 4, we show how these rules are implemented to generate specific types of lexical and syntactic constructions to convey information concisely.

This approach to generation allows STREAK to incrementally produce the complex sentences required for summarization by opportunistically adding optional historical information into simple sentences generated as a first draft. Example output sentences for STREAK illustrating how this works is shown in Fig. 2. Here, five different revision tools are applied in sequence, each adding in new information.

As shown in Fig. 3, there are five main modules in STREAK: the fact generator, the sentence planner, the lexicalizer, the sentence reviser and SURGE. The fact generator, which is still at the design stage,† will take as input the game boxscore augmented by a database of historical statistics and will produce as output a list of essential facts that must be included and a list of floating facts to convey opportunistically. Each fact is a conceptual network encoded as a feature structure (an example of such a network is given in Fig. 7). The fact generator thus has the task of conceptual summarization.

---

* Taken from the UPI newswire.
† The current implementation takes hand coded symbolic input like the input shown in Fig. 15.

1. **Initial draft (basic sentence pattern)**: "Hartford, CT -- Karl Malone <u>scored</u> 39 points Friday night as the Utah Jazz defeated the Boston Celtics 118 94."

2. **adjunctization**: "Hartford, CT -- Karl Malone **tied a season high with** *39 points* Friday night as the Utah Jazz defeated the Boston Celtics 118 94."

3. **conjoin**: "Hartford, CT -- Karl Malone tied a season high with 39 points **and Jay Humphries added 24** Friday night as the Utah Jazz defeated the Boston Celtics 118 94."

4. **absorb**: "Hartford, CT -- Karl Malone tied a season high with 39 points and Jay Humphries **came off the bench** *to add 24* Friday night as the Utah Jazz defeated the Boston Celtics 118 94."

5. **nominalization**: "Hartford, CT -- Karl Malone tied a season high with 39 points and Jay Humphries came off the bench to add 24 Friday night as the Utah Jazz **handed** the Boston Celtics **their sixth straight home** *defeat* 118 94."

6. **adjoin**: "Hartford, CT -- Karl Malone tied a season high with 39 points and Jay Humphries came off the bench to add 24 Friday night as the Utah Jazz handed the Boston Celtics their **franchise record** sixth straight home defeat 118 94."

Fig. 2. Incremental generation of a complex sentence using various revision tools.

Linguistic summarization is carried out in STREAK by the next three modules: sentence planner, lexicalizer and sentence reviser. The sentence planner takes as input the flat conceptual network containing all essential facts and maps it onto a semantic tree which represents overall sentence structure. The lexicalizer then maps the semantic tree onto a lexicalized skeletal syntactic tree; in the process open-class words* and overall sentence structure are determined.

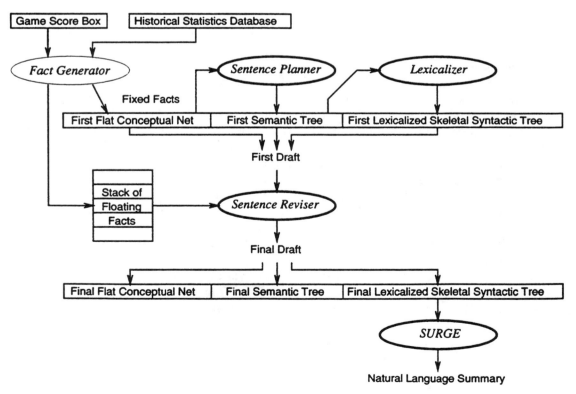

Fig. 3. An overview of STREAK's architecture.

---

* Open-class words are words from a syntactic category that contain an unlimited number of different words (e.g. nouns). In contrast, closed-class words are from a category that contains a small set of different possible words (e.g. prepositions).

Both the sentence planner and the lexicalizer are implemented through functional unification, using FUF.

The sentence reviser takes as input both the draft (note that the draft encodes both meaning, in the semantic tree, as well as any words or syntactic structures that will be used, in the thematic feature structure) and the list of potential facts. It consists of a revision rule interpreter with a set of revision rules drawn from the corpus analysis. The interpreter is also written in FUF. The output of the sentence reviser is a final draft incorporating both the essential facts of the first draft and as many potential facts that could be added following the domain, linguistic and space constraints encoded in the revision rules. To keep the rules general, they indicate only *where* and *how* to attach the new fact onto the draft. The precise wording and syntactic form of the attached phrase are chosen by re-calling the sentence planner and the lexicalizer in context from the reviser. After revision, the actual natural language text is produced by extracting the lexicalized structure from the final draft and unifying it with SURGE. All four linguistic summarization modules are fully implemented. For more details on the implementation of STREAK see Robin (1994).

3.2. *Automated documentation of planning engineer activity*

Jointly with Bellcore, we are developing a system, PLANDOC, that will document the activity of planning engineers as they study telephone routes.† Planning engineers currently use a software tool, the Bellcore PLAN system, that helps them derive a 20-year plan based on growth forecasts and economic constraints. Documentation of the activity is helpful for informing managers who are responsible for authorizing expenditures as well as for auditors and external regulators. PLANDOC takes as input a trace of the engineer's interaction with PLAN and produces a 1–2 page summary.

The telephone network planning engineer's job is to derive a capacity expansion (relief) plan specifying when, where, and how much new copper, fiber, multiplexing and other equipment to install in the local network to avoid facilities exhaustion. PLAN first automatically derives a plan for a route using economic constraints only. The engineer then uses PLAN to refine this plan using information about any company strategic policies (e.g. conversion to fiber), intangibles in the route (e.g. crowded manholes preventing further installations), and any long or short term economic constraints. During this interaction the engineer can experiment with hypothetical scenarios, exploring the results of different possible changes. Management will check that all possibilities have been explored before approving a particular plan for change. This is but one way in which the PLANDOC system is important; in providing a summary of the engineer's activity, it can show managers that other possible changes were explored and rejected as not beneficial.

We based development of PLANDOC on a user-needs analysis (see Kukich *et al.*, 1993), including a set of model narratives written by an experienced planning engineer. This corpus provided a general model for the documentation, beginning with a summary of the plan produced by PLAN alone, followed by a summary of the engineer's refinements to this plan, and concluding with a summary of the plan recommended by the engineer (which usually includes elements of the program generated plan and human refinements). Currently, PLANDOC can produce the refinement summary (one paragraph from a refinement summary is shown in Fig. 4) and we are beginning work on opening and closing summaries of the report.

PLANDOC's architecture, which is shown in Fig. 5, draws on our previous text generation and report generation work (McKeown, 1985a, Kukich, 1983) and includes a fact generator, a discourse planner, a lexicalizer, and a sentence generator. Input to PLANDOC is a trace of the engineer's activity with PLAN. It indicates, in table format, the different types of changes to the route the engineer experimented with and how this affects overall cost. Input for a single refinement scenario is shown in Fig. 4 along with the summary paragraph generated. Since the

---

† PLANDOC is being developed collaboratively with Karen Kukich and Neal Morgan of Bellcore and James Shaw, Jacques Robin, and Jong Lim of Columbia University.

PLAN Tracking Information:
Sample fact generator Input

1. RUNID fiberall FIBER 6/19/93 act yes
2. FA 1301 2 1995
3. FA 1201 2 1995
4. FA 1401 2 1995
5. FA 1501 2 1995
6. ANF co 1103 2 1995 48
7. ANF 1201 1301 2 1995 24
8. ANF 1401 1501 2 1995 24
END. 856.0 670.2

PLANDOC Output:

Run-ID: FIBERALL

This saved fiber refinement included all DLC changes in RUNID ALLDLC. RUNID FIBERALL demanded that PLAN activate fiber for CSAs 1201, 1301, 1401 and 1501 in 1995 Q2. It requested the placement of a 48-fiber cable from the CO to section 1103 and the placement of 24-fiber cables from section 1201 to section 1301 and from section 1401 to section 1501 in the second quarter of 1995. For this refinement, the resulting 20 year route PWE was $856.00K, a $64.11K savings over the BASE plan and the resulting 5 year IFC was $670.20K, a $60.55K savings over the BASE plan.

Explanation of Input:

Facts 2-5 are all fiber activations (FA). The second column for these facts indicates the site (e.g., CSA 1301 for line 2), the third indicates the quarter (quarter 2 for all of them) and the fourth column, the year. These three lines are all generated as the second sentence of the summary. Lines 6-8 are all cable placements (indicated by the code ANF). Column 2 indicates the starting section where the cable is placed (realized by "from section" in the summary), column 3 the ending section, column 4 the quarter, column 5 the year, and column 6 indicates the number of fibers in the cable. Facts 6-8 are realized as the third sentence of the summary.

Fig. 4. PLANDOC input and output.

PLAN system is implemented in C and most of PLANDOC is implemented in Lisp, a fact generator module* serves as an interface between PLAN and PLANDOC. The fact generator produces a fact in the form of a semantic feature structure for each refinement action in a PLAN tracking report. In Fig. 6, a fact corresponding to a single line of PLANDOC input is shown along with the part of the sentence generated for this fact.

Fig. 5. An overview of PLANDOC's architecture.

---

* Written in C by N. Morgan.

```
INPUT:

RUNID fiberall FIBER 6/19/93 act yes
FA 1301 2 1995

Fact Generated by PLANDOC:

((cat fact)
 (admin ((PLANDoc-fact-name RFA)        ; administrative information
         (track-tag FA)                 ; providing unique identifiers
         (seq-num 19)
         (runid r-fiberall)
         (prev-runid r-alldlc)
         (status act)
         (saved yes)))
 (class refinement)                     ; indicates that this is an engineer's refinement
 (ref-type FIBER)                       ; equipment is of type fiber
 (action activation)                    ; fiber will be activated
 (csa-site 1301)                        ; site of activation
 (date ((year 1995) (quarter 2)))))     ; date of activation

Sentence Generated by PLANDOC:

RUNID FIBERALL demanded that PLAN activate fiber for CSA 1301
in the second quarter of 1995.
```

Fig. 6. PLANDOC input and corresponding fact.

This set of facts is first passed to an *ontologizer*,* that enriches each fact with semantic knowledge from PLAN's domain. The enriched facts are then passed to a discourse planner,† whose job is to determine which information in the facts should appear in the various paragraphs and to organize the overall narrative. For our intitial prototype, we have focused only on the generation of paragraphs that summarize refinement actions and not on the generation of the paragraphs that summarize the base plan and the final plan. Thus, the discourse planner's task is to combine individual facts to produce the input for complex sentences. The output of the discourse planner is a 'condensed' set of complex facts, each still a semantic feature structure.

As in STREAK, the lexicalizer module‡ maps the semantic feature structure representing the fact onto a lexicalized thematic structure. It thus chooses the overall sentence form, open-class words and syntactic features associated with the words and does so while maintaining constraints imposed by the discourse planner. Finally, this lexicalized structure is unified with SURGE to produce the full syntactic tree, which is linearized to yield an English sentence. PLANDOC is fully implemented for refinement summaries and will be tested with actual users over the next several months.

Just as for STREAK, one major issue for PLANDOC in generating the refinement summaries is to combine individual facts into a single sentence. If separate sentences were generated for each input fact, the resulting summary would be quite verbose and repetitive. PLANDOC uses a top-down, recursive method, which is complementary to STREAK's use of revision, for this problem. It uses discourse knowledge to look ahead for facts that have equivalent features, combining them into a single complex fact. The resulting complex fact is then passed to the lexical chooser. While making word choices, the lexical chooser also selects a complex sentence structure using conjunction. It determines which pieces of the sentence can be deleted since they occur in another part of the conjunction, thus producing a concise sentence.

---

* Written in FUF by J. Robin and J. Shaw.
† Written in Lisp by J. Robin and J. Shaw.
‡ Written in FUF by J. Shaw with input from J. Robin, D. Radev, J. Lim, M. Elhadad and D. Horowitz.

4. LINGUISTIC SUMMARIZATION DEVICES

Summaries are necessarily much shorter in length than the full text they summarize. This can be achieved in part through conceptual summarization by leaving out inessential information. But more information can be conveyed if the summary language is concise, packing in as many facts as possible into a short amount of space. In this section, we show the language constructions our systems use to convey information concisely for this task of linguistic summarization.

A summary generator is given as input a set of facts to convey. In our systems, these facts are divided into two classes: essential (must be included) and potential (include if possible). For example, in STREAK game results are essential while the historical significance of the results can potentially be included. In PLANDOC, the refinements eventually used in the proposed plan are essential, while those that were explored and rejected are potential. It is the job of the language generator to determine both where in the summary to place each fact and how to realize it in English. A simplistic approach, for example, might realize each fact as a sentence. Such a scheme would tend to produce a verbose text, as some information may be repeated over several facts.

In this section, we show how a single word can convey multiple facts, how multiple modifiers can be used to pack information into a single sentence, how conjunction with ellipsis can be used to convey multiple facts concisely, and finally, how referring expressions can be abridged to save space for other facts.

4.1. Single word, multiple facts

In some cases, two facts can be merged into one sentence by selecting a word that can simultaneously convey two or more pieces of information (*content units*) contained in the two facts. This is usually only the case if some information is repeated in both facts. Usually, the word conveying more than one content unit is a verb and the information that is repeated from one fact to the next appears as arguments to the verb. We term this situation *content conflation*.

For example, consider the corpus sentence:

> *"Portland outlasted Utah 101 97."*

Both the fact that Portland won and the fact it was a tight game in which Portland took the decisive advantage only at the very end are conflated in the single verb *"to outlast"*. Without using such a semantically rich verb, a much longer paraphrase, would have been needed:

> *"Portland defeated Utah 101 97, in a tight game where the lead kept changing hands until late in the fourth quarter."*

This type of conflation is the simplest case since it involves a single word choice which does not affect the rest of the sentence. For more detail on simple content conflation, see Elhadad and Robin (1992). In more complex cases, content conflation is possible only if it is accompanied by some re-organization of the rest of the sentence's content.

As an example of conflation requiring reorganization, consider the situation, again in the case of sport summaries, where the system is given two related facts, shown as two networks in Fig. 7. If these facts were each realized as separate sentences, the top one would produce the sentence:

> *"Karl Malone scored 39 points."*

while the bottom one would produce

> *"Karl Malone's 39 point performance is equal to his season high."*

Note that several pieces of information are repeated from one fact to the next; the player is the same and the same score is mentioned. The new information included in the second fact is the *"season high"* and the fact that his score is *"equal"* to the season high. These two facts can

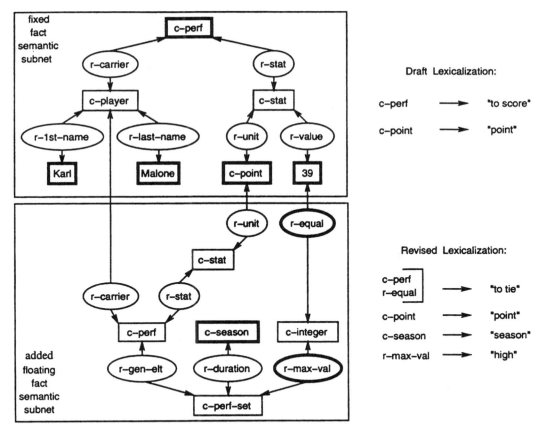

Fig. 7. Input and lexicalization of sentence revised by adjunctization.

be conveyed simultaneously by choosing the verb "*tie*" to produce the single sentence:

"*Karl Malone tied his season high with 39 points.*"

In this sentence, the verb "*tie*" simultaneously conveys that Malone scored these 39 points and that they equal the season high.

STREAK combines these two facts using its draft and revision approach. On first pass, it generates the draft "*Karl Malone scored 39 points.*" saving a representation of both the conceptual fact and its various intermediate linguistic representations. Note that this fact is fixed and must appear in the summary as it conveys the most significant player statistic.

On second pass, it uses a revision rule that adds the two new facts at the same time to the draft by selecting a new verb and placing the object of the tie (i.e. the season high) as the object of the new verb, yielding:

"*Karl Malone tied his season high.*"

This displaces the object of the old verb (the score); in order to include it, it is made into an adjunct, in this case a prepositional phrase that conveys the quantity of the score yielding the full sentence: "*Karl Malone tied his season high **with 39 points**"*. The mapping from the concepts and relations of the networks* for both the draft and revised sentences is indicated at the right of Fig. 7. "*tie*" conveys both the "c-perf" concept which was conveyed by "*to score*" in the draft and the added "r-equal" relation.

The revision rule is called *adjunctization of object into instrument*, precisely because it selects a new verb with new object and makes the old object into an instrument adjunct. More generally, we call *adjunctization* any revision where a verb argument (**Bc2**) becomes an adjunct to accommodate new content (**Vf** and **Ac**) as shown in Fig. 8.

---

* Respectively prefixed by "c-" and "r-".

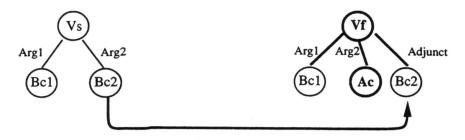

Fig. 8. General adjunctization rule.

4.2. Modification

Another way to combine two facts into a single sentence is by realizing one fact as a modification of some element of the first. In this case, the first fact forms a simple sentence, with its action as the verb of the sentence. If the two facts both refer to the same element, which is an argument of the verb, then the second fact can be expressed more compactly by making it a modifier of the verb argument. Consider, for example, the following situation from the sports domain: a player scores many points and it is all the more remarkable because he played the game only as a reserve. The scoring action and his reserve status correspond to two distinct facts in the generator's input. A system with no other linguistic summarization abilities than straightforward pronominalization would have to convey these two facts by two sentences, e.g.:

"Jay Humphries scored 24 points. He came in as a reserve."

Instead, the content of the second sentence can be compactly conveyed by adding a modifier up front in the first:

*"**Reserve** Jay Humphries scored 24 points."*

This revision is achieved by using the rule called *nominal-rank adjoin of pre-modifier* since it adds a modifier at the beginning of a noun phrase (i.e. nominal rank). This rule has syntactic constraints in that the information shared across facts must appear as a noun phrase in the first sentence and that the second fact must be expressed as a pre-modifier. It has no semantic constraints since it can apply to any facts that meet these conditions. In general, any rule involving the simple addition of an optional dependent constituent (**Ac**) is called an *adjoin* as shown in Fig. 9.

Like conflation, there are both simple cases of modification (the *adjoin* revision just presented), and more complex cases where the modification can occur only after some sentence content reorganization.

Nominalization is an example of a revision rule involving a complex modification. It replaces a meaning carrying verb (**Vf**) in the draft sentence, with a collocation consisting of a support verb (**Vs**) plus a noun (**Nf**], where the noun is a nominalization of the original verb. This type of revision allows additional modifiers to be added onto the nominalization in subsequent revisions. For example, in revising sentence 4 into sentence 5 in Fig. 2, the verb structure "X *defeat* Y" is replaced by the collocation "X *hand* Y *a defeat*." Once nominalized, *"defeat"* can then be pre-modified by the phrase *"their sixth straight home"* providing historical background.

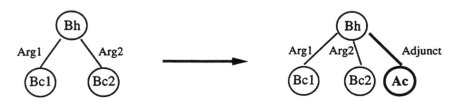

Fig. 9. General adjoin rule.

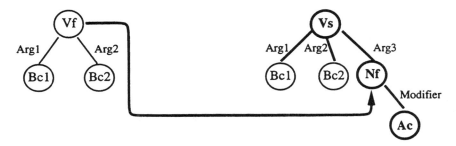

Fig. 10. General nominalization rule.

This rule embodies both a syntactic and lexical constraint on adding in new information modifying an action; only if there is a nominal synonym to the verb describing the action can this revision rule be selected. The general structural schema of this revision is shown in Fig. 10.

The FUF conjunctions encoding this revision are shown in Figs 11 and 12. The first precondition in the nominalization rule shown in these figures constrains its application to clauses of the form "WINNER verb LOSER" where:

(1) The verb is a full-verb realizing the result itself (this is indicated by the chain of REALZ features in Fig. 12, starting from the process feature of the syntactic tree—the one where the draft verb is specified—down to the BEAT role relation of the corresponding conceptual network). This is a lexical constraint matched by the class of verbs including "to beat", "to defeat", "to triumph against" etc.

```
;;; Revision rule for nominalization
(def-conj nominalization
  (preconditions
   (;; Applies to draft clauses headed by a full verb conveying the game result
    (old-draft ((:& basic-game-result-clause)))

    ;; Can be used to add a losing streak from the floating fact stack
    (floats-top ((:& losing-streak-extension)))))))

  (actions
   ((delete {new-draft})   ;; delete the matching draft clause

    ;; Replace it by the frame of a transfer of possession clause headed by
    ;; a support verb e.g., ``WINNER hand LOSER      a defeat''
    ;;                                possessor possessed (nominalized)
    ;;                      agent            affected
    (insert ((surfsemcat rhetor)
             (struct hypotax)
             (root ((surfsemcat rhetor)
                    (struct event)
                    (root transf-poss)))))
            {new-draft sem-tree})

    ;; Locally call the lexicalizer on this new clause frame to choose a
    ;; support verb to head it.
    (lexicalize {new-draft sem-tree} {new-draft synt-tree})

    ;; Copy the fixed predicate modifiers and participants of the clause,
    ;; from the original clause.
    (copy {old-draft sem-tree rels score} {new-draft sem-tree rels score})
    ...
    < more copy actions not shown here for agent and affected roles >
    ...
    ;; Locally call the phrase planner and lexicalizer to realize the possessed
    ;; role of the new clause containing the nominalized game result
    (plan {floats-top} {new-draft sem-tree args possessed})
    (lexicalize {new-draft sem-tree args possessed}
                {new-draft synt-tree participants possessed}))))))
```

Fig. 11. FUG implementation of nominalization revision rule.

```
;; Precondition pattern for basic clauses realizing the game result and
headed by a
;; full-verb e.g., ``WINNER defeat LOSER SCORE''
(def-conj basic-game-result-clause
  (synt-tree
   ((cat clause)
    ; 1. VERB IS A FULL VERB REALIZED BY 1A. BELOW
    (process ((realz {sem-tree root concept})))
    (participants ((agent ((realz {sem-tree root args agent})))
                   (affected ((realz {sem-tree root args affected}))))))
    (predicate-modifiers ((score ((realz {sem-tree rels score}))))))))
  (sem-tree
   ((surfsemcat rhetor)
    (struct hypotax)
    (root
     ((surfsemcat encyclo)
      ; 1A. THIS IS JUST A POINTER TO 4. BELOW
      (concept {concept-net results rels result role})
      ; 2. AGENT IS WINNER
      (args ((agent
              ((surfsemcat encyclo)
               (realz {concept-net results rels result args winner})))
      ; 3. AFFECTED IS LOSER
             (affected
              ((surfsemcat encyclo)
               (realz {concept-net results rels result args loser}))))))))
      (rels ((score ((surfsemcat encyclo)
                     (realz {concept-net results entities score})))))))
  (concept-net
   ((deepsemcat entity)
    (concept game)
    (results
     ((entities ((host ((deepsemcat entity) (concept team)))
                 (visitor ((deepsemcat entity) (concept team)))
                 (score ((deepsemcat entity) (concept score)))))
      ; 4. VERB MUST BE CHOSEN FROM SYNONYMS OF ``BEAT''
      (rels ((result ((deepsemcat relation)
                      (role beat)
                      (args ((winner {concept-net results ents host})
                             (loser {concept-net results ents host})))))))))))))))))
```

Fig. 12. FUG implementation of nominalization revision rule.

(2) The winner relation is realized by an AGENT participant in the syntactic tree (this is a semantic constraint)

(3) The loser relation is realized by an AFFECTED participant in the syntactic tree (this is a semantic constraint)

This combination of semantic, syntactic and lexical constraints are shown in detail in the feature conjunction BASIC-GAME-RESULT-CLAUSE. The second precondition is that a losing streak is present in the stack of floating facts. In practice, nominalization can apply to other pairs ⟨draft form, new-content-type⟩ though only one is shown here.

The first nominalization action is to delete the clause to revise from the new-draft (which is initially a copy of the old draft). This clause is replaced by a transfer of possession clause frame (e.g. as "to hand," "to give," "to bring"). The lexicalizer is then called from the reviser to realize the head verb of this frame. The participants and predicate modifiers that are unchanged by the revision are then copied in turn from the old draft to the new draft (in this case, the AGENT and AFFECTED). Then the phrase planner is called on the floating fact to incorporate it into the draft. The resulting plan fills the POSSESSED role in the new clause frame. The lexicalizer is then called on this phrase plan and produces a new POSSESSED role whose head is a nominal synonym of the old draft head verb (e.g. "a defeat," "a loss"). At the surface form level the successive effects of this series of action on a particular draft could be for example:

- precondition matched: "... while Chicago defeated New York 99–84."
- delete action: "... while"
- insert and perform the first lexicalize action: "... while ... handed"
- copy actions: "... while Chicago handed New York ... 99–84"

- plan and perform the second lexicalize action: "... while Chicago handed New York their third straight defeat 99–84"

4.3. Conjunction

A common way to combine separate facts into a single sentence is to use conjunction (i.e. a list of constituents separated by the word "*and*" or "*or*"). In order to use conjunction, there must be a common piece of information occurring across all facts. Both PLANDOC and STREAK use conjunction. PLANDOC handles conjunction through discourse planning, while STREAK uses revision.

For PLANDOC, conjunction with ellipsis is the primary means of creating a concise summary. Its discourse planner includes a fact combining stage, where it collects facts with common information (in PLANDOC, information in facts is represented as feature structures, so common information would be features shared across facts). It primarily looks for facts with the same action and for these facts, notes which features in the separate facts are equivalent. It creates a new fact, with the features separated into those that are *common* to all facts and those that are *distinct* in each. Creating a sentence that contains conjunction is complex primarily because the number of different feature combinations in facts is large and each different combination of common and distinct groupings results in a different kind of conjunction. Depending on which information is common across facts, different amounts of the sentence can be *elided* (i.e. removed) in adjoining clauses.

Figure 13 shows four different examples of conjunction. Each example includes a pair, where the first part of the pair shows the facts combined using conjunction, but with no ellipsis. The second part of the pair gives the same example, but with the common information across facts left implicit on subsequent mention. These examples show that the amount of information that is elided varies tremendously. In the first example, all information is common to the facts except for the CSA site. A conjunction of nominals, each denoting one site can therefore be used following "*for*", resulting in the eight facts being very concisely expressed by only a single clause instead of eight.

Examples 2–4 show how the different combinations of common and distinct information can get quite complex and yet still result in a conjoined sentence. In Example 2, all CSA's were activated for the same date except one, but they could be successfully combined by using two layers of conjunction. The third example shows a situation where two features are in distinct (in Example 1 only the CSA site was distinct). Finally, in the fourth case, only the refinement and the action is the same, but all other features are different. This results in almost full sentences appearing in each clause of the conjunction.

We have implemented a general algorithm which groups together input features having the same value, so that as many separate messages as possible can be collapsed into a single message. In the first step, messages with the same action are identified and grouped together for possible coordination, called *common-action group*. Since the action is realized in a verb form or nominalization in the sentence, this means that the action will be common across all clauses. Depending on which of the remaining features (in the group of messages with common action) are common or distinct, one or more of the roles (e.g. subject, object, complement) will be conjoined. Next PLANDOC determines whether conjunction can be contained within one constituent [preferable because there is less chance for ambiguity (Quirk *et al.*, 1985)] or whether conjunction must be treated as between full clauses requiring deletion in the final sentence of common constituents. To do this, PLANDOC identifies any subsets of the messages in the current *common-action group* which differ by only one feature. These subsets are immediately collapsed into a single message where the distinct features are made into a list, and the resulting sentence will contain conjunction within the constituent realizing this feature. Example 1, Fig. 13, illustrates this case. Here, conjunction is contained within a noun phrase that realizes the list of CSA sites.

When more than one message remains in the *common-action group* after this collapsing, then more than one feature is distinct and conjunction must be done across the clause as a whole. To determine how to form groups of the remaining messages, PLANDOC determines which feature

Example 1:

- RUNID R-DLC1 activated ALL-DLC for CSA 8105 in the first quarter of 1994 and
  RUNID R-DLC1 activated ALL-DLC for CSA 8107 in the first quarter of 1994 and
  RUNID R-DLC1 activated ALL-DLC for CSA 8113 in the first quarter of 1994 and
  RUNID R-DLC1 activated ALL-DLC for CSA 8118 in the first quarter of 1994 and
  RUNID R-DLC1 activated ALL-DLC for CSA 8121 in the first quarter of 1994 and
  RUNID R-DLC1 activated ALL-DLC for CSA 8126 in the first quarter of 1994 and
  RUNID R-DLC1 activated ALL-DLC for CSA 8128 in the first quarter of 1994 and
  RUNID R-DLC1 activated ALL-DLC for CSA 8132 in the first quarter of 1994.

- RUNID R-DLC1 activated ALL-DLC for CSAs 8105, 8107, 8113, 8118, 8121, 8126,
  8128 and 8132 in the first quarter of 1994.

Example 2:

- This refinement activated fiber for CSA 4109 in the first quarter of 1995 and
  this refinement activated fiber for CSA 4114 in the first quarter of 1995 and
  this refinement activated fiber for CSA 4211 in the first quarter of 1995 and
  this refinement activated fiber for CSA 4403 in the first quarter of 1995 and
  this refinement activated fiber for CSA 4502 in the first quarter of 1995 and
  this refinement activated fiber for CSA 4104 in the second quarter of 1995.

- This refinement activated fiber for CSAs 4109, 4114, 4211, 4403 and 4502 in the
  first quarter of 1995 and for CSA 4104 in the second quarter of 1995.

Example 3:

- This refinement used a cutover strategy of GROWTH for CSA 1401 and
  this refinement used a cutover strategy of ALL for CSA 1318 and
  this refinement used a cutover strategy of MIN for CSA 1001.

- This refinement used a cutover strategy of GROWTH for CSA 1401, of ALL for CSA
  1318 and of MIN for CSA 1001.

Example 4:

- It requested the placement of a 48-fiber cable from the CO to section 1103 in the
  second quarter of 1995 and it requested the placement of 24-fiber cables from section 1201 to section 1301 in the second quarter of 1995 and it requested the
  placement of 24-fiber cables from section 1401 to section 1501 in the second
  quarter of 1995.

- It requested the placement of a 48-fiber cable from the CO to section 1103 and the
  placement of 24-fiber cables from section 1201 to section 1301 and from section
  1401 to section 1501 in the second quarter of 1995.

Fig. 13. Conjunction and ellipsis in PLANDOC.

is shared by the greatest number of remaining messages. The remaining messages are then grouped into subsets where each subset has the same value for the feature just identified. This allows the most concise sentence to be generated because the greatest number of common constituents can be deleted in the sentence. Finally, the messages are sorted by the date feature so that the conjoined clauses appear in temporal order (Quirk *et al.*, 1985). This algorithm can be summarized in the following steps:

(1) Group messages by common action
(2) For each common-action group:
    (a) collapse any messages which differ by one feature into a single message

    (b) if more than one message remains:
        (i) determine which feature is shared across most messages
        (ii) sort messages by most common shared feature to form subgroups
        (iii) within each subgroup, sort again by most common shared feature of subgroup, repeating until all nested subgroups have been sorted.
        (iv) sort by date feature so that clauses are conjoined in temporal order.

To see how this works, consider Example 4. Here, there are three distinct features, equipment type (with values of 48-fiber cable, 24-fiber cable, and 24-fiber cable), from-section (with values of CO, section 1201, and section 1401), and to-section (with values of 1103, 1301, and 1501). Of these, equipment type has the largest number of shared values across messages (2 shared values, 24-fiber cable) while the other features have no shared values. Thus, two conjoined clauses are formed, where the second has an embedded conjunction. Next each common feature is deleted. Action is common to all messages so only appears in the first clause ("it requested"), while "the placement of 24-fiber cables" is deleted in the last clause. The clauses are ordered so that the simplest (i.e. with fewest messages and/or number of distinct features) is placed first. This avoids sentences that are difficult to understand because very complex constituents must be processed first in the conjunction. In such difficult sentences, the subject of the first clause is also the subject of the second clause, but is separated from the second clause by many words due to the complex constituent. This creates difficulty in understanding because the reader must remember the subject while processing all the intervening material before finally getting to the verb. For technical writing and proscriptive approaches, this is described as a situation to avoid (Gopen & Swan, 1990; Quirk et al., 1985).*

Eillipsis in conjunction is difficult to handle because without careful control, it can give rise to ambiguity. Ambiguity can be triggered by *surface form factors* like ordering of movable constituents and comparative length of adjacent constituents (Quirk et al., 1985; Gopen & Swan, 1990). Overuse of ellipsis can also result in sentences difficult to comprehend. Such overuse is illustrated by the following example:

"This refinement extended fiber from fiber hub 8107 to CSAs 8128, 8126, 8121 and 8113, from fiber hub 8107 and the CO to CSAs 8105 and 8120 and from the CO to CSAs 8118 and 8107} **in 1994 Q1** *and from the CO to CSA 8120* **in 1994 Q3, with both the active fibers and the protection fibers placed on the primary path."**

This sentence conveys a complex feature sharing pattern that occurred in the PLANDOC domain. It is not only barely intelligible but also ambiguous: it is unclear what preceeding portion of the sentence each boldfaced prepositional phrase modifies. For example, both the active and protection fibers could have been placed on the primary path only for the last extension (i.e. to CSA 8120) or they could have been placed on the primary path for all extensions. PLANDOC prevents sentences such as this from being generated. Currently this is done by blocking conjunction for message types which include too many conjoined features such as the one in this example. We are working on devising a general linguistic constraint which would selectively disallow conjunction between very complex constituents. This might be done by counting the number of messages being conjoined and/or the number of distinct features within each message or the number of embedded conjunctions within clauses, disallowing those where the count is too high.

As an alternative strategy to PLANDOC's, STREAK relies on explicit surface form criteria to avoid generating sentences too hard to read. After each revision adding a new piece of information in the draft, the complexity of the draft is checked against the maximum complexity observed in the model corpus of the human-written summaries. Two criteria are used to define this complexity: the number of words, whose observed maximum is 45 and the depth of syntactic embedding, whose observed maximum is 10. This complexity check occurs right before the final sentence is generated. If the last revision has pushed the draft over one of these

---

* It should be noted that although there is a good deal of literature on conjunction, much of it addresses issues involving competence rather than performance (the latter being closer to the constraints on processing complexity that we seek).

two thresholds, this last revision is then undone before the output is displayed. This constraint applies to any complex linguistic construction, whether or not it uses conjunction.

4.4. Abridged references

When facts get packed into the same sentence, it is sometimes the case that the same piece of information must be referred to more than one time. The summary can be made more concise by making a second reference to the same object shorter.

In PLANDOC this is done in the discourse planner by examining the content of the summary generated so far (in natural language, this is often termed "the previous discourse"). If the object was first referred to in the previous sentence, PLANDOC generates a shorter reference using just the head of the original noun phrase, changing the determiner as well. For example, on first reference to a refinement, PLANDOC would use the full refinement identifier as in "*Refinement 2A193*". On second reference in the subsequent sentence, PLANDOC generates "*This refinement.*" On third and subsequent references, PLANDOC uses a pronoun, "*it.*" PLANDOC uses essentially the most *recent mention* algorithm for interpreting anaphora (Hobbs, 1985), but reversed for generation.

STREAK can shorten a reference as part of revision. For example, suppose that it generates the draft sentence:

"*San Antonio, TX—David Robinson scored 32 points Friday night lifting the San Antonio Spurs to a 127 111 victory over* <u>the Denver Nuggets.</u>",

To this, STREAK chooses to add a fact about past results of the Denver Nuggets using conjunction. Then it will generate:

"*San Antonio, TX—David Robinson scored 32 points Friday night lifting the San Antonio Spurs to a 127 111 victory over* <u>Denver</u> **and handling** <u>the Nuggets</u> **their seventh straight loss**".

In this revised sentence the original reference to the losing team is shortened from the default form "*the Denver Nuggets*" to just "*Denver*". The second reference added by the conjunction can then become just "*the Nuggets*". This avoids a redundant and verbose form like:

?"*San Antonio, TX—David Robinson scored 32 points Friday night lifting the San Antonio Spurs to a 127 111 victory over* <u>the Denver Nuggets</u> **and handing** <u>the Denver Nuggets</u> **their seventh straight loss**".

This also exemplifies how maintaining proper style while adding new content necessitates changing the existing draft. It also allows a more balanced division of the referent properties than is the case if a more traditional pronoun is used as second reference:

"*San Antonio, TX—David Robinson scored 32 points Friday night lifting the San Antonio Spurs to a 127 111 victory over* <u>the Denver Nuggets</u> **and handing** <u>them</u> **their seventh straight loss**".

5. CONCEPTUAL SUMMARIZATION

Conceptual summarization requires determining the content of the summary, and to a certain extent, its organization. When summarizing data, the task involves determining which data are important enough to include in the summary. When summarizing text, the task is to determine which facts or characteristics of the text are important. Whether information is considered important will vary depending on the goal of summarization. For example, if the goal is to give the reader enough information to determine whether or not to read the full text, the summary might be closer to an *indicative* abstract (Borko, 1975), including more information about text characteristics (e.g. its length, style, etc.). In contrast, if the goal is to produce a shorter version of the text which the reader can read in place of the text itself, then the key content of the text is more important resulting in a summary much like an *informative* abstract (Borko, 1975). Here again, depending on the reader's goals, key content can vary. For example, one sports fan might be more interested in tracking the achievements of a particular player, while another may want to track game results of all teams within an entire league.

For our applications, we are interested in the production of informative summaries. If there were a full text (e.g. a full newspaper article on the basketball game), the summary could be read in place of the full text. Thus, conceptual summarization must determine what key content should be conveyed. One of our claims is that the line between information that should or should not appear in a summary is fuzzy. If a summary could be longer, perhaps more information could be included. Our approach, therefore, involves a gradation of essential information to interesting information that could be included if space exists, but need not. We divide information into two classes, that which *must* appear, and potential information, which *may* be included if there is room. Potential information is ordered from more important to less important. Exactly how this information could be automatically generated is dependent on the domain and is discussed separately for STREAK and PLANDOC below.

Determining what information goes into these two classes (essential and potential) is part of conceptual summarization. But, as we just described in the previous section, determining which potential information actually gets included in a summary is done during linguistic summarization. Using both conceptual and linguistic constraints to fully determine the content of the summary is a unique contribution of our work. In this section we focus on the construction of these two classes of information. While we have not implemented conceptual summarization for STREAK, we describe our design and show how implementation is quite feasible.

Once we have the facts, then the techniques we have developed allow the generation of concise summaries. If the facts are obtained from a text, these same techniques are needed and can be used for certain kinds of text summarization tasks, namely informative summaries. To do this, the task of conceptual summarization could be handled in either one of two ways. Either a natural language interpretation system could process the full text, producing a set of facts representing text meaning. From this set of fact, a conceptual summarizer could select the subset that convey the key content, depending on the reader's interest. Alternatively, the bulk of the conceptual summarization task could be embedded in the interpretation system which, instead of "understanding" the full text, could instead extract only the facts of interest. Given the state of the art of natural language intepretation, the second alternative appears more feasible at this point in time and, in fact, is possible for certain domains and text types (e.g. newspaper articles on terrorism) as demonstrated by the ARPA message understanding systems (e.g. Krupka *et al.*, 1992). Integrating a summary generator such as described here with the output of ARPA message understanding systems would allow the production of informative summaries of full text newspaper articles on terrorist events where the summaries contain only specific information such as type of terrorist event, victims, perpetrators, etc., regardless of the range of information included in the article.

In the remainder of this section, we describe the task of conceptual summarization for STREAK and PLANDOC.

5.1. Conceptual summarization in STREAK

We determined which information was essential and which could potentially be included in the summary through the corpus analysis of newspaper basketball reports. Our first observation in the analysis was that all reports followed the *inverted pyramid structure with summary lead* where the most essential facts are included in the first sentence (Fensch, 1988). We used the lead sentences (800 in total) in the corpus to guide determination of summary content. We noted that all 800 lead sentences contained the game result (e.g. *"Utah beat Miami 105–95"*), its location, date and at least one final game statistic: the most remarkable statistic of a winning team player. These constitute the essential facts as they consistently appear in a fixed location in the report.

These facts can be obtained from the tabular formatted box score statistics. A box-score is a

ORLANDO MAGIC					24	24 (48)	21 (69)	25 (94)		
		fg	3pt-fg	ft	rb					
Players	mn	m-a	m-a	m-a	o-t	bl	st	as	to	pf	tp
Catledge	44	8-15	0-0	0-0	4-11	0	3	3	2	3	16
Reynolds	27	3-9	1-1	2-2	0-2	1	1	1	1	3	9
Roberts	16	4-7	0-0	1-2	2-6	2	0	1	1	5	9
Vincent	22	4-12	0-0	0-0	3-6	0	1	3	4	0	8
Anderson	30	6-10	0-0	2-4	1-2	0	1	1	0	2	14
Kite	22	2-4	0-0	0-0	3-4	0	0	0	0	2	4
O.Smith	26	4-11	0-0	1-2	0-1	0	2	1	0	2	9
Skiles	26	8-15	0-3	5-5	1-2	0	4	7	1	3	21
Scott	14	1-7	0-1	2-2	0-0	0	0	0	1	1	4
Je. Turner	4	0-1	0-0	0-0	0-1	0	0	1	0	3	0
Williams	9	0-1	0-0	0-0	0-1	0	0	0	0	0	0
Team totals	240	40-92	1-5	13-17	14-36	2	12	18	12	24	94
Team %		.435	.200	.765							

HOUSTON ROCKETS					20	25 (45)	31 (76)	23 (99)		
		fg	3pt-fg	ft	rb					
Players	mn	m-a	m-a	m-a	o-t	bl	st	as	to	pf	tp
Johnson	38	4-10	0-1	2-4	2-8	1	2	4	1	3	10
Thorpe	40	5-11	0-0	4-4	5-10	0	0	2	1	3	14
Olajuwon	33	6-16	0-0	5-6	3-14	8	2	4	3	6	17
Maxwell	42	4-14	3-9	3-4	0-3	0	1	5	3	3	14
K.Smith	38	12-15	1-1	3-3	1-4	0	2	9	6	0	**28**
Rollins	14	0-0	0-0	0-0	1-2	1	0	0	0	2	0
Floyd	19	2-5	1-2	7-8	0-3	0	0	4	4	2	12
Herrera	8	1-3	0-0	2-4	0-1	0	0	0	1	2	4
Jo. Turner	5	0-0	0-0	0-0	0-1	0	0	0	1	2	0
Bullard	3	0-0	0-0	0-0	0-0	0	0	0	0	0	0
Team totals	240	34-74	5-13	26-33	12-46	10	7	28	20	21	99
Team %		.549	.385	.788							

ORLANDO, Fla. (UPI) – Kenny Smith scored 28 points Sunday night to pace the Houston Rockets to a 99-94 victory over Orlando, **giving the Magic their league-high 10th straight loss.**

Hakeem Olajuwon contributed 17 points, 14 rebounds and eight blocked shots before fouling out with 3:15 remaining in the game.

The Magic led 48-45 at halftime, *but Houston outscored Orlando 23-12 in the first eight minutes of the third quarter to take the lead for good.*

Smith converted 12 of 15 shots from the field and dished out nine assists **to give the Rockets their sixth win in eight meetings with Orlando.**

Scott Skiles provided spark of the bench with 21 points, seven assists and four steals for the Magic, **which lost for the 14th time in 15 games.**

Orlando was outrebounded 46-36 and shot just 43.5-percent from the field. **The Magic have dropped their last six home games.**

Fig. 14. Standard box score and corresponding natural language report.

table containing a standard set of statistics for one game. In daily newspapers, there is one box-score accompanying each game report. An example box-score with the corresponding report is given in Fig. 14. In this report, fine-grained statistics *not* available in the box-score are emphasized by an *italic* font (historical information is, as usual, emphasized by **a boldface** font). Such finer grained statistics come from complete game charts (Anderson, 1985). Box-scores are available on-line through newswire and sport statistic computer services, whereas game charts

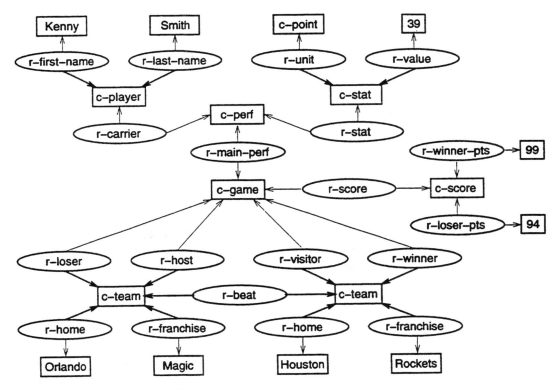

Fig. 15. Symbolic input for facts in box score.

are not.* Therefore, only box-scores constitute a realistic statistical input for a report generation system at this point in time.

For input to the summary generator, we need to convert purely quantitative data to a symbolic form that is suitable for content planning and that represents the meaning of numeric values (e.g. whether a numeric score is a win or a loss). Thus, the box score input is represented as a flat conceptual network that expresses relations between what were the columns and rows of the table. The symbolic representation of two facts (Kenny Smith's significant statistic and the game result) is given in Fig. 15. This appears as fixed information in the first sentence of the report and appears in the box score as the last column of the 5th row entry in the Houston Rocket's table (Smith's statistic) and the heading of the two tables (game result and score). The symbolic form explicitly identifies winner and loser along with the scores. Currently, STREAK accepts this symbolic form as input. While the conversion from numeric, tabular form to symbolic, conceptual net has not yet been implemented, it would be very straightforward.

In addition to fixed, essential facts, input to STREAK also contains a symbolic representation of potential facts. We used the most commonly occurring floating facts that we found in the corpus:

- Other notable final game statistics of individual players (e.g. "*Stockton finished with 27 points*").
- Game result streaks (e.g. "*Utah recorded its fourth straight win*").
- Extremum performances such as maximums or minimums (e.g. "*Stockton scored a season-high 27 points*").

The first of these is termed "new information" and can be obtained from the box-score statistics. Box-score statistics are the most common type of new information. It was the sole type of new information in 50.2% of the corpus sentences.† New statistics which are not fixed (i.e. other than the most significant player statistic) can be obtained directly from the box-score and placed on the list of potential information.

---

* To the best of our knowledge.
† Note also in Fig. 14 that most of the information conveyed in the report comes directly from the box-score.

The second two types of potential information are historical. They place current game results and player statistics in historical context, underscoring their significance. The fact generator will ultimately query a database of historical statistics to retrieve for each new statistic a set of related historical statistics. In the sports domain, access to such historical databases through a modem is offered by several companies that specialize in such services. This historical data is used to assess the relevance of the new data and vice-versa. Thus, a new statistic will be ranked higher on the potential fact list if it is historically significant and the historical facts that best relate to significant new statistics will be ordered higher.

Note that the inclusion of historical information in report generation triggers a combinatorial explosion of the number of relevant propositions. This explosion is due to the fact that the historical context multiplies the dimensions along which to evaluate the significance of each input statistic. Consider, for example, a player's scoring statistic. Ignoring the historical context there are basically only two ways in which this statistic can be significant: when compared to the scoring statistics of all the other players in the game (game-high) and when compared to the scoring statistics of his teammates only (team-high). However, such a statistic can be *historically* significant in a combinatorially explosive number of ways: when compared to that player's scoring average (or high or low) over the season (or over his entire career or since he joined his current team, etc.), when compared to the highest scoring performance of any player on his team (or on any team in a given division, conference, etc.) this season (or over the last 10 games, or ever) while playing at home (or on the road) against a particular opponent (or against any opponent) etc.

Such facts can be determined by comparing a statistic or game result against varying periods of times and against different groups of players. While we have not implemented this, it could be done by encoding a systematic search for maximums, minimums, and consecutive sequences of similar results. Because of the sheer number of historical facts, any such fact is likely to be of similar relevance as many others. Therefore, content production results in a much larger set of candidate propositions with many more shades of relative importance. This makes content selection much harder. General rules based on purely domain grounds (e.g. if a player scores more than 20 points or if he scores more than anybody in his team, then include his scoring in the report) can be used to provide some ordering of the facts.

However, there are still likely to be too many facts to include in the final report. Other factors need to be considered. One such factor is whether the possible forms of the candidate propositions can be combined with the draft summary in cohesive and stylistically felicitous surface forms. The ability to convey historical information thus entails the ability *to perform final content selection under surface form constraints*. Thus, while conceptual summarization can generate and order potential new and historical facts, linguistic summarization must be called into play to determine which of these will actually be included.

5.2. Conceptual summarization in PLANDOC

Conceptual summarization in PLANDOC is currently much simpler than in STREAK, although this will change once we begin generating the base plan and proposed plan paragraphs of the full report along with enriched refinement paragraphs.

The current refinements summary is intended to provide information about the scenarios explored by the engineer that led to the proposed final plan. Thus, the essential facts are those refinements which the engineer made and included in the final plan. Recall that the engineer may also experiment with refinements to the base plan and finally, reject these refinements if she decides they are not optimal for any reason. For example, the engineer may wish to test some hypothetical scenarios to show management that other possibilities were explored but rejected because they were not optimal. Alternatively, the engineer may just want to get a feel for the route before seriously beginning making changes to the system generated plan (the base plan). Refinements which were tried but not included in the final plan are potential candidates for inclusion in the summary. Whether the refinement is included depends on whether it is a

The BASE plan for this route calls for the following actions in the first 10 years of the study: (1) CSA 6501 is activated for DLC in 1992Q1; (2) CSA 6122 and CSA 6131 are activated for fiber in 1993Q1 with 150mb FOT's placed; (3) CSA 6501 is activated for fiber in 1995 with a 150mb FOT; and (4) 35 lines are transferred from copper to DLC in CSA 6801. There are no copper terminations, coarse gauge cable or duct placements in the first 10 years of the study. The BASE plan 20 year route PWE is $855K and the 5 year IFC is $463K.

Fig. 16. One model base plan summary.

plausible alternative to the final plan which management will want to know about. This is very domain specific information which is not currently encoded anywhere in the system (and since it relies heavily on human expertise, would be quite difficult to encode). Only the planning engineer knows why she tried and rejected any refinements. Thus, in our current version of the system, we ask the planning engineer to indicate which refinement scenarios should be included in the summary when a report is requested.

In the final version of the system, output will include an introductory paragraph summarizing the base plan (i.e. the plan which the system produced), enriched refinement summary paragraphs (i.e. that include additional facts related to refinement actions), and a closing paragraph that summarizes the proposed plan (i.e. that indicates which base plan elements were included and which refinements were included). We expect that determining the content of these additional paragraphs and sentences will require some domain heuristics. Knowledge engineering techniques such as interviewing planning experts and analyzing human-generated model summaries will be required to devise such heuristics. These heuristics could then be used to identify salient facts from among all those available in the data representing PLAN's base plan results, and to categorize those facts as essential or potential facts. Once facts have been identified and categorized, the linguistic summarization devices already in use for both STREAK and PLANDOC can be applied. We have just begun to analyze a small sample of model summaries.

Figure 16 provides an example of the kind of information one expert felt should be included in a base plan summary paragraph. This example is informative with respect to both potential heuristics for conceptual content inclusion and useful linguistic summarization devices. Conceptually, this summary suggests heuristics such as "limit essential facts to those occurring within the first 10 years of the study", "mark as essential all facts related to activations, DLC transfers and placements", and "create negation facts for those actions that are notable by their absence" (e.g. no coarse gauge cable placements or duct placements). Linguistically, note the use of the colon-enumeration format for concise expression of similar facts. Note also the use of the *General Adjunctization Rule* in items (2) and (3) by which a placement fact is succinctly folded into an activation sentence via a "with" clause. Item (3) achieves further conciseness by eliding the subordinate verb "placed". Finally, the common feature *negation* allows three facts to be combined and ellipsis to be used in the negation sentence.

In our corpus of human-generated refinement summaries, we found that refinement paragraphs were sometimes enriched with "non-refinement" sentences, i.e. statements that referred to facts that were *not* among those in the input trace of the refinement scenario in process. Two such non-refinement sentences are shown in **boldfaced** type in Fig. 17.

The first non-refinement sentence refers to facts that would be found in the route model database; the second refers to a fact found in the base plan data; other non-refinement sentences we've encountered refer to facts found in previous refinement scenarios. Since non-refinement facts do not appear in the trace of the refinement scenario currently in process, PLANDOC's content planner must proactively seek out these facts from the total pool of route model facts, base plan facts and previous (and perhaps subsequent) refinement facts, and it must do so intelligently. That is, it must exploit both domain heuristics and discourse structure knowledge to determine when and how a non-refinement fact might be appropriately included. One such

After starting over with the BASE plan, this refinement demanded a fiber activation for CSA 2551 in the first quarter of 1994. **CSA 2551 is an existing DLC site with 180 conditioned copper pairs and 0 spare.** ...

RUN-ID DLC94 activated CSA 4111 for DLC in 1994 Q4. **CSA 4111 was activated in 1997 in the BASE plan.** ...

Fig. 17. Enriched refinement summary paragraphs.

current fact in focus". In this case three common features and one contrastive feature with the current fact in focus". In this case three common features are CSA-site (4111), action (activation), and equipment (DLC) and one contrastive feature is date. This heuristic could also be invoked by a *contrastive* rhetorical relation (McKeown, 1985b; Mann, 1984). The first non-refinement example above employs the *General Adjunctization Rule* to concisely express two facts.

The closing paragraph, i.e. the proposed plan summary, will essentially serve as a summary of the entire previous text. Due to length restrictions it most likely will only be able to contain the most important changes from both the base plan and the engineer refinements. For these summaries, domain heuristics can be used to indicate which types of refinements are more important than others. In addition, linguistic summarization techniques can be used to condense the final version. One clear issue in the organization of proposed plan summaries is the need for decisions about what information should be included in the summary to be influenced by how information can be grouped together in a single sentence. In order to convey information more concisely, similar refinements are often grouped together and short phrases that can refer to the group selected, usually using conjunction and ellipsis. Thus, for example, in one of our model summaries shown in Fig. 18, the summary groups together a set of refinements which activated a specific type of equipment and uses a nominalization to refer to them ("*DLC activations*"). Thus, as is the case in the refinements summary, wording and syntactic constraints will determine what information gets included in the summary and where. However, unlike the current implementation, the system needs to be able to determine which refinements should not be mentioned and when additional information should be included. For example, the summary should mention aspects of the BASE plan which are recommended and it may sometimes need to provide supporting information from other databases that justifies the recommended plan.

6. RELATED WORK

The research presented in this paper concerns two subareas of generation: report generation, relevant to both PLANDOC and STREAK, and revision-based generation, relevant to STREAK. We compare previous work in each of these two subareas with our approach in what follows.

The refinement "fib_2551" is the best solution for this route. This plan includes the BASE plan DLC activations of CSA 2907 in 1997 and CSA 2119 in 1998. It also includes the BASE plan fiber activation of CSA 2317 in 1994Q4. ...

Fig. 18. Portion of a model proposed plan summary.

6.1. Report generation

At least four previous systems use natural language to summarize quantitative data: SEMTEX (Roesner, 1987), LFS (Iordanskaja *et al.*, 1992), FOG (Bourbeau *et al.*, 1990) and ANA (Kukich, 1983).

SEMTEX and LFS each generate summaries of labor market statistics, SEMTEX generates German text; LFS generates bilingual French/English reports. SEMTEX does both conceptual and linguistic summarization, each in a separate module. The conceptual module takes raw labor market statistics as input and outputs a list of frame structures representing the text's content. The frame structures are converted to functional structures representing thematic and lexical information by SEMTEX's linguistic module. SEMTEX's functional structures are similar to but less detailed than those of STREAK and PLANDOC. A surface generator converts SEMTEX's functional structures to linearized German text. SEMTEX's linguistic module emphasizes the need for conciseness in summaries by using ellipsis to avoid repetition of redundant information whenever possible, e.g. information about the time period concerned. However, it does not make systematic use of conjunction as does PLANDOC. LFS is similar to SEMTEX in that both are implemented for similar domains and produce summaries of similar content and style (Iordanskaja *et al.*, 1992). However, the focus in LFS is on the use of Meaning-Text Theory and lexical functions (Mel'cuk, 1981) that allow for the computation of collocations and semantically related lexemes, resulting in a system that employs systematic paraphrasing. Important types of conjunction and ellipsis are also covered in its extensive grammar, but the full range of linguistic summarization techniques we describe here is not a focus of their work.

FOG generates marine weather forecasts from meteorological data and remains to date the only generator in everyday industrial use. ANA generates stock market reports from updates arriving on the half hour of financial index values. FOG performs only *conceptual* summarization, by picking only a few facts among the large amount of input data available. It does not perform *linguistic* summarization, discussed in this paper: it generates many short sentences in a telegraphic style in which fluency is essentially a non-issue.

This is in contrast with ANA whose main theme was the generation of multiple clause sentences fluently combining several related facts. ANA performs both conceptual and linguistic summarization. It achieves a high degree of fluency for fairly complex sentences by relying on a phrasal lexicon. The entries in this lexicon are phrases, comprising up to 8 words, simultaneously realizing several facts in an idiomatic and concise way. The advantage of this approach is that it circumvents the identification of the complex constraints that influence the generation of these phrases. It has two drawbacks. First, it cannot exploit summarization potential lying below the clause rank such as the nominalization, head noun modification or nominal conjunction examples presented in this paper. Second, it makes scaling up the paraphrasing power prohibitively costly, since it requires the hand-coding of a combinatorially explosive number of phrases.

In the two systems presented here, STREAK and PLANDOC, the lexicon entries are individual words or collocations, each realizing one to three fine-grained content units. Phrases that were stored as a whole in ANA's lexicon are instead dynamically built at generation-time. Though other generation systems have used such a compositional approach (McKeown *et al.*, 1990; Dale, 1992; Elhadad, 1993a), PLANDOC and STREAK are the first to exploit it to perform pervasive linguistic summarization. By using revision in addition to a word-based lexicon, STREAK takes this compositional approach one step further, resulting in a recognized benefit of compositionality: enhanced expressive flexibility and reduced scale-up cost. However, such extreme compositionality also involves an increase in the overall complexity of the generation process.

6.2. Revision

Previous work viewed revision uniquely as a way of improving stylistic quality while preserving content. Analyzing a corpus of work sessions from professional editors (Meteer,

1991) presented an interesting set of revision operations to leave draft content intact while improving its style. She did not attempt to implement these operations in a generator (Inui *et al.*, 1992) presented a generation system in which similar types of content-preserving revisions are implemented.

In STREAK, revision is viewed as a way to gradually and opportunistically improve informative content of the report while keeping it short and concise. This view brings together revision with another line of research: incremental generation (Joshi, 1987; De Smedt, 1990). This line of research, however, limited itself to study only elaborations that *preserve* the linguistic form of the draft. The most sophisticated revision tools of STREAK, such as nominalization with adjoin discussed above, show that it is often necessary to *change* the linguistic form of the draft in order to accommodate additional background facts in the most compact way. STREAK is unique in that it performs revisions that alter both the content *and* the linguistic form of the draft and simultaneously improves both the coverage and compactness of the summary.

7. CURRENT DIRECTIONS

For STREAK, we have looked at the portability of the revision based approach by doing an analysis of summaries in another quantitative domain, the stock market. This analysis showed that many of STREAK's revision rules could be directly used in this domain. For PLANDOC, we are currently turning our attention towards the generation of summaries of PLAN's base plan and of the final recommended plan, as described earlier. We are also beginning a new summarization application, the generation of full text summaries, using input from natural language information extraction systems. In this section, we discuss these directions briefly.

7.1. Portability of STREAK's revision based approach

While the use of revision to generate concise, compact summaries appears promising, we were interested in determining whether any of the specific revision rules we had identified could be used when moving to a new domain. In particular, we were curious whether the rules could be used directly for similar domains or whether they were specific to sports reports.

To assess the degree of domain dependence of the revision rules we abstracted from our analysis of sports summaries, we looked for examples of their use in stock market summaries. Use of a revision rule in a corpus can be identified by the simultaneous presence of:

(1) A simple sentence whose content types and form match the triggering conditions of the rule.
(2) A more complex sentence whose content types and form can be derived from the simple one by applying the rule.

For example, the rule *Nominalization with Ordinal Adjoin* was originally abstracted from the following pair of sports sentences:

- "*helping Detroit defeat Indiana 114 112*"
- "*helping the Milwaukee Bucks* **hand** *the Denver Nuggets* **their fourth straight defeat,** *115–98.*"

Here, the verb "*to defeat*" is nominalized in order to modify it by an ordinal pre-modifier providing the historical context of the defeat in just two words, something that could not have been done as concisely by directly modifying the verb or clause. The rules for this revision was presented in Section 4.2.

This tool is used in the stock market as well, as demonstrated by the following pair of corpus sentences:

- "*the Tokyo stock market plunged*"
- "*the Tokyo stock market* **posted its third consecutive decline**"

where the verb *"to plunge"* is nominalized into the noun *"decline"* also because the latter can be concisely modified with streak information (*"third consecutive"*).

This portability evaluation was partially automated by using CREP (Duford, 1993), a software tool that retrieves corpus sentences matching a regular expression of words and/or parts-of-speech tags. We used such expressions to approximate the basic and revised sentence patterns characterizing each revision rule observed in the sports domain. CREP was run on a corpus of over 18,000 sentences in the financial domain compiled from several newswires.

The revision rules identified in the sports domain form (and are implemented as) a hierarchy characterizing the observed transformations at various degrees of specificity. On top of this hierarchy sits nine general syntactic transformations such as *nominalization, adjunctization, adjoin, conjoin,* etc. At this coarse grain, was found that portability was 100%: all nine of these general transformations were used at least once in our test financial corpus. Each transformation is refined down the hierarchy in terms of the syntactic category and semantic roles of each constituent involved, yielding more specific revision rules such as *adjunctization of object NP into instrument PP, adjoin of non-finite clause to NP,* etc. At this finer grain, portability fell to 71.4%. For example, no usage of *adjoin of <u>non-finite</u> clause to NP* was found in our financial corpus even though cases of *adjoin of <u>relative clause</u> to NP* were found.* The most specialized rules incorporate stylistic transformations such as abridged references in addition to syntactic ones. Such transformations tend not to port very well. Consider, for example, the strategy for abridging references presented in Section 4.4. It relies on the fact that in the sports domain all entities have compound names (e.g. "Denver Nuggets", "Shaquille O'Neal") different parts of which can be used unambiguously in different references for the targeted audience, i.e. sports fans. This is not the case for all financial entities. Nevertheless, even at this finest grain, a majority of revision rules (51.9%) were portable.

This is a very encouraging result for the portability potential of STREAK to other summarization domains and more generally for the potential of scaling up the revision-based generation approach. For an in-depth presentation of this portability assessment see Robin (1994).

7.2. *Generating summaries from news articles*

Given the recent results of the natural language information extraction systems developed under ARPA's message understanding conferences (MUC-4, 1992) along with recent advances in natural language generation, the stage is now set for text summarization. Information extraction systems use natural language analysis to extract key facts from the newspaper articles in a given domain. For example, when applied to articles about terrorism, these systems extract facts such as the victim, the perpetrator, the level of confidence, the source, the time, the location, etc. If these facts were passed as input to a natural language summarizer such as the ones we have discussed here, it would be possible to produce summaries of news articles in specific domains. This is a task which we have begun to work on.†

Input to our system will be a set of articles on a single event. The generation system will use the set of templates produced by the information extraction system for each article. We are currently using the published "correct" answers during development as planned input for our system.‡ In any case, this means the summarization system will be used to produce a textual summary, where the input facts have been extracted form a text. From our initial analysis of a corpus of articles used for the message understanding system evaluation, there seems to be several ways the input articles can vary. For example, the sources (e.g. AP newswire vs Reuters) can vary while the account of the event is essentially the same. Alternatively, the sources may

---

* Note that a larger financial corpus may have contained such cases. The results reported here are thus lower bounds on portability.
† This work is being carried out by Dragomir Radev.
‡ Evaluations of these systems are carried out by comparing system output with "correct" answers that have been prepared ahead of time by hand by the evaluation committee. It is these answers that we are using.

be different and the accounts contradictory. Perhaps the most interesting case is when the source is the same, but the time of the account varies. In this scenario, the articles relate a changing view of the same event over time.

In addition to the dimensions along which the articles can vary, we have also noted that summaries take advantage of general knowledge that tends to be fixed over time. This may or may not be explicitly mentioned in the input news article. Even if it is, the summarizer must be able to distinguish between new facts about an event (what is being reported) and facts that remain constant over time and set the stage for the article. For example, assassination of an official may be reported along with the fact that he is President of his country. We are exploring whether a distinction between these kinds of facts is similar to the distinction between essential facts (game results) and potential (historical significance) in the basketball domain. Here, we suspect that well-known, facts that have been true for some period of time and serve to set the stage for the "news" may function similarly to historical information; they get included if they fit and if they can be folded into the draft. Note that in some cases, such facts may be essential, but they still may be more easily conveyed in modifier form.

While this summarization domain involves summarizing of qualitative data and the work we have reported here involves summarizing quantitative data, note that once input has been produced in symbolic form (that is, once the conceptual summarizer has completed its task), there is nothing in our approach that is dependent on quantitative input. Linguistic summarization only presupposes that the input will include a list of essential facts and a list of potential facts; whether or not potential facts are included in the summary depends on how they can be realized and the form of the draft, criteria that can be applied to any form of input fact. However, simply interfacing a message understanding system with summarizers such as we describe will neither fully resolve the text summarization problem nor result in a full system. First, an integration of these two types of systems will produce a restricted class of summaries. The summaries will be informative and can only include information extracted by the message understanding system. Note that if information on a terrorist event can be extracted from the article, the summary will convey only that information regardless of whether the article was about a terrorist event or not. Thus, if the article included a digression on a terrorist event in the course of relating some other story, the summary will include no information on that other story. Another problem that must be addressed in developing a fully integrated text summarization system from these two existing systems is knowledge abstraction. Generalizations from individual facts extracted from separate articles may result in a single fact which adequately and more concisely conveys the several individual facts. This is part of what we are working on.

Our work is still at early stages, but we have noted the different forms of summaries that can be used depending on the kinds of generalizations that can be made about the input facts. We will explore integrating the approaches taken in STREAK and in PLANDOC so that the summarization system can use both discourse planning and revision in combination to produce the summaries.

8. CONCLUSION

Our work identifies problems unique to concise summarization of different types of information and demonstrates an approach that has been successfully implemented in two separate systems. Underlying our approach is the basic tenet that summary generation requires a different approach than used in traditional language generation. Summaries attempt to fit as much information as possible into as short a space as possible. Developing a system that can do this requires changing the generation process. We have shown that the following features are essential to a summary generator:

- A summary generator must be able to opportunistically add information to the summary, incrementally building complex sentences.
- The addition of new information can be triggered by the surface form of an existing text, along with semantic constraints. Thus, the syntax or words used in an existing text can allow or disallow the addition of specific new information.

- Producing a concise summary is dependent on finding concise constructions that take advantage of similarities between information already in the text and new facts, thus compactly expressing new facts through small changes to existing sentences.
- Opportunistic addition of information implies a division of information into essential information that *must* appear in the summary and additional facts that are added *if possible*.

In both domains, the examples illustrate that selection of information to include in a summary can depend on lexical and syntactic constraints. In STREAK, the wording of the draft summary can determine whether information gets included at all in the final version, e.g. addition of an optional fact can be triggered by a verb which can be nominalized. In PLANDOC, choosing what optional facts to include and how to order them depends on whether they can be concisely conjoined using ellipsis. Influence of wording and surface form on the inclusion and ordering of information is quite unique to our work; previous generation systems used content planning (McKeown, 1985a; Hovy, 1991; Moore & Paris, 1989; Paris, 1987) that relied on rhetorical strategies, relations or planning about the user's knowledge to determine the content and organization of a text. These are all reasoning strategies that rely on conceptual information only and ignore the text surface form.

This approach of incrementally adding in information as it fits makes it possible for a generator to produce the complex sentences required in summaries. Sentences of almost 50 words in length can be generated, much longer than sentences produced by any previous language generation system. Moreover, these sentences are generated from individual words* and use concise linguistic forms. This happens since the summary generator chooses various modifying constructions that gradually add information and build up the summary sentences to full length.

In this paper, we described four main constructions that could be used to concisely add information, exploiting repetitions across facts; these included the selection of a single word to simultaneously convey multiple pieces of information, the selection of modifiers to convey full facts, the use of conjunction along with ellipsis to group together similar facts while deleting repetitions, and the use of abridged references when multiple references to the same object are required.

STREAK and PLANDOC use different, but complementary, approaches to the task of opportunistically adding information based on linguistic constraints. STREAK uses revision to incrementally add information, constructing a full draft of essential facts, and using revision rules that encode lexical, syntactic and semantic constraints to determine how to fold in new information to the draft. PLANDOC embodies a more traditional language generation approach, using discourse planning to look ahead and gather together facts that can be combined in systematic ways using conjunctions of various different syntactic constitutents, reasoning about how to delete repetitions. Ultimately, these two approaches can be combined to yield a more complete approach to summarization. STREAK's approach allows local changes within a sentence, while PLANDOC's can pull information together from distant parts of its text plan using long distance knowledge to make modifications. Both local and discourse knowledge must eventually be coordinated in the summarization task.

Finally, both applications illustrate the feasibility of summarizing input data as opposed to full text. In both domains, the input is currently readily available as data. For STREAK, box scores for a game are accessible from online services; for PLANDOC, input data is drawn from an existing application that planning engineers currently use in production at various regional companies. Summarization is thus practical today, without also having to carry out the difficult task of interpreting texts in the domain. Moreover, the summarization techniques we have developed are general. Were information to be extracted from a text using natural language interpretation, the same summarization techniques we have described here could be applied to produce a natural language summary of a text. In fact, as we have described in Section 7 we believe that today's technology is currently poised for a breakthrough in this area; by using the

---

* As opposed to hard-wired phrases.

output of information extraction systems developed in ARPA's message understanding program, which can extract key facts from news articles in restricted domains, and feeding this information as input to a summary generator we could see the realization of full text summarization for a limited class of summary types, namely informative summaries conveying specific types of key content.

Acknowledgements—This work was supported in part by Bellcore through sponsored research agreement *Bellcore CU01403301, by a joint grant from DARPA and ONR under contract N00014-89-J-1782, by NSF GER-90-24069, and by New York State Center for Advanced Technology Contract NYSSTF-CAT(91)-053 and NYSSTF-CU50947301. We would like to acknowledge the contributions of James Shaw in the development of conjunction in PLANDOC and for his continuing work on this system.

REFERENCES

Anderson, D. (1985). *Contemporary sports reporting.* Chicago, Ill.: Nelson–Hall.

Appelt, D. E. (1985). *Planning English sentences. Studies in natural language processing.* Cambridge: Cambridge University Press.

Borko, H. (1975). *Abstracting concepts and methods.* New York: Academic Press.

Bourbeau, L., Carcagno, D., Goldberg, E., Kittredge, R., & Polguere, A. (1990). Bilingual generation of weather forecasts in an operations environment. *Proceedings of the 13th International Conference on Computational Linguistics.* COLING.

Cox, J. (1993). Text-analysis server to simplify queries. *Communication Week.*

Dale, R. (1992). *Generating referring expressions.* Cambridge, Mass.: ACL-MIT Press Series in Natural Language Processing.

Danlos, L. (1986). *Studies in Natural Language Processing. The linguistic basis of text generation.* Cambridge University Press.

DARPA Software and Intelligent Systems Technology Office (1992). *Proceedings of the Fourth Message Understanding Conference.*

De Smedt, K. J. M. J. (1990). IPF: an incremental parallel formulator. In R. Dale, C. S. Mellish, & M. Zock (Eds), *Current research in natural language generation.* New York: Academic Press.

Duford, D. (1993). CREP: a regular expression-matching textual corpus tool. New York: Technical Report. Columbia University.

Elhadad, M. (1993a). *Using argumentation to control lexical choice: a unification-based implementation.* Doctoral dissertation, Computer Science Department, Columbia University.

Elhadad, M. (1993b). FUF: The universal unifier – user manual, version 5.2. Technical Report. Columbia University.

Elhadad, M., & Robin, J. (1992). Controlling content realization with functional unification grammars. In R. Dale, H. Hovy, D. Roesner, & O. Stock (Eds), *Aspects of automated natural language generation.* Berlin: Springer.

Feiner, S., & McKeown, K. R. (1991). Automating the generation of coordinated multimedia explanations. *IEEE Computer, 24*(10), 33–41.

Fensch, T. (1988). *The sports writing handbook.* Hillsdale, N.J.: Erlbaum.

Gopen, G. D., & Swan, J. A. (1990). The science of scientific writing. *American Scientist,* (78), 550–558.

Hobbs, J. R. (1985). Ontological promiscuity. *Proceedings of the 23rd Annual Meeting of the ACL.* ACL.

Hovy, E. (1985). Integrating text planning & production in generation. *Proceedings of the 9th International Joint Conference on Artificial Intelligence.* IJCAI.

Hovy, E. (1988). *Generating natural language under pragmatic constraints.* Hillsdale, N.J.: Erlbaum.

Hovy, E. (1991). Approaches to the planning of coherent text. In C. Paris, W. Swartout, & W. C. Mann (Eds), *Natural language generation in artificial intelligence and computational linguistics,.* Amsterdam: Kluwer Academic.

Inui, K., Tokunaga, T., & Tanaka, H. (1992). Text revision: A model and its implementation. In R. Dale, E. Hovy, D. Roesner, & O. Stock (Eds), *Aspects of automated natural language generation,* Berlin: Springer.

Iordanskaja, L., Kim, M., Kittredge, R., Lavoie, B., & Polguere, A. (1992). Generation of extended bilingual statistical reports. *Proceedings of COLING-92.* COLING.

Jacobs, P. (1985). PHRED: A generator for natural language interfaces. *Computational Linguistics, 11*(4), 219–242.

Joshi, A. K. (1987). The relevance of tree-adjoining approach to generation. In G. Kempen (Ed.), *Natural language generation: New results in artificial intelligence, psychology and linguistics.* Amsterdam: Ninjhoff.

Kay, M. (1979). Functional grammar. *Proceedings of the 5th Annual Meeting of the Berkeley Linguistic Society.*

Krupka, G. R., Jacobs, P. S., & Rau, L. F. (1992). GE NLToolset: Description of the system as used for MUC-4. *Proceedings of the Fourth Message Understanding Conference (MUC-4).* San Mateo, Calif.: Kaufmann.

Kukich, K. (1983). The design of a knowledge-based report generation. *Proceedings of the 21st Conference of the ACL.* ACL.

Kukich, K., McKeown, K., Morgan, N., Phillips, J., Robin, J., Shaw, J., & Lim, J. (1993). User-needs analysis and design methodology for an automated documentation generator. *Proceedings of the Bellcore/BCC Symposium on User-Centered Design: "People and Technology".* Piscataway, N.J.

Mann, W. C. (1983). An overview of the PENMAN text generation system. Technical Report. Marina del Rey, Calif.: ISI.

Mann, W. C. (1984). Discourse structure for text generation. Technical Report. Marina del Rey, Calif.: Information Sciences Institute.

Matthiessen, C. M. (1991). Lexicogrammatical choice in text generation. In C. Paris, W. Swartout, & W. C. Mann (Eds),

Natural language generation in artificial intelligence and computational linguistics. Amsterdam: Kluwer Academic.

Maybury, M. T. (1990). Using discourse focus, temporal focus and spatial focus to generate multisentential text. *Proceedings of the 5th International Workshop on Natural Language Generation.* Pittsburgh, Pa.

McCoy, K. F. (1986). The ROMPER system: Responding to object-related misconceptions using perspective. *Proceedings of the 24th Annual Meeting of the ACL.* New York: Association of Computational Linguistics.

McDonald, D. (1983). Description directed control: Its implications for natural language generation. In B. Grosz, K. Sparck-Jones, & B. Webber (Eds), *Readings in natural language processing.* San Mateo, Calif.: Kaufmann. Also in *Computers & Mathematics, 9*(1).

McKeown, K. R. (1985a). *Studies in natural language processing. Using discourse strategies and focus constraints to generate natural language text.* Cambridge University Press.

McKeown, K. R. (1985b). The need for text generation. Technical Report. Columbia University.

McKeown, K. R., & Swartout, W. R. (1987). Language generation and explanation. In J. Traub, B. Grosz, B. Lampson, & N. Nilsson (Eds), *Annual Review of Computer Science.* Palo Alto, Calif.: Annual Reviews Inc.

McKeown, K. R., Robin, J., & Tanenblatt, M. (1993). Tailoring lexical choice to the user's vocabulary in multimedia explanation generation. *Proceedings of the 31st Annual Meeting of the Association for Computational Linguistics.* Columbus,. Ohio.

McKeown, K. R., Elhadad, M., Fukumoto, Y., Lim, J. G., Lombardi, C., Robin, J., & Smadja, F. A. (1990). Text generation in COMET. In R. Dale, C. S. Mellish, & M. Zock (Eds), *Current research in natural language generation.* New York: Academic Press.

Mel'cuk, I. A. (1981). Meaning-text models: A recent trend in Soviet linguistics. *The Annual Review of Anthropology.* (10).

Meteer, M. (1991). The implications of revisions for natural language generation. In C. Paris, W. Swartout, & W. C. Mann (Eds), *Natural language generation in artificial intelligence and computational linguistics.* Amsterdam: Kluwer Academic.

Meteer, M. W., McDonald, D. D. , Anderson, S. D., Forster, D., Gay, L. S., Huettner, A. K., & Sibun, P. (1987). Mumble-86: Design and implementation. Technical Report. Amherst, Mass.: University of Massachussets at Amherst.

Moore, J. D., & Paris, C. L. (1989). Planning text for advisory dialogues. *Proceedings of the 27th Annual Meeting of the Association for Computational Linguistics.* Vancouver, B.C.: Association for Computational Linguistics.

Paice, C. (1990). Constructing literature abstracts by computer: techniques and prospects. *Information Processing & Management, 1*(2), 171–186.

Paris, C. L. (1987). *The use of explicit user models in text generation: Tailoring to a user's level of expertise.* Doctoral dissertation, Columbia University.

Quirk, R., Greenbaum, S., Leech, G., & Svartvik, J. (1985). *A comprehensive grammar of the English language.* London: Longman.

Rambow, O., & Korelsky, T. (1992). Applied text generation. *Proceedings of the 3rd Conference on Applied Natural Language Processing.* Trento, Italy: Association for Computational Linguistics.

Rau, L. F. (1987). Information retrieval in never-ending stories. *Proceedings of the Sixth National Conference on Artificial Intelligence.* Seattle, Wash.: Morgan Kaufmann.

Reiter, E. B. (1991). A new model for lexical choice for open-class words. *Computational Intelligence,* (7).

Robin, J. (1993). A revision-based generation architecture for reporting facts in their historical context. In H. Horacek, & M. Zock (Eds), *New concepts in natural language generation: Planning, realization and systems.* London: Pinter.

Robin, J. (1994). *Revision-based generation of natural language summaries: corpus-based analysis, design, implementation and evaluation.* Doctoral dissertation, Computer Science Department, Columbia University.

Robin, J., & McKeown, K. R. (1993). Corpus analysis for revision-based generation of complex sentences. *Proceedings of the National Conference on Artificial Intelligence,* Washington, D.C.

Roesner, D. (1987). SEMTEX: A text generator for German. In G. Kempen (Ed), *Natural language generation: New results in artificial intelligence, psychology and linguistics.* Amsterdam: Martinus Ninjhoff.

Rubinoff, R. (1988). A cooperative model of strategy and tactics in generation. Presented at the *Workshop on Natural Language Generation.*

Suthers, D. (1991). A task-appropriate architecture for explanation. *Computational Intelligence, 7*(4), 315–333.

Wahlster, W., Andre, E., Hecking, M., & Rist, T. (1989). WIP: Knowledge-based presentation of information. Technical Report. Saarbruecken: German Research Center for Artificial Intelligence.

Wolz, U., McKeown, K. R., & Kaiser, G. (1989). Automated tutoring in interactive environments: A task centered approach. *Journal of Machine Mediated Learning.*

Zukerman, I., & Pearl, J. (1986). Comprehension-driven generation of meta-technical utterances in math tutoring. *Proceedings of AAAI-86.* Philadelphia, Pa.

17

GENERATING SUMMARIES FROM EVENT DATA

MARK T. MAYBURY

Artifical Intelligence Center, The MITRE Corporation, Mail Stop K329, 202 Burlington Road, Bedford, MA 01730, U.S.A.

Abstract—Summarization entails analysis of source material, selection of key information, condensation of this, and generation of a compact summary form. While there have been many investigations into the automatic summarization of text, relatively little attention has been given to the summarization of information from structured information sources such as data or knowledge bases, despite this being a desirable capability for a number of application areas including report generation from databases (e.g. weather, financial, medical) and simulations (e.g. military, manufacturing, economic). After a brief introduction indicating the main elements of summarization and referring to some illustrative approaches to it, this article considers specific issues in the generation of text summaries of event data. It describes a system, SumGen, which selects key information from an event database by reasoning about event frequencies, frequencies of relations between events, and domain specific importance measures. The article describes how SumGen then aggregates similar information and plans a summary presentation tailored to a stereotypical user. Finally, the article evaluates SumGen performance, and also that of a much more limited second summariser, by assessesing information extraction by 22 human subjects from both source and summary texts. This evaluation shows that the use of SumGen reduces average sentence length by approx. 15%, document length by 70%, and time to perform information extraction by 58%.

Keywords: Automated summarization, Natural language generation, Importance, Condensation, Aggregation, Tailored summarization, Automated abstracting

1. INTRODUCTION

An effective summary distills the most important information from a source (or sources) to produce an abridged version of the original information for a particular user(s) and task(s). Automated summarization from a source text encompasses at least four distinct types of processing: (1) analysis of the source text, (2) identification of important source elements, (3) condensation of information, and (4) generation of the resulting summary presentation (see Fig. 1). In contrast to some pipe-line architectures of the summarization process, observation of human abstractors suggests these processes occur concurrently and are co-constraining (Endres-Niggemeyer, 1993). For example, in human abstracting, just as the structure of the source and the abstractor's knowledge of the domain can influence processing and the structure of the resulting summary (Friedrich, 1993), so too the specification of the resulting summary itself (its type, length, contents) also affects the kind and depth of processing that occurs (Cremmins, 1993).

1.1. Source interpretation

Despite this observed complexity in human summarization, some of the simplest automatic summarization techniques work surprisingly well. For example, Mead Data Central's *Searchable Lead*™ simply selects an extract by taking the first 60, 150, or 250 words from a source up to a sentence boundary and achieves an over 90% "acceptability" rating by users. To a great extent, this success results from the journalistic nature of the sources in which the most important information is located at the beginning of each text. To mitigate the limited

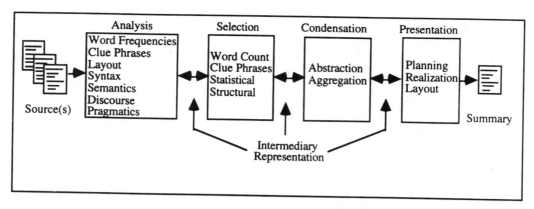

Fig. 1. Summarization processes.

applicability of this approach, the ANES (Automatic News Extraction System) system (Rau *et al.*, 1993) weighs and heuristically selects sentences following term frequency analysis. Using similar sources and human evaluators, however, it achieves a 75% "acceptability" rating. Determining what is acceptable, in general evaluating summaries, remains an important research area which we discuss in Section 4.

Other types of source analysis techniques identify clue phrases (e.g. "the most important", "the key idea") (Paice, 1981), use knowledge-based techniques such as frames, scripts, or rules to detect and elide commonplace material (DeJong., 1979, Tait, 1982; Fum *et al.*, 1985), or recognize and exploit rhetorical structure in source texts (Ono *et al.*, 1994). Still others use a combination of techniques (e.g. word frequencies, clue words, syntactic information), as in the AND Corporation's SUMMA system (Polanyi, 1993). Sparck Jones (1993) performed several types of more sophisticated analyses by hand (using Rhetorical Structure Theory, story grammars, predicate-argument structures, scripts and frames, and intentions) and found that while all yielded plausible results, none appeared completely satisfactory, suggesting some combination of them might support summarization more effectively. As we describe in this article, we have discovered benefit to combinations of importance determination, condensation, and generation techniques for material summarization.

As Fig. 1 indicates, once a source has been analyzed and transformed into some kind of intermediary representation (e.g. a predicate-argument structure, rhetorically structured propositions), important information needs to be identified. As the figure suggests, this can be accomplished by simply counting the number of words in the source as done in *Searchable Lead™*, by exploiting word-frequency distributions (Luhn, 1958), by referring to the elements identified in the first stage of analysis (e.g. clue phrases), by measuring frequencies of concepts mentioned in the text (Fum *et al.*, 1985), or by reasoning about the rhetorical structure of source text (Ono *et al.*, 1994). Determining what is important is influenced by the source and its relevance to a particular information need or query, the task (e.g. search, overview, evaluate), the properties of the user (e.g. level of expertise in the subject matter, reading skills, cultural expectations), the discourse history (in interactive settings), and the desired product. In Sections 2 and 3, we present a method for determining importance using a combination of event frequencies, frequencies of relations between events, and domain knowledge.

The selected information may then need to be condensed. This can be achieved either by abstraction or aggregation. For example, in an attempt to abstract away from the underlying events and states of a story, Lehnert (1981) suggested a number of "plot units" (e.g. problem resolution by intentional means, trade, and honored request) which were configurations of "positive" events, "negative" events, and "neutral" emotional states. This is related to plan recognition, which attempts to identify a subsuming event(s) that best explains observed events. In addition to abstracting away from particulars, other research has focused on techniques to aggregate information (Dalianis & Hovy, 1993). Still others have built hierarchical thematic graphs based on statistical measures of concept occurrence (Reimer & Hahn, 1988).

1.2. Summary generation

The final step of automated summarization as shown in Fig. 1 is the presentation of information to the user. This entails planning the presentation, realizing it (e.g. as text, graphics, animation, coordinated multimedia), and laying this out. Relatively few systems have focused on generation in support of summarization. Some systems avoid generation altogether for source material that they cannot process, presenting extracts of the source amidst machine generated summary (Tait, 1982).

Systems that do employ generation tend to employ simple techniques. For example, Goldman's BABEL (1975) within MARGIE produced stories by translating underlying conceptual dependency structures, compactly explaining complex conceptual structures by using a rich lexicon that could distinguish similar concepts (e.g. "drink" vs "guzzle"). Meehan's (1976) TALE-SPIN traced the goal stack of simulated agents to tell their story. In contrast to these story generators, which perform little explicit summarization, many domain specific report generators have been developed guided by analysis of corpora of human-produced narratives. For example, Kukich's (1983) ANA generates stock market reports (regarding the trend and volume of the industrial average) by collecting semantically related messages concerning 10 specific market issues such as "closing market status", "volume of trading", "mixed market" and "interesting fluctuations." Using domain specific rules, some of these messages are inferred (e.g. if the market closed up but the number of declines exceeded the number of advances for the day, then the market was mixed). A relatively simple "discourse organizer" groups and selects messages by prioritizing important messages such as indicators hitting record highs. Important messages are then realized using a phrasal lexicon of just under 600 entries. Similarly, Kittredge et al., (1986) use a sublanguage approach in RAREAS to produce Canadian weather reports. The sublanguage includes knowledge about the importance of content such as the fact that warnings preceded normal weather or that sentence groupings follow the order WINDS > CLOUD-COVER > PRECIPITATION > FOG&MIST > VISIBILITY. Of course these fixed importance rank orders may need to be modified for users with differing interests (e.g. weather reports for flying vs boating vs camping).

These sublanguage approaches can be contrasted with systems that represent explicit *text grammars* (domain specific schemata) such as Li et al.'s, (1986) system which produces two types of reports, a current status report and a discharge report, by accessing facts from a Stroke Consultant expert system. For example, the top level rule for a stroke case report is:

Case_Report → Initial_Information + Medical_History + Physical_Examination +

Laboratory_Tests + Final_Diagnosis + Outcome

The Initial_Information portion of this rule includes patient information, described by the rule:

Patient_Information → Registration_Number + Age + Handedness + Race + Sex

The right-hand side of the Patient_Information rule consists of leaf nodes which refer to information in the stroke knowledge base. In addition to being domain dependent, this text grammar does not have an explicit indication of the relative importance of information in the report that could be exploited for summarization. And while researchers have developed domain independent text schemata for descriptive texts (McKeown, 1985), these too, like the aforementioned text grammars and sublanguages, are "compiled" plans that indicate *what* and *when* content should appear in a text but not *why*, so the ability to tailor summaries to individual contexts or users [however, see Paris (1988)] as well as the ability to reason about summary purposes is not possible.

As is evident by the above report generators, selection, condensation and generation might occur directly from an intermediary representation (e.g. application events), without reference to a source text. Indeed, none may exist. In the two application systems we have investigated this is the case, although in our joint venture domain we have access to the source text from which information has been previously extracted. In contrast to previous work, however, this article describes the application of both domain dependent and domain independent strategies for selection and aggregation. We further utilize plan-based presentation mechanisms to generate summary presentations that can be user and situation tailored. This differs from

Table 1. Event summarization techniques

	Technique	Strengths	Weaknesses
S E L E C T	1. Importance (of events)	Relatively easy to implement; intuitive	Domain dependent; requires acquisition from experts; context dependent
	2. Importance (of event attributes or semantic roles)	Easy to implement; intuitive	Domain and context dependent; application must represent and reason about semantic roles and associated data; requires knowledge acquisition from experts
	3. Link analysis	Takes advantage of type and number of semantic relations among events and states; domain independent	Requires semantic relations in application; need mechanisms to capture event/state network; assumes isolated events unimportant
	4. Statistical Analysis (e.g. word frequencies, event frequencies)	Easy to implement; domain independent; computationally inexpensive; easy to identify statistical outliers (in current set of events or historically)	Relies on law of large numbers to measure event distributions, can overlook significant events embedded in large numbers of events of similar type
C O N D E N S E	5. Abstraction	Enables summarization across events; elides details	Requires semantic hierarchy of events and more complex reasoning about abstraction; risk loss of precision and coherency by eliding details
	6. Aggregation (semantic or linguistic)	Requires less presentation space and time for same content (e.g. using adverbials to combine similar events)	Requires identifying and integrating similar events into a single utterance; can lose details of combined entities
P R E S E N T	7. Presentation	Context (task, time, space, topic) can be exploited to both reduce content and increase coherency; different media types (e.g. text vs graphics, maps) may shorten elapsed time of presentation; different rhetorical structures and/or communicative plans can elide information	Requires representing and reasoning about context, media, and/or rhetoric; rhetorical tactics limited to rhetorically structured prose

McKeown's (1993) investigation which utilizes a plan-and-revise architecture that incrementally "packs" information into linguistic constituents.

We now turn to the main focus of this article, summarizing events. Event data may originate not only from an input text but also from other sources such as events entered manually into a database, real-world events captured directly by sensors, or events simulated in a virtual world. After we outline a taxonomy of techniques for event summary generation, we describe our use of aggregation to compress events by grouping similar objects or events. The article concludes by describing our approach to summary generation and evaluating the results of two implemented summarization prototypes.

2. TECHNIQUES FOR EVENT SUMMARIZATION

There are several classes of techniques for summarizing events from simulations or other event-oriented application systems (including databases of previously extracted information). We describe these techniques in turn, illustrating the use of several of them in two application systems for which we have developed summarization components. Table 1 outlines the

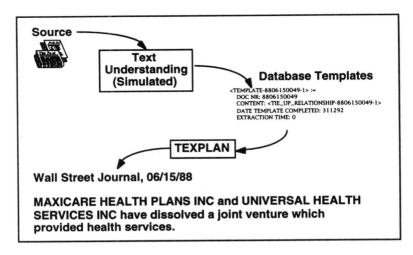

Fig. 2. Summarizing joint ventures.

strengths and weaknesses of these techniques which support the selection, condensation, and presentation tasks of Fig. 1. Techniques include exploiting the importance of events (and their associated characteristics), analyzing the types and numbers of links (i.e. semantic relations) between events, analyzing statistical distributions of events, abstracting more general events from collections of events, aggregating related events, and controlling the presentation of events. These techniques are not mutually exclusive, nor do we claim they are a complete set, rather they serve as a starting point for further refinement. We illustrate and discuss each of these in turn.

Implicit in the stock market, weather, and medical report generators described in the previous section is a notion of the importance of types of events or information. In these report generators, the domain specific importance of information is used to govern content selection and presentation order. Analogously, human-produced newspaper reports typically attempt to capture the key characteristics of some event (i.e. who, what, when, where, how, and why) in the leading or "topic" sentence or paragraph.

Importance is a domain and context specific measure of the relative significance of an event, and can refer either to particular events, characteristics of events, or classes of events. For example, Fig. 2 illustrates a prototype developed in our laboratory by Sam Bayer that takes the human-generated object-oriented answer key templates from the ARPA Message Understanding Conference (MUC-5) joint venture information extraction task and, using a linguistic realizer re-engineered from TEXPLAN (Maybury, 1991a), generates a sentence indicating the type, partners, and status of joint venture(s) found in the source (template). The partner names and status of the joint venture are generated by directly looking up values in slots in the templates; its type is determined using a table lookup, indexed by the Standard Industrial Code of the product or service found in the templates. While simple in design, this approach illustrates the power of pre-specified identification of important domain information (both from the text, which requires information extraction techniques, and from the detailed resulting slots and values within templates, which requires selection as done by TEXPLAN). Of course, this strength is also its greatest weakness: the type, partners, and status of the joint venture may or may not be the most significant joint venture characteristics for every reader or task. For example, one user may be interested in the financial values of the joint ventures whereas another may be interested in joint ventures with particular partners or kinds of partner. Nevertheless, the ability to capture a knowledge-level characterization of interest provides a deeper representation of user interest than the Boolean keyword approach described in Fum *et al.* (1986).

This complexity of determining which characteristics of an event or set of events are most significant or which combination of characteristics makes an event significant is also apparent in a land air combat (LACE) simulation we have studied (Anken, 1989). Domain experts indicate that events dealing with bombings or missile launches are, in general, more significant

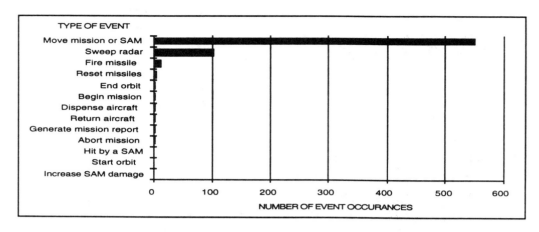

Fig. 3. Battle simulator event frequencies.

than movement events. And yet certain kinds of movements in certain contexts may be very important (e.g. those leading up to a bombing, or those resulting in strategic repositioning of assets). Just as classes of events can be specified as significant, so too particular events or patterns can be identified as significant (e.g. a bombing followed by an explosion; bombings of particular kinds of facilities). Importance is not only context dependent, but also in the eye of the beholder. For example, stereotypically, military operations staff are concerned with strike missions, close air support missions, and so on; logisticians care about refueling, resupply, and transportation missions; intelligence users care about enemy forces, their type, size, location, and activities. In addition to these broad classes of user interests, there are many other perspectives which could govern content selection (air vs ground vs sea; friendly vs enemy). Also, for particular event classes, there may be semantic roles associated with types of events that domain specialists deem more important than others (e.g. the target and weapon associated with a bombing event). This is the approach used in the joint venture summarizer. Finally, event characteristics (e.g. its location, size, number of participants) may also indicate significance. While we have found event importance to be effective for summarizing a battle simulation, it is domain specific and does not take advantage of context.

In contrast to selecting events based on semantic patterns, domain independent event selection techniques include frequency analysis of events and frequency analysis of relations between events. In the latter case, the relative importance of a particular event is determined by the amount and type of links between it and other events. The assumption is that, for example, events that enable or cause many other events should be more significant than events that are isolated from all other events. An even more basic method, particularly useful when analyzing a large pool of events, is to simply count the number of different types of events, the times they occur, and so on, and from this determine event frequency occurrences. The assumption is that in simulations or other event-oriented applications, events that occur frequently tend to be less significant than those that occur infrequently. Conversely, in the analysis of source texts, the assumption is that events that are *mentioned* more frequently are more indicative of the source content and, hence, more significant.

Consider, for example, Fig. 3 which charts occurrences of different types of events from our battle simulator. General frequencies are obvious (e.g. movement events occur many more times frequently than other events, more missiles are fired than hits occur). Because of the object-oriented nature of the simulation, we can consider specializations of these classes of events to identify other patterns, for example, all ground vs air movements, only strike mission movements, and so on.

It is not only important to determine if events occur with statistically significant frequency. We must also analyze their distribution over time. Many events compressed over a small time frame may indicate important activity, whereas events that occur with constant frequency or periodicity may be more "common" and hence less significant. Figures 4 and 5, for example,

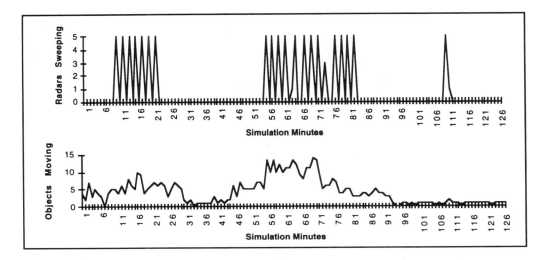

Fig. 4. Radar sweep and movement frequency over 129 min of simulation time.

plot frequencies of several different kinds of events from a typical run of our simulation. While some events occur at a steady state of frequency, others occur intermittently. If we assume frequent or commonplace events are less interesting, these histograms become a first indicator of what might be interesting or not in a domain. For example in our battle simulator, long-range radar are frequently sweeping, Surface to Air Missile (SAM) sites are always repositioning themselves, and aircraft are always flying point-based ingress/egress routes and so these events, independent of context, are deemed uninteresting and are not reported (see Fig. 4). In contrast, missile firings and hits are less frequent, thus key events (see Fig. 5). Finally, in domains in which histories can be captured [e.g. previous runs of simulations, previous period financial transactions), we can capture average event occurrences over time and use these to identify variations from the norm. This could include matching event histories with probability dist:ibution functions (e.g. normal, poisson, exponential) which could then be used to detect variations. We also can correlate frequencies of various event classes with one another, detecting potential causal or temporal relations when we are unable to introspect the underlying simulation or events. For example, we might detect that aircraft always produce mission reports after they return. Note that Fig. 4 suggests as correlation between movement and radar activity, an indicator of a possible causal relation. Indeed, in the underlying simulation, aircraft

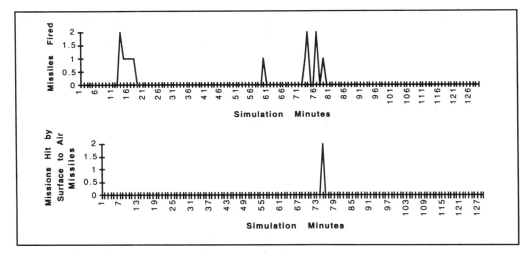

Fig. 5. Missile fire and hit frequencies over 129 min of simulation time.

movements stimulate radar sweeping. This type of analysis is useful if the application system does not represent or provide access to underlying relationships. Finally, in addition to considering different classes of events, we can analyze events with particular agents, characteristics, and so on, to identify patterns.

In addition to selecting information, it may need to be condensed (see Table 1). *Abstraction*, takes a series of events and replaces them with a single event. Lehnert's (1981) "plot units" are a general case of this. A domain specific example, in our battle simulation, is that a number of movement events followed by missiles firing then an aborted mission event can be abstracted into a foiled attack event. That is, a number of subevents can be described by an overarching event. This abstraction can be accomplished either by using pattern-matching techniques or plan-recognition. While potentially very powerful, there can be significant additional cost to build the abstraction machinery to support this, complicated by the need to validate that more general events are meaningful to the addressee. Moreover, leaving out information reduces detail, potentially increasing vagueness and ambiguity. The trick is to discover the "right" level of abstraction for the user(s).

A related condensation technique, *aggregation*, identifies similar events that can be unified into a single description. For example, two events that share a semantic agent, patient, instrument and so on, can be expressed in a single utterance. For example, if two missions are fired upon at the same time our battle report generator simply states "Site-A and Site-D *simultaneously* fired a missile at offensive counter air mission 102" using a temporal adverbial to relate the events. This technique both reduces the amount of space and time required to report the two events and increases the local cohesion of the text.

While the previously mentioned techniques focus on constraining and/or compressing the amount of information to be presented (by selection or condensation), there are also presentational techniques which can help shorten the length of time or space required to express information. First, we can exploit the context set by previous utterances in a dialogue. In our report generator we use the notions of temporal, spatial, and topical focus (Maybury, 1991b) so that after a context is originally set, subsequent references are related to these. For example, we use linguistic constructs such as tense and aspect and temporal adverbs (e.g. "and then", "three minutes later") to convey temporal relations between events without providing exact details of event times which nonetheless can be inferred by the user from context. Similarly, spatial adverbials [e.g. "four miles west (from here)"] eliminate detailed spatial description. Finally, if an event has already occurred and been reported, by using the adverbial "again" (as an anaphoric event reference) we reduce the amount of detail expressed about the event, shortening the resulting presentation.

In contrast to text-only summaries, selecting a particular medium (e.g. text vs graphics) in which to realize information can reduce the amount of time (possibly also space) required to present a given set of content. For example, spatial information (e.g. locations, routes, movements) can be more rapidly displayed and perceived graphically than textually (Bieger & Glock, 1986). Thus, while not summarizing the content, this can achieve the effect of reducing the time for (user) perception and possibly also enhance comprehension. The use of alternative media to present information (e.g. tabular comparisons vs textual comparisons) requires further investigation, particularly with respect to different summarization purposes and the speed and accuracy of performing different cognitive tasks. For example, tables are prefered for looking up information about exact values of event attributes whereas a scatter plot is more effective for performing trend analysis over time (as in Figs 4 and 5).

Finally, a very intriguing summarization technique is to utilize the rhetorical or intentional structure of the presentation to select what to include or exclude. This can be contrasted with *analysis* of source structure, as in Sparck Jones (1993) and Ono *et al.*, (1994). Assume an event has been determined to be significantly important to warrant description in the resulting summary. We could begin describing the event with a term definition, in particular, the identification of the superclass and differentia or distinguishing characteristics of the entity. Only then, space and time providing, would specifics about the components or different classes of the event be detailed. Similarly, in narrative, elaboration of background and/or setting often proceeds the communication of a sequence of events. By identifying the key rhetorical elements

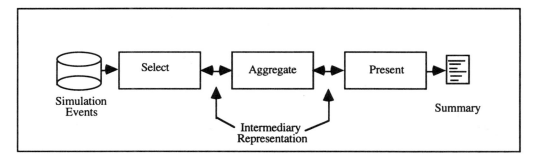

Fig. 6. SumGen: a summary generator.

[the "nucleus" in Rhetorical Structure Theory terms (Mann & Thompson, 1987)] and the larger rhetorical and intentional strategies, we might begin to identify domain independent rhetorical and intentional techniques for summarization. Eliding background material or supporting details which the addressee cannot infer, of course, runs the risk of loss of coherence in the resulting summary.

We have discussed multiple techniques for selecting, condensing, and presenting information in support of automated summarization of events. Each approach has its strengths and weaknesses and the choice among these is application dependent. Moreover, our limited experience suggests that a mix of techniques (e.g. performing some statistical analysis of event occurrence coupled with some domain specific knowledge of importance) produces better results than using individual techniques in isolation. We next describe a summary generation prototype that employs several of these techniques, and addresses the crucial event selection step already assumed performed in the simple joint venture summarizer described earlier.

3. SumGen: A SUMMARY GENERATOR

The above observations result in part from our experiments summarizing events from an object-oriented battle simulation (Anken, 1988). Our summary generator, SumGen, is part of a larger text planning system, TEXPLAN (Maybury, 1991a), which has been ported to several application systems. In the battle simulation application, as Fig. 6 illustrates, the generator takes as input time stamped event messages from the simulator which it then selects, aggregates, and presents as a battle summary. The simulation run is initiated by a battle planning system which, in the example we will describe, has planned an air strike attack ($\#\langle$air-strike-10$\rangle$).

Depending upon the nature of the simulation run and how frequently event occurrences are sampled, each run results in several hundred to over seven thousand messages passed between simulation objects. Because of this, we set a sampling threshold based upon empirical tests, ranging from sampling events every clock second to sampling them every 60 clock seconds. Figure 7 illustrates a set of simulation events in their original message form, including a time-stamp, message, and sender. For example, the first event can be glossed as "At time 2774438460, the 50th Tactical Fighter Wing Operations Center asked mission OCA100 to begin execution".

Unfortunately, sampling events every 60 clock seconds is still too large to present as a summary or even as a full report. It therefore must be pruned by selecting only the most important events. First, the messages are parsed into a semantic network of events, each event containing attribute slots such as the type of event, its time and place of occurrence as well as role slots indicating the agent, recipient, instrument, and so on of the event. The *agents* of the resulting events are missions (e.g. strike, refueling), organizations (e.g. refueling wing) or attacking forces (e.g. MOBILE-SAM-2).

Event selection from the event network is guided by an *importance metric* which measures the significance of an event relative to other events in the simulation. Importance is a function

```
(2774438460 (ASK OCA100 BEGIN MISSION EXECUTION) WOC-50-TACTICAL-FIGHTER-WING-)
(2774438460 (ASK 50-TACTICAL-FIGHTER-WING- DISPENSE 4 F-16 AIRCRAFT) OCA100)
(2774439140 (ASK MOBILE-SAM2 FIRE A MISSILE AT OCA100) CLOCK)
(2774439140 (ASK MOBILE-SAM1 FIRE A MISSILE AT OCA100) CLOCK)
(2774439180 (ASK RFL100 BEGIN MISSION EXECUTION) WOC-1ST-REFUELING-WING)
(2774439180 (ASK 1ST-REFUELING-WING DISPENSE 1 KC-135 AIRCRAFT) RFL100)
(2774439199 (ASK OCA100 ABORT MISSION) EINSTEIN)
(2774439200 (ASK MOBILE-SAM2 FIRE A MISSILE AT OCA100) CLOCK)
(2774439320 (ASK MOBILE-SAM2 FIRE A MISSILE AT OCA100) CLOCK)
(2774439963 (ASK OCA100 END MISSION) OCA100)
(2774439963 (ASK 50-TACTICAL-FIGHTER-WING- RETURN F-16 AIRCRAFT NIL AND NIL) OCA100)
(2774439963 (ASK OCA100 GENERATE POST-MISSION REPORT) OCA100)
(2774440194 (ASK RFL100 START ORBIT) RFL100)
(2774441100 (ASK SSM100 BEGIN MISSION EXECUTION) WOC-52-TACTICAL-FIGHTER-WING)
(2774441100 (ASK 52-TACTICAL-FIGHTER-WING DISPENSE 2 F-4J AIRCRAFT) SSM100)
(2774441700 (ASK OCA101 BEGIN MISSION EXECUTION) WOC-52-TACTICAL-FIGHTER-WING)
(2774441700 (ASK 52-TACTICAL-FIGHTER-WING DISPENSE 4 F-16 AIRCRAFT) OCA101)
(2774441880 (ASK SSM100 ABORT MISSION) SSM100)
(2774441900 (ASK HAINA-B FIRE A MISSILE AT SSM100) CLOCK)
(2774442600 (ASK RFL100 END ORBIT) RFL100)
(2774442680 (ASK ALLSTEDT-C FIRE A MISSILE AT OCA101) CLOCK)
(2774442686 (ASK SSM100 END MISSION) SSM100)
(2774442686 (ASK 52-TACTICAL-FIGHTER-WING RETURN F-4J AIRCRAFT NIL AND NIL) SSM100)
(2774442686 (ASK SSM100 GENERATE POST-MISSION REPORT) SSM100)
(2774442740 (ASK ALLSTEDT-C FIRE A MISSILE AT OCA101) CLOCK)
(2774442740 (ASK ALLSTEDT-B FIRE A MISSILE AT OCA101) CLOCK)
(2774442799 (ASK OCA101 ABORT MISSION) EINSTEIN)
(2774442920 (ASK ALLSTEDT-B FIRE A MISSILE AT OCA101) CLOCK)
(2774442920 (ASK ALLSTEDT-C FIRE A MISSILE AT OCA101) CLOCK)
(2774443040 (ASK ERFURT-A FIRE A MISSILE AT OCA101) CLOCK)
(2774443160 (ASK HAINA-B FIRE A MISSILE AT OCA101) CLOCK)
(2774443220 (ASK HAINA-B FIRE A MISSILE AT OCA101) CLOCK)
(2774443924 (ASK OCA101 END MISSION) OCA101)
(2774443924 (ASK 52-TACTICAL-FIGHTER-WING RETURN F-16 AIRCRAFT NIL AND NIL) OCA101)
(2774443924 (ASK OCA101 GENERATE POST-MISSION REPORT) OCA101)
(2774446036 (ASK RFL100 END MISSION) RFL100)
(2774446036 (ASK 1ST-REFUELING-WING RETURN KC-135 AIRCRAFT NIL) RFL100)
(2774446036 (ASK RFL100 GENERATE POST-MISSION REPORT) RFL100)
```

Fig. 7. Battle event messages (time, message, sender).

of:

(1) the frequency of occurrence of simulated events in the event/state network
(2) the kind and amount of links or relations associated with an event or state in the event network
(3) domain specific knowledge of importance

The first measure reflects the notion, introduced in the previous section, that frequent or commonplace events are potentially less interesting. Perhaps the simplest metric measures, for each event E, the frequency of E with respect to all other event occurrences:

$$\text{Relative frequency of } E = \frac{\text{Number of occurrences of event } E}{\text{Total number of event occurrences}}.$$

Thus, the higher the ratio the more routine, hence less significant, the event. This gets more complicated when addressing the issue of what constitutes an equivalent event (e.g. exact vs partial matches). Maybury (1995) details a similarity metric used to measure partial object equality.

The second measure, also previously discussed, is a link analysis heuristic, concerning issues such as does the event achieve a main goal of a key agent in the simulation, and does it motivate, enable, or cause a number of events or states to occur (i.e. how many and what type of links and/ or relations to other events does it have in the event network). One of the simplest measures of links or relations between events is to count their frequency of occurrence, possibly weighting these according to the type of link or relation and using this as another mechanism for rank ordering domain events in terms of implied significance. If we let Significance(R) indicate the *a priori* relative significance of relation R (e.g. cause vs enable) on a scale of 0–1, and let EVENTS and RELATIONS, respectively, be the set of all events and relations in the domain (assuming for simplicity two argument relations), then a relative frequency of relations for event E, weighted by relation type, is computed by counting a weighted average of the number of relations involving event E, divided by the weighted average of all event relations that occur:

$$\text{Relative relation frequency for } E = \frac{\text{Weighted average \# of relations involving } E}{\text{Weighted average \# of relations for all events}}$$

where the weighted average number of relations involving event E is:

$$\sum_{R \in \text{RELATIONS}} \sum_{EV \in \text{EVENTS}} \text{Significance}(R) * R(E, EV).$$

That is, for all relations involving event E, multiply the significance of that relation, Significance(R), with the total number of times in which E occurs in that relation. When this is divided by a similar measure for all domain events, this will yield a relative ranking of events in terms of frequency of relations weighted by their importance. Note we can similarly measure the frequency of event occurance in the second argument of a relation, i.e. $R(EV, E)$ where, for example, event E is caused by (as opposed to causes) event EV.

For events that occur equally frequently and have similar link/relation distributions, a domain specific order of importance is used (offensive air attack > SAM suppression > refueling > transportation; where > indicates greater importance). If necessary, we can compute a weighted average of the results of these measures. Having determined the relative importance of events, a threshold can be applied to elide events or even classes of events that do not exceed a certain level of importance.

After determining which events will remain in the summary, SumGen then condenses the events using aggregation. Equivalent events are aggregated (e.g. if three missiles are fired from the same agent at the same target at the same time). Similar events that occur simultaneously but have different semantic agents are also aggregated (e.g. if two missiles are fired from different missile sites at the same target at the same time). The original events are deleted from the representation and an aggregated event replaces them. Finally, all events are grouped by the mission they relate to (e.g. air strike, refueling).

Following aggregation, the overall organization of the resulting narrative is planned using a communicative-act based text generator (Maybury, 1991a, 1992) that sequences the report first by topic (e.g. mission OCA100), then chronologically within topic, resulting in a multiparagraph summary report. The missions are ordered by the number of important events associated with them so that missions with the most amount of important events are described first, those with the least last. In equivalent cases, the domain specific preference order is used (i.e. air attack > SAM suppression > refueling > transportation; where > indicates precedence).

Figure 8 illustrates the resulting hierarchical report plan which consists of an overall communicative action of the system narrating to the user the event sequence in the last run of the simulation. This is accomplished by first introducing via description the air strike that initiated the simulation (by defining the type of air strike and its constituent missions) and second by chronologically narrating events (narrate-sequence) that occur grouped by particular missions. Each leaf node in the tree, a speech act (e.g. inform), will ultimately be realized as a (possibly multimedia) utterance in the resulting presentation. Figure 9 shows the final text that is generated from this communication plan: an introductory paragraph followed by chronological recounting of events associated with particular missions. Cohesion, i.e. local connectivity, is aided by linguistic devices such as temporal adverbials (e.g. "in the meantime", "three minutes later") and anaphoric expressions ("its ingress route"). At the same time, these devices provide a more compact expression by relying upon context for resolution, as mentioned previously.

While the summary in Fig. 9 is a succinct and coherent report of the several thousand events that occurred in the previous run of the simulation, it still may be too lengthy for some or all users. Because both the content and structure of the summary were automatically planned, we

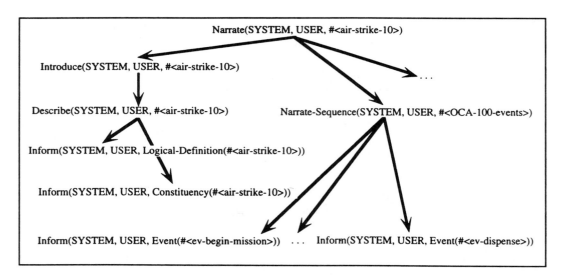

Fig. 8. Battle report communication plan.

can control either or both of these. For example, by encoding user preferences in the constraints
of the plan operators that produce the communication plan of Fig. 8, we can select particular
elements of the communication plan to convey to the user, such as the air strike description
realized as paragraph one in Fig. 9. Similarly, we can produce (paragraph length) summaries that
focus on a particular agent(s) in the simulation (e.g. transportation missions) by modulating the

```
Air-strike 10 was an attack against Alpha-Delta airfield in sector 32umv7035 on
Tuesday December 2, 1987.  Air-strike 10 included three Offensive Counter Air Missions
(OCA100, OCA101, and OCA102), one SAM Suppression Mission (SSM444), one Transportation
Mission (TRANS250), and one air refueling mission (RFL109).

Offensive Counter Air Mission 100 began mission execution at 8:20 Tuesday December 2,
1987.  902TFW-F-16c dispensed four aircraft for Offensive Counter Air Mission 100.
Eight minutes later Offensive Counter Air Mission 100 began flying its ingress route.
Three minutes later Allstedt-B and Allstedt-C simultaneously fired a missile at
Offensive Counter Air Mission 100.  And fifty-nine seconds later Offensive Counter Air
Mission 100 was ordered to abort its mission.  One second later Allstedt-C and
Allstedt-B again simultaneously fired a missile at Offensive Counter Air Mission 100.
Two minutes later Allstedt-B again fired a missile at Offensive Counter Air Mission
100.  Then one minute later Erfurt-A fired a missile at Offensive Counter Air Mission
100.  Then two minutes later Haina-B fired a missile at Offensive Counter Air Mission
100.  Seven minutes later Offensive Counter Air Mission 100 ended its mission.  It
generated its post-mission report.

In the meantime SAM Suppression Mission 444 began mission execution at 8:30 Tuesday
December 2, 1987.  126TFW-F-4g dispensed one aircraft for SAM Suppression Mission 444.
SAM Suppression Mission 444 began flying its ingress route.  Thirteen minutes later
Mobile-SAM1 fired a missile at SAM Suppression Mission 444.  Then fifty-nine seconds
later SAM Suppression Mission 444 was ordered to abort its mission.  And then one
second later Mobile-SAM2 fired a missile at SAM Suppression Mission 444.  One minute
later Mobile-SAM2 and Mobile-SAM1 simultaneously fired a missile at SAM Suppression
Mission 444.

In the meantime Offensive Counter Air Mission 101 began mission execution at 8:41
Tuesday December 2, 1987.  900TFW-F-4c dispensed four aircraft for Offensive Counter
Air Mission 101.  Then seven minutes later Offensive Counter Air Mission 101 began
flying its ingress route.  Then ten minutes later it bombed its target.  It began
flying its egress route.  Thirty-Six minutes later it ended its mission.  It generated
its post-mission report.

Meanwhile Transportation Mission 250 ...
```

Fig. 9. Battle report summary.

```
Air refueling mission 100 began mission execution at 8:46::40 Tuesday Decem
2, 1987.  513TAW-SAC-Rotational-KC-135 dispensed one aircraft for Air Refue
Mission 100.  Air Refueling Mission 100 began flying its ingress route.
Eighteen minutes later it started its refueling orbit.  Twenty-Six minutes
it ended its refueling orbit.  It began flying its egress route.
```

Fig. 10. User tailored battle report summary.

event selection criteria, thus producing a summary tailored to a stereotypical user (e.g. logistician). For example, Fig. 10 shows a summary of the same simulated battle, however, the user topic of interest is indicated as only refueling missions. In this case all other missions are elided by the selection mechanism—the aggregation and presentation mechanisms remain unchanged—resulting in the final refueling summary shown in Fig. 10.

4. EVALUATION

In order to attempt to validate the benefits but also uncover the limitations of the SumGen (as applied to battle summarization) and joint venture summarizer, we designed an experimental study involving 22 subjects. Participants were asked to read long and summarized versions of the LACE battle simulation output and retrieve the names, participants, time and duration of all missions that appeared in the text. In addition, each subject was asked to extract information from original and summary versions of eleven randomly selected joint venture documents from a pool of 748 *Wall Street Journal*, Mead, and Promt documents. Specifically, subjects were asked to extract the type, partners and status of all joint ventures mentioned in the text. It is important to note that the evaluation of SumGen reults are more important than those of the joint venture summarizer as the former included both event selection and condensation whereas the latter assumed that an information extraction component had already selected relevant joint venture events, significantly simplifying the summarization task.

For each of the sources, original (long) and summary (short) texts, Fig. 11 reports the average results for time to complete the extraction task (measured in seconds), and the precision and

	LACE	Mead	WSJ	Promt	Average
Average Time for Task (seconds)					
Original Documents	362.5	392.8	323.3	124.3	300.7
Summary Documents	153.7	126.3	125.5	78.6	121.0
Average Document Length (words)					
Original Documents	437.0	606.3	581.0	343.3	491.9
Summary Documents	127.0	45.3	54.0	30.8	64.3
Average Sentence Length (words)					
Original Documents	12	29	23	24	21.9
Summary Documents	11	24	17	14	16.6
Average Precision (% correct)					
Original Documents	1.00	1.00	0.91	1.00	0.98
Summary Documents	0.99	1.00	0.99	1.00	0.99
Average Recall (% retrieved)					
Original Documents	1.00	0.92	0.81	1.00	0.93
Summary Documents	0.95	0.99	0.98	0.96	0.97

Fig. 11. Original vs summary documents by source. In the LACE domain, original documents refer to documents generated after event selection and condensation. Summary documents refer to user tailored summaries as exemplified in Fig. 10. Prior to the development of SumGen, one sentence was generated for each simulation event, resulting in report lengths of up to 7000 sentences and more. In other sources, the original documents refer to human generated sources whereas the summary documents are generated from MUC-5 joint venture templates.

	LACE	Mead	WSJ	Promt	Average
Time Reduction	57.6%	67.8%	61.2%	36.8%	55.8%
Document Length Reduction	70.9%	92.5%	90.7%	91.0%	86.3%
Sentence Length Reduction	14.6%	15.9%	23.8%	40.8%	23.8%

Fig. 12. Percentage reductions from original to summary texts.

recall performance of subjects. Figure 11 also reports average document length (number of words) and average sentence length (number of words per sentence) in the evaluated collections, the latter giving a limited indication of document complexity. The percentage based comparison shown in Fig. 12 summarizes our overall findings comparing original and summarized texts showing the reduction in processing time. document length, and sentence length. The length reductions for LACE approximate the 70–76% reduction reported by Ono *et al.* (1994) for scientific and technical texts but are surpassed by the joint venture texts by 20%. It should be noted, however, that Ono *et al.*'s approach determines key sentences based on rhetorical-based analysis of source text and has neither the advantage of a detailed knowledge base of information to be summarized (their technique is claimed to be dependent only upon rhetorical relations in the source text) nor a specific and narrow query with which to further limit the summary, both of which provide significant leverage for reduction in our domains.

One observation from the data is that, as might be expected, there is a high correlation between time to complete an information extraction task and the length of the document, both in original documents (0.79 where 1.0 indicates full correlation and −1.0 opposite correlation) and summary documents (0.83). Figure 13 depicts this relationship. Also, the original texts tend to have slightly longer sentences than the summaries (see Fig. 14). The time required to process short, summary texts was negatively correlated with precision (−0.57) and recall (−0.47) as was the length of text (-0.49 and −0.57 correlation with precision and recall, respectively), indicating the more time spent on short texts and the longer texts are, the lower the accuracy for information extraction. While average recall was improved in the summary texts over the original documents by 4.3% (0.97 vs 0.93), the average precision was nearly equivalent (0.99 vs 0.98). A small amount of precision and recall errors in handling the summary documents were a result of incomplete database templates and/or information left out during the selection process, rather than human failure during the extraction task. Finally, the average sentence length was negatively correlated with time (−0.90), i.e. readers proportionally spent less time on longer sentences and more on shorter ones [contrast Fig. 13 with Fig. 14(a)], which in part may account for slightly better average precision and recall performance with shorter documents.

The precision and recall results depicted in Fig. 14 can be contrasted with those reported by Will (1993), who evaluated human and machine performance on information extraction tasks using a corpus of 120 English microelectronics texts and found domain expert humans able to

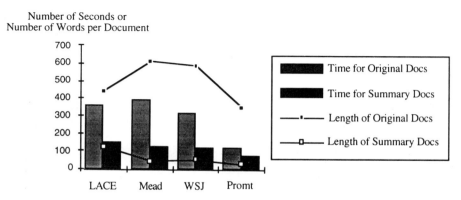

Fig. 13. Correlation of average time for task performance and length of documents.

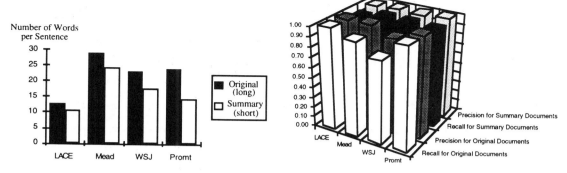

Fig. 14. (a) Sentence lengths. (b) Precision/recall for original and summaries.

perform on average 79% in recall and 82% in precision, exceeding computer based information extraction precision and recall but not speed. While our performance results appear on the surface to improve upon these, there are important differences in our domains (microelectronics vs joint ventures and battle simulation), human subjects (Will's experts vs our novices), and task (Will's task involved much more detailed information extraction and considered only human generated source, not also machine generated summaries). Evaluation of user's subjective assessment of the quality of the summaries could be performed in a future study, however, we believe the task speed and accuracy metrics (i.e. precision and recall) remain key indicators of system utility.

While the summarization techniques we have investigated work well in both the mission simulation and joint venture domains, we have not validated their broad applicability across many domains nor tested the value of varying summary length, apart from tailoring output to stereotypical user classes for the LACE simulator. Nonetheless, the approach taken in SumGen is primarily domain independent and should be feasible in many other event-oriented applications such as weather event summarization, financial event summarization, computer network and/or road traffic summaries.

5. FUTURE RESEARCH

Evaluation of summaries remains an important research topic, and, among other things, this evaluation needs be tied to the purpose of the summarization. One obvious purpose is to convey less information—selecting only the most significant information. As our LACE application demonstrates, this could result in a more indicative summary (e.g. the orginal LACE report describing the overall simulation activities) versus an informative summary (e.g. the user tailored summaries which target specific information). In both cases, this may entail trading off detail for conciseness, risking loss of coherence. Doing this effectively may also require reasoning about the inferability of information from compact expression by the addressee, requiring detailed user modeling. Another purpose of a summary may be to convey a given amount of information in less space (i.e. in fewer words or pictures) or in a shorter time period. These latter purposes might be achieved by condensation or presentation techniques such as those discussed above. What makes a good summary for who and for what purpose remains an important issue.

While we have considered tailoring event selection to particular stereotypical users, several questions remain, such as do different classes of users or characteristics of users require different kinds of summaries, in content or form? Or do different interaction needs (e.g. limited space, time, or attention) require distinct summaries? Another important area for future work is the use of rhetorical and linguistic techniques for analysis and generation to support summarization. A combination of techniques appears promising for analysis (Sparck Jones, 1993)—we might expect the same to be true for generation.

In summary, this paper outlines several techniques for summarization and aims to stimulate readers to consider experiments combining techniques as we have done. Both analysis of human produced summaries and evaluation of machine generated summaries should help identify the direction for further research to help refine the initial taxonomy of summarization techniques we have outlined and illustrated herein.

Acknowledgements—I am indebted to Judy Sider, Sam Bayer, David Day, Angel Acensio, and Nick Pioch for developing and extending the report generator and presentation planning system in which several of the above ideas were explored. This work also benefited from interaction with participants at the Dagstuhl Summarization workshop, in particular the processing view characterized in Fig. 1. I thank the reviewers and editors for their detailed comments. Finally, I am appreciative to the many individuals who generously volunteered to be subjects in the evaluation.

REFERENCES

Anken, C. S. (1989). LACE: Land Air Combat in Eric. Rome Air Development Center TR 89-219.

Bieger, G. R., & Glock, M. D. (1986). Comprehending spatial and contextual information in picture-text instructions. *The Journal of Experimental Education, 54*(4), 181–188.

Cremmins, E. (1993). Valuable and meaningful text summarization in thoughts, words, and deeds. In B. Endres-Niggemeyer, J. Hobbs, & K. Sparck Jones (Eds), *Preprints of Summarizing Text for Intelligent Communication. Dagstuhl Seminar Report 79* (p. 20), Schloss Dagstuhl, Germany.

Dalianis, H., & Hovy, E. (1993). Aggregation in natural language generation. In *Proceedings of the Fourth European Workshop on Natural Language Generation* (pp. 67–78), Pisa, Italy.

DeJong, G. F. (1979) Skimming stories in real time: An experiment in integrated understanding. Research Report #158, Yale University, New Haven, Conn.

Endres-Niggemeyer, B. (1993). A naturalistic models of abstracting. In B. Endres-Niggemeyer, J. Hobbs, & K. Sparck Jones (Eds), *Preprints of Summarizing Text for Intelligent Communication. Dagstuhl Seminar Report 79* (pp. 21–25), Schloss Dagstuhl, Germany.

Fum, D., Guida, G., & Tasso, C. (1985). Evaluating importance: A step towards text summarization. *Proceedings of the 9th International Joint Conference on Artificial Intelligence* (pp. 840–844), Los Angeles, Calif.

Fum, D., Guida, G., & Tasso, C. (1986). Tailoring importance evaluation to reader's goals: A contribution to descriptive text summarization. In *Proceedings of the 11th International Conference on Computational Linguistics (COLING-86)* (pp. 256–259), University of Bonn, Germany.

Friedrich, H. F. (1993). Training of reductive text learning strategies. In B. Endres-Niggemeyer, J. Hobbs, & K. Sparck Jones (Eds), *Preprints of Summarizing Text for Intelligent Communication. Dagstuhl Seminar Report 79* (pp. 28–31), Schloss Dagstuhl, Germany.

Goldman, N. M. (1975). Conceptual generation. In R. C. Schank (Ed.), *Conceptual Information Processing.* Amsterdam: North-Holland.

Kittredge, R., Polguère, & Goldberg, E. (1986). Synthesizing weather forecasts from formatted data. In *Proceedings of the 11th International Conference on Computational Linguistics (COLING-86)* (pp. 563–565), University of Bonn, Germany.

Kukich, K. (1983). Design of a knowledge-based report generator. In *Proceedings of the 21st Meeting of the Association for Computational Linguistics* (pp. 145–150), Cambridge, Mass.

Li, P., Evens, M. & Hier, D. (1986). Generating medical case reports with the linguistic string parser. *Proceedings of the Fifth National Conference on Artificial Intelligence (AAAI-86)* (pp. 1069–1073), Philadeliphia, PA.

Lehnert, W. G. (1981). Plot units and narrative summarization. *Cognitive Science, 4,* 293–331.

Luhn, H. P. (1958). The automatic creation of literature abstracts. *IBM Journal, April,* 159–165.

Mann, W. C., & Thompson, S. A. (1987). Rhetorical structure theory: Description and construction of text structures. In G. Kempen (Ed.), *Natural Language Generation* (pp. 85–95). Dordrecht: Martinus Nijhoff.

Maybury, M. T. (1991a). *Planning multisentential English text using communicative acts.* Ph.D. dissertation, University of Cambridge, England. Available as Rome Air Development Center TR 90-411, In-House Report (1990) and as a Cambridge University Computer Laboratory TR-239 (1991).

Maybury, M. T. (1991b). Topical temporal and spatial constraints on linguistic realization. *Computational Intelligence, 7*(4), 266–275.

Maybury, M. T. (1992). Communicative acts for explanation generation. *International Journal for Man–Machine Studies, 37*(2), 135–172.

Maybury, M. T. (1995). Using similarity metrics to determine content for explanation generation. *Expert Systems with Applications, 8*(4), 513–525.

McKeown, K. (1985). *Text generation.* Cambridge: Cambridge University Press.

McKeown, K. (1993). Generating the complex sentences of summaries using syntactic and lexical constraints: Two applications. In B. Endres-Niggemeyer, J. Hobbs, & K. Sparck Jones (Eds), *Preprints of Summarizing Text for Intelligent Communication*, Dagstuhl Seminar Report 79, Schloss Dagstuhl, Germany.

Meehan, J. R. (1976). *The Metanovel: Writing stories by computer.* Ph.D. dissertation, Yale University TR 74, New Haven, Conn.

Ono, K., Sumita, K., & Miike, S. (1994). Abstract generation based on rhetorical structure extraction. In *Proceedings of 15th International Conference on Computational Linguistics (COLING '94)* (pp. 344–348), Kyoto, Japan.

Paice, C. D. (1981). The automatic generation of literature abstracts: An approach based on the identification of self-indicating phrases. In R. N. Oddy, S. E. Robertson, C. J. van Rijsbergen, & P. W. Williams (Eds), *Information Retrieval Research* (pp. 172–191). London: Butterworths.

Paris, C. L. (1988). Tailoring object descriptions to a user's level of expertise. Computational Linguistics, 14(3), 64–78.

Polanyi, L. (1993). Linguistic dimensions of text summarization. In B. Endres-Niggemeyer, J. Hobbs, & K. Sparck Jones (Eds), *Preprints of Summarizing Text for Intelligent Communication*, Dagstuhl Seminar Report 79 (pp. 64–70) Schloss Dagstuhl, Germany. [Presentation given described SUMMA.]

Rau, L., Brandow, R., & Mitze, K. (1993). Domain-independent summarization of news. In B. Endres-Niggemeyer, J. Hobbs, & K. Sparck Jones (Eds), *Preprint of Summarizing Text for Intelligent Communication*, Dagstuhl Seminar Report 79 (pp. 71–75), Schloss Dagstuhl, Germany.

Reimer, U. & Hahn, U. (1988) Text condensation as knowledge base abstraction. In *Proceedings of the Fourth Annual Conference on Artificial Intelligence Applications* (pp. 338–344), San Diego, Calif. New York: IEEE.

Sparck Jones, K. (1993). What might be in a summary? In G. Knorz, J. Krause, & C. Womser-Hacker (Eds), *Proceedings from Information Retrieval 93: Von der modellierung zur Anwendung* Universitätsverlag Konstanz (pp. 9–26).

Tait, J. (1982). Automatic summarising of English texts. Computer Laboratory TR 47, Cambridge University.

Will, C. (1993). Comparing human and machine performance for natural language information extraction: Results for English microelectronics from the MUC-5 evaluation. In *Proceedings of the Fifth Message Understanding Conference (MUC5)* (pp. 53–67).

Section 5

Evaluation Methods

The problem of evaluating text summarization is a very deep one, and serious questions remain concerning the appropriate methods and types of evaluation. There are a variety of possible bases for comparison of summarization system performance, e.g., summary to source, system to human-generated summary, system to system. In general, methods for evaluating text summarization approaches can be broadly classified into two categories. The first is an *extrinsic* evaluation, in which the quality of a summary is judged based on how it affects the completion of some other task. The tasks have included humans determining the relevance of documents to topics (e.g., Jing et al. 1998; Tombros et al. 1998; Mani and Bloedorn, Section 6) as well as humans answering questions based on reading the summaries (e.g., Maybury Section 4, Merlino and Maybury Section 6).

The second category is an *intrinsic* evaluation, where humans judge the quality of the summarization directly based on analysis of the summary. This can involve user judgments of fluency of the summary (Minel et al. 1997), coverage of stipulated "key/essential ideas" (Paice and Jones 1993), or similarity to an "ideal" summary (e.g., Edmundson, Section 1, see also Kupiec et al. Section 2). Measures of fluency can address language complexity (e.g., word and sentence length), presence of dangling anaphors, preservation of structured environments like lists or tables, grammatical and stylistic features, etc. Many of these fluency measures can be detected by automatic means. Judging coverage of key ideas is more subjective, even if humans agree in advance as to what constitutes the set of key ideas.

The problem with matching a system summary against an ideal summary is that the ideal summary is hard to establish. The human summary may be supplied by the author of the article, by a judge asked to construct an abstract, or by a judge asked to extract sentences. There can be a large number of generic and user-focused abstracts that could summarize a given document, just as there can be many ways of describing something. The lack of uniqueness of the ideal abstract extends to extracts as well, as is borne out by the paper by Rath et al. in this section.

In addition, when a judge is required to extract sentences from a full-source text to construct an ideal summary, which sentences become part of the summary depends in part on what instructions are given to the judge. She may be told to extract every sentence worthy of inclusion in a summary, or to extract just the best 10% or 20% of the sentences. Further, her judgment may not be required to be a boolean one; she might be required to rate sentences in terms of "most important," "moderately important," or "unimportant," as Marcu describes in his paper in Section 5. In addition, she may be required to rank either the extracted sentences or all of the sentences. Finally, she may be required to extract clauses or paragraphs instead of sentences.

As might be expected, these different compression instructions can make a considerable difference in what gets extracted. For example, consider the case where the most salient concept A in a document is expressed by two sentences $s1$ and $s2$, with $s1$ or $s2$ alone failing to express A. Assume there's a next-to-most salient concept B in that document, which is expressed by a single sentence $s3$. Now, a one-sentence summary of the document will extract $s3$, while a two-sentence summary will extract $s1$ and $s2$. In this example, sentences extracted at the lower compression do not include sentences extracted at the higher compression.

A further blow to the idea of an ideal summary is that there is evidence of low agreement among humans as to which sentences are good summary sentences. The paper by Salton et al. in Section 6 indicates that subjects showed only 46% overlap in their extracts when asked to extract at least 5 paragraphs from each of 50 articles from an encyclopedia. The results obtained by Rath et al. in this section are similar in spirit. However, such results are not fatal to the possibility of constructing an ideal summary. For one thing, there have been several recent studies of sentence extraction that indicate that while judges may not agree on all of the sentences to be included in a summary, they may agree somewhat better on the most important sentences to include, e.g., Marcu's paper in Section 3, which deals with texts from *Scientific American*, and Jing et al. (1998) on news text. Also, it is possible to merge information from multiple summaries constructed by humans (e.g., choosing sentences judged unanimously to be worthy of inclusion in a summary, or judged summary-worthy by a majority of subjects).

The papers included in this section have evaluation as a primary focus, and reflect a wide spectrum of approaches. The first paper, by Rath et al., is a classic paper that shows that different abstractors may produce very different summaries, and that an abstractor given the same document after eight weeks may produce a substantially different summary. In the first section, the authors avail of five different word frequency- and distribution-based sentence selection programs such as those described in Luhn's article in Section 1. They contrast the performance of these algorithms with one another and with sentence selection by humans. In these experiments, 6 subjects were asked to pick the 20 most representative sentences from 10 *Scientific American* articles. They found there was considerably more variability among the human subjects than among the machine summaries and very little agreement between human and machine selections. In particular, whereas the six subjects agreed upon an average of only 1.6 sentences per article out of the 20 sentences (i.e., only 8% of the data was unanimously agreed upon), this rose to 6.4 sentences agreed upon by a majority of 5 out of 6 subjects (i.e., 32% of the data was agreed upon by this majority). In contrast, the 5 machine methods agreed upon an average of 9.2 sentences out of the first 20; 17 out of 20 were agreed upon by 4 out of 5 machine methods. There was very little agreement between sentences selected by humans and machines. The authors point to the need for future studies that factor out sources of variability caused by, e.g., multiple topics and less well-edited sources.

In the second part of the article, Resnick tested the reliability of 5 students in extracting 20 of the most representative sentences from six randomly ordered Scientific American articles. Eight weeks later the test was repeated but students were also asked to mark those sentences they had selected previously. The subjects exhibited low reliability, selecting the same sentences only 55% of the time on average and correctly identifying those they had selected previously only 64% of the time. Both human and machine selections differ significantly from randomness. They conclude that the lack of inter- and intra-subject reliability suggests there may be many equally representative sets of sentences for any given article.

The next paper by Brandow, Mitze, and Rau describes the design and evaluation of the ANES system, which was developed at General Electric in the early 1990's. The approach uses term and sentence weighting based on *tf.idf*, with words below a particular weight threshold being excluded. To address the dangling anaphor problem, sentences that begin with certain anaphors are excluded. For continuity, sentences without signature words lying between two sentences containing signature words are selected; also, the first (or second) sentence of a paragraph is added to the summary if the second (or third) sentence of a paragraph contains signature words.

ANES was evaluated in an intrinsic evaluation. Judges were asked to assess how "acceptable" short extracts of new stories were, given the full source of the article. This acceptability judgment was made based on fluency and coverage measures of the sort described above. The extracts were 50-, 150-, and 250-words long. ANES was deemed acceptable 68% to 78% of the time (the percentages vary for different lengths of abstracts). In comparison against Searchable Lead, a leading-text system from Mead Data Central (which just extracts the initial part of the text), the latter was deemed acceptable 87% to 96% of the time, outperforming ANES. The few cases where leading-text abstracts were unacceptable could be attributed to anecdotal, human-interest style lead-ins, documents that contained multiple news stories, and stories

with unusual structural/stylistic features, including lists, tables, questions and answers, etc.

The preference for leading text might serve as a cautionary tale for sentence extraction methods used on newswire texts. Indeed, leading text tends to be more coherent, since there are no out-of-context extracts. However, while certain trends are obvious from Brandow et al's data, it should be borne in mind that this study does not report any statistical analysis of the results. Further, it is unclear whether leading text serves a useful function in other genres, in longer summaries, or in user-focused summaries of documents where the query-relevant information isn't at the beginning.

The above two papers were intrinsic evaluations carried out with a small number of subjects. In contrast, the remaining two papers deal with extrinsic evaluations.

The paper by Morris et al. reports on an extrinsic evaluation in a task of question-answering. The authors picked four Graduate Management Admission Test (GMAT) reading comprehension exercises. The exercises were multiple-choice, with a single answer to be selected from answers shown alongside each question. There were eight questions for each exam, with five possible answers shown for each question. The authors measured how many of the answers the subjects got correct under different conditions, including a full-text condition (where the subjects were shown the original passages), an extract condition (where the subjects were shown automatically generated generic extracts from the passages), an abstract condition (where the subjects were shown a generic human abstract of about 25% compression created by a professional abstractor instructed to create informative abstracts), and a control no-text condition (where the subjects had to pick the correct answer just from seeing the questions, without seeing the passages themselves). The extract condition included as a baseline a random 25% sentence selection without replacement, as well as 20% and 30% extracts generated by a sentence-weighting algorithm based on Edmundson's (Section 1) method using presence of fixed phrases, title words, high-frequency "thematic" words, and sentence location in the paragraph. Unfortunately, a leading text baseline wasn't used.

The results show that the performance of the 20% and 30% extracts and the informative abstract were comparable to the full-text, with only the random and no-text condition being significantly below the full-text performance. This suggests that summaries can be very effective in certain tasks as substitutes for full-text.

The final paper by Firmin and Chrzanowski describes an initial "dry-run" of the TIPSTER evaluation of text summarization systems, conducted in 1997 (a formal evaluation with detailed statistical analyses was carried out in 1998 and will be published at the end of 1998; see Mani et al (1998)). The evaluation is especially notable because it is the first large-scale evaluation of text summarization systems conducted by someone other than a developer of those systems. The evaluation is an extrinsic task-based evaluation, measuring the impact of summarization on performance time and accuracy in assessing relevance. The experimental hypothesis is that use of summarization saves time in relevance assessment in certain tasks, without impacting accuracy.

In the first "adhoc" task, subjects are asked to judge whether a text (which could be a user-focused indicative summary or a full-text - the subject isn't told which) is relevant or irrelevant to a query. In the second "categorization" task, a text (which could be a "generic" indicative summary or a full-text) is judged as to whether it belongs in one of five mutually exclusive subject categories, or "none of the above." The accuracy of the subject in determining relevance of a document to a query or category is scored in terms of the "ground-truth" relevance judgments used in the TREC conferences (Harman and Voorhees 1996), which are standard evaluations of information retrieval systems conducted by the U.S. government. The texts were typically short (2,000-15,000 characters in length), and were all newswire texts. In each task, summaries were of two types: fixed-length (10% of source) and best-length (where there was no restriction on summary length). As a leading text baseline to compare against the first 10% of the document was used.

In addition to finding that summaries take less time in relevance assessment decision-making than full-text, the authors found that the 10% fixed-length user-focused and generic summaries were not significantly more accurate than the leading text baseline method. For user-focused summaries, they confirm the trend observed with intrinsic evaluations of generic summaries in Brandow, Mitze and Rau's paper, suggesting that the query-relevant material is often at the beginning of the article. Variable-length summaries, on the other hand, were always significantly faster than full-text; they were also not significantly different in accuracy from full-text, and significantly more accurate than the fixed-length summaries.

In conclusion, there are a number of fundamental problems that crop up in designing evaluations of text summarization systems, on which these papers provide insights:
- Creating tasks for extrinsic evaluations that adequately model real-world situations and information needs. It is often hard to mirror real tasks and at the same time construct controlled experiments. Ideally, these would be tasks that are onerous for humans (and which may or may not be easy for them), but which computers can perform very fast.
- Preparing instructions for human summarizers in intrinsic evaluations. For example, details such as

whether they are asked to construct a summary, to assign a score to each full-text sentence, or to merely select certain portions of the full-text, as well as the particular compression rate (ratio of summary length to source length) they are expected to target and whether they construct extracts or abstracts makes a great difference in terms of what gets included in a summary.
- Ensuring that the task is not biased towards a particular summarization technology (e.g., where extracts are likely to perform better than abstracts) or genre (e.g., including a variety of text genres beyond news and scientific text), or length of text (e.g., many evaluations are based on newswire texts, which are often already quite concise.)
- Designing a controlled experiment with enough data and subjects to provide statistically sound results. Often, the resources required for this can be prohibitive. Sometimes, it may be useful to prefer an assessment by experts to a controlled experiment.
- Arriving at adequate metrics of summarization accuracy or efficiency.

References

Harman, D., and Voorhees, E.M. 1996. *The Fifth Text Retrieval Conference (TREC-5)*, Technical Report, SP-500-238, National Institute of Standards and Technology, Gaithersburg, Maryland.

Jing, H., R., Barzilay, R., McKeown, K., and Elhadad, M. Summarization evaluation methods: Experiments and analysis. In *Working Notes of the AAAI Spring Symposium on Intelligent Text Summarization*, Spring 1998, 60-68. Menlo Park, Calif.: AAAI Press.

Mani, I., Firmin, T., House, D., Chrzanowski, M., Klein, G., Hirschman, L., Sundheim, B., and Obrst, L., "The TIPSTER Text Summarization Evaluation": Final Report, November 1998, http://www.tipster.org/.

Minel, J., Nugier, S., and Piat, G. How to appreciate the quality of automatic text summarization. In *Proceedings of the ACL/EACL'97 Workshop on Intelligent Scalable Text Summarization*, Madrid, July 1997, 25-30.

Paice, C., and Jones, P. 1993. The Identification of Important Concepts in Highly Structured Technical Papers. In *Proceedings of the Sixteenth Annual International ACM SIGIR Conference on Research and Development in Information Retrieval (ACM-SIGIR'93)*, 69-78.

Tombros, A., Sanderson, M., and Gray, P. Advantages of query biased summaries in information retrieval. In *Working Notes of the AAAI Spring Symposium on*

Intelligent Text Summarization, Spring 1998, 44-52. Menlo Park, Calif.: AAAI Press.

18
The Formation of Abstracts By the Selection of Sentences

Part I. Sentence Selection By Men and Machines[1]

G. J. RATH, A. RESNICK, and T. R. SAVAGE

International Business Machines Corporation
Yorktown Heights, New York

Auto-abstracting techniques based on high-frequency words show an extremely small variation among themselves in the selection of sentences to form abstracts. Human selection of sentences, although less variable than chance expectancy, is considerably more variable than the machine methods. There was very little agreement between the subjects and machine methods in their selection of representative sentences.

The basic method of automatically generating abstracts described by Luhn (2) and Savage (3), involved selecting a subset of representative sentences from a document by formulas based on word frequency and distribution. The comparison of which sentences humans would select from the same documents seemed to be an appropriate part of an experimental study of abstracting procedures. The purpose of this study was to determine the inter-subject differences, the inter-machine program differences, and the man-machine differences with respect to the selection of sentences.

• Method

Six subjects were given 10 *Scientific American* articles and were asked to pick the 20 most representative sentences from each. Once the subjects had picked the 20 sentences of the documents, they were told to rank those sentences in the following manner: Pick the single sentence which would best represent the article; rank as second that sentence which added to the first sentence is most representative of the article. Continue this procedure until all 20 sentences are ranked.

The 10 *Scientific American* articles which the subjects read were analyzed according to 5 auto-abstracting programs on the IBM 704, and the score for each sentence was prepared. The five machine methods differ only in the manner in which the individual sentences are evaluated. The basic statistical procedure is to select from each document all those words which occur more often than the mean frequency of occurrence for that document. These "high-frequency" words are then traced back to the sentences in which they occurred and their positions noted. Each method then assigns a score to each sentence based on the number and position of the high-frequency words it contains.

The first method divides the square of the number of high-frequency words by the number of words in the sentence which occur between the first high-frequency word and the last. The second method divides the product of the square of the number of high-frequency words and the divisor of the first method by the total number of words in the sentence minus the number of high-frequency words, plus one.

The third method adds to the number of high-frequency words a total derived by considering all gaps (occurrences of non-high-frequency words) between high-frequency words and adding for each gap 2^{-n} where n is the number of words in the gap. The fourth method simply sums the "9's" complement of the number of words in each gap in the sentence.

The fifth method divides the result of method three by the square root of the number of words in the sentence. Captions and headings were ignored in the analysis even though some were picked by both the subjects and the machine programs.

• Results

The number of agreements among subjects in picking specific sentences was tabulated and compared with a Poisson Approximation to the expected agreements in a random selection. The same analysis was done among

[1] Hugh Fallon and Marjorie Saxon did the programming for this experiment. This research was partially supported by the Department of the Army Contract # DA-49-083 OSA-2109. Permission is granted for reproduction, publication, use and disposal, in whole or in part, by and for the United States Government.

the five auto-abstracting programs. The subjects agreed more than expected at the .05 level on the basis of random selection, while the auto-abstracting programs agreed beyond the .001 level.

The distribution of sentence selection over the paragraphs was analyzed. Neither the subjects nor the auto-abstracting programs distributed their selections randomly as measured by a chi square at the .05 level. The length of a paragraph does not seem to be the determining factor in whether sentences are selected in that paragraph by either man or machine.

Baxendale (1) found that "topic sentences" usually were the first and last sentences in a paragraph. The selection of "topic sentences" by the five subjects and five machine methods was analyzed. The results were that 37% of the sentences in the entire document population were first or last sentences, i.e., "topic sentences." Forty-seven percent of the sentences selected by the subjects were "topic sentences," while 33% of the machine selected sentences were "topic sentences."

The subjects and machine preferences for different quarters of the article based on the location, where sentences were selected including their ranks, were compared by the Spearman Coefficient of Concordance. For the subjects and machines there were no significant differences between the ranks of the first and second quarters, or the ranks of the third and fourth quarters. The subjects, however, prefer the first half of the document over the last half, while the opposite is true for the machine method. Each sentence the subject picked was scored by Method 5. The mean value of the 20 sentences for each article was within one standard deviation of the mean of the article calculated by Method 5. The auto-abstracts are the upper extreme of the range of scores by their nature. The combined mean scores for the subjects in each article plus the equivalent mean score for the auto-abstract calculated by Method 5 are shown in Figure 1.

All 6 subjects agreed upon an average of only 1.6 sentences per article out of the 20 sentences each subject selected from each article. However, an average of 6.4 sentences out of the 20 sentences selected by each subject were agreed upon by 5 out of 6 subjects.

In looking at the machine methods, it was found that all 5 methods agreed upon an average of 9.2 sentences out of the first 20 sentences selected per article. While, if the number of machine methods selecting the same sentences is reduced to 4 out of 5, the agreement increases to 17.0 sentences per article, i.e., 17 out of the 20 sentences selected by the machine methods were agreed upon by 4 out of the 5 machine methods.

The mean number of sentences per article upon which all 6 subjects and all 5 machine methods agreed was 0.2. Reducing the criterion to 5 out of 6 subjects and 4 out of 5 machine methods, the number of man-machine agreements becomes 1.7 sentences per article.

If the 6 subjects' selections are compared to the first 40 sentences selected by each of the 5 machine methods

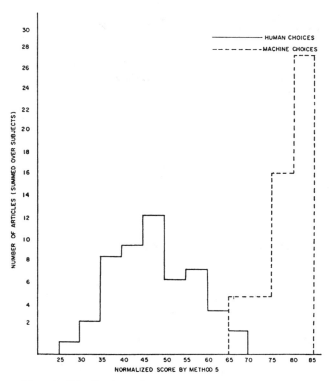

FIG. 1—Distribution of number of articles against mean score of the 20 sentences selected by man and machine. The abscissa is calculated by Method 5 and normalized to a percentage by dividing by the maximum sentence score for each article. The number of articles in each score category is summed over all subjects.

rather than just the first 20 sentences, the average number of man-machine agreements per article becomes 0.4 sentences. When the criterion is reduced to 4 out of 5 machine methods and 5 out of 6 subjects, an average of 2.7 sentences per article was found to be in agreement between man and machine.

• Discussion

The analysis shows that both the human selected sentences and the program selected sentences differ significantly from randomness. There is a wide range of individual differences between the human subjects, while the 5 methods yield very small differences in the sentences chosen. There was very little agreement between the subjects and the machine methods on the sentences selected as being representative.

The human and machine differ regarding their selection of "strategic sentences" (1). The results would seem to indicate that humans and machines are indifferent to the selection of "strategic sentences" evidently feeling that they are not "representative" sentences.

Other studies have indicated that automatic abstracting methods can be made to vary more than the present results would indicate. One procedure to accomplish this is to select other than high-frequency words as those on which the sentence analysis is based. Another source of variation appears when the documents abstracted are less well-edited or discuss a number of different topics. Therefore, if further development of auto-abstracting is contemplated, it would appear that the emphasis should be placed on these factors rather than the sentence evaluation procedures.

• Summary

Auto-abstracting techniques based on high-frequency words show an extremely small variation among themselves in the selection of sentences. Human selection of sentences, although less variable than chance expectancy, is considerably more variable than machine methods. There was very little agreement between the subjects and machine methods in their selection of representative sentences.

References

1. BAXENDALE, P. B. 1958. Machine-made index for technical literature—an experiment. *IBM Journal of Research and Development.* 2 October, p. 354.
2. LUHN, H. P. 1958. The automatic creation of literature abstracts. *IBM Journal of Research and Development.* 2 April, p. 159.
3. SAVAGE, T. R. November, 1958. The preparation of auto-abstracts on the IBM 704 data processing system. *IBM Research.*

Part II. The Reliability of People in Selecting Sentences

A. RESNICK

*International Business Machines Corporation
Yorktown Heights, New York*

Although subjects exhibited some reliability in selecting representative sentences, the resultant reliability was low. The lack of inter- and intra-subject reliability seems to imply that a single set of representative sentences does not exist for an article. It may be that there are many equally representative sets of sentences which exist for any given article.

Considerable interest has been expressed and effort expended in attempting to prepare abstracts automatically by means of computers as suggested by Luhn (1) and Savage (2). In so doing, it is hoped a useful tool may be offered to research workers so that they may make inroads into the vast volume of scientific literature which appears annually.

Suggestions have been made that in attempting to prepare these abstracts one should, perhaps, try to emulate the human abstractor.

The purpose of this study was to test the reliability of humans in preparing abstracts by selected "representative" sentences from the document to be abstracted. The automatic abstracting programs have all involved the selection of "representative" sentences.

• Procedure

Five students from The King's College, Briarcliff Manor, New York, were given six articles in random order from the *Scientific American*. They worked independently and on one article at a time. They were given the following instructions:

1) You will be asked to read several articles from the *Scientific American* magazine.

2) Read each article thoroughly to become acquainted with its content.

3) Then go back through the article and select 20 sentences which you feel are the most representative of the content of that article.

4) After having selected the 20 sentences which you

felt were most representative and written them down, you are to select the one sentence which you feel is most representative of the entire article.

5) You will place this sentence at the top of your list and then select a second sentence which you believe, combined with the first, best represents the article. You will continue this process until all the sentences that you have chosen are ranked according to their representativeness.

6) Do not select captions or titles.

Eight weeks later, the subjects were given the same six articles in random order and given similar instructions but, in addition, they were instructed not to attempt to select sentences which they had selected previously unless they felt they were still representative; and after selecting 20 sentences, indicate with an asterisk (*) any sentences which they felt they had selected previously.

• Results

One aspect of the experiment was the subjects' ability to recall sentences which they had previously selected. The subjects' responses are classified into four possible alternatives:

1) Correctly identifying a sentence previously selected
2) Incorrectly identifying a sentence previously selected
3) Correctly identifying a sentence which had not been selected previously
4) Incorrectly identifying a sentence which had not been selected previously.

The percentage response for each alternative is presented in Table 1. The subjects were able to identify a sentence they had previously selected 42.5% of the time.

Kendall's Rank Correlation Coefficient tau (τ) (3) was utilized to obtain an estimate of the subjects' reliability in both selecting the same sentences and in ranking them for each of the six articles. The distribution of (τ's) for the five subjects over the six articles is presented in Table 2. The mean of this distribution was .47.

In determining the significance of the (τ's), it was found that all except one of the 30 (τ's) were significant at the .05 level.

It was hypothesized that the observed values of (τ) might be dependent upon the number of sentences within each article, since it would appear that the sentences could be more consistently selected from shorter articles. The number of sentences per article ranged from 78 to 171 sentences. Using Spearman's Rank Difference Correlation Method, this hypothesis was rejected at the .05 level.

An analysis of variance performed on the data in Table 3, i.e., the percentage of sentences selected by the subjects on the second trial which were the same

TABLE 1. Mean percentage of responses of five subjects making selections of 20 "representative" sentences two months apart from each of six articles. During the second selection the subjects were asked to indicate whether or not they had chosen each sentence two months earlier

	Sentence correctly identified	Sentence incorrectly identified
Sentence previously selected	42.5%	13.1%
Sentence not previously selected	21.7%	22.7%

TABLE 2. Correlation between selections two months apart of 20 "representative" sentences from six articles by five subjects. Table entries are values of Kendall's (τ)

Articles	Subjects				
	A	B	C	D	E
1	.50	.31	.44	.29	.79
2	.47	.30	.52	.38	.60
3	.32	.71	.45	.44	.63
4	.27	.74	.67	.49	.54
5	.33	.36	.49	.33	.49
6	.32	.54	.44	.04*	.78

* Not significant at .05 level.

TABLE 3. Percentage of sentences selected on second trial which were the same as those selected on the first trial

Subjects	Articles					
	A	B	C	D	E	F
1	60%	55%	45%	45%	40%	40%
2	45	50	75	80	45	60
3	60	65	55	70	55	50
4	45	55	55	55	40	15
5	80	70	70	60	55	80

as those selected on the first trial, indicated that the differences between individuals was significant, but the differences between articles was not significant at the .05 level.

In looking at all six articles and the sentences selected from each article by all five subjects, it was observed that an average of only 2.7 sentences per article was selected by all the subjects on the first trial and 2.5 sentences per article on the second trial. If the number of subjects selecting the same sentence is lowered to

4, 5.0 sentences are agreed upon per article on the first trial and 7.5 sentences on the second trial.

• Discussion and Conclusion

The results indicate that although the subjects exhibited some reliability in selecting representative sentences, the resultant reliability was low. There was a significant difference between subjects but not between articles as determined by the percentage of sentences which were selected on the second trial and which were the same as those selected on the first trial.

Each subject on the average selected the same sentences only 55% of the time, i.e., selected the same sentences on the second trial as on the first. They were able to correctly identify their previous selection 64% of the time.

The lack of inter- and intra-subject reliability seems to imply that a single set of representative sentences does not exist for an article. It may be that there are many equally representative sets of sentences which exist for any given article.

References

1. LUHN, H. P. 1958. The automatic creation of literature abstracts. *IBM Journal of Research and Development.* 2 April, p. 159.
2. SAVAGE, T. R. November, 1958. The preparation of auto-abstracts on the IBM 704 data processing system. *IBM Research.*
3. SIEGEL, S. 1956. *Nonparametric statistics.* McGraw-Hill, New York.

19

AUTOMATIC CONDENSATION OF ELECTRONIC PUBLICATIONS BY SENTENCE SELECTION

RONALD BRANDOW,[1] KARL MITZE[2] and LISA F. RAU[3],*

[1]Information Technology Laboratory, GE Corporate Research and Development, Schenectady, NY 12301, U.S.A., [2]3RD Millenium Inc., 1 River Road, Carlisle, MA 01741, U.S.A., and [3]SRA Corp., Arlington, VA 22201, U.S.A.

Abstract—As electronic information access becomes the norm, and the variety of retrievable material increases, automatic methods of summarizing or *condensing* text will become critical. This paper describes a system that performs domain-independent automatic condensation of news from a large commercial news service encompassing 41 different publications. This system was evaluated against a system that condensed the same articles using only the first portion of the texts (the *lead*), up to the target length of the summaries. Three lengths of articles were evaluated for 250 documents by both systems, totalling 1500 suitability judgements in all. The outcome of perhaps the largest evaluation of human vs machine summarization performed to date was unexpected. The lead-based summaries outperformed the "intelligent" summaries significantly, achieving acceptability ratings of over 90%, compared to 74.4%. This paper briefly reviews the literature, details the implications of these results, and addresses the remaining hopes for content-based summarization. We expect the results presented here to be useful to other researchers currently investigating the viability of summarization through sentence selection heuristics.

1. INTRODUCTION

Automatic summarization of text is a worthy goal of NLP, however it challenges the field in ways that related areas (e.g. machine translation, extraction of information from text, and interfaces) do not. This is because in order to achieve readable, appropriate summaries, a system must (1) understand the content of a text at a fairly deep level, (2) be able to ascertain the relative importance of the material, and (3) generate coherent output. Any one of these three things is currently beyond the state of the art for anything more than demonstration systems or systems significantly constrained in their domain (either subject matter or grammatical or lexical variability).

Automatic summarization can be used commercially for three separate functions. First, condensed versions of the documents can function as stand-alone mini-documents or executive summaries. In this case, the information in the summary should be maximally *informative*. Second, condensed versions of full documents can serve as a preview format to support a retrieval decision on the full text of the article. Here, the summary should contain information *indicative* of the content of the full document. Finally, summaries can improve the precision of text search, as searching against a condensed version decreases the chance that spurious text will match a query. In this application, the summary need not be shown to the user, thereby relaxing constraints on the readability and coherence for this application.

We decided to experiment with simple techniques to determine how acceptable condensed versions of news articles could be constructed from extracting whole sentences from the input text. The recently completed system, called ANES (Automatic News Extraction System), performs domain-independent summarization of news documents.

This system took a representative sample of news material, encompassing the three general

* This paper was prepared while Lisa Rau was on an NSF Visiting Professorship for Women grant (NSF GER-9350134), hosted by the Computer and Information Sciences Department at the University of Pennsylvania. Correspondence regarding this paper and requests for reprints should be sent to Lisa Rau.

categories of news wires, magazines and newspapers, from 41 publications, and output condensed versions into lengths of 60, 150, and 250 words (independent of initial article length).

The prototype effort was geared towards accomplishing a number of objectives in addition to the demonstration of the functionality. In particular:

Source-independent: The prototype was designed to be publication-source-independent to reduce the software maintenance costs. This objective is also important to ensure that the summary generation system performs adequately for a wide variety of sources to maximize the potential utility of the software.

Extensible: The system was designed so that publication-specific or product-specific summaries could be generated. The base configuration operates in a publication-independent mode, but contains the infrastructure to add special conditions to tailor summaries to either particular types of articles or particular types of information requests.

Flexible: The system was designed so that the user could vary parameters to change the system's performance, such as the length and type of summary generated.

Intelligent: ANES was designed to identify certain types of documents, e.g. question/answer, speeches, op-ed pieces, tables, and embedded lists of various kinds. Additionally, ANES determines, *a priori*, whether it is possible to generate an acceptable condensed version from a given document based upon the structural features of the document.

Copyright Compliance: Only deletion of text was performed, while retaining grammaticality to avoid any copyright restriction violations or other legal issues involving manipulation of the source material while retaining the existing copyright.

We start with a brief review of the literature, and then detail the implementation and the evaluation of the results.

2. RELATED RESEARCH

Since its beginnings, automatic text summarization has been performed primarily by the selection of sentences from the original document (Luhn, 1958; Rath *et al.*, 1961; Edmundson, 1964). Although attempts have been made to utilize Natural Language (NL) text condensation approaches (Rau *et al.*, 1989; Allport, 1988; Marsh *et al.*, 1984), they generally required the selection of a narrow domain and the availability of domain knowledge. These shortcomings have made NL approaches to text condensation currently infeasible for generic text condensation tasks.

The state of sentence selection-based text condensation was advanced by improvements introduced by Paice (1990): textual cohesion, balance, and coverage. Textual cohesion was attained mainly by the resolution of anaphora; whether an anaphoric sentence was selected for the summary depended upon the number of additional sentences which needed to be included to properly resolve the anaphor. Textual balance and coverage were achieved by the prejudicial selection of sentences based upon the location of the sentences in the original document.

Even with these improvements, there still remain problems identified by Edmundson (1964) in both the conceptual content (presentation and length of summary) and evaluation (summary's acceptability and/or usefulness). These problems were addressed by Morris *et al.* (1992) who empirically determined, using a variety of short texts taken from GMAT reading comprehension tests, that the optimal informative summary length was somewhere between 20 and 30% of the original document length; at these lengths, it was found that summaries conveyed a similar amount of information as the original document. Although the experiment was limited in scope, it suggests an optimal size for text consideration via sentence selection.

Most recently, Johnson *et al.* (1993) took a related approach to that taken in ANES. In this system, inclusion of sentences for the abstract was based on indicator phrases (an approach we initially planned but later abandoned). Sentences were then discarded because anaphora were detected. The anaphora detection heuristics are quite similar to ANES, but more extensive. The major differences between the two systems are:

(1) The Johnson system required manual markup of the input texts, identifying non-

textual material and marking paragraph boundaries; an impossible requirement for a commercial system.

(2) The system relied on the identification of cue (or *indicator*) phrases to pick out sentences likely to contain important material. This approach can work for narrow kinds of texts, especially scientific articles such as this system was developed for, but is inappropriate for domain-independent summarization.

(3) Their approach requires a fairly complex pre-processing system to tag texts by part-of-speech, including the use of a parser to perform disambiguation of tags.

(4) It was not clear how many texts the system was evaluated on, although the paper suggests this figure to be between one and ten, and clearly not large enough to support any general conclusions.

ANES continues the work in automatic text condensation via sentence selection but varies from previous work in two important respects: (1) domain range and significance of the evaluation in both size and nature and (2) automatic identification of when a document is capable of being summarized in a meaningful way. ANES is able to generate acceptable summaries from a myriad of publication sources and types. Currently it has been used to generate summaries from paper, magazine and wire publication types and from 41 different publication sources. Additionally, ANES has the ability to determine, *a priori*, whether an acceptable summary can be generated from a particular document; documents from which acceptable summaries cannot be automatically generated are flagged for human summary generation.

3. PROTOTYPE DESCRIPTION

The ANES system was designed and implemented to contain core technologies that could be applied outside the particular application of extracting news, and be easily reconfigured to alter performance along a number of different dimensions. In addition, the system was designed to require no maintenance upon the addition or change of publications going through the system, although periodic retraining is desirable.

Our initial technical approach was similar to that taken by Johnson *et al.* (1993). In addition to constructing summaries by extracting whole sentences from the source documents, Johnson used as an indicator of key content such phrases as *The objective of this study is* or *The findings from our research show*. After analyzing the source material we were to summarize, however, it rapidly became clear that indicator phrases of this type were heavily source document-dependent and could not generalize across the entire range of material being summarized.

The process of summary generation we settled on has four major constituents: statistical corpus analysis, signature word selection, sentence weighting, and sentence selection. These are briefly described here.

3.1. Statistical selection of signature words

ANES utilizes individual word statistics to determine the sentences of interest. Through statistical analysis of a representative corpus, the typical frequency of occurrence of words averaged across representative publications is generated; this information is used to calculate individual word weights, which in turn are used to determine *signature* words.

A 70 Megabyte sample of text consisting of 20,997 documents from 41 distinct publications was used to gather word and document statistics. The statistical analysis of this corpus was performed off-line as a batch process, prior to extract (summary) generation.

During extract generation, ANES selects sentences for the summary by utilizing a list of signature words. Individual word weights are calculated by employing a term frequency times inverted document frequency method [$tf * idf$ (Salton & McGill, 1983)]. For each word in a document, the system computes a weighted measure of the frequency of that word using the following formula:

$$tf * idf = \frac{term\ frequency}{document\ frequency}$$

where

$$term\ frequency = \log_2 \left(\frac{words\ in\ corpus}{occurrences\ of\ term\ in\ corpus} \right)$$

$$document\ frequency = \log_2 \left(\frac{words\ in\ document}{occurrences\ of\ term\ in\ document} \right).$$

The above formula has the desirable attributes that low corpus frequency words have higher weights; increasing the frequency in a document increases the weight of a word. This identifies the words in a document that are relatively unique (hence, signature) to that document.

Words whose *tf * idf* weight suggest that they could convey topical information are identified and the headline words which are infrequent (i.e. their occurrence in the corpus falls below an empirically chosen frequency threshold) and are not already represented by a signature word are added. This extended list of signature words represents words that are likely to indicate topic or convey other important information. There is no limit on the number of signature words used for a given document. All topical signature words exceeding an empirically determined significance threshold and all infrequent headline words are included.

The process of identifying words that indicate topic is fundamentally subjective. Nonetheless, we believe that the method used here succeeded in identifying the salient words in the stories. The issues in increasing the relevant content of the output summaries are mainly in the sentence selection heuristics as opposed to modifications of the signature word generation. There are a wide variety of methods to make this process more complicated (morphology, name recognition, collocation analysis, etc.), however based on our own experiments, we did not believe they would contribute significantly to an improved choice of sentences for increased content of the summaries.

3.2. Sentence selection

Sentence selection chooses the sentences that will become the final document summary. Sentence weighting determines which sentences contain information relating to the main ideas in the document based on the previously identified signature word list. Each sentence's weight is computed by summing the weights of the individual signature words present in the sentence; the sentence weights are used to choose the summary sentences. For each document, a set of sentences is chosen based on a number of factors, such as: the presence of signature words in the sentence; its location in the document; the presence of words signaling anaphora;[†] the target length of the extract, and the type of extract to be generated.

Sentences which contain signature words are grouped into sequences of sentences based upon adjacency. To enhance readability, single sentences which contain no signature words but separate sequences of sentences containing signature words are also included. Likewise, the first one or two sentences of a paragraph are also added when the second or third sentence, respectively, of the paragraph contains signature words. These heuristics implement constraints to maximize the text summary's coherence and cohesion.

ANES continues to add sentences to the summary until the length of the summary, in words, is within ± 10 words of the desired word count.

---

† Sentences which begin with certain anaphoric references are automatically disqualified from selection in order to avoid "dangling" references.

4. PROTOTYPE TESTING AND RESULTS

An independent 70 Megabyte training text sample consisting of 20,849 documents, along with a "regression set" data sample were used for development testing. The "regression set" data sample, consisting of 95 documents requiring 517,544 bytes, was used as a constant data set to track the improvement in the system from week to week.

After the development phase was completed, ANES was formally tested in two ways. First, an evaluation of the acceptability of the summaries was performed. This was followed by an evaluation of the retrieval performance using the summaries as indices into the full text.

4.1. Acceptability evaluation

The formal test of ANES involved generating document summaries of 60, 150 and 250 words for a test set of 250 representative documents (a total of 750 document summaries). These 250 documents were not included in any of the previously used corpora. The ANES summaries were compared to those generated by a system, based on a Mead Data Central commercial product called *Searchable Lead*, that outputs sentences, in order, until the target summary length is achieved.

Acceptability judgments were rendered by experienced news analysts using content and readability guidelines established in advance from a variety of industry sources and standards (rather than task-based or product-related criteria). Each extract was read and judged independently by at least one analyst, with the corresponding full-text document serving as the basis for judging acceptability of extract content.

The final results of comparing the acceptability of the ANES summaries and leading-text summaries for the 250 document evaluation corpus is given in Table 1. The final performance rating ranged from 68 to 78%, in rough agreement with the last informal development phase testing performance rating of 61% and the rate of improvement of the system during previous development testing.

Seven of the 250 test data documents (2.8%) were composed of multiple topics. ANES correctly identified three out of these seven documents as being unextractable; the remaining multi-topic documents were not identified and resulted in unacceptable extracts.

One important and unexpected result of this evaluation was that the leading-text summaries received significantly higher acceptability ratings than the summaries generated by our statistical/heuristic system. However the evaluation was not task-based, so it is possible that different kinds of results would have been obtained in an end-use, operational environment. Another important point regarding this evaluation, applying to both types of extracts, is that most summaries judged less-than-perfect *would not be detectable as such to a user*. This is because the user is not considering the question "is this a good summary of the full text?". The user assumes this to be the case, and might only doubt the assumption when confronted with a summary that completely misses the point or is not comprehensible. In order to determine the true acceptability of the system, an operational, task-based evaluation must still be performed. Note also that the news genre by its very nature is arguably biased toward lead-based summarization, whereas other genres might be less amenable to such a technique.

Table 2 provides further detail on the reasons for which ANES and leading-text summaries were judged unacceptable. Examples of readability problems might include dangling references,

Table 1. Final evaluation results

Summary length	ANES acceptable	ANES unacceptable	Lead acceptable	Lead unacceptable
60	171 (68%)	79 (32%)	191 (87%)	33 (13%)
150	191 (76%)	59 (23.6%)	232 (93%)	18 (7%)
250	196 (78%)	54 (22%)	241 (96%)	9 (4%)
Overall	558 (74%)	192 (26%)	690 (92%)	60 (8%)

Table 2. Categorization of errors

Summary type	Readability	Content	Content and readability	Erroneous flagging
ANES	51 (27%)	96 (50%)	33 (17%)	12 (6%)
Leading-text	3 (5%)	57 (95%)	0 (0%)	—

excessive choppiness, premature sentence termination, etc. Content problems are problems related to the adequacy of treatment in the extract of the subject matter of the full-text document (e.g. inadequate, misleading, or skewed representation of the full-text document's subject matter). Erroneous flagging errors are misjudgments on the part of the system as to the extractability of particular documents (most of these errors resulted when the system mistakenly decided that a document had too many tables to allow a reasonable extract to be created).

The majority of the leading-text summary rejections (95%) were due to content problems compared to 67% ANES summaries rejected for this reason. The few leading-text summary readability errors were due to sentence boundary recognition problems. As the leading-text system copied sentences, in order, from the original document, this high proportion of content-related rejection can only be explained by the presence of "anecdotal" and other peripheral material in the leading sentences of the documents (Table 4 provides empirical support for this argument). Anecdotal, or other human-interest type information is a journalistic style often used as a lead-in to newspaper-style stories.

Further analysis of the rejected leading-text summaries revealed that 45% of these rejected summaries were rejected due to anecdotal information; ANES produced acceptable summaries in 37% of the cases where the corresponding leading-text summaries were rejected due to the presence of anecdotal information. These results suggest that a combined ANES/leading-text system can achieve a higher acceptability rate.

Achieving higher acceptability is primarily limited by the constraint that ANES be publication-independent, although somewhat higher accuracies could be achieved by continuing refinements within the existing framework. The publication-independent limitation forced the implementation to be intelligent enough to automatically identify certain types of documents, e.g. question/answer sessions, speeches, op-ed pieces, tables, and embedded lists of various kinds, as opposed to hard-coding the special conditions that identify these documents. Generic pattern-based cues were used to accomplish this identification.

4.2. Summary rejection analysis

Table 3 details the percentage of the total failures for each summary length for the ANES and leading-text summaries. As can be seen from the table, the largest percentage of rejected leading-text summaries were 60 word; a 46% decrease in rejections was attained with 150 word summaries with another 50% decrease achieved with the 250 word summaries. This improvement ratio is not unexpected given the relatively simple approach utilized to generate the leading-text summaries and the nature of the test documents.

However, the ANES summaries do not show as pronounced a drop in rejected summaries with length; in fact, the rejection rate of the 150 and 250 word ANES summaries are very similar. This result can be attributed to the technology used and the attempt to retrieve

Table 3. % Total failures by summary length

	60	150	250
ANES	41.15	30.73	28.12
Leading-text	55.00	30.00	15.00

Table 4. Leading-text summary rejections

	60	150	250	Total*
≤ 750	16 (48%)	8 (44%)	4 (44%)	28 (47%)
>750 and ≤ 1250	6 (18%)	3 (17%)	3 (33%)	12 (20%)
>1250	11 (33%)	7 (39%)	2 (22%)	20 (33%)
Total	33	18	9	60

*Note that it was possible under the conditions of the evaluation for a short summary of a document to be accepted while a longer summary for the same document was rejected. This did in fact occur fairly frequently for ANES summaries, albeit rather infrequently for leading-text summaries. Recall that acceptability judgments were provided independently for each extract, regardless of size.

information from disparate portions of the document and reassemble it into a coherent summary.

Although the ANES summaries do not show the pronounced variability with respect to summary length, they also do not match the high rate of acceptability achieved by the leading-text summaries (ANES's 74.4% acceptability rate versus the leading-text technology's 92% rate). Given the superior acceptability of the leading-text summaries, our future work in text summarization will revolve upon improving the acceptability of the leading-text summaries. To that end, the analysis was performed primarily on the rejected leading-text summaries with analysis of rejected ANES summaries being performed to gauge the effectiveness of its intelligent features.

Because the text corpus was composed mainly of generic public consumption documents, it was assumed that the writing style and information dissemination would be fairly regular. Since we generated fixed length summaries of 60, 150 and 250 words, according to Morris *et al.*, who reported that the optimal summary length is between 20 and 30% of the original document length, the optimal original documents would have had lengths between 200 and 300 words, 500 and 750 words, and 833–1250 words for 60, 150 and 250 word summaries, respectively. Because we elected to count summaries which consisted of the entire document as acceptable, analyzing documents of < 300 words as a single category would probably lead to misleading results for 250 word, and possibly 150 word summaries. To mitigate this effect somewhat, the analysis was performed for only 3 document lengths: ≤ 750 words, >750 and ≤ 1250 words, and >1250 words.

In Table 4, the leading-text summary rejection frequency by summary length and document length is given. As can be seen from the table, the summaries of documents ≤ 750 words in length accounted for approx. 47% (28/60) of the rejected summaries. Although documents of this length accounted for approx. 71% of the total test documents (with the documents between 750 words and 1250 words accounting for 17% and documents >1250 words, 12%), this high rejection rate was unexpected. However, the 33% rejection rate seen for long length documents (those >1250 words) was not unexpected; for these documents none of the generated summaries would have been of the optimal length. Likewise the 20% rejection rate seen for medium length documents (those documents >750 and ≤ 1250 words) agrees very closely with its expected rejection rate given its percentage (17%) of the test corpus.

Given the nature of the corpus—general public interest documents—it was thought that leading-text summarization would yield better results for smaller documents with increasingly higher rejections rates as the document length increased. For these document types, usually the shorter the document, the more relevant the leading information as opposed to a longer document which has more words to convey the information. From the analysis, this assumption appears to be incorrect.

Upon further analysis, the unacceptable leading-text summaries were divided into 3 broad categories: multiple topic, anecdotal, and other. The "multiple topic" category includes those documents which were composed of multiple unrelated articles. The "anecdotal" category includes documents whose leading sentences and/or paragraphs contain mainly anecdotal

Table 5. Leading-text summary rejection breakdown

Document length	Multiple topics	Anecdotal	Other	Total
≤ 750	11	6	11	28
>750 and ≤ 1250		7	5	12
>1250	3	12	5	20
Total	14	25	21	60

information. The other category encompasses all of the remaining unacceptable documents (documents dominated by tables, lists, questions and replies, and other unusual structural or stylistic features).

Table 5 shows the division of the leading-text summary rejections by document length and rejection category. Approximately 65% (39/60) of the rejections are attributed to multiple topic document or a document with anecdotal leading sentences/paragraphs. The elimination of these rejections would increase the overall leading-text summary acceptance rate to 97.2%, an increase of 5.2%.

ANES was designed with intelligent features to detect these conditions. Table 6 gives the number of leading-text summaries ANES correctly identified as unextractable (i.e. no acceptable extract of the specified size could be generated, due to the presence of interfering structural or stylistic features detected programmatically by the system). As can be seen from the table, the current ANES technology correctly detected 16 of 39 documents for which unacceptable leading-text summaries were generated. Instances where the system wrongly classified summaries as unextractable are summarized in Table 2 under the heading "Erroneous Flagging". Additionally, although the ANES multiple topic detection algorithm would have increased the summary acceptability percentage slightly, it correctly identified all of the multiple topic documents with 250 words and less. This is explainable due to the current dependence on the length of the original document in the algorithm to automatically detect unextractable documents; modifying the algorithm to remove this dependency should result in the correct detection of many if not all of the documents.

Furthermore, ANES was designed to detect certain document styles, mainly question and answer formatted documents with or without leading speeches.

4.3. Retrieval effectiveness evaluation

In addition to the acceptability evaluation, a small experiment was conducted to explore the potential benefit of using the ANES summaries to enhance the accuracy of (Boolean-based) document retrieval. The Searchable Lead product mentioned earlier was introduced expressly for the purpose of enhancing search precision, so part of the experiment included a comparison of the relative effectiveness of using ANES summaries versus leading-text summaries for this purpose.

Twelve queries representative of typical users' queries were used to retrieve documents from a full-text test sample equivalent in size and composition to the training sample described earlier. Each document retrieved for each query was evaluated by the creator of the query and

Table 6. Articles ANES correctly identified as unextractable

	Multiple topic			Anecdotal			Total
	60	150	250	60	150	250	
≤ 750	1	2	1	3	1		8
>750 and ≤ 1250				2	1	1	4
>1250				2	1	1	4
Total	1	2	1	7	3	2	16

Table 7. Summary and full text precision results

	60	150	250	Average
ANES	45%	46%	46%	45%
Leading text	50%	47%	44%	47%
Full text	—	—	—	37%

Table 8. Summary and full text relative recall results

	60	150	250	Average
ANES	42%	59%	67%	56%
Leading text	46%	57%	71%	58%
Full text	—	—	—	100%

judged either relevant or irrelevant to the information need represented by the query. The same queries were then run against ANES and leading-text summaries created from the test sample, with relevance judgments again being made for every retrieved document. Independent evaluations were conducted for the three summary lengths described earlier (60, 150, and 250 words), using ANES summaries and leading-text summaries.

In addition to computing average precision across queries and summary sizes, a relative recall measure was also computed to assess the loss of recall that generally attends an increase in precision in real-world retrieval systems. Due to the large size of the sample, it was beyond the scope of available resources to determine absolute recall across the entire sample. Thus, in order to have some basis for comparing impact on recall using the various summary types, it was assumed that the relevant documents returned from the full-text queries represented all relevant documents in the sample (i.e. Boolean retrieval against the full-text sample was assumed to have 100% recall).† Recall results computed under this assumption were dubbed "relative recall" results.

Tables 7 and 8 present precision and relative recall results from this experiment. Keep in mind that only twelve fairly simple Boolean queries were run against the sample for each summary type and size, so these results are only indicative of general trends and cannot be used to make fine distinctions between the various text condensation methods represented.

Two results stand out from this experiment. First, using the programmatically generated summaries from the experiment clearly improves retrieval precision significantly, but at the cost of a dramatic loss in recall (acceptable for certain applications, unacceptable for others). Second, the leading-text summaries once again proved just as useful for this purpose as the ANES summaries.

A comparative analysis of the leading-text and ANES answer sets reveals an average overlap of approx. 80% in relevant documents and an average overlap of approx. 65% in irrelevant documents. One possible explanation for this disparate result is that both methods (i.e. extracting leading text and extracting statistically important pieces of text) do a reasonably good job of finding relevant sections of text (which are likely to be very similar between the two methods), but since the two methods take text from different parts of a given document, surrounding irrelevant text will differ substantially between the two methods and will result in the retrieval of a wider variety of irrelevant documents.

The purpose of this analysis was to get some indication of whether a combination of the two extraction methods could support higher retrieval accuracy. Straightforward arithmetic extrapolation from these results would seem to indicate that using the union of the answer sets from the two methods as a basis for retrieval would hurt precision more than it would improve recall, while using the intersection of the answer sets from the two methods would improve precision more than it would hurt recall (assuming that recall and precision are assigned equal weight).

Overall, however, this is probably an academic question, since given the levels of recall and precision exhibited here, the magnitude of the potential improvement in accuracy would probably not be worth the cost of applying these two extraction methods to the corpus to be searched, inverting the resulting extracts, and searching against both extracts for each document. On the other hand, these results suggest that there may be some advantage in a non-Boolean retrieval system to using a weighting scheme that assigns higher weights to statistically

---

† The summary-based queries did not retrieve any documents that the full-text queries failed to retrieve, although it was possible for such a situation to arise given the use of phrases and proximity connectors in some of the queries.

significant words that appear in the leading text of a news document. We are currently investigating this hypothesis.

Several issues and directions for future work remain open. For example, it would be interesting to perform a similar experiment using more complex Boolean queries, or using a non-Boolean retrieval engine. It might also be worthwhile doing a more detailed experiment to determine the relative improvement using ANES summaries versus leading-text summaries for documents of different lengths or genres.

5. LESSONS LEARNED

There are several significant lessons to be learned from this experiment. First, the superior performance of the Lead-based system indicates the importance of well-connected text in constructing summaries that will be read from start to finish. Even when the ANES summary is more informative or indicative than the Lead, it is judged unacceptable if comprehension is impeded by awkward transitions or dangling references. It is an open question to what extent a maximally informative or indicative summary can be constructed based on sentence extraction methods alone, if the resulting summary is to contain no readability problems.

These results also give data on the percent of times, in these types of texts (newspapers, wires, magazines), that a valid summary of the content is present in the beginning of the text. Before this analysis was performed, we had no measure of this figure, although we assumed it would be much lower. We hope that these experimental results can be a caution to other researchers currently taking the sentence selection approach to constructing summaries.

Second, although the Lead system outperforms the ANES system, our final acceptability range of 68–78% rating is encouraging, given the non-task driven evaluation, and the significant additional functionality in the approach. This method allows for variable length summarization, as well as goal-directed summaries. A goal-directed summary that is particularized to a specified information need or goal a user is seeking; something the Searchable Lead-based system cannot do. ANES can implement this functionality by factoring the terms *specific to a user's goals* into the list of signature words. In the future, this type of function should allow for highly individualized summaries to be maximally responsive to a user's information need.

Moreover, an analysis of the failures of the ANES system and the successes of the Lead-based system point to immediate improvements by weighting the sentences appearing in the beginning of the stories more heavily, and focusing our efforts on detecting those cases where taking the first portion of the stories does *not* yield a good summary.

Finally, recent work by others (Johnson *et al.* 1993) has come up with more complete heuristics to estimate the likelihood that a sentence contains an anaphoric reference not resolved within the sentence. These heuristics fit very well into the current ANES architecture and should substantially decrease the readability problems due to dangling references. Note however, that we still have no good estimate of the impact that eliminating sentences with dangling references will have on the resulting content of the summary. Conversely, we have no estimate of how including sentences that resolve dangling references in the summary impact our ability to then choose potentially more contentful sentences due to length restrictions. These questions can only be answered by additional experimentation and evaluation.

We believe that our "weak method" of generating summaries based on statistical indications of topic and heuristic methods of ensuring coherence and cohesion can yield viable automatic systems to condense text to arbitrary lengths with respect to *ad hoc* user goals while retaining domain-independence. Our approach should apply to other genres of texts where the first few paragraphs do not contain a good summary as well.

6. CONCLUSIONS

ANES was an experiment in automatically summarizing news using a combination of statistical and heuristic methods. The most surprising result of the experiment was the adequacy of producing summaries consisting only of the first sentences in a story. Although the evaluators were not task-driven (i.e. their judgements of adequacy were not with respect to task, but application-independent), we suspect that this type of summary is suitable for many purposes.

In spite of the difference in performance between the two methods, we are encouraged by the acceptability that was achieved with the statistical/heuristic method. The acceptability results of the Lead-based system will be used to modify the heuristics of the ANES system to weight leading information more heavily.

REFERENCES

Allport, D. (1988). The ticc: Parsing interesting text. In *Second Conference on Applied Natural Language Processing* (pp. 211–218).

Edmundson, H. P. (1964). Problems in automatic abstracting. *Communications of the ACM, 7*(4), 259–263.

Johnson, F. C., Paice, C. D., Black, W. J., & Neal, A. P. (1993). The application of linguistic processing to automatic abstract generation. *Journal of Documentation and Text Management, 1*.

Luhn, H. P. (1958). The automatic creation of literature abstracts. *IBM Journal of Research and Development, 2*(2), 159–165.

Marsh, E., Hambuger, H., & Grishman, R. (1984). A production rule system for message summarization. In *Proceedings of the National Conference on Artificial Intelligence*.

Morris, A. H., Kasper, G., & Adams, D. (1992). The effects and limitations of automated text condensing on reading comprehension performance. *Information Systems Research, 3*(1), 17–35.

Paice, C. D. (1990). Constructing literature abstracts by computer: Techniques and prospects. *Information Processing & Management, 26*(1), 171–186.

Rath, G. J., Resnick, A., & Savage, T. R. (1961). The formation of abstracts by the selection of sentences. *American Documentation*, 139–141.

Rau, L. F., Jacobs, P. S., & Zernik, U. (1989). Information extraction and text summarization using linguistic knowledge acquisition. *Information Processing & Management, 25*(4), 419–428.

Salton, G., & McGill, M. (1983). *An introduction to modern information retrieval*. New York: McGraw-Hill.

The Effects and Limitations of Automated Text Condensing on Reading Comprehension Performance

Andrew H. Morris*   *formerly of Department of Information and Management Sciences*
College of Business
Florida State University
Tallahassee, Florida 32306

George M. Kasper   *Department of Information Systems and Quantitative Sciences*
College of Business Administration
Texas Tech University
Lubbock, Texas 79409

Dennis A. Adams   *Department of Decision and Information Sciences*
College of Business Administration
University of Houston
Houston, Texas 77204

The optimal amount of information needed in a given decision-making situation lies somewhere along a continuum from "not enough" to "too much". Ackoff proposed that information systems often hinder the decision-making process by creating information overload. To deal with this problem, he called for systems that could filter and condense data so that only relevant information reached the decision maker. The potential for information overload is especially critical in text-based information. The purpose of this research is to investigate the effects and theoretical limitations of extract condensing as a text processing tool in terms of recipient performance. In the experiment described here, an environment is created in which the effects of text condensing are isolated from the effects of message and individual recipient differences. The data show no difference in reading comprehension performance between the condensed forms and the original document. This indicates that condensed forms can be produced that are equally as informative as the original document. These results suggest that it is possible to apply a relatively simple computer algorithm to text and produce extracts that capture enough of the information contained in the original document so that the recipient can perform as if he or she had read the original. These results also identify a methodology for assessing the effectiveness of text condensing

* Andrew Morris died in May 1989 of cancer. The research reported here was started as his doctoral thesis. All that is good in the manuscript can be attributed to Andy. Those who knew him recognize that this article only began to demonstrate his potential.

schemes. The research presented here contributes to a small but growing body of work on text-based information systems and, specifically, text condensing.

Text-based information systems—Text condensing—Abstracting/extracting—Performance

Introduction

The optimal amount of information needed in a given decision-making situation lies somewhere along a continuum from "not enough" to "too much" (Schroder et al. 1967). Over two decades ago, Ackoff (1967) proposed that information systems (IS) often hinder the decision-making process by creating information overload. To deal with this problem, he called for systems that could filter and condense data so that only relevant information reached the decision maker. In the years since Ackoff's challenge, the rapid growth of the information processing industry has reinforced the importance of filtering and condensing data. However, as Rappaport (1968) was quick to note, the danger of over-filtering and over-condensing also exists.

The potential for information overload is especially critical in text-based information (Hiltz and Turoff 1985). Communication is arguably the most critical and time consuming process in organizations (Culnan and Bair 1983; Rice and Bair 1984); it is a vital supporting routine that permeates the process of problem solving and decision making (Mintzberg et al. 1976). Yet, the amount of attention that a manager can devote to any single form or source of information is extremely limited (Kahneman 1973), and organizations can perform only a finite amount of information processing. Computer-mediated communication systems (CMCS) are rapidly becoming commonplace and, if the history of computing is any indication, they will result in an increase in the volume of text messages. Denning (1982) described the increase of *unwanted* computer mail as "electronic junk." Tools to control electronic communication must be in place to prevent the potential deluge (Hiltz and Turoff 1985). Unless practical filtering and condensing tools are developed, this increase is likely to place an excessive strain on the very limited resource of managerial attention (Denning 1982).

In addition to the increasing volume of communication generated within the organization, there exists an overwhelming and growing number of potential sources of information external to the firm; again, the majority of which are in the form of text. Resource and technological limitations (Blair and Maron 1985; Blair 1990) force managers to restrict their scanning activities to a very small subset of the potential sources of external information (El Sawy 1985). This can adversely affect performance as executives in successful organizations have been shown to engage in broader and more effective scanning activities than do their counterparts in poorer performing firms (Daft et al. 1988). Information systems that can "pre-scan" potential sources and identify sources of information have been developed (Jacobs and Rau 1990). Despite the obvious need and potential benefits, text condensing has proven to be a very difficult problem and has received very little attention from information systems (IS) researchers. As used here, text condensing refers to any text summary or reduction, and two approaches exist: (1) an "extract" is a summary based on a set of sentences or phrases selected virtually verbatim (allowing for very minor modifications) from a document; and (2) an "abstract" refers to a summary that restates the original document in a more concise manner.

The purpose of this research is to investigate the effects and theoretical limitations of extract condensing as a text processing tool in terms of recipient performance. Specifically, the effectiveness of applying a relatively simple extract technique to text-based information is assessed in terms of reading comprehension. Based on the library science literature, an efficient extracting algorithm for condensing text is empirically tested to determine the extent of reduction that results in effective message comprehension.

In the next section, current approaches to text-based processing are reviewed. This is followed by a discussion of text condensing techniques. Next, hypotheses are developed and empirically investigated. Specifically, a relatively simple algorithm for extracting text is developed, and the limits of its effectiveness are empirically investigated. Finally, the results of the work are summarized, and recommendations and conclusions are presented.

Background

The application of computers to the problem of information overload and, in particular, text processing is not new. Luhn (1958b) was probably the first to propose a computer-based "business intelligence system" designed to automatically produce "auto-abstracts" and to selectively disseminate information based on "action-point profiles." Later, Ackoff (1967) formalized this position, arguing that the purpose of information systems is to filter and condense information. To filter is to disseminate by deciding between relevant and irrelevant information; whereas condensing reduces relevant information to a more compact, summarized form. Filtering might combine the use of automatic routing schemes (Tsichritzis 1984), perhaps based on search strategies (Blair 1984), system-maintained profiles of the user's area(s) of interest (Luhn 1958a, b; Ewusi-mensah 1981) and already available automatic indexing systems (van Rijsbergen 1979, Dillon and Gray 1983, Salton 1989), which are able to classify documents according to the topic(s) addressed within them. Filtering can be aided by condensing (Swanson 1977). Condensing text, however, appears to be a much more difficult task. When a human condenses text (i.e., creates an abstract), he or she must understand the essence of what is explicitly stated as well as that implied in the document (Cremmins 1982). Designing computer-based systems that "understand" the content of a document has proven to be very difficult. However, it may not be necessary to wait until efficient artificial intelligence-based natural language processing systems that mimic the human's abstracting abilities are available before systems to effectively condense text can be employed.

Text Processing Systems

Most systems designed to *process*[1] text-based information fall in two categories: (1) systems that are intended to support document archival and retrieval and (2) systems that are primarily intended to support organizational communication functions. Identified as "document-based systems" by Swanson and Culnan (1978), the first category includes automated bibliographic databases (e.g., ERIC, ABI/INFORM), image processing (e.g., Image Plus), on-line text searching systems (e.g., SCISOR), hypertext systems (e.g., Hypercard), and other document archival and retrieval systems. The second category, organizational communication systems, is characterized by CMCS (Kerr and Hiltz 1982).

---

[1] This specifically excludes systems that aid in *creating* text such as word processors, style critiquing systems, spelling checkers, and others.

Document-based systems differ from those that process alphanumeric data in several important ways. Focusing on the distinction between document and data retrieval, Blair (1984) identifies four differences: the way the retrieval is answered, the relation between the formal request and user satisfaction, the factors that influence retrieval speed, and the criterion for successful retrieval. In data retrieval a query is deterministic, while a document retrieval query is nondeterministic. Rather than answering a specific question, document retrieval is indirect providing a set of documents that are *likely* to contain the desired information. This uncertainty makes document retrieval fundamentally a trial-and-error process (Swanson 1977). This lack of specificity also makes the efficiency of document retrieval less dependent on the speed of the system and more dependent upon the user's decisions. In terms of the criterion used to evaluate system performance, Blair states that, for data-based systems, performance is measured by correctness: the system responds with the right answer to a factual question. For document-based systems, the performance criterion is utility: the system must provide a response that is useful to the person requesting the information. Brookes (1983) also recognizes that the meaning of text is often ambiguous and thus difficult for automated systems to process, a problem well known to researchers in natural language processing.

Extensive research on document-based systems has been conducted in the area of library science, but relatively little attention has been paid to document processing by business and IS researchers (Swanson and Culnan 1978; Schwartz et al. 1980; Slonim et al. 1981). One of the most significant trends in information processing is the growth of CMCS (Kiesler et al. 1984), and most IS research that addresses text-based information processing falls into this category. Surveys of major business firms have consistently projected significant growth of CMCS well into the next decade (Kolodziej 1985, Kriebel and Strong 1984, Dickson et al. 1984, Brancheau and Wetherbe 1987, Adams and Weiss 1989). The application of CMCS has important implications for text-based information systems in that much of the basic technology for transmitting text (computer networks, protocols, communication equipment, etc.) is already in place. What remains is for advances to add value to these systems by providing, among other things, text condensing and filtering tools.

Text Condensing

Conceptually, the efficacy of text condensing is founded in statistical information and control theory (Wiener 1961) and, in particular, related developments in human information processing such as complexity theory (Schroder et al. 1967), information redundancy, and information overload. In an early review of the sciences of management, Goode (1958) identifies the relationship between Wiener's work and the human's capacity to process information:

> . . . the capacity [of an individual] to accept information, act on it, and put out a response, rises linearly at first, then less quickly, and after reaching a peak performance does not continue at peak, but falls off rapidly . . . remind[s] [me] of Wiener's discussion of the performance of a telephone exchange . . . (pp. 369–370).

This inverted U-shaped relationship exists between the quantity of information provided to a decision maker and his or her performance (Schroder et al. 1967, Chervany and Dickson 1974, Davis and Olson 1985, p. 237). "Information processing by 'people in general' . . . reaches a maximum level at some level of environmental complexity . . ." (Schroder et al. 1967, p. 36) beyond which information overload is experienced and performance actually deteriorates. Directly related to information overload and human information processing performance is redundancy.

Communication rarely, if ever, exists without redundancy. Redundancy occurs when more data are transmitted than are strictly required to convey the information (Davis and Olson 1985, p. 206). While redundant data can be used for error detection and correction, an objective of text condensing is the elimination of redundancy without reducing human information processing performance (i.e., successful communication). In fact, based on entropy theory, Shannon (1951) estimated that printed English has a redundancy of about 75 percent. Confirmed by Burton and Licklider (1955), this suggests a theoretical limit to nonexpository text condensing. In these studies, subjects were presented with a series of texts ranging from zero to 10,000 letters and were required to continue guessing until they named the next letter in the text correctly. Burton and Licklider found that, from 32 to 10,000 characters, there was no difference in the subject's ability to predict the next letter; the constraint imposed by 10,000 preceding letters is no different than that imposed by 32. Beyond 32 characters, the relative redundancy of written English is approximately 75 percent. "Written English does not become more and more redundant as longer and longer sequences are taken into account" (Burton and Licklider 1955, p. 652). Whether this is simply a reflection of printed English's redundancy of characters and words as suggested by Kibby (1980) or extends to message comprehension is unknown. However, for text-based information systems it suggests a measure of condensing, a theoretical limit to the effectiveness of extraction, beyond which expository abstracting is necessary.

Abstracting

The best known form of text condensing is the abstract—an abbreviated, accurate representation of the contents of a document (American National Standards Institute 1979).[2] Three main types of abstracts are generally recognized: indicative, informative, and critical (Borko and Bernier 1975, Weil 1970, Cremmins 1982). Briefly, the indicative (sometimes called descriptive) abstract describes what the text is about and helps the reader decide if the original full text should be consulted; the informative abstract tries to summarize the information in the text so that the reader will not need to consult the full text; and the critical abstract evaluates the text, expressing the reviewer's opinion of the original document. Because relatively few applications require critical abstracts, and because the technology needed to provide this subjective assessment is beyond that needed to produce the other two types of abstracts, research in automated text condensing has focused on the development of informative abstracts.

Automated Text Condensing

Until recently, automated text condensing has received relatively little research attention (Jacobs and Rau 1990). Three reasons have been suggested for this. First, if the original full text must first be physically entered into the computer, the cost effectiveness of automated condensing is questionable. However, Paice (1977, p. 144) predicted that when the input inefficiencies were resolved, "the interest in automatic extracting will be revived." Since then, optical character readers have become

---

[2] An excellent review of the ANSI standard on abstracts can be found in Cremmins (1982).

more sophisticated and less expensive, and fewer source documents are entered into the computer by hand. At the same time, more text is being created with the aid of computers, and therefore is already available in a computer-readable form for condensing.

A second issue influencing research in automated text condensing techniques is the lack of an objective measure of the quality of the reduction. Without such a measure, there is no guide for judging the success of a condensing technique. However, while literary quality remains largely a subjective issue, the information quality of a reduction can be objectively assessed by, for example, comparing reading comprehension performance of the condensed reduction to that of the original document.

Finally, two approaches to automated text condensing exist: (1) using natural language processing techniques to construct a map of the knowledge in a document from which an abstract is produced; and (2) employing an algorithmic system to extract important sentences and phrases from the document. Natural language processing requires syntactic, semantic and pragmatic knowledge. Syntactic knowledge is comprised of the rules for structuring a language, while semantic and pragmatic knowledge are increasingly domain specific (Hale et al. 1991). Analysis of syntax is relatively domain independent, and several important syntax-based systems have been built (Taylor and Krulee 1977, Miller 1980, Miller et al. 1981, Heidorn et al. 1982). Probably the best known of these is EPISTLE (Heidorn et al. 1982, Schriber 1983). Unfortunately, the use of syntax alone sometimes results in totally incorrect interpretations, particularly of idiomatic phrases such as "he threw the book at me" (Smeaton and van Rijsbergen 1986). Largely because of the knowledge domain constraints, systems that can fully analyze the semantic information of a broad domain of free text have been beyond the scope of technology (Epstein 1985), and are likely to remain so for the foreseeable future. The few prototype systems that do make use of semantic knowledge require an understanding of the subject-domain's "deep" knowledge, and are restricted to a single, typically very narrow domain (Smeaton and van Rijsbergen 1986). In a recent article, for example, Jacobs and Rau (1990) discuss a state-of-the-art natural language system which parses every word in a sentence, identifying linguistic structures and mapping these structures into a conceptual framework such as a semantic network. This very resource intensive process is capable of processing financial news at about six stories per minute with 80 to 90 percent recall (the proportion of relevant material retrieved) and precision (the proportion of retrieved materials that are relevant) in constrained texts. However, it "would also produce almost nothing useful, for instance, in reading the entire *Wall Street Journal*" (Jacobs and Rau 1990, p. 96).

The resource requirements of semantic-based condensing systems have been and will remain for the foreseeable future, a serious limitation to the application of this approach. However, even if resources suddenly became available and semantic-based condensing systems were a reality, research and development of extracting techniques would remain important for several reasons. First, if extracts can be produced that are informationally equivalent to the original text, these more efficiently produced extracts could be used directly in many cases. If the subjective literary quality of these informationally equivalent reductions was critical, they could be used as an intermediate product to be refined by a semantic-based system to a more literary pleasing, abstract equivalent, reduction. Moreover, even if literary refinement is essential, it may not require very intelligent processing because relatively simple rule-based parsing techniques can greatly improve the readability of extracts (Paice 1981).

Second, for many applications, literary refinement may not be needed for extract produced reductions to be just as effective as semantic-based reductions, particularly if the objective of the condensing operation is to enhance the user/manager's ability to scan internal and/or external sources of information. Finally, compared to syntax and semantic-based systems, extracting algorithms are much less domain dependent and are not prone to dramatic, sometimes complete, errors in interpretation such as those associated with idiomatic phrases.

Extracting

Mathematical and statistical information can be derived from text and used in the condensing process. Based on the frequency and relative position of nontrivial words in a document, many of the early so-called automated abstracting systems actually produced extracts. Luhn (1958a, b) pioneered this work with a system designed to produce "auto-abstracts," extracts consisting of sentences selected verbatim from the original document (Weil 1970). Extensive reviews of mathematical models of text can be found in Edmunson (1977, 1984).

During the 1960s, Edmunson and Wyllys (1961) and Edmunson (1964, 1969) developed four methods of weighting sentences for extract selection. Briefly, the Location method uses the position of the sentence in the document as an indication of its importance, and is based on the work of Baxendale (1958), who found that so-called "topic sentences" are most likely to occur as either the first (85%) or the last (7%) sentence in a paragraph. The Cue method uses a dictionary of pragmatic words such as "significant" and "purpose" to weight and select sentences to include in the extract. The Key Word method selects sentences for extracting based on the relative use of nontrivial words found in the document. Finally, the Title method uses non-trivial words in the title and subtitles as indicative of the sentence's relative importance to the extract. Based on subjective and statistical similarity ratings, Edmunson (1969) attained the best results when these methods were used in combination.

Perhaps the most successful extracting system was developed in the 1970s and reported by Rush et al. (1971), Mathis et al. (1973), and Pollock and Zamora (1975). Called ADAM (Automatic Document Abstracting Method), this system was based primarily on the Cue method, applied through a list known as a "word control list" (WCL). A WCL contains terms that when present in a sentence increase or decrease the likelihood that it will be included in the extract. Negative terms, such as "for instance," "perhaps," and "possible," imply a sense of qualification or hedging, or a statement of obvious fact or known research, or pertain to a peripheral topic. Positive words and phrases that increase the likelihood of a sentence being selected for extraction include "it was found," "results," and "conclusion." Parenthetical material is removed.

The subjective literary quality of extracts has never been as good as a well-written abstract (Bernier 1985, Cremmins 1982). To improve the quality of these reductions, Paice (1981) described an extracting approach that uses exophoric references to identify clusters of sentences that should be treated as a unit. Exophoria are words within a sentence that require reference to material in some other sentence(s) for resolution; the most common example of this is a pronoun that has its antecedent in previous text. To resolve exophoria, the sentence(s) containing the material referred to should also be included in the reduction. Thus, a sentence to be extracted serves as a nucleus around which all or a segment of the extract is developed, greatly reducing the sometimes disjointed appearance of extracts. Commenting on extracting, Paice (1981, p. 172) states:

> The possibility of producing abstracts by computer has not received very much attention. There are perhaps two main reasons for this. First, it appears that the production of well-constructed abstracts is an artificial intelligence problem, and therefore unlikely to be either feasible or worthwhile until well into the future; the alternative of picking sentences here and there in a document is a rather unattractive proposition. Second, the cost of key-punching texts for input into an abstracting program can hardly be justified—especially since the program will then in effect discard most of the text which has been so laboriously prepared. It now appears that the first of these objections is exaggerated—reasonable-looking abstracts can often be produced by quite "unintelligent" programs—while with advances in technology the second problem should soon disappear.

Research Hypotheses

To assess the theoretical limits and effectiveness of extracting as an approach to text condensing, three hypotheses were investigated. To assess whether the theoretical level of redundancy in printed English also holds for reading comprehension performance, extracts of varying degrees of reduction were produced. This was done by varying the extracting algorithm's stopping rule to produce reductions containing approximately 30% and 20% of the original text. Formally, this question can be stated in the null form as:

$H1_0$. *In terms of reading comprehension, no difference in performance exists between the original document and extracts containing 20% or 30% of the original document.*

Failure to reject $H1_0$ would indicate that extracts containing 20% or 30% of the original document are equally effective surrogates for the original document. This would suggest that Shannon's and Burton and Licklider's estimate of the redundancy of printed English is limited to prediction of character or word sequence, but does not hold for message comprehension and more informative chunks of information such as sentences. On the other hand, rejecting $H1_0$ would indicate that printed English is less redundant in terms of message comprehension than expected. Finally, rejecting $H1_0$ for the 20% extracts but finding no difference in performance between the 30% extracts and the original document would suggest that to condense text beyond the redundancy limit of 75% requires natural language processing and the production of informative abstracts. This can be stated in the null form as:

$H2_0$. *In terms of reading comprehension performance, there is no difference between the informative abstract whose length is less than 75% that of the original document and the extracts (20% and 30%).*

As discussed below, to produce the high quality informative abstracts expected of future very intelligent condensing systems, a human expert was employed. Failure to reject $H2_0$ would suggest that there is no difference in reading comprehension performance between the informative abstracts and the algorithm-produced extracts.

Finally, because these abstracts and extracts represent only a fraction of the length of the original text, they "rarely equal and never surpass the information content of the basic document" (Cremmins 1982, p.3). Yet, the literature also supports the argument that quality reductions might actually enhance the subject's comprehension of the information contained in the original document, because the concise and summarized presentation sufficiently reduces distracting information that would otherwise impede performance through information overload. Stated in the null form, the hypothesis of interest is:

$H3_0$. *In terms of reading comprehension performance, there is no difference between the condensed forms (abstract and extract) and the original document.*

Failure to reject the null hypothesis would indicate that the condensed forms are of sufficient quality that reading comprehension scores are not significantly reduced in the condensing treatments. If there is a significant treatment effect, then it will be necessary to examine the nature of the effect more carefully by constructing contrasts that investigated the differences between the specific treatments of interest. Collectively, these hypotheses begin to investigate the limits of text condensing, an issue that Ackoff (1967) argued was a critical function of information systems, but has been mostly ignored by IS.

Experimental Design

The effectiveness of text condensing is a function of the message, the condensing procedure, and the recipient. In the experiment described here, an environment is created in which the effects of text condensing are isolated from the effects of message and individual recipient differences. To isolate individual differences, a blocked design in which each subject receives all treatments of interest was used. This takes advantage of the statistical power inherent in multiple measures of the same unit (Horton 1978), as each block consists of a nonrepeating combination of all treatments. To prevent any carryover effect from confounding the results, all possible treatment orderings occurred an equal number of times in the experimental design. Each treatment consisted of either some condensed form or the original text followed by a reading comprehension test designed to assess the subject's understanding of the original full-length document. Because the subject served as the block, receiving more than one treatment, it was necessary that different text appear within the block; otherwise, the learning effect would overwhelm any other effect. The different texts were also ordered and assigned within the experimental design across treatments. The final treatment/text combinations, shown in the appendix, result in a partially balanced incomplete block design that provides a powerful test of the hypothesis and has been used in other studies (Morris 1988, Kasper and Morris 1988, Hale and Kasper 1989).

Treatments

In total, six treatments were administered: four condensing treatments, a no-extract treatment consisting of only the reading comprehension questionnaire and no text, and the original full-length text. Each block of the research design contained the four condensing treatments. Written by an expert, one treatment consisted of a high quality informative abstract of the text. The other three treatments were extracts. Two of these were extracts generated by the algorithm described below: one containing approximately 20% and the other about 30% of the original document. The third extract was generated by selecting sentences at random from the text. Each of these is discussed further below.

Full Text Treatment

Four passages were randomly selected from a set of twelve sample Graduate Management Aptitude Test (GMAT) reading comprehension tests (Educational Testing Service 1986). These tests averaged 453 words, ranging in length from 430 to 470 words and covered very diverse topics, including: medieval literature, 18th-century Japan, minority-operated businesses, and Florentine art. A well-known indicator of the difficulty of reading material, the Fog Index (Gunning 1968) was calculated for each passage. Considered an estimate of the educational grade level required to read and understand a passage, the index ranged from 15.5 to 18.9, indicating that the selected passages were all about the same level of relatively moderate difficulty. The use of moderately difficult passages was intentional in an effort to encourage treatment differences.[3]

Informative Abstract Treatment

To produce the high quality abstracts expected of future very intelligent condensing systems, a human expert (a professional abstracter) was employed. The expert was never shown the reading comprehension questions. He was simply instructed to produce informative abstracts. The four abstracts ranged in length from 90 to 129 words, with an average of 106 words or 23% of the original documents.

Extract Treatments

Three extract treatments were developed. To produce extracts containing 20% and 30% of the original full-length document an algorithm that combined and developed the approaches discussed earlier was used. The basic structure of the extracting algorithm consisted of three phases: (1) remove parenthetic material, (2) determine the sentence weights for the remaining material, and (3) build the extract by selecting the highest weighted sentences and resolving the exophoric references.

In the first phase, a three-step process is used to remove all parenthetic material. First, all text contained within parentheses or between a pair of dashed lines is removed. Second, any material contained within a pair of commas where the second comma is followed immediately by a verb or verb form, or by an infinitive, is assumed to be parenthetic and is deleted. Third, "padding" expressions such as "in fact," "indeed," "of course," "in any case," etc., are deleted.

The second phase in the procedure is to determine a weight for each sentence. Based on Edmunson's (1969) work, a simple summate of weighting functions is used that can be easily adjusted to reflect both the content of the document and user requirements. The variables used in the summate are: (1) the number of nontrivial title and subtitle words found in the sentence, (2) the number of words in the sentence that is in each of the categories of the WCL, (3) binary indicators to designate the first and the last sentences in a paragraph, and (4) a count of the high-frequency nontrivial words contained in the sentence (the definition of high frequency is also a parameter). A matrix containing the values of each variable for each sentence is constructed, and a vector of parameter weights is then applied, producing the vector of sentence weights.

---

[3] Other tests of reading comprehension exist. For example, cloze is a widely accepted measure of reading comprehension; however, it has been seriously questioned, especially in this type of application (Kibby 1980). According to Kibby, cloze may only measure the subject's ability to predict the next word in the text, rather than comprehend the meaning of the whole message.

The third phase in the procedure is to build the extract. This is accomplished by (1) adding the highest weighted as-yet-unselected sentence to the extract; (2) checking to see if this sentence has any exophoric references, and, if so, adding the referenced sentence(s) in the order of their weights to the extract; (3) recursively resolving the exophoric references of sentences added in step (2); and (4) counting the number of words in the sentences selected for the extract thus far and returning to step (1) if the count is less than the stopping rule. Before this algorithm can be applied, the parameter weights must be established. Working with four passages used in a earlier study (Kasper and Morris 1988), one of the researchers adjusted the parameter weights until the algorithm produced reasonable extracts; however, little effort was spent "optimizing" the weights, as only two iterations were performed. In a production system, these terms and weights would be adjusted to reflect the user's interests and the position, role, and function performed for the organization.

Based on Shannon's and Burton and Licklider's theoretical estimates of the redundancy in printed English, stopping rules were selected to produce extracts greater than and less than the theoretical reduction limit of 25% of the original without loss of information. The intent was to produce two sets of extracts: one set consisting of approximately 30 percent of the original document, and a second set containing about 20 percent of the original document, the latter exceeding the theoretical limits of nonexpository reduction. These are hereafter referred to as 30% extracts and 20% extracts, respectively.

According to the extracting algorithm, once a sentence is selected, sentences related through exophoric references are also selected without checking the stopping parameter until all exophoria is resolved. Therefore, the length of the extracts could not be predetermined exactly, as is the case with words or character sets. On average, the 30% extracts contained 31% of the original document, plus or minus 5%. The 20% extracts contained an average 19.2% of the original document, ranging from 19% to 21%. The extracts bounded both sides of the theoretical limit of 75% reduction very closely. Because the passages were randomly selected and the algorithm applied strictly as developed, no modifications or other original texts were considered.

To provide a control and a further assessment of the effectiveness of the abstract and the 20% and 30% extract algorithm, reductions produced by a totally "unintelligent" procedure were developed. These extracts were produced by randomly selecting sentences without replacement from the original full-length text until the reduction consisted of at least 25% of the original document. Once this amount was exceeded, the sentences were arranged by the order of their occurrence in the original document. This process resulted in random extracts that contained on average 26% of the words in the original document.

No-Extract Treatment

To provide a control and to investigate the possibility that the examination questions themselves contained information, a no-extract treatment was developed. The no-extract treatment contained only the examination questions and no other information. Like each of the other treatments, the no-extract treatment consisted of eight multiple-choice questions, each containing five possible responses.

Subjects

A total of 72 graduate students participated in the study. These students represented three classes of 24 students that elected to participate in the study. These

TABLE 1

Sample Means, Variances and Standard Errors by Treatment
for the Dependent Variable: Percent Reading Comprehension

	Percentage Score ($N = 72$)		
Treatment Levels	Mean ($n = 24$)	Variance	Standard Error
No Extract	0.346	0.011	0.021
Random Extract	0.489	0.047	0.044
20% Extract	0.552	0.031	0.036
30% Extract	0.609	0.017	0.026
Full Text	0.620	0.040	0.041
Abstract	0.630	0.024	0.031

subjects are appropriate for the task of reading and comprehending a text passage because the GMAT is intended to be administered to the same population. To motivate their performance subjects were given monetary prizes and class credit based on their performance.

Procedures

One of the three groups of 24 students was assigned the no-extract treatment. In this treatment no extract was given and only the examination questions were administered to the 24 subjects. At the other extreme, the full-length original text was administered to a second group of 24 subjects. Finally, a third group of 24 subjects was given all four condensing treatments according to the design described in the appendix. The groups as a whole were randomly assigned one of the three treatment regimes and the subjects within a group were randomized. However, because the data were collected in a classroom setting, complete randomization was not possible. Each group of subjects completed their assigned treatment(s) in a single session. At the beginning of the experiment, subjects were given a set of instructions. Next, the treatment(s) were administered. All treatments were administered on paper, and subjects with text to read were instructed not to return to the text once they began answering the questions. Each examination consisted of eight multiple-choice questions, each containing five possible responses. The subject's percentage correct score on these examinations served as the dependent variable for analysis.

Analysis and Results

Table 1 presents the sample means, variances, and standard errors for the dependent variable for each treatment level. Because each question had five multiple choice answers, the probability of a correct response without any information was 0.20 (a random guess). However, as the data show, all the treatments, even the no-extract treatment, exceeded this value by a considerable amount.

As can be seen from the data in Table 1, the mean performance by treatment is consistent with expectations. Ranked by decreasing order of performance, the treatment means are: informative abstract, original full text, 30% extract, 20% extract, random extract, and no extract. These results are consistent with Burton and Licklider's findings and suggest that the 75% limit to reduction may also hold for text condensing based on sentence extraction.

The analysis of variance for this data, including the type III sum of squares tests for

TABLE 2

Analysis of Variance for Reading Comprehension Performance

Source	df	Sum of Squares	F-value	R-square
Model	86	4.007	2.00**	0.751
Subject	66	1.849	1.20	
Passage	3	0.252	3.61*	
Treatment	3	0.287	4.11*	
Passage × Treatment	9	0.158	0.75	
Error	57	1.326		
Total	143	5.333		

** = alpha ≤ 0.01; * = alpha ≤ 0.05 level of significance.

the main effects and passage by treatment interaction model, is presented in Table 2. These results show that both the passage and treatment effects are significant at the alpha = 0.05 level; however, neither the subject nor the passage by treatment interaction is significant. The latter indicates that the relative performance of the treatment levels remained the same across passages and that no single passage accounted for these results.

To investigate the nature of the treatment effect, mean differences were computed and are presented in Table 3. For each comparison, the difference between the means is presented. Based on the least significant difference (LSD), a test of the hypotheses of equal means was computed for each comparison.

An examination of the mean differences in Table 3 shows that all the treatments including the random extract performed significantly better than the no-extract treatment. The data also show that the performances of the condensing treatments—the 20% extract, the 30% extract, and the informative abstract—were no different from that of the original full-text. Only the random, and the no-extract treatment means were significantly below the full-text treatment mean. Likewise, both the 30% extract and the informative abstract performed better than the randomly produced extract. However, the 20% extract mean performance was not significantly different from

TABLE 3

Treatment Level Mean Differences (Row-Column)

	Treatment Levels				
	No Extract	Random Extract	Full Text	Abstract	30% Extract
Random Extract	0.143**				
Full Text	0.273**	0.130**			
Abstract	0.284**	0.141**	0.010		
30% Extract	0.263**	0.120**	−0.010	−0.021	
20% Extract	0.206**	0.063	−0.068	−0.078	−0.057

df = 57 for all comparisons.
Least Significant Difference (LSD) for alpha ≤ 0.01 = 0.118, alpha ≤ 0.05 = 0.088.
** The hypothesis of equal means is rejected at alpha ≤ 0.01 level of significance.

that of the random extract treatment. Yet, there was no difference in performance between the two extract treatments, the two extract treatment levels and the original full text, and the two extract treatment levels and the informative abstract.

Collectively, these comparisons suggest that it is possible to produce extracts that exceed the 75% redundancy limit. Consistent with Brookes (1983), these results might also reflect the subjects' ability to compensate, in this case interpolating information from the 20% extract, and even the random treatment. In sum, $H1_0$ cannot be rejected; in terms of reading comprehension, the data show that no difference in performance exists between the original document and extracts containing 20% or 30% of the original document. Likewise, $H2_0$ cannot be rejected; in terms of reading comprehension performance, the data show no difference between the informative abstract and either the 20% or the 30% extracts. Apparently, the extract algorithm produced extracts that were as informative as the human-expert produced abstracts.

Finally, $H3_0$ cannot be rejected; the data show no difference in reading comprehension performance between the condensed forms (abstract and extract) and the original document. This indicates that condensed forms can be produced that are equally as informative as the original document. While not significant, the mean performance of the informative abstract treatment actually exceeded that of the original document treatment, suggesting that quality reductions might actually enhance the subject's comprehension of the information contained in the original document. Failure to reject the null hypotheses, however, reflects a strict interpretation of the results. The results also show that the mean performance of the 20% extract was not statistically different than the random extract treatment. This may be a reflection of the loss of information as the 20% extract exceeded the 75% redundancy level of printed English or this may indicate that the random extracts were particularly informative. Support for the latter is provided by the finding that the random extract performed significantly better than the no-extract treatment.

Summary and Conclusions

Collectively, these results suggest that it is possible to apply a relatively simple computer algorithm to text and produce extracts that capture enough of the information contained in the original document so that the recipient can perform as if he or she had read the original. In this study, subjects performed as well reading extracts as they did reading the original full length text, even though the text was relatively difficult and the measure of performance, reading comprehension, was intended to be very discriminating. Under less discriminating conditions, where the objective is to provide a more general overview of the original document or to help the reader decide if the full text should be consulted, these results indicate that the extracting algorithm would produce reductions containing more information than that needed for the task. Moreover, these results were achieved over an atypically broad set of problem domains (medieval literature, 18th-century Japan, minority business opportunities, and Florentine art). It seems unlikely that the typical business user would encounter such a diverse set of domains on any regular basis, nor does it seem reasonable to expect any condensing technique using a single set of parameters, including any future natural language-based abstracting system, to perform any better over such a diverse set of topics. As the breadth of topics is narrowed, the extracting algorithm could be tuned and thus potentially produce even better reductions.

The reader should note that the "abstract" at the beginning of this paper is actually an extract that was generated using the algorithm discussed here. In this case, the algorithm was modified slightly to reflect the academic research nature of the article. For example, slightly more emphasis was placed on introductory and summary sections than on the intervening text. In addition, this paragraph was excluded from analysis. The extract itself was not modified after extraction.

In terms of reading comprehension, these results also failed to support Shannon's and Burton and Licklider's estimate that printed English has a redundancy of about 75 percent. Reductions of 80% were shown to be effective in this study. These results support Kibby's (1980) suggestion that the 75 percent prediction rate of Shannon and Burton and Licklider may simply reflect printed English's redundancy of characters and words and does not extend to information units or chunks into message comprehension. As both Kibby (1980) and Brookes (1983) have observed, these results might also reflect the subjects' ability to compensate and interpolate information from text. Compensation and interpolation increase with experience in the subject matter. The diversity of the topics used in this study probably understated this ability. One might expect that experienced people in the domain of the condensed text might need even less text to attain a high level of comprehension.

These results also have implications for designers of natural language processing systems. It is important to realize that the extracting algorithm is not without intelligence. Mathematical information has (Edmunson 1977, 1984) and is currently (Jacobs and Rau 1990) being used to process text. However, much of the effectiveness of the extracting algorithm used here can be attributed to its resolution of exophoria. This resulted in the identification of clusters of sentences that were treated as a single information unit. In this way, sentences served as a nucleus around which all or a segment of a mapping of the information or semantic content of the message was developed. For natural language processing researchers this suggests that rather than focusing on words as the unit of analysis, much more effective and efficient systems might result from constructing a conceptual framework such as semantic networks at an information unit level (e.g., the sentence). The results of this study suggest that the resolution of exophoria is a very powerful technique for mapping the linguistic structure of information units such as groups of sentences.

These results also identify a methodology for assessing the effectiveness of text condensing schemes. Future text condensing schemes must produce reductions that contain less than 80% of the original full-length text and produce reductions that result in reading comprehension performance that is equal to or exceeds that attained from the original full-length document. Quality reductions might actually enhance the subject's comprehension of the information contained in the original document, because the concise and summarized presentation sufficiently reduces distracting information that would otherwise impede performance through information overload. Such a finding is supported by research in condensing numerical data (Chervany and Dickson 1974).

While these results are informative, both in practice and theory, several limitations of the research should be noted. First, the subjects were university students, but there is no reason to expect that their reading comprehension varies greatly from that of the "real world" population. A second more severe limitation of the study is the type of passage used in the research—difficult and relatively short. The use of easier to read, more typically constructed communication may influence the findings. Also, the lengths of the original passages used here were all about 450 words. While this length is consistent with many business magazine articles and reading comprehension examinations, many documents are much longer. Although short, the length of the passages used in this study is consistent with newspaper[4] and magazine columns and short stories (Neff 1990, Mandell 1987, Peterson and Kesselman-Turkel 1987), as well as frequently used business correspondence such as letters, memoranda and short reports (Kirtz and Reep 1990). However, the use of relatively short documents probably understated the true difference between the extracts, particularly the 20% extracts, and the random treatments.[5] A third limitation is that the abstracts were, as part of the research design, not expository, likely understating the potential performance of the abstracting treatment. Despite these limitations, a number of implications for text-based information systems research and practice can be drawn.

Demonstrating that a relatively simple text condensing algorithm can be used to generate highly effective reductions, these results suggest a number of important research questions. Text condensing techniques are represented as a continuum ranging from randomly generated extracts to critical abstracts. This research developed one extracting algorithm, but others may prove more appealing. Future research should also investigate the degree to which the subjects' ability to compensate, interpolating information from that provided, is related to text condensing and the maximum reduction possible without loss of information.

In summary, more than 20 years ago Ackoff argued that condensing is critical for dealing with information overload, especially when the information is in the form of text. As the volume of text being transported by information systems increases, so will the potential for information overload. To deal with this problem, efficient and effective text condensing techniques will become essential. The research presented here suggests one near-term approach for dealing with this growing problem and an approach for assessing the effectiveness of future condensing schemes. The research presented here contributes to a small but growing body of work on text-based information systems and, specifically, text condensing.*

[4] For example, on Thursday, January 31, 1991, a total of 164 general, international, financial and Washington news articles, commentaries and standing feature columns were transmitted by the United Press International (UPI) wire service. The average word count of these articles was approximately 524. (Word counts were obtained by the authors from Dialog Information Services.)

[5] Because the original passages consisted of from 15 to 20 sentences, the probability of randomly selecting a sentence from the document that was also selected by the extracting algorithm was great, thereby understating the difference between the extract and random treatments. In fact, approximately 20 percent of the extract sentences were also included in the random reduction.

* Barbara Gutek, Associate Editor. This paper was received on February 7, 1991 and has been with the authors 2 months for 1 revision.

Appendix. Order and Combination of Treatments and Passage in Experimental Design

Subject	Position 1	Position 2	Position 3	Position 4
49	Random Extract, D	Abstract, C	20% Extract, B	30% Extract, A
50	Random Extract, C	Abstract, D	30% Extract, B	20% Extract, A
51	Random Extract, B	20% Extract, D	Abstract, A	30% Extract, C
52	Random Extract, A	20% Extract, B	30% Extract, C	Abstract, D
53	Random Extract, A	30% Extract, D	Abstract, B	20% Extract, C
54	Random Extract, D	30% Extract, A	20% Extract, C	Abstract, B
55	Abstract, D	Random Extract, C	20% Extract, A	30% Extract, B
56	Abstract, C	Random Extract, B	30% Extract, D	20% Extract, A

Appendix (continued)

Subject	Position 1	Position 2	Position 3	Position 4
57	Abstract, B	20% Extract, A	Random Extract, C	30% Extract, D
58	Abstract, A	20% Extract, B	30% Extract, D	Random Extract, C
59	Abstract, B	30% Extract, C	Random Extract, A	20% Extract, D
60	Abstract, B	30% Extract, A	20% Extract, D	Random Extract, C
61	20% Extract, D	Random Extract, B	Abstract, C	30% Extract, A
62	20% Extract, C	Random Extract, A	30% Extract, D	Abstract, B
63	20% Extract, C	Abstract, D	Random Extract, A	30% Extract, B
64	20% Extract, A	Abstract, C	30% Extract, B	Random Extract, D
65	20% Extract, B	30% Extract, C	Random Extract, D	Abstract, A
66	20% Extract, C	30% Extract, B	Abstract, A	Random Extract, D
67	30% Extract, D	Random Extract, B	Abstract, A	20% Extract, C
68	30% Extract, C	Random Extract, A	20% Extract, B	Abstract, D
69	30% Extract, B	Abstract, D	Random Extract, C	20% Extract, A
70	30% Extract, A	Abstract, C	20% Extract, D	Random Extract, B
71	30% Extract, D	20% Extract, A	Random Extract, B	Abstract, C
72	30% Extract, A	20% Extract, D	Abstract, C	Random Extract, B

A–D = the passages; subjects 1–24 were administered the No Extract treatment (i.e., questions only) and subjects 25–48 received the original Full Text treatment.

References

Ackoff, R. L., "Management Misinformation Systems," *Management Science,* 14, 4 (1967), B147–156.

Adams, D. A. and I. R. Weiss, "Organizational Connectivity Systems: Is the Function Being Effectively Managed?," *Data Base,* 20, 1 (1989), 16–20.

American National Standards Institute, Inc., *American National Standard for Writing Abstracts,* ANSI, Inc., New York, 1979.

Baxendale, P. B., "Machine-Made Index for Technical Literature—An Experiment," *IBM Journal of Research and Development,* 2, 4 (1958), 354–361.

Bernier, C. L., "Abstracts and Abstracting," in *Subject and Information Analysis,* E. D. Dym (Ed.), Marcel Dekker, Inc., New York, 1985.

Blair, D. C., *Language and Representation in Information Retrieval,* Elsevier Science Publications, Amsterdam, 1990.

————, "The Data-Document Distinction in Information Retrieval," *Communications of the ACM,* 27, 4 (1984), 369–374.

———— and M. E. Maron, "An Evaluation of Retrieval Effectiveness for a Full-Text Document Retrieval System," *Communications of the ACM,* 28, 3 (1985), 289–299.

Borko, H. and C. L. Bernier, *Abstracting Concepts and Methods,* Academic Press, New York, 1975.

Brancheau, J. C. and J. C. Wetherbe, "Key Issues in Information Systems Management," *MIS Quarterly,* 11, 1 (1987), 23–45.

Brookes, C. H. P., "Text Processing as a Tool for DSS Design," in *Processes and Tools for Decision Support,* H. G. Sol (Ed.), North-Holland Publishing Company, Amsterdam, 1983, 131–138.

Burton, D. and J. Licklider, "Long-Range Constraints in the Statistical Structure of Printed English," *American Journal of Psychology,* 68 (1955), 650–653.

Chervany, N. L. and G. W. Dickson, "An Experimental Evaluation of Information Overload in a Production Environment," *Management Science,* 20, 10 (1974), 1335–1344.

Cohen, J., *Statistical Power Analysis for the Behavioral Sciences,* (Revised Ed.), Academic Press, New York, 1977.

Cremmins, E. T., *The Art of Abstracting,* ISI Press, Philadelphia, 1982.

Culnan, M. J. and J. H. Bair, "Human Communication Needs and Organizational Productivity: The Potential Impact of Office Automation," *Journal of the American Society for Information Science,* 34, 3 (1983), 215–221.

Daft, R. L., J. Sormunen and D. Parks, "Chief Executives Scanning, Environmental Characteristics, and Company Performance: An Empirical Study," *Strategic Management Journal,* 9, 2 (1988), 123–139.

Davis, G. D. and M. H. Olson, *Management Information Systems: Conceptual Foundations, Structure, and Development,* (Second Ed.), McGraw-Hill, Inc., New York, 1985.

Denning, P., "Electronic Junk," *Communications of the ACM,* 25, 3 (1982), 163–165.

Dickson, G. W., R. L. Leitheiser, J. C. Wetherbe and M. Necis, "Key Information Systems Issues for the 1980's," *MIS Quarterly,* 8, 3 (1984), 135–159.

Dillon, M. and A. S. Gray, "FASIT: A Fully Automated Syntactically Based Indexing System," *Journal of the American Society for Information Science,* 34, 2 (1983), 99–108.

Edmunson, H. P., "Problems in Automatic Abstracting," *Communications of the ACM,* 7, 4 (1964), 259–263.

———, "New Methods in Automatic Extracting," *Journal of the ACM,* 16, 2 (1969), 264–285.

———, "Statistical Inference in Mathematical and Computational Linguistics," *International Journal of Computer and Information Sciences,* 6, 2 (1977), 95–129.

———, "Mathematical Models of Text," *Information Processing and Management,* 20, 1–2 (1984), 261–268.

——— and R. E. Wyllys, "Automatic Abstracting and Indexing—Survey and Recommendations," *Communications of the ACM,* 4, 5 (1961), 226–234.

Educational Testing Service, *The Official Guide for GMAT Review,* Graduate Management Admissions Council, Princeton, NJ, 1986.

El Sawy, O. A., "Personal Information Systems for Strategic Scanning in Turbulent Environments: Can the CEO Go On-Line?," *MIS Quarterly,* 9, 1 (1985), 53–60.

Epstein, S. S., "Transportable Natural Language Processing Through Simplicity—The PRE System," *ACM Transactions on Office Information Systems,* 3, 2 (1985), 107–120.

Ewusi-mensah, K., "The External Organizational Environment and Its Impact on Management Information Systems," *Accounting, Organizations and Society,* 6, 4 (1981), 301–316.

Goode, H. H., "Greenhouses of Science for Management," *Management Science,* 4, 4 (1958), 365–381.

Gunning, R., *The Technique of Clear Writing,* (Revised Ed.), McGraw-Hill, New York, 1968.

Hale, D. P., J. E. Hurd and G. M. Kasper, "A Knowledge Exchange Architecture for Collaborative Human-Computer Communication," *IEEE Transactions on Systems, Man, and Cybernetics,* (1991) (forthcoming).

——— and G. M. Kasper, "The Effect of Human-Computer Interchange Protocol on Decision Performance," *Journal of Management Information Systems,* 6, 1 (1989), 5–20.

Heidorn, G. E., K. Jensen, L. A. Miller, R. J. Byrd and M. S. Chodorow, "The EPISTLE Text-Critiquing System," *IBM Systems Journal,* 21, 3 (1982), 305–326.

Hiltz, S. R. and M. Turoff, "Structuring Computer-Mediated Communication Systems to Avoid Information Overload," *Communications of the ACM,* 28, 7 (1985), 680–689.

Horton, R. L., *The General Linear Model,* McGraw-Hill, Inc., New York, 1978.

Jacobs, P. S. and L. F. Rau, "SCISOR: Extracting Information from On-Line News," *Communications of the ACM,* 33, 11 (1990), 88–97.

Kahneman, D., *Attention and Effort,* Prentice-Hall, Inc., Englewood Cliffs, NJ, 1973.

Kasper, G. M. and A. H. Morris, "The Effect of Presentation Media on Recipient Performance in Text-Based Information Systems," *Journal of Management Information Systems,* 4, 4 (1988), 25–43.

Kerr, E. B. and S. R. Hiltz, *Computer-Mediated Communication Systems: Status and Evaluation,* Academic Press, New York, 1982.

Kibby, M. W., "Intersentential Processes in Reading Comprehension," *Journal of Reading Behavior,* 12, 4 (1980), 299–312.

Kiesler, S., J. Siegel and T. M. McGuire, "Social Psychological Aspects of Computer-Mediated Communication," *American Psychologist,* 39, 10 (1984), 1123–1134.

Kirtz, M. K. and D. C. Reep, "A Survey of the Frequency, Types, and Importance of Writing Tasks in Four Career Areas," *The Bulletin,* 53, 4 (1990), 3–4.

Kolodziej, S., "Where Is the Electronic Messaging Explosion?," *Computerworld Focus,* 19, 41A (October 16, 1985), 21–23.

Kriebel, C. H. and D. M. Strong, "A Survey of the MIS and Telecommunications Activities of Major Business Firms," *MIS Quarterly,* 8, 3 (1984), 171–178.

Luhn, H. P., "The Automatic Creation of Literature Abstracts," *IBM Journal of Research and Development,* 2, 2 (1958a), 159–165.

———, "A Business Intelligence System," *IBM Journal of Research and Development,* 2, 4 (1958b), 314–319.

Mandell, J., *Magazine Writers Nonfiction Guidelines,* McFarland and Company, Inc., Jefferson, NC, 1987.

Mathis, B. A., J. E., Rush and C. E. Young, "Improvement of Automatic Abstracts by the Use of Structural Analysis," *Journal of the American Society of Information Science*, 24 (1973), 101–109.

Miller, L. A., "Project EPISTLE: A System for the Automatic Analysis of Business Correspondence," *Proceedings of the First Annual National Conference on Artificial Intelligence*, Stanford University, 1980, 280–282.

————, G. E. Heidorn and K. Jensen, "Text-Critiquing with the EPISTLE System: An Author's Aid to Better Syntax," *AFIPS Conference Proceedings*, AFIPS Press, Arlington, VA, 1981, 649–655.

Mintzberg, H., D. Raisinghani and A. Theoret, "The Structure of 'Un-structured' Decision Processes," *Administrative Science Quarterly*, 21, 2 (1976), 246–275.

Morris, A. H., "Supporting Environmental Scanning and Organizational Communication with the Processing of Text: The Use of Computer-Generated Abstracts," Unpublished Ph.D. Dissertation, Texas Tech University, 1988.

Neff, G. T., 1991 *Writer's Market: Where and How to Sell What You Write*, Writer's Digest Books, Cincinnati, OH, 1990.

Paice, C. D., *Information Retrieval and the Computer*, MacDonald and Jane's, London, 1977.

————, "The Automatic Generation of Literature Abstracts: An Approach Based on the Identification of Self-indicating Phrases," in *Information Retrieval Research*. Oddy, R. N., Robertson, S. E., van Rijsbergen, C. J., and Williams, P. W. (Ed.), Butterworths, London, 1981.

Peterson, F. and J. Kesselman-Turkel, *The Magazine Writer's Handbook*, Dodd, Mead and Company, New York, 1987.

Pollock, J. J. and A. Zamora, "Automatic Abstracting Research at Chemical Abstracts," *Journal of Chemical Information and Computer Science*, 15, 4 (1975), 226–232.

Rappaport, A., "Management Misinformation Systems—Another Perspective," *Management Science*, 15, 4 (1968), B133–136.

Rice, R. E. and J. H. Bair, "New Organizational Media and Productivity," in *The New Media*, R. E. Rice (Ed.), Sage Publications, Beverly Hills, CA, 1984, 185–215.

Rush, J. E., R. Salvador and A. Zamora, "Automatic Abstracting and Indexing. II. Production of Indicative Abstracts by Application of Contextual Inference and Syntactic Coherence Criteria," *Journal of the American Society for Information Science*, 22 (1971), 260–274.

Salton, G., *Automatic Text Processing: The Transformation, Analysis, and Retrieval of Information by Computer*, Addison-Wesley, Reading, MA, 1989.

Schriber, J., "Move Over, Strunk and White," *Forbes*, (August 15, 1983), 100–101.

Schroder, H. M., M. J. Driver and S. Streufert, *Human Information Processing*, Holt, Rinehart, and Winston, New York, 1967.

Schwartz, R., J., Fortune and J. Horwich, "AMANDA: A Computerized Document Management System," *MIS Quarterly*, 4, 3 (1980), 41–49.

Shannon, C. E., "Prediction and Entropy of Printed English," *Bell Systems Technical Journal*, 30 (1951), 50–64.

Slonim, J., L. J. MacRae, W. E. Mennie and N. Diamond, "NDX-100: An Electronic Filing Machine for the Office of the Future," *Computer*, (May 1981), 24–36.

Smeaton, A. F. and C. J. van Rijsbergen, "Information Retrieval in an Office Filing Facility and Future Work in Project Minstrel," *Information Processing and Management*, 22, 5 (1986), 135–149.

Swanson, D. R., "Information Retrieval as a Trial-and-Error Process," *Library Quarterly*, 47, 2 (1977), 128–148.

Swanson, E. B. and M. J. Culnan, "Document-Based Systems for Management Planning and Control: A Classification, Survey, and Assessment," *MIS Quarterly*, 2, 4 (1978), 31–46.

Taylor, S. L. and G. K. Krulee, "Experiments with an Automatic Abstracting System," in *Information Management in the 1980's, Proceedings of the ASIS Annual Meeting. Vol.* 14, Knowledge Industry Publications, White Plains, NY, 1977, 83.

Tsichritzis, D., "Message Addressing Schemes," *ACM Transactions on Office Information Systems*, 2, 1 (1984), 58–77.

van Rijsbergen, C. J., *Information Retrieval*, (2nd Ed.), Butterworths, London, 1979.

Weil, B. H., "Standards for Writing Abstracts," *Journal of the American Society for Information Science*, 21, 5 (1970), 351–357.

Wiener, N., *Cybernetics or Control and Communication in the Animal and the Machine*, (2nd Ed.), The MIT Press and John Wiley & Sons, Inc., New York, 1961.

An Evaluation of Automatic Text Summarization Systems

Thérèse Firmin and Michael J. Chrzanowski

Department of Defense
9800 Savage Road
Ft. Meade MD 20755-6000
{tfirmin,mjchrza}@romulus.ncsc.mil

Abstract

This paper discusses the importance of evaluation for automatic text summarization systems and the results of one such experiment conducted with the participation of six key researchers in the field. Efforts such as this will help us to learn more about the utility of automatically summarized data and effective metrics for evaluation.

1. Introduction

The explosion of on-line textual material and the advances in text processing technology have provided an important opportunity for broad application of text summarization systems. Many techniques for deriving summaries from full text documents have already been implemented, and several commercial summarization products are already available. The summaries generated by these systems are potentially useful in a variety of settings.

Many different types of evaluations have been undertaken in an attempt to better understand the utility of these systems. These evaluations have typically been conducted by system designers and were focused on the specific type of summary created by that system. They include many types of intrinsic evaluations, which focus on the quality of the summary and extrinsic evaluations, which focus on the task (McKeown 1998). The intrinsic evaluations strive for a gold-star summary, which is believed to be the best summary possible of a given text. The task-based evaluations have been tied to information retrieval tasks and relevance judgments for a set of documents. None of these evaluations are perfect, but they all provide information and feedback which allow researchers to continue to improve their systems. Previous evaluations are described further in section 3. They provided an excellent basis for the design of the dry run evaluation discussed in this paper, which was intended to be a multiple system, tasked-based evaluation.

In 1997, the Defense Advanced Research Projects Agency (DARPA) expanded the TIPSTER program to include the development and evaluation of full text summarization systems. TIPSTER is a DARPA initiative with participation from multiple U. S. Government agencies and research and commercial institutions to push the state of the art in the text processing technologies of information retrieval, information extraction, and text summarization. This new text summarization effort will, in part, evaluate the output of various systems' approaches with respect to specific summarization tasks and provide feedback to their developers. It was a natural extension of the existing research and there was a previous history of successful evaluations for both information retrieval (the Text REtrieval Conference) and information extraction (the Message Understanding Conference).

2. Concepts of Text Summarization

Although summaries of texts may be described in many ways, we will limit our discussion here to the concepts of intent, focus and coverage.

Intent describes the potential use of the summary, which can be indicative, informative or evaluative. Indicative summaries provide just enough information to judge the relevancy of the corresponding full text or give a brief indication of its central topic. Informative or substantive summaries serve as substitutes for the full documents, retaining important details while reducing the amount of information presented to the user. Evaluative summaries capture the point of view of the author on a given subject.

Focus refers to the scope of the summary, either generic or query-relevant. A generic summary is based on the main theme or themes of a document whereas a query-relevant summary is constructed around a particular topic of interest as indicated by the recipient of the summary.

Coverage refers to whether the summary is based on a single document or multiple documents relating to the same subject matter.

Much of the historical work in automatic text summarization has been geared toward the creation of indicative, generic summaries of single documents. For example Luhn (1958), Edmundson (1969), Johnson et al. (1993) and Brandow, Mitze and Rau (1995) all generated this type of summary, although their approaches have included different combinations of statistical and linguistic techniques. Luhn (1958) considered frequency of word occurrence within a document and the position of the word in a sentence.

Edmundson (1969) looked at cue words, title and heading words, and structural indicators. Johnson et al. (1993) used indicator phrases. Brandow, Mitze and Rau (1995) applied sentence weighting using signature word selection. Most of these approaches claim some degree of domain independence; however they have been tested only on a specific type of data, such as newspaper articles (Brandow, Mitze and Rau 1995) or technical literature (Edmundson 1969).

More recently, the scope of research efforts has expanded to include informative, user-directed, and multi-document summaries. Reimer and Hahn (1988), Maybury (1993), and McKeown and Radev (1995) used knowledge-based approaches to generate informative summaries that can serve as substitutes for the original document.

The expansion in focus to include user-directed summaries has been influenced by research in the information retrieval (IR) community on passage-based retrieval, as in the work of Knaus et al. (1996). Aone et al. (1997) have combined advances in statistical learning algorithms and user-customization, allowing the user to affect the content of the generic summaries by manipulating sentence extraction features.

The potential for multi-document summarization as proposed by the work of Strzalkowski (1996) and Mani and Bloedorn (1997a) is based in part on advances in related areas of natural language processing (NLP) such as information retrieval and information extraction.

3. Previous Evaluations

During the course of their development, most of the above systems were subject to some form of evaluation. Many of these evaluations relied on the presence of a human-generated target abstract or the notion of a single "best" abstract. However, there is fairly uniform acceptance of the belief that any number of acceptable abstracts could effectively represent the content of a single document. Human-generated abstracts attempt to capture the central ideas of a document using the terminology of the document, similar to a generic summary. There might be more than one sentence or phrase that captures the essence of an idea. Neither sentence might be preferable over the other, but only one is necessary to create a good summary. The comparisons made between these human-generated and machine-generated summaries were intended primarily for the developers' own benefit in order to improve their system. They evaluate the technology itself, rather than the utility of the technology for a given task. There have been other evaluations that focus on specific tasks and potential uses of automatic summaries, but usually only with respect to a single system and a limited document set.

Many different techniques have been applied to intrinsic evaluations, which judge the quality of summaries. Edmundson (1969) compared sentence selection in automatic abstracts to target abstracts and performed a subjective evaluation of their content. Johnson et al. (1993) proposed matching a template of manually generated key concepts with the concepts included in the abstract and performed one sample abstract evaluation. Paice and Jones (1993) used a set of statistics to determine if the summary effectively captured the focal concepts, the nonfocal concepts, and conclusions of the full text. Brandow, Mitze and Rau (1995) had news analysts evaluate summaries generated using complex heuristics based on statistical and NLP techniques to summaries based on the initial sentences (called the "lead" summaries) of the document. They discovered that, overall, experienced news analysts felt that the lead summaries were more acceptable than the summaries created using sophisticated NLP techniques.

Kupiec et al. (1995) calculated the percentage of sentence matches and partial matches between their automatic summary and a manually generated abstract. The main problem with this type of evaluation is its reliance on the notion of a single "correct" or "best" abstract. Since many different representations of a document can form an effective summary, this can be a misleading measure. There have been several recent studies, however, that indicate that while judges may not agree on all of the sentences to be included in an abstract or summary, they do agree on the most important sentences to include and on which sentences should definitely be excluded (Marcu, 1997; McKeown, 1998).

In extrinsic or task-oriented evaluations, the information retrieval notion of relevance of a document to a specific topic is a common metric for assessing the acceptability of summaries. This type of evaluation is often conducted in conjunction with other more intrinsic evaluations. Miike et al. (1994) analyzed key sentence coverage, similar to the Kupiec test. They also conducted an IR-based task, recording timing and precision/recall statistics of relevance decisions based on summaries for a domain-specific summarizer. Five judges reviewed the top 10 editorial-style documents retrieved from the IR system for relevance. Miike et al. found that for selecting relevant documents returned as a result of an IR query, summaries have similar precision and recall scores to full text documents while taking only 80% of the time.

More recently, Mani and Bloedorn (1997b) generated precision/recall and timing measures for an information retrieval experiment using a graph search and matching technique and learned that their summaries were effective enough to support accurate retrieval. They also included some feedback from the judges in response to questions about the desired length of the documents being reviewed and the usefulness of the text in deciding relevance. For this test, there were four judges, four queries and 1200 documents total. Some of this feedback information was incorporated into the dry run evaluation.

In a set of experiments conducted shortly after the dry run evaluation, Jing et al. (1998) studied the performance of both human-generated summaries and the output of three different automatic summarizers. In their intrinsic evaluation, they compared sentences selected by human abstractors with each other and with sentences selected by the systems. Shorter summaries had greater agreement in sentence selection in this experiment, possibly reflecting the essential nature of the information found in the shorter summaries.

They also conducted an extrinsic evaluation using summaries as a back end to an information retrieval system. The summaries were created at 10% and 20% of the length of the full text. The baselines were keywords and human-generated summaries. Assessors determined the relevance of the summary to the query. Jing et al. recorded time required to read the text, accuracy of decision, and confidence of decision. The summaries did not perform as accurately as the full text, although they did save time. The human-generated summaries took proportionally less time to read than the summaries of different lengths, possibly because the text was more cohesive. This experimental setup is very similar to a task in the dry run evaluation, although smaller in scale.

4. TIPSTER Evaluation

As part of the TIPSTER Phase III Text Program, in the fall of 1997 the U. S. Government conducted a dry run of an extrinsic, task-based evaluation of automatic summarization systems. The dry run was limited to TIPSTER Phase III summarization contractors: Carnegie Group Inc., Cornell University, GE Research and Development, New Mexico State University, the University of Pennsylvania and the University of Southern California-Information Sciences Institute.

The goals of the dry run evaluation were to:

- judge summarization systems independently on their applicability to a given task (rather than as a comparison of systems),

- gain a better understanding of the issues involved in building and evaluating summarization systems and

- guide the direction of the research to requirements of real world tasks.

The evaluation focused on the end-user utility of summaries. It included two primary user-oriented tasks: categorization and adhoc* retrieval. The summaries were treated as indicative summaries of a single document. For the categorization task, the focus was on generic summaries; for the adhoc task, the focus was on user-directed (query relevant) summaries. We selected these tasks for the initial evaluation to get an early indication of the utility of the technology and to provide feedback to the participants on their respective approaches.

The Text REtrieval Conferences (TREC) played a crucial role in the summarization evaluation by serving as a successful evaluation model and by providing data in the form of documents, topics and relevance judgments.

TREC is a large-scale evaluation of full text retrieval systems. Participants are provided topics and a large corpus of full text documents. For the primary TREC adhoc task, they must return a set of the top 200 documents retrieved by their information retrieval system using the topic as the statement of user need. All documents returned as a result of this query are pooled together. The same assessor who drafted the initial topic reviews the resulting pooled document set and determines the relevance of each document. Precision and recall scores for each participant are calculated based on relevance of the documents in the set of top 200 they provided versus the entire set of relevant documents submitted by all participants.

The data for the summarization evaluation was generated from the same TREC/TIPSTER collection. This collection, which is all in English, consists of SGML-formatted documents from the Wall Street Journal, AP news wire, Ziff-Davis, the Federal Register, and the Department of Energy publications (Harman 1995).

The TREC documents range a great deal in length. For the summarization evaluation we used only those documents between 2,000 and 15,000 characters in length with an average length of 4,765 characters.

The TREC topics, as described in Harman (1995), reflect user need statements. They characterize, in varying levels of detail, what constitutes a relevant document for a given query. For the summarization evaluation, we chose topics from both the detailed TREC-1 and 2 sets and the more informal TREC-3 set. The detailed topics included title, description and narrative fields whereas the informal topics included only the title and the description.

The relevance decisions made by an assessor for a given topic and document set serves as the ground truth for all TREC evaluations. For the

---

* Following the convention established in the Text REtrieval Conferences, adhoc is spelled as a single word.

summarization evaluation, since the tasks selected are dependent on both the TREC topics and the relevant document sets, this was an appropriate set of data for an initial evaluation and served as our ground truth as well.

4.1 Categorization Task

The goal of the categorization task was to evaluate generic summaries to determine if the key concept in a given document was captured in the summary. The real-world activity represented by the categorization task was that of a person manually routing or filtering information who must quickly decide whether a document contains information about any of several related topic areas. For the evaluation, the major variable was the presentation of the document: full document, lead-line summary, or generic, system-generated summary. Lead-line summaries were selected as the baseline because they have been shown in the past to be as acceptable as summaries generated using sophisticated techniques (Brandow, Mitze and Rau 1995). The lead-line summaries consisted of the initial 10% of the document length with word completion. We felt that in order to demonstrate the utility of summaries, performance of the automatic summaries must be significantly better than lead sentence summaries

The TREC topics were the discriminating categories for the evaluation. The topics selected were all in the subject area of government regulations. In accordance with the task we were simulating, all documents in a broad subject area, such as government regulations, were displayed to a user, who then must distribute them into various categories based on their content. The following topics were used for the dry run evaluation:

115   Impact of the 1986 Immigration Law
161   Acid Rain
164   Generic Drugs - Illegal Activities by Manufacturers
167   Regulation of the showing of violence and explicit sex in motion picture theaters, on television, and on video cassettes
175   NRA Prevention of Gun Control Legislation

Two of the topics, 164 and 175, were selected because they included references to named entities. Named entities are references to people, locations and organizations and represent specific detailed information that might be useful in summary creation. These entities were expected to be referenced in the full text of the document. This provided variety in the queries and allowed us to address the capabilities of more information extraction or NLP-oriented approaches. The remaining topics were a subset of the area of government regulations, but with no other specific criteria.

The topics were used to generate the set of documents to be summarized by the participants and subsequently categorized by the assessors. We selected 200 documents retrieved by a TREC system for each topic. Using TREC relevance data, we tried to select those documents returned within the top 200 system hits for a topic, which resulted in a mixture of 43% relevant and 57% nonrelevant documents. No document occurred in more than one set. The TREC topics, document sets, and relevance data were used as ground truth decisions during the dry run evaluation. This allowed us to use existing data for generation of the precision/recall metrics. We assumed that if a TREC assessor found a full text document to be relevant to a topic, a good summary of that document should also appear relevant to an assessor. We had a different set of assessors, but compared their decisions to the ground truth previously established by the TREC assessors.

The resulting documents were randomly mixed and provided to the evaluation participants. The topics were not provided. The participants were directed not to determine the original topics either manually or automatically. Summarization systems developed by the participants automatically built generic summaries of each document.

The full text document and the lead sentences of the document (up to 10% of the document length) were used as baselines. Each participant was allowed to submit two summaries. One was a maximum of 10% of the original document length - the *fixed* summary, and the other was the optimal summary of the document that the system could produce – the *best* summary. The summaries provided by the participants, the baseline lead summaries and the full text documents were mixed together, resulting in a total of 14 versions of a single document.

The complete document set was randomly divided among 15 assessors who were professional information analysts. Each assessor read a summary or document and categorized it into one of the five topic areas or "none of the above". No assessor read more than one version (summary or full text) of a single document, and each assessor completed one set of 100 documents and summaries. The assessor's decision-making process was timed.

4.2 Adhoc Task

The goal of the adhoc task was to evaluate query-relevant summaries to determine if each summary effectively captured the information sought by the user, as indicated by the topic.

The real-world activity represented by this task was that of a person doing adhoc retrievals using an information retrieval system who must determine quickly and accurately the relevance of a retrieved document. For the evaluation the major variable was the nature of the document: full document, lead summary, or query-relevant summary. Lead-line summaries again were used as a baseline for comparisons.

The data used for this task were similar to and in the same proportions as the categorization task: five topics and approximately 200 documents per topic. The topics were selected to provide variety for the summarization systems and the assessors, while not duplicating any of the topics used in the categorization task.

110	Black Resistance Against the South African Government
132	"Stealth" Aircraft
138	Iranian Support for Lebanese Hostage-takers
141	Japan's Handling of its Trade Surplus with the U. S.
151	Coping with Overcrowded Prisons

Topics 110 (South Africa), 138 (Iran) and 141 (Japan) were the entity-based topics. As with the categorization task, the entity-based topics included references to people, locations and organizations and the relevant documents were expected to include similar information. There was a mixture of 42% relevant and 58% nonrelevant documents in the resulting document sets.

For this task, both the topics and corresponding document sets were provided to the participants. Summarization systems developed by the participants automatically built a summary using the topic as the indication of user interest. Each participant was again allowed to submit two summaries: the *fixed* (10%) summary and the *best* (variable length) summary of the document.

Assessors worked with one topic at a time. All summaries received from the participants for a given topic, along with the full text and the lead summaries, were combined into a single group, randomly mixed, and divided among the assessors in 1000 document sets. Each assessor reviewed a topic, then read each summary or document and judged whether it was relevant to the current topic. No assessor read more than one representation of a single document in order not to bias the relevance decision. Fourteen assessors were assigned to this task, although some assessors worked on both the categorization and the adhoc task.

4.3 Summary Presentation

For both tasks, the participants had four days from the receipt of the text data to generate summaries. The submissions were limited to ASCII text, following a specified document type definition (DTD) which included tags for the document, a participant identifier, a document identifier, a title, a summary, and a query number (adhoc task only). The data could be presented in a format of the participant's choosing within the range of readable ASCII text. No

additional formatting was allowed (e.g., highlighting, boldfacing, or underlining). Although in system implementation, data presentation will play a vital role, in order to evaluate each summary on the same criteria formatting was prohibited. Only the <TEXT> portion of the summary was presented to the user. Headlines were not included in the display.

4.4 Results Analysis

We selected both quantitative and qualitative criteria as points for evaluation. The quantitative measures included precision, recall, compression (of *best* summaries only) and time required for assessment. The qualitative measures addressed preferred length, intelligibility and usefulness of the summaries. During the initial design of the evaluation, a sufficient number of documents, topics, and assessors were determined to ensure statistical significance of the results.

4.4.1 Quantitative Measures. The TREC relevance assessments were used as ground truth for the relevance of each full text document to the topic. These relevance judgments can be considered either positive (judged relevant) or negative (judged nonrelevant). The summaries based on each document were further judged to be either relevant or nonrelevant to the same topic. These relevance judgments of the summaries fall into four distinct classes, as indicated in Table 1 below.

Full Text	Summary	Outcome	Notation
Relevant	Relevant	True Positive	TP
Nonrelevant	Relevant	False Positive	FP
Relevant	Non-relevant	False Negative	FN
Nonrelevant	Non-relevant	True Negative	TN

Table 1: Basis for scoring summaries against full text

4.4.1.1 Precision, Recall and F-score. Precision and recall address documents classified as true positive. *Precision* (P) measures the percentage of correctness for the total number of summaries judged by the summary assessors to be relevant. That is, from the pool of summaries judged to be relevant, how many actually were (based on ground truth)? It incorporates the two relevant summary assessment classes (*TP, FP*) in the equation $P=TP/(TP+FP)$.

Recall (R) measures the percentage of correctness for judgments made by the summary assessors for full text documents judged to be relevant. From the pool of full text documents judged to be relevant, how many of the corresponding summaries were similarly judged? It incorporates the two relevant full text assessment classes (*TP, FN*) in the equation

R=TP/(TP+FN).

F-score (F) is a composite score that combines the precision and recall measures in the equation **F=(2*P*R)/(P+R)**. Precision, recall and F-score are calculated according to a common IR metric initially described in van Rijsbergen's text **Information Retrieval** (van Rijsbergen 1975). Van Rijsbergen advocated using a β factor to weight the relative importance of precision and recall in the formula

$$E = 1 - (1+\beta^2)*P*R / (\beta^2*P+R)$$

Using a β of 1 weights these measures equally and results in the formula for a composite F-score.

Table 2 lists the precision, recall, and F-score for each dry run participant across all topics and documents for the adhoc and categorization tasks.

	Adhoc			Categorization		
Part	P	R	F	P	R	F
1	.55	.45	.49	.71	.45	.55
2	.50	.60	.54	.69	.44	.53
3	.55	.56	.55	.76	.41	.53
4	.52	.63	.56	.69	.51	.58
5	.54	.46	.49	.77	.41	.53
6	.57	.41	.47	.81	.21	.33

Table 2: Individual participant (Part), precision (P), recall (R), and F-scores (F)

Table 3 lists the overall performance on each type of document displayed to the assessor (full text, *best* length summary, *fixed* length summary and lead summary. These results are statistically significant to .05 with the exception of *fixed* to baseline performance and full text to *best* performance.

Type of Document	Accuracy (F)
Full Text	.60
Best Summary	.52
10% Fixed Summary	.45
10% Lead Summary	.43

Table 3: Overall adhoc F-score across document types

4.4.1.2 Compression and Norm-f. *Compression* (C) measures length of a summary relative to the length of the full text and is derived from the equation $C=N_s/N_n$ where N_s is the number of characters in the summary and N_n is the number of characters in the full text document. Only the characters in the <TEXT> portion of the documents are counted, excluding white space. Compression was calculated per document, rather than per test set. Degree of compression was then used as a factor in assessing performance of individual systems.

Fixed Length Summaries. The participants were required to submit a 10% *fixed* length summary of the original document. If a summary exceeded 10%, it

was truncated to the required length, allowing for word completion. The scores for the 10% summaries varied by participant, but were similar to the baseline lead summary, which was also limited to 10%. Table 4 lists the F-scores by participant for the *fixed* length summaries for both the categorization and the adhoc tasks.

Participant	F-Score /Categ	F-Score /Adhoc
1	.40	.39
2	.39	.47
3	.40	.47
4	.40	.42
5	.38	.35
6	.32	.40

Table 4: Participant scores for 10% summaries

Best Length Summaries. The participants were also encouraged to submit a 'best' summary which were not limited in length. These summaries varied a great deal in the length relative to the full text of the document. Most participants submitted summaries that stayed consistently within a narrow range of the original document length (e.g., 10% or 25%) for their system. Some, however, used this flexibility to generate summaries that ranged anywhere from 14% to 67% of the length of the original. The degree of compression did not correlate directly to system performance as measured by the F-score. Table 5 lists participant F-scores for *best* length summaries for the adhoc and categorization tasks.

Participant	F-Score	Avg Comp	Range of Comp
1	.47	.25	.22-.29
2	.52	.40	.14-.67
3	.52	.25	.24-.26
4	.53	.34	.28-.40
5	.47	.23	.15-.27
6	.46	.10	.09-.11

Table 5: Participant scores and compression ratios for *best* summaries for the adhoc task

Recognizing that shorter summaries are preferred to longer summaries (as long as correctness is maintained), a normalizing measure, *Norm-f* (*NF*) combines the F-score and the degree of compression in the equation **NF=(1-C)*F**. Since shorter is considered preferable, the 1's complement of compression is used so that higher scores are better, consistent with the precision, recall and F-scores.

With the compression factor incorporated into the scoring data, the relative performance of the systems changes considerably for the adhoc task, as shown in Table 6.

	Categorization				Adhoc			
Part	F	Rank	NF	Rank	F	Rank	NF	Rank
1	.53	1	.39	1	.47	4	.35	5
2	.54	5	.31	5	.52	2	.33	6
3	.52	2	.39	2	.52	2	.39	2
4	.57	4	.34	4	.53	1	.36	3
5	.50	3	.35	3	.47	4	.36	3
6	.31	6	.28	6	.46	6	.41	1

Table 6: Individual participant F and NF scores.

Time Required. Assessors were timed as they made their decisions and were instructed to take breaks only when in feedback mode. Some extreme values indicate that this was not always the case, and these data points were not included in the final results. There are clear trends in the time required to read the documents presented to the assessors. Full text documents consistently take the longest to read, the baseline and the 10% summaries the shortest. The *best* summaries fall between these two extremes. The results are summarized in Table 7.

Type of Document	Time Required (seconds)
Full Text	68.17
Best Summary	36.87
Fixed 10% Summary	24.16
Lead 10% Summary	23.20

Table 7: Time required across document types

4.4.1.3 Problems with the Standard Measures. Precision and recall measures are commonly used in information retrieval evaluations. The IR evaluation problem differs from the summarization system evaluation in fundamental ways. Consequently, as applied above, precision, recall and F-score may not be the most appropriate measures for a summarization system evaluation.

In the IR problem, the goal of the IR system is to select those documents from a corpus which are relevant to a specific query. Some documents within the corpus are relevant to the query and many are not. The IR system will select some combination of relevant and nonrelevant documents. The results can be described similarly to the summarization evaluation, as seen in Table 8, below.

Document	IR System Determination	Results
Relevant	Relevant	True Positive
Nonrelevant	Relevant	False Positive
Relevant	Nonrelevant	False Negative
Nonrelevant	Nonrelevant	True Negative

Table 8: Basis for IR scoring

This similarity appears to suggest that the use of the precision and recall measures is appropriate to the summarization problem.

In the IR problem, an initial determination of relevance is made and that decision is maintained consistently for each system being evaluated. The operation is binary and is universal to all systems.

In the summarization evaluation problem, the relevance of the full text document has been determined at the time the summarization system operates on it. Summarization systems modify the full text document with many possible resulting summaries. Many of these summaries may be relevant and many may be nonrelevant. Each summarized version of a document is then judged by a different assessor with a potentially different interpretation of the relevance criteria for a topic.

Even if assessors were able to agree on relevance criteria and decisions, other problems exist. In an IR evaluation, precision measures the percentage of relevant documents in a set retrieved as a result of a query. Clearly, this measures the preciseness of the system.

In the summarization evaluation, precision measures how well the system is able to summarize relevant documents in a relevant way without summarizing nonrelevant documents in a way that *appears* relevant. That is, precision in the summary evaluation measures the system's ability to extract relevant information from relevant documents while not extracting information that appears to be relevant from nonrelevant documents.

In an IR evaluation, recall measures how many relevant documents of the total relevant document set a system is able to retrieve. This is clearly an important measure for IR systems which, in combination with precision, gives a workable measure of a system's effectiveness.

For summarization, recall measures how well the system is able to capture the relevant content of a document. It measures a system's ability to extract relevant information from documents known to contain relevant information. Consider, however, the case of a long document that contains only a small text portion relevant to a given topic. Should the document be considered relevant to the topic? If the document should be considered topic relevant, should the generic summary (as produced for the categorization task) include the relevant section? If not, the produced summary will be judged as nonrelevant, resulting in a false negative adversely affecting recall. If the document should be considered not relevant to the topic, should the query-specific summary (as produced for the adhoc task) include the relevant section? If so, the produced summary will be judged as relevant, resulting in a false positive and adversely affecting precision.

4.4.1.4. Alternative Measures

False Positives and Recovery. The generation of a relevant summary from a nonrelevant document, which produces a false positive result, may be considered good behavior in a query-based summarization system. There are several reasons why a false positive might occur: 1) The TREC assessor might have made an initial error in judgment, 2) The summarization assessor might disagree with the TREC assessor, or 3) The summary might have captured the relevant part of a document that causes the IR system to retrieve it in the first place. It is this last possibility that makes the false positives interesting. If the TREC topic is not the main subject of the document, this relevant section might have been obscured so that the article appeared to be nonrelevant.. If a query-relevant summarization system is able to recover these relevant sections, the use of such systems can be very advantageous, particularly with longer documents The measure Recovery (RCVR) described in the formula **RCVR=FP/(FP+TN)** measures this characteristic by providing positive evaluation metrics which rewards finding relevant documents. Recovery is referred to as fallout in the IR community where it measures those documents returned by a system which are not relevant against the set of nonrelevant documents (van Rijsbergen 1979).

Negative Recall and Catf. For the categorization task, a summarization system should:

1) create summaries of relevant documents which are judged relevant as measured by Recall - R

2) create summaries of nonrelevant documents which are judged nonrelevant

Negative recall (*RNEG*), defined as **RNEG=TN/(TN+FP)** is a measure of the second condition.

Note that negative recall is concerned with how a summarization system handles nonrelevant documents.

One possible way to combine these measures to determine performance on the categorization task can be described as **CATF = (2*R*RNEG)/(R+RNEG)**.

Adhf. For the adhoc task, a summarization system should:
1) create summaries of relevant documents such that they are judged relevant (Recall, R) and
2) extract any available topic-relevant information from nonrelevant documents (Recovery, RCVR).

One possible way to combine these measures to determine performance on the adhoc task can be described as **ADHF = (2*R*RCVR)/(R+RCVR)**.

The results of these measures are summarized in Table 9 below.

Parti-cipant	Recall	RCVR	RNEG	ADHF	CATF
1	.45	.23	.76	.30	.57
2	.60	.37	.62	.46	.61
3	.56	.36	.63	.44	.59
4	.63	.38	.61	.47	.62
5	.46	.27	.72	.34	.56
6	.41	.21	.78	.28	.54

Table 9: Individual participants' alternative scores

Assessor Tendencies and the Effect on Results. In judging the relevance or nonrelevance of summaries and full texts for the evaluation, individual assessors of the dry run texts displayed widely varying tendencies to judge the items relevant or nonrelevant. Some of the faster readers were far more likely to judge an item as nonrelevant. It is possible that in their attempt to process the items quickly, they did not recognize shorter sections of relevant material. Analysis of the effect of assessor tendencies on the various measures discussed above yielded the following conclusions.

Effect on Recall. As the assessor tendency to judge most items nonrelevant moves toward a tendency to judge more items relevant (i.e., their relevant tendency increases), recall improves from very low to very high for the following reasons.

In the case where the assessor tends to judge most items as nonrelevant (as often happened with the faster assessors) there will be very few true positives (since there will be very few positives). The number of false negatives will be correspondingly high, since the remaining documents are being judged nonrelevant when many of them are actually relevant.

In terms of recall (**TP/(TP+FN)**): R=(low number)/(same low number + some high number) results in a recall score approaching 0.

If the assessor tended to judge most items relevant, there will be many more true positives but false negatives will be very low, since there are very few documents judged nonrelevant. Therefore: R=(high number)/(same high number + some low number) and recall will be high (approaching 1).

Effect on Precision. The effect on precision is slightly more complex. In the case where the assessor tends to judge most items nonrelevant, one might assume that the assessor is very discriminating about what is relevant. Most of the assessments would be correct and in terms of precision (**TP/(TP+FP)**), P=TP/(TP+almost 0) and precision would approach 1.

In the extreme case where an assessor judged all items relevant, there would be as many true positives as there were relevant documents in the set with the remaining being false positives. Therefore, precision would equal the distribution of relevant and nonrelevant documents.

In the summary evaluation conducted, having a large, diverse group of assessors leveraged the effect of individual assessor tendencies. Should some fundamental change in the approach of assessors to the relevance judgments cause a shift in the tendencies to either relevant or nonrelevant, the resulting scores would be affected.

4.4.2 Qualitative Feedback.

After making a relevance determination or categorization decision, the assessor was then asked to rate each document according to preferred length, intelligibility, and perceived usefulness. This was the feedback section of the evaluation and was not included in the timing computations. Preferred length was described in terms of shorter/just right/longer, intelligibility as low/OK/fine, and usefulness as low/medium/high. The assessors were also given a free text comment field in which they could provide additional feedback.

Length. The assessors were not told that they were judging summaries. They frequently found the full text documents to be too long, the baseline and *fixed* 10% summaries to be too short, and the *best* summaries the appropriate length. This is encouraging in that it suggests that if the summarization systems correctly select the appropriate sentences to generate the summary, the resulting summaries would be an acceptable replacement for the full text.

Intelligibility. The *best* summaries were considered more intelligible than the baseline or 10% summaries, although they did not rate as consistently high as the full text.

Usefulness. Usefulness was generally equated to relevance. Eighty-four percent of the documents judged to be not relevant were also not useful. Both the preferred length and intelligibility scores for the *fixed* and baseline summaries were probably affected by the presentation of these summaries. Because of the rules for creating the shorter summaries, the text was cut off mid-sentence most of the time, resulting in incomplete documents that caused some confusion for the assessors. Table 10 summarizes the scores for the qualitative measures across participants for the adhoc task.

Partici-pant	Pref Length	Intelligi-bility	Useful-ness	Com-pression
1	2.02	2.25	1.40	.25
2	1.91	2.21	1.55	.40
3	2.0	2.24	1.55	.25
4	1.88	2.27	1.56	.34
5	2.14	2.03	1.39	.23
6	2.34	2.03	1.28	.10

Table 10: Qualitative ratings for adhoc task

Preferred Length – (1) shorter, (2) just right, (3) longer

Intelligibility – (1) poor, (2) OK, (3) fine

Usefulness – (1) low, (2) medium, (3) high

Comments. The free text comments provided some interesting feedback as well. Many summaries were considered too vague or lacking in detail, suggesting that the assessors did not feel comfortable making relevance decisions with minimal information, or with information that was unsubstantiated in the text that was available to them.

Summary Analysis. After combining all of the data generated by the above measures, we then studied the sentence selection patterns of each system. All systems in the dry run extracted complete sentences from the full text to generate the summary. This is not expected to remain the case in future evaluations. We looked at the following parameters in relation to precision, recall and F-score:

1. sentence position in the document,
2. sentence position in a paragraph and
3. paragraph position in a document.

The data used for this analysis were based on all summaries by a participant for a given topic. Clear patterns emerged for each of the different systems, but there were no trends that indicated how sentences should be selected positionally to create an acceptable summary. Most participants tended to include the first sentence in the document. This occurred in approximately 57% of the cases for the adhoc task and 68% of the cases for the categorization task. One participant tended to select sentences only from the initial part of the document. For those documents where the information relevant to the topic occurred later in the document, this approach was less effective. Systems that routinely selected sentences from further in a document had higher accuracy scores; however since these trends covered all documents in a set, it is likely that the first sentence or paragraph was also included. It is impossible to detect from this set of data which sentences might have contained the relevant information.

Several systems selected complete paragraphs. This approach did not necessarily improve overall scores, but those systems did fair slightly better in the 'intelligibility' ratings in comparison to those that extracted isolated sentences.

The tasks selected for the dry run relied on individual judgments of relevance, which are inherently subjective. Each assessor creates an individual definition of relevance, usually while reading through the set of texts. We attempted to overcome this obstacle by sheer numbers, using 26 assessors reviewing more than 14,000 documents. There were many cases where assessors disagreed on the relevance of a summary, however, we can make some very general observations.

- Often one sentence captures the vital detail that makes a document relevant. That sentence alone, however, does not make a summary relevant. The summary needs to have sufficient detail for the assessor to be able to determine the scope of the document.

- Several participants provided keyword lists drawn from the document, with the intention that the keywords would help the assessor make the correct decision. Instead, based on frequent comments in the feedback section, these keywords were often considered distracting.

4.5 Lessons Learned

The dry run evaluation provided a first step toward a large-scale summarization evaluation. While it will take some time to work out an evaluation that is acceptable to most parties, we believe it moves us in the right direction. Several changes will be made based on the outcome of and reaction to the first evaluation. Some will be incorporated immediately and become part of the formal evaluation to be held in the spring of 1998. Others will be addressed in future evaluations as time and resources permit.

4.5.1 Immediate Changes
1. Improve variability of topics and document sets.

The number of topics for both tasks needs to be increased. Performance varied by topic, but it was not along the lines of entity-based versus non-entity-based topics. More data are needed to learn the factors that affect performance on different topics. In order to study the effect of different topics, 20 topics will be used for the next evaluation for the adhoc task. For the categorization task, this large number of topics is infeasible, due to the other requirements imposed on the task and topic selection, but it will be expanded to include ten topics. Those topics will be grouped into two subject domains. For each task, the number of documents per topic will be reduced, resulting in the same total number of one thousand documents per task.

2. Provide more specific instructions to assessors.

The assessors were informed only that they were determining relevance or categorizing documents. They were not aware that most of the documents were summaries, some of which were truncated to meet the 10% maximum length requirement. During the next iteration of the evaluation, we will test the theory that if the assessors are cognizant of the actual task of judging indicative relevance of summaries, their decisions will be different. The nature of indicative summaries is not to capture all relevant details of a summary, but only enough for the user to judge whether the full text is relevant. Therefore, it is

appropriate that the decisions are made on this basis.

3. Provide more specific instructions to participants.

Participants will not be allowed to use any statistics generated from the test corpus in the creation of generic summaries. We are using a small set of one thousand documents and such analysis impacts the independent nature of those summaries. They will, however, be allowed to work with the entire corpus from which the documents are drawn.

4.5.2 Future Changes
1. Reduce reliance on comparisons with TREC.

We rely heavily on the TREC relevance assessments and do not currently have the resources to create another pool of relevant documents. To improve inter-assessor agreement for the summarization decisions, assessors will be provided an opportunity to review sample relevant and nonrelevant documents for each topic as a group and come up with a more coherent definition of relevance. While this will not overcome any disagreement with the TREC assessors, it should create a more cohesive environment for this evaluation. The assessments and resulting scores can then be more readily compared with each other.

2. Include additional analysis.

Resources permitting, we will analyze the summaries by genre to find out if performance varies along those lines.

3. Design a more suitable task for generic summaries.

The categorization task was not particularly effective as a measure of the acceptability of generic summaries. With the TREC relevance data, it is not necessarily the case that the main topic of a document directly matches the TREC query. Perhaps a better measure would be to devise a list of focal and nonfocal concepts, as was done in Paice and Jones (1993), and determine how well the summary captures these concepts. This would best be done on an individual document basis, however, which is an extremely labor-intensive and subjective task. The categorization task will be repeated one final time in an evaluation open to all interested participants, and will be replaced with a more appropriate measure following that effort.

5. Conclusions

The dry run evaluation generated a great deal of interesting and useful data. Hopefully subsequent evaluations will demonstrate which algorithms show promise for different tasks. This does not directly translate, however, into resources that can be used by interested parties to improve their systems. There is a great deal of interest in creating such resources that will allow researchers progressively to improve their systems. The evaluation to be held in the spring of 1998 will incorporate a question-and-answer task that will address informative summaries. A by-product of this task will be model summaries for the set of documents that are being evaluated. If possible, this resource will be made available following the evaluation.

While the dry run tasks help to demonstrate the utility of summaries as they exist today, there are many improvements that can be made to the quality of the summaries, such as emphasizing cohesion in sentence selection or sentence generation, and topic coverage across the set of topics mentioned within a document. Subsequent evaluations should also address these issues.

5.1 Impact on the Future

Interest in summarization is high. This will likely be the case for the foreseeable future. It is evident in the growing number of commercial products that incorporate this technology and in the interest of both managers and end-users in these products. It is useful for all parties to have a common forum such as an open evaluation that will encourage researchers to share ideas, compare and contrast techniques and further advance the state of the art in this important field.

Acknowledgments

We are grateful for the support of DARPA and the TIPSTER community in sponsoring and participating in this initial evaluation. It was conducted with the expertise and assistance of key members of the MITRE Corporation, Dr. Inderjeet Mani, David House and Dr. Lynette Hirschman, and with the advice and assistance of Donna Harman (National Institute for Standards and Technology) and Beth Sundheim (Space Systems Command).

References

Aone, C.; Okurowski, M. E.; Gorlinsky, J.; and Larsen, B. 1997. A Scalable Summarization System Using Robust NLP. In *Intelligent Scalable Text Summarization*, 66-73. Madrid, Spain.: Association for Computational Linguistics.

Brandow, R; Mitze, K; and Rau, L. F. 1995. Automatic Condensation of Electronic Publications by Sentence Selection. *Information Processing and Management*, 31(5):675-685.

Church, K. W., and Rau, L. F. 1995. Commercial Applications of Natural Language Processing. *Communications of the ACM*, 38(11):71-79.

Edmundson, H. P. 1969. New Methods in Automatics Abstracting. *Journal of the ACM*, 16(2): 264-285.

Endres-Niggemeyer, B.; Hobbs, J.; and Sparck Jones, K. 1993. Summarizing Text for Intelligent Communication. In *Dagstuhl Seminar Report*, IBFI GmbH, Schloss Dagstuhl, Wadern, German.

Galliers, J. R. and Sparck Jones, K. 1993. Evaluating Natural Language Processing Systems. University of Cambridge Computer Laboratory Technical Report No. 291, Computer Laboratory, University of Cambridge.

Harman, D. 1993. Overview of the First Text Retrieval Conference (TREC-1). In *TREC-2 Proceedings*, Gaithersburg, Maryland. Morgan-Kaufman Publishers.

Harman, D. 1996. Overview of the Fourth Text Retrieval Conference (TREC-4). In *The Fourth Text Retrieval Conference (TREC-4)*, pages 1-24, Gaithersburg, Maryland. Morgan-Kaufman Publishers.

Jing, H.; McKeown, K.; Barzilay, R.; and Elhadad, M. 1998. Summarization Evaluation Methods: Experiments and Analysis. In *American Association for Artificial Intelligence 1998 Spring Symposium Series, Intelligent Text Summarization*, 60-68. Stanford, Calif.

Johnson, F. C.; Paice, C. D.; Black, W. J.; and Neal, A. P. 1993. The Application of Linguistic Proceessing to Automatic Abstract Generation. *Journal of Document and Text Management*, 1(3): 215-241.

Knaus, D.: Mittendorf, E.; Schauble, P.; and Sheridan, P. 1996. Highlighting Relevant Passages for Users of Interactive SPIDER Retrieval System. In *The Fourth Text Retrieval Conference (TREC-4)*, 233-238, Gaithersburg, Maryland.: Morgan Kaufman Publishers.

Kupiec, J; Pedersen, J.; and Chen, F. 1995. A Trainable Document Summarizer. In *SIGIR '95*, 68-73, Seattle, Washington.

Luhn, H. P. 1958. The Automatic Creation of Literature Abstracts. *IBM Journal*, 159- 165.

Mani, I., and Bloedorn, E. 1997. Multidocument Summarization by Graph Search and Matching. In *Proceedings of the American Association for Artificial Intelligence-97*, Providence, Rhode Island.

AAAI Press.

Mani, I., and Bloedorn, E. 1997. Summarizing Similarities and Differences Among Related Documents. In Proceedings of the Computer Assisted Information Retrieval Conference (RIAO). 373-387. Montreal, Canada. Centre de Hautes Etudes Internationales d'Informatique Documentaires and the Center for the Advanced Study of Information Systems, Inc.

Marcu, D. 1997. From Discourse Structures to Text Summaries. In *Intelligent Scalable Text Summarization*, 82-88. Madrid, Spain. Association for Computational Linguistics.

Maybury, M. T. 1993. Automated Event Summarization Techniques. In Dagstuhl Seminar Report, 100-108, IBFI, GmbH, Schloss Dagstuhl, Wadern, Germany.

McKeown, K., and Radev, D. R. 1995. Generating Summaries of Multiple News Articles. In *SIGIR '95*, 74-82, Seattle, Washington.

Merchant, R. 1993. Tipster Program Overview. In *Tipster Text Program*, 1-2, Fredericksburg, Virginia. Morgan-Kaufman Publishers.

Merchant, R. 1996. Tipster Phase III. In *TIPSTER Text Phase III Kickoff Workshop*, Columbia, Maryland.

Morris, A. H.; Kasper, G. M.; and Adams, D. A. 1992. The Effects and Limitations of Automated Text Condensing on Reading Comprehension Performance. *Information Systems Research* 3(1):17-35.

Miike, S.; Itoh, E.; Ono, K; and Sumita, K. 1994. A Full-Text Retrieval System with a Dynamic Abstract Generation Function. In *SIGIR '94*, 152-161. Seattle, Washington.

Paice, C. D., and Jones, P. A. 1993. The Identification of Important Concepts in Highly Structured Technical Papers. In *SIGIR '93*, 69-77.

Rath, G. J.; Resnick, A.; and Savage, T. R. 1961. The Formation of Abstract by the Selection of Sentences. *American Documentation*, 139-143.

Reimer, U., and Hahn, U. 1988. Text Condensation as a Knowledge Base Abstraction. *In IEEE Conference on AI Applications*, 338-344.

Strzalkowski, T. 1996. Robust Natural Language Processing and User-Guided Concept Discovery for Information Retrieval, Extraction, and Summarization Tipster Phase III. In *TIPSTER Text Phase III Kickoff Workshop*, Columbia, Maryland.

Sundheim, B. 1995. Overview of the Results of the MUC-6 Evaluation. *In Sixth Message Understanding Conference (MUC-6)*, 13-31, Columbia, Maryland. Morgan Kaufman Publishers.

Taylor, S. 1996. TIPSTER Text Program Overview. In *TIPSTER Text Phase II*, Tysons Corner, Virginia.

van Rijsbergen, C. J. 1979. Information Retrieval. Woburn Massachusetts. Butterworths.

Section 6

New Summarization Problem Areas

With the growth in availability of on-line information, and increased access to different forms of such information, two new summarization problem areas have been growing in interest: multi-document summarization, and multimedia summarization.

We first discuss *Multi-document Summarization*. Here the number of documents to be summarized can range from large gigabyte-sized collections, to small collections, to just pairs of documents, and different methods may be needed for these different size ranges. There are many possible ways of characterizing relationships among documents, including part-whole relationships (e.g., chapters in a book, hyperlinked documents, or "webs" of on-line information), differences of detail (a news story which explores a previous story in more detail), differences of perspective (different commentaries on an event), and temporal trends (e.g., developments in a hostage crisis). In general, there are many challenges in this emerging area including:

- Identifying algorithms which scale up to large-size collections
- Eliminating redundancy of information across documents
- Exploiting orderings among documents in intelligent ways
- Making use of effective presentation and visualization strategies to represent relationships.

There has been a growing amount of recent research examining this problem, including the use of lists of named entities (people, organizations, places) across documents to characterize content. Of particular interest is the work by Carbonell et al. (1997) in which multi-document summarization is offered as a post-retrieval filter on hits returned from a search engine. Their "Maximal Marginal Relevance" approach exploits a re-ranking parameter which allows a system to slide between relevance to a query and diversity (and lack of redundancy) from the hits seen so far.

The first two papers on multi-document summarization exploit a connectivity model: the more strongly connected a text unit is to other units, the more salient it is. In the first paper by Salton, Singhal, Mitra, and Buckley, paragraphs from one or more documents are compared in terms of similarity, using a measure based on similarity of vocabulary. Those paragraphs above a particular similarity threshold are linked to form a "text relationship map" graph. Paragraphs which are connected to many other paragraphs (i.e., "bushy nodes" in the graph) are considered salient. Summaries can then be generated by

traversing a path along links, and extracting text from each paragraph along the path.

In their evaluation, Salton et al. compare these summaries against human summaries. To construct the latter, the authors had two subjects extract by hand at least 5 most important paragraphs from each of 50 articles from an encyclopedia against manual abstracts. On the average, they found that for each article about 47% of the paragraphs deemed important by both the subjects were found by the system. Interestingly, they also found that the 2 subjects showed only 46% overlap in their extracts, reiterating once again the trend found by Rath et al. in their paper in Section 5.

The second paper by Mani and Bloedorn explores other cohesion relationships to construct user-focused multi-document summaries. They use a graph representation whose nodes are term occurrences and whose edges are cohesion relationships (proximity, repetition, synonymy, hypernymy, and coreference) between terms. The approach is therefore also related to the discourse-based approaches in Section 3, in particular that of Barzilay and Elhadad, and the paper by Boguraev and Kennedy. However, the coreference relations Mani and Bloedorn consider are limited to cases where proper names refer to the same entity, rather than the more general case of anaphoric reference involving pronouns or definite noun phrases. As in the paper by Aone et al. in Section 2, terms can include words, phrases and proper names. Given a user's query, a spreading activation algorithm explores links in from occurrences of query terms in each document's graph, to determine what information in each document is relevant to the query. The activated regions are then compared to extract query-related terms common to the documents, and query-related terms unique to each document. Sentences are then extracted based on weights of terms that are common (or unique). To minimize redundancy across extracts, sentence extraction can greedily cover as many different common (or unique) terms as possible. The authors explore a variety of presentation strategies, and present detailed results regarding the algorithmic complexity and performance of their programs.

Overall, the technique used by Mani and Bloedorn is more complex than the approach used by Salton et al., and perhaps may be especially effective when the coreference model is extended to include pronominal anaphora. The resolution of this kind of anaphora in unrestricted texts is a very active research area (see also Boguraev and Kennedy's paper in Section 3), where more developments are expected in the near future.

As mentioned earlier, information extraction systems can be used to fill templates from text for pre-specified kinds of information, such as terrorist incidents. In the third paper, by McKeown and Radev, relationships between different news stories are established by comparing and aggregating templates using various operators. Each operator takes a pair of templates and yields a more salient merged template, which can be compared with other operators. When applied to texts describing terrorist incidents, the *contradiction* operator compares two templates that have the same incident location but where the incident originated from different sources, and identifies slots which have different values in each template. In the synthesis phase, the summarizer then uses text generation techniques to express the contradiction. Other operators include *agreement* and the *superset* operator, which fuses summaries together.

These latter examples are very striking and show great promise in the exploitation of semantic relationships in multi-document summarization. However, it is worth noting that these techniques only apply to documents for which such templates can be reliably filled. The earlier approaches in this section, which work on unrestricted documents, cannot pinpoint such semantic relationships, using instead coarser representations of relationships in terms of term weight comparisons. There are also many intermediate levels of analysis; for example, one can construct models of all the named entities (e.g., people, organizations, places) that occur in a collection of documents, and use that to group documents in interesting ways[1]. In general, one might expect that on longer documents, the best compression can be obtained by knowledge-level comparisons.

The second emerging area is that of *Multimedia Summarization*, i.e., summarization where the input and/or output need not be text. This is a new area with research work in a very early stage, but, with the growing availability of multimedia information in our computing environments, likely to be the most important of all. Two broad cases can be distinguished based on input and output: cases where source and summary are in the same media, and cases where the source is in one media, the summary in the other. Techniques may leverage cross-media information in fusing across media during the analysis or transformation phases of summarization, or in integration across media during synthesis. An interesting example of this leveraging is found in the work of Takeshita et al. (1997) who select representative images from video by analyzing the topic structure (specific to the genre and the Japanese language) of the accompanying closed-captioned text.

The paper by Merlino and Maybury describes a study of presentation techniques for summarization of video news broadcasts. Their Broadcast News Navigator (BNN)

system provides a tool for searching, browsing and summarizing TV news broadcasts. In BNN, information extracted from the audio (silence, speaker changes), video (anchor and logo detection), and text (anchor-reporter handoffs) is used to discover news stories, somewhat analogous to the use of cue phrases in text summarization as key indicators of the relative importance of content. The system uses a variety of presentation techniques based on analysis of the accompanying closed-captioned text as well as the video, which results in a discourse segmentation of the news. Their extrinsic evaluation looks at two different tasks: *identification*, a relevance assessment task, and *comprehension*, a reading comprehension task. In each task, each subject is required to answer 10 questions, while being exposed to exactly one of ten different presentation strategies. These strategies included presentation of multimedia summaries, full-source closed-captioned text, and the full video. The atomic summary presentation methods using closed-captioned text include topic summaries ("theme" terms - usually single words - extracted using Oracle's Context product), lists of proper names, and a single sentence summary (extracted by weighting occurrences of proper name terms). They also exploit direct summarization of the video, using an automatically extracted key frame (presented along with news source and date). In addition, there are a number of compound, mixed-media presentation strategies, which combine one or more video and textual strategies.

On the comprehension task, none of the strategies came out winning, in terms of being close to the "ideal" position of high-accuracy, low-time in a graph of accuracy against time. However, on the identification task, it was found that the best performance in terms of most accuracy and least time occurred with mixed media presentations. This was as accurate as viewing the video, while requiring about one third of the time to make the relevance assessment. Overall, these results suggest that increased integration across media can lead to more effective summaries.

The final paper by Futrelle addresses the problem of summarizing diagrams, such as the line drawings found in scientific and technical text. This is an exciting area in which there has been very little work to date. Futrelle's contribution discusses the requirements in different phases of the summarization task. In the analysis phase of summarization, structural descriptions of the diagram are constructed, along with analysis of text in the diagram, in the caption, as well as in the running text. The transformation phase produces summary diagrams by selecting one or more figures from a document (analogous to sentence extraction), distilling a figure to simplify it (analogous to elimination by text compaction), or merging multiple figures (analogous to merging and aggregation of text). The final synthesis phase involves generation of the graphical form of the summary diagram. Implementation methods to date are confined to diagram parsing. Futrelle illustrates these methods with respect to a variety of

---

[1] In more recent work, (McKeown et al. 1998) have studied some of the challenges in comparing recommended treatments for a patient across multiple medical articles.

different diagrams: a table of images, a flow chart, a set of 2-dimensional data plots, and a block diagram. The author points out that in comparison with summarization of text, it is relatively difficult to carry out domain-independent summarization of diagrams; however, some general methods based on the overall topological and geometrical organization of a diagram can be used. Further progress in this field is dependent on having diagrams available in vector form along with associated meta-data, rather than as raster images. In addition, a corpus of full-text with diagrams along with summaries of those diagrams could be extremely useful.

Overall, the field of multimedia summarization allows for many new possibilities. The summarization of movies or figures in text can make possible much more efficient and finer-grained access to such information. One might also consider other kinds of media, such as music. Many different varieties of information presentation and visualization methods can play a role here. Improved availability of meta-information related to non-textual media, as well as improved analysis of such media, will further contribute to the maturing of this area, since there are limits to what can be leveraged from the textual component of multimedia information sources. Once the analysis of these other media improves, further challenges in this field include being able to deal with degenerate input (e.g., text produced by automatic transcription of audio using speech recognition), and the development of improved methods for cross-media information fusion and integration. It is worth noting that multimedia summarization may require synthesis of new text, e.g., in the case of diagram summarization, revision of labels, captions, and running text. There is also an open question as to when and where textual summaries of multimedia data are appropriate.

There are a few other new areas which are not addressed in this book, but which are of active research interest. These include:

- Multilingual summarization, where the source could be the same or different language than the target summary, is of considerable interest.
- Hybrid multisource summarization, where information can come from both structured data (i.e., databases) as well as document collections. For example, McKeown et al.'s basketball summarizer in Section 3 used as input structured data of tables of basketball scores; one can imagine integrating that sort of information with extracted information from the latest news stories on particular games or players.

In conclusion, multi-document, multilingual, and multimedia summarization will become increasingly important areas of research and application as our global village becomes increasingly digital. Our challenge is to harness the knowledge gained over the previous forty years together with robust, corpus-based, evaluation-driven approaches to make the necessary advances required to address the new problems.

References

Carbonell, J., Geng, Y., and Goldstein, J. 1997. Automated Query-Relevant Summarization and Diversity-Based Reranking. In *Proceedings of the IJCAI'97 Workshop on AI in Digital Libraries*, Fifteenth National Conference on Artificial Intelligence (IJCAI'97), Nagoya, Japan.

McKeown, K., Jordan, D. A., and Hatzivassiloglou, V. 1998. Generating Patient-Specific Summaries of On-Line Literature. In *Working Notes of the AAAI Spring Symposium on Intelligent Text Summarization*, Spring 1998, 34-43. Menlo Park, Calif.: AAAI Press.

Takeshita, A., Inoue, T., and Tanaka, K. 1997. Topic-based Multimedia Structuring. In Maybury, M., ed., *Intelligent Multimedia Information Retrieval*. Cambridge, MA: AAAI/MIT Press.

22

AUTOMATIC TEXT STRUCTURING AND SUMMARIZATION

GERARD SALTON, AMIT SINGHAL*, MANDAR MITRA and CHRIS BUCKLEY

Department of Computer Science, Cornell University, Ithaca, NY 14853-7501, U.S.A.

Abstract—In recent years, information retrieval techniques have been used for automatic generation of semantic hypertext links. This study applies the ideas from the automatic link generation research to attack another important problem in text processing—*automatic text summarization*. An automatic "general purpose" text summarization tool would be of immense utility in this age of information overload. Using the techniques used (by most automatic hypertext link generation algorithms) for inter-document link generation, we generate *intra-document* links between passages of a document. Based on the intra-document linkage pattern of a text, we characterize the structure of the text. We apply the knowledge of text structure to do automatic text summarization by passage extraction. We evaluate a set of fifty summaries generated using our techniques by comparing them to paragraph extracts constructed by humans. The automatic summarization methods perform well, especially in view of the fact that the summaries generated by two humans for the same article are surprisingly dissimilar. © 1997 Elsevier Science Ltd

1. BACKGROUND

The World Wide Web (WWW) has now emerged as the standard platform for information dissemination. There has been an exponential growth in the amount of information available on the Web. Good hypertext linking between different information items on the Web can help a user in successfully navigating through the colossal amount of information available on the Web. When the information space is as large as the Web, it is impossible for people to manually link a text (for example, their home page) to all the "appropriate" information related to the text. Tools for automatic discovery of hypertext links can be useful in this environment. Methods for automatic text linking have been proposed in recent years (Allan, 1996; Bernstein, 1990; Furuta *et al.*, 1989; Salton *et al.*, 1991). These techniques can be used to find articles related to a text; links can then be created to the discovered articles, if appropriate.

Most methods for automatic hypertext link generation use techniques from the field of Information Retrieval (Salton, 1989; Salton & McGill, 1983). Information retrieval is aimed at retrieving useful documents in response to a user query from a large collection of articles. One can also view the information retrieval task as the task of finding articles that are semantically related, or "linked", to the user query. If the user query in this task is replaced by the text, or the text excerpt, for which we intend to automatically generate links, information retrieval techniques can be adapted for automatic link generation (Allan, 1995). This process can be especially helpful as a "link proposer". Based on information retrieval techniques, several links can be proposed to users interested in linking their text to other related texts on the Web. Users can then create links to all the related texts they deem important.

Typically, in information retrieval, each text or text excerpt is represented by a vector of weighted terms of the form $D_i = (d_{i_1}, d_{i_2}, \ldots, \ldots, d_{i_l})$ where d_{i_k} represents an importance weight for term T_k attached to document D_i. The terms attached to documents for content representation purposes may be words or phrases derived from the document texts by an automatic indexing procedure, and the term weights are computed by taking into account the occurrence characteristics of the terms in the individual documents and the document collection as a whole (Salton & McGill, 1983). Assuming that every text or text excerpt is represented in vector form

---

* To whom all correspondence should be addressed (E-mail: singhal@cs.cornell.edu).

as a set of weighted terms, it is possible to compute pairwise similarity coefficients, showing the similarity between pairs of texts, based on coincidences in the term assignments to the respective items. Typically, the vector similarity might be computed as the inner product between corresponding vector elements, that is, $Sim(D_i, D_j) = \sum_{k=1}^{t} d_{i_k} d_{j_k}$, and the similarity function might be normalized to lie between 0 for disjoint vectors and 1 for completely identical vectors (Salton, 1989).

The similarity between two text vectors is based upon the vocabulary overlap between the corresponding texts. If the similarity between two vectors is large enough to be regarded as non-random, we can say that the vocabulary-matches between the corresponding texts are meaningful, and the two texts are "semantically related". We can then introduce a "semantic" hypertext link between the two texts (Salton et al., 1991). For example, if a passage from one Web page is used as one vector, and its similarity to other texts on the Web is computed based on vector inner product, the top few texts can be proposed to a user as potential links. Users can then decide on what proposed links are really pertinent to their text. One problem with links thus generated is the lack of the *type* or the *context* of a link. Users can be asked to assign types or context to various links, or an automatic technique for link typing can possibly be used for this (Allan, 1996).

Based on the above principle, we can generate pairwise links between a group of articles. A link indicates that the linked texts are semantically related; the group of articles and the pairwise links can then be placed on a graph to obtain a *text relationship map* (Salton & Allan, 1993). Figure 1 shows a typical text relationship map for six texts included in the Funk and Wagnalls encyclopedia (Funk & Wagnalls, 1979) dealing with the general topic of Nuclear Energy. The documents appear as nodes (vertices) in the graph of Fig. 1, and a link (branch) appears between two nodes when the similarity between two texts is sufficiently large. The similarity threshold used to build the map of Fig. 1 is 0.01. Any similarity below the (low) threshold of 0.01 can be caused by random word matches between texts, and should not be considered a valid semantic hypertext link. Figure 1 shows that the similarity measure between documents 17012 and 17016 (Nuclear Energy and Nuclear Weapons) is a high 0.57, whereas no significant similarity exists between 8907 (Nuclear Fission) and 22387 (Thermonuclear Fusion). This indicates that

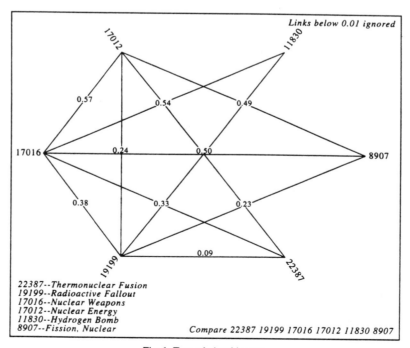

Fig. 1. Text relationship map.

documents 17012 and 17016 are semantically well related, whereas documents 8907 and 22387 don't share much content.

In this study, we take the above idea (used to generate automatic hypertext links) and apply it to attack another important problem in modern day information environments—*automatic text summarization*. To reduce the amount of information that people have to deal with everyday, techniques for automatic text summarization are desired. Text summarization in *unrestricted text domains* still remains a hard and elusive problem. This study is an attack on this problem using ideas from the automatic hypertext link generation research. Instead of generating the traditional inter-document links between various documents, we use the automatic link generation techniques to generate *intra-document* links, i.e. links between various paragraphs (or sentences) of an article. By placing the paragraphs and the intra-document links on a text relationship map, it is possible to visualize the structure of a document. Automatic techniques can then be devised to discover the abstract structure of a text (Furuta, 1989; Salton *et al.*, 1991). This text structure, in turn, can be used to generate better text summaries by passage extraction.

For example, Fig. 2 shows a paragraph relationship map for encyclopedia article 21385 entitled "Smoking". The paragraph similarity threshold used to generate the map of Fig. 2 is 0.20, that is, paragraph similarities smaller than 0.20 do not appear as a link on the map. Various elements of text structure are immediately desirable from a paragraph-relationship map such as that of Fig. 2. For example, the importance of a paragraph for conveying the content of the text might be related to the number of incident branches of the corresponding node on the map. A central node (paragraph) might then be characterized as one with a large number of associated links. For article 21385, the most central paragraphs are then paragraphs 3, 6, 9, 13, and 14. It is also visible from Fig. 2 that paragraphs 15 and 16 are somewhat disjoint from the rest of the nodes. This might indicate that these two paragraph deal with some aspect of smoking, not covered well in the rest of the text; indeed these two paragraphs are about support and counseling to quit smoking, whereas the rest of the article deals with the health effects of smoking.

We use such heuristics to gain a better understanding of the text structure. We then use this understanding of text structure in automatic text summarization by passage extraction (Salton *et*

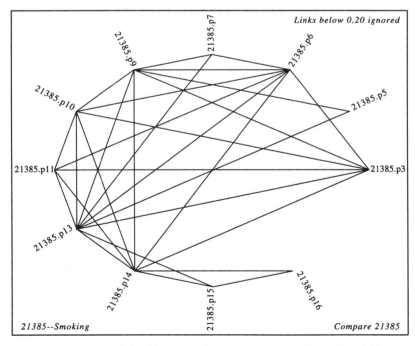

Fig. 2. Paragraph relationship map (smoking—16 paragraphs, 29 links above 0.20).

al., 1994a). For example, we can extract the few most central paragraphs (where centrality of a paragraph may be measured as the number of its links) of an article, and present them to a user in place of the entire article. Since well linked paragraphs convey the contents of an articles well, this heuristic can be used to present the main points of an article in little text.

2. TEXT SEGMENTATION

One important structural property of most texts is their use of multiple functional (or semantic) units. Each unit in a text serves an important purpose in conveying the entire document content to a reader. For example, a text might have a unit that introduces the text, another unit that presents the main idea of text,..., another unit that concludes the text. We are interested in automatically locating such functional units in a text. In principle, the section break-up of an article should indicate this structure; however, oftentimes the sectioning information is not available to a text processing system. (There are numerous articles on the Web that have no structural mark-up to demark sections.) Also, many authors might break one semantic unit into two or more sections, or they might write a section which actually consists of two or more semantic units (Hearst & Plaunt, 1993; Salton *et al.*, 1994b). In this study, we develop techniques that can work across texts, irrespective of the presence or absence of structural mark-up. Of course, if structural mark-up is available, our system can be improved by making use of that information. Our techniques bear some resemblance to the topic–sub-topic structuring techniques of Hearst and Plaunt (Hearst & Plaunt, 1993), but our main aim in this work is to use text structuring for better text summarization as opposed to improving ranked retrieval, as proposed by Hearst and Plaunt.

Based on the paragraph relationship maps generated using automatic hypertext linking techniques (as shown in Fig. 2), a functional unit will be well linked internally, that is, all its paragraphs will have good semantic links to each other, but they will have poor linkage to the surrounding text. In studying the structure of written texts, we are interested in identifying such text pieces that exhibit internal consistency but can be distinguished from the remainder of the surrounding text. When a passage is well linked internally, but is not substantially linked to the surrounding text, chances are that the passage deals with a coherent topic within the article, and forms a functional unit in the text. Such structural knowledge about an article can be effectively used for generation of comprehensive text summaries.

A text relationship map obtained by intra-document text linking may be used to isolate text passages that are functionally homogeneous. We call these passages *text segments*. A text segment is a contiguous piece of text that is well linked internally, but largely disconnected from the adjacent text. Typically, a segment might consist of introductory material, or cover the exposition and development of the text, or contain conclusions and results (Salton *et al.*, 1996). To obtain text segments, we study the linkage pattern of the intra-document links. If a sequence of paragraphs has very few links to the preceding text, chances are that the paragraphs are starting a new unit in the text. Also, if a sequence of paragraphs is not linked well to the paragraphs immediately following the sequence, chances are that these paragraphs are ending a coherent functional unit in the text. Based on such observations, we can isolate the various functional units of a text.

To obtain the text segments, it is necessary to find gaps in the connection pattern between adjacent paragraphs in a text relationship map. However, as the example of Fig. 3 shows, it is often difficult to find obvious gaps in the connection pattern. Since we are interested in analyzing the "local" linkage pattern to detect breaks in the flow of text, we can simplify the text relationship map by considering only the local connections between paragraphs, i.e. connections between the paragraphs located in close proximity to each other. When the long-distance links— those spanning more than five adjacent paragraphs—are eliminated from the map of Fig. 3, the reduced map of Fig. 4 is obtained showing an obvious break down into five disconnected segments: 170416.p3 to p8, 17016.p9 to p21, 17016.p23 to p35, 17016.p39 to p47, and 17016.p48 to p54.

One aspect of such text segmentation is the use of a threshold value to decide whether a link

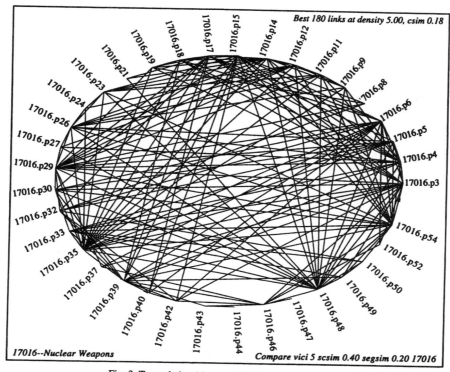

Fig. 3. Text relationship map (17916 nuclear weapons).

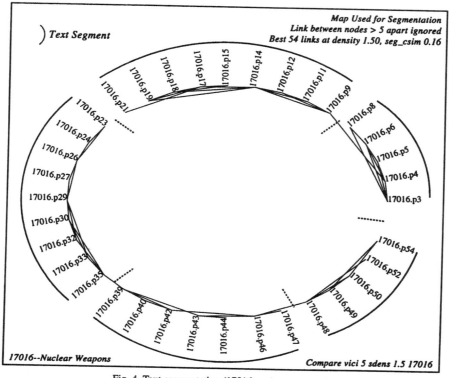

Fig. 4. Text segmentation (17016 nuclear weapons).

should be considered a valid semantic link or not. It is possible that a threshold value that is well suited for one article might not be well suited for another. Even though in practice a blanket threshold value of about 0.20 works well for segmentation, we have recently replaced the use of a threshold for segmentation by a *map density* parameter. For example, using a density parameter of 1.5 in Fig. 4, we select the best $1.5 \times n$ local links on the map, where n is the number of paragraphs on the map. We have observed that the density parameter is quite stable across articles for generating text segments.

3. TEXT SUMMARIZATION

As the amount of textual information available electronically grows rapidly, it becomes more difficult for a user to cope with all the text that is potentially of interest. Automatic text summarization methods are therefore becoming increasingly important. Consider the process by which a human accomplishes this task. Usually, the following steps are involved (Brandow *et al.*, 1995):

1. understanding the content of the document;
2. identifying the most important pieces of information contained in it;
3. writing up this information.

Given the variety in the kinds of available information, it would be useful to have domain-independent, automatic techniques for doing this. However, automating the first and third steps for unconstrained texts is currently beyond the state of the art (Brandow *et al.*, 1995). Thus, the process of automatic summary generation reduces to the task of *extraction*, i.e. we use heuristics based upon a detailed statistical analysis of word occurrence to identify the text-pieces (sentences, paragraphs, etc.) that are likely to be most important to convey the content of a text, and concatenate the selected pieces together to form the final extract[1] (Earl, 1970; Luhn, 1958). Techniques for sentence extraction have been proposed in several earlier studies (Brandow *et al.*, 1995; Kupiec *et al.*, 1995; Luhn, 1958; Paice, 1990). In other studies, the paragraph is chosen as the unit of extraction (Salton *et al.*, 1994a, 1996). It was expected that since a paragraph provides more context, the problems of readability and coherence that were seen in the summaries generated by sentence extraction would be, at least partially, ameliorated.

A text summary can be generated by selectively extracting important paragraphs from the text. This could be accomplished by automatically identifying the important paragraphs on a text relationship map and traversing the selected nodes in text order to construct an extract, or *path*. In dealing with text traversal, it is necessary to distinguish the so-called global paths that operate on a complete text from paths restricted to some substructure, such as paths within a segment. In either case, many different traversal orders can be considered, the most important being as follows.

3.1. Bushy path

The *bushiness* of a node on a map is defined as the number of links connecting it to other nodes on the map. Since a highly bushy node is linked to a number of other nodes, it has an overlapping vocabulary with several paragraphs and is likely to discuss topics covered in many other paragraphs. Such paragraphs are desirable in a summary, and are good candidates for extraction. When paragraphs that are linked to many other paragraphs of the article are extracted, the summaries obtained are quite comprehensive, i.e. the coverage of the subject matter of the article is good. A global bushy path is constructed out of the n most bushy nodes on the map, where n is the targeted number of paragraphs in the summary. These nodes are arranged in chronological order, i.e. the order in which they appear in the original document, to form the summary.

---

[1] Henceforth, the term *summary* is used in this sense of a representative extract.

3.2. Depth-first path

The nodes on a bushy path are connected to a number of other paragraphs, but not necessarily to each other. Therefore, while they may provide comprehensive coverage of an article, they may not form a very coherent (readable) extract. To avoid this problem, we use the following strategy to build depth-first paths: start at an important node—the first node or a highly bushy node are typical choices—and visit the next most similar node at each step. Note that, only the paragraphs that follow the current one in text order are candidates for the next step. Since each paragraph is similar to the next one on the path, abrupt transitions in subject matter should be eliminated, and the extract should be a coherent one. However, since the subject matter of the paragraphs on the path is dictated to some extent by the contents of the first paragraph, all aspects of the article may not be covered by a depth-first path (Salton & Singhal, 1995; Salton *et al.*, 1996).

3.3. Segmented bushy path

Some articles contain short segments dealing with a specialized topic. The paragraphs in such a segment would be well connected to each other, but poorly connected to other paragraphs. A bushy path would not include these paragraphs, and would thereby completely exclude an aspect of the subject matter covered in the article. A segmented bushy path attempts to remedy this problem. It is obtained by constructing bushy paths individually for each segment and concatenating them in text order. At least one paragraph is selected from each segment. The remainder of the extract is formed by picking a number of bushy nodes from each segment in proportion to its length. Since all segments are represented in the extract, this algorithm should, in principle, enhance the comprehensiveness of the extract (Salton *et al.*, 1996).

Consider, as an example, the 20% global text traversal path for encyclopedia article 78 (Abortion) shown in Table 1. This article has two clearly separated segments (see Fig. 5). The article starts out by defining abortion and furnishing other facts about abortion, and then moves on to talk about the legality of abortion and how sensitive this topic has become in recent times. The segmentation map of Fig. 5 contains 15 nodes. Hence, the 20% paths will include 3 paragraphs. The global bushy extract shows that the main aspects of the topic are indeed covered by the extract; however, all the paragraphs included in the global extract appear in segment 1 where the facts of abortion are discussed. This summary completely misses the legality aspect of this article. An alternative traversal path, also consisting of three paragraphs, is presented in Table 2. Here an additional requirement is added that some paragraph must be chosen from each segment. This leads to the addition of paragraph 21 from segment 2, dealing with certain legal

Table 1. 20% Global bushy path: encyclopedia article 78 (Abortion).

-Path Length 3-
-Path Summary-
78. p3   78. p5   78. p9 : S1

-Paragraph 78. p3-
Abortion, termination of pregnancy before the fetus is capable of independent life. When the expulsion from the womb occurs after the fetus becomes viable (capable of independent life), usually at the end of six months of pregnancy, it is technically a premature birth.

-Paragraph 78. p5-
Abortion may be spontaneous or induced. Expelled fetuses weighing less than 0.45 kg (16 oz) or of less than 20 weeks' gestation are usually considered abortions.

-Paragraph 78. p9-
The most common symptom of threatened abortion is vaginal bleeding, with or without intermittent pain. About one-fourth of all pregnant women bleed at some time during early pregnancy, however, and up to 75% of these women carry the fetus for the full term. Treatment for threatened abortion usually consists of bed rest. Almost continuous bed rest throughout the pregnancy is required in some cases of repeated abortion, and vitamin and hormone therapy also may be given. In addition, surgical correction of uterine abnormalities may be indicated in certain cases of repeated abortion.

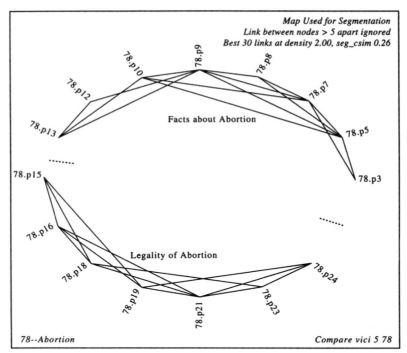

Fig. 5. Text relationship map.

aspects of the abortion problem. The new extract gives a full picture of what this article is about. Such a requirement broadens the coverage of an extract, but may also introduce some lack of coherence in the final text traversal. In general, as the focus of discourse changes from one segment to the next, a paragraph traversal path may never be totally smooth.

Possible solutions consist in actually supplying some transition material between different

Table 2. Equivalent traversal within segments: encyclopedia article 78 (Abortion)

-Total Path Length (over all segments) 3-
-Path Summary-
78. p5 78. p9 : S1
78. p21 : S2

-15% Bushy path in segment 1 (degree>=14)-
-Paragraph 78. p5-
Abortion may be spontaneous or induced. Expelled fetuses weighing less than 0.45 kg (16 ozs) or of less than 20 weeks' gestation are usually considered abortions.

-Paragraph 78. p9-
The most common symptom of threatened abortion is vaginal bleeding, with or without intermittent pain. About one-fourth of all pregnant women bleed at some time during early pregnancy, however, and up to 75% of these women carry the fetus for the full term. Treatment for threatened abortion usually consists of bed rest. Almost continuous bed rest throughout the pregnancy isrequired in some cases of repeated abortion, and vitamin and hormone therapy also may be given. In addition, surgical correction of uterine abnormalities may be indicated in certain cases of repeated abortion.

-15% Bushy path in segment 2 (degree>=12)-
-Paragraph 78. p21-
Opponents of the 1973 Supreme Court ruling, arguing that a fetus is entitled as a person to constitutional protection, attacked the decision on a variety of fronts. State legislative bodies were lobbied for statutes narrowing the implications of the decision and circumscribing in several ways the mother's ability to obtain an abortion. A nationwide campaign was instituted to amend the Constitution to prohibit or severely restrict abortion. Right-to-life groups also engaged in grass-roots political activity designed to defeat abortion proponents and elect abortion opponents. Abortion became, rather than simply a legal and constitutional issue, one of the major political and social controversies of the late 1970s and the '80s. Many state legislatures responded with a succession of statutes imposing additional procedural burdens on women who sought abortions; federal court decisions holding these new statutes unconstitutional usually followed each legislative initiative.

Table 3. Important traversal path properties

	Importance of initial paragraph	Coherence/comprehensiveness
Global central path	Usually starts with important early paragraph	Not coherent because adjacent paragraphs may be unrelated
Segmented bushy path	May lose important first paragraph because of need to include material from other segments	Not coherent but more comprehensive than global central path
Depth-first path	Starts with important first paragraph	Not comprehensive but more coherent than central paths, may be specialized to important subtopic.

segments taken from the available text material to provide a more unified treatment for the text content. A summary of traversal path properties appears in Table 3. As the Table indicates, within each segment, the depth-first path provide a maximum of coherence because pairs of adjacent paragraphs exhibit the required minimal similarity. Global central paths, on the other hand, tend to be more comprehensive than depth-first paths. This suggests that within each segment, the traversal order be tailored to depth-first or global central traversal orders. Since the emphasis in the discourse may change between adjacent segments, greater coherence will be obtained by supplying transition materials to introduce new material covered by the added segments. This leads to the following text traversal prescription:

1. maintain important first paragraphs from global central path;
2. add other paragraphs in depth-first or global central orders within text segments;
3. supply more coherence by using transition materials introducing the topics covered by the various segments.

Good transition paragraphs are normally those exhibiting high similarities with the initial extracted paragraphs in a segment. For the example of article 78 (Abortion), the first extracted paragraph in segment 2 is 78.p21 (see Table 2). A good transition paragraph is therefore an early paragraph of segment 2 that relates highly with paragraph 21. For document 78 (Abortion), it turns out that paragraph 18 has a much higher similarity with paragraph 21 than any other early paragraph in segment 2 of document 78 [similarity (78.p18, 78, p21) =0.4880]. This suggests that paragraph 78.p18 be added to the standard traversal order ahead of paragraph 78.p21.

Table 4 shows a final text traversal order for the example of article 78 (Abortion), starting with paragraph 3 (from the global central path), and continuing with paragraphs 7 and 9 (depth-first path in segment 1). This is followed by the transition material from paragraph 18 introducing the 1973 "Roe vs Wade" decision by the U.S. Supreme Court, and finally ending with paragraph 21 which is the representative from segment 2 in the path within segments of Table 2.

In standard selective text traversal, texts can be traversed entirely, or alternatively, it is possible to concentrate on particular segments that may cover relevant subject matter. The text summarization question can be treated by methods similar to those used for text traversal, except that more emphasis is placed on comprehensiveness of the resulting extract. In general, a 20% global path should be adequate for most purposes; alternatively, an equivalent path within segments, with extracts being concatenated in the normal text (or segment) order, should provide a comprehensive picture.

Summaries, consisting of selected paragraph excerpts, plus appropriate transition materials between segments, should give high performance for the vast bulk of simply structured documents, i.e. documents with a few topics discussed sequentially. However, even when the text structure is complex, i.e. the document has numerous topics and the author switches from one topic to another and picks up the previous topics later, experimental evidence suggests that useful, readable output is obtainable. Consider, for example, the encyclopedia article 24411 (World War 1). Here, the various topics are intermeshed, covering variously the Western Front (Belgium, France), the Eastern Front (Russia), and the Southern Front (Serbia, Turkey). In addition, auxiliary topics are covered by specialized segments.

The sample traversal order for segment 1 (beginning of World War 1) is shown in Table 5. The significant paragraphs consist of paragraphs 22, 32, and 36, preceded by the transition paragraphs 3 and 21. As the example indicates, this excerpt provides a nearly perfect summary of the situation at the beginning of the War. Segment 3 of this document is a specialized segment, covering the activities of U.S. President Woodrow Wilson prior to the entry of the United States in the War. The significant paragraph in this case, is paragraph 55 preceded by the transition material of paragraph 53. The complete summary is once again well-constructed as shown in the sample of Table 6.

In conclusion, central node paths within segments appear to offer reasonable solutions to the text summarization problem. Greater coherence can be supplied by adding relevant transition materials at the beginning of the various segments. Ultimately, completely smooth and comprehensive summaries will be difficult to build by pure text extracting methods. However, from a practical viewpoint, the text extraction system appears to provide rapid text reading, and easily comprehensible text extracts.

4. EVALUATION OF TEXT SUMMARIZATION

Since the goal of our summarization schemes is to automate a process that has traditionally been done manually, a comparison of automatically generated extracts with those produced by

Table 4. Final modified traversal path for article 78 (Abortion).

-Paragraph 78.p3-

Abortion, termination of pregnancy before the fetus is capable of independent life. When the expulsion from the womb occurs after the fetus becomes viable (capable of independent life), usually at the end of six months of pregnancy, it is technically a premature birth.

-Paragraph 78.p7-

It is estimated that some 25% of all human pregnancies terminate spontaneously in abortion, with three out of four abortions occurring during the first three months of pregnancy. Some women apparently have a tendency to abort, and recurrent abortion decreases the probability of subsequent successful childbirth.

-Paragraph 78.p9-

The most common symptom of threatened abortion is vaginal bleeding, with or without intermittent pain. About one-fourth of all pregnant women bleed at some time during early pregnancy, however, and up to 75% of these women carry the fetus for the full term. Treatment for threatened abortion usually consists of bed rest. Almost continuous bed rest throughout pregnancy is required in some cases of repeated abortion, and vitamin and hormone therapy also may be given. In addition, surgical correction of uterine abnormalities may be indicated in certain cases of repeated abortion.

a) Paragraph 78.p3: global central path. Paragraphs 78.p7, p9: depth-first path in segment 1.

-Paragraph 78.p18-

In the U.S., legislation followed the world trend. Fourteen states adopted the moderately restrictive type of abortion law between 1967 and 1972. Alaska, Hawaii, New York, and Washington legislated abortion on request with few restrictions. In 1973, the United States Supreme Court declared unconstitutional all state statutes but the least restrictive type. Noting that induced early abortions had become safer than childbirth and holding that the word person in the United States Constitution does not include the unborn, the Court defined, within each of the three stages of pregnancy, the reciprocal limits of state power and individual freedom:

b) Transition material to introduce section 2.

-Paragraph 78.p21-

Opponents of the 1973 Supreme Court ruling, arguing that a fetus is entitled as a person to constitutional protection, attacked the decision on a variety of fronts. State legislative bodies were lobbied for statutes narrowing the implications of the decision and circumscribing in several ways the mother's ability to obtain an abortion. A nationwide campaign was instituted to amend the Constitution to prohibit or severely restrict abortion. Right-to-life groups also engaged in grass-roots political activity designed to defeat abortion proponents and elect abortion opponents. Abortion became, rather than simply a legal and constitutional issue, one of the major political and social controversies of the late 1970s and the '80s. Many state legislatures responded with a succession of statutes imposing additional procedural burdens on women who sought abortions; federal court decisions holding these new statutes unconstitutional usually followed each legislative initiative.

c) Paragraph 78.p21 from central path in segment 2.

Table 5. Text summary for segment 1, article 24411 (World War 1: 107 paragraphs).

Global central path in segment 1 (**24411.p3-24411.p39**): p22, p32, p36

Transition material between the initial paragraph of Segment 1 (24411.p3) and the initial paragraph of central path in Segment 1 (24411.p22): 24411.p21. Sim(24411.p3, 24411.p22) = 0.2742, Sim(24411.p21, 24411.p22) = 0.2746

Paragraph 24411.p3: World War I, military conflict, from 1914 to 1918, that began as a local European war between Austria-Hungary and Serbia on July 28, 1914; was transformed into a general European struggle by declaration of war against Russia on August 1, 1914; and eventually became a global war involving 32 nations. Twenty-eight of these nations, known as the Allies and the Associated Powers, and including Great Britain, France, Russia, Italy, and the United States, opposed the coalition known as the Central Powers, consisting of Germany, Austria-Hungary, Turkey, and Bulgaria. The immediate cause of the war between Austria-Hungary and Serbia was the assassination on June 28, 1914, at Sarajevo in Bosnia (then part of the Austro-Hungarian Empire; now in Bosnia and Hercegovina), of Archduke Francis Ferdinand, heir-presumptive to the Austrian throne, by Gavrilo Princip (1893-1918), a Serb nationalist. The fundamental causes of the conflict, however, were rooted deeply in the European history of the previous century, particularly in the political and economic policies that prevailed on the Continent after 1871, the year that marked the emergence of Germany as a great world power.

Paragraph 24411.p21: On July 28 Austria declared war against Serbia, either because it felt Russia would not actually fight for Serbia, or because it was prepared to risk a general European conflict in order to put an end to the Greater Serbia movement. Russia responded by partially mobilizing against Austria. Germany warned Russia that continued mobilization would entail war with Germany, and it made Austria agree to discuss with Russia possible modification of the ultimatum to Serbia. Germany insisted, however, that Russia immediately demobilize. Russia declined to do so, and on August 1 Germany declared war on Russia.

a) Transition Material between Beginning of Segment and Initial Paragraph of Central Path.

Paragraph 24411.p22: The French began to mobilize on the same day; on August 2 German troops traversed Luxembourg and on August 3 Germany declared war on France. On August 2 the German government informed the government of Belgium of its intention to march on France through Belgium in order, as it claimed, to forestall an attack on Germany by French troops marching through Belgium. The Belgian government refused to permit the passage of German troops and called on the signatories of the Treaty of 1839, which guaranteed the neutrality of Belgium in case of a conflict in which Great Britain, France, and Germany were involved, to observe their guarantee. Great Britain, one of the signatories, on August 4 sent an ultimatum to Germany demanding that Belgian neutrality be respected; when Germany refused, Britain declared war on it the same day. Italy remained neutral until May 23, 1915, when, to satisfy its claims against Austria, it broke with the Triple Alliance and declared war on Austria-Hungary. In September 1914 Allied unity was made stronger by the Pact of London, signed by France, Great Britain, and Russia. As the war progressed, other countries, including Turkey, Japan, the U.S., and other nations of the western hemisphere, were drawn into the conflict. Japan, which had made an alliance with Great Britain in 1902, declared war on Germany on August 23, 1914. The United States declared war on Germany on April 6, 1917.

Paragraph 24411.p32: On the eastern front, in accordance with the plans of the Allies, the Russians assumed the offensive at the very beginning of the war. In August 1914 two Russian armies advanced into East Prussia, and four Russian armies invaded the Austrian province of Galicia. In East Prussia a series of Russian victories against numerically inferior German forces had made the evacuation of that region by the Germans imminent, when a reinforced German army commanded by General Paul von Hindenburg decisively defeated the Russians in the Battle of Tannenberg, fought on August 26-30, 1914. The four Russian armies invading Austria advanced steadily through Galicia; they took Przemysl and Bukovina, and by the end of March 1915 were in a position to move into Hungary. In April, however, a combined German and Austrian army drove the Russians back from the Carpathians. In May the Austro-German armies began a great offensive in central Poland, and by September 1915 had driven the Russians out of Poland, Lithuania, and Courland, and had also taken possession of all the frontier fortresses of Russia. To meet this offensive the Russians withdrew their forces from Galicia. The Russian lines, when the German drive had ceased, lay behind the Dvina River between Riga and Dvinsk (Daugavpils), and then ran south to the Dnestr River. Although the Central Powers did not force a decision on the eastern front in 1914-15, the Russians lost so many men and such large quantities of supplies that they were subsequently unable to play any decisive role in the war. In addition to the Battle of Tannenberg, notable battles on this front during 1914-15 were the First Battle of the Masurian Lakes (September 7-14, 1914), and the Second Battle of the Masurian Lakes (February 7-21, 1915), both German victories.

Paragraph 24411.p36: Turkey entered the war on October 29, 1914, when Turkish warships cooperated with German warships in a naval bombardment of Russian Black Sea ports; Russia formally declared war on Turkey on November 2, and Great Britain and France followed suit on November 5. In December the Turks began an invasion of the Russian Caucasus region. The invasion was successful at its inception, but by August 1915 the hold that Turkish forces had gained had been considerably reduced. Turkish pressure in the area, however, impelled the Russian government early in 1915 to demand a diversionary attack by Great Britain on Turkey. In response, British naval forces under the command of General Sir Ian Hamilton bombarded the Turkish forts at the Dardanelles in February 1915, and between April and August, two landings of Allied troops took place on the Gallipoli Peninsula, one of British, Australian, and French troops in April, and one of several additional British divisions in August. The Allied purpose was to take the Dardenelles; however, strong resistance by Turkish troops and bad generalship on the part of the Allied command resulted in complete failure. The Allied troops were withdrawn in December 1915 and January 1916 (see Gallipoli Campaign).

b) 20% Central Path in Segment 1.

Table 6. Text summary for specialized segment 3, article 24411 (World War 1).

24411: World War I (107 Paragraphs)

Segment 3: **3 paragraphs**: 24411.51, p53, p55
(Specialized Segment: President Woodrow Wilson).

-Paragraph 24411.p53-

In 1916 President Woodrow Wilson of the U.S., at that time a neutral nation, attempted to bring about negotiations between the belligerent groups of powers that would in his own words bring peace without victory. As a result of his efforts, and particularly of the conferences held in Europe during the year by Wilson's confidential adviser, Colonel Edward M. House, with leading European statesmen, some progress was at first apparently made toward bringing an end to the war. In December the German government informed the U.S. that the Central Powers were prepared to undertake peace negotiations. When the U.S. informed the Allies, Great Britain rejected the German advances for two reasons: Germany had not laid down any specific terms for peace; and the military situation at the time (Romania had just been conquered by the Central Powers) was so favorable to the Central Powers that no acceptable terms could reasonably be expected from them. Wilson continued his mediatory efforts, calling on the belligerents to specify the terms on which they would make peace. He finally succeeded in eliciting concrete terms from each group, but they proved irreconcilable.

a) Transition Material to Segment 3
(Sim(24411.p53, 24411.p55) = 0.2956)

-Paragraph 24411.p55-

Wilson still attempted to find some basis of agreement between the two belligerent groups until a change in German war policy in January 1917 completely altered his point of view toward the war. In that month Germany announced that, beginning on February 1, it would resort to unrestricted submarine warfare against the shipping of Great Britain and all shipping to Great Britain. German military and civil experts had calculated that such warfare would bring about the defeat of Great Britain in six months. Because the U.S. had already expressed its strong opposition to unrestricted submarine warfare, which, it claimed, violated its rights as a neutral, and had even threatened to break relations with Germany over the issue, Wilson dropped his peacemaking efforts. On February 3, the U.S. broke diplomatic relations with Germany and at Wilson's request a number of Latin American nations, including Peru, Bolivia, and Brazil, also did so. On April 6 the United States declared war on Germany.

b) Central Path in Segment 3

---

humans would provide a reasonable evaluation of these methods. We assume that a human would be able to effectively identify the most important paragraphs in an article. If the set of paragraphs selected by an automatic extraction method has a high overlap with the human-generated extract, the automatic method should be regarded as effective.

Thus, our evaluation method takes the following form: a user submits a document to the system for summarization; in one case, the system presents a summary generated by a person; in the other, it produces an automatically generated extract. The user compares the two summaries—manual and automatic—to his/her own notion of an ideal extract. To evaluate the automatic methods, we compare the user's "satisfaction" in the two cases.

Fifty articles were selected from the Funk and Wagnalls Encyclopedia (Funk & Wagnalls, 1979). For each article, two extracts were constructed manually (by two different subjects), a total of 100 extracts. The following instructions were given to those who constructed the manual extracts:

> Please read through the articles. Determine which n paragraphs are the most important for summarizing this article. $n = $ MAX [5, 1/5th the total number of paragraphs (round to the next higher number for fractions)]. Mark the paragraphs which you chose.

We used a total of nine subjects; each summarized 11.11 (100/9) articles on an average. Seven of our subjects were graduate students in computer science. One of the subjects was a researcher in computer science, and the last subject was an administrative aide in our department. All subjects came from a similar academic background, and the articles being summarized were general non-scientific articles. The same article was presented to two different subjects chosen randomly,[2] and the overlap between the two summaries was studied. Space restrictions prohibit us from providing more specific data on the overlap between various subjects, or overlap for different articles.

---

[2]We ensured that any particular subject was not overburdened.

The resulting database of 100 summaries was used in the final evaluation of the automatic methods. Summaries were then automatically generated for the 50 articles, using each of the three paths—global bushy paths, depth—first paths, and segmented bushy paths. In each case, the automatic and manual extracts had the same number of paragraphs.[3]

5. RESULTS AND DISCUSSION

The evaluation of the automatic algorithms was based on the amount of overlap between the automatic and the manual extracts. This overlap was compared to the overlap between the two manual extracts. As explained above, an algorithm for paragraph extraction may be regarded as satisfactory if it produces a similar overlap with one of the manual extracts as the other manual extract.

For each automatic procedure, four quantities were computed:

1. *Optimistic evaluation*: since the two manual extracts for an article are different, the amount of overlap between an automatic and a manual extract depends on which manual extract is selected for comparison. The optimistic evaluation for an algorithm is done by selecting the manual extract with which the automatic extract has a higher overlap, and measuring this overlap.
2. *Pessimistic evaluation*: analogously, a pessimistic evaluation is done by selecting the manual extract with which the automatic extract has a lower overlap.
3. *Intersection*: for each article, an intersection of the two manually constructed summaries is generated. The fact that the paragraphs in this intersection were deemed important by both the readers suggests that they may, in fact, be the most important paragraphs in the article. We compute the percentage of these paragraphs that is included in the automatic extract.
4. *Union*: we also calculate the percentage of automatically selected paragraphs that is selected by at least one of the two users. This is, in some sense, a precision measure, since it provides us with a sense of how often an automatically selected paragraph is potentially important.

Table 7 shows the overlap for the two manual extracts, and the above measures averaged over all 50 articles, for the bushy, depth-first, and segmented bushy extracts. In addition to using these three methods, extracts were also generated for the articles by selecting the required number of paragraphs at random. The evaluation results for these random extracts are also shown in the table. Random selection of paragraphs serves as the weakest possible baseline. If an algorithm does not perform noticeably better than a random extract, then it is certainly doing a poor job of summarization.

5.1. Manual extracts

The most unexpected result of our experiment was the low level of agreement between the two human subjects. The overlap between the two manual extracts is only 46% on an average,

Table 7. Evaluation measures for automatic extraction methods

Overlap between manual extracts: 46%				
Algorithm	Optimistic (%)	Pessimistic (%)	Intersection (%)	Union (%)
Global bushy	45.60	30.74	47.33	55.16
Global depth-first	43.98	27.76	42.33	52.48
Segmented bushy	45.48	26.37	38.17	52.95
Random	39.16	22.07	38.47	44.24

[3]Different users could count paragraphs differently. Thus, for a few articles, the lengths of the two manually generated summaries were different. In such cases, the automatic procedures took the average of these two lengths as the target length for the extract.

i.e., an extract generated by one person is likely to cover 46% of the information that is regarded as most important by another person. This ratio suggests that two humans disagree on more than half the paragraphs that they consider to be critical. In addition, the first paragraph of these encyclopedia articles is a general introduction to the article and is often selected by both subjects—in 50% of the cases in which the intersection between the two users' extracts is a single paragraph, this paragraph is the first one. This increases the chances of overlap between the two manual extracts. If we exclude this special paragraph from the article, the overlap figures for two humans will be even worse.

The lack of consensus between users on which paragraphs are important can be explained as follows. On a first reading, users earmarked certain paragraphs as important. Some of these paragraphs were then eliminated, in order to reduce the extract to the stipulated size. Often, the choice between which paragraphs to keep and which to exclude was a difficult one, and in such situations, some arbitrariness is bound to creep in.

5.2. Automatic extracts

Table 7 indicates that global bushy paths produce the best extracts. 55% of the paragraphs selected by the process were considered important by at least one user. Optimistically speaking, a global bushy path may be expected to agree 45.60% with a user. This number is at par with the agreement between two humans (45.81%). This result is reassuring in terms of the method's viability for generating good extracts, since the scheme performs as well as a human. On an average (generated by taking the mean of the optimistic and pessimistic measures), the global bushy paths cover 38% of the information regarded important by a human.

About 47% of the paragraphs deemed important by both users are included in the bushy extract for an article. This figure is somewhat disheartening. We expected a better coverage of these vital paragraphs by our extracts. A further study of these paragraphs might reveal some properties that users look for in a paragraph to decide its importance. It might then be possible to automate this selection process. We also identified the articles for which the intersection of the two user summaries is a single paragraph. For 78% of these articles, this paragraph was included in the bushy path. This figure was 67% and 56% for depth-first and segmented bushy paths, respectively.

Segmented bushy paths perform worse than expected. This is because the first paragraph of an article is very often selected by users, and segmented bushy paths occasionally omit this paragraph. This results in a decrease in the overlap between automatic and manual extracts. In contrast, the other paths are *guaranteed* to include the first paragraph, and perform better. But, in general, the performance of segmented bushy paths was satisfactory (45.48% overlap with the user in the optimistic method). Similarly, the performance of the depth-first path was also satisfactory. All paths achieved the minimum requirement of performing significantly better than a random extract.

Extracts produced by selecting the first few paragraphs of the articles also performed comparably. This agrees with the observations in the study by Brandow and others (Brandow *et al.*, 1995). News reports, used in the study (Brandow *et al.*, 1995), frequently contain a leading paragraph that summarizes the story contained in the rest of the report. Likewise, in the encyclopedia articles used in this study, the first paragraph usually defines the topic, and provides a general outline about it.

To sum up: interpreted in light of the fact that the overlap between the two manual extracts is, on an average, 46%, and given the enormous reduction in the amount of resources required[4], our results indicate that automatic methods for extraction compare very favorably with manual extraction—the optimistically calculated overlaps being 46% for bushy paths, 44% for depth-first paths, and 45% for segmented bushy paths.

---

[4]The system took about 15 minutes to produce 150 summaries, 3 summaries for each of 50 articles. A human would require about 10 minutes to produce a summary for a typical article from this set.

6. CONCLUSIONS

The internal structure of a text can be analyzed by decomposing the text into its constituent pieces and grouping these pieces together according to their functionality in the text. This knowledge of text structure can be exploited for producing comprehensive text summaries by automatic passage extraction. In view of the fact that extracts generated by two humans for the same article are surprisingly dissimilar, the performance of the automatic text summarization methods is acceptable. Even though this observation calls into question the feasibility of producing perfect summaries by simple passage extraction techniques, given the unavailability of other effective domain-independent summarization tools, we believe that this is a reasonable, though imperfect, alternative.

Acknowledgements—This study was supported in part by the National Science Foundation under grant IRI 9300124. We thank Nawaaz Ahmed, David Fielding, Nicholas Howe, S. Ravikumar, Cynthia Robinson, and Divakar Vishwanath for generating extracts for the articles used in the evaluation process. We are especially thankful to the anonymous referees for their most valuable comments on the earlier draft of this paper.

REFERENCES

Allan, J. (1995). Automatic hypertext construction. Ph.D. Dissertation (Technical Report TR 95-1484), Computer Science Department, Cornell University, Ithaca, NY.

Allan, J. (1996). Automatic hypertext link typing. *Hypertext '96*, The Seventh ACM Conference on Hypertext (pp. 42–52). New York: Association for Computing Machinery.

Bernstein, M. (1990). An apprentice that discovers hypertext links. In A. Rizk, N. Streitz, & J. Andre, (Ed.). *Hypertexts: Concepts, Systems and Applications, Proceedings of the European Conference on Hypertext* (pp. 212–223). Cambridge: Cambridge University Press.

Brandow, R., Mitze, K., & Rau, L. (1995). Automatic condensation of electronic publications by sentence selection. *Information Processing and Management, 31*(5), 675–685.

Earl, L. (1970). Experiments in automatic extracting and indexing. *Information Storage and Retrieval, 6*(4), 313–334.

Funk & Wagnalls (1979). *Funk & Wagnalls new encyclopedia*, 29 volumes, 25000 encyclopedia articles. New York: Funk & Wagnalls.

Furuta, R. (1989). An object-based taxonomy for abstract structure in document models. *Computer Journal, 32*(6), 492–504.

Furuta, R., Plaisant, C., & Shneiderman, B. (1989). A spectrum of automatic hypertext constructions. *Hypermedia, 1*(2), 179–195.

Hearst, M. A., & Plaunt, C. (1993). Subtropic structuring for full-length document access. In *Proceedings of the Sixteenth Annual International ACM SIGIR Conference on Research and Development in Information Retrieval* (pp. 59–68). New York: Association for Computing Machinery.

Kupiec, J., Pedersen, J., & Chen, F. (1995). A trainable document summarizer. In *Proceedings of the Eighteenth Annual International ACM SIGIR Conference on Research and Development in Information Retrieval* (pp. 68–73). New York: Association for Computing Machinery.

Luhn, H. P. (1958). The automatic creation of literature abstracts. *IBM Journal of Research and Development, 2*(2), 159–165.

Paice, C. (1990). Constructing literature abstracts by computer: techniques and prospects. *Information Processing and Management, 26*(1), 171–186.

Salton, G. (1989). *Automatic text processing—the transformation, analysis and retrieval of information by computer.* Reading, MA: Addison-Wesley Publishing Co.

Salton, G. & Allan, J. (1993). Selective text utilization and text traversal. In *Proceedings of Hypertext '93* (pp. 131–144). New York: Association for Computing Machinery.

Salton, G., & McGill, M. (1983). *Introduction to modern information retrieval.* New York: McGraw Hill Book Co.

Salton, G., & Singhal, A. (1995). *Selective text traversal.* Technical Report, TR 95-1549, Department of Computer Science, Cornell University, Ithaca, NY.

Salton, G., Buckley, C., & Allan, J. (1991). *Automatic structuring of text files.* Technical Report TR 91-1241, Computer Science Department, Cornell University, Ithaca, NY.

Salton, G., Allan, J., Buckley, C., & Singhal, A. (1994a). Automatic analysis, theme generation and summarization of machine-readable texts. *Science, 264*, 1421–1426.

Salton, G., Allan, J., & Singhal, A. (1994b). Automatic text decomposition and structuring. *Information Processing and Management, 32*(2), 127–138.

Salton, G., Singhal, A., Buckley, C., & Mitra, M. (1996). Automatic text decomposition using text segments and text themes. *Hypertext '96*, The Seventh ACM Conference on Hypertext (pp. 53–65). New York: Association for Computing Machinery

23

Summarizing Similarities and Differences
Among Related Documents

INDERJEET MANI, ERIC BLOEDORN

imani@mitre.org, bloedorn@mitre.org
The MITRE Corporation, W640
11493 Sunset Hills Road
Reston, VA 22090, USA.

Abstract.

In many modern information retrieval applications, a common problem which arises is the existence of multiple documents covering similar information, as in the case of multiple news stories about an event or a sequence of events. A particular challenge for text summarization is to be able to summarize the similarities and differences in information *content* among these documents. The approach described here exploits the results of recent progress in information extraction to represent salient units of text and their relationships. By exploiting meaningful *relations* between units based on an analysis of text cohesion and the *context* in which the comparison is desired, the summarizer can pinpoint similarities and differences, and align text segments. In evaluation experiments, these techniques for exploiting cohesion relations result in summaries which (i) help users more quickly complete a retrieval task (ii) result in improved alignment accuracy over baselines, and (iii) improve identification of topic-relevant similarities and differences.

Keywords: Text summarization, information retrieval, natural language processing.

1. Introduction

With the mushrooming of the quantity of on-line text information, triggered in part by the growth of the World Wide Web, it is especially useful to have tools which can help users digest information content. Text summarization attempts to address this problem by taking a partially-structured source text, extracting information content from it, and presenting the most important content to the user in a manner sensitive to the user's needs. Clearly, some sort of summarization is indispensible for dealing with these massive and unprecedented amounts of information. Now, in many modern information retrieval applications, a common problem which arises is the existence of multiple documents covering similar information, as in the case of multiple news stories about an event or a sequence of events. A particular challenge for text summarization is to be able to summarize the similarities and differences in information *content* among these documents.

A variety of approaches exist for extracting content for multi-document summarization, which vary in the extent of domain dependence. In constrained domains, e.g., articles on terrorist events, natural language message understanding systems can extract relationships between entities, such as the location and target of a terrorist event. Such relationships can be used to identify areas of agreement and disagreement across texts [34]. For arbitrary text, such techniques do not apply, and instead, word-based content representations have traditionally been exploited (e.g., [49]). However, as recent progress in information extraction reveals (e.g., [39]), it is possible to extract not just salient words but also phrases and proper names from unrestricted text in a highly scalable manner. As a result, such extraction techniques are now being exploited in general purpose information retrieval tools (e.g., [10], [16], [18], [42], [56]).

The focus of the work described here is to provide a tool for analyzing document collections such as multiple news stories about an event or a sequence of events. Given a collection of such documents, the tool can be used to detect and align similar regions of text among members of the collection, and to detect relevant differences among members. It is worth noting here that the context-sensitive aspect of summarization is particularly important in this task. Depending on the users' interest, there may be many different sets of similarities and differences. Our summarization approach represents context in terms of a topic, which is a set of words which can be drawn from a user query or profile. Given a topic and a pair of related news stories, our method identifies salient regions of each story related to the topic, and then compares them, summarizing similarities and differences. Until now, only portions of this approach have been described [29], [30]. In this more detailed paper, we present our approach in more general terms, and include additional experimental data and techniques.

2. Overall Approach to Summarization

We will first clarify the variety of summarization being considered here. In general, there are many varieties of automatic summarization. A classical distinction (e.g., [40]) is that a summary can be "indicative", used to alert the user as to what the source is about (thus helping her decide whether the source might be worth reading) or it can be "informative", attempting, within the constraints of the particular compression desired, to stand in place of the source. A summary can also be "evaluative" [55] offering a critique of the source, as in a book review. In some situations (e.g., a scientific abstracting service), a high degree of fluency and connectedness of the summary text may be called for; in contrast, when a summary is used merely as a gist, more fragmentary or less connected text may suffice. A summary can be in the form of an extract, or an abstract; it can stand by itself, or it can be linked to the source or to more detailed summaries. A summary can cover a single source, or multiple sources. Finally, the audience for a summary can vary. Traditionally, abstracts were written by authors or by professional abstractors with the goal of dissemination to a particular - usually broad - readership community. These "generic" abstracts were traditionally used as surrogates for full-text. As our computing environments continue to accommodate increased full-text searching, browsing, and personalized information filtering, "user-focused" abstracts, which are customized to the user's interests, have assumed increased importance. As will be made clear, we report here on techniques for generating user-focused, indicative, moderately fluent, extract-based summaries for multiple sources.

Automatic text summarization can be characterized as involving three phases of processing: analysis, refinement, and synthesis[1]. The analysis phase builds a representation of the source text. The refinement phase transforms this representation into a summary representation, condensing text content by selecting salient information. The synthesis phase takes the summary representation and renders it in natural language using appropriate presentation techniques.

In our approach, the analysis phase builds a representation based on domain-independent information extraction techniques. Text items such as words, phrases, and proper names are extracted and represented in a graph. In particular, nodes in the graph represent word instances at different positions, with phrases and names being formed out of words. The refinement phase exploits cohesion relationships (to be discussed below) between term instances to determine what is salient. Finally, the synthesis phase takes the set of salient items discovered by the refinement phase, and uses that set to extract text from the source to present a summary.

Of course, if we are able to discover, given a topic and a pair of related documents, salient

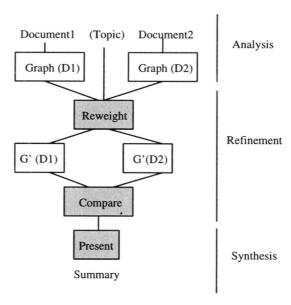

Fig. 1. Multi-document Summarization Approach

items of text in each document which are related to the topic, then these salient items can be compared to establish similarities and differences between the document pair. This forms the basis for a general scheme for multi-document summarization. As shown in Figure 1, given a pair of documents, the Analysis phase builds a graph for each document. In the Refinement phase, salient nodes in each graph related to the topic are discovered, using a spreading activation search of the graph. The set of activated (i.e., reweighted) nodes for each graph are then compared; comparing just these salient items results in fewer comparisons than comparing the entire body of the two texts. Finally, the result of this comparison is used in a synthesis phase to extract sentences. Thus, given a pair of related news stories about an event or a sequence of events, the problem of finding similarities and differences becomes one of comparing text items which have been activated by a common topic. This allows different comparisons to be generated, based on the choice of common topic.

The overall approach in Figure 1 extends easily to comparing sets of documents rather than pairs, with some restrictions on the presentation strategies in the synthesis stage. In this paper, we explore several different synthesis techniques in multi-document summarization, including identifying similarities and differences and aligning text across multiple documents. While the former method applies to sets of documents, the latter (as will be explained in Section 7.2.3) is more suited to pairwise comparison.

Although our interest here is in user-focused summaries, the overall approach can be extended to deal with "generic" summaries. In that case, in Figure 1, instead of reweighting based on a query (using spreading activation), we weight the nodes based on a conventional weighting metric, such as tf.idf. The comparison and presentation steps in Figure 1 (after applying a segment finding operation on these graphs, described in Section 6.2) remains as in the user-focused case, allowing for generic summaries to be produced.

These summarization techniques yield useful summaries when applied to large quantities of unrestricted text, of the kind found on the World Wide Web. To investigate the degree of scalability of the approach, we investigate measures of algorithmic time and space complexity, timing results, and evaluation metrics for effectiveness. The approach has been embedded in an information retrieval tool which allows the user to issue queries to Internet search engines running queries against the World Wide Web. The user can choose any set of hits to summarize. The system offers a set of common terms, which the user can select one or more from, to constitute the common topic.

For such applications, summarization needs to be able to help users minimize reading time on longer documents, to enable them to quickly select relevant information, and discard irrelevant information. In such situations, the summaries need not be highly polished, but must be intelligible enough to stand on their own to be archived or linked in for later perusal.

3. Distinguishing Features of Our Approach

Our summarization approach in Figure 1 has three main distinguishing features:

1. We explicitly identify commonalities and differences across documents. This may be contrasted with approaches such as [43], where (queries and) documents are matched for similarity, with statistically prominent terms in each document being highlighted. Among the advantage of identifying commonalities and differences is that in addition to the commonalities telling us what information is salient with respect to the topic in the entire set, the differences tell us what's unique about each document. Thus, if the set of documents is ordered, say, in chronological order, the differences for the latest document tells us what's *novel* in it (with respect to the current topic). Novelty, in turn, is rather fundamental to summarization, and the ability to distinguish what's new from a sequence of similar documents retrieved for a query is of practical value.

2. We are able to identify the salience of different *regions* of text in a document with respect to a query. This is in keeping with the assumption underlying much summarization research that location and linear order of text items are important (e.g., [15], [26], [41]) in determining what's salient. This might be achieved by a passage-level relevance ranking approach [5]. However, choosing the best window size for identifying passages is a problem, whether one uses fixed-length overlapping windows, or "discourse" windows (e.g., sentences, paragraphs, sections). If the window size is too small, one may end up with a set of adjacent windows which individually contribute little relevance information but which as a whole are highly relevant. If the window size is too large, it may include too much irrelevant information[2]. Instead of using a fixed window size, or paying the increased time complexity of varying the window size dynamically, we use a text representation which assigns weights to different positions of a term (these term occurrences correspond to nodes in the graph representation). Further, identifying regions in each document relevant to the query allows us to compare just those regions, reducing the set of items to be compared for commonalities and differences.

3. Finally, we explore a model of text which takes into account how connected items in the text are. This therefore explores a similar model of connectivity to the approach of [49] and [51], where the strength of links (in their case based on similarity) between different text units is used to identify salient text units in one or more documents. However, instead of just using a cosine-similarity measure between word-based vectors for fixed-size text units, we assign weights to different word occurrences based on "cohesion" links between these occurrences, discovered in part based on information extraction techniques.

The cohesion relations considered here include synonym/hypernymy relations, repetition, adjacency, and coreference. Cohesion itself is an abstract notion, expressing the intuition that certain relations help make the text "hang together", and in some sense cause portions of the text to "be about the same thing" [37][3]. While it is as a result a rather imprecisely defined concept, the linguistic devices grouped under text cohesion are directly observable. (Cohesion is often contrasted with *coherence*, which is a relation between larger units of text, typically sentences and clauses, which has to do with macro-level, deliberative structuring of the text, e.g., represented by text schemas and rhetorical structures [27], [31], [32], [35], [57]). In keeping with trends of improved information extraction capabilities, cohesion also appears to be a renewed focus of interest among researchers in the text summarization field, e.g., [4], [8], [6]. Various cohesion relations are also of considerable interest in identifying topic shifts, e.g., [6], [24].

This cohesion approach is one way to allow term occurrences which are indirectly related to the topic to emerge as salient; in turn this allows them to be candidates for comparison across documents. As these cohesion relations are represented as edges in the document's graph, the topology of the graph can be used to compute salience, using a spreading activation search algorithm. While spreading activation has been used in information retrieval [50], [12] and text summarization [46], [3] to search hand-created semantic nets or networks derived from thesauri, the focus here is on directly activating the richly structured graph for the text. In contrast to summarization approaches such as [46], which use information extraction techniques to build graphs for text about specific events such as corporate takeovers, the graphs built here apply to unrestricted text.

To conclude this section, our summarization approach is distinguished from others as follows. We use a graph representation which explicitly represents position and linear order of text items. The connectivity of text based on robustly-extracted linguistic relations between word occurrences is used to compute a salience function for the text as a whole with respect to a particular topic. Text regions deemed salient by this method are then used to address summarization of sets of documents with respect to a topic.

4. Representing Meaningful Text Content

As shown in Figure 2, each node is a word *instance*, and has a distinct input position. Associated with each such node is a record characterizing the various features of the word in that position (e.g., absolute word position, position in sentence, weight). As shown in part 1 of the figure, a node can have adjacency links (ADJ) to textually adjacent nodes, SAME links to other instances of the same word, and other semantic links (represented by *alpha*). PHRASE links tie together strings of adjacent nodes which belong to a phrase (part

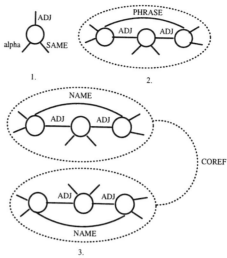

Fig. 2. Graph Representation

2). In part 3, we show a NAME link, as well as the COREF link between subgraphs, relating positions of name instances which are coreferential. NAME links can be specialized to different types, e.g., person, province, etc. In our work, the *alpha* links are restricted to synonymy and hypernymy among words.

This representation is highly flexible, and general enough to encompass more fleshed-out linguistic representations; new relationships can be threaded easily into the graph. This results in a level of sentential analysis where words are grouped, where possible, into names and phrases, which in turn can make up a sentence. This representation allows for a degree of graceful degradation; in the worst case a sentence is just made up of a sequence of words.

Using this graph representation, the weights of nodes in the graph can be represented as an *activation vector*, as follows. A text D_i can be represented as a vector of weights $(wp_{i1}, .., wp_{ik}, .., wp_{in})$ where wp_{ik} is the weight of word position k in text i. In the initial activation vector, a given term has the same weight for all occurrences (positions). Given a topic T, the activation vector for D_i can be reweighted favoring term occurrences related to the topic, using the spreading activation techniques described in Section 6. Further reweighting is achieved by clipping the activation vector, as described in Section 6.2. A graph is implemented as an adjacency list, which requires $B.N$ storage, where N is the

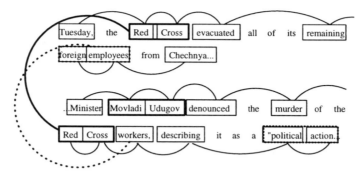

Fig. 3. Graph Example. Names and phrases are grouped together. Dark edges: COREF; Light edges: ADJ; dotted edges: hypernym.

number of nodes in the graph and B is the maxmimum branching factor of a node. In practice B is observed to be small (maximum observed = 7, average = 3.5), so the graph requires $O(N)$ storage.

A sample graph is shown in Figure 3[4]. We also introduce here Figure 4 (Appendix), which serves as an example used throughout this paper to illustrate some of our observations about multi-document summarization. It shows the text (some of which is elided for reasons of space) of two related articles. The article in the left column is from the Associated Press (AP), the one in the right is from Reuters. Relevant subgraphs discussed in the paper are sketched. Some alignments between the two texts are shown boxed.

5. Tools for Building Meaningful Content Representations

The construction of text graphs for use in summarization requires at minimum a component for associating words with sentence and paragraph positions. We use a sentence and paragraph tagger which contains a very extensive regular-expression-based sentence boundary disambiguator [1]. Next, weights are computed for the words in the text. We use tf.idf [54] weighting, though any sensible weighting scheme could be substituted; here use is made of a reference corpus derived from the TREC [23] corpus. The weight $tf.idf_{ik}$ of term k in document i is given by:

$$tf.idf_{ik} = tf_{ik} * (ln(N) - ln(df_k) + 1) \qquad (1)$$

where tf_{ik} = frequency of term k in document i, df_k = number of documents in the reference corpus in which term k occurs, N = total number of documents in the reference corpus.

It should be mentioned that the weights here are used for two purposes: first, as a filtering mechanism in extracting phrases (as described next), and second, to provide initial weights for occurrences of query terms in the text, for use by the spreading activation search for query-related text regions (described in Section 6). Before beginning the spreading activation phase, the weights of all terms other than query terms are zeroed out; it is the spreading activation itself which determines the final weights based on the initial weights of query term occurrences. As a result, the main overall impact of the initial weighting scheme is in determining the heights of the "peaks" (i.e., occurrences of query terms) in the eventual distribution of weights of terms across text positions in the document. As a result, the summarization is not particularly sensitive to the particular weighting scheme; other weighting schemes have also been used effectively in our approach, including G^2 statistics [13]. Nor is the summarization particularly sensitive to different scaling factors used to normalize the tf_{ik} frequency; among the scaling factors we have used is the maximum frequency of any term in the document.

The remaining component tools include phrase extraction, name extraction, and synonym and hypernym extraction. The summarization algorithms described in this paper can work without all of these, but the use of these tools provides more structure to the graph, allowing use of these content-based features in summarization. To support phrase finding, MITRE's Alembic part-of-speech tagger [1] is invoked on the text. This tagger uses the rule-sequence learning approach of [9][5]. Names and relationships between names are extracted from the document using SRA's NameTag [25], a MUC6-fielded system. Phrases are extracted from the text using the word weights and part-of-speech and punctuation features. Finally, synonyms and hypernyms are extracted for the words using WordNet [38]. "Function" words, it should be noted, are stripped out using a stoplist, except where they occur within extracted names and phrases.

The name extraction techniques are now quite standard; for more details see [1], [25]. In what follows, we discuss the phrase and synonym/hypernym extraction analysis tools in more detail.

5.1. Phrase Extraction

Phrases are useful in summarization as they often denote significant concepts. In our application, phrases are of interest as summary descriptors rather than as index terms. Thus, we are not interested in extracting components of phrases, or syntactic variants of phrases; we require only a single phrase to describe a phrase-denoted concept. In general, one would prefer phrases which are as specific as possible; this is approximated by preferring longer phrases. Finally, we prefer phrases to be different from one another, to represent more of the conceptual content of the document. Our phrase extraction method finds candidate phrases using robust finite-state parsing techniques. We use several patterns defined over part-of-speech tags. One pattern, for example, uses the maximal sequence of one or more adjectives followed by one or more nouns. The weight of a candidate phrase is the average of the tf.idf weights of non-function (or content) words in the phrase, plus a factor β which adds a small bonus in proportion to the length of the phrase. We use a contextual parameter θ to avoid redundancy among phrases, by selecting each term in a phrase at most once in a window w. The size of the window is application dependent; our typical setting for news stories is

the whole document. The weight of a phrase W of length n content words in document i is:

$$wt(W, i) = \beta(n) + \frac{\sum_{k=1}^{n} \theta(ik) * tf.idf_{ik}}{n} \qquad (2)$$

where $\theta(ik)$ is 0 if the word has been seen before in the window, and 1 otherwise.

5.2. Synonym and Hypernym Extraction

We now discuss the extraction of synonym and hypernym links. These are extracted using WordNet 1.5 [38]. Our algorithm takes every distinct word in the graph which is identified as a noun by the part-of-speech tagger, and looks up its synonyms and immediate hypernyms. First, if the word has an entry in a lookup table, that is used; otherwise, WordNet lookup is performed, with any hits being cached in the lookup table. Whenever a pair of words has a synonym or immediate hypernym link, an edge is drawn between all its instances. Although words tend to be highly polysemous in WordNet, no sense-disambiguation is carried out. Thus, even if a pair was linked by a very rare noun sense, the edge would be present on the graph. The reasoning is that automatic word sense disambiguation (e.g., distinguishing among different noun senses) within a text is quite hard. Further, an experiment described below suggests that investing in such an algorithm may not be worthwhile, as most of the synonyms found (using the part-of-speech method) are "correct".

For the texts in Figure 4, we have good links like *captive ⇔ prisoner, head ⇔ chief ⇒ leader, ambassador ⇒ diplomat, assault ⇔ attack, residence ⇒ house, reception ⇒ party*[6]. Examples of bad links due to lack of sense disambiguation are *sister ⇒ member, head ⇔ question*.

To get a better handle on the performance of this method, we conducted a small experiment to examine precision of synonym linking over 17 articles (11986 words) with 510 synonym links in all. The articles were drawn from a collection of Internet news articles (where each article was on a different topic). (More details of the collection are described in Section 9.2.) A synonym link was judged correct if the linked pair of words appeared to have the same sense, given the context in which they each appeared in the article. As mentioned earlier, our algorithm takes every distinct word in

Table 1.   Precision of 510 synonym links using two different techniques

Guessing "noun"	Part-of-speech tagging
.51 (264 links)	.67 (342 links)

the graph which is identified as a noun by the part-of-speech tagger, and looks up its synonyms and immediate hypernyms in WordNe'. To compare with what would happen without part-of-speech tagging, we used a "dumb" baseline of treating every word to be looked up as a noun, leaving WordNet to do the rest. Table 1 shows the results under these two conditions. It can be seen from Table 1 that over two-thirds of the synonym links were correct using noun lookup in WordNet based on part-of-speech tagging, whereas guessing noun every time resulted in only about half the synonym links being correct. (In this experiment, the part-of-speech tags were correct in $78/87 = 89.65\%$ of the cases involving synonyms.) This shows a substantial positive impact due to part-of-speech tagging. It is also worth noting that of the correct guesses found, 20.17% ($69/342$) were simply morphological variants (noun inflections) found by WordNet (e.g., *protest* $\Leftrightarrow$ *protests*).

However, synonyms by themselves may sometimes be misleading in terms of establishing cohesion. That's because a synonym link between a pair of nouns does not imply that their containing noun phrases are coreferential. For example, for the AP text in Figure 4, we have *hostage* $\Rightarrow$ *captive* $\Leftrightarrow$ *prisoner*; however, in that text, "the remaining captives" refers to people taken hostage by the rebels, whereas, "the prisoners" refers to rebels imprisoned by the government. In the above experiment, only 32 of the correct synonym links (6.27% of the total) were cases where referring NPs containing the nouns were not coreferential. To exclude these would require extremely robust techniques for recognition and resolution of pronominal and definite noun phrase anaphora (i.e., not just proper-name coreference), e.g., as are beginning to be explored in the MUC-6 coreference task [39]. These figures suggest that even if one succeeded in doing so, it would not be a big win in terms of accuracy improvement.

While these accuracy figures are suggestive, more statistically interesting inferences can only be drawn from a much larger-scale experiment. Also, judgments of synonymy can be quite del-

icate; studies of agreement in judgments across subjects is clearly needed. Finally, the evaluation of a synonym component by itself does not tell us that much about its impact on the overall task of summarization. Clearly, one might expect spurious synonym links to lead the spreading activation search of the graph (to be discussed next) astray, but the size of such a possible effect is unclear.

In the course of working with synonyms, we also explored a more general semantic distance measure between words, based on the relative height of the most specific common ancestor class of the two words, i.e., the most specific common hypernym synset (synonym set) in Wordnet, subject to a context-dependent class-weighting parameter. This approach proved not to give good results, as the technique turned out to be oversensitive to the structure of the thesaurus. The approach of Resnick [47] gets around this by using information content rather than height of the class, where the information content of a synset is related to the probability of the synset and all its subordinates (hyponyms) occurring in a large reference corpus. This approach, when implemented by us, turned out to be very expensive to compute at run-time. Smeaton [53] has addressed this issue, by compiling out, based on Resnick's statistic, a very large table (150,000,000 word pairs) of semantic distances. While Smeaton [53] reports interesting results in image caption retrieval using this table (in combination with a particular query-caption matching metric), the scale of the compilation effort required and the uncertainty of whether it would meet our needs kept us from pursuing it further.

6.   Discovering Topic-Related Text Regions

6.1.   Finding Topic-Related Text Regions Using Spreading Activation

Given a topic that expresses the user's interest, the refinement phase of processing begins by computing a salience function for text items based on their relation to the topic. A spreading activation algorithm (derived from [12]) is used to find nodes in the graph related to topic nodes.

```
Algorithm Spread(Graph, Topic):
 Input := words(Topic);
 sort(Input);
 while (Continue?(Output))
    [Node := first(Input);
     insert(Output, Node);
     Succs := ActivateSuccs(Node, Graph);
     while (Succs)
        [insert(Input, pop(Succs));]]
Algorithm ActivateSuccs(Node, Graph):
 while (<Node1, Edge> := edges(Node, Graph))
    [Node1.wt
       = max(Node1.wt, (Node.wt * Edge.wt));
     if (type(Edge) = ADJ)
        [Node1.wt
           = ScaleDist(Node1, Node, Node1.wt).]]
```

The method, which corresponds to a strict best-first search of the graph, begins by adding the nodes matching the given query terms onto an input priority queue, which is kept sorted by decreasing weight[7]. The method then iterates until a terminating condition is reached, taking the first node off the input priority queue and placing it on the output, and then finding successor nodes linked to the current node in the graph and inserting them into the input priority queue. The weight of a successor node is a function of the source node weight and the link type weight. Each different link type has a dampening effect on the source node weight. Since the graph may have cycles, the weight of a successor node is determined by the strongest path to the node. Thus, the successor node weight is the maximum of its new weight and its old weight. ScaleDist returns an exponential function of the text distance between the input nodes. In the termination condition, *Spread* halts if either the number of output nodes is greater than a threshold t_1, or if a slope-based test succeeds.

The slope-based test is as follows. At each iteration of the outer while loop in *Spread*, we maintain the total activation weight of the nodes taken off the input priority queue so far. We compute, for that iteration, the change in activation weight compared to 40 iterations ago, which, di-

vided by the window size of 40, gives us the slope for the change between this iteration and the 40-iterations-previous one. If the standard deviation of the last 40 slopes is less than 0.1, the test succeeds.

The spreading activation is constrained so that the activation decays by link type and text distance. We use the following ordering of different link types, with earlier links in the ordering being heavier (and thus having less dampening effect) than later links:

$$SAME > \ COREFERENCE > \ NAME \\ > PHRASE \qquad > ALPHA > \qquad ADJ \qquad (3)$$

For ADJ links, successor node weight is an exponentially decaying function of current node weight and the distance between nodes. Here distances are scaled so that travelling across sentence boundaries is more expensive than travelling within a sentence, but less than travelling across paragraph boundaries. For the other link types, the successor weight is the product of link weight and current node weight.

As an example, the sentence-level plot of the activation weights for a Reuters article, where the weight at a given sentence position is calculated as the average of its constituent word weights, is shown in Figure 4. The results after spreading, given the topic *Tupac Amaru*, are shown in Figure 5. The spreading has changed the activation weight surface, so that some new related peaks (i.e., local maxima) have emerged (e.g., sentence 4), and old peaks have been reduced (e.g., sentence 2, which had a high tf.idf score, but was not related to *Tupac Amaru*). The exponential decay function is also evident in the neighborhoods of the peaks.

The worst-case algorithmic time complexity of Algorithm *Spread* can be calculated as follows. Assume there are N nodes in the graph and the maximum branching factor of a node is B. The initial sort of the Input priority queue takes at most $Nlog(N)$ time. The test for the termination condition is bounded by some constant k_1. The code in the while loop in *Spread* runs for at most N iterations. In each iteration, we sum the constant cost k_2 of picking the first element and putting it on the output, the cost $log(N)$ of insertion into the priority queue, and the cost of *Acti-*

vateSuccs. The code in the while loop in *Activate-Succs* runs at most B times; each time the operations are bounded by some constant k_3. *Spread*'s while loop thus takes $(k_1 + k_2 + Bk_3 + logN)$ time. Thus the worst case time complexity of *Spread* is $NlogN + N(k_1 + k_2 + Bk_3 + logN) = O(BN + NlogN)$. Since $B < 8$, this gives the algorithm close to $NlogN$ performance.

The space complexity is as follows. *Spread* allocates an Input priority queue of size N, where N is the number of nodes in the graph, and an output list. At each step of *Spread*'s while loop, no more than B nodes (where B is the maximum branching factor) are added to Input, with one node being removed. So, the Input requires $B(N - 1)$ storage, with the Output requiring no more than the output threshold t_1 storage. The register *Succs* in *ActivateSuccs* reuses B elements of storage at each call. So the total worst case space allocation is $B(N-1)+t_1+B = O(N)$, assuming, as above, that B is a constant.

6.2. Filtering Activated Regions by Segment Finding

As defined by [51], a text segment is "a contiguous piece of text that is linked internally but largely disconnected from the adjacent text". While the goal of the spreading activation is to reweight the nodes of the graph based on a topic, the goal of the segment finder is to select segments from the reweighted graph. This reduction of the search space is useful in increasing the speed of the system to find similarities and differences and align text segments. The segment finder uses the words of the topic to locate specific nodes in the graph which has first been reweighted by spreading activation. Depending on the parameters given it will define a segment as either all nodes with a weight within a user-defined delta of each peak value (the depth parameter), or it will output all nodes within a user-defined distance in the text from each peak (the width parameter). In the former case, which corresponds to a horizontal clipping of the activation signal, one or more text segments, each of whose words has values within the particular delta of the peak value, will be generated. In the latter case, which corresponds to sampling of the signal, the number of segments is

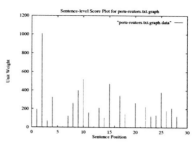

Fig. 4. Sentence-level Activation Weights from Raw Graph (Reuters news)

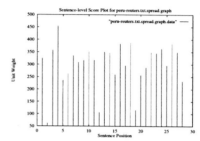

Fig. 5. Sentence-level Activation Weights from Spread Graph (Reuters news; topic: *Tupac Amaru*)

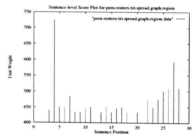

Fig. 6. Sentence-level Activation Weights after Segment Finding (Reuters news; topic: *Tupac Amaru*)

less than (in case the width encompasses a neighboring peak) or equal to the number of peaks. The clipping involves sorting the nodes by weight and then filtering the nodes above a threshold; the clipping thus has an algorithmic time complexity of order $O(NlogN)$ for a graph of size N nodes, and a space cost of order $O(N)$ (assuming nondestructive sorting).

Figure 6 and Figure 7 shows the results of segment finding on the activation weights in the Reuters and AP articles, using the default depth of 90. The segment-finder has removed 163 word-nodes from the Reuters graph (43% reduction) and 88 words (21% reduction) from the AP news article. Note that the amount of reduction varies with the topology of the surface generated by the

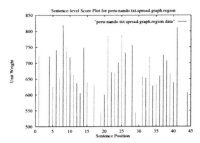

Fig. 7. Sentence-level Activation Weights after Segment Finding (AP news; topic: *Tupac Amaru*)

activation function. Where highly active nodes are uniformly distributed in the text, clipping will result in much less reduction than in cases where there are only a few distinct peaks. The result of this is that some of the sentences are eliminated (sentences 1, 2, 12, 19 and 21) and the weight of the remaining sentences is increased. The important aspect of this reduction is that although it significantly reduced the number of words being compared, it left nodes with strong associations to *Tupac Amaru* (where the group is mentioned by name, e.g., sentence 4), and also those with less obvious associations (e.g., nodes in sentence 26 - a sentence about a past U.S. collaborator of the MRTA).

It is worth noting that this segment-finding approach differs substantially from previous approaches. For example, in contrast to [51], [24], these text segments are not generated by directly comparing blocks of text (problems with block sizes were discussed earlier). In addition, the segments correspond to potentially variable-sized neighborhoods around the peaks. Finally, unlike approaches such as [24] which use segments to discover topic shifts in text, the segments here are simply used to further restrict the set of salient terms.

6.3. *Examples*

We will now discuss an example, to illustrate the kinds of links discovered by the spreading activation. Of course, this does not tell us much about aggregate behavior over texts in general. See Section 8 for performance data on arbitrary newswire culled from the World Wide Web, and Section 9 for evaluation. Algorithmic complexity measures for *Spread* and and segment finding have been dis-

cussed; corresponding measures for remaining algorithms will also be offered.

Our use of spreading activation allows us to find word occurrences which are indirectly related to the query. Unlike traditional information retrieval approaches [50], [12], however, the final link weights are determined by the number and type of links in the graph. For example, the Reuters sentence 4 plotted in Figure 5 and shown in Figure 4 might have been found via an information retrieval method which matched on the query *Tupac Amaru* (allowing for *MRTA* as an abbreviated alias for the name). However, it would have not found other information related to the *Tupac Amaru*: In the Reuters article, the spreading method follows an ADJ link from *Tupac Amaru* to *release* in sentence 4, to other instances of *release* via the SAME link, eventually reaching sentence 13 where *release* is ADJ to the name *Victor Polay* (the group's leader). In an Associated Press (AP) article describing the same event, a thesaurus link becomes more useful in establishing a similar connection: it is able to find a direct link from *Tupac Amaru* to *leaders* (via ADJ) in sentence 28, and from there to its synonym *chief* in sentence 29 (via ALPHA), which is ADJ to *Victor Polay*.

Of course, this cohesive relation could also be found more directly if the system could correctly interpret the expressions *its chief* in the AP article and *their leader* in the Reuters article. This raises the question of finding stronger evidence as to how effective the spreading activation is in finding salient topic-related items. In Section 9, we report on experiments which each confirm that the spreading activation is effective in summarization.

7. Summarizing Multiple Documents

7.1. *Finding Commonalities and Differences*

We now describe our algorithm for finding similarities and differences. Given a set of documents, the goal is to find their relevant shared and distinguishing terms with respect to a topic. Once text segments are found, only nodes belonging to such segments are considered in building Commonalities and Differences; all other nodes are zeroed out. The set of common words given activated, clipped graphs $G'_1 \ldots G'_n$ is computed by Algorithm Compute-Common:

```
Algorithm Compute-Common(G'_1 ... G'_n):
 for k = 1..n
 [Words[k] = sort-alpha(nodes(G'_k));]
 # sort-alpha removes duplicates
 # remembering only the best weighted occurrences
 # and their weights
 # Words[k] =< t_1, w_1 > ... < t_m, w_m >
 # where t_i <_α t_{i+1}, 1 ≤ i ≤ m
 # where m is the number of distinct words in G'_k.
 Row-indices = intersection(Words[1]...Words[n]);
 # Contains terms from intersection, remembering
 weights
 # Row-indices preserves the alphabetic sorting
 # from Words
 Column-indices = 1...k;
 # Common.Words = Row-indices
 #Common.Docs = Column-indices;
 Common = build-matrix(Row-indices, Column-indices);
```

Note that Common contains only distinct terms, not term occurrences. Common is represented as a term-document matrix, where the weight of each distinct term in a document is the highest weight of any of its occurrences in that document, normalized by the maximum weight of any term in that document.

Differences, which are computed at the same time as Common, are defined as follows:

$$Differences = (G'_1 \ldots \cup G'_n) - Common.Words \quad (4)$$

These Differences are differences in query-related information.

Algorithm *Compute-Common* carries out K sorting operations to build $Words$, where K is the number of graphs being compared. If the graph with the most nodes has N nodes, the building of $Words$ costs $O(KN log N)$. The intersection operation involves intersection of K lists each of length N in the worst case, which costs $K.N$. This gives us $O(KN log N)$ worst case time complexity for *Compute-Common*. The algorithm uses $O(N)$ space for the sorting and $O(KN)$ space for the Common matrix.

7.2. Presentation Strategies

7.2.1. Overview
The kinds of presentation strategies used in the synthesis stage of summarization will vary with the application. However, since very little attention has been paid to this in discussions of multi-document summarization, we illustrate here a range of presentation strategies.

1. A very simple strategy for synthesis of multi-document summaries is to avoid computing commonalities and differences, and instead to simply rank sentences in each document based on weights of contained words, and then to merge the rankings to get multi-document extracts. However, such an approach will not guarantee that higher-ranked sentences in the merged ranking reflect common information among the documents. The presentation strategies we discuss here, therefore, rely on identification of terms in Common and Differences.

2. In *cross-document sentence extraction*, discussed in Section 7.2.2, the best sentences containing words in Common are selected from the set of documents based on the total weight of such words. Likewise, the best sentences containing words in Differences are selected from the set of documents based on the total weight of such words. The two are presented separately, as similarities and differences. When there is a chronological ordering in the set of documents, the differences are presented in terms of what's new in the latest document (with respect to the current topic).

3. In *cross-document sentence alignment*, discussed in Section 7.2.3, pairs of sentences, one from each document (the alignment algorithm is restricted to document pairs), are ranked for coverage of common words.

4. Finally, in Section 7.2.4, we discuss techniques where fragments are extracted instead of sentences. These include "bag-of-terms" presentation strategies, as well as generation of well-formed sentence fragments.

5. Of course, other presentation methods are also possible, e.g., "graphical" displays where we plot documents in a collection so that documents closer together in the plot have more terms in Common. We have not implemented

these graphical strategies, but suggest them to indicate the wide space of possible presentation strategies.

7.2.2. Cross-Document Sentence Extraction

The presentation strategy used to cover similarities and differences then simply outputs the set of sentences covering the terms in Common and the set of sentences covering the terms in Differences, highlighting the relevant terms in each, and indicating which document the sentence came from. This technique is what we call FSD (for Find Similarities and Differences):

```
Algorithm FSD(Common):
  For each doc k in Common.Docs
  [for each sentence p in doc k
    [score(p,k);]]
```

Sentence selection is based on the coverage of nodes in Common and Differences. Sentences are selected based on the average activated weight of the covered words: The score $score(p,k)$ for sentence p in document k (i.e., sentence s_{pk}) in terms of coverage of Common is:

$$score(p,k) = \frac{1}{|c(p,k)|} \sum_{i=1}^{|c(p,k)|} weight(w_i k) \qquad (5)$$

where $c(p,k) = \{w | w\epsilon(Common.Words \cap s_{pk})\}$ and $weight(w_i k)$ is the weight of term i in document k in (the term-document matrix) Common.

The score for Differences is similar. The user may specify the maximal number of non-zero-weighted sentences in a particular category (common or different) to control which sentences are output.

The worst case time complexity of FSD is as follows. Let N be the most number of *distinct words* in any of the input graphs. The cost of the intersection operation to build $c(p,k)$ is bounded by $k_1 logN$, where k_1 is the maximum sentence length, since the $Common.Words$ is sorted alphabetically. The summation in Equation 5 iterates for k_1 times at most, with each iteration having unit cost. The computation of $score(p,k)$ is invoked, in the worst case, for all the sentences in all the documents i.e., KN/k_2 times, where k_2 is the minimum sentence length, and K is the number of graphs. The worst case time complexity of FSD is therefore $K(N/k_2)(k_1 + k_1 logN) = O(KNlogN)$. Holding the sentence scores requires (N/k_2) stor-

age, with $c(s)$ using k_1 storage; this gives us $k_1 + (N/k_2) = O(N)$ storage cost for the algorithm.

It is possible to enhance FSD to ensure that all the commonalities in Common are represented in the summary. This could of course be done by outputting all sentences which contain common words, but this might yield many sentences which each cover the same subset of common words. Instead, it is possible to find smaller subsets of the sentences containing common words, which would reduce the redundancy of information content. We try to find such a subset in the enhanced version, called Algorithm *Greedy-FSD*:

```
Algorithm Greedy-FSD(Common):
while (not-empty(Common.Words))
  [FSD(Common);
   top-s = pop(Sentences);
   Common.Words = rest(Common.Words, top-s);
   output(top-s);]
```

Here, we score all the sentences using Equation 5, then pick the best-scored one, remove the terms covered in Common by that sentence (the *rest* operator in the algorithm), then rescore all remaining sentences using the new Common, and repeat until Common or the set of remaining sentences is empty.

The while loop in *Greedy-FSD* runs as many times as $|Common.Words| = N$ in the worst case, where N is the most number of *distinct words* in any of the input graphs. The first step is given by the complexity of FSD. The "removal" of the current sentence's words from Common is bounded by k_1, the maximum sentence length, and the popping of the set of sentences has some small constant cost $k4$. So, the worst case time complexity of *Greedy-FSD* is $N(k4 + k_1 + K(N/k_2)(k_1 + k_1 logN)) = O(KN^2 logN)$, where k_2 is the minimum sentence length and K is the number of graphs. The *Greedy-FSD* enhancement is thus relatively expensive compared to Algorithm *FSD* in terms of worst case time complexity, and as a presentation strategy, is useful when maximum compression is desired at the expense of (potentially) increased time. The space cost of *Greedy-FSD* is given by the cost of *FSD* plus the length of the output, which is no longer than $|Common|$, i.e., the space cost is $O(N)$.

To illustrate the behavior of FSD, consider the application of FSD to the extracted segments in Figure 6 (the Reuters article) and the extracted segments in Figure 7 (an AP article of the same date describing the same hostage crisis). The extracted segments had 42 words in Common, out of 180 words for the first article's segments and 326 for the latter article's segments. The algorithm extracts 24 commonalities, with the commonalities with the strongest associations being on top. Among the high scoring commonalities and differences are the ones shown in Figure 4, where the words in Common are in bold face. The algorithm discovers that both articles talk about *Victor Polay* (e.g., the Reuters sentence 13 mentioned earlier, and the AP sentence 29 shown in Figure 4). A similar point could be made about the *Fujimori* sentences. Notice that the system is able to extract commonalities without *Tupac Amaru* being directly present. Regarding differences, the algorithm discovers that the AP article is the only one to explain how the rebels posed as waiters (sentence 12) and the Reuters article is the only one which told how the rebels once had public sympathy (sentence 27).

7.2.3. *Cross-Document Sentence Alignment*

In aligning news stories, we directly compare text units from one text with text units from the other. Here, we have in general a choice between aligning segments or sentences, in the former case outputting sentences by completing (say) to the nearest sentence boundary. In this method, rather than comparing one unit and outputting another, we chose to consistently align sentences, where the weights of words which are not part of a text segment are zeroed out.

```
Algorithm Align(Common):
For each sentence p in Common.doc1
[for each sentence q in Common.doc2
 [score = score-overlap(p, q);
  if (best-match-row[p] < score)
   [best-match-row[p] = q;]
  if (best-match-col[q] < score)
   [best-match-col[q] = p;]]]
For each sentence p in Common.doc1
[q = best-match-row[p];
 if (best-match-col[q] = p)
```

```
[then output(<p, q>);]]
```

The algorithm ranks pairs of sentences, one member from each document, for coverage of common words. First, as before, once a pair of graphs has been spread and clipped, terms in Common are computed. Only sentences containing terms in Common are considered. The basic one-to-one algorithm matches pairs of sentences based on their degree of overlap, where the overlap between a sentence pair is the total activation weight of terms common to both. Thus, given a pair of sentences s_1 and s_2, s_1 is scored for overlap with s_2 using Equation 5 with $S = Common \cap s_1 \cap s_2$ being used instead of *Common*. Once all the pairs are scored for overlap, the algorithm imposes a "symmetry check", picking the sentence pairs $< s_i, s_j >$ such that s_i's best overlapping alignment is with s_j, and s_j's best overlapping alignment is with s_i.

This overlap measure is somewhat insensitive to relative differences in weights, making it somewhat less precise than one that is more sensitive to the relative weights, such as cosine similarity [48]. Section 9.2 explores the use of cosine similarity further, offering some experimental results using cosine similarity as the sentence matching metric. Our experience indicates a tradeoff exists between higher recall of common terms (emphasized by the word overlap measure) and higher precision (emphasized in this case by cosine similarity).

The worst case time complexity of this algorithm is as follows. Let S_1 be the number of sentences in the first document, and S_2 be the number of sentences in the other. To perform the one-to-one sentence alignment of the two documents, in the worst case the algorithm considers $S_1.S_2$ pairs. Each pair is measured for the degree of overlap by computing an intersection costing no more than k_1, where $k_1 =$ the maximum sentence length. The symmetry check takes $min(S_1, S_2)$ time. So, the worst case time complexity of the algorithm is $S_1 S_2 k_1 + min(S_1, S_2)$. Now, $S_1 = N_1/k_2$ and $S_2 = N_2/k_2$, where N_1 is the number of distinct words in the first graph, N_2 is the number of distinct words in the second graph, and k_2 is the minimum sentence length. Thus we have the worst case time complexity as $((N_1/k_2)(N_2/k_2)k_1) + min(N_1/k_2, N_2/k_2)$. Letting $N = max(N_1, N_2)$, this gives $O(N^2)$ time complexity. The space complexity is given by the space required to store each maximum value for each row and column in a matrix of size $S_1.S_2$, which requires $S_1 + S_2 = O(N)$ storage.

Given *Align*'s quadratic worst case time complexity on document pairs, it is not particularly scalable, and it becomes even more computationally expensive to extend it to align sentences for every pair of documents in a set. Further, it is hard to for the user to interpret alignments between more than one pair at a time. Therefore, we have restricted its use to a document pair at a time. However, our experience shows that the algorithm is surprisingly useful in various applications, e.g., on static collections of news articles about related events. It is able to discover both obvious cases where the two articles use very similar sentences to describe a common event, as well as, in a large number of cases, ones where the sentences are rather different.

Figure 4 shows the top two one-to-one alignments from the AP-Reuters pair. Here the alignments are shown boxed, with overlap terms in bold font. The first alignment's sentences, which do not mention the topic *Tupac Amaru*, are near the top in both documents. The algorithm often aligns initial texts, because the initial texts often use similar terms to encapsulate a story. A comparison of alignment methods is described in Section 9.2.

7.2.4. *Extracting Fragments instead of Sentences*
In the above presentation strategies, the presentation unit is the sentence. However, while a sentence may have a certain degree of coverage of terms in Common (or Differences) (and therefore of terms related to the topic by cohesion relations) there will be other words in the presented sentence which aren't related to the topic. Some of these words may be function words, but others may not. Presenting units smaller than a sentence is thus often useful. One "bag-of-terms" presentation strategy is to present lists of words, phrases, and proper names relevant to the multi-document summary. These can be straightforward presentations of terms in Common and Differences, or they can be presentations of sentences extracted by other presentation modes (i.e., FSD and alignment). For example, terms in Common in the documents can be highlighted, much as salient terms

are highlighted in [43]. There are also certain applications which call for well-formed, more connected extracts, but where, given a particular target compression rate, we would like to pack the available space more efficiently. We will now illustrate its use in multi-document alignment, although it is applicable to FSD and other presentation modes.

Once we have aligned pairs of sentences, the synthesis component can choose to extract fragments rather than full-sentences. Given a (soft) reduction factor (e.g., 25% of full-text), the system picks off terms from Common from the reweighted positional term vector, and then extracts a context window around each selected term occurrence. The context window extraction is based on taking a minimal window (2-3 words) around each selected term occurrence (by itself not likely to yield well-formed fragments) and extending the context towards a boundary. The tests for a boundary uses patterns involving part-of-speech and punctuation features. Overlapping contexts are then merged by merging their context windows. The patterns are rather trivial at this point (e.g., extend to the right until the last noun in a noun group, or punctuation characters) but with more data analysis we expect to come up with a more definitive set of such patterns. This "middle-out" method allows for fine-grained control in summary output, cuts out potentially irrelevant sentence material and therefore packs the summary rather better with salient terms. This becomes useful in fitting a larger number of alignments (each of which can be rendered in fewer words than two full sentences) within the length limits required by the reduction factor for the summaries. Figure 8 illustrates this. The sentence number from which each fragment is drawn is shown alongside the fragment; the pairs are presented in decreasing order of degree of overlap. Terms in Common are boldfaced. This particular summary shows a reduction of 28% over the corresponding full-sentence summary.

8. Performance

We now measure the timing performance of the algorithms on Internet news sources. All results are cpu time on a sparc10 with a 55 MHz clock

Topic: arrest
Doc1: (AP) **Man Held** by N. **Korea** Found Dead; 12/19/96
Doc2: (New York Times) **Man Held** as Spy in North **Korea** Is a Suicide; 12/19/96
xxxxxxxxxxxxxxxxxxxxxxxxxxxxxxxxxxxxxxxxxxxxxxxxx
(13)... Hunziker had said he entered communist **North   Korea** from China "out of curiosity and to **preach**   the **Gospel** ." ...
(17)... American said he was in **North   Korea** because he wanted to **preach** the Gospel . ...
xxxxxxxxxxxxxxxxxxxxxxxxxxxxxxxxxxxxxxxxxxxxxxxxx
(27)... Evan refused to **talk** about his **time** in **North   Korea** ...
(46)... interviews, preferring not to **talk** about his **time** in **North   Korea** . ...
xxxxxxxxxxxxxxxxxxxxxxxxxxxxxxxxxxxxxxxxxxxxxxxxx
(20)... **Hunziker** had four **outstanding   arrest   warrants** for failing to comply with earlier court orders, such as getting evaluated for **alcohol** and **drug** abuse and attending ...
(7)... pursuit of him on three **outstanding   arrest   warrants** , or personal demons of drugs and alcohol . ...
xxxxxxxxxxxxxxxxxxxxxxxxxxxxxxxxxxxxxxxxxxxxxxxxx
(3)... (AP) **Evan C. Hunziker** would never say much about the three **months** he was **held** in **North   Korea** as a **spy** suspect before diplomatic negotiations won his **release** just in time for **Thanksgiving** . ...
(4)... **month** after basking in the **Thanksgiving** Eve glow of **release** from **North   Korea** , where he was **held** as a **spy** and threatened with execution, **Evan   Hunziker** was found Wednesday ...
xxxxxxxxxxxxxxxxxxxxxxxxxxxxxxxxxxxxxxxxxxxxxxxxx
(5)... office ruled the **death** a suicide . ...
(53)... police said they considered the **death** a suicide . ...

Fig. 8.   Alignment Examples using Fragment Extraction

speed. In Figure 9, we show the number of nodes in the graph as a function of document size. Figures 10-13 show the times to compute the graph, spread, segment-finding using clipping, and total time. The times are plotted against document size. As can be seen, the time performance of these algorithms appears to be approximately linear in document size.

Next, we measure the timing performance of the algorithm to find common nodes between two graphs, described earlier in Section 7.1. This is shown in Figure 14. As can be seen from these figures, the time to find common nodes is approxi-

mately linear in the size of the documents. Finally, in Figures 15,16 and 17, we show the performance of *FSD*, *Greedy-FSD*, and *Align*, respectively.

9.   Evaluation

9.1.   Overview

Text summarization is still an emerging field, and serious questions remain concerning the appropriate methods and types of evaluation. There is little consensus as to what basis is best for

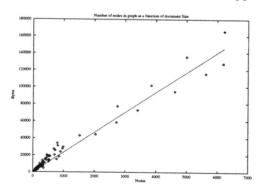

Fig. 9.   Number of nodes in graph as function of document size

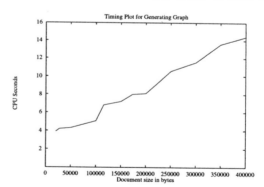

Fig. 10.   Time to build graph as a function of document size

comparison, e.g., summary to source, machine to human-generated, system to system. In comparing against human summaries, reports of low inter-annotator agreement over what should be included in a summary (e.g., [45], [36]) raise questions about the appropriateness of a "gold standard" for sentence extraction.

In general, methods for evaluating text summarization approaches can broadly classified into two

categories. The first is an extrinsic evaluation in which the quality of the summary is judged based on how it affects the completion of some other task. The second approach, an intrinsic evaluation, judges the quality of the summarization directly based on user judgements of informativeness, coverage, etc. In our evaluation we per-

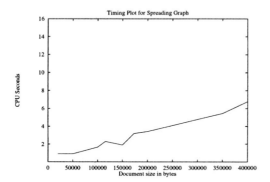

Fig. 11. Spread Time as a function of document size

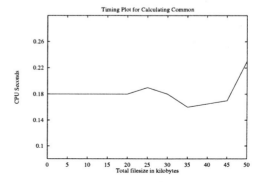

Fig. 14. Time to find common nodes as a function of combined document pair size

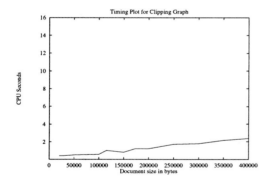

Fig. 12. Clip Time as a function of document size

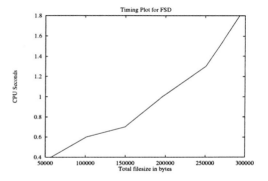

Fig. 15. Time for FSD as function of combined document pair size

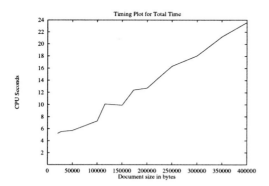

Fig. 13. Total time (graph+spread+clip) as a function of document size

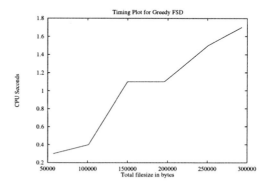

Fig. 16. Time for Greedy-FSD as function of combined document pair size

Table 2. Information about Sources Being Aligned

Name	Source	Headline
Peru	AP	Rebels in Peru hold hundreds of hostages inside Japanese diplomatic residence
	Reuters	Peru rebels hold 200 in Japanese ambassador's home
Evangelist	New York Times	Man Once Held As Spy In North Korea Is A Suicide
	Washington Post	Man Held By N. Korea Found Dead
Chechnya	Washington Post	Gunmen Kill Aid Workers In Chechnya
	New York Times	6 Red Cross Aides Slain in Chechnya, Imperiling Peace

Table 3. Alignment Comparison Results

Article Pair	RAW	RAWPOL	SPREAD	RAW-CLIP	RAWPOL-CLIP	SPREAD-CLIP
Peru	10	25	11	37	20	44
Evangelist	15	27	24	21	20	27
Chechnya	15	13	14	14	17	12
Average	13.3	21.7	16.3	24	19	**27.7**

formed both type of experiments. Evaluation experiments based on the intrinsic method are discussed in Section 9.2.

We believe the objective evaluation measures we introduce in Section 9.3 represents a significant step forward in terms of empirically demonstrating the utility of summarization in a practical information retrieval task. This method has since been adopted as a standard method for summarization evaluation in the U.S. government's TIPSTER program [22]. However, it is important to stress that our evaluations, while obtaining statistically significant results, are on small datasets.

9.2. Comparison of Weighting Methods in Cross-Document Alignment

In this experiment, six different schemes for reweighting words within the sentence were compared: 1) tf.idf (RAW), 2) tf.idf with weights increased for proper names by a constant factor (RAWPOL), 3) spreading (SPREAD), 4) raw

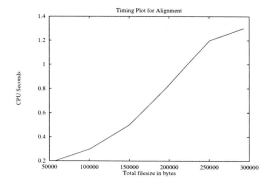

Fig. 17. Time for Align as function of combined document pair size

tf.idf after removal of low-weight terms (RAW-CLIP), 5) clipping after RAWPOL (RAWPOL-CLIP) and 6) clipping after spreading (SPREAD-CLIP). In all these schemes, we used cosine similarity instead of the overlap measure, as it allows for more standard baselines. Three different document pairs were used here for evaluation, as shown in Table 2. These pairs were selected from a larger collection of pairs of articles on international events culled from searches on the World Wide Web, including articles from Reuters, Associated Press, the Washington Post, and the New York Times. Pairs were selected such that each member of a pair was closely related to the other, but by no means identical; the pairs were drawn from different geopolitical regions so that no pair was similar to another. In the Peru pair only the precision of the top ten sentence pairs is calculated. For the other pairs precision is calculated for all output sentence pairs (on average 50 sentence pairs for Evangelist and 60 for Chechnya). For each document pair the assigned weighting method was applied to each text and the single best match for each sentence was output. The goal of this experiment was to measure the ability of the alignment method to find correct alignments (those that are both correctly aligned and relevant to the user's given topic). Alignment correctness was determined by a human judge.

In Table 3, we see that all of the reweighting schemes outperform the baseline tf.idf measure for these tasks and that the highest average results are obtained with the method which uses spreading and clipping. The results with spreading alone (SPREAD) were also better on average than tf.idf (RAW) with the greatest difference on the Evangelist pair, but small differences on the other pairs. The removal of words using clipping resulting in improvements (on average) for the RAW and SPREAD based methods, but not for the RAWPOL. Clipping results in the most reduction when the differences between minimum and maximum word weights is greatest. This suggests that the proper name weight increment in RAWPOL may have been too large, causing more words, and sometimes useful words, to be removed. These results are only suggestive; conclusive results would require experimenting with a much larger data sample.

9.3. Effectiveness of Spreading Activation

In addition to the intrinsic evaluation of alignments, we also carried out an extrinsic evaluation, where we evaluated the usefulness of spreading in the context of an information retrieval task. In this experiment, subjects were informed only that they were involved in a timed information retrieval research experiment. In each run, a subject was presented with a pair of query and document, and asked to determine whether the document was relevant or irrelevant to the query. In one experimental condition the document shown was the full text, in the other the document shown was a summary generated with the top 5 weighted sentences. Subjects (four altogether) were rotated across experimental conditions, but no subject was in both conditions for the same query-document pair. We hypothesized that if the summarization was useful, it would result in savings in time, without significant loss in accuracy.

Four queries (204, 207, 210, and 215) were preselected from the TREC [23] collection of topics, with the idea of exploiting their associated (binary) relevance judgments. A subset of the TREC collection of documents was indexed using the SMART retrieval system from Cornell [11]. Using SMART, the top 75 hits from each query were reserved for the experiment. Overall, each subject was presented with four batches of 75 query-document pairs (i.e., 300 documents were presented to each subject), with a questionnaire after each batch. Accuracy metrics include precision (percentage of retrieved documents that are relevant, i.e., number retrieved which were relevant/total number retrieved) and recall (per-

centage of relevant documents that are retrieved, i.e., number retrieved which were relevant/total number known to be relevant).

In Table 4, we show the average precision and average recall over all queries (1200 relevance decisions altogether). The table shows that when the summaries were used, the performance was faster than with full-text (F=32.36, p < 0.05, using analysis of variance F-test), without significant loss of accuracy. While we would expect shorter texts to take less time to read, it is striking that these extracts are effective enough to support accurate retrieval. In addition, the subjects' feedback from the questionnaire (shown in the last three rows of the table) indicate that the spreading-based summaries were found to be useful.

10. Conclusion

This summarization approach exploits the results of recent progress in information extraction to represent salient units of text and their relationships. By exploiting meaningful *relations* between units based on text cohesion and the *perspective* from which the comparison is desired, the summarizer can pinpoint similarities and differences and align text extracts across articles. In evaluations, these techniques for exploiting cohesion relations result in summaries which helped users more quickly complete a retrieval task, which resulted in improved alignment accuracy, and which improved identification of topic-relevant similarities and differences. Our approach is highly domain-independent, even though we have illustrated its power mainly for news articles. However, despite these encouraging outcomes, we are also painfully aware that the field of summarization has still a long way to go, and that these methods only touch the surface of the problem. It is our hope that this paper will spur discussion and future work in this area. In the future, we expect to investigate incorporation of co-occurrence statistics, e.g., [14], [17], [19], [20], [52], and also to further investigate temporal sequences of stories, to summarize changes over time.

Table 4. Summaries versus Full-Text: Task Accuracy, Time, and User Feedback

Metric	Full-Text	Summary
Accuracy (Precision, Recall)	30.25, 41.25	25.75, 48.75
Time (mins)	**24.65**	**21.65**
Usefulness of text in deciding relevance (0 to 1)	.7	.8
Usefulness of text in deciding irrelevance (0 to 1)	.7	.6
Preference for more or less text	"Too Much Text."	"Just Right."

Acknowledgements

We would like to thank Barbara Gates for helping generate performance data, and David House and Gary Klein for help with the evaluation experiments. We are also grateful to two anonymous referees for their helpful comments.

Appendix

Topic: Tupac Amaru   Associated Press   Reuters

1.1:Rebels in Peru hold hundreds of hostages inside Japanese diplomatic residence

1.2: Copyright Nando.net Copyright The Associated Press

1.3:*U.S. ambassador not among hostages in Peru

1.4:*Peru embassy attackers thought defeated in 1992

1.5:LIMA, Peru(Dec 18, 1996 05:54 a.m. EST) Well-armed guerilas posing as waiters and carrying bottles of champagne sneaked into a glittering reception and seized hundreds of diplomats and other guests.

1.6:As police ringed the building early **Wednesday**, an excited rebel **threatened** to start killing the **hostages**.

...

1.9:They demanded the release of their jailed comrades in the Tupac Amaru rebel movement.

...

1.11:The group of 23 rebels, including three women entered the compound at the start of the reception, which was in honor of Japanese Emperor Akihito's birthday.

1.12:Police said they *slipped* through *security* by *posing* as *waiters, driving* into the *compound* with *champagne* and *hors d'oeuvres.*

...

1.17:Another guest, BBC correspondant Sally Bowen said in a report soon after her release that she had been eating and drinking in an elegant marquee on the lawn when the explosions occurred.

...

1.19:"The **guerillas** stalked around the **residence** grounds **threatening** us: 'Don't lift your heads up or you will be shot."

1.24:**Early Wednesday** , the rebels threatened to kill the remaining captives.

...

1.25: "We are clear: the liberation of all our comrades, or we die with all the hostages," a rebel who did not give his name told a local radio station in a telephone call from inside the compound.

...

1.28:Many leaders of the Tupac Amaru which is smaller than Peru's Maoist Shining Path movement are in jail. 1.29:Its chief Victor Polay, was captured in June 1992 and is serving a life sentence, as is his lieutenant, Peter Cardenas.

1.30:Other top commanders conceded defeat and surrendered in July 1993.

1.32: President Alberto Fujimori, who is of Japanese ancestry, has had close ties with Japan.

1.33: Among the hostages were Japanese Ambassador Morihisa Aoki and the ambassadors of Brazil, Bolivia, Cuba, Canada, South Korea, Germany, Austria and Venezuela.

...

1.38:**Fujimori** whose sister was among the **hostages released, called** an **emergency cabinet meeting** today.

1.39: Aoki, the **Japanese ambassador,** said in **telephone calls** to **Japanese** broadcaster NHK that the **rebels** wanted to talk directly to **Fujimori.**

...

1.43:According to some estimates, only a couple hundred armed followers remain.

...

2.1: Peru rebels hold 200 in Japanese ambassador's home

2.2:By Andrew Cawthorne

2.3:LIMA-Heavily armed guerrillas **threatened** on **Wednesday** to kill at least 200 **hostages**, many of them high-ranking officials, held at the Japanese ambassador's residence unless the Peruvian government freed imprisoned fellow rebels.

2.4:"If they do not release our prisoners, we will all die in here," a guerilla from the Cuban-inspired Tupac Amaru Revolutionary Movement (MRTA) told a local radio station from within the embassy residence.

2.9:President Alberto Fujimoro put the number of hostages at 200 in a telephone conversation with Japan's Prime Minister Ryutaro Hashimoto.

...

2.13:The rebels said they had 400 to 500 comrades in jail and said their highest priority was release of Victor Polay, their leader who was imprisoned in 1992. 2:14 They also called for a review of Peru's judicial system and direct negotiations with the government beginning at dawn on Wednesday.

...

2.19 They are *freeing* us to *show* that they are not doing us any *harm,"* said one *woman.*

...

2.22:The attack was a major blow to Fujimori's government, which had claimed virtual victory in a 6-year war on communist rebels belonging to the MRTA and the larger and better-known Maoist Shining Path.

...

2.26:The MRTA called Tuesday's *operation "Breaking The Silence."*

2.27:Although the MRTA gained support in its early days in the mid-1980s as a Robin Hood-style movement that robbed the rich to give to the poor, it lost public sympathy after turning increasingly to kidnapping, bombing and drug activities. 2.28:**Guerilla** conflicts in **Peru** have cost at least 30,000 lives and $25 billion in damage to the country's infrastructure since 1980.

Fig. A.1. Texts of two related articles. The top 5 salient sentences containing words in Common have these common words in bold face; likewise, the top 5 salient sentences containing words in Differences have these words in italics. Alignments are shown boxed.

Notes

1. There is some degree of consensus on this, though it is not entirely standard. [55] characterizes summarization in terms of a three-phase model, but chooses the term 'transformation' rather than 'refinement'. [33] assumes a four-phase model, where what we are calling 'refinement' is split into 'selection' and 'condensation'.

2. As [28] shows, in applying the TextTiling work of [24] to closed-captioned news broadcasts, it is hard to make do with a single block size; the block size must be small enough to catch relatively small topics, and yet large enough for the similarity metric to be useful.

3. In general, the relations grouped under 'text cohesion' as used by [21] include linguistic devices such as anaphora, ellipsis, conjunction and lexical relations such as reiteration, synonymy, hypernymy, and conjunction.

4. Repetition links are not evidenced in the example.

5. In terms of accuracy, when trained on about 950,000 words of Wall Street Journal text, the tagger obtained 96% accuracy on a separate test set of 150,000 words of WSJ [1].

6. Here the symbol $\Rightarrow$ stands for a hypernym link, $\Leftrightarrow$ for a synonym link.

7. The matching uses stemming based on [44].

References

1. Aberdeen, J., Burger, J., Day, D., Hirschman, L., Robinson, P., and Vilain, M., "MITRE: Description of the Alembic System Used for MUC- 6", Proceedings of the Sixth Message Understanding Conference (MUC-6), Columbia, Maryland, November 1995.

2. Abracos, J. and Pereira Lopes, G., Statistical Methods for Retrieving Most Significant Paragraphs in Newspaper Articles, in Mani, I., and Maybury, M., eds., Proceedings of the ACL/EACL'97 Workshop on Intelligent Scalable Text Summarization, Madrid, Spain, 11 July 1997, pp. 51-57.

3. Alterman, R., "A Dictionary Based on Concept Coherence", Artificial Intelligence, 25, 1985, pp. 153-186.

4. Aone, C., Okurowski, M.E., Gorlinsky, J., and Larsen, B., "A Scalable Summarization System using Robust NLP", in Mani, I., and Maybury, M., eds., Proceedings of the ACL/EACL'97 Workshop on Intelligent Scalable Text Summarization, Madrid, Spain, 11 July 1997, pp. 66-73.

5. Callan, J.P., "Passage-Level Evidence in Document Retrieval", Proceedings of SIGIR'94, p. 302-310, 1994.

6. Barzilay, R., and Elhadad, M., "Using Lexical Chains for Text Summarization", in Mani, I., and Maybury, M., eds., Proceedings of the ACL/EACL'97 Workshop on Intelligent Scalable Text Summarization, Madrid, Spain, 11 July 1997, pp. 10-17.

7. Baxendale, P.B., "Man-made index for technical literature: an experiment", IBM Journal of Research and Development, 2, 4, 1958, pp. 354-361.

8. Boguraev, B., and Kennedy, C., "Salience-based Content Characterization of Text Documents", in

Mani, I., and Maybury, M., eds., Proceedings of the ACL/EACL'97 Workshop on Intelligent Scalable Text Summarization, Madrid, Spain, 11 July 1997, pp. 2-9.

9. Brill, E., "Some advances in rule-based part-of-speech tagging", Proceedings of the Twelfth National Conference on Artificial Intelligence (AAAI-94), Seattle, August 1-4, 1994, pp. 722-727.

10. Broglio. J, and Croft. B, "Query Processing for Retrieval from Large Text Bases", ARPA Human Language Technology Workshop, 1993.

11. Buckley, B., "The Importance of Proper Weighting Methods", ARPA Human Language Technology Workshop, 1993.

12. Chen, C.H., Basu. K, and Ng. T, "An Algorithmic Approach to Concept Exploration in a Large Knowledge Network", Technical Report, MIS Department, University of Arizona, Tucson, AZ, 1994.

13. Cohen, J.D., "Hilights: Language- and Domain-Independent Automatic Indexing Terms for Abstracting", Journal of the American Society for Information Science, 46, 3, 162-174, 1995. See also vol. 47, 3, 260 for a very important erratum.

14. Deerwester, S., Dumais, S.T., Furnas, G.W., Landauer, T.K., and Harshman, R., "Indexing by Latent Semantic Analysis", Journal of the American Society for Information Science, 41, 6, pp. 391-407.

15. Edmundson, H.P., "New methods in automatic abstracting", Journal of the Association for Computing Machinery, 1969, 16, 2, pp. 264-285.

16. Evans, D., "The Clarit Project", Technical Report, Laboratory for Computational Linguistics, Carnegie Mellon University, 1991.

17. Evans, D.A, Ginther-Webster, K., Hart, M., Lefferts, R.G., and Monarch, I.A., "Automatic indexing using selective NLP and first-order thesauri", Proceedings of RIAO'91, 2, pp. 624-643.

18. Evans, D., and Zhai, C., "Noun Phrase Analysis in Unrestricted Text for Information Retrieval", Proceedings of ACL-96, Cambridge, MA, June 1996.

19. Grefenstette, G., "Use of syntactic context to produce term association lists for text retrieval", Proceedings of the Fifteenth Annual International ACM SIGIR Conference on Research and Development in Information Retrieval, 1992, pp. 89-97.

20. Grefenstette, G., "Explorations in Automatic Thesaurus Discovery", Kluwer, Boston, 1994.

21. Halliday, M. and Hasan, R., "Cohesion in Text", 1996, London, Longmans.

22. Hand, T. F., "A Proposal for Task-Based Evaluation of Text Summarization Systems", in Mani, I., and Maybury, M., eds., Proceedings of the ACL/EACL'97 Workshop on Intelligent Scalable Text Summarization, Madrid, Spain, 11 July 1997.

23. Harman, D., ed., "An Overview of the Third Text Retrieval Conference", National Institute of Standards and Tehnology, NIST Special Publication 500-225, 1994, Gaithersburg, MD.

24. Hearst M., "Multi-Paragraph Segmentation of Expository Text", Proceedings of ACL-94, Las Cruces, New Mexico, 1994.

25. Krupka, G., "SRA: Description of the SRA System as Used for MUC-6", Proceedings of the Sixth Message Understanding Conference (MUC-6), Columbia, Maryland, November 1995.

26. Kupiec, J., Pedersen, J., and Chen, F., 1995, "A Trainable Document Summarizer", Proceedings of ACM-SIGIR'95, Seattle, WA, pp. 68-73.

27. Liddy, E.R., "The discourse-level Structure of Empirical Abstracts: An Exploratory Study", Information Processing and Management, 1991, 27, 1, 55-81.

28. Mani, I., House, D., Maybury, M., and Green, M,, "Towards Content-Based Browsing of Broadcast News Video", in Maybury, M., ed., Intelligent Multimedia Information Retrieval, AAAI/MIT Press, 1997.

29. Mani, I., and Bloedorn,. E., "Summarizing Similarities and Differences Among Related Documents", Proceedings of RIAO-97, Montreal, Canada, June 25-27, 1997, pp. 373-387.

30. Mani, I., and Bloedorn, E., "Multi-document Summarization by Graph Search and Merging", Proceedings of the Fourteenth National Conference on Artificial Intelligence (AAAI-97), Providence, RI, July 27-31, 1997, pp. 622-628.

31. Mann, W. C. and Thompson, S, A., Rhetorical Structure Theory: Toward a functional theory of text organization. Text, 8, 3, 1988, pp. 243-281.

32. Marcu, D., "From discourse structures to text summaries", in Mani, I., and Maybury, M., eds., Proceedings of the ACL/EACL'97 Workshop on Intelligent Scalable Text Summarization, Madrid, Spain, 11 July 1997, pp. 82-88.

33. Maybury, M., "Generating Summaries from Event Data", Information Processing and Management, 31, 5, 1995, pp. 735-751.

34. McKeown, K., and Radev, D., "Generating Summaries of Multiple News Articles", Proceedings of ACM-SIGIR'95, Seattle, WA.

35. Miike, S., Itoh, E., Ono, K., and Sumita, K., "A Full-Text Retrieval System with a Dynamic Abstract Generation Function", Proceedings of ACM-SIGIR'94, Dublin, Ireland.

36. Mitra, M., Singhal, A., and Buckley, C., "Automatic Text Summarization by Paragraph Extraction", in Mani, I., and Maybury, M., eds., Proceedings of the ACL/EACL'97 Workshop on Intelligent Scalable Text Summarization, Madrid, Spain, 11 July 1997.

37. Morris, J., and Hirst, G., "Lexical Cohesion Computed by Thesaural Relations as an Indicator of the Structure of Text", Computational Linguistics, 17, 1, pp. 21-43, 1991.

38. Miller, G., "WordNet: A Lexical Database for English", Communications of the ACM, 38, 11, pp. 39-41, 1995.

39. MUC-6, Proceedings of the Sixth Message Understanding Conference (MUC-6), Columbia, Maryland, November 1995.

40. Paice, C, "Constructing Literature Abstracts by Computer: Techniques and Prospects, Information Processing and Management, 26, 1, pp. 171-186, 1990.

41. Paice, C. and Jones, P., "The Identification of Important Concepts in Highly Structured Technical Papers", Proceedings of ACM-SIGIR'93, Pittsburgh, PA.

42. Paik, W., Liddy, E., Yu, E., and McKenna, M., 1993, "Categorizing and Standardizing Proper Nouns for Efficient Information Retrieval", Proceedings of the ACL Workshop on Acquisition of Lexical Knowledge from Text, Ohio State University, June 1993.

43. Pearce, C., and Nicholas, C., "TELLTALE: Experiments in a dynamic hypertext environment for degraded and multilingual data", JASIS, 47, 4, 263-275, 1996.

44. Porter, M.F., "An Algorithm For Suffix Stripping", Program, 14, 3, July 1980, pp. 130-137.

45. Rath, G.J., Resnick, A., and Savage, T.R., "The formation of abstracts by the selection of sentences", American DOcumentation, 12, 2, 1961, pp. 139-143.

46. Rau, L., Knowledge Organization and Access in a Conceptual Information System, Information Processing and Management, 23, 4, 269-283, 1987.

47. Resnick, P., "Selection and Information: A Class-Based Approach to Lexical Relationships", Ph.D. Dissertation, 1993, University of Pennsylvania, Philadelphia, PA.

48. Salton, G., "Automatic text processing - the transformation, analysis, and retrieval of information by computer", Addison-Wesley, Reading, MA, 1989.

49. Salton, G., Allan J., Buckley C., and Singhal A., "Automatic Analysis, Theme Generation, and Summarization of Machine-Readable Texts", Science, 264, June 1994, pp. 1421-1426.

50. Salton G. and Buckley C., "On the Use of Spreading Activation Methods in Automatic Information Retrieval", Technical Report 88-907, Department of Computer Science, Cornell University, 1988.

51. Salton, G., Singhal A., Buckley C., and Mitra M., "Automatic Text Decomposition Using Text Segments and Text Themes", Cornell University Technical Report TR 95-1555, Nov. 17, 1995.

52. Schutze, H.M and Pedersen, J.O., "A Cooccurrence-Based Thesaurus and Two Applications to Information Retrieval", Proceedings of RIAO'97.

53. Smeaton, A.F., and Quigley, I., "Experiments on Using Semantic Distances Between Words in Image Caption Retrieval", Proceedings of ACM-SIGIR'96, Zurich, Switzerland.

54. Sparck-Jones, K., "A Statistical Interpretation of Term Specificity and Its Application in Retrieval", Journal of Documentation, 28, 1, 11-20, 1972.

55. Sparck-Jones, K., "Summarizing: Where are we now? Where should we go?", in Mani, I., and Maybury, M., eds., Proceedings of the ACL/EACL'97 Workshop on Intelligent Scalable Text Summarization, Madrid, Spain, 11 July 1997.

56. Strzalkowski, T., "Natural Language Information Retrieval: TIPSTER-2 Final Report", TIPSTER Text Program (Phase II), 1996, pp. 143-148.

57. Van Dijk, T. A., "News as Discourse", Lawrence Erlbaum, Hillsdale, NJ, 1988.

58. Voorhees, E.M., "Using WordNet to Disambiguate Word Senses for Text Retrieval", Proceedings of the Sixteenth Annual International ACM SIGIR Conference on Research and Development in Information Retrieval, Pittsburgh, PA, June, 1993, pp. 171-180.

Generating Summaries of Multiple News Articles

Kathleen McKeown and Dragomir R. Radev

Department of Computer Science
Columbia University
New York, NY 10027
{kathy,radev}@cs.columbia.edu

Abstract

We present a natural language system which summarizes a series of news articles on the same event. It uses summarization operators, identified through empirical analysis of a corpus of news summaries, to group together templates from the output of the systems developed for ARPA's Message Understanding Conferences. Depending on the available resources (e.g., space), summaries of different length can be produced. Our research also provides a methodological framework for future work on the summarization task and on the evaluation of news summarization systems.

Keywords: Natural language summarization, Natural language generation, Summarization of multiple texts

1 Introduction

In this age of information overload, the ability to automatically summarize news stories would allow readers more ability to control the quantity of text that they read. Given the accuracy of current information retrieval systems, a typical search request returns many irrelevant documents. This is especially true for newswire information, since there are typically many articles on the same event. Online summaries could aid readers in determining if they want to access and read the full news articles as well as allow them to get the gist of the reported event by reading the summary only. While some previous approaches use statistical techniques to extract one or more sentences from the text which can serve as a summary with modest success (e.g., [Rau *et al.* 1994; Paice 1990; Economist 1994]), summarization in general has remained an elusive task. In this paper, we present a system, SUMMONS (SUMMarizing Online NewS articles), to summarize full text input using templates produced by the message understanding systems developed under the ARPA human language technology program [MUC 1992]. Unlike previous approaches, our system summarizes a *series* of news articles on the same event, producing a paragraph consisting of one or more sentences. Our research focuses on techniques to summarize how the perception of an event changes over time, using multiple points of view over the same event or series of events.

Our system attempts to generate fluent text from sets of templates that contain the salient facts reported in the input texts. To produce these templates, we rely upon the ARPA message understanding systems. These systems accept full text as input, extracting specific pieces of information from a given newspaper article. To test our system, we used the templates produced by systems participating in MUC-4 [MUC 1992], available from the Linguistic Data Consortium (LDC), as input. MUC-4 systems operate on the terrorist domain and extract information by filling fields such as perpetrator, victim, and type of event, for a total number of 25 fields. In addition, we filled the same template forms by hand from current news articles for further testing[1]. Note that while our system uses templates as input, if it were integrated with one of the existing message understanding systems, the resulting larger system would automatically produce summaries of raw text in a modular way.

Our work provides a methodology for developing summarization systems, identifies planning operators for combining

---

[1] Answer templates or system output from later MUC and TIP-STER conferences were not available to us.

information in a concise summary, and uses empirically collected phrases to mark summarized material. While critics of summarization have argued that it would be difficult to both develop principled summarization techniques and evaluate summarization systems, our approach indicates otherwise. We have collected a corpus of newswire summaries that we used as data for developing the planning operators and gathering a large set of lexical constructions used in summarization and which will eventually aid in a full system evaluation. Since news articles often summarize previous reports of the same event, we collected a corpus of articles which included short summaries of previous articles.

We used this corpus to develop both the content planner (i.e., the module which determines what information to include in the summary) and the linguistic component (i.e., the module which determines the words and surface syntactic form of the summary) of our system. We used the corpus to identify operators which are used to combine information; this includes techniques for linking information together in a related way (e.g., identifying changes, similarities, trends) as well as making generalizations. We also identified phrases that are used to mark summaries and used these to build the system lexicon. An example summary produced by the system is shown in Figure 1. This paragraph summarizes four articles on the World Trade Center bombing, using two different operators. The second sentence shows a contradiction between sources (Reuters and Associated Press) on the number of victims. The final sentence shows a refinement because the initial report did not contain information about the perpetrator. The resulting summary text uses lexical cues such as "however," "exactly," and "finally" to mark summary material.

In the afternoon of February 26, 1993, Reuters reported that a suspected bomb killed at least five people in the World Trade Center. However, Associated Press announced that exactly five people were killed in the blast. Finally, Associated Press announced that Arab terrorists were possibly responsible for the terrorist act.

Figure 1: Use of multiple operators.

While the system we report on is fully implemented, our work is still at early stages. We need to increase the robustness of the system, which currently includes 7 different planning operators, a testbed of 60 input templates, and can produce content for all pairs of related input templates but fully lexicalized summaries for approximately 20 cases. Nonetheless, our work at this point shows that full text summarization using symbolic techniques is possible. It provides a methodology for increasing the vocabulary size and the robustness of the system using a collected corpus, and moreover, it shows how summarization can be used to evaluate the message understanding systems, identifying future research directions that would not be pursued under the current MUC evaluation cycle[2]. Due to inherent difficulties in the summarization task, our work is a substantial first step and provides the framework for a number of different research directions.

In the following sections, we provide a description of the components of SUMMONS, then turn to the planning operators for summarization, and a detailed discussion of the

summarization algorithm showing how summaries of different length are generated. We provide examples of the summarization markers we collected for the lexicon and close by showing the demands that summarization creates for interpretation.

2 Overview of the system

SUMMONS is based on the traditional language generation system architecture [McKeown 1985; McDonald and Pustejovsky 1986; Hovy 1988]. A typical language generator is divided into two main components, a content planner, which selects information from an underlying knowledge base to include in a text, and a linguistic component, which selects words to refer to concepts contained in the selected information and arranges those words, appropriately inflecting them, to form an English sentence. The content planner produces a conceptual representation of text meaning (e.g., a frame, a logical form, or an internal representation of text) and typically does not include any linguistic information. The linguistic component uses a lexicon and a grammar of English to perform its task. The lexicon contains the vocabulary for the system and encodes constraints about when each word can be used. As shown in Figure 2, SUMMONS' content planner determines what information from the input MUC templates should be included in the summary using a set of planning operators that are specific to summarization and to some extent, the terrorist domain. Its linguistic component determines the phrases and surface syntactic form of the summary. The linguistic component consists of

- a lexical chooser, which determines the high level sentence structure of each sentence and the words which realize each semantic role, and

- the FUF (Functional Unification Formalism) [Elhadad 1991; Elhadad 1993] sentence generator, which uses a large systemic grammar of English, called SURGE[3] [Halliday 1985; Elhadad 1993; Robin 1994] to fill in syntactic constraints, build a syntactic tree, choose closed class words, and eventually linearize the tree as a sentence.

Input to SUMMONS is a set of templates, where each template represents the information extracted from one or more articles by a message understanding system. We restricted the domain to articles on terrorism, since this was what was available from the LDC. However, the hand-constructed templates included terrorist events such as the World Trade Center bombing, the Hebron Mosque massacre, and airline hijackings, which may or may not have been handled by the original message understanding systems. We also created by hand a set of templates unrelated to real newswire messages which we used for testing some techniques of our system. We enriched the templates for these cases by adding four slots: the primary source, the secondary source and the times when both sources made their reports[4]. We find having the source of the report immensely useful for summarization, because there are often conflicts between different reports of an event and these can indicate the level of confidence in the report, particularly as reports change over time.

---

[2] Currently, participating systems in the ARPA message understanding program are evaluated on a regular basis. Participants are given a set of training text to tune their systems over a period of time and their systems are tested on unseen text at follow-up conferences.

[3] FUF is a sentence generator that follows the functional unification paradigm, whereas SURGE is a large-scale surface generation grammar of English built on top of FUF.

[4] primary source - usually a direct witness of the event, and secondary source - most often a press agency or journalist, reporting the event.

For example, if many sources all report the same incidents for a single event, it is more likely that this is the way the event really happened, while if there are many contradictions between reports, it is likely that the facts are not yet known. We assume that some other system has selected a reasonable set of templates, or articles, to summarize; that is, input should contain a set of templates which report on the same event. The articles may be written at any point in time and may be written by the same or many sources.

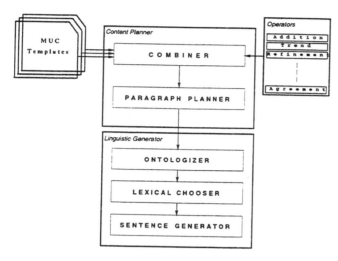

Figure 2: System Architecture.

Output is a paragraph consisting of one or more sentences, where the length of the summary is controlled by a variable input parameter. At this point, we have no theory on how to determine the length of a summary, but assume that like any good paper writer, given more space, SUMMONS can use it to include more information. Information is rated in terms of importance, where information that appears in only one article is given a lower rating and information that is synthesized from multiple articles is rated more highly. When space allows, SUMMONS may choose to include the base facts from two separate articles as well as the conclusion that can be drawn from both, while given less space, only the summarizing fact would be included.

Development of SUMMONS was made easier because of the language generation tools and framework available at Columbia University. No changes in the FUF sentence generator were needed. In addition, the lexical chooser and content planner were based on the design used in the PLANDoc automated documentation system, developed jointly with Bellcore to summarize the activities of telephone planning engineers [McKeown *et al.* 1994]. In particular, we used FUF to implement the lexical chooser, representing the lexicon as a grammar as we have done in many previous systems (e.g., [Elhadad 1993; Robin 1994; McKeown *et al.* 1993; Feiner and McKeown 1991]), and thus the main effort was in identifying the words and phrases needed for the domain. The content planner, implemented in PERL, features several stages, as does the PLANDoc system. It first groups messages together, identifies commonalities between them, and notes how the discourse influences wording by setting realization flags. Before lexical choice, SUMMONS maps the templates into the FD formalism expected as input to FUF and uses a domain ontology (derived from the ontologies represented in the message understanding systems) to enrich the input.

The main point of departure for SUMMONS is in the stage of identifying what information to include and how to group it together, as well as the use of a corpus to guide this and later processes. In PLANDoc, successive messages are very similar and the problem is to form a grouping that puts the most similar messages together, allowing the use of conjunction and ellipsis to delete repetitive material. For summarizing multiple news articles, the task is almost the opposite; we need to find the differences from one article to the next, identifying how the news has changed. Thus, the main problem was the identification of summarization strategies, which indicate how information is linked together to form a concise and cohesive summary. As we have found in other work [Robin 1994], what information is included is often dependent on the language available to make concise additions. Thus, using a corpus summary was critical to identifying the different summaries possible.

3 Methodology: collecting and using a summary corpus

In order to produce plausible and understandable summaries, we used available on-line corpora as models, including the Wall Street Journal and current newswire from Reuters and the Associated Press. Our corpora contain about 2 MB of news articles. We have manually grouped articles in threads related to single events or series of similar events.

From the so collected corpora we extracted manually, and after careful investigation, several hundred language constructions which we found relevant to the types of summaries that we want to produce. Some examples of such phrases are included in Figures 7–9. In addition to the summary cue phrases collected from the corpus, we also tried to incorporate as many phrases as possible that have relevance to the message understanding conference domain. Due to domain variety, such phrases were essentially scarce in the newswire corpora and we needed to collect them from other sources (e.g., modifying templates that we acquired from the summary corpora to provide a wider coverage).

Since one of our goals has been conciseness, we have tried to assemble small paragraph summaries which in essence describe a single event and its change over time, or a series of related events with no more than a few sentences.

4 Summary operators for content planning

We have developed a set of heuristics derived from the corpora which decide what types of simple sentences constitute a summary, in what order they need to be listed, as well as the ways in which simple sentences are combined into more complex ones. In addition, we have specified which summarization-specific phrases are to be included in different types of summaries.

We attempt to identify a preeminent set of templates from the input to the system. This set needs to contain a large number of similar fields. If this holds, we can merge the set into a simpler structure, keeping the common features and marking the distinct features as Elhadad [1993] and McKeown *et al.* [1994] suggest.

At each step, a summary operator is selected based on existing similarities between messages in the database. This operator is then applied to the input templates, resulting in a new template which combines, or synthesizes, information from the old. Each operator is independent from the other and several can be applied in succession to the input templates. Each of the seven major operators is further subdivided to cover various modifications of its input and output. Figure 3 shows part of the rules for the Contradiction operator.

$$((\#TEMPLATES == 2)\&\&$$
$$(T[1].INCIDENT.LOCATION == T[2].INCIDENT.LOCATION)\&\&$$
$$(T[1].INCIDENT.TIME < T[2].INCIDENT.TIME)\&\&...$$
$$(T[1].SECSOURCE.SOURCE\mathrel{:}= T[2].SECSOURCE.SOURCE)) ==>$$
$$(apply("contradiction", "with-new-account", T[1], T[2]))$$

Given two templates, if INCIDENT.LOCATION is the same, the time of first report is before time of second report, the report sources are different, and at least one other slot differs in value (this rule not shown), apply the contradiction operator to combine the templates.

Figure 3: Rules for the Contradiction operator.

A summary operator encodes a means for linking information in two different templates. Often it results in synthesis of new information. For example, a generalization may be formed from two independent facts. Alternatively, since we are summarizing reports written over time, highlighting how knowledge of the event changed is important and thus, summaries sometimes must identify differences between reports. A description of the operators we identified in our corpus follows, accompanied by an example of system output for each operator. Each example primarily summarizes two input templates, as this is the result from applying a single operator once. More complex summaries can be produced by applying multiple operators on the same input, as shown in the introductory example.

4.1   Change of perspective

When an initial report gets a fact wrong or has incomplete information, the change is usually included in a summary. In order for this operator to apply, the source field must be the same, while the value of another field changes so that it is not compatible with the original value. For example, if the number of victims changes, we know that the first report was *wrong* if the number goes down, while the source had *incomplete information* (or additional people died) if the number goes up. The first two sentences from the following example were generated using the change of perspective operator. The initial estimate of "at least five people" killed in the incident becomes "exactly five people":

The afternoon of February 26, 1993, Reuters reported that a suspected bomb killed at least five people in the World Trade Center. Later, Reuters announced that exactly five people were killed in the blast.

4.2   Contradiction

When two sources report conflicting information about the same event, a contradiction arises. A summary cannot report either of them as true, but can indicate that the facts are not clear. The number of sources that contradict each other can indicate the level of confusion about the event. Note that the current output of the message understanding systems does not include sources. However, SUMMONS could use this feature to report disagreement between output by different systems. A summary might indicate that BBN determined that 20 people were killed, while NMSU determined only 5 were killed. The difference between this example and the previous one on Change of Perspective is

the source of the update. If the same source announces a change, then we know that it has realized a change in the facts. Otherwise, an additional source presents information which is not necessarily more correct than the information presented by the earlier source.

The afternoon of February 26, 1993, Reuters reported that a suspected bomb killed at least five people in the World Trade Center. However, Associated Press announced that exactly five people were killed in the blast.

4.3   Addition

When a subsequent report indicates that additional facts became known, this is reported in a summary. Additional results of the event may occur after the initial report or additional information may become known. The operator determines this by the way the value of a template slot changes (up for numbers).

January 1st 1994, Reuters announced that three terrorists killed four civilians in the first assault. Later, Reuters reported that three people were killed in the second assault. A total of seven people were killed in the two assaults.

4.4   Refinement

In subsequent reports a more general fact may be refined. Thus, if the location is originally reported to be New York City, it might later be noted as a particular borough of New York. Or, if a terrorist group is identified as Palestinian, later the exact name of the terrorist group may be determined. Since the update is assigned a higher value of "importance", it will be favored over the original message in a shorter summary. Sentence 3 from the introductory example was generated using the refinement operator, since the responsibility for the terrorist act was attributed to Arab terrorists, whereas earlier reports did not include perpetrator information.

Finally, Associated Press announced that Arab terrorists were possibly responsible for the terrorist act.

4.5   Agreement

If two sources agree on the facts, this will heighten the reader's confidence in their veracity and thus, agreement between sources is usually reported.

The morning of March 1st 1994, UPI reported that a man was kidnapped in the Bronx. Later, this was confirmed by Reuters.

4.6   Superset

If the same event is reported from different sources and all of them have incomplete information, it is possible to combine information from them to produce a more complete summary.

According to UPI, three terrorists were arrested in Medellin last Tuesday. Reuters announced that the police arrested two drug traffickers in Bogota last Wednesday. A total of five criminals were arrested in Colombia last week.

4.7 Trend

There is a trend if two or more messages reflect similar patterns over time. Thus, we might notice that three consecutive bombings occurred at the same location and summarize them into a single sentence. This is the only operator which is not implemented in the current version of the system.

4.8 No information

Since we are interested in conveying information about the primary and secondary source of a certain piece of news, which are generally trusted sources of information, we ought to pay attention also to the lack of information from a certain source when such is expected to be present. For example, it might be the case that a certain news agency reports a terrorist act in a given country, but the authorities of that country don't give out any information. An example of use of the *no information operator* is given in Figure 8.

5 Algorithm

The algorithm used in the system to sort, combine, and generalize the input messages can be described as follows:

5.1 Input

At this stage, the system receives a set of templates from the Message Understanding Conferences or a similar set of messages from a related domain. All templates are described as lists of attribute/value pairs (see Figure 5). These pairs are defined in the MUC guidelines [MUC 1992].

5.2 Preprocessing

This stage includes the following substages:

- The templates are sorted in chronological order. A later stage will take care of their conceptual ordering.

- Messages that have obviously been incorrectly generated by a MUC system are identified and filtered out by hand.

- A database of all fields and messages is created. This database is used later as a basis for grouping and collapsing messages.

- All irrelevant fields or fields containing bad values are manually marked as such and don't participate in further analyses.

- Knowledge of the source of the information is marked as the specific Message Understanding System for the site submitting the template if it is not present in the input template. Note that since the current Message Understanding Systems do not extract the source, this is the most specific we can be for such cases.

5.3 Heuristic combination

The template database is scanned for interesting relationships between templates. Such patterns trigger reordering of the templates and modification of their individual "importance" values. As an example, if two templates are combined with the "Refinement" operator, the "importance" value of the combined message will be greater than the sum of the individual "importances" of the constituent messages. At the same time, the values of these 2 messages are lowered (still keeping a higher value on the later, more correct of the two). All templates directly extracted from the MUC output are assigned an initial importance value of 100. Currently, with each application of an operator, we lower the value of a contributing individual template by 20 points and give any newly produced template that combines information from already existing contributing templates a value greater than the sum of the values of the contributing templates after those values have been updated. Furthermore, some operators reduce the importance values of existing templates even further (e.g., the refinement operator reduces the importance of chronologically earlier templates by additional increments of 20 points because they contain outdated information). These values were set empirically and future work will incorporate a more formal approach. Thus, the final summary is likely to contain only the combined message if there are restrictions on length. It can also contain all three of them if length restrictions are considerably lax. The value of the "importance" of the message corresponds also to the position in the summary paragraph, as more important messages will be generated first.

Each new template contains information indicating whether its constituent templates are obsolete and thus no longer needed. Also, at this stage the global coverage vector (a data structure which keeps track of which templates have been already combined and which ones are still to be considered in applying operators) is updated to point to the messages which are still active and can be further combined. This way we make sure that all messages still have a chance of participating in the actual summary.

The resulting messages are combined into small "paragraphs" according to the event or series of events that they describe. Each paragraph can then be realized by the linguistic component. Each set of templates produces a single paragraph.

5.4 Discourse planning

Given the relative importance of the messages included in the database after the Heuristic Combination stage, the content planner is called to organize the presentation of information within a paragraph. It looks at consecutive messages in the database, marked as separate paragraphs from the previous stage, and assigns values to "realization switches" [McKeown *et al.* 1994] which control local choices such as tense and voice. They also govern the presence or lack of certain constituents to avoid repetition of constituents and to satisfy anaphora constraints.

5.5 Format conversion

All messages included in the database and augmented through the content planner are sent to a so-called "lispize" module which converts the records of the message database[5] into FUF Functional descriptions (FD's) [Elhadad 1993].

---

[5] All database access functions are written in PERL. Acknowledgments to its creator, Larry Wall.

5.6 Ordering of templates and linguistic generation

In order to produce the final text, SUMMONS carries out the following steps:

- Templates are sorted according to the order of the value of the "importance" slot. Only the top templates are realized. Messages with higher importance values appear with priority in the summary if a restriction on length is specified.

- An intermediate module, the ontologizer, converts factual information from the message database into data structures compatible with the ontology of the MUC domain. This is used, for example, to make generalizations (e.g., that Medellin and Bogota are in Colombia).

- The lexical chooser component of SUMMONS is a functional (systemic) grammar which emphasizes the use of summarization phrases originating from the summary corpora.

- The surface generation from the augmented message FD's is performed using SURGE and FUF. We have written additional generation code to handle paragraph-level constructions (the summarization operators).

6 An example of system operation

This section describes how the algorithm is applied to a set of 4 templates by tracing the computational process that transforms the raw source into a final natural language summary. Excerpts from one of the four input news articles are shown in Figure 4.

> An explosion apparently caused by a car bomb in an underground garage shook the World Trade Center in lower Manhattan with the force of a small earthquake shortly after noon yesterday, collapsing walls and floors, igniting fires and plunging the city's largest building complex into a maelstrom of smoke, darkness and fearful chaos.
> The police said the blast killed at least five people and left more than 650 others injured, mostly with smoke inhalation or minor burns.

Figure 4: Excerpts from the initial newswire and newspaper articles.

The four news articles result in four different templates which correspond to four separate accounts of the same event and will be included in the set of templates from which the template combiner will work. Initially, all four templates will be given equal importance. Since two of the templates contain similar information, they will be replaced by a single one (actually, one of the two will be assigned a negative "importance" so that it will be ignored in the later stages). In this case, the incident type, the location, and the date are the same in the two templates and therefore, the heuristic combiner will replace them with a single template. Since there are no other templates that need to have their "importance" values adjusted, the factor used in ordering the output will be chronological order.

Let's now consider the first two templates in the order that they appear in the list of templates (note, however, that the output example in Figure 1 covers all three relevant templates). These templates are shown in Figure 5 and Figure 6 respectively. They are generated manually from the input newswire texts. Information about the primary and secondary sources of information (PRIMSOURCE and SECSOURCE) is added. Due to lack of space, only a few template slots are shown. The differences in the two templates (which will trigger certain operators) are shown in **bold face**.

MESSAGE: ID	TST-COL-0001
SECSOURCE: SOURCE	**Reuters**
SECSOURCE: DATE	**26 FEB 93**
	EARLY AFTERNOON
INCIDENT: DATE	26 FEB 93
INCIDENT: LOCATION	WORLD TRADE CENTER
INCIDENT: TYPE	BOMBING
HUM TGT: NUMBER	**AT LEAST 5**

Figure 5: Template for newswire article 1.

MESSAGE: ID	TST-COL-0002
SECSOURCE: SOURCE	**Associated Press**
SECSOURCE: DATE	**26 FEB 93 19:00**
INCIDENT: DATE	26 FEB 93
INCIDENT: LOCATION	WORLD TRADE CENTER
INCIDENT: TYPE	BOMBING
HUM TGT: NUMBER	5

Figure 6: Template for newswire article 2.

The different values of SECSOURCE:SOURCE and SEC-SOURCE:DATE in the two message templates trigger the activation of the contradiction operator. That operator makes use of the fact that there has been an apparent change in the number of victims (more specifically, the **perception** of this change between two sources of information, in this case, two SECSOURCEs). By looking at the diverging values as well as the times of the two reports, the content planner, activates the contradiction operator and decides that:

- the information contained in the second template should follow the first one.

- there is a logical connection between the two templates in that a value of one field changes over time. Accordingly, the content planner includes an appropriate realization switch for the second template which will be used by the lexical chooser module.

On the other hand, the lexical choice component of the linguistic module will make the following word choices specifically related to summarization:

- Since the "with-new-account" realization switch is present, the linguistics module will include an appropriate connective (in this case "later").

- Because of the change in the value of a specific field (in this case, "HUM TGT: NUMBER"), a cue phrase "exactly" will be inserted.

The different operators specify what combinations of values in certain template fields are used in the output.

7 Phrases used in summarization

Phrases used in summarization, such as connectives, and explicit examples of summarization phrases were collected from newswire corpora. Some example summarization phrases taken from the corpora and implemented in the system are shown below. The sequence in Figure 7 illustrates the use of summary cues, shown in italics, as well as the use of two operators, *addition* and *no information*. This sequence is a short summary appearing in a later article, highlighting changes. The sequence in Figure 8 illustrates the heavy reliance on multiple sources and disagreement between them to aid in conveying the level of confidence in what is actually known. This sequence also illustrates the *no information* operator; the text explicitly mentions that certain information was not reported, when all other indications lead one to expect it should have been. Finally, Figure 9 shows a sequence of text from an earlier article and the summary sentence which appeared in a later article, with summary cue phrases italicized. These are but a few examples from our collection.

> ... *another* ten people were killed ...
> Reuters *didn't confirm* the shooting
> *in addition* to this killing.

Figure 7: Summary cues.

> NICOSIA, Cyprus (AP) – Two bombs exploded near government ministries in Baghdad, but there was no immediate word of any casualties, Iraqi dissidents reported Friday. There was no independent confirmation of the claims by the Iraqi National Congress. Iraq's state-controlled media have not mentioned any bombings.

Figure 8: Multiple sources disagree.

> **Sentences from earlier article:**
> The bodies of three men and a woman were pulled from the bay. The men were not immediately identified. Authorities were trying to identify the woman, Bergen said...
>
> **Summary sentence in later article:**
> In *the most serious incident of the year,* four people drowned...

Figure 9: Summary cues.

8 Related work

There has been very little work on automatic text summarization primarily because it requires substantial capabilities in both interpretation and generation, and it is only recently that systems have reached these levels. In order to avoid solving the full natural language problem and to allow summarization in arbitrary domains, some researchers have applied statistical techniques to the summarization task [Rau et al. 1994; Paice 1990; Economist 1994]. This approach can be better termed extraction, rather than summarization, since it attempts to identify and extract key sentences from an article using statistical techniques that identify important phrases using various statistical measures. Such an

approach can only work if there are sentences contained in the article which already serve as a summary. While this approach appears to have had modest success in some domains [Economist 1994], Rau reports that statistical summaries of individual news articles were rated lower by evaluators than simply using the lead sentence or two from the article. Paice [Paice 1990] also notes that problems for this approach center around accidentally including any pronouns which have no previous reference in the extracted text or, in the case of extracting several sentences, of including incoherent text when the extracted sentences are not consecutive in the original text and don't naturally follow one another. Paice has developed techniques for modifying the extracted text to replace unresolved references. Note, in any case, that these approaches cannot handle the task that we address, summarization of multiple articles, since this requires information about similarities and differences across articles.

Work in summarization using symbolic techniques has tended to focus more on identifying information in text that can serve as a summary (e.g., [Young and Hayes 1985; Rau 1988; Hahn 1990]) as opposed to generating the summary, and often relies heavily on scripts (e.g., [DeJong 1979; Tait 1983]). One exception is work at Cambridge University on identifying strategies for summarization [Sparck Jones 1993] which studies how various discourse processing techniques (e.g., rhetorical structure relations) can be used to both identify important information and form the actual summary. While promising, this work does not involve an implementation as of yet, but provides a framework and strategies for future work.

9 Future work

The prototype system that we have developed serves as the springboard for research in a variety of directions. First and foremost is the need to use statistical techniques to increase the robustness and vocabulary of the system. Since we were looking for phrasings that signal summarization in a full article that includes other material as well, for a first pass we found it necessary to do a manual analysis in order to determine which phrases were used for summarization. In other words, we knew of no automatic way of identifying summary phrases. However, having an initial seed set of summary phrases might allow us to automate a second pass analysis of the corpus by looking for variant patterns of the ones we have found. By using automated, statistical techniques to find additional phrases, we could increase the size of the lexicon and use the additional phrases to identify any new summarization strategies to add to our stock of operators.

By creating a corpus of summaries, we are now prepared to do a quantitative evaluation of the system. The best way to do the evaluation would be to run a message understanding system on earlier articles in a sequence of articles on the same event to create a set of templates as input and then score the automatically generated summary against the existing summaries in the corpus articles[6]. Scoring must rate the summary generator both on operators and phrasing, measuring coverage (did the generator use as wide a range of operators as occurred in the test corpus?) and match (did the generator use the same operators for a given set of input

---

[6] We would need to use a reserved portion of the corpus as test material, a portion which was not used in the original system development. In order to get a large enough test corpus, we would need to collect additional articles, but this is not difficult given the number of online news services.

templates as were used in the corpus?). Since there is choice in how several articles are summarized, evaluation would need to use different summaries found in the corpus for the same earlier articles and rate the generated summary against these multiple models (see [Hatzivassiloglou and McKeown 1993] for an evaluation metric using multiple models).

Our summary generator could be used both for evaluation of message understanding systems by using the summaries to highlight differences between systems as well as for identifying weaknesses in the current systems. We have already noted a number of drawbacks with the current output, which makes summarization more difficult, giving the generator less information to work with. For example, there is only sometimes indication in the output that a reference to a person, place, or event is identical to an earlier mention; there is no connection across articles. The source of the report is not included. Finally, the structure of the template representation is somewhat shallow, being closer to a database form than a knowledge representation. This means that the generator's knowledge of different features of the event and relations between them is somewhat shallow. An ideal solution would be to team with a message understanding project so that advances in interpretation and in generation could be influenced by demands and restrictions on each side.

We also plan to incorporate a multilingual component to our system so that we can generate summaries of the same series of articles in multiple languages. Our goal is to add a FUF grammar in one other language to start and to develop the content planning and lexicalization components so that they facilitate making choices in multiple languages simultaneously.

In addition to generation in multiple languages, one might expand the system to handle templates produced from news articles in multiple languages. Since the structure of the templates is not language-dependent, one might try to incorporate an understanding system in another language that would generate templates compatible with the ones used as input by our system.

10 Conclusions

Our prototype system demonstrates the feasibility of generating summaries of a series of news articles on the same event, highlighting changes over time. The ability to automatically provide summaries of textual material will critically aid in effective use of the internet in order to avoid overload of information. We show how planning operators can be used to synthesize summary content from individual templates, each representing a single article. These planning operators are empirically based, coming from analysis of existing summaries, and allow for the generation of concise summaries. Our framework allows for experimentation with different length summaries and for the combination of multiple, independent summary operators to produce more complex summaries.

Our system was developed under somewhat primitive conditions, without the ability to access and change the interpretation component of the system, without access to the full set of current output produced by message understanding systems, and without an existing corpus of summaries. Consequently, our results include the development of a methodological framework to ease future implementation of news summarization systems; this includes collecting the summary corpus, structuring it around threads of articles on the same events with later articles including summaries,

and identifying summarizing phrases. This seed work will allow us to apply automated techniques (e.g., [Smadja 1991; Smadja et al. 1995; Robin 1994]) to further corpus analysis since we now have a database of lexical phrases that are used to mark summary material. By identifying the characteristics of these phrases, we can use this seed set to guide and control further automatic analysis. Such a corpus will also allow for evaluation of the generated summaries; development of an evaluation procedure will require additional work to develop a set of good metrics.

Acknowledgments: We wish to thank Jacques Robin and James Shaw for the help using FUF and SURGE as well as for some hints from their work on the PLANDoc system. We are also grateful to Vasileios Hatzivassiloglou for his thoughtful comments. This work was partially supported by NSF Faculty Award for Women GER-90-2406.

References

G.F. DeJong. *Skimming stories in real time: an experiment in integrated understanding.* PhD thesis, Computer Science Department, Yale University, 1979.

Short Cuts. Science and Technology Section. *Economist,* 17:85–86, December 1994.

M. Elhadad. FUF: The universal unifier - user manual, version 5.0. Technical Report CUCS-038-91, Columbia University, 1991.

M. Elhadad. *Using argumentation to control lexical choice: a unification-based implementation.* PhD thesis, Computer Science Department, Columbia University, 1993.

S. Feiner and K.R. McKeown. Automating the Generation of Coordinated Multimedia Explanations. *IEEE Computer,* 24(10):33–41, October 1991.

U. Hahn. Topic parsing: accounting for text macro structures in full-text analysis. *Information Processing and Management,* 26:135–170, 1990.

M.A.K. Halliday. *An Introduction to Functional Grammar.* Edward Arnold, London, 1985.

V. Hatzivassiloglou and K.R. McKeown. Towards the Automatic Identification of Adjectival Scales: Clustering Adjectives According to Meaning. In *Proceedings of the 31st Conference of the ACL,* Columbus, Ohio, 1993. Association for Computational Linguistics.

E.H. Hovy. Planning Coherent Multisentential Text. In *Proceedings of the 26th Annual Meeting of the Association for Computational Linguistics,* Buffalo, N.Y., June 1988. Asscoication for Computational Linguistics.

D.D. McDonald and J.D. Pustejovsky. Description-directed natural language generation. In *Proceedings of the 9th IJCAI,* pages 799–805. IJCAI, 1986.

K.R. McKeown, J. Robin, and M. Tanenblatt. Tailoring lexical choice to the user's vocabulary in multimedia explanation generation. In *Proceedings of the 31st Annual Meeting of the Association for Computational Linguistics,* Columbus, Oh., June 1993.

K.R. McKeown, K.K. Kukich, and J. Shaw. Practical Issues in Automatic Documentation Generation. In *Proceedings of the ACL Applied Natural Language Conference*, Stuttgart, Germany, October 1994.

K.R. McKeown. *Text Generation: Using Discourse Strategies and Focus Constraints to Generate Natural Language Text*. Cambridge University Press, Cambridge, England, 1985.

Message Understanding Conference (MUC). *Proceedings of the Fourth Message Understanding Conference (MUC-4)*. DARPA Software and Intelligent Systems Technology Office, 1992.

C. Paice. Constructing Literature Abstracts by Computer: Techniques and Prospects. *Information Processing and Management*, 26:171–186, 1990.

L.F. Rau, R. Brandow, and K. Mitze. Domain-Independent Summarization of News. In *Summarizing Text for Intelligent Communication*, pages 71–75, Dagstuhl, Germany, 1994.

L.F. Rau. Conceptual information extraction and information retrieval from natural language input. In *Proceedings RAIO-88, Conference on User-Oriented, Content-Based, Text and Image Handling*, pages 424–437, Cambridge, MA, 1988.

J. Robin. *Revision-Based Generation of Natural Language Summaries Providing Historical Background*. PhD thesis, Computer Science Department, Columbia University, 1994.

F. Smadja, K.R. McKeown, and V. Hatzivassiloglou. Automatic Development of Bilingual Lexicons. *Journal of Computational Linguistics, to appear*, 1995.

F. Smadja. *Retrieving Collocational Knowledge from Textual Corpora. An Application: Language Generation*. PhD thesis, Department of Computer Science, Columbia University, New York, NY, 1991.

K. Sparck Jones. What might be in a summary? In *Proceedings of Information Retrieval 93: Von der Modellierung zur Anwendung*, pages 9–26, Universitatsverlag Knstanz, 1993.

J.I. Tait. *Automatic summarising of English texts*. PhD thesis, University of Cambridge, Cambridge, England, 1983.

S.R. Young and P.J. Hayes. Automatic classification and summarization of banking telexes. In *Proceedings of the Second Conference on Artificial Intelligence Applications*, pages 402–408, 1985.

25

An Empirical Study of the Optimal Presentation of
Multimedia Summaries of Broadcast News

Andrew Merlino and Mark Maybury
Advanced Information Systems Center
The MITRE Corporation
202 Burlington Road
Bedford, MA 01730, USA
{andy, maybury}@mitre.org
http://www.mitre.org/resources/centers/advanced_info/

Abstract
We present results of a controlled experiment aimed at discovering, through empirical user evaluation, the optimal mix of media for automatically generated news summaries. Utilizing MITRE's Broadcast News Navigator news on demand system, we explore mixing visual, linguistic, and graphical elements (in ten different combinations) to support user tasks of detecting and extracting information from news. We report how different mixes can improve user precision, recall, timeliness, and perceived quality of interaction.

1. Introduction

The proliferation of multimedia sources (e.g., broadcast news, surveillance video, and video conference sessions) is driving a requirement for automated processing of video, including indexing and summarization. While there has been extensive work in single channel information processing and visualization (Christel 1995; Ding and Marchionini 1997) such as the audio, video (Zhang et al 1995), and closed caption text channels of video, more recent efforts have focused on multi-channel multimedia processing systems that automatically segment, extract, summarize and visualize multimedia information (e.g., Hauptmann and Smith 1995; Merlino et al. 1997). For example, MITRE's Broadcast News Navigator (BNN) (Merlino et al. 1997) utilizes image, speech, and language processing to segment, extract, index, and summarize broadcast news. BNN extracts multiple media elements from the source content, which then can be utilized to generate mixed media presentations.

This raises an issue of what the optimal mix is of media elements (i.e., keyframes, keywords, key entities, key subjects, key sentences) for which sources, users, and information analysis tasks (e.g., browse, search, extract, compare). Given an interactive context, we have an even richer environment in which multiple presentations may be exploited both for different data, tasks, and users and at different times within different tasks. This paper reports on a task-based evaluation that empirically measures usage of BNN, which provides multiple types and levels of news abstracts.

As illustrated in Figure 1, BNN processes video by discovering frame, shot (frame sequences), and story elements (Yeo and Yeung 1997) using a suite of previously reported multistream analysis algorithms. A simplified view is that users will want to perform different tasks at different levels of abstraction (e.g., trend analysis or retrieval of stories, extraction of particular details from particular frames or shots). Our hypothesis is that different mixed media presentations (combinations of audio, video, text or derived media elements) will yield more effective and efficient interaction for different task requirements such as analysis, retrieval, or extraction. For example, at the most abstract level, users may wish to analyze trends over time, such as the frequency or severity of events occurring in the world. Figure 2 illustrates a trend analysis of a month of news from BNN that enables a user to visualize the large increase in stories of President Clinton and Monica Lewinsky on August 18, i..e., related to President Clinton's deposition to the Grand Jury about Monica Lewinsky (this display actually dynamically scrolls down the most frequent named entities across selected sources and time).

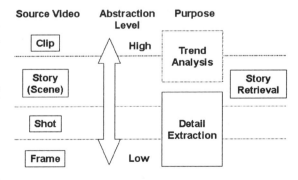

Figure 1. Video Abstraction Levels

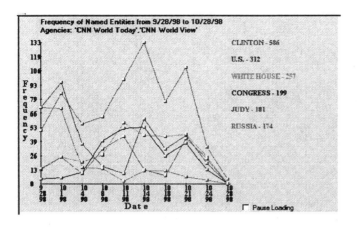

Figure 2. Trend Analysis of Named Entities

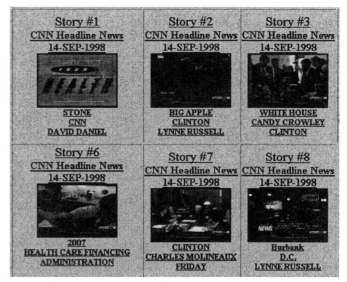

Figure 3. Story Skim

However, users often have more focused interests and tasks. For example, Figure 3 illustrates a BNN "Story Skim" wherein given a query, a user is presented with a list of retrieved stories, each represented by the source and date, an automatically extracted key frame and the three most frequent named entities (people, organizations, locations) mentioned in the stories, as extracted automatically by MITRE's Alembic workbench (Aberdeen et al. 1995). While viewing a story skim, the user can click on a key frame to view the story details. Figure 4, illustrates a "Story Details" display, which consists of a key frame, topics, named entities, one-line summary, and access to the caption and video source of the detected story by clicking on the closed caption symbol or key frame, respectively.

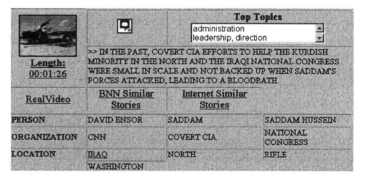

Figure 4. Story Details

Given the automated processing and extraction of key elements in the source video, what is the most effective mix of elements in what form for different kinds of content, tasks and users? To begin to answer this question, this paper reports on an empirical evaluation of a range of mixed media presentation methods for different content and tasks. We first describe the basic mixed media presentation alternatives we evaluated. We next describe the experimental design. Finally we report and discuss our results.

2. Mixed Media Presentation Methods

In addition to the compound "Story Skim" and "Story Detail" views which include multiple extracted elements from the source video (e.g., keyframe, key closed caption sentence, named entities), we can also present only the constituent parts. For example, Figure 5 shows a BNN display of keyframes and Figure 6 shows the list of the three most frequent named entities in each story.

Figure 5. Key Frames

Story #1	Story #2	Story #3
CNN Prime News 06-JAN-1998	CNN Prime News 06-JAN-1998	CNN Prime News 06-JAN-1998
SONNY 1964 CHER	CALIFORNIA CNN DON	DON DUE LAKE TAHOE
Story #6	Story #7	Story #8
CNN Prime News 06-JAN-1998	CNN Prime News 06-JAN-1998	CNN Prime News 06-JAN-1998
SONNY CHER PALM SPRINGS	CNN DOUG ROSE MICHAEL KENNEDY	CODE CNN JOIE
Story #11	Story #12	Story #13
CNN Prime News 06-JAN-1998	CNN Prime News 06-JAN-1998	CNN Prime News 06-JAN-1998
WHITE HOUSE AMERICAN ASSOCIATION OF RETIRED AVA	MORRIS 1400 ALABAMA	RITZ DENVER DODI FAYED

Figure 6. Three Named Entities

In addition to showing only the three most frequent named entities, an alternative view is a list for each story of all unique named entities found (Figure 7) or a one line summary (Figure 8), extracted based on sentence location and frequency of statistically significant named entities within an automatically segmented news story (see Maybury and Merlino, 1997 for details). The text summaries can be described in terms of intent (i.e. indicative or informative), focus (i.e., generic or query relevant summary) and coverage (i.e. based on a single document or multiple documents) (Firmin and Chrzanowksi, this volume). In this evaluation we used indicative, generic, single-document summaries. In an alternative presentation, the user is presented with all of the Oracle Context generated topics, called "themes", for the story in a scrollable box (Figure 9). The richest presentation method is termed "Full Details" in which the user has hypertext access to both of the previously mentioned skim and story details presentation. Upon selection of a key frame in the skim view, the user is presented the story detail view.

Story #1	10-DEC-1997	CNN Prime News	
LOCATION	RUSSIA		
PERSON	BORIS YELTSIN		
Story #2	10-DEC-1997	CNN Prime News	
LOCATION	RUSSIA		
ORGANIZATION	NATIONAL TRANSPORTATION SAFETY BOARD	TWA	
Story #3	10-DEC-1997	CNN Prime News	
LOCATION	MOSCOW	MAGADAN	RUSSIA
	RUSSIAN FAR EAST	SWITZERLAND	
PERSON	RUSSIAN PRESIDENT BORIS YELTSIN		

Figure 7. All named entities

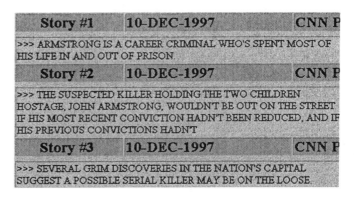

Figure 8. One line Summary

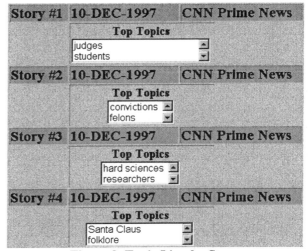

Figure 9. Topic Lists by Story

Finally, we can provide the user with access to the entire source, either viewing the full closed caption text (Figure 10) or viewing a digital VCR-like viewer of the video itself (Figure 11).

> JOIE: SOME VERY BAD WEATHER COMING UP FOR SOME OF THE COUNTRY. LET'S START IN THE SOUTHWEST, AN AREA OF LOW PRESSURE, WARM MOISTURE FROM THE GULF OF MEXICO, THUNDERSTORMS POSSIBLE FROM THE SOUTHEAST, BEHIND THE COLD AIR, THOUGH, WHERE THAT COLD FRONT IS, YOU'RE GOING TO SEE SNOW, ALL THE WAY TO COLORADO. THERE ARE NUMEROUS WINTER STORM WATCHES. IF YOU'RE IN HILL CITY, LET'S GO FROM KANSAS DOWN TOWARDS OKLAHOMA, FROM ALBUQUERQUE, SNOW IS IN THE FORECAST AND THEN IF YOU GO TO THE SOUTHEAST, RAIN SHOWERS AHEAD OF THAT SYSTEM, YOU'RE GOING TO SEE THE THUNDERSTORMS WITH THE GREEN HERE, THE DARK GREEN, INDICATING HEAVY RAIN SHOWERS WITH THE POSSIBILITY OF INSTABILITY IN THE ATMOSPHERE. YOU'RE GOING TO SEE THUNDERSTORMS WITH THAT. YOU MIGHT EVEN SEE SOME TORNADOES. HOPEFULLY THAT WILL NOT OCCUR. IT GOES ALL THE WAY OVER TO FLORIDA. HEAVY DOWN POURS.

Figure 10. Closed Captioned Source

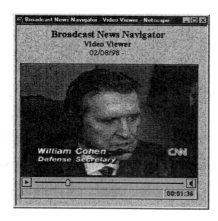

Figure 11. Video Source

3. Experimental Design

For this paper, our hypothesis is that some mix of the above multimedia story summaries will minimize the user viewing time and maximize accuracy in the tasks of identifying stories (i.e. identification) and extracting facts from stories (i.e. comprehension). The test set included (single topic) stories and associated questions dealing with people, organizations, locations and topics.

In order to explore optimal presentation methods for identification and comprehension tasks, 20 users[1] were individually asked two sets of ten questions shown in Figure 12. The questions were displayed in a web interface and the users recorded their responses on a paper-based standardized response form. The recorded times were obtained by having the users use a stopwatch. The user started the watch after the presentation method was displayed on the screen and stopped it after answering the question.

The first ten questions required the user to identify those stories within a given pool that satisfied the given request (e.g., find stories about a person, place, thing, or topic) whereas in the second 10 questions the user was asked to extract certain facts from the presentations. Mixed media presentation methods (the ten different types) and the size of the story pools were varied for each user and each question. For example, user one answered question one with presentation methods A, user two answered question one with presentation method B and so on up to user ten who answered question one with presentation method J. Thus, all ten presentation methods were used for each question but with different users. To vary the presentation methods per user, user one answered question two with presentation method B,

user two answered question two with presentation method C and so on up to user ten who answered question two with presentation method A. To avoid ordering bias among the identification and comprehension tasks, ten users were given the identification test first followed by the comprehension test. The other ten users were given the tests in the reverse order.

As a training exercise to familiarize each user with each presentation method, each user was given a ten question pre-test containing examples of all presentation methods for a mix of identification and comprehension tasks. These training results are not reported in this paper. The training times varied based on users' experience level. We further ran a three-user trial run prior to the evaluation to refine the evaluation procedure (e.g., we added original video and text sources to serve as a baseline and discovered and corrected network latency by moving video to local networks to avoid interference with timing results). During the experiments we measured the time to perform tasks, accuracy of task performance and user satisfaction. After completing each section of identification and comprehension, users were asked to rate their satisfaction with each of the mixed media presentation methods on a scale of 1-10 (i.e. 1 for least satisfied and 10 for most satisfied). The complete test was designed to take 60 minutes.

In each question, we measured speed of the respondent, and later calculated the following performance measures:

tp (true positive) = number of stories correctly classified as belonging to the event

fp (false positive) = number of stories incorrectly classified as the event

fn (false negative) = number of stories belonging to the event but not classified as such

tn (true negative) = number of stories correctly classified as not belonging to the event

Following Yang et al. (1998), these measures were used to compute the metrics of recall, precision, error, miss ratio, fallout, and F score (a balanced average of precision and recall) as follows:

recall = tp/(tp+fn); if tp+fn > 0, otherwise undefined

precision = tp/(tp+fp); if tp+fp > 0, otherwise undefined

error = (fp+fn)/(tp+fp+fn+tn)

miss ratio = fn/(tp+fn); if tp+fn > 0, otherwise undefined

fallout = fp/(fp+tn); if fp+tn > 0, otherwise undefined

F Score = (2*recall*precision)/(recall+precision)

---

[1]In this article the terms "subject" and "user" are used interchangeably.

Identification Questions	Type of Question
1) What stories are about weather?	Topic
2) What stories are about Sonny Bono?	Person
3) What stories are about Mo Vaughn?	Person
4) What stories are about Michael Carneal?	Person
5) What stories are about Boris Yeltsin?	Person
6) What stories are about Tony Blair?	Person
7) What stories are about aircraft accidents?	Topic
8) What stories are about Iran?	Location
9) What stories are about the United Nations?	Organization
10) What stories are about the Pentagon?	Organization
Comprehension Questions	
1) What position does Louis Freeh hold?	Person
2) What British Bank manages the Diana, Princess of Wales memorial fund?	Organization
3) Who heads the U.N.s hunt for IRAQs weapons?	Person
4) What animal is protected by the endangered species act?	Topic
5) What country is going through financial problems?	Location
6) How many people were killed by the floods in Somalia?	Topic
7) Who announced an initiative to persuade Americans to give the gift of life?	Person
8) What did the United States Government propose for organic food?	Topic
9) What disease has been detected in Europe again?	Topic
10) What country is the Roman Catholic Church asking to make Christmas a public holiday?	Location

Figure 12. Story Identification and Comprehension Questions

An answer key was developed for each question by the first author.

4. Results for Identification Task

For the identification task, the number of stories presented for each question varied as shown in Table 1 as did the resulting average precision, recall and overall time to answer the questions across the 20 users. On average, approximately fourteen stories were presented for each question, the average precision was 89%, average recall was 74%, and average time to identify relevant stories from the presented set was 25 seconds. The number of stories presented and the mean precision were not correlated (Pearson R = .19[2]). The number of stories presented and the mean recall were weakly correlated (Pearson R = .46). The number of stories presented and the time to complete the task were highly correlated (Pearson R = .89). Therefore, the final column normalizes time by the number of stories presented.

Question	# Stories Presented	# Relevant Stories	Mean Time (Seconds)	Mean Normalized (Secs/Story)
1	27	7	172.85	6.40
2	20	8	159.15	7.96
3	29	1	129.65	4.47
4	5	2	49.8	9.96
5	16	5	117.95	7.37
6	7	1	52.95	7.56
7	3	2	30.2	10.07
8	15	14	122.75	8.18
9	8	6	58.5	7.31
10	11	2	110.55	10.05
Mean			100.44	7.93
Std. Dev.			49.40	1.78

Question	Mean Precision	Std. Dev. Precision	Mean Recall	Std. Dev. Recall
1	0.93	0.10	0.71	0.39
2	1	0	0.66	0.29
3	0.86	0.23	0.9	0.31
4	0.69	0.13	0.73	0.41
5	0.91	0.17	0.82	0.3
6	0.97	0.13	0.8	0.41
7	0.93	0.27	0.63	0.48
8	0.98	0.03	0.85	0.22
9	0.98	0.07	0.66	0.35
10	0.64	0.3	0.65	0.4
Mean	0.89	0.14	0.74	0.36
Std. Dev.	0.13	0.10	0.10	0.08

Table 1. Number of Stories Presented during Identification Task

---

[2]The significance level $\alpha = .05$ throughout this paper.

Table 2 illustrates the precision and recall based on the technical (software developer) and non-technical (technical support) evaluators. It is noted that the sample size for the non-technical evaluation group is small. Although the standard deviation is slightly higher for non-technical evaluators, the non-technical precision was noticeably lower than their technical counterparts. The recall was very similar. Both groups have many years of computer system exposure.

Type/of Evaluator	No.	Precision Mean	Precision Standard Deviation	Recall Mean	Recall Standard Deviation
Software Developers	18	0.94	0.16	0.66	0.44
Technical Support	2	0.82	0.29	0.62	0.48

Table 2. Precision and Recall based on Evaluator Type

Table 3 illustrates the overall results by media type for the identification task[3]. Averaging across all presentation methods, users identify relevant news stories (video segments) with 82% precision and 70% recall, requiring 6.92 seconds per story, as above. Task performance varied according to presentation method and, in some cases, the number of stories presented to the user.

Observation 1: No difference in accuracy between most mixed media presentations and original video. Users can find stories with most mixed media summary presentations (story details and full details) as accurately as they can by reviewing the full source video; there is no significant difference between these mixed media and video on Precision, Recall, and F-score[4]. (The other mixed media presentation, story skim, is significantly less accurate in recall and just below the threshold for being significantly different in F-score). Moreover, the mean F Scores for these two mixed media presentations were significantly higher than for certain individual media element presentations (e.g., all named entities, key frames). As a reminder to the reader, story details and full details contained links to the original closed caption text and video.

Observation 2: Less is more. A related finding is that presenting less information to the user can enable them to discover content not only quicker but just as accurately. It took significantly less time to identify relevant stories looking

[3]The HSD score is the minimum value for a difference between means to be significant at $\alpha = .05$, as determined by Tukey's HSD test.
[4]Discrepancies between the F-score and the Precision and Recall values in Table 3 are due to the fact that when the user didn't put down a response, the recall was scored as 0 and the F-score wasn't computed.

at only the 3 most frequent named entities (i.e., people, organizations, and locations) in the story than looking at the story details (2.08 vs. 10.23, HSD=4.734), while their F-scores weren't significantly different (.82 vs. 94, HSD=.138). Similarly, there is a statistically significant time reduction for identifying stories with a one line summary extract than with the full text of the story (3.57 vs. 13.58 seconds/story, HSD = 4.734). The F score differences (.86 vs. .84, HSD = .138) were not (quite) statistically significant. This corroborates the empirical finding by Maybury (1995) that users spend less time and perform at least as accurately in extracting information from news summaries than from source articles. A corollary to observation 1 and 2 is that minimal amounts of mixed media elements should outperform individual single long elements.

Summary (See Example Figure)	Precision Mean	Precision St. Dev.	Recall Mean	Recall St. Dev.	F-Score Mean	Time (Secs/-Story)
Story Details(4)	0.93	0.15	0.97	0.06	0.94	10.23
Video(11)	0.94	0.16	0.94	0.15	0.93	24.53
Topic (9)	0.95	0.15	0.73	0.40	0.92	6.41
Full Details (3 & 4)	0.91	0.14	0.96	0.14	0.92	8.28
Summary (8)	0.88	0.26	0.77	0.26	0.86	3.57
Text (10)	0.80	0.22	0.81	0.34	0.84	13.58
3-Named Entities (6)	0.88	0.27	0.60	0.43	0.82	2.08
Skim (3)	0.93	0.13	0.74	0.32	0.81	3.69
All Named Entities (7)	0.81	0.20	0.68	0.43	0.78	3.54
Key Frame (5)	0.84	0.32	0.21	0.29	0.54	3.42
Mean	0.82	0.19	0.70	0.27	0.78	6.92
Standard Deviation	0.25	0.07	0.25	0.12	0.22	6.66
Tukey's HSD (.05)	0.105		0.153		0.138	4.734

Table 3. Accuracy and Time for Identification Task

Observation 3: Source Quality Matters. The average precision for the story identification task was significantly higher while watching the video versus reading the associated closed caption text (.94 vs. .80, HSD = .105). The average word error rate in the closed caption text sources is over 12.5%. This error rate accounts for some of this error.

Observation 4: Key-frames have poor Recall. As Table 3 illustrates, the recall values for key frames were significantly lower than the other presentation methods. This is likely a consequence of BNN's use of a simplistic key frame extraction heuristic. As one user commented "Key frames would work better if they had something to do with the story rather than the anchor shot."

The two graphs in Figure 13 depict precision versus time (13a) and recall versus time (13b), respectively, for various presentation methods (note the scale differences). The ideal performance is where time is minimized and precision and recall are maximized (upper left-hand corners of the graphs). Notice that video source and text closed captions had the longest average task times as expected. The overall accuracy results are perhaps most clearly viewed in the precision vs. recall chart shown in Figure 14. On average, the Story Details, Full Details and Video presentation methods form a significantly better group on the Recall and Precision chart. In contrast, Text, Summary, Topic, Story Skim, All Named Entities and 3 Named Entities presentation methods have lower recall or precision, or both.

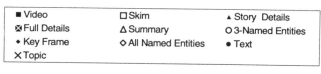

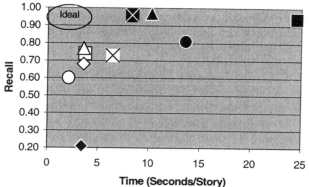

Figure 13b. Recall vs. Time

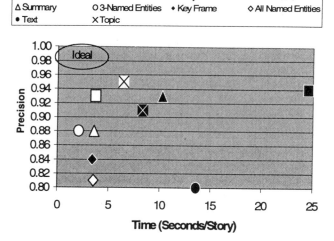

Figure 13a. Precision vs. Time

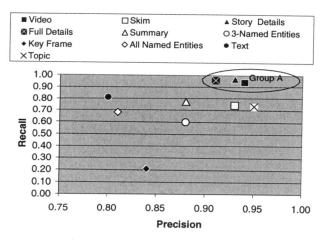

Figure 14. Average Precision vs. Average Recall (Identification Task)

5. Results for Comprehension Task

In contrast to the story identification task, in which a user is given a set of stories from which to select the relevant ones, the comprehension task measures how quickly and accurately a user can extract a specific fact from a given story (e.g., who was mentioned or what happened in a story). No partial credit was given for any of the answers, including synonyms. Only exact matches were accepted as being correct. For the story comprehension task (the ten questions for which were shown above in the bottom half of Figure 12) the average miss ratio was 0.43. On average, answering comprehension questions took 50% longer to perform (4.32 seconds per question/story) than story identification (2.18 normalized seconds per story), which we expect given the latter is a relevance judgment as opposed to retrieval of a specific fact.

Observation 1: There were three groups of presentation methods within the miss ratio. As seen in Table 4, there are three significantly different groups in the average miss ratio column (HSD = .235). The first group consisted of the key frame presentation method. Not one question out of 20 was correctly answered with this presentation method. The second group consisted of story skim, all named entities, 3 named entities, topic and summary. The average miss ratio for this group ranged from 0.65 to 0.55. The third group consisted of text, full details, story details and video. The average miss ratio for this group ranged from 0.10 to 0.00.

Observation 2: There are three groups of presentation methods for the average time. As seen in Table 4, there are three significantly different groups in the average time column (HSD=6.23). The first group consists of the video presentation methods. The second group consists of story details, text, full details, skim and topic presentation methods. The last group consists of the low density key frame, all named entities, 3 named entities and summary presentation methods. A corollary to observation 1 and 2 is that there is a high negative correlation (Pearson R = -0.857) between the miss ratio and time columns.

Presentation Method	Miss Ratio	Time (Seconds)
Key Frame	1.00	8.95
3 Named Entities	0.65	8.26
All Named Entities	0.65	8.95
Story Skim	0.65	17.58
Summary	0.55	7.05
Topic	0.55	16.58
Full Details	0.10	21.05
Text	0.10	23.55
Story Details	0.05	26.65
Video	0.00	33.30
Mean	0.43	17.19
Std. Dev.	0.34	8.96
Tukey (.05)	0.235	6.23

Table 4. Average Comprehension Results

Figure 15 graphically depicts results of the comprehension task, contrasting average user miss ratio with the average time to answer questions given different presentation types. As we might also expect, presentation methods containing less displayed information (i.e. 3 Named entities, Key Frame, All Named Entities, Skim[6] and Summary), required less time on

average than full source or composite presentations (e.g., full details, video). The times along the x-axis are the actual values in seconds for each presentation type (e.g., question answering took on average 7.05 seconds for one line summary texts whereas video took on average 33.3 seconds).

As annotated in Figure 15, the ideal presentation would have a low miss ratio and low time (bottom left hand corner). The high negative correlation between miss ratio and time suggests this ideal may not be reachable. One group, group A, on the graph consisting of text, video, full and story details, represents the low error, high time presentation alternative. In contrast to group A, group B includes summary and named entity presentation alternatives, require about a third or quarter the time, but with a significantly higher error rate. The skim and topic alternatives shown in Group C provide the same level of error rates as those in Group A but require about twice as much time. Presumably the presentations in Group A and B did not include sufficient factual details required to answer the comprehension questions. Overall, the users took on average 64 minutes to perform the identification and comprehension tasks.

6. User Preferences

After each test, users were asked to subjectively assess their preference for particular presentation strategies, 1 indicating least preferred, 10 the most preferred. Results averaged across all users are shown in Table 5. For the comprehension tasks, the average user preferred to use the story details or full details presentation methods. The average rating for these two methods (8.2) is higher than the average rating of the others (4.0). These two methods were preferred in the identification task although other methods rated higher. The average rating for the two methods (7.8) is higher than the average rating of the others (5.2).

---

[5]Skim took significantly less time than video (17.58 vs. 33.30, HSD=6.23) but wasn't significantly different in time from Full Details (21.05).

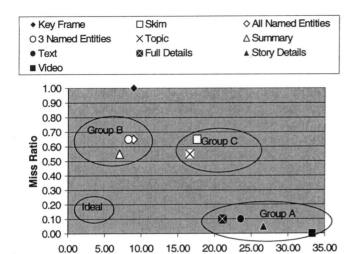

	◆ Key Frame	□ Skim	◇ All Named Entities
	○ 3 Named Entities	✕ Topic	△ Summary
	● Text	⊠ Full Details	▲ Story Details
	■ Video		

Figure 15. Miss Ratio vs. Time: Comprehension Task

Visualization Method	Comprehension		Identification	
	Mean Rating	St. Dev. Rating	Mean Rating	St. Dev. Rating
3-Named Entities	2.22	1.80	5.12	2.34
All-Named Entities	3.50	2.87	6.29	2.02
Full Details	8.33	1.94	7.78	2.10
Key Frame	2.11	2.35	3.17	2.73
Skim	3.28	2.52	4.72	2.19
Story Details	8.11	2.40	7.88	2.50
Summary	4.06	2.58	5.94	2.26
Text	6.33	2.74	5.24	2.14
Topic	4.17	2.92	5.53	2.60
Video	6.50	1.86	5.61	2.33
Mean	4.86	2.40	5.73	2.32
St. Dev.	2.30	0.41	1.39	0.23

Table 5. User Rating of Presentation Methods

7. Discussion

The most significant overall finding is that mixed media summaries (story details and full details) are the most effective presentation for story retrieval and comprehension tasks. As one user remarked: "I liked the Story Details and Full details visualization methods because lots of information is displayed and one can easily glance through it for content and images. In addition, all information can be obtained by watching the video clip or reading the transcript. Full details visualization method was a bit nicer since there was a little visual summary at the top which prevented unnecessary scrolling." A related finding is that giving the user less

information (e.g., 3 named entities versus the entire story details) can enhance processing time without significantly affecting accuracy. With larger data sets, users exhibit higher precision with the skimming presentation technique, enabling them to more quickly scan larger amounts of content than by reviewing raw video or data.

The accuracy of the underlying extraction algorithms significantly influenced the outcome. For example, closed caption data errors (ranging from 2-20% word error rates), simplistic key frame selection heuristics as well as including only 1 key frame per story, and simple summarization algorithms result in data errors which reduce user performance. Another interference factor was the need for users to scroll down topics, only two of which were displayed for each story in a scrolling list (see Figure 9). A future study should present all topics to see if this has an effect on timing and accuracy. Also, half of the identification questions were concerned with people, two with organizations, two with general topics, and only one with a location. Future studies should explore the less frequently investigated ones, especially topics.

Finally, comprehension task performance is highest for story details and full details as well as with the text or video source. Users' preference for story details and full details is consistent with the time and quality of results they are able to achieve with these methods. Other results, however, are task dependent. For example, topic displays apparently fared better in the identification task than in the comprehension task as they provide a good mechanism for determining "aboutness".

8. Conclusion and Future Work

We have illustrated the efficacy of multimedia summaries of broadcast news. By controlled "ablation" experiments in which users were given random presentations of individual and mixed media summaries, we have discovered which presentation methods are most effective for which sizes of data and types of tasks (e.g., story identification vs. comprehension). We have also identified those summary presentation elements within the existing BNN system that require enhancement to increase precision and recall, especially key frames and, to a lesser extent, named entities.

This study opens a number of new avenues for additional investigation. In addition to extending the number of users involved in such an evaluation, future testing should focus on assessing any preferences for particular presentation methods based on job function (e.g., secretary vs. engineer vs. manager), experience level (e.g., years, hours/day using a computer), and type of content. One possible extension is to measure user confidence ratings in assessments in addition to preferences as a number of users indicated higher levels of confidence in different presentation types.

Within this study, we focused on stories that contained only one topic and very few proper names. This study can be expanded to evaluate presentation methods for stories that contain more than one topic. Within this study, because of the limited number of questions per proper name type, we did not study the optimal presentation methods to be used for tasks in which the user is searching for an individual person, organization or location.

More expertly crafted presentations should also be explored. For example, we could minimize unused space in the named entity (Figure 7) and topic (Figure 9) displays, eliminate scrolling in the topic display, and minimize metadata repetition (See Figures 6 and 8) to improve search and selection tasks. We could also improve the textual summaries by using summary lengths that are appropriate to each document (Jing et al 1998). We could also design more effective hypermedia displays. More fundamental means of information encoding are also possible. A related, important area is the visualization of very large data sets, such as that suggested by the (dynamic) named entity trend analysis display in Figure 2 and by related work in our group on large scale relevancy visualization (Mitchell, Day, and Hirschman 1995, Smotroff et al. 1995) as well as content visualization (Chase et al, 1998).

Finally, as the BNN system is currently being extended to include spoken language transcription for non-closed captioned sources, this will require additional testing given errors introduced by these processes.

9. Acknowledgments

We thank the evaluators for their willing participation and generous feedback following the experiments. We also thank the anonymous referees for numerous comments which helped improve the paper.

References

Aberdeen, J., Burger, J., Day, D., Hirschman, L., Robinson, P., and Vilain, M. 1995. Description of the Alembic System Used for MUC-6. In Proceedings of the Sixth Message Understanding Conference, 141-155. Advanced Research Projects Agency Information Technology Office, 6-8. Columbia, MD.

Chase, P., D'Amore, R., Gershon, N., Rod Holland, R., Hyland, R., Mani, I., Maybury, M., Merlino, A., and Rayson, J.. 1998. Semantic Visualization. In Pustejovsky, J. and Maybury, M. (eds) Working notes of the COLING-ACL '98 Workshop on Content Visualization and Intermedia Representation, Montreal, August 1998, pp 52-62.

Christel, M. 1995. Addressing the Contents of Video in Digital Library. Electronic Proceedings of the ACM Workshop on Effective Abstractions in Multimedia. San Francisco: California, November 4, 1995. http://wwww.cs.tufts.edu/~isable/christel/christel.html

Ding, W. and Marchionini, G. A Study on Video Browsing Strategies. Human Computer Interaction Lab Technical Reports, 14th Annual Symposium and Open House, Friday May 30th, 1997, University of Maryland.

Firmin, Therese and Chrzanowski, Michael, An evaluation of Automatic text summarization systems, this volume.

Hauptmann, A. and Smith, M. 1995. Text, Speech, and Vision for Video Segmentation: The Informedia Project. In Maybury, M. (editor) Working notes of International Joint Conference on Artificial Intelligence-95 Workshop on Intelligent Multimedia Information 17-22. Montreal, Canada.

Jing, H., Barzilay, R., McKeown, K., Elhadad, M., Summarization Evaluation Methods: Experiments and Analysis, in working Notes of the AAAI Spring Symposium on Intelligent Text Summarization, Spring 1998, Technical Report, AAAI, 1998, pp. 60-68.

Maybury, M. T. (ed.) 1997. *Intelligent Multimedia Information Retrieval.* Menlo Park: AAAI/MIT Press. (http://www.aaai.org:80/Press/Books/Maybury-2/)

Maybury, M. T. 1995. Generating Summaries from Event Data. *International Journal of Information Processing and Management: Special Issue on Text Summarization.* 31(5): 735-751.

Maybury, M., Merlino, A., and Rayson, J. 1997. Segmentation, Content Extraction and Visualization of Broadcast News Video using Multistream Analysis. In Proceedings of the AAAI Spring Symposium, Stanford, CA.

Maybury, M. and Merlino, A. 1997. Multimedia Summaries of Broadcast News. International Conference on Intelligent Information Systems. Bahamas, 8-10 December, 422-429. IEEE Press.

Merlino A., Morey, D. and Maybury M. 1997. "Broadcast News Navigation using Story Segments", Proceedings of ACM Multimedia '97. Seattle, WA, November 8-14, 381-391.

Mitchell, R., Day, D., and Hirschman, L. 1995. Fishing for Information on the Internet. In Proceedings for Visualization '95 Symposium on Information Visualization, Atlanta GA, October 1995, 105-111.

O'Connor, B. C. 1991. Selecting Key Frames of Moving Image Documents: a Digital Environment for Analysis and Navigation. *Microcomputers for Information Management*. 8(2): 119-133.

Rao, R., Pedersen, J., Hearst, M, Mackinlay, J., Card, S., Masinter, L., Halvorsen, P. K & Roberston G. 1995. Rich Interaction in Digital Video Library. *Communications of the ACM*, 38(4): 29-39.

Smotroff, I., Hirschman, L., and Bayer, S. 1995.Integrating Natural Language with Large Dataspace Visualization.I Adam, N. and Bhargava, B. (eds), *Advances in Digital Libraries, Lecture Notes in Computer Science*, Springer Verlag. 209-224.

Yang, Y.; Carbonell, J.; Allan, J.; Yamron, J. 1998. Topic Detection and Tracking Detecting Task. Broadcast News and Transcription Workshop, February 8-11, 1998.

Yeo, Boon-lock and Yeung, Minerva M. 1997. "Retrieving and Visualizing Video", *Communications of the ACM*, December 1997, 40(12): 43-52. Zhang, H. J., Low, C. Y., Smoliar, S. W., and Zhong, D.Video Parsing, Retrieval, and Browsing: An Integrated and Content-Based Solution. In Proceedings of ACM Multimedia '95 15-24. San Francisco, CA.

26

Summarization of Diagrams in Documents

Robert P. Futrelle

College of Computer Science 161CN, Northeastern University
360 Huntington Ave., Boston, MA 02115
futrelle@ccs.neu.edu, http://www.ccs.neu.edu/home/futrelle/

Abstract

Documents are composed of text and graphics. There is substantial work on automated text summarization but almost none on the automated summarization of graphics. Four examples of diagrams from the scientific literature are used to indicate the problems and possible solutions: a table of images, a flow chart, a set of x,y data plots, and a block diagram. Manual summaries are first constructed. Two sources of information are used to guide summarization. The first is the internal structure of the diagram itself, its topology and geometry. The other is the text in captions, running text, and within diagrams. The diagram structure can be generated using the author's constraint-based diagram understanding system. Once the structure is obtained, procedures such as table element elision or subgraph deletion are used to produce a simpler summary form. Then automated layout algorithms can be used to generate the summary diagram. Current work on parsing and automated layout are briefly reviewed. Because automated diagram summarization is a brand-new area of inquiry, only the parsing phase of the approach has been fully implemented. Because of the complexity of the problem, there will be no single approach to summarization that will apply to all kinds of diagrams.

1. Introduction

Documents are composed of text and graphics. But virtually all summaries and excerpts of documents available today are in text form exclusively. Including graphics in summaries would address this imbalance, but raises obvious questions as to how such graphics summaries could be generated. There is essentially no literature on the summarization of graphics. This paper is a first foray into this unexplored territory. It focuses on *diagrams*, which are line drawings such as data plots or block diagrams.

The overall plan of this paper is to first present a set of four examples of diagram summarization, all constructed manually, using diagrams from the science and engineering literature. Since the summaries are constructed manually, they represent, in a sense, the ideal summarization that we would like an automated system to achieve. We then go on to discuss what would be involved in automating the process of summarizing diagrams, illustrated with the same four example diagrams. As part of this we discuss the computational results we have achieved so far on extracting structural information from diagrams by constraint-based parsing. The four diagrams have been chosen to represent a cross-section of the types of problems that arise in diagram summarization.

Assuming that structural descriptions can be obtained, either from parsing or as metadata furnished by the author of the document, the problem then becomes one of *selecting* one or a few figures from a document, or *distilling* a figure (simplifying it), or *merging* multiple figures. The last two approaches require the generation of a new figure that did not previously exist, so results in the fields of automated layout and graph drawing are discussed to see how those methods can be brought to bear on distillation and merging. The overall process then is one of *analysis* to develop structural descriptions, the production of *summaries of the descriptions*, and finally the *generation* of the graphical form of the summary diagram.

Throughout we assume that the diagram of interest is vector-based, as contrasted with a raster image. Summarization of raster images involves an entirely different set of problems including image processing and segmentation, topics not treated here.

Our work on diagram summarization so far has been to develop systems that can automatically discover diagram content by visual parsing. It is this content that must be analyzed, along with related text, to produce summary figures that then have to be laid out and displayed. Because we have not yet developed automated systems to produce reduced or summary versions of diagram content, our discussion has to be viewed as an initial exploration of the nascent field of diagram summarization. It attempts to lay out the research and implementation problems that must be solved in order for working systems to be built. We hope that this paper serves as both a catalyst and a guide for this new domain. One inspiration for this work is the rapidly increasing availability of electronic documents on the World-Wide Web and elsewhere as well as the profusion of formats, such as PDF (Adobe Systems Incorporated, 1996) for whole documents, PGML for vector graphics, XML (World-Wide Web Consortium, 1998) for metadata, that make it possible to access and manipulate the contents of these documents for information extraction and summarization. The availability of these documents and the needs of users to access them efficiently motivates the current work on summarization in general, and this paper on diagram summarization in particular. A useful discussion of the structure needed to fully exploit scientific documents appears in (Fateman, 1997), with additional discussion and web links at http://http.cs.berkeley.edu/~fateman/MVSD.html. Fateman uses mathematical notation as his example and discusses the problems of representing visual appearance, syntax (structure), and semantics, all issues that have to be dealt with in diagram summarization.

Our work on diagram parsing and this discussion of summarization focuses on the scientific and technical literature. The figures in such documents tend to be strongly information-bearing, as contrasted with figures in newspapers and magazines that are often more topical and indicative, e.g., a picture of some unidentified people applauding at a concert.

At first blush it might seem that the text accompanying figures could be exploited to guide diagram summarization, but as we explain below, this is often not the case — the diagram itself must be analyzed. This means that we cannot always take advantage of lexical resources and text statistics that are so helpful in text summarization.

2. Manually Constructed Diagram Summarization Examples

2.1 Example #1: Distilling a table of images

The first example is drawn from a paper about OCR (Ho and Baird, 1997) that has eleven figures in it, many multi-part and one occupying an entire page. The paper is about building parameterized defect models for the appearance of characters and training systems on very large collections of characters generated by the models, and assessing their performance. Some of the figures show the degraded characters that are synthesized, but most show statistical results of their analyses. An informative summary should probably include one figure that shows examples of the degraded characters. The figure we have chosen is their Fig. 7, shown in our Fig. 1a below. The running text in the article offers the following support for this decision,

> "...The key contributors to scanning and printing noise are the three parameters blur ..., thrs ..., and sens .... These will be our primary concern. Figure 7 illustrates these effects."

The choice of this figure is a *selection process* but we will not dwell on that process at this point. On examining the figure, we can see that it is possible to reduce it to a more compact summary form, by manipulating its graphics content and its caption. The graphics content, with ten sample images in each of three rows, offers more detailed information than is necessary in a summary. The summarized form, shown in Fig. 1b, elides the eight intermediate examples, and indicates them with ellipsis. In summarizing the caption, the detailed numerical values can be omitted, giving the caption in Fig. 1b. This collapsing of the set of graphical items is a *distillation process*.

Example #1 does include *images* in tabular positions, but our approach to summarization for this example treats them as anonymous items, with no internal structure.

In Fig. 1 and throughout the remainder of the paper, we have adopted the convention that figures reproduced from other sources are surrounded by a border; if the original caption is included, it is contained within the same border. This is also true of figure/caption pairs that represent summaries such as Fig. 1b. Additional captions of our own are placed outside the borders. The full text of the original captions is included in all four example figures.

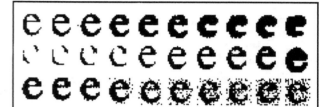

Fig. 7. Effects of blurring, thresholding, and pixel sensitivity. Images are created with **blur** varying from 0.0 to 3.6 by 0.4 (top row); **thrs** varying from 0.9 to 0.0 by -0.1 (middle row); and **sens** varying from 0.0 to 0.9 by 0.1 (bottom row).

Figure 1a, Example #1. This figure shows three monotonic sequences of degraded characters arranged in tabular form (Ho and Baird, 1997). The appearance of the characters is not discussed in the original paper, since their appearance is evident on viewing the figure.

Fig. XX. Effects of blurring, thresholding, and pixel sensitivity (parameters **blur**, **thrs**, and **sens**).

Figure 1b. A manually constructed summary figure and caption for Fig. 1a. Each horizontal sequence in Fig. 1a shows a monotonic progression that is captured by the extreme values in this figure summary.

2.2 Example #2: Distilling a Flow Chart

Flow charts are common diagrams in many fields. They are often candidates for distillation because they contain minor steps that can be omitted in a summary. The flow chart in Fig. 2a shows the link of events leading from DNA to the synthesis of a protein. A normal path is shown on the left and an abnormal one on the right.

chart (Richardson, 1997) includes two initial stages, a binary split, and then four additional stages in each of the two pathways. Biologically, the key element is the addition of a certain substance, "ODN", in the right-hand pathway which leads to the synthesis of an abnormal and non-functioning receptor protein compared to the normal left-hand pathway.

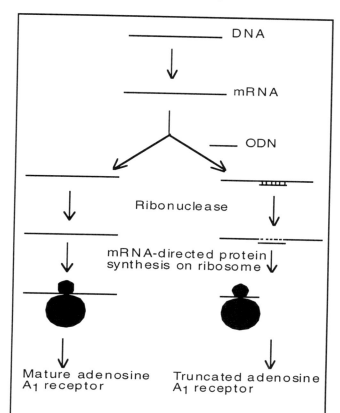

Figure 2 Nyce and Metzger have used antisense oligodeoxynucleotides (ODNs) to selectively inhibit the synthesis of adenosine A$_1$ receptors in rabbit lungs. Transcription of messenger RNA from the gene for the A$_1$ receptor is followed by synthesis of the receptor protein on ribosomes. The ODN consists of deoxynucleotides that are linked by phosphorothioate linkages (which confer stability to DNA-degrading enzymes). The ODN hybridizes by Watson-Crick base-pairing to the mRNA, to generate a substrate for ribonucleases, particularly RNase H, which degrade the RNA protion of the hybrid. ODNs must be long enough to hybridize only to the mRNA of interest, they need to be stable and they must be able to enter cells and activate ribonucleases. As the mRNA no longer encodes the full-size protein, fewer receptors are synthesized, and the normal turnover of the adenosine A$_1$ receptor reduces the total number of receptor molecules.

Figure 2a, Example #2. The topology of this flow

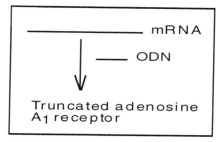

Figure 2b. A manually generated summary of Fig. 2a. The essence of the process is that ODN interferes with subsequent processing of the mRNA, leading to an abnormal protein. That is all that is retained in this simple summary.

Both the caption and the running text mention "ODN" extensively. Apposition tells us that ODN is the abbreviation used for "antisense oligodeoxynucleotide", and "antisense" is another prominent term, included also in the title of the article. This makes the right-hand branch of the flow chart, and ODN in particular, the most salient part of the diagram. The summary retains the arc with the ODN label, omits the common initial node and omits all intermediate states between the mRNA node and the final node. Since the left-hand path in Fig. 2a is normal and conventional, it is not particularly informative and is omitted in the summary.

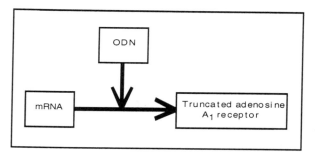

Figure 2c. A stylistically distinct rendering of the summary in Fig. 2b. This contains essentially the same information as the Fig. 2b. But the different style makes it difficult for a reader to first look at the summary and then go to the full paper where the full figure (2a) is presented, because of the horizontal organization versus the vertical organization of the original, rectangular nodes instead of the horizontal line nodes of the original, etc. A summary in the style

of Fig. 2b would be strongly preferred on these grounds.

2.3 Example #3: Merging for Contrast

Summarizing large collections of numerical data from experiments or complex simulations is an intrinsically difficult problem. The example, in Figs. 3a and 3b shows the *merging* parts of two different diagrams into a single one.

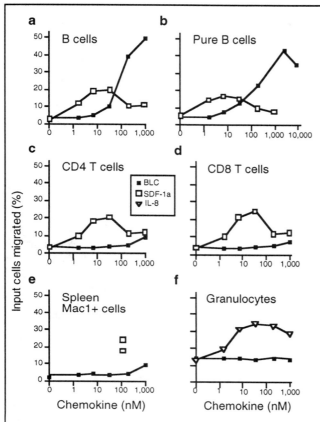

Figure 3 Chemotactic activity of BLC on leukocyte subtypes. Results are expressed as the percentage of input cells of each subtype migrating to the lower chamber of a transwell filter. Panels show migration of: **a**, B cells; **b**, purified B cells; **c**, CD4+ T cells; **d**, CD8+ T cells; **e**, monocytes/macrophages; **f**, granulocytes, towards BLC. Positive controls are SDF-1α (**a-e**) and IL-8 (**f**). ....

Figure 3a, Example #3. This contains the first six of eight subfigures from Fig 3 in (Gunn, et al., 1998) and the corresponding portions of the original caption.

The primary point made in the article in which the material in Fig. 3a appears is that the researchers have discovered a substance that specifically affects (attracts) B cells (a class of motile blood cells) but not T cells and other major classes of blood cells. This can be pointedly summarized in a single figure that selects the portions of two of the data plots that show the contrasting behavior, e.g., plots **a** and **c**. The merged graph is shown in Fig. 3b.

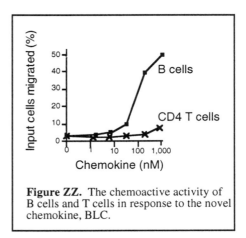

Figure ZZ. The chemoactive activity of B cells and T cells in response to the novel chemokine, BLC.

Figure 3b. This data plot contains the significant contrasting portions of Fig. 3a, parts **a** and **c**. We created the caption within this summary figure in the style normally used in biology research papers.

2.4 Example #4: Distilling a Large Block Diagram

Flow charts are typically DAGs, whereas block diagrams can have numerous interconnections and cycles. The example here is a block diagram for a video signal compression system (Bhatt, Birks and Hermreck, 1977), Fig. 4b. It is interesting to note that the original figure is in color, with eight distinct colors used for the various blocks. The colors for the various blocks are chosen essentially at random, with little regard to grouping them by functionality. This is apparent for example in a set of three source-to-transmitter figures earlier in the original article. In two of the figures the video camera icon is light blue and in the third it is a mustard color, an arbitrary difference for items with identical roles.

3. Automated Summarization of Diagrams

This section discusses the goals of automation and the important concepts that underlie the work. It also gives a brief overview of the important aspects of diagram content, from syntactic structure to semantic associations with real-world entities.

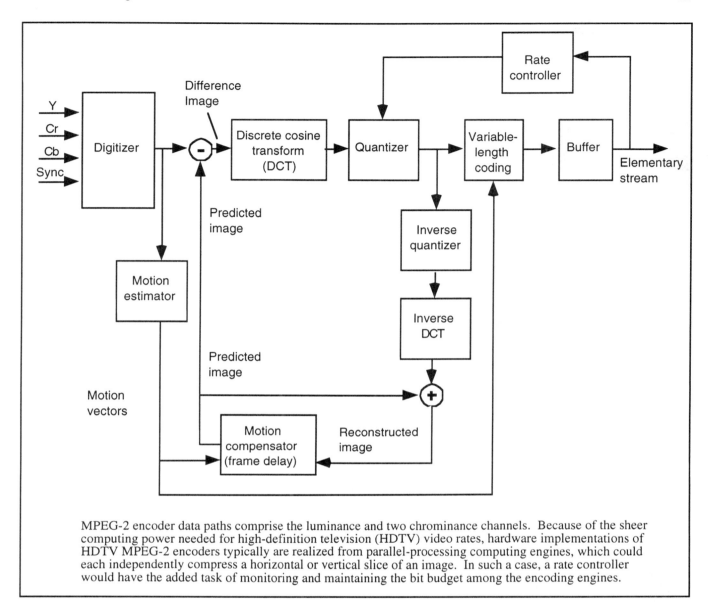

MPEG-2 encoder data paths comprise the luminance and two chrominance channels. Because of the sheer computing power needed for high-definition television (HDTV) video rates, hardware implementations of HDTV MPEG-2 encoders typically are realized from parallel-processing computing engines, which could each independently compress a horizontal or vertical slice of an image. In such a case, a rate controller would have the added task of monitoring and maintaining the bit budget among the encoding engines.

Figure 4a, Example #4. A large block diagram. The summary in Fig. 4b merges all the units below the primary upper backbone into a single composite unit.

3.1 Goals of Automation

One of the goals of any summarization system is to generate summaries in real time or, operating in batch mode, produce summaries at the rate at which the corpus of interest grows. That is, the methods should scale to realistically useful tasks. Our diagram parsing system currently parses a typical diagram (100 to 200 vector elements), in about 10 seconds. Let us assume, for the sake of argument, that the full summarization process would take about 30 seconds. Since there are 32M seconds/year, such a system could process 1M diagrams/year. This would be a sizable fraction of the scientific and technical diagrams published per year, estimated from article counts gathered from databases such as *BIOSIS* and the *Engineering Index* (totaling over 1M documents/year).

Another goal is to develop summarization techniques that are relatively domain-independent. This is possible in text summarization, because corpus statistics are able to reveal major terms in the discussion, and the linear organization of the text can also be used, e.g., selecting the first sentences of section-leading paragraphs. It is more difficult to do domain-independent summarization for diagrams. We do suggest below that in some cases, the

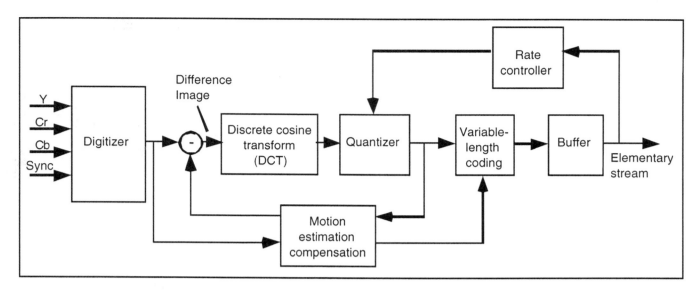

Figure 4b. A summary of Fig. 4a focusing on the horizontal "backbone" connecting the system input on the left to the output on the right. The choice of the text in the "black box" node at the bottom is a text summarization task.

overall topological and geometrical organization of a diagram may be exploited for domain-independent summarization.

3.2 Background for Automation

There is a collection of concepts and a standard terminology for them, some of it derived from text-based document analysis, that we will use in the discussions which follow. Documents can be characterized by their *genre* (journal article, newspaper article, book, etc.) and their *domain* (operating systems, microbiology, etc.). Text is essentially *propositional*, presenting statements in natural language that can be mapped into formalisms such as the predicate calculus. Language draws from a huge store of lexical entities that map words to meaning. In contrast, graphics is *analogical*, using spatial structures as the information-carrying elements (Sloman, 1995). Graphics and language are different *modalities*, because they require distinct interpretation functions, whereas both may rendered in the same *medium*, e.g., on the printed page (Stenning and Inder, 1995). Graphics can be divided into *veridical* entities, such as photographs and drawings of real-world structures, and *abstract diagrams* such as flow charts or data plots, but for the most part, diagrams are built up from relatively content-free items such as lines, curves, and closed regions such as polygons, which are (only roughly) analogous to the orthographic characters making up words. In graphics, there are also *conventional* classes of symbols, such as arrows, tick marks, error bars, corporate logos, and standard traffic signs (FHWA, 1997) that are learned elements of the visual lexicon.

It is useful to distinguish the general term, *graphics,* which contrasts with *text,* from specific subclasses such as

figures which are instances of graphics in documents; *diagrams* which are line drawings; and *images* which are raster-based. There are distinct *classes* of diagrams such as x,y data plots, pie charts, vertex/edge graphs, gene diagrams, etc.

The text associated with figures can be in *captions* or in the *running text*, or *included* within the figures. *Metadata* is normally propositional material that is available in an index or other data structure or is generated, that gives additional information about diagram structure and content, but is not always made available for viewing by the reader of an electronic document. *Tables* are hybrids of text and graphics. Summarization of text or graphics can be *indicative* or *informative* (Paice, 1990). The former presents material that indicates the subject domain (such as the audience picture we mentioned earlier), while the latter contains information which plays a substantive role in the document.

Additional concepts include the *purpose* of summarization which can include the intended *audience*, and a chosen *emphasis*, which can focus on methods, results, judgments, or matters in dispute. The choice of these can influence the type of summarization that is constructed.

3.3 Diagram Content

It is possible to define grammars and parsing strategies to produce structured descriptions of the contents of diagrams. In this section the basic structure of diagrams and its interpretation at the syntactic and semantic levels is described, using the examples in Fig. 5. Further details on the parsing approach are given in the next major section on diagram understanding.

The raw content of a diagram is the collection of vector primitives that make it up, the lines, curves, polygons, and text, each with their specific numerical parameters. For summarization to work, a description of the diagram is needed that codifies the objects, and their functional, geometrical, and topological relations, e.g., the fact that an object is a node in a block diagram that contains certain text and that is contacted on left by an oriented edge (indicated by an arrowhead). The edge may in addition emanate from another node or have a free end, etc.

The syntax and semantics of diagrams has strong overlaps with the related natural language concepts, but there are major differences. In language, the *model* of the logical form of an utterance is normally a collection of real-world entities existing outside language per se. But the basic objects in a figure can be viewed as having a physical existence of their own, e.g., marks on paper. More formally, the axioms of geometry and their associated computational algorithms (for length, distance, orthogonality, etc.) can be used to extend the meaning of geometrical objects in the formalism, allowing arbitrary geometrical calculations to discover or test relations among sets of objects. Graphical knowledge has been characterized as *vivid knowledge* (Levesque, 1987; Levesque, 1992), first-order languages which only contain ground atomic sentences, are universally quantified over the domain, and have other "concrete" properties. Entailment in such languages has been shown to be tractable. The limitation of this view is that though the graphical elements themselves are so restricted, the real-world entities to which they refer have no such constraints.

The approach above forms the basis for grammars that describe complex graphical objects. Fig. 5a shows a simple data plot, whose analysis by such a grammar identifies the scale lines with their tick marks, tick mark labels, and axis labels. The less orderly curve in the space delimited by the two axes is the data.

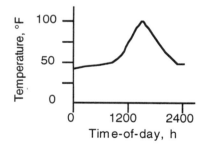

Figure 5a. Basic syntax: E.g., identification of the basic components, the x and y scale structures, and the data curve.

At the next level, in Fig. 5b, the world coordinates of the data points can be extracted, i.e., in units of degrees Fahrenheit and the time in hours. At this level there need be no explicit representation of the semantics of time or temperature.

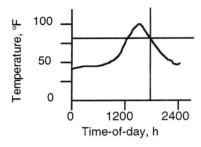

Figure 5b. Lowest semantic level: Numerical values of world coordinates, e.g., 79° at 1800 h.

Additional computations can yield useful information that is still domain-independent, e.g., the maximum value achieved by the data set, Fig. 5c. (The operations in Figs. 5b and 5c could be applied in either order.)

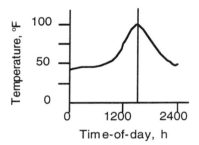

Figure 5c. Numerical analysis semantics: "Day's maximum of 100° reached at 1520 h"

Finally, an interpretation can be developed at a much higher level in which the information in the plot is related to real-world situations outside the diagram proper, in this case a statement about the affect of such temperatures on crop viability, Fig. 5d. Such an interpretation goes beyond diagram analysis per se, but could play a significant role in deciding whether or not to include information from particular diagrams in a document summary.

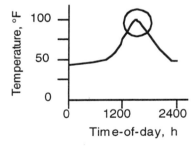

Figure 5d. Real-world semantics: "Reaching this temperature may cause some crop damage because of the current drought conditions"

4. Diagram Understanding

This section discusses our work on diagram parsing as well as work by others on the problem. Parsing is the first stage of the diagram summarization process, producing the structural descriptions that are the input to later stages.

4.1 The Diagram Understanding System (DUS)

Parsing a diagram generates a syntactic description, a parse tree. The parse structures we consider here are based on approaches to parsing that we have pursued using *context-based constraint grammars* (Futrelle, 1985; Futrelle, 1990; Futrelle, Carriero, Nikolakis and Tselman, 1992a; Futrelle and Kakadiaris, 1991; Futrelle, et al., 1992b; Futrelle and Nikolakis, 1995). Our system is called the *Diagram Understanding System* or DUS. A typical production in a DUS grammar for x,y data plots describes a collection of x-axis tick marks and their associated horizontal scale line, such as in our figures 3a,b and 5a-d, by the following production,

```
X-Ticks -> Ticks X-Line
   (X-Line)
   (Ticks (touch X-Line ?)
      :constraints
         (> (number-of Ticks) 2))
```

In the X-Ticks production, the body of the production states the order of analysis (X-Line followed by Ticks) and states the constraints on the constituents —in this case that the number of Ticks be greater than 2. The term (touch X-Line ?) specifies that the items that can be considered in analyzing the Ticks production are restricted to a *context*, the set of objects that *touch* the X-Line already identified. The context functions as an *inherited attribute* in the sense of (Knuth, 1968). X-Line is defined by another production, as is Ticks, a *set object*,

```
Ticks -> Set ( Line )
   (:element-constraints
      (vertp Line)
      (short Line))
   (:constraint horiz-aligned))
```

In the Ticks production there are constraints on the individual elements of the set given by :element-constraints, as well as a constraint on the set as a whole, that its members be horizontally aligned with one another. A potential ambiguity of the Ticks rule is that the any subset of the vertical lines touching the horizontal one would be a legal instance. This ambiguity is avoided by a meta-rule that chooses the *maximal* (largest) set satisfying the constraints.

A simple diagram that would be an instance of this rule is shown in Fig. 6.

Figure 6. This structure is an instance of the X-Ticks grammar rule that describe it as a set of short vertical

lines that are horizontally aligned and touching a long horizontal line.

In addition to inherited attributes, there are *synthesized attributes* (Knuth, 1968) in the DUS formulation that are passed from a production to a higher-level node in which the constituent appears. An example would be the computation of the midpoint of a line, passed upwards as the value of an explicitly named attribute.

The efficiency of our system is aided by the use of context which restricts the search, as well as the order of construction of the constituents as stated in the rules. There are many computations of geometrical relations such as *near* and *aligned* that have to be done as parsing proceeds. These are speeded up by a preprocessing phase that builds an index, a spatially associative structure (SPAS). SPAS is a pyramid of square arrays covering the diagram space at varying levels of resolution, down to resolution of about one character width (Futrelle, 1990). It is created in a preprocessing stage before parsing proper begins. Each square element lists all graphical objects that occupy or pass through the region. Thus, to find the objects near to a given one, only a local search in the SPAS index is needed. Computations of geometrical relations between simple objects such as straight lines or complex objects such as Bezier curves are all done in the same uniform way when using SPAS. Memoization is also used to enhance performance (Norvig, 1991).

Parsing in the DUS is implemented as a constraint satisfaction problem which, among other things, makes it straightforward to allow objects to be *shared*, i.e., to participate in more than one distinct structure in the same parse. Sharing is quite common in graphics. For example, the y-axis (ordinate) tick mark numerical labels in Fig. 3a are shared across a pair of plots, and the y-axis label on the left is shared by all six plots. Sharing allows us to analyze each of the six plots as a complete plot with full tick marks and a label without having to explicitly include sharing in the grammar. The parse of each of the six subplots in Fig. 3a can be treated as a tree structure even though it is technically a DAG because of the shared constituents.

Sharing allows another powerful type of analysis in which a single diagram is simultaneously analyzed in two different ways, all in terms of common objects rather than by two distinct analyses that later have to be brought into concordance. This is useful for example if one part of the analysis is stated in topological terms, e.g., the connectivity of a flow chart or block diagram, and another simultaneous analysis describes the spatial organization, e.g., the two lower vertical columns of nodes in the flow chart of Fig. 2a.

One issue that arises in a general-purpose retargetable system such as the DUS is how it should behave when presented with an arbitrary unknown diagram. We could attempt to parse the figure with a succession of grammars, each specialized to a different class of diagrams. A more efficient way to proceed would be to write a grammar that had in it a collection of simple productions that describe common "signatures" of certain classes of diagrams, such as scale lines, arrows, tick-marks, back-bone structures, labeled boxes, etc. A preponderance of any one of these or of some subset of them in the resulting parse would greatly restrict the full-fledged grammars that would then be appropriate to use for more detailed analyses.

The DUS is implemented in Common Lisp / CLOS (Macintosh Common Lisp) and every constituent, whether a primitive (Line) or a higher-level one (Data-Plot) is an instance of a class of that name, with slots that include its constituents (RHS). The parsing proceeds top-down and the result is one or more solution objects of the start-node, which in turn contain constituents, etc., all CLOS instances. Detailed performance figures exist only for older machines (Futrelle and Nikolakis, 1995; Nikolakis, 1996), and scaling up from these, we expect that current machines should parse a typical diagram of 100 to 200 primitives, which is the size of a typical published data plot, in 10 seconds or less. The system is also being ported to Unix. So far, we have working grammars for x,y data plots, linear gene diagrams, and finite-state automata (Nikolakis, 1996).

Genesis of the DUS. Before reviewing other approaches to diagram parsing, it is worth explaining the strategy we employed to develop the DUS system, which gives it a very different character than other systems. The reason this discussion is relevant to the diagram summarization problem is that we intend to apply the same philosophy to the development of efficient and effective approaches to automated diagram summarization. Practically all other systems for parsing visual languages have grown from the extensive conceptual base and formalism developed for string languages, e.g., natural language and programming languages. Our approach began by studying thousands of published diagrams in a variety of scientific and technical publications. From that study we saw the great importance of repeated elements and thus the need for sets in our formalism. We also realized that there is a major distinction between *background* and *foreground* elements in informational diagrams. Background elements are those that are arranged in simple low-complexity patterns, e.g., with aligned repeated elements, such as tick marks. The background is called the *framework* in (Kosslyn, 1994). We then wrote algorithms that could discover and give structure to background elements very efficiently. Items not in the background constitute the foreground, the high-content or informational items, e.g., the non-uniformly positioned data points in a data plot. Our computational strategy was then extended to handle the foreground elements, ignoring the previously discovered background elements. Once this efficient computational system was in place, its procedural face was systematically transformed, using Lisp macros, to the essentially declarative form of the current DUS. Thus our system is the result of placing a declarative face on a fundamentally efficient underlying parsing engine, rather than attempting to efficiently parse grammars using strategies that are based ultimately on string language techniques.

4.2 Previous Work on Diagram Understanding

Now that we have described the DUS approach to diagram structure discovery, we will briefly discuss some of the other work in the field, generally know as *visual language parsing*. Reviews of this field can be found in Nikolakis' thesis (Nikolakis, 1996) and in the extensive recent review (Marriott, Meyer and Wittenburg, 1998) with 201 references. Given this amount of past work, our discussion is necessarily quite selective. Our approach falls under the general rubric of *attributed multiset grammars*. The constituents in these grammars may have geometric and semantic attributes associated with them. Productions contain constraints over the attributes of RHS constituents. Other approaches to parsing include logical and algebraic formalisms (Marriott, Meyer and Wittenburg, 1998). The primary statement that can be made about visual language parsing is that the demands of the problem are so great that the approaches needed to deal with them go beyond those that are theoretically and computationally tractable. This means that the utility of the approaches is very dependent on their design, their implementation, and the class of graphical items that they are expected to analyze. This is precisely the reason that our own approach was developed by focusing first on the efficient parsing of real diagrams, and only later on declarative formalisms and formal analysis (Nikolakis, 1996). Interestingly, in the extensive review we have already mentioned (Marriott, Meyer and Wittenburg, 1998), the analysis of published diagrams is hardly touched on as an application, in spite of their great volume and their importance in all of scientific communication. In the same vein, there has been little concern over parsing diagrams with hundreds of elements and essentially no systematic performance studies in this domain. The great utility of parsing systems such as the DUS is that they can be retargeted, applied to a variety of diagram types by simply changing the grammar. The only systems that have been built for truly large diagrams are hand-crafted, non-retargetable systems for problems such as interpreting drawings of telephone central office equipment racks ("distributing frames") (Luo, Kasturi, Arias and Chhabra, 1997), architectural drawings (Ah-Soon and Tombre, 1997), etc.

Comparison of a DUS and CMG example. Though developed from different points of view, it is interesting to compare a portion of a DUS grammar for a state diagram with the corresponding production in constraint multiset grammars (CMG) (Marriott, 1994). The DUS grammar includes context restrictions and sets and explicitly states the sequence of constituent processing. The CMG grammar is purely declarative.

DUS:

```
********** < TRANSITIONS > *************
Transition  ->  A-state_1  Labeled-arrow
                 A-state_2
  (Labeled-arrow)
  (A-state_1
    (touch (leave-pt (arrow Labeled-arrow)) '?))
  (A-state_2
    (touch (reach-pt (arrow Labeled-arrow)) '?));

Transitions -> Set ( Transition );
```

CMG:

```
TR:transition ::= A:arrow, T:text
  where exists R:state, S:state where
  T.midpoint close_to A.midpoint
  R.radius=distance(A.startpoint,R.midpoint),
  S.radius=distance(A.endpoint,S.midpoint)
  and TR.from=R.name, TR.to=S.name.
```

4.3 Diagram Syntax, Semantics, and Style

Syntax and Semantics. Stripped to its essentials, the DUS generates a parse tree for a diagram. But as the earlier examples make clear, both the DUS and CMG grammars are couched in terms of constituents whose semantic roles are evident from their names. Here is a list of some of the constituents in our grammars that makes this clear. For state machines: Init-state, Transitions, Final-states, Labeled-arrow, A-state. For gene diagrams: Gene, Gene-body, Gene-title, Backbone, Segment. For data plots: XY-Data-Plot, X-Axis, Y-Axis Data, Data-Lines, Data-points, etc. Though writing grammars in this way might appear to solve the semantics problem, extending the coverage to a greater variety of diagram classes and domains could result in a proliferation of grammars that each try to solve the semantics role problem in a single step. For example, a graph could represent an organizational chart, a network diagram, a chemical process flow chart, etc. A better way to deal with such variety would probably be to have a grammar with more neutral terms, followed by a semantic interpretation process tuned to the domain. This would parallel natural language semantic formalisms more closely.

Style. In Fig. 2c we demonstrated what could happen if the details of the style and layout of the original diagram were not followed in constructing a summary. The reader who then went from the summary to the full document and its figures would find the transition disorienting. This situation could be even worse for a complex diagram such as the block diagram summary of Fig. 4b. Due to its complexity there are a large number of different ways in which the summary could be laid out on the page (vertically for example!) which would have the same topology but a radically different appearance.

In order to maintain as much style constancy as possible, it is necessary to capture the stylistic and layout information of the original in the diagram understanding step and preserve it during the summarization and generation process. A related problem is discussed in the automated graph drawing literature. Graph drawing sometimes proceeds incrementally, as the user adds new vertices. If the automated layout of the graph were recomputed from scratch each time a new vertex was added, its appearance could change radically at each step. So some graph drawing algorithms attempt to preserve as much of the layout as possible when redrawing after insertion which allows the user to maintain a rather constant "mental map" of the graph (Misue, Eades, Lai and Sugiyama, 1995).

Most visual language parsing systems pay little or no attention to the stylistic aspects of diagrams. In our DUS work, the vector-based diagram data that we parse is derived from postprocessing Postscript files, themselves generated from diagrams that we have created using drawing applications such as Canvas. These retain all style information such as line widths, fonts, color, etc. Our parsing work has for the most part ignored the style information, but clearly it is available and could be used in the later generation phase. The locations and therefore the relative locations of various objects is an integral part of diagram parsing, so that layout information is always available.

There is a more complex problem that must be faced in capturing layout information for later use in generation, which is that the description of the necessary topological, content, and layout information might be difficult to represent simultaneously in a single parse. It might be necessary to build additional tools to extract the variety of types of information needed from a single parse. But as we described earlier, the constraint-based approach of the DUS, and sharing in particular, allows more than one type of analysis to proceed simultaneously, with the various results all using the same objects where appropriate.

5. Automated Diagram Generation

Diagram summarization often involves the *generation* of a diagram, once the summarized structure for the diagram is developed. There are three important aspects of the problem of generating diagrams. The first is the art and science of good graphics design which prescribes guidelines for the use of graphics elements and their layout in space in ways that make the presentation of information clear and unambiguous (Cleveland, 1994; Kosslyn, 1994; Tufte, 1985; Tufte, 1990; Tufte, 1997). The second is the collection of common systems that generate much of the graphics produced today. These are exemplified by systems such as spreadsheets that have built-in data plot generation capabilities. In these systems, the style of the plot is selected from a small set of examples and some portion of the data in the spreadsheet is used to generate a data plot containing it. This is normally not a difficult task, because the system designers retain total control over the specifications of each of the supported styles. The third aspect is the work of the graph drawing community, which is primarily concerned with drawing large vertex/edge graphs under certain constraints such as minimizing the number of crossings or minimizing the number of right-angle bends (for drawings using only vertical and horizontal edge segments). There have been a number of annual graph drawing symposia, dealing with these issues, e.g., (DiBattista, 1997). Beyond these approaches to the generation of graphics, there is a good deal of research today on scientific visualization and the presentation of large datasets such as the collections of documents returned by retrieval systems. This work is less directly applicable to the problem of summarizing already existing diagrams, the primary concern here.

The field of automated graphics design and layout is even more active than visual language parsing. An excellent recent review of just the constraint-based approaches to such problems has more than 200 references (Hower and Graf, 1996). The early work in this field used algebraic (Mackinlay, 1987) and rule-based approaches (Seligmann and Feiner, 1991), but there is now substantial work based on constraints (Graf, 1998). The readings volume containing the last-mentioned reference reprints nine other papers on the topics of automated graphics design and layout (Maybury and Wahlster, 1998).

Constraint-solving algorithms have been developed with special attention to the problems of interactive graphics input including constraint hierarchies (Borning, Freeman-Benson and Wilson, 1992), and incremental constraint solving (Freeman-Benson, Maloney and Borning, 1990).

Generation for Summarization. The important and obvious point to note at this juncture is that the DUS diagram parsing system is itself constraint-based, so the grammars already go a long way towards specifying the constraints on generation. The major difference between diagram summarization and most of the constraint-based layout and design problems is that we focus on the *reduction* of diagrams rather than *additions* to them, though this is not a profound difference. In fact, it is reasonable, particularly with complex graphs, to reduce them a node at a time, allowing the system to maintain the same general layout, solving only an incremental constraint problem at each step. One major addition to our formalism that would be required to move it from parsing to generation would be to add quantitative preferences. A simple example of where this would be needed would be in the generation of tick marks in a data plot. In parsing a data plot, any number of tick marks would be acceptable, but in generation, some minimal spacing of a few mm and a total number of the order of ten to twenty tick marks would be typical design parameters.

The problem of automated layout can be computationally quite demanding, e.g., for label placement (Christensen, Marks and Shieber, 1995), but the diagram summarization problem should be able to take account of the many details embodied in the original diagram(s) to be summarized. From the original diagram it can obtain box

dimensions, font size, line widths, arrowheads, alignments, etc., and reuse these as much as possible. In the discussion below of automated techniques that could be applied to our example diagrams, we will make more specific suggestions.

6. The Relations of Text and Graphics

One of the first suggestions that researchers in text summarization make in discussions about the problem of diagram summarization is to exploit the text associated with diagrams, especially captions. But this approach is fraught with problems, as we explain and illustrate in this section.

6.1 Figure Captions.

The style and content of figure captions varies widely across the range of scholarly journals. Surveying current academic periodicals revealed the following: The biological literature, and to a large extent all scientific literature that reports the results of experiments, has substantial captions, averaging over 100 words in length. The first portion of each caption is typically a noun phrase that serves as a title. A few publications, such as the *Biochemical Journal*, separate the figure title from the caption text. Engineering and Physics tend to have only noun phrase captions from about 3 to 15 words in length. Mathematics is the extreme, in many cases having only figure numbers and no captions whatsoever. Linguistics journals often number figures (such as parse trees) just as all other presented items, with sequential parenthesized numbers in the margins and no captions. The humanities and social sciences, business, and clinical medicine have few figures but may include tables. Examples of typical brief figure captions from the information retrieval literature include, "System Architecture", "Hierarchical feature map", and "Average Improvement in Precision", each quoted in its entirety.

In spite of the paucity of significance information in many figure captions, they can represent a useful division of the set of figures in a document, and can be useful in the *selection* form of summarization, when only one or two figures are selected to be included in the summary, either in their original form or in summarized form. For example, the title portions of the four figures in the original article corresponding to our example #3 are: "Expression pattern of BLC mRNA in mouse tissues.", "BLC sequence and alignment with other protein sequences.", "Chemotactic activity of BLC on leukocyte subtypes.", and "BLR-1 mediated calcium mobilization and chemotaxins in response to BLC." In a system in which the reader states some particular aspect that he or she would like to see emphasized in a summary, titles such as this could be useful guides for an automated selection process.

It might seem that lengthy figure captions, where they are available, would be excellent indicators of figure content and significance. Surprisingly, this is rarely the case. Virtually all lengthy captions that we have studied in the scientific literature are associated with the presentation of experimental data in the accompanying figures. These captions focus on the detailed conditions under which the data was gathered, or label the specific data subsets shown. They rarely contain any language that evaluates or explains the significance of the figure content.

Publications intended for wide audiences, such as *National Geographic*, are the only ones that appear to put significant content in figure captions. This is presumably done to present information in smaller "chunks" by allowing individual figures and their captions to be understood by the casual reader without their having to read the accompanying article in detail. Many popular publications do not even use figure numbers, making it difficult to refer to specific figures from the running text. Many popular magazines such as *Time* or *Scientific American,* and most newspapers, have "stand-alone" figure-caption pairs and never specifically refer to the figures in the running text at all.

The conclusion of the preceding analysis is that for most of the scientific and technical literature we can look for certain details in captions, but all comments as to the substance and significance of figure content will have to be found in the running text. As we have already emphasized, there will be important aspects of figure content that are not explained anywhere in the text of a document, since their content is obvious when looking at the figure.

6.2 Examples of Figure Captions

Example #1. In Fig. 1a, the "Effects" in the original caption are self-evident when viewing the figure. It is far more appropriate to simply look at them than to read a textual description of them.

Example #2. Fig. 2a appeared in an article in the *news and views* section of the journal *Nature*. These short pieces appear in the early pages of each issue and discuss the significance and interesting points of full technical papers that appear later in the same issue. As such, each *news and views* piece is written in an accessible and somewhat pedagogical style. The original 200 word caption in Fig. 2a explains the overall process of protein synthesis and how it was blocked by the addition of ODN in the experiments reported. Natural language analysis of this caption could markedly aid the summarization processing of the figure.

Example #3. The original 100 word caption in Fig. 3a has a somewhat informative initial title phrase, "Chemotactic activity of BLC on leukocyte subtypes." Most of the remainder of the caption deals with the experimental procedures and specifies the particular cell types used. The only particularly informative phrases in the caption refer to the control experiments whose results are contained in subfigures g and h, which we have not reproduced. The most significant results, which are presented in subfigures a-f of Fig. 3a and summarized in our Fig. 3b, are not explicated in the caption at all. In this regard, this caption

is quite typical of figure captions throughout the biological literature.

Example #4. *IEEE Spectrum* is that organization's most widely distributed publication, covering topics of interest to all members in carefully edited form with extensive color illustrations. It is a popular technical magazine. Consistent with this role, the captions are normally rather informative. The caption in Fig. 4a begins abruptly with a sentence that serves as a less than optimal figure title. It begins, "MPEG-2 encoder data paths comprise the luminance and two chrominance channels." It does not state that the figure is in fact a block diagram, though this is immediately obvious from the figure. The caption does not discuss the contents of the diagram per se but mentions the hardware implementation of it as well as changes that would need to be made to accommodate specialized hardware. We have to conclude that this caption would not be particularly helpful in the diagram summarization process.

6.3 What Running Text Says About Diagrams

When figure content is explicated in text, we have seen that little of it is to be found in figure captions; it is in the running text (if anywhere!). So we turn to a discussion of the running text of our four examples where we will find more useful information referring to figure content. The utility of this information is tempered by the complexity of the text, the same complexity met in attempting to do text summarization. Often there is only one or a few explicit references in the running text to a specific figure. But the discussion of the topics related to the figure may be still be extensive and distributed throughout the document.

Example #1. We have already quoted a significant item drawn from the running text in our first discussion of this example, Fig. 1a, viz.,

> "...The key contributors to scanning and printing noise are the three parameters blur ..., thrs ..., and sens .... These will be our primary concern. Figure 7 illustrates these effects."

There are two marker phrases in the running text excerpt that emphasize the importance of the material in their Fig. 7 (our Fig. 1a): "The key contributors .. are ...", and, "... our primary concern." This is followed by the definitively worded figure reference sentence, "Figure 7 illustrates these effects." If this text is to be used to evaluate the importance of the figure, the referent of "these effects" would have to be identified. This is not a trivial problem because there is no obvious "effect-like" term in the preceding sentences, only "contributors", "parameters" and a prior use of "These", which itself needs to have its referents identified.

Example #2. Since this figure (2a) has an extensive and useful caption, the content of the running text is less critical. The article has two figures, of which Fig. 2a is the second. The first mention of it in the running text is in the initial sentence of the third paragraph, about 1/3 of the way through the 900 word article. The sentence is, "ODNs act by sequence-specific hybridization to messenger RNA (Fig. 2)." The sentence which follows it parallels the content of our manually generated summary, Fig. 2b. The sentence is, "They then selectively prevent the translation of the RNA message into protein, and promote degradation of the message by ribonucleases." Some of the details presented in the original figure, Fig. 2a, are omitted in this summary sentence, suggesting that they can be omitted in a summary figure. Though this informal analysis is reasonable on the surface, it has inherent dangers – for example there may be important material in a figure that should be included in a summary figure but is so visually obvious that it is not discussed in the text.

Example #3. This figure (3a) has a weakly informative caption, as we have discussed, so the running text needs to be looked at closely. The article is a *letter to nature*, so it is short and packed with information, with figures covering micrography, gels results, DNA and amino acid sequences and comparisons, the eight-part figure we are discussing, and a final seven-part figure. The first two sentences that mention our figure (their Fig. 3) contain exactly the contrast displayed in our summary figure, 3b, viz.,

"BLC induced a strong chemotactic response in B cells in experiments using either total spleen lymphocytes (Fig. 2a) or purified B cells (Fig. 2b)."

and

"In contrast, BLC showed limited activity towards T cells carrying CD4 or CD8 antigens (Fig. 2c, d)."

In our summary, we chose to display the first item of each pair, **a** and **c**, but any pairing would have sufficed (one from a or b and the other from c-f). This is evident from the plots we have shown in Fig. 3a. So in this case at least, the running text has elements in it with significant marker items, "strong .... response", "In contrast", and "limited activity". These could guide an automated diagram summary system in achieving the summary diagram we produced manually in Fig. 3b.

Example #4. Our Fig. 4a appears in a two-page spread, a sidebar (distinguished by a light blue background), in the middle of a full article. The article figures are numbered, but the four in the sidebar have no figure numbers. Some are referred to in the running text positionally, e.g., "[see top left diagram, opposite]", but the figure we have chosen is not referred to explicitly in the running text at all. Without explicitly stating that the figure is being discussed, about one-third of the way through, it mentions the "digitizer", the left-most item in the block diagram. The discussion next mentions the DCT block, then the quantizer. The discussion then moves to the form of the signals within the encoder, with occasional mentions of other blocks in the diagram, e.g., the motion estimator and the two "inverse" blocks. Eventually, most of the blocks are described. There is no obvious emphasis on particular blocks or links in the running text, either by frequency of occurrence or by emphasis terms, so there is little to guide

automated summarization of the block diagram.

6.4 Text Included within Diagrams

Text within diagrams is common, ranging from data plot axis labels to text overlaid on images. It is distinct from captions and running text in that it is normally positioned within the diagram to indicate its role. Included text can play a number of distinct roles. Our example #1 has no included text so it is omitted from this part of the discussion.

Example #2. The various text items within Fig. 2a play four distinct roles. The top two text items label vertices (nodes) in the flow chart, the two horizontal lines, indicated by their adjacency and horizontal alignment with the lines. The next text item, "ODN", which labels an edge of the graph, indicates that a certain substance is introduced at the point in the process between the mRNA and the topmost right node below "ODN". The text "Ribonuclease" is aligned with and between the two arrows, indicating that it is associated with the transition between the vertices on each side (shared), rather than vertices proper. The same analysis applies to "mRNA-directed protein synthesis on the ribosome" below it. Finally, the two text items at the very bottom of the figure constitute vertices in themselves and both identify and describe the vertices (protein products as the end result of processing). In our summary diagram, Fig. 2b, the three text items play three distinct roles, the same roles they play in the original, Fig. 2a.

Example #3. In this set of data plots, Fig. 3a, the text items play five distinct roles. The six characters, a-f, label the six separate plots to allow efficient reference in the caption and running text. Their position is a *customary* one, lying slightly outside and above each plot. This prevents them from being confused with the shared ordinate label for the six plots, "Input cells migrated (%)". Another customary position for such letter labels is in the position occupied by the cell descriptor text, e.g., "B cells". The text within the key box identifies the three different types of data points, "patches" in (Kosslyn, 1994). The abscissa labels, "Chemokine (nM)", are duplicated, each being shared by the three plots above them. The numerical text labeling the ordinate tick marks, 0-50, is shared across two horizontally aligned plots, but the abscissa tick labels are repeated for all six plots (and differ for graph b). Our summary plot, Fig. 3b, is a single item requiring no sharing of text and has text in three roles. The role of the cell descriptor text has changed from one associated with an entire (sub)plot to one in which the two data sets are separately labeled. (A key could also have been used.)

Example #4. A block diagram, like a flow chart, is often replete with text, labeling every block. Of course, we have seen a flow chart, example #2, in which some nodes are purely graphical. In the block diagram of Fig. 4b, text labels either the blocks (vertices) or the links between them (directed edges). In one case, in the upper left, the text "Difference Image" labels a *call-out*, used because there is no space in which to insert the text appropriately. Call-outs are frequently used to solve these layout "real estate" problems. Our summary diagram, Fig. 4b, uses text in the identical roles, including using the same call-out. Unlike the prior flow chart example, #2, the function of the link labels is to denote the data flowing between the processing or buffer nodes. In the flow chart, the link labels play a complementary role, indicating the *processing* occurring between the nodes that leads from one substance or configuration to the next.

7. Diagram Summarization Procedures

In this section we will discuss the structures (parses) generated for each original diagram of the four examples, the transformations done to produce summary structures, and the process of generating the resulting summarized diagram. Each diagram presents us with a new set of problems. The algorithms and other automation procedures used below have not yet been implemented in running code. Rather, the procedures are spelled out explicitly and the manipulations are done by hand. Of course the DUS has been used to produce full parses of similar diagrams in the past.

We have chosen to ignore the problem of text summarization required to synthesize new captions for diagram summaries. This is a topic unto itself, discussed in all the other papers in this volume. Text summarization in the context of diagram summarization is not simple, because the text summaries have to be concordant with the material that is presented in the summary diagrams, which may be a subset of the old or contain newly synthesized items, e.g., the new composite vertex at the bottom of the block diagram summary, Fig. 4b. The referent problem also arises whenever any summarization of the running text refers to figures that no longer are included or refers to material within a figure that has been altered or deleted.

7.1 Distilling Figures

Numerically parameterized sequences, Example #1. Fig. 1a contains three parallel sequences of items (ten simple images) each parameterized by a monotonic sequence of numerical parameter values.

In order for our diagram parsing approach to produce a useful structure for Fig. 1a, we will assume that the figure is made up of 30 small images. A grammar rule would be written describing a regular rectangular array using the horizontally and vertically aligned constraints. At this point the knowledge from the caption would need to be used, the fact that each row contains results for changes in a single degradation parameter. Combining the structure and caption information would allow the system to perform a sequence elision procedure, retaining only the extreme instances (and possibly the fifth or sixth instance to represent the intermediate appearances). The elided structure would be built using the same parse representation as the original. Using quantitative

parameters from the original figure, the summary figure could be constructed, Fig. 1b. An alternate approach would be to specify the summary as the original minus a sequence of deletions of the intermediate items in each row. Then an incremental constraint solver would "slide" the outer items toward the middle, producing a reduced form through a series of minimal changes.

The manual summary elides the eight intermediate images in each row, yielding Fig. 1b. This procedure could fail to produce correct results in many instances. It is often the case for such parameterized sequences that the most important items appear at intermediate values of the parameter, rather than at the extremes (minimum or maximum) values. For example, for living systems, optimal viability and growth is achieved at intermediate values of temperature, salinity, pH, etc. Ordinary data plots such as in example #3, Fig. 3a, commonly show such behavior, so an algorithm that produced a summary by only reporting values of the dependent data items at extreme values of the independent parameter value would often fail.

The article in which Fig. 1a appeared is concerned with synthesizing defective character images and then evaluating the performance of OCR systems trained on the images. Conceptually, it is clear to a manual summarist that increasing values of the image defect parameters induce a monotonic change in the quality of the images. Thus the extreme values, the "best" and "worst" items, are quite adequate as a summary. On reading the text it appears that it would be difficult to extract this type of information from it to guide an automated summarization process. The conservative approach would be to include the extreme parameter value items as well as one item corresponding to an intermediate parameter value. Choosing the value appropriately in an automated way, rather than just choosing the mean or median, may be problematic.

7.2 Graph Reduction

When graphs such as flow-charts or block diagrams are represented as standard directed vertex-edge structures, there are topological reduction procedures that can be applied to distill them to simpler form. Because they are based entirely on topology, these methods are domain independent. We define one such reduction procedure, *link-subgraph-deletion (LSD)*, and apply it to two of our diagrams. In LSD we identify certain subgraphs of a larger graph as shown in Fig. 7a. Each such subgraph is a *meganode*, a set of vertices which is allowed to have only a single entering edge and a single exit edge. Otherwise it may have arbitrary internal connectivity. The vertices that precede and follow the subgraph, a and b, can have arbitrary additional connectivity, indicated schematically in Fig. 7a. The graph is reduced by deleting the entire subgraph, resulting in Fig. 7b. The new edge between a and b now receives an ordered pair of labels, e and f. The LSD procedure uses the *maximal* 2-connected subgraphs between nodes since, for example, a simple linked list would contain many 2-connected subgraphs.

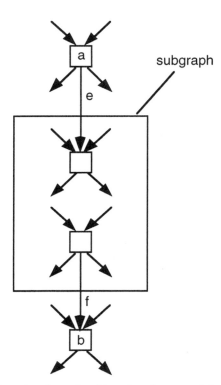

Fig. 7a. A subgraph of restricted connectivity that is deleted by the link subgraph deletion procedure (LSD), resulting in the graph shown in Fig. 7b.

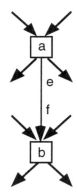

Figure 7b. The graph resulting from the deletion of the subgraph in Fig. 7a. The a-to-b edge is now labeled with the ordered pair of labels from the original.

Application of LSD to Example #2. The application of the link subgraph deletion procedure to the molecular flow chart of example #2 results in the distilled version of Fig. 8a. Parsing the original graph requires a grammar describing a graph, one that allows a vertex to be a text item (the two vertices at the bottom of the original graph). This would require a slight extension of the grammars previously used in the DUS for parsing state-machine diagrams. Another portion of the parse would be needed to

capture the vertical geometric arrangement of the diagram. The parse result would be walked to discover its topology, which could then be reduced by LSD. The resultant structure would be used to generate the summary diagram using the geometrical arrangement and numerical parameters of the original. Note that the object-based formulation in the DUS makes it relatively easy to reposition items and sets of items in space, so that for example, the first vertex and its "DNA" label could be repositioned as a unit to its final position in the summary diagram, as could the mRNA vertex and label, the branching edge and its ODN label, etc.

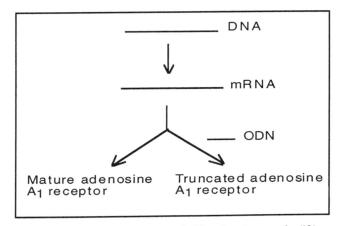

Figure 8a. Summary of Fig. 2a (example #2) produced by application of the link subgraph deletion (LSD) procedure, a domain-independent algorithm based entirely on graph topology. Compare with the simpler manual summary in Fig. 2b.

The original figure, 2a, contained 10 vertices and 9 edges. The algorithm-based summary in Fig. 8a contains 4 vertices and 3 edges, whereas the "optimal" manual summary of Fig. 2b contains only 2 vertices and 1 edge. The material in Fig. 8a that does not appear in the manual summary are the vertices for DNA at the top and the "Mature ... " item on the lower left, as well as their two connecting edges. The caption and running text in the original article contain 10 references to ODN as well as 5 to RNA, but only 1 reference to DNA. This could be taken as grounds for further automated pruning of Fig. 8a to delete the DNA node and its link as was done in the manual summary. It is also the case that in biology, the synthesis (transcription) of RNA from a DNA template is so commonplace that it hardly bears mention. The text describing the normal versus the abnormal (truncated) receptors is more complex and does not yield useful word-count data for, e.g., "mature" versus "truncated". This suggests that the best that an automated summarization procedure might be able to accomplish is the diagram shown in Fig. 8b, with 3 vertices and 2 edges.

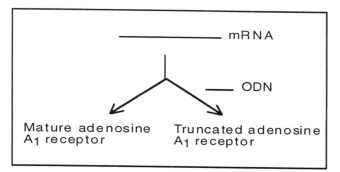

Figure 8b. A automated summary that might be produced using text analysis to discover salient concepts (terms) in the caption and running text for the original figure. Starting with the automated summary in Fig. 8a, the lack of evidence for the importance of the DNA-labeled vertex has been used to delete it and its accompanying edge.

7.3 Merging Figures

Compare and Contrast — Data in Example #3. The datasets in example #3, Fig. 3a are significant because they demonstrate a contrast between two types of behavior that is evident when certain subsets of the data are compared. The running text of the article places great emphasis on the compound, "BLC", mentioning it explicitly more than 50 times in the 3000 word article. It is introduced in the abstract in the sentence, "Here we describe a novel chemokine, B-lymphocyte chemoattractant (BLC), that is strongly expressed in the follicles of Peyer's patches, the spleen and lymph nodes." This simple statistic by itself could lead an automated system to focus on the BLC-related data sets within Fig. 3a (the black squares). Even the simplest statistical analysis of the BLC-related data sets would reveal that the data behavior in plots a and b, related to B cells, is significantly different from the corresponding behavior in plots c, d, e, and f. This would allow an automated procedure to select a pair of strongly contrasting data sets such as the two shown in the manually constructed summary of Fig. 3b, taken from Fig. 3a, plots a and c.

Though the preceding argument is attractive, it will be difficult to test the utility of such approaches without extensive application of automation algorithms to a variety of examples. Many published datasets are more equivocal than those in Fig. 3a, making it difficult to find clear-cut contrasts. But scientists continually strive to design experiments and data presentation procedures that make the significance of data strikingly clear.

The automated procedure for building the summarization in this example would start with a parse of the six plots. The parse distinguishes the background scale lines and their annotations from the data points and lines proper. We'll assume that analysis of the text and data has resulted in the choice of the appropriate datasets in a and c. Constructing the resultant summary plot could then be

done by bringing together and aligning a few large constituents: the x and y scale lines from plot a or c, the BLC dataset from plot a, the BLC dataset from plot c, the y scale label from the left, the x scale label from the bottom below plot e, the "B cells" label from plot a, and the "CD4 T cells" label from plot c.

7.4 Role of Layout in Summarization Decisions

Example #4, a Large Block Diagram. This block diagram, Fig. 4b, is difficult to deal with because as a graph it has a high level of connectivity (only one small link subgraph). This makes it difficult to argue that some particular portion of it should be favored for retention or for reduction/deletion. As we stated earlier, the running text accompanying the figure discusses most of the blocks with equal emphasis.

What can be used to drive the decision-making process for an automated summarization algorithm for this figure is its *geometrical layout*. Viewing the diagram as a complex flow chart, a signal processor, it has signal input on the upper left, the video stream entering the digitizer, and signal output, the compressed signal, on the upper right, after the buffer. There are six horizontally aligned blocks spanning the space between signal input and output (we must count the "+" item as a legitimate vertex). The edges between them are all directed to the right, making the set a linear chain, with numerous "side" connections. All blocks above and below the horizontal sequence are involved with feedback and feedforward controls related to image motion and rate throttling.

Initially the automated analysis would proceed much as in the previous graph example, in this case allowing vertices to be rectangles with internal text labels. Walking the parse structure would again construct a representation of the graph topology. Using the geometrically identified horizontal backbone, a dual analysis of the geometry and topology would indicate that there are four edges leaving the backbone from below and two from above. This would identify the subgraphs to be collapsed. The summary redrawing could use all the elements from the backbone, unchanged as well as the block above the backbone, all in unmodified form. The only actual synthesis required would be that of the new lower block. Even in this case, the identical contact points of the four lower edges with the backbone elements could be used. That is, the algorithm would attempt to maintain the "mental map" of the original as much as it could in the summary. Incremental constraint solving could aid in the process.

8. Discussion and Summary

Clearly, the problem of summarizing diagrams in documents is a complex and multi-faceted one. The variety and complexity of diagrams and their multifarious relations to text will require a variety of summarization strategies — there will be no single approach that will apply across the board. Reviewing the problems of automated summarization for our four examples, we see that example #1 required the collapsing of a tabular set of images that was numerically parameterized. Example #2 allowed us to delete an internal "meganode" in a graph. Example #3 dealt with the selection and merging of numerical data from a collection of x,y data plots. Example #4 was a complex block diagram in which the summary was guided by the geometrical structure (layout) of the original. The role of text in guiding the automation for these examples was itself complex, and we did not attempt to investigate that aspect in much detail.

Essentially nothing has been done in this new field of diagram summarization, save some interesting work on multimedia, e.g., (Maybury and Merlino, 1997). Our own work has progressed to the point that we can parse a wide variety of diagrams efficiently, producing structured descriptions that are the input required by any automated diagram summarizer. This paper has used four examples, explored in depth, to describe how the summarization process might work, including the description of simple topological and elision algorithms. We felt that a thorough-going discussion of examples was needed because diagram summarization is such a new idea that most readers would not be able to fall back on any prior knowledge of the topic — this paper is in many ways, a "first" in its field. We hope that it has laid out a practical agenda for exploring the problem in greater breadth and depth and building practical systems.

The world is hardly ready for the application of automated diagram summarization because too few documents contain graphics in vector form that could serve as input to the first parsing stage. That is, most diagrams available today in PDF and HTML formatted documents are in raster form, as images, even though many were originally created as vector diagrams! But in 1998 there has been a surge in proposals to the World-Wide Web Consortium for various vector graphics standards (World-Wide Web Consortium, 1998), so that documents could contain more structured graphics, including *metadata* which describes the internal content of graphics items, using, for example, XML (World Wide Web Consortium, 1997).

Indeed, once we consider the possibility of including extensive metadata about diagrams within electronic documents, we can question how much of the complex analysis strategies we have discussed would be necessary. It should be possible to build intelligent authoring systems (IAS), applications that would allow the author to develop documents that include metadata about diagrams, and text for that matter. For a discussion of IAS strategies for text, see (Futrelle and Fridman, 1995). There is nothing new about metadata. Virtually anything beyond normal sequential natural language text can properly be called metadata. Web hyperlinks are an obvious example, but so are bibliographic citations, references to specific figures, etc. Authors already include such metadata in the papers they write. The only question is, what other types of metadata might they agree to include in the future? Diagram metadata could include information that would indicate which diagram would be the one to retain in a summary, if only one were to be included, or at a more detailed level, which parts of a diagram would be suitable for a summary. The goal of a good IAS would be to make the inclusion of this type of additional information as effortless as possible for the already overworked author.

More and more major publications in science and various technical fields are moving online. Because of this, the desire to have the graphics in them treated as first-class content will spur the development of better formats, more metadata, and graphics manipulation systems such as diagram summarizers.

Acknowledgments

The author wishes to thank Tyler Chambers who was involved with and very helpful in developing the first draft of this paper. Thanks also to three anonymous reviewers whose insight and knowledge markedly transformed the original. Thanks finally to Carolyn S. Futrelle for her editing suggestions.

References

Adobe Systems Incorporated (1996). *Portable Document Format Reference Manual*. Version 1.2.

Ah-Soon, C. and Tombre, K. (1997). Variations on the Analysis of Architectural Drawings. In ICDAR 97 (*Fourth Intl. Conf. on Document Analysis and Recognition*), (pp. 347-351). Ulm, Germany: IEEE Computer Soc.

Bhatt, B., Birks, D. and Hermreck, D. (1977). Digital television: making it work. *IEEE Spectrum*, **34**(10), 19-28.

Borning, A., Freeman-Benson, B. and Wilson, M. (1992). Constraint Hierarchies. *LISP and Symbolic Computation*, **5**(3), 223-270.

Christensen, J., Marks, J. and Shieber, S. (1995). An Empirical Study of Algorithms for Point-Feature Label Placement. *ACM Trans. on Graphics*, **14**(3), 203-232.

Cleveland, W. S. (1994). *The Elements of Graphing Data* (Revised Edition ed.). Summit, NJ: Hobart Press.

DiBattista, G. (Ed.). (1997). *Graph Drawing*: Springer.

Fateman, R. J. (1997). More Versatile Scientific Documents. Extended Abstract. In ICDAR 97 (*Fourth Intl. Conf. on Document Analysis and Recognition*), (pp. 1107-1110). Ulm, Germany: IEEE Computer Soc.

FHWA (1997). *Manual on Uniform Traffic Control Devices (MUTCD)*. Washington, DC: Federal Highway Administration — U. S. Dept. of Transportation. http://www.ohs.fhwa.dot.gov/devices/mutcd.html.

Freeman-Benson, B., Maloney, J. and Borning, A. (1990).

An incremental constraint solver. *Communications of the ACM*, **33**(1), 54-63.

Futrelle, R. P. (1985). A Framework For Understanding Graphics In Technical Documents. In Expert Systems in Government Symposium (pp. 386-390): *IEEE Computer Society*.

Futrelle, R. P. (1990). Strategies for Diagram Understanding: Object/Spatial Data Structures, Animate Vision, and Generalized Equivalence. In *10th International Conference on Pattern Recognition*, (pp. 403-408): IEEE Press.

Futrelle, R. P., Carriero, C., Nikolakis, N. and Tselman, M. (1992a). Informational Diagrams in Scientific Documents. In *AAAI Spring Symposium on Reasoning with Diagrammatic Representations*, (pp. 185-188). Stanford University.

Futrelle, R. P. and Fridman, N. (1995). Principles and Tools for Authoring Knowledge-Rich Documents. In *DEXA 95 (Database and Expert System Applications) Workshop on Digital Libraries*, (pp. 357-362). London, UK.

Futrelle, R. P. and Kakadiaris, I. A. (1991). Diagram Understanding using Graphics Constraint Grammars. In S. G. Tzafestas (Eds.), *Engineering Systems with Intelligence - Concepts, Tools and Applications* (pp. 73-81). Boston, MA: Kluwer Academic Press.

Futrelle, R. P., et al (1992b). Understanding Diagrams in Technical Documents. *IEEE Computer*, **25**(7), 75-78.

Futrelle, R. P. and Nikolakis, N. (1995). Efficient Analysis of Complex Diagrams using Constraint-Based Parsing. In ICDAR-95 (*Intl. Conf. on Document Analysis & Recognition*), (pp. 782-790). Montreal, Canada.

Graf, W. H. (1998). Constraint-Based Graphical Layout of Multimodal Presentations. In M. T. Maybury & W. Wahlster (Eds.), *Readings in Intelligent User Interfaces* (pp. 263-285). San Francisco: Morgan Kaufmann.

Gunn, M. D., et al (1998). A B-cell-homing chemokine made in lymphoid follicles activates Burkitt's lymphoma receptor-1. *Nature*, **391**(1669), 799-803.

Ho, T. K. and Baird, H. S. (1997). Large-Scale Simulation Studies in Image Pattern Recognition. *IEEE Trans. on Pattern Analysis and Machine Intelligence*, **19**(10), 1067-1079.

Hower, W. and Graf, W. H. (1996). A Bibliographical Survey of Constraint-Based Approaches to CAD, Graphics Layout, Visualization, and Related Topics. *Knowledge-Based Systems*, **9**(7), 449-469.

Knuth, D. E. (1968). Semantics of Context-Free Languages. *Mathematical Systems Theory*, **2**, 127-145.

Kosslyn, S. M. (1994). *Elements of Graph Design*. New York: W. H. Freeman.

Levesque, H. J. (1987). Making Believers out of Computers. *Artificial Intelligence*, **30**, 81-108.

Levesque, H. J. (1992). Logic and the Complexity of Reasoning. *J. of Philosophical Logic*, **17**, 355-389.

Luo, H., Kasturi, R., Arias, J. F. and Chhabra, A. (1997). Interpretation of Lines in Distributing Frame Drawings. In ICDAR 97 (*Fourth Intl. Conf. on Document Analysis and Recognition*), (pp. 66-70). Ulm, Germany: IEEE Computer Soc.

Mackinlay, J. D. (1987). Automating the Design of Graphical Presentations of Relational Information. *ACM Trans. Computer Graphics*, **5**(2), 110-141.

Marriott, K. (1994). Constraint Multiset Grammars. In Visual Languages 94: *IEEE Computer Soc.*

Marriott, K., Meyer, B. and Wittenburg, K. (1998). A Survey of Visual Language Specification and Recognition. In K. Marriott & B. Meyer (Eds.), *Visual Language Theory* : Springer Verlag.

Maybury, M. and Merlino, A. (1997). Multimedia Summaries of Broadcast News. In *Conference on Intelligent Information Systems*.

Maybury, M. T. and Wahlster, W. (Ed.). (1998). *Readings in Intelligent User Interfaces*. San Francisco: Morgan Kaufmann.

Misue, K., Eades, P., Lai, W. and Sugiyama, K. (1995). Layout Adjustment and the Mental Map. *J. Visual Languages and Computing*, **6**, 183-210.

Nikolakis, N. (1996) *Diagram Analysis using Equivalence and Constraints*. Ph.D. thesis, Northeastern University.

Norvig, P. (1991). Techniques for Automatic Memoization with Applications to Context-Free Parsing. *Computational Linguistics*, **17**(1), 91-98.

Paice, C. D. (1990). Constructing literature abstracts by computer: Techniques and prospects. *Information Processing & Management*, **26**(1), 171-186.

Richardson, P. J. (1997). Blocking adenosine with antisense. *Nature*, **385**(20 February), 684-685.

Seligmann, D. D. and Feiner, S. (1991). Automated Generation of Intent-Based 3D Illustrations. *Computer Graphics*, **25**(4), 123-132.

Sloman, A. (1995). Musings on the Roles of Logical and Non-Logical Representations of Intelligence. In B. Chandrasekaran, J. Glasgow & N. H. Narayanan (Eds.), *Diagrammatic Reasoning. Cognitive and Computational Perspectives* (pp. 7-32). Menlo Park, CA, Cambridge, MA: AAAI Press, MIT Press.

Stenning, K. and Inder, R. (1995). Applying Semantic Concepts to Analyzing Media and Modalities. In B. Chandrasekaran, J. Glasgow & N. H. Narayanan (Eds.), *Diagrammatic Reasoning. Cognitive and Computational*

Perspectives (pp. 303-338). Menlo Park, CA, Cambridge, MA: AAAI Press, MIT Press.

Tufte, E. R. (1985). *The Visual Display of Quantitative Information*. Cheshire, CT: Graphics Press.

Tufte, E. R. (1990). *Envisioning Information*. Cheshire, CT: Graphics Press.

Tufte, E. R. (1997). *Visual Explanations*. Cheshire, CT: Graphics Press.

World Wide Web Consortium (1997). *Extensible Markup Language (XML)*. http://www.w3.org/XML/.

World-Wide Web Consortium (1998). *Technical Reports (covering XML, PGML)*. http://www.w3c.org/TR/.

Index